New Horizons in Reading

John E. Merritt, *Editor*
The Open University
Milton Keynes, England

Proceedings of the
Fifth IRA World Congress on Reading
Vienna, Austria
August 12-14, 1974

International Reading Association
800 Barksdale Road
Newark, Delaware, United States of America

Contents

139189

Foreword

The International Reading Association has sponsored five World Congresses on Reading—the first in Paris in 1966, the second in Copenhagen in 1968, the third in Sydney in 1970, the fourth in Buenos Aires in 1972, and the fifth in Vienna in 1974. The Hofburg Congress Center in Vienna was the site for the fifth congress, August 12-14, 1974. Registrants numbered 876 from 33 countries and every continent.

John E. Merritt of the Open University, Milton Keynes, England, was the chairman of the committee which planned the program and provided the list of speakers. The result was truly remarkable for its breadth of coverage, its satisfaction of both sophisticated researchers and practitioners, its presentation of established practices and new challenges in theory, and its provision for specialist working parties to focus on specific problems, bringing insights from research and experience in different parts of the globe. The Congress provided an environment for the creation of ideas as well as for the exchange of knowledge and experience.

Hence, the International Reading Association is greatly indebted to John Merritt and his committee for bringing individuals from every continent closer to a global understanding of the reading process and its cultivation. We are doubly indebted to John Merritt for having assembled in this volume some of the papers from the Fifth IRA World Congress on Reading to share with those who did not attend and to remind those who did attend of the stimulation of that event.

The reading of *New Horizons in Reading* and the other IRA World Congress Proceedings listed below should prepare you for, and entice you to attend, the Sixth IRA World Congress on Reading to be held in Singapore, August 17-19, 1976.

> *Reading: A Human Right and a Human Problem*, edited by Ralph Staiger and Oliver Andresen
>
> *Improving Reading Ability Around the World*, edited by Dorothy Bracken and Eve Malmquist
>
> *Reading for All*, edited by Robert Karlin

A Spanish version of *Reading for All*, entitled *Lectura Para Todos*, edited by Professor J. Ricardo Nervi, is available from the IRA Latin American Office: Asociacion Internacional de Lectura, Avenue de Mayo 749, Piso 7 Of. 73, Buenos Aires, Argentina.

Remember: To be a full reader you must have a global appetite!

Constance M. McCullough, *Past President*
International Reading Association
1975-1976

ACKNOWLEDGEMENTS

The editor would like to thank Dianna Moylan, B.A. (Open), Course Assistant, Open University, for her work on the index. The editor would also like to thank Lloyd Kline and Faye Branca for their help and guidance at various stages throughout publication. Appreciation goes, of course, to all of the contributors to this volume. Not all of the excellent papers that were presented at the Fifth IRA World Congress in Vienna could be included here and acknowledgement must also be made to those speakers whose papers were not adopted in this particular publication. Finally, it must be said that in view of all this excellent support, any blemishes in this volume must be laid firmly at the door of the editor.

JEM

Introduction

The purpose of the World Congress is to provide an opportunity for members of the International Reading Association in different countries to share ideas about the nature of the reading process and ways of improving reading standards throughout the world. The formal presentations at this Congress have two purposes. Primarily they are intended to provide a focus for discussion, since discussion is perhaps the most important part of the proceedings; in their printed form, however, they are intended to provide a resource to stimulate further thinking and action long after the participants have dispersed.

This volume contains a limited selection of the papers presented and these are grouped into six relatively discrete areas. Naturally, the papers cannot provide an exhaustive coverage of each topic of importance in each of these areas. Their purpose, rather, is to provide important new perspectives on familiar problems, and to draw attention to problems which have not previously been clearly recognized or adequately defined—hence the title *New Horizons in Reading*.

Part One—Reading: an expanding concept. In many countries the concept of reading has not yet developed beyond a recognition of some of the more obvious problems which face the apprentice reader in tackling the printed code. Even where the concept of reading is more advanced, however, there are many aspects of the reading process which are as yet underemphasized, and others which are largely unexplored. The papers in Part One are intended to draw attention to some of these aspects. They provide new horizons in terms of our understanding of what we need to teach. The final paper in Part One draws attention to the need to gain a comparative perspective in looking at reading—and this, of course, is one of the most important reasons for organizing a world congress.

Part Two—Some implications for the reading curriculum. Any development in our ideas about goals in teaching reading must lead to a reexamination of the reading curriculum; the arrangements we make in each area of the curriculum for the development of reading skills and interests. This will involve an examination of the plans we may make to achieve our goals, the methods we may adopt in seeking to implement these plans, and various ways of evaluating what we actually do so that we can strive continuously to develop a more effective reading curriculum. The papers in Part Two provide a stimulus for thinking in each of these areas.

Part Three—Writing systems: some comparative perspectives. Many different kinds of code could be devised to represent the ideas which, for various reasons, we record in printed form. Symbols can be used not only to represent speech sounds, but may also be used to represent morphemes, words, or quite complex ideas. It is important to bear in mind this wide range of possibilities when looking at any particular writing system or when comparing different kinds of writing systems. The papers in Part Three draw attention to some of the advantages and disadvantages of some existing systems. The first three papers provide perspectives on the different kinds of writing system in use in Japan. In doing so, they help to provide perspective on other orthographies so that we may see more clearly some of their relative advantages and disadvantages. The other papers in Part Three provide additional viewpoints on some of the problems raised in the earlier papers, but in terms of more familiar writing systems.

Part Four—The printed media: a question of standards. Generally speaking, we take our writing system as "given." Attempts to alter writing systems in any substantial way tend to meet with limited success, and so we concentrate our attention on helping the reader to cope with the systems as they are. Other aspects of the printed word lie, to some extent, within our control. For example, we can at least reject printed material which does not satisfy certain criteria. The more often we do so, the more likely it is that those aspects which concern us will be modified in the desired direction. Part Four is concerned with the kinds of criteria we might select in trying to establish standards to guide us in making such decisions.

Most studies in this area have been concerned with different aspects of readability. The development of programmed texts, however, has stimulated an increased concern about the conceptual structure of the normal text, and also any underlying assumptions that may have been made concerning the reader's previous level of understanding. Beyond this lies the whole problem of validity of content—the extent to which a particular text provides a basis for accurate appraisal of the area covered, and ways in which a text may tend to obscure or distort rather than clarify important issues. These, too, must be considered, and the papers in this section are intended to stimulate debate among those who have not yet given detailed attention to such issues.

Part Five—Special problems and special approaches. The problem of raising standards of reading is highly complex when viewed in the context of a fairly homogeneous population. It is naturally much more complex in the context of the vast range of individual differences that exist in any society. The papers in Part Five examine some of the teaching and organizational approaches that are currently being explored for dealing with special problems at various age-levels. The last two papers provide information about existing standards and their correlates. One of these papers relates to standards of reading in the United Kingdom and the other to standards in the fifteen countries studied in the IEA survey.

Part Six—Raising teaching standards. If we are to improve teaching standards we must have a reasonably clear idea about what those standards are. We must be able to define or describe in some way the more critical aspects of teacher performance. We also must be sure that we can evaluate competence in each of these critical aspects in some reasonably effective and not too obtrusive way. We must be able to provide training programmes that enable the teacher to achieve relevant competencies, instead of merely encouraging the acquisition of examination-passing techniques. We must also ensure that those competencies are fully exercised in teaching situations. No small task. This, however, is the greatest challenge, and the papers in this section give an indication of some of the thinking that must be done if we are to improve standards of teaching and, hence, standards of reading.

A FINAL COMMENT

There are those who think that there is nothing difficult about teaching reading. They will cite all those examples of parents who, without training, have been successful in teaching their own children to read; they will point out, quite rightly, that many preschool children virtually teach themselves, given a little help from siblings; and they will remind us that the underattaining 18-year-old is often more effective in helping other children to learn to read than is the highly qualified reading specialist.

Unfortunately, there is another side to the coin. We do not know, for example, how many retarded readers are produced by those parents who are overdemanding, overanxious, or misguided in their approach. We do know, on the other hand, that children can teach themselves (how else would they learn?). We also know that the incentive to learn and the materials for learning are not universally available in every home, so the school must compensate in a variety of ways. We know, too, that insight into a child's difficulties is a prerequisite for providing suitable help; and we recognize that the retarded student may have considerable intuitive understanding of these difficulties as a result of his own experience. The more highly qualified the educator, the less likely it is that he has ever experienced similar difficulties. Unless we are going to advocate that only the retarded should become teachers, however, we must surely provide a much more sophisticated form of teacher education—not a more simpleminded approach. In particular, we must engineer a much closer relationship between theory and practice, rather than dismiss theory as irrelevant, or dismiss the thoughtful teaching of good practice as mere "tips for teachers."

Those who dismiss the problem airily are all too often first class teachers themselves. Because they have been relatively successful, they often assume that this was a direct result of the methods they used—methods they selected quite intuitively. These teachers then tend to advocate the universal adoption of their own particular methods, ignoring the fact that many other equally successful teachers may use quite different methods. What they do not appreciate is that no single method, nor collection of methods, brought about their success. Success was due, instead, to their professional judgment of when to use which method with which student, group, or class. Judgment is manifestly not present in every teacher in equal degree, and we can only seek to develop it by means of courses which provide practical experience in making such judgments within the context of a sound understanding of relevant theoretical considerations. The teacher is not an artisan who needs only to be taught a few tricks. If he is to be entrusted with responsibility for educating children, he must be a fully trained professional; he must be sensitive to the needs of his pupils and aware of his own need to continue developing professional skills. Indeed, the best teacher is one who realizes how much more he has to learn. It is hoped that the contents of this book will provide a stimulus for all those educators in schools and colleges throughout the world who fall within this category.

JOHN E. MERRITT

PART ONE

Reading: An Expanding Concept

Straws in the Wind

Constance M. McCullough, Emeritus
San Francisco State University
San Francisco, California
United States of America

The history of reading instruction is evident all around the world. In some places it is still thought that all one needs to do to teach reading is to teach the symbols which represent the sounds or the ideas of the language. It is a very dangerous practice to stop with that level of literacy. The reader can then become a parrot who broadcasts ideas he does not really think through. He can become unwittingly a tool in the hands of an enemy. It does not behoove any nation to stop with that kind of literacy, or even to introduce it if that is where it will stop.

In some countries in the world, reading is *used* rather than taught, once the symbols are learned. The subskills which would support the further development of comprehension are assumed, not taught. The textbook is read aloud and the grasp of ideas is assumed. Questions on the author's meaning are not asked. Differences of opinion are not invited, and the teacher never knows what may be puzzling the student or how he might be helped.

Even in countries where textbooks are designed to stress comprehension, children's perceptions of reading are not entirely satisfactory. Studies in Scotland, New Zealand (2), and North America have shown that young children taught to read for as long as a year still may not be able to identify a word, a letter, the beginning of a sentence, or the letter which stands for the first sound in the word. They think that reading is saying what the print represents.

This kind of evidence reveals that not only have we failed to match instruction with the reading task, we ourselves have had and have transmitted a distorted and limited idea of the reading process.

In a massive and expensive national effort in the United States to improve the reading ability of the poorer readers, great stress was laid on sound-symbol correspondences and word recognition. The gain was disappointing.

In a large group of beginning reading studies using different methods of instruction, the finding was that method made less difference than the quality of the teacher. Something the successful teachers were doing was not a part of teacher education.

Robert Thorndike's, *Reading Comprehension Education in Fifteen Countries* (9), showed that the cultural opportunities of the home were the best predictors of reading comprehension scores, and that the reading comprehension scores were generally good predictors of student scores on tests of science and literature. In developing countries, the mean scores were so low that errors on fact questions were no less numerous than errors on questions requiring inference. The younger Hindi speaking children in India read relatively better than the children of other developing countries, and better than would have been expected from the scores of the students tested at higher educational levels. I could not help remembering when I saw this that a special effort was made eleven years ago (6) in Indian teacher education and in the publishing of textbooks to stress cognition and reading comprehension. Perhaps the new program for standards one through five in Hindi reading was reflected here.

It took Piaget to stun the world with the central importance of cognition. It took Carol Chomsky and others (1) to break the myth that children have a mastery of the grammar of their language on entrance to school. Now many research scholars are working on these two areas of strength for the development of reading comprehension.

While neurologists implant devices in the brain to discover clues to its operation, computer scientists build computer systems for problem solving. Herbert Simon of the Carnegie-Mellon Institute in Pittsburgh, is trying to find out how problem-solving by the human brain differs from that of manmade computers (8). He gives a student a prose passage on a social problem and then tapes what the student says he is thinking as he tries to solve it. While Simon's research is rewarding, he knows that even the student may be unconscious of some of the thinking he does, and the brain itself refuses to be interviewed. When asked why he confines his material to problem-solving, Professor Simon says, "Because it is the most important thing man does."

The field of anthropology had a shock several years ago in the work of Alexander Marshack, *The Roots of Civilization* (5), which is in itself a fascinating study in problem-solving. Like Heinrich Schliemann, Marshack was not a trained specialist in the field he was to invade. It all started with marks on a prehistoric tool. Marshack knew that the earlier manlike anthropoids were nomadic hunters who took their tools from one campsite to another and who survived by anticipating the location of herds of their prey. The herds, in turn, were following their food, and so it became important to know when certain plants in certain places would be ripe for the herds to use. Seasons of the year were basic knowledge for the solution of the hunter's problem.

Marshack found that the border marks on the tool showed under magnification that they were not made by the same instrument. These could have been made at successive campsites or on different occasions. With dogged persistence he discovered that these marks corresponded to the phases of the moon. Other tools which he analyzed bore marks accounting for a thirteen month year. Marshack's discovery pushed back the history of symbol-writing, symbol-reading, and symbol-teaching tens of thousands of years, as well as the sophistication of language needed to express it. The code on the tool was the key to survival, born of an awareness of time, comparison and contrast, cause and effect, classification, logical reasoning: highly motivated reading matter read with cognitive appraisal of current environmental conditions.

Primitive man who painted the interiors of caves where he took refuge from the killing temperatures of the Ice Age was not just another interior decorator. His drawings of pregnant animals and phallic symbols were not the work of someone who had no television set. Marshack's microscope showed that the marks thought to be phallic symbols were forms of plants and flowers which attracted the animals at a certain time of year. Where and when those plants developed foliage, he would find the animals.

How strange that we should have neglected the cognitive core of reading, that we should have thought grammar was for writing and speaking, not central to the understanding of what was read. How strange that we did not realize the need for a language-related cognitive readiness, that we taught all children alike, whether the language of the book was their mother tongue or an unfamiliar language in an unfamiliar code.

In 1974, the United States Supreme Court ruled (3) that a school requiring a child to read English was to be held responsible for providing prior instruction in English. Even primitive man would have understood that. The more civilized we become, the longer it seems to take us to see the obvious. Yet I wonder how many countries have still to make like decisions.

In *Reading Research Quarterly* Williams (11) reviews theories and models of learning to read. She makes the statement that present-day theorists seem to be moving toward the view that reading is both a complex cognitive skill, the goal of which is obtaining information, and a complex language system.

In his book, *What Shall We Teach?* Merritt (7) points out that competent management is a matter of making intelligent decisions about goals, designing adequate plans, implementing those plans skillfully, and developing from the new base line that has been achieved.

If we take as our new base line the definition of reading which Dr. Williams stated, that reading is both a complex cognitive skill and a complex language system, we then must decide on goals.

What can we expect of the child who comes to reading? He brings a degree of mastery of his mother tongue. The utterances he hears around him which he has learned to associate with certain meanings, feelings, and intentions on the part of the speakers come in some kind of rhythm, but the groupings of run-together words give him no warning of a page of symbolic ideas as in Chinese or a page of separated words as in English. As a reader he is going to have to group the ideas or words just as a speaker would. So part of his job is to decide which ideas or words belong together. One of the ways the teacher would implement this would be to ask questions which the phrases answered. A child who does not speak the language of the school will not be able to do this.

The child's previous experiences will have provided him with concepts and labels. Initial reading or listening experiences which feature these known ideas will make it easier for him to be a thinker as he reads, an anticipator of what the author is going to say. It is good for children to guess what will happen next and to have many different plausible suggestions with many different defenses of them, so that the child will know many ways to anticipate the next step in a sequence and the effect for a cause (10).

In the development of new concepts the teacher can introduce a ritual of language (How does the duck feel? He's soft. He's smooth. He's fluffy.)—all sentences of sensory attribute; (What can he do? He can run. He can fly. He can walk wobbly.)—all sentences of behavior attributes; (What happens when he swims? He pushes the water and the water makes waves. When you give him some grain? He pecks at the grain. He eats it up.)—cause and effect. Some day, the teacher hopes, similar sentences, by their very form, will help the child expect and recognize an attribute, a condition of cause and effect, and so forth.

In children's writing, similar stress can be achieved. (My dog likes me because. . . . My Mother likes me because. . . . I scratch his back. I feed him. I help her. I'm good.)

The ultimate goal of our teaching is for the child to become a skillful reader.

The skillful reader has had many language-related experiences in which he has communicated his ideas and feelings and listened to the language invention of others. His concepts are rounded, so that he has many things to say about a given concept. This being so, he is ready for the directions an author may take in relation to a concept. Suppose he is reading to see whether the author is still on the subject or passing to another subject (as one must read when the author is enumerating, with one or more sentences devoted to one subject). When he ceases to encounter words and phrases usually associated with the subject, he thinks that point number two has arrived.

The skillful reader is alert to what I call the mismatching of ideas. *The fence runs around the field.* Everybody knows that fences stand still. The mismatch or incongruity signals the figurative use of the word *runs*, and actually now a commonplace use of *run*. Or take this sentence: *The king stamped his foot and flew to the ceiling.* "Kings don't fly," thinks the reader. "This is fiction. This is fancy." If the reader is not good at making comparisons, he will miss these signals; but the skillful reader doesn't. So he notices the cognitive relationships among ideas such as part-whole, classification, definition, comparison, ordering, enumeration, causation.

The goal of the reader, unless he has a special goal of his own, is to discover the author's focus, whether it be on laws, principles, theories, concepts, problems, events, objects, or living things.

In this search he notes the author's patterns of reasoning, such as inductive, deductive, convergent, divergent, syllogistic. He asks questions as he reads, corrects his mistaken hunches and proceeds to generate new ones.

What are the clues to the author's focus? The reader must notice main ideas, examples, elaboration, and application of ideas. But he can't discover these just by being told to find them. What makes a main idea main? What vectors point to it? What examples contribute to it? What elaboration expands it? What applications prove its generality?

These relationships among ideas are revealed through semantic and syntactical relationships among words, phrases, clauses, sentences, and paragraphs (4).

Additional aids are signs such as capitalization, bold type, italics, punctuation, footnotes, headings and sub-headings, indentation, paragraphing, space allotment, and illustrations.

As the good reader observes these elements and their interrelationships, he decides on the author's intent, such as to describe, to persuade, or to evaluate. He notes the author's nature as revealed by his language, his citing of experiences, his feelings, attitudes, and cognitive skills. The feelings and attitudes of the reader are in turn stimulated by the author, and the reader who wishes to be objective often bends over backwards to resist having his own preconceptions color his acceptance of new information and his inferences based upon it.

With all of these observations and experiences with the organization and direction of the author's thought, as well as the way he has expressed it, the skillful reader operates on the author's message to achieve literal comprehension, to deduce implications and possible applications, to assess the message in relation to previous knowledge, and to store in memory whatever he prefers.

The amazing truth is that all of this is done so rapidly that it cannot be recounted in a valid sequence. The other day I was typing an address. I wrote "Oldman's Traditional School." It should have been "Oldman's *Transitional* School." My head and hands had completely betrayed what my eyes were registering. My head knew that old men tend to be traditional, and that the next transition for them is something to delay.

The answer to reading comprehension will be not one answer but many answers in congenial relationship, and it will require a world of scholarship and dedication and cooperation to achieve. Reading comprehension is our responsibility and cannot be achieved solely through the child's recognition of symbols and the teacher's asking questions or the book's giving the answers. Whether the teacher is a person or instructional material, the teacher's role is to clarify the process. This is enough challenge to light the years ahead and to make those of us who have been in this work a long time wish we were just beginning.

REFERENCES AND NOTES

1. Chomsky, Carol. *The Acquisition of Syntax in Children from 5 to 10*, Research Monograph 57. Cambridge, Massachusetts: MIT Press, 1969.
2. Clay, Marie. *Reading: The Patterning of Complex Behavior*. Auckland, New Zealand. Heinemann Educational Books, 1972.
3. Decision of United States Supreme Court on Education of Chinese Speaking Children in San Francisco, 1974.
4. Hodges, Richard, and Hugh Rudorf (Eds.). *Language and Learning to Read*. Boston: Houghton Mifflin, 1972.
5. Marshack, Alexander. *The Roots of Civilization*. New York: McGraw-Hill, 1972.
6. McCullough, Constance, and others. *Preparation of Textbooks in the Mother Tongue*. Newark, Delaware: International Reading Association, 1967.
7. Merritt, John. *What Shall We Teach?* London: Ward Lock Educational Limited, 1974.
8. Simon, Herbert. Talk delivered in Chicago at the Convention of the American Educational Research Association, April 1974.
9. Thorndike, Robert L. *Reading Comprehension Education in Fifteen Countries*, International Studies in Evaluation III. Stockholm, Sweden: Malmquist and Wiksell, 1973; also John Wiley and Sons.
10. Tinker, Miles, and Constance McCullough. *Teaching Elementary Reading* (4th ed.). Englewood Cliffs, New Jersey: Prentice-Hall, 1974.
11. Williams, Joanna. "Learning to Read: Theories and Models," *Reading Research Quarterly*, 8 (Winter 1973), 121-146.

Literal Comprehension: A Reevaluation

Amelia Melnik
University of Arizona
Tucson, Arizona
United States of America

"It is not a small or unworthy task to learn what the book says."
—Thorndike (8)

THE CONUNDRUM OF COMPREHENSION

The subject of comprehension, whether in discussion or in publication, is likely to be characterized by confusion and contradiction, if not chaos. Why should this be so? Why, after more than fifty years of study, have we failed to achieve a comprehensive common understanding and precise terminology to confirm and communicate our present state of knowledge of the operational and developmental nature of comprehension?

Can it be that we have approached our comprehension of comprehension on the assumption that it consists of a series of separate skills which operate in some sequential order? Without questioning this assumption, we have gone on to dissect and categorize its various facets into an endless array of isolated minuscule fragments to such a degree that, as Edgar Dale said, "We suffer from hardening of the categories" (1). And, inevitably, the professional literature fills to overflow with diverse definitions, a multiplicity of levels and labels, an endless list of comprehension skills and subskills, and now, more recently, a plethora of muddled models which illuminate little more than our ignorance.

Would our knowledge of comprehension today be more precise and profound had our studies begun with the assumption that the two major interacting components of reading—the reader and the printed media—involve multiple interacting variables that operate *simultaneously* within, between, and among one another in unique and varied relationships that can only be uncovered through intensive case studies and longitudinal research? This view was reinforced in the Summer 1974 issue of the *Reading Research Quarterly* devoted to reporting 369 investigations in reading during the previous year. In their concluding summary, the editors state (9):

Conceivably, we have erred in the types of designs and statistical procedures we've used in the past and continue to use. Perhaps for purposes of the reading field, we need to look at other ways of approaching problems than through the classical designs commonly employed. Possibly better answers may come through venturing into other, "looser" research. Few intensive case studies appear in the literature. Longitudinal studies of various kinds are almost non-existent. As one views reading research, much of it seems to be a hit and run type. We rush in to administer 14 tests, collect 2 minutes of information from each child in an individual interview, and then correlate these data, making grand generalizations about the nature of reading.

Maybe we haven't solved our problems or answered many questions because we have attempted to be too rigorous in applying our statistical procedures. Rigor comes in many forms, including mortis. Perhaps a fresh breath, a new view is needed. Observational studies, case reports of an intensive nature, historical research, depth interviews, Piaget-type experimentation, broadly based evaluation studies may all help us to understand the reading process more fully. If nothing else, they might permit us to view reading from a different perspective—and possibly we need that different viewpoint now.

But even beyond these limitations, should not scholarship in reading follow the problem-solving pattern and culminate in *application*—the test of use? Knowledge gained through research will remain little more than inert information until the step of application becomes an integral part of research design. There is need to remind ourselves of the wisdom of Woodrow Wilson's admonition: "We need to take the truth out of the cupboards and put it in the hearts and minds of men who stir abroad," for, today, the chasm between our "knowin's and doin's" lies deep and broad.

Perhaps a historical perspective may illuminate the direction of our pursuits and provide a path through which we may confute the conundrum of comprehension.

"READING AS REASONING"—AN HISTORiCAL PERSPECTIVE

In 1917 E. L. Thorndike published his now classic study, "Reading As Reasoning: A Study of Paragraph Mistakes," which was reprinted in the *Reading Research Quarterly* in 1971 as the subject of commentary. One of the most widely quoted studies in all of reading research, Thorndike derived significant insights into the nature of comprehension through his perceptive analysis of pupils' responses to questions relating to simple paragraphs. His conclusions initiated a major departure from exclusive emphasis on precise pronunciation and oral reading to a greater awareness and concern for comprehension and silent reading. In his commentary on this study, Otto concluded that "While the influence of Thorndike's article is undeniable, its practical impact is questionable at best" (4). Why? Where have we erred?

Perhaps in these past 57 years we ourselves have limited our own comprehension of Thorndike's report primarily to theoretical academic discussions of 1) his description of the nature of reading (which readers delight in improving upon) and 2) his research design (which others delight in disparaging) to the complete neglect of his concluding statement of recommendations. Perhaps, if given the opportunity today, Thorndike himself might well classify these responses in his overpotency and underpotency categories of comprehension errors.

In any case, Thorndike (8) concluded his report with the following statement:

> It is not a small or unworthy task to learn what the book says. In school practice it appears likely that exercises in silent reading to find the answers to questions, or to give a summary of the matter read, or to list questions which it answers, should in large measure replace oral reading.

Baffling as it may seem, critics today take exception to Thorndike's statement, "It is not a small or unworthy task to learn what the book says." The critics' own literal comprehension of the statement is revealed in their disparaging comments deriding questions such as "What does the book say?" claiming that it promotes nothing more than literal comprehension and fosters factual responses, memorization, and convergent thinking.

However, even out of context of this study, it is reasonable to infer that in his open-end question Thorndike was suggesting that all aspects and levels of comprehension are involved in a response to "What does the book say?" How else could Thorndike have derived his description of the dynamics of reading as

> . . . a very elaborate procedure, involving a weighing of each of many elements in a sentence, their organization in the proper relations one to another, the selection of certain of their connotations and the rejection of others, and the cooperation of many forces to determine the final response.

Perhaps those of us who have become enamoured with the aims of critical and creative reading have lost sight of the need for the literal level of comprehension as the foundation for operating on successive levels of comprehension. For, as John Dewey said, "You can have facts without thinking, but you cannot have thinking without facts."

Is it not also reasonable to suggest that in analyzing his subjects' responses, Thorndike derived significant insights into the nature of reading comprehension which led him to conclude that "It is no small or unworthy task to learn what the book says"? Fortunately, there have been a few voices in the wilderness who have recognized the deceptive simplicity of Thorndike's open-end question and have employed it as a free-response technique in their study and teaching of comprehension.

EXPLORATION THROUGH THE FREE-RESPONSE TECHNIQUE

In 1942, Strang published *Explorations in Reading Patterns* (7), a study she described as

> . . . a transition from the statistical analysis of masses of data to the insightful analysis of intensive case studies. In a sense, it is a hybrid, and it is at present in the unhappy state of not having entirely extricated itself from the influence of one parent or given wholehearted devotion to the other. Its preference for the case study approach, however, is obvious.
>
> Through the case study method the interrelation of many factors—accessibility of reading material, its content, the reader's predispositions, and his observed responses—can be most adequately studied . . . .

In this study, Strang was the first to employ, among other techniques, the free response question, "What did the author say?" and reported that

> . . . the freely written response to the three articles gave more significant information about the way people read, what they get out of their reading, and how effective they are in communicating to others the knowledge thus gained than any other single item in the entire procedure.

Based on her insightful analysis of subjects' responses in relation to the structure of the articles, Strang developed a rating scale to objectively assess the adequacy of these subjects' varying levels of comprehension and the skills they employed in their reading.

In 1957, Gray and Rogers (2) published their study, *Maturity in Reading*, in which they concurred with procedures encouraging the use of the free response and less dependence on formally structured (objective-type) questions. Accordingly, they state that

> . . . this change would insure more information about the respondent as a person and keener insight concerning his interaction with specific reading materials in given reading situations. It also appeared to be more likely to provide insight into the nature of the respondent's use of reading and his level of competence in reading than an approach which depended on formally structured objective questions.

From their analysis of responses, Gray and Rogers elaborated and further developed Strang's rating scale for assessing the levels of adequacy of reading comprehension of their subjects. Both investigators concluded that through the free response keener insight was gained regarding the interaction between the reader and the reading material in given reading situations.

Using the free response technique with Harvard students, Perry reported in 1959 that, although on standardized tests these students surpassed 85 percent of the freshmen students in the United States, when asked to write a short statement of what the chapter they had read was about, only one in a hundred—a total of 15—were able to do so. Perry's observations (5) led him to conclude that:

> As a demonstration of obedient purposelessness in the reading of 99 percent of Harvard freshmen we found this impressive.
> ... what the students lack is not mechanical skills but flexibility and purpose in the use of them.

From the observations of these investigators, it is clear that the free response technique, such as the open-end question "What did the author say?" elicits the single most revealing picture of the reader's comprehension, i.e., his judicious selection of significant ideas, related one to another, and to his past and present knowledge and experience. More specifically, from an analysis of responses to this question, it is possible to obtain evidence of the following facets of comprehension (3):

1. The reader's approach to a reading passage.
2. His tendency to relate ideas rather than to merely seize on isolated details.
3. His ability to uncover the author's pattern of thought.
4. His ability to organize and show the relationship among ideas.
5. His tendency to relate what he reads to other knowledge he has gained and to life experiences and needs.
6. His tendency to let his emotions or biases and prejudices influence his comprehension.
7. His ability to adjust his method and rate of reading according to his purpose and the type of printed media.

If these are the goals of comprehension, then the question is, "Through what procedures may we employ the free response technique to improve comprehension at all levels of reading development?"

STEPS TO EFFECTIVE TEACHING

A group procedure, fusing diagnosis-instruction-practice into a single ongoing process currently identified as diagnostic teaching, was developed in 1960 by Melnik (3) for improving the reading of social studies material of junior high school students.

It begins by asking students to state the reading goals or aims they wish to achieve to further improve their reading. Next they are asked to state their responses to the question, "What reading skills help you to understand and remember what you read?"

Then they are asked to read a passage from a social studies textbook that is typical of the material they are expected to read in their classes. After reading the passage, with no direction from the teacher and in whatever time they require, they write their answer to the question "What did the author say?" without referring to the text. They also answer a number of multiple-choice questions, each designed to identify a particular comprehension skill for which each option indicates a particular type of comprehension error. A third free response question, asking them to apply the knowledge they have gained from their reading, is included to provide evidence of creative reading.

As soon as the students have answered these questions, each individual has before him the data for self-appraisal. They mark their own performance. They rate their responses to "What did the author say?" on a ten point scale developed to reflect the author's pattern of thought. They analyze the kind of errors they made on multiple-choice questions. During each of these steps, instruction and guidance are provided through discussion in which reference is continually made to 1) the content of the selection, 2) its organizational structure of thought, and 3) the typographical clues which clarify the author's message for evidence to justify differences of opinion or rating.

Practice on similar material immediately follows this self-appraisal and instructional phase of the procedure, while the students are specifically motivated to learn how to improve their performance. Practice in systematically employing Robinson's Survey Q3R technique (6) with their daily assignments is also provided.

Later, the whole procedure is repeated on another similar passage. After the second exercise is completed and analyzed, the students are able to note the progress they have made. A third repetition of the procedure produces marked improvement.

After completing the third exercise, the students were asked to evaluate their experience with this teaching procedure. Of all the features in the procedure, the students without exception stated that analyzing their response to the question "What did the author say?" had helped them most.

This appraisal-instruction-practice-evaluation procedure bridges the gap between teaching and testing. It provides opportunity for practice and progress geared to the wide range of individual differences in reading in the typical classroom situation. It relieves the teacher of the time-consuming burden of grading papers by herself by providing the students with a concrete guide to appraise their own performance. Through this procedure students' increased understanding of the comprehension process enables them to become more flexible, purposeful, and searching readers.

Perhaps today, in a day and age of technological, synthetic, prepackaged reading programs, we need more procedures which integrate personalized insights with relevant know-how which will enable both teachers and pupils to replace the humdrum in the conundrum of comprehension with an internalized realization of the meaning, use, and purpose of reading.

REFERENCES
1. Dale, Edgar. "Things to Come," *Newsletter*, 34 (1969).
2. Gray, William S., and Bernice Rogers. *Maturity in Reading: Its Nature and Appraisal*. Chicago: University of Chicago Press, 1956, 59.
3. Melnik, Amelia. "The Improvement of Reading Through Self-Appraisal," unpublished doctoral dissertation, Teachers College, Columbia University, New York, 1960, 40-41.
4. Otto, Wayne. "Thorndike's 'Reading as Reasoning': Influence and Impact," *Reading Research Quarterly*, 6 (Summer 1971), 439.
5. Perry, William G. "Students' Use and Misuse of Reading Skills: A Report to the Faculty," in Amelia Melnik and John Merritt (Eds.), *Reading: Today and Tomorrow*. London: University of London Press, 1972, 374, 372.
6. Robinson, Franklin P. *Effective Study*. New York: Harper and Row, 1961.
7. Strang, Ruth. *Explorations in Reading Patterns*. Chicago: University of Chicago Press, 1942, 5, 78.
8. Thorndike, E. L. "Reading As Reasoning: A Study of Mistakes in Paragraph Reading," in Amelia Melnik and John Merritt (Eds.), *Reading: Today and Tomorrow*. London: University of London Press, 1972, 30, 20.
9. Weintraub, Samuel, et al. "Summary of Investigations Relating to Reading July 1, 1972 to June 30, 1973," *Reading Research Quarterly*, 9 (1973-1974), 245-246.

Miscue Analysis: Theory and Reality in Reading

Kenneth S. Goodman
University of Arizona
Tucson, Arizona
United States of America

More than ten years ago this researcher set himself a simple task: He wished to examine, from the perspective of modern linguistics, what happened when people read. It seemed logical to ask subjects to read material they had not seen before, so that what they did could be analyzed.

This examination of oral reading is not new. Analysis of reading errors in oral reading has been going on for several decades. What is new is the linguistic perspective which is applied. Error analysis had largely followed two assumptions. First, it was assumed that oral reading should be accurate and therefore that errors represented undesirable events in reading. Second it was assumed that errors grew from weaknesses or deficiencies in the reader. The number of errors was counted but little attention was given to qualitive differences among miscues or their effects.

In miscue analysis, from the very beginning, reading has been treated as a language process, the receptive aspect of written language and therefore the parallel process to listening. The reader is regarded as a user of language, one who constructs meaning from written language.

Everything the reader does is assumed to be caused in this linguistic process. Unexpected events in oral reading thus reveal the way the reader is using the reading process itself. The term error is a misnomer then, since it implies an undesirable occurrence. The term miscue has emerged instead. A miscue is any observed oral response (OR) to print which does not match the expected response (ER). Miscue analysis reveals the reader's strengths and weaknesses and provides a continuous window on the reading process.

In this last sense miscue analysis is a uniquely powerful tool in linguistic and psycholinguistic research since it makes it possible to monitor a language process continuously as it proceeds.

Shifting the focus in this analysis from errors as undesirable phenomena to be eliminated to miscues as the by-product of the reading process has made possible a revolution in viewpoint in which both the reader and the reading process may be regarded positively. The reader, particularly of a native language, may be regarded as a competent user of language whose language competence is reflected in miscues produced as a proficient reader and at all stages of acquisition of reading proficiency.

By moving away from a simplistic view that reading must be accurate we are able to see, through miscues, how the efficient and effective reader operates. We can further define effectiveness in reading as the ability to construct a message (comprehend) and define efficiency as the ability to use the least amount of available cues necessary to get to the meaning. Miscues are produced in efficient reading but they are likely to either leave meaning unaffected or be corrected by the reader. As efficiency increases, frequency of miscues tends to decrease; but this is the result and not the cause of efficiency.

AN EMERGING MISCUE TAXONOMY

In early miscue research we sought simple cause-effect relationships. We began to recognize that there were graphic cues from the perception of the print itself, phonic cues which relate print to speech, syntactic cues which derive from the structure of the language, and semantic cues from the meaning. But we looked for a one-to-one cause-effect relationship. We tried to classify some miscues as grapho-phonic (combining the first two since the cues are the same), some as syntactic, some as semantic. We soon became aware that we could not fragment the process of reading, that every event involved the use of all three systems. Consider this example:

> Text Wait a *moment*.
> Reader Wait a *minute*.

The reader substitutes *minute* for *moment*. The observed response (OR) looks like and sounds like the expected response to some extent. But *minute* and *moment* also have the same grammatical function and mean the same thing. All of the three sorts of cues and their interactions contribute to the miscue. Furthermore the reader who is American is more likely to use *minute* than *moment* which the British writer has used. So the reader has shown that the influence of dialect is also at work.

A taxonomy for the analysis of oral reading miscues has emerged over a period of years in a series of studies. Each miscue is examined by asking a number of questions about the relationship of expected to observed response. All relevant questions are answered independently. What emerges then is the pattern of how the cuing systems are used in ongoing reading.

Here are the questions which are asked:
1. Is the miscue self-corrected by the reader?
2. Is the reader's dialect involved in the miscue?
3. How much graphic similarity is there between ER and OR?
4. How much phonemic similarity is there?
5. Is the OR an allolog of the ER? *Typing* and *typewriting* are allologs of the same word. Contractions are also allologs.
6. Does the miscue produce a syntactically acceptable text?
7. Does the miscue produce a semantically acceptable text?
8. Does a grammatical retransformation result from the miscue?
9. If the miscue is syntactically acceptable, how much is syntax changed?
10. If the miscue is semantically acceptable, how much is meaning changed?
11. Is intonation involved in the miscue? In English, changed intonation may reflect change in syntax, meaning, or both.
12. Does the miscue involve the submorphemic language level?
13. Does the miscue involve the bound morpheme level?
14. Does the miscue involve the phrase or free morpheme level?
15. Does the miscue involve the phrase level?
16. Does the miscue involve the clause level?
17. What is the grammatical category of the OR?
18. What is the grammatical category of the ER?
19. What is the relationship between function of ER and OR?
20. What influence has the surrounding text (peripheral visual field) had on miscues?
21. What is the semantic relationship between ER and OR word substitutions?

Miscue analysis using this taxonomy is suitable for depth research on small numbers of subjects. Typically, our research has involved 3-6 subjects selected because they have common characteristics. These subjects are asked to read one or more full selections. In our most recent research our subjects have been asked to read two stories. Comparing profiles on both stories adds to the depth of our insights into the process.

A simpler form of miscue analysis dealing with only the more significant questions has been developed by Yetta M. Goodman and Carolyn Burke. This form has been used in some research studies, but it is designed for use by teachers and clinicians as a diagnostic tool. It also has found wide use in teacher education as a means of helping preservice and inservice teachers to understand the reading process.

PSYCHOLINGUISTICS AS A BASE FOR STUDY OF READING

Reading and listening are receptive language processes. Speaking and writing are generative, productive, language processes. The reader or the listener is actively involved in the reconstruction of a message. He must comprehend meaning in order to be considered successful.

Meaning is not a property of the graphic display. The writer has moved from thought to language, encoding his meaning as a graphic display just as the speaker moves from thought to language encoding his meanings as a phonological sequence. The reader decodes the graphic display and reconstructs meaning.

Whether one wishes to understand reading as a process to teach initial literacy or to help readers become more effective, one must start from a base of psycholinguistics, the study of the interrelationships of thought and language. All the central questions involved in reading are psycholinguistic questions, because reading is a process in which language interacts with thought. Psycholinguistics is foundational to all understanding of the reading process.

In research and instruction, learning to read has been commonly equated with learning to match an alphabetic orthography with its oral language counterpart. Reading instruction has frequently either been minimal, considered to be complete once the orthography is mastered, or endlessly repetitious and barren for those learners who persist in not acquiring correspondences between oral and written language. Skills have been taught on the basis of tradition with no insight into their relationship to the basic function of reading, reconstructing the message. The result is the most common, persistent, and disabling reading problem in all cultures: people who have learned to respond orally to print but who cannot or do not comprehend what they are reading. Reading becomes a print-to-speech short circuit. Those who cannot get meaning from written language are just as functionally illiterate as those who never received instruction.

A PSYCHOLINGUISTIC THEORY OF READING ENGLISH

A theory and model of the reading process has grown out of research with young American readers of English. The theory has evolved as a means of interpreting the differences between OR and ER in order to understand the process of reading.

Behavior, whether linguistic or any other, is the end product of a process. The external behavior is observable and serves as an indicator of the underlying competence. Behavior can be observed but it cannot be understood without some theory of how it is produced. Seemingly identical behaviors may result from very different processing. Very different behaviors may prove closely related if they are seen within a theoretical framework.

Comparison of OR and ER in miscues is a powerful means of inferring the process readers are using in dealing with specific reading tasks. When reading is as expected, the process is not discernible, but when it has produced miscues, then the information used by readers and the ways in which they use it may be seen.

The following is the beginning of a short story as read by five relatively proficient readers aged 13-15. It will serve to illustrate the miscue phenomena and to introduce the theory of the reading process.

Miscues of Five Readers

Subject 1.

> It must have been around mid-
> night when I drove home, and as I ap-
> proached the gates of the bungalow I
> switched off the head lamps of the car *lights*
> so the beam wouldn't swing in through *on*
> the window of the side bedroom and
> wake Harry Pope,

Subject 2.

> It must have been around mid-
> night when I drove home, and as I ap-
> proached the gates of the bungalow I
> switched off the head lamps of the car *2.lights*
> so the beam wouldn't swing in through
> the window of the side bedroom and
> wake Harry Pope.

Subject 3.

> It must have been around mid-
> night when I drove home; and as I ap- *As*
> proached the gates of the bungalow I
> switched off the head lamps of the car *lights*
> so the beam wouldn't swing in through
> the window of the side bedroom and
> *where* *was—*
> wake Harry Pope.

Subject 4.
It must have been around midnight when I drove home, and as I approached the gates of the bungalow I
switched off the head lamps of the car
so the beam wouldn't swing in through
the window of the side bedroom and
wake Harry Pope.

Subject 5.
It must have been around midnight when I drove home, and as I approached the gates of the bungalow I
switched off the head lamps of the car
so the beam wouldn't swing in through
the window of the side bedroom and
wake Harry Pope.

The first phenomenon which can be seen here is a common tendency among these readers to substitute *lights* for *lamps* in line four. The two words start with the same sound and letter but the relationship between the words is clearly semantic. Unless one assumes some kind of pervasive habitual association between these two words, one must conclude 1) that the readers are anticipating what they will in fact see, and 2) that they are more likely to expect *lights* than *lamps*. Notice, in fact, that subject 2 says *lamps*, rejects that in favor of *lights*, and then goes back to *lamps*. This is a good example of the reading process at work. This British writer has used the term *head lamps*. Our American subjects prefer the term *headlights* and have already predicted it. Subsequent graphic input, however, contradicts the prediction. Some of the readers reprocess, however they have already gotten the meaning from the initial processing and must have done so before they said *lights* if it is meaning which influenced their choices.

The words which are omitted by these five readers offer more insights into the process. *As* in line two is omitted by two readers, one of whom corrects. *In* in line five is omitted by three readers, one of whom corrects. Subject 1 substitutes *on* for *in*.

If we examine these for both cause and effect these insights emerge:

As may produce miscues (unexpected responses) because it follows *and* and introduces a dependent clause which precedes the independent

Miscue Analysis

clause it relates to. That requires that the *as* clause be processed, stored, and held until the following clause is processed before the meaning is fully clear. Omission of *as* changes the structure so that the hitherto dependent clause is independent conjoined by *and* to the preceding independent clause. A problem is then created since now there is no signal left as to the relationship between the new independent clause and the clause starting with *I* at the end of line three. The omission of *as* creates a sequence with an unacceptable grammatical structure. The reader who corrected seemed aware of this problem before he was aware of the precise omission because he repeated *and I* three times before a successful correction. The reader who did not correct inserts a conjunction *and* before *I* in line three producing parallel independent clauses.

Subject three omits *and* before *as* on line two. This conjunction turns out to be optional since the prior clause is independent.

The omission of *in* before *through* on line five results in little loss of semantic or syntactic information. The readers appeared to omit an element perhaps redundant in their American dialects. One substitutes *on* for *in* which may be more likely in her dialect in this context.

Subject five replaces *of the side bedroom* with *at the side of the bedroom*. In doing so he makes a minor change in the meaning but produces a new structure which is both meaningful and grammatical.

Subject three moves even farther away from the text at the end of the paragraph. He substitutes *where Harry Pope was* for *and wake Harry Pope*. Apparently he expected it to conclude with *sleeping*. He realizes his expectation is not borne out and regresses, reprocesses and corrects.

The miscues of these readers can not be explained by viewing reading as a process of sequential letter or word identification. If it were so, then miscues would be more evenly distributed and be confined to words or word parts.

Even with the one word in this paragraph that did cause some recognition problems, *bungalow*, the problems cannot be seen simply as letter-sound (phonics) or word recognition based. It may be that the problem comes from a mismatch between the reader's definition (and concept) of a bungalow and the writer's. Americans commonly use bungalow to refer to a very modest house or vacation home. Furthermore we can't be sure that those readers who exhibited no difficulty with *bungalow* understood its use by this author in this context.

Several key concepts about the reading process are required to begin to explain the miscues of these readers.

1. Anticipation or prediction is an important part of the reading process.

2. Readers process syntactic or grammatical information as they

read and this plays an important role in their ability to predict what they have not yet seen or processed.

3. Meaning is the end product of the reading process and effective readers are meaning-seekers.

4. Meaning is also input in the reading process. The success of the reader in comprehending is largely a function of the conceptual and experiential background he brings to the task and which his processing of the writer's language evokes in him.

5. Graphic information (letters, letter constituents, and patterns of letters) is by no means the sole input in the reading process. Nor is the matching of such information to phonological information a necessarily significant part of the reading process.

6. Accuracy in oral reading is not a prerequisite to effective reading. Comprehension is the basic goal and a focus on accuracy may be counterproductive.

The reader must begin with this graphic display and somehow decode it in such a way that he reconstructs the author's message.

Any passage may be analyzed for letters, words or meaning. The last focus is a much more efficient one in that the amount of information needed to get to the meaning is far less than if words or letters must be first analyzed. Thus, to be both *effective* and *efficient*, reading must be focused on meaning.

An effective, efficient reader uses the least amount of information necessary to reconstruct the writer's message. This is only possible if he is able to sample from available cues those which are most productive, that is, those that carry the most information. To do so he must use strategies which he develops that make it possible to predict and guess at the other available information without actually processing it. The reader's knowledge of the grammatical system of the language and the constraints within that system as well as the semantic constraints within the concepts dealt with constitute the parameters within which the reader's strategies are operating.

To get from print to meaning, the reader must treat the graphic display as a surface representation of an underlying structure. He must not only process the graphic display as a grammatically structured language sequence but he must assign an underlying or deep structure in order to process the interrelationships between clauses.

Consider, for example, the paragraph cited above as read by these subjects. This paragraph is a single sentence composed of clauses combined in complex ways so that the meaning of the whole is more than that of any one clause. Rewritten as a string of one clause sentences which express about the same meaning, it might read like this:

It must have been around midnight. I drove home at midnight. I approached the gates of the bungalow. (at the same time) I switched off the headlamps of the car. (in order that) The beam wouldn't swing in through the window of the bedroom. The bedroom was at the side. (in order that) The beam wouldn't wake Harry Pope.

The reader must deal with an underlying structure by interpreting signals in the surface structure because meaning relates not to the surface structure but to underlying structure.

The writer has produced the graphic display starting with meaning, assigning a deep grammatical structure, then transforming this deep structure by use of transforming rules and subsequently applying a set of orthographic rules to produce a surface representation in the form of a graphic display.

This process is much the same as speaking except that the final rules are orthographic rather than phonological. In use, the graphic display and oral language are alternate surface representations of the deep structure. Writing is not a secondary representation of speech. This is obvious in nonalphabetic writing systems. It is no less true in alphabetic systems even though there are direct relationships between the two surface representations.

The alphabetic systems are economical in that they are able to use a small number of symbols in patterned combinations to express an unlimited number of meanings, just as oral language does. And using the oral language symbols as a base for the written symbols is both convenient and logical. But if readers found it necessary to identify letters and match them with sounds or even identify word shapes and match them with oral names, then efficient reading would be slower than speech. But efficient readers use distinctive features of letters to move from print to deep structure and meaning. Their ability to identify letters or words they have read *follows* rather than *precedes* their assignment of deep structure and meaning. Once they know what they have read they also know the words they have read and their spellings. In this manner they *appear* to identify graphic elements much more rapidly than they could actually do so.

Essentially the same deep language structure underlies both speech and writing. There are, of course, different circumstances in which oral and written language are used. The former is much more likely to be in a situational context which may be indicated by gesture or which need no explanation. Written language, on the other hand, is most often abstracted from the situations it deals with. It must create its own setting and be a much more complete representation of the message to achieve effective communication. But these differences are more those of use than of process.

The reader samples the three systems of cues in order to be aware of and predict surface structure and induce deep structure and meaning.

The reader responds to what he sees or what he thinks he sees. His experience with and knowledge of the graphic symbols (letters), spelling patterns, sequencing rules and redundancies set up expectations. He is able to use distinctive features to form perceptual images which are partly the result of what he expects to see.

Subject five thought the name was *Henry* rather than *Harry*. The two names differ graphically in very minor ways. She had no reason to reject that having produced it since it fits both meaning and grammar constraints.

A minimum amount of syntactic information, that *as* is a marker of a clause for example, makes it possible to predict a surface structure and almost simultaneously begin to induce an underlying structure. Punctuation, part of the graphic cue system, comes mostly at the end of sequences in English and therefore is of little use except as a check on prediction. One must predict the pattern in order to process subsequent elements.

For a proficient reader to get directly to meaning he must draw on his knowledge of the patterns, rules, constraints, and redundancies of the grammatical system.

Even beginning readers in our research substitute *a* for *the*, an indication that they use grammatical as well as graphic cues. As the surface structure is predicted, the rules by which that structure is linked to the underlying deep structure are evoked and serve as additional cues.

Because of the limited number of patterns, the constraints within these patterns (only certain elements may follow certain others), and the redundancy of language (every cue does not carry a new bit of information) a reader is able to sample those cues which carry the most information and predict whole patterns on that basis.

Sampling, selecting, and predicting are basic aspects of reading. They require development by the reader of comprehension strategies which control the choice and use of cues and keep the reader oriented to the goal of reading which is meaning.

When miscues effect meaning the reader must be aware that they do and correct. He uses a set of confirmation strategies as he proceeds. He asks himself 1) whether he can predict a grammatical sequence on the basis of information processed, 2) whether he can assign a decodable deep structure, and 3) whether what he has decoded as meaning in fact makes sense.

As he continues to process information he is constantly alert to information which contradicts his prediction. As long as subsequent information confirms, he proceeds. If any contradictory information is encountered he must reprocess to reconcile the conflicting information. This may require a new hypothesis about what is coming. The problems with *as* that our subjects had and their subsequent responses illustrate this process at work.

Reading then becomes a sample, predict, test, confirm, and correct when necessary process.

The constant concern for meaning as output makes meaning input as well. The deep structure must be decodable, the reader must know whether what he had decoded makes sense. Furthermore, experience and concepts must be evoked to create a semantic context and a set of semantic constraints which correspond to the syntactic constraints.

Memory functions as a kind of highly cross-referenced lexicon feeding the most appropriate referential meaning into the processing to complete the set of semantic cues.

No person, however literate, is ever able to read all that is written in his native language. The ability to read any selection is a function of the semantic background one brings to it. Without substantial meaning input, effective reading is not possible. Literacy is by no means a constant for any individual for all reading tasks.

NEW VIEWS OF OLD QUESTIONS

Miscue analysis and the psycholinguistic view of reading suggest the need for reconsidering old issues. Here, a few of these can only be listed. In each case the traditional view seems to be at odds with this new view.

1. Where should reading instruction begin? Not with letters or sounds but with whole real relevant natural language we think.
2. What is the hierarchy of skills that should be taught in reading instruction? We think there is none. In fact, in learning to read as in learning to talk, one must use all skills at the same time.
3. Why do some people fail to learn to read? Not because of their weaknesses but because we've failed to build on their strengths as competent language users.
4. What should we do for deficient readers? Build their confidence in their ability to predict meaning and language.
5. Can anyone learn to read? Yes, we say. Anyone who can learn oral language can learn to read and write.

SOME NEW QUESTIONS

There is still a lot to be learned about reading. Many new questions emerge as reading is seen from a new vantage point.

1. How does the difference in grammatical structure of different languages influence the reading process?
2. How does the reading process differ in nonalphabetic writing systems?
3. How do variations among readers in conceptual development influence their reading and their comprehension?
4. Can methods be devised for teaching people to read languages they don't speak? This question is of particular importance in countries where college texts are in languages other than the national language.

Perhaps the most basic question we need to ask is how can we put these new scientific insights to use in achieving the goal of universal literacy.

Reading Flexibility: A Neglected Aspect of Reading Instruction

Theodore L. Harris
University of Puget Sound
Tacoma, Washington
United States of America

No one can gainsay that the development of functional literacy among the peoples of the world is an objective of prime importance. Yet the attainment of this objective has created problems in such a country as the United States where an enormous amount of time, energy and money has been expended without a satisfactory resolution of an adequate level of literacy in several million pupils. It is to this problem that current efforts spearheaded by the Right to Read division in the United States Office of Education are addressed on a nationwide basis.

But if there is a right to read, surely there is a right to be a flexible reader. A flexible reader is one whose command of reading processes enables him to successfully integrate three important variables in the reading act: his purpose for reading, the material which he reads, and his speed of reading. The purposes for reading may be externally or internally guided. The materials for reading may vary in difficulty, style, appeal, and a host of other factors. Yet the speed with which one reads with comprehension appropriate to varied purposes and materials is the crucial mark of the flexible reader. Such a conception is not inconsistent with the original concept of the Right to Read advanced by former United States Commissioner of Education Allen. While he stressed such things as the ability to read and the desire to read, his statement was not limited just to the rudiments of reading. On the contrary, his conception of the Right to Read embraced all levels of reading ability and all levels of schooling from young adult to adult. Thus I believe the Right to Read must likewise embrace the more sophisticated levels of reading development as well as the basic aspects of functional literacy. Developing more flexible readers in our school population is therefore a basic right if they are to function effectively in society.

There is, however, another reason for considering that flexibility in reading is a fundamental part of basic reading instruction. Conceivably, basic reading programs which have not given due attention to the concept of variability in reading purposes and tasks, whether internally or externally motivated, may be a contributing factor to many reading failures. That is, the conventional beginning orientation to careful, systematic and detailed reading in which total recall is the virtue to be rewarded may, if continued, soon become counterproductive in developing an adaptable, flexible reader. This matter may be of concern to other countries as well as to the United States.

My interest in this topic stems from several sources. One reason is because of my involvement in an extended cooperative research study (4) on this topic. A second reason is the perennial controversy surrounding the proper role of reading speed. We have, for example, the extended debates on the merits of the use of films and machines versus classroom procedures for developing reading speed, and the questionable claims of the commercial purveyors of rapid reading courses, both of which beg the question of the concept of flexibility. An example of this is this advertisement from a magazine (12):

DOUBLE YOUR READING SPEED IN ONE WEEK!
by Martin K. Roan

Finish an entire novel in a single evening! Slash through a business report in 60 seconds! Read a complete magazine article in 3 minutes! And what's more, understand twice as much—and remember twice as much!

A more important reason, however, is my feeling that there is still a fundamental lack of understanding among teachers about the speed component in reading and how to handle it. This is well illustrated by the almost unfailing response teachers make to this question: "Which is more important in reading, speed or comprehension?" When the question is put in this way, the answer is predictable: "Comprehension." Teachers know this is the right answer because textbooks tell them so. I suggest that such an answer is neither sufficient nor accurate.

First let us examine the notion of effective reading speed. Buswell (2), in the 1930s in his research on *How Adults Read,* considered speed of reading to be essentially a matter of perceptual efficiency in attaining minimal levels of comprehension. Using eye-movement photography, he demonstrated the marked inefficiency in reading among adults whose eye fixations were excessive and whose span of recognition was narrow. Out of his laboratory at the University of Chicago came the first reading pacers which were designed by film projection and by sliding plates to force more rapid speed of recognition. He demonstrated some success in reducing perceptual inefficiency and hence in improving reading speed in his subjects. He likewise proposed that a goal of the schools should be to produce readers capable of reading 500 words per minute. Forty years have passed. How much progress have we made toward such a goal? Very little.

Perhaps one reason that we have not moved more rapidly toward such a goal is due to a different conception of the nature of effective reading speed held by another professor at the same institution, William S. Gray. He believed that reading speed was not simply a matter of perceptual efficiency but of interpretive speed. Gray argued that the concept of reading speed involved more complex comprehension or thinking processes than Buswell admitted. He insisted that speed of reading comprehension, not mere perceptual fluency, should be the ultimate criterion. His view has largely prevailed in reading instruction. In my opinion, however, this view has also led to a disproportionate emphasis upon the virtues of thorough comprehension to the detriment of a realistic instructional emphasis upon flexible and efficient reading speeds *with* comprehension.

The nature of materials has also been shown to influence reading speed. Early experiments by Judd and Buswell (8) in the 1920s demonstrated that mature good readers vary their speed according to the nature and difficulty of the materials. Later, in the 1940s Blommers (1) showed that good junior high school comprehenders varied their reading speeds according to the difficulty of the materials. Poor comprehenders did not; they kept on plodding away at the same speed. Blommers' study is of particular interest because of the age group studied, the controls placed on the difficulty of materials, and the fact that speed of comprehension was defined as the time taken to successfully find the answer to a specific question.

The important role of purpose in reading was acknowledged as early as 1908 by Huey (7) in his succinct statement that even mature readers "read by phrases, words, or letters as we may serve our purpose best." In the 1960s Henderson (6) showed that pupils can be taught to identify their own purposes for reading and vary their reading speed accordingly. Similarly, in the research (4) with which I was associated, nine, ten, and eleven-year-olds were able to intelligently self-select their own instructional sequences from among passages to be read for one of three reading purposes and vary their reading speed accordingly in attaining such purposes.

Thus we may see that there are conflicting notions about what speed of reading itself involves. Indeed, there are formidable problems in measuring successive samples of a person's speed of reading as Rankin (10) has recently noted. I would particularly stress the point that reading speed is relative to what you are reading and what you want to get out of it. Furthermore, the key to the efficient use of reading speed is flexibility in its application. I believe we should disabuse ourselves once and for all that reading speed is an absolute factor. It is not, many prevailing notions and reading programs to the contrary. One way to illustrate the absurdity of thinking about reading speed in an absolute sense is to enjoy with me a satirical piece which I ran across several years ago entitled "Confessions of the World's Fastest Reader" (9), reprinted below by permission of *Saturday Review* and the author.

The way you do rapid reading is to forget the old way and start at the top of the page and read right down the middle, taking in what you can out toward the edges of the page or column. You start taking in blocks of words, then blocks of several lines, then paragraphs, and finally you are gulping whole pages—at least the center part of the pages.

By the time I finished my third course in rapid reading I was racing along at the unbelievable speed of 4,900 words a minute. And the fourth course saw me more than triple that rate to achieve an unheard-of 18,000 words a minute. "That's equivalent to space travel at 18,000 miles an hour," the rapid reading man said gleefully.

I was missing a page now and then, a chapter here and there, but my speed had never been better. Confidentially, 18,000 words a minute is a terrifying speed, even for reading, like being chased down a dark hall by howling banshees. Still, nobody had ever read this fast before. I was ready for the big test.

My reading marathon, lasting five days, was held under the auspices of the National Institute of Space Age Reading (NISAR). I began at 6 a.m. on Monday, warming up with the Koran and the Bible. I was near the end of the New Testament, at twenty-nine minutes out, before I hit orbital speed of 18,000 words a minute.

The collected works of Shakespeare I went through in fifty-five minutes flat. I was burning along now at roughly a million words an hour. I felt some weightlessness that interfered with comprehension, but it did not affect speed.

Next came *War and Peace*, finished in forty minutes. At 9 a.m. just past my three-millionth word, I had a ten-minute break and a cup of coffee. Thirty other famous novels followed. With thirty minutes out for lunch, I stopped the first day at 4:10 p.m., having soared through 9,600,000 words in nine hours and forty minutes.

That first day was really a warm-up for a long, grueling three days—from beginning to end of the *Encyclopaedia Britannica*. Reading twelve hours a day—Tuesday, Wednesday, and Thursday—I blasted through 39 million words in thirty-six hours.

Friday was easier. In the home stretch I was more relaxed, though weightlessness of the head continued to bother my comprehension. A ten-volume set of selected poetry was polished off in thirty minutes. Then came twenty "Great Books" that kept me rocketing along for three hours. Ten fat books on the Civil War, one day's publishing output, occupied me for an hour and a half, at the end of which I stopped for lunch. Soon I was back in orbit again.

I was preparing to land now, the finish line in view. In a little less than two hours I orbited through Winston Churchill's six-volume set of *The Second World War*. "Their Finest Hour" lasted only sixteen minutes.

At the end of Churchill I began to fire mental retro-rockets to slow my speed. These "retros," as they are called, are gimmicks worked out by the rapid reading experts. You begin occasionally to point little mental jets of vision out toward the edges of the page, picking up fringe words and ideas. It works beautifully.

At a somewhat slower pace, perhaps 10,000 words a minute, I flashed through Carl Sandburg's multi-volume life of Abraham Lincoln, crossing the finish line at 1:10 p.m. with the Gettysburg address. In fifty-two hours I had read 54,500,000 words—a feat no other human being had ever accomplished.

Here's a tiny example of what reading is like at that speed Starting at the top—down through the middle, you know—the Gettysburg Address comes through like this: "Years ago in on of what should consecrate dead to we the living who to be from which resolve God people by." A great speech, I say.

When I was officially declared the world's fastest reader, the reporters present kept asking me these silly questions. What did I get out of such a fantastic reading bout?

"Don't be pre-atomic," I told them. "This is the space age, man! I read those books I always wanted to read. And I got a world speed record out of it, didn't I?"

What did I get in the way of meaning, understanding, enjoyment? Nothing. I get my kicks from TV.

Seriously, though, we still need to ask the question "Is reading speed an important component in the reading act?" I believe it is. Otherwise, why do we have crash programs in speed reading in high schools, in colleges, among adults—whether they be doctors, engineers, or salesmen? Clearly, far too many people have not learned to read efficiently the materials their needs and purposes demand, to say nothing of their inability to vary their reading speed. I am inclined to believe that Buswell's suggestion that schools seek to develop average reading speeds of 500 words per minute is both realistic and necessary for certain purposes and for certain types of materials. We still need to ask such questions as "Do schools and teachers recognize speed as an important component in reading instruction?" "Are schools and teachers working to produce flexible readers?" and "How highly valued is efficiency in the reading act?" As late as 1963, there was no published evidence that United States schools produce flexible readers.

There is, however, more recent research evidence that flexibility in reading speed can be taught to nine-year-olds in the United States. This was the purpose of the cooperative research project on the experimental development of variability of reading speed conducted by the

Laboratory of Research in Basic Skills at the University of Wisconsin and published in 1965 (4). In this study we worked with three specified purposes for reading: reading for the main idea, reading to find a specific fact, and reading for the sequence of ideas. In seeking materials for training and testing we first went to textbooks in the hope of finding appropriate passages. It may interest you to know that we found virtually none that was suitable for our purposes. We found that in order to control such passages for length, difficulty, and content appropriate for each of the three reading purposes, we had to write materials according to rigid specifications. For example, each paragraph to be read for the main idea had to have only one clearly distinguishable main idea. When sufficient passages were available, training sessions were set up with small groups of the seventy-two carefully selected fourth grade pupils who were reading at or above grade level in order to teach them the concept of each of the three reading purposes. In order to measure speed of comprehension accurately, we set a criterion of 100 percent comprehension which was measured as the actual amount of time taken, including time for rereading, to read for comprehension. Three different types of tests for comprehension were devised which were relevant to each of the three reading purposes.

Several results of this study were most interesting. Our original hypothesis was that the children we were working with would have a relatively invariant, generalized speed set in reading as such research as was available might indicate. Apparently, however, in our training session we did such a good job of clarifying the different purposes for reading that on pretesting, these children did vary their speed to a certain extent. This finding was unexpected but reassuring. The more salient finding was that, with only two weeks of short daily training sessions, our nine-year-olds learned to vary their speed of reading significantly according to reading purpose. Furthermore, they retained this flexibility in varying reading speed according to purpose three weeks later. The actual gains in reading speed for each purpose were approximately 40 percent as a result of training, and further gains were also evident on our retention tests three weeks later. We also found that these children were able to adjust their reading speeds to reading purposes significantly differently according to the style of the passage; expository materials rather than narrative materials usually produced the greatest speed increments. The greatest improvement in reading speed was in relation to the reading purposes of reading for the main idea and reading to find a specific fact. Some evidence was otherwise gained that these children became more accurate in predicting their reading speeds for the reading purpose with which they were most familiar, reading for the sequence of ideas. Similar results, however, were not found for reading for the main idea or for reading to find a specific fact.

Since this study and a follow-up study (5) by our research group, involving the transfer effects of such training to speed variability in reading longer selections of several paragraphs, demonstrate nicely that flexibility in reading can be encouraged and developed quite readily if specific attention is given to this matter, there are, I believe, a number of implications for the development of flexibility of reading by teachers. One thing we can do is to examine textbooks and other matter, such as newspapers and magazines, to identify materials suitable for differentiated purposes for reading and seek to identify with pupils reading speeds appropriate to such purposes and materials. Certainly we can begin by asking ourselves, "Is the purpose/speed relationship the same for fiction, history, mathematics, and poetry? Should it be the same for each of these?" A second thing we can do is to examine the specific characteristics of materials themselves that may affect reading speed and thus require a flexible adjustment on the part of the reader. We may look for such characteristics as the vocabulary burden of a passage; specifically, the proportion of difficult and abstract ideas in a passage. We may look for elements of writing style to which adjustments may be made. For example, is the passage a theorem to be understood, or a descriptive narrative passage to be savored? A former colleague of mine once remarked that he spends most of his time trying to get his students to slow down their reading speed. In this case, the reason was fairly obvious; he was a professor of statistics. We may also examine materials to determine whether the language patterns are familiar or unusual. Such characteristics as these and others need to be considered by both teacher and pupil in making the proper adjustment to the reading of such materials.

A third thing that we can do is to be extremely careful to evaluate only those aspects of reading comprehension that are really pertinent to the reading purpose and, for that matter, to the nature of the material read. In this respect I think we should be more critical of typical textbook comprehension questions. They should be carefully examined in terms of their relevance to their teaching purposes. They should also be examined for similar relevance to the reading purposes of the pupils. I suggest that it is also particularly important that we distinguish between relevant detail and the many extraneous "filler-type" detailed questions often found in connection with certain passages in textbooks. If such questions are not appropriate, then appropriate ones should be invented and used. A fourth thing that is implied from the study I have cited in some detail is that we can surely begin developing efficiency and attaining flexibility in reading early in schooling, perhaps as early as the command of fundamental reading skills is attained. But we must also continue to stress adaptation of reading speed to reading purposes and materials continuously throughout schooling if such flexibility is to function effectively then and later. The development of flexible readers is not a stop and go proposition; it is a matter of continued application. Finally, and perhaps most importantly, we must get across the idea of importance of flexibility in reading speed to the pupil in terms he can understand. Our ultimate goal should be to make the pupil more self-reliant in determining his own reading purposes, more aware of the salient characteristics of materials to which he should attend, and more skillful in gauging and using appropriate reading speeds. There is evidence that this can be done relatively early in the process of learning to read.

In the preceding presentation, I have deliberately emphasized only one of several concepts of reading flexibility (the given task-oriented purpose) in order to judge whether children age nine can be taught to vary their reading speeds when selection difficulty is controlled and full comprehension is required. The affirmative reaction after two short weeks of specific training strongly suggests that such children have unsuspected capabilities for learning flexible reading habits; or, perhaps more properly stated, for displaying the ability to vary reading speed when they understand and accept the idea that different purposes and materials make different comprehension demands, some of which may be attained more efficiently and rapidly than others. It would seem, in other words, that the relatively inflexible reading habits so common in the early years, habits which may become firmly crystallized in later years, really represent a psychological "set" toward the reading act which is encouraged by typical early reading practices and signal to the learner to read slowly enough to provide for all detailed comprehension contingencies.

Further evidence that nine-year-olds can vary their reading speed when they know the type of questions they will be asked, is reported by Samuels and Dahl in a forthcoming article (11). They demonstrate that reading a practice selection for a given purpose only, either general or detailed understanding, produced significant differences in reading speed on a subsequent test selection. This study gives additional evidence that the potential for developing early reading flexibility—for becoming aware of and using purposes wisely, for becoming sensitive to the comprehension demands of different types of materials, for being selective and efficient in controlling reading speed—is already present in many children who are reading up to their expectancy whether they reveal this flexibility in the ordinary demands of the classroom. If these studies can be documented by further studies, possibly with eight-year-olds, I submit that we should work to replace a relatively invariant reading speed set with one that is variable and responsive to the reading needs of pupils. We should do this much earlier than in the past. We cannot afford to wait until the invariant set of the inflexible reader is so ingrained in older pupils that it is then difficult and costly to alter.

REFERENCES

1. Blommers, Paul J. "Rate of Comprehension of Reading: Its Measurement in Relation to Comprehension," *Journal of Educational Psychology*, 35 (1944), 449-472.
2. Buswell, Guy T. *How Adults Read*. University of Chicago, 1937.
3. Harris, Theodore L., educational collaborator. "Adjusting Your Reading Speed." Coronet Films.
4. Harris, Theodore L., and others. *Experimental Development of Variability in Rate of Reading in Grades 4, 5, and 6*. U.S. Office of Education Cooperative Research Project, No. 1755, University of Wisconsin, 1965.
5. Harris, Theodore L., and others. *Transfer Effects of Training Intermediate Grade Pupils to Adjust Reading Speed to Reading Purpose*. USOE Cooperative Research Project No. 3137, University of Wisconsin, 1966.
6. Henderson, Edmund H. "A Study of Individually Formulated Purposes for Reading," *Journal of Educational Research*, 1965, 438-441.
7. Huey, Edmund Burke. *The Psychology and Pedagogy of Reading*. New York: Macmillan, 1906.
8. Judd, Charles H., and Guy T. Buswell. *Silent Reading: A Study of the Various Types*. Chicago: University of Chicago, 1922.
9. Owsley, Clifford D. "Confessions of the World's Fastest Reader," *Saturday Review*, June 9, 1962.
10. Rankin, Earl F. *The Measurement of Reading Flexibility*. Newark, Delaware: International Reading Association, 1974.
11. Samuels, S. Jay, and Patricia Dahl. *Verbal Communication* (in press).
12. *True Magazine*, December 1973.

Reading as a Comparative Process

Ralph C. Staiger
International Reading Association
Newark, Delaware
United States of America

As all of us know, there are many ways to look at reading. It is a fascinating process, ability, constellation of skills, tool, aspect of language, or area of study—depending upon your vantage point. Among many other things, reading is also a comparative process in several ways, which I shall try to explore in this paper. It should be considered an exploratory rather than an exhaustive treatment.

Although reading has been called "a linguistic guessing game," it includes far more than guessing. The term has attracted some attention, and the definition particularly appears to appeal to some who are not familiar with the many ramifications of reading and who are satisfied by an oversimplified description. If we view reading as a comparative process, perhaps we can consider that reading heavily involves discrimination, which may lead to comparison, which may lead to memory, which hopefully leads to evaluation and sometimes to action.

Discrimination is a comparative exercise which is basic to reading. As a person learns his mother tongue, and indeed a second or additional language, he must discriminate first between or among the sounds of the language, and, later, the structure and patterns of the language. Some languages, especially in the Orient, use tones— Chinese and Thai— which complicate the discrimination process for a Westerner unaccustomed to these shadings of sounds. In Africa, clicks are used as a part of the sound system. This also complicates things for those of us who are unfamiliar with such sounds. The umlaut in German changes vowel sounds strangely for the English speaker. English, of course, is a dreadful language for the foreigner to learn, especially when he speaks a language in which the sound system corresponds fairly regularly with the written language. The reason for the difficulty of English is, of course, its orthography's relation to the sounds of the spoken language. Soffietti (2) indicated that while the Italian language has 24 letters in its alphabet, it has only 26 separate sounds. English, he estimated, has 26 letters, but about 250 sounds which can be represented by various combinations of those letters.

Anyone learning to read must make many orthographic discriminations. Some examples of difficult discriminations for young learners of English are the **b/p/d** letters, which it is estimated are confused by 70 percent of beginning readers; **m** and **w** appear to be confusing to speakers of other languages who take up English.

Discriminations among words or ideographs can also be considered a part of the learning-to-read process. In English, the words which Lin Yutang called "the small coin of language" offer particular difficulty. These are the *who, what, which, where, when, this, that, then, those* words. Who has not—and I am talking about experienced readers—confused words like *conscious* and *conscience* as he reads half-thinking in a newspaper, only to realize that he has failed to discriminate between the two when he gets to the end of the sentence?

Discriminating among ideas starts early and continues throughout life. I recall when I learned the difference between the meanings of street, road, highway, and boulevard. No doubt, you can recall a similar discrimination among words in your experience; and some visitors in Vienna are learning the difference between Strasse and Gasse. And in Vienna's Hofburg Center, the SALT Talks took place. The differences among *cease fire, armistice, disarmament* and *peace* are important to the future of mankind.

Memory is a very important aspect of reading as a comparative process, and also a very mysterious one. It may sometimes by a product of practice and overlearning. There is evidence that the readers of the Tom Swift/Enid Blighton/Karl May type of books are likely to become good readers of more substantial fare, perhaps from practice. But motivation can also play a critical role in memory. How else can we explain the phenomenal ability of some individuals to remember batting averages or football team standings, as well as the ability to retain, with little effort, scientific or technical information. Some persons who have eidetic imagery or photographic memory are difficult to explain in the present state of our psychological knowledge.

We do know that memory permits high-level comparisons, whether they be between baseball or football players, stories, literary genre, or historical data. The philosopher Santayana called this to our attention when he reminded us that those of us who do not read history are doomed to repeat the past. Reading is a phenomenon which provides us with part of our cultural memory and enables us to use information in comparable situations, if we will take the trouble to do so.

Another state in reading as a comparative process, and a very necessary step in high-level literacy, is evaluation. It is essentially a means of making decisions by use of the reading tool. Evaluation can be done at the level of prices and products; at the level of arguments—political, social, philosophical—and in the comparison of texts. In scholars, this is often a lifetime work. A. E. Houseman, who is remembered as a poet, spent most of his life analyzing classical texts. In journalism, a news story is not always directly related to a speech. Recently Andre Maulraux was interviewed (1), and he suggested that if St. Augustine, Voltaire, and Albert Einstein were in a discussion of the development of ideas, St. Augustine and Voltaire could have understood one another, but they could not have dealt with Einstein's ideas.

It seems to me that every educated person must use reading as a comparative process. The way it will be used will be dependent upon the intellectual curiosity and capacity of the reader; the degree to which comparative reading has been expected in his development, in school and outside school; the depth of interest he has in a topic; and the availability of materials.

The gauntlet has been thrown down to us as parents, to create a desire for our children to use reading as a comparative process, and to provide as many materials and incentives for them as is possible; and most importantly, the gauntlet has been thrown down to us as teachers. At every school level, the amount and quality of comparative reading done by the students is in part a reflection of the teacher.

We have our work cut out for us.

REFERENCES
1. *Newsweek, The International Newsmagazine,* August 12, 1974, 24-25.
2. Soffietti, James P. "Why Children Fail to Read," *Harvard Educational Review,* 25, No. 2, 63-84.

Reading Skills—What Reading Skills?

Arthur De W. Smith
Training Research and Development Station
Prince Albert, Saskatchewan, Canada

The literature of research in reading contains almost countless studies, models, theories, and strategies dealing with the various problems of what to teach, how to teach, how to test reading skills and how to determine readability levels. The literature embraces many diverse areas including comparative studies in the teaching of reading, special population studies such as the handicapped and ethnic groups, language development studies for those acquiring a new language, and basic research studies dealing mainly with various physical phenomena in reading as well as with verbal learning and information processing.

The aim of this paper is to examine the communications skills which are actually used in the performance of occupational work and to briefly comment on the implications of these skills insofar as they affect reading strategies and standards.

The term *communications skills* in this paper includes the skills of reading, writing, talking and listening. Excluded from this paper are those interpersonal skills which are also used in communications, such as eye contact, body posture, role distance, and other verbal and nonverbal attending skills.

GENERIC SKILLS RESEARCH

The generic skills project is a research study being carried out in Canada to determine those overt and covert behaviors which are fundamental to the performance of many tasks and subtasks carried out in a wide range of occupations. Generic skills include many of the concepts and skills generally referred to as mathematics skills, communications skills, reasoning skills, interpersonal skills, procedural skills, and motorsensory skills. The study is aimed at the needs for adult education and training.

Complete details of the study are included in the publications by Smith (5, 6), and by Smith, et al. (7).

SKILLS	PHASE I 27 OCCUPATIONS N - 680 SASKATCHEWAN			PHASE II 37 OCCUPATIONS N - 970 CANADA		
	a	b	c	a	b	c
READING COMPREHENSION						
Literal	94%	94%	27/27	91%	96%	37/37
Interpretive	64%	61%	27/27	70%	73%	20/37
Evaluative				21%	27%	4/37
TYPES OF READING						
Forms	89%	89%	27/27	82%	82%	37/37
Notes				87%	84%	34/37
Letters	91%	93%	27/27	65%	67%	32/37
Memos				82%	83%	34/37
Books and Manuals	85%	85%	27/27	80%	81%	36/37
Charts and Tables	61%	65%	21/27	53%	56%	23/37
Graphs	22%	29%	5/27	18%	20%	6/37
Scales	64%	64%	24/27	49%	54%	31/37
Scale Drawings	40%	37%	14/27	46%	44%	16/37
Assembly Drawings	-	-	-	40%	42%	11/37
Schematic Drawings	-	-	-	33%	33%	9/37
WRITING						
External Letters				21%	20%	9/37
Form Letters	44%	46%	23/27	14%	12%	6/37
Single Paragraph Letters				9%	10%	5/37
Internal Memos				27%	25%	13/37
Short Notes	70%	71%	24/27	45%	44%	19/37
Notes from Conversation				45%	44%	19/37
Forms: Phrases	83%	82%	27/27	72%	76%	37/37
Sentences	57%	57%	26/27	34%	41%	17/37
Paragraphs	41%	45%	25/27	19%	26%	7/37
Reports: Information	46%	49%	17/27	22%	23%	12/37
Recommendation	26%	30%	10/27	20%	21%	5/37
Technical	10%	13%	0/27	14%	13%	2/37

Codes: a - Percentage of workers who said they use the skill.

b - Percentage of supervisors who said that the skill is used by the workers.

c - Ratio of occupations who use the skill.

Plate 1. Reading and Writing Skills

SKILLS	PHASE I 27 OCCUPATIONS N - 680 SASKATCHEWAN			PHASE II 37 OCCUPATIONS N - 970 CANADA		
	a	b	c	a	b	c
LISTENING COMPREHENSION						
Literal	99%	99%	27/27	100%	100%	37/37
Interpretive	73%	70%	26/27	86%	87%	33/37
Evaluative				25%	28%	7/37
TALKING (ONE TO ONE) COMPREHENSION						
Give Job Directions	83%	78%	27/27	80%	75%	37/37
Give Job Information	96%	92%	27/27	94%	90%	37/37
Ask Job Questions	97%	92%	27/27	95%	94%	37/37
Debate with: Fellow Workers	91%	89%	27/27	80%	73%	37/37
Supervisors	94%	94%	27/27	81%	84%	36/37
Customers	-	-	-	54%	47%	20/37
Persuasive Conversation	-	-	-	6%	5%	2/37
Diverting Conversation	-	-	-	71%	65%	33/37
GROUP DISCUSSIONS						
Give Directions/Information	44%	49%	20/27	38%	30%	7/37
Give Persuasive Talks	-	-	-	5%	5%	1/37
Participate	-	-	-	40%	42%	11/37
Control	-	-	-	11%	15%	2/37
TALKS TO AUDIENCE						
Factual	6%	12%	-	9%	7%	2/37
Persuasive	-	-	-	6%	5%	2/37
INTERVIEW/COUNSEL						
Information Centered	-	-	-	15%	14%	4/37
Problem Centered	-	-	-	27%	26%	8/37
GIVE ON JOB						
Instruction	-	-	-	77%	71%	36/37
Demonstration	-	-	-	76%	72%	37/37

Codes: a - Percentage of workers who said they use the skill.
b - Percentage of supervisors who said that the skill is used by the workers.
c - Ratio of occupations who use the skill.

Plate 2. Listening and Talking Skills

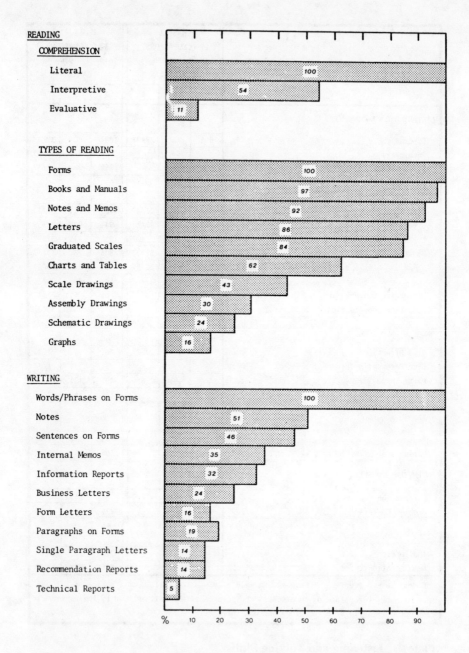

READING

COMPREHENSION
- Literal — 100
- Interpretive — 54
- Evaluative — 11

TYPES OF READING
- Forms — 100
- Books and Manuals — 97
- Notes and Memos — 92
- Letters — 86
- Graduated Scales — 84
- Charts and Tables — 62
- Scale Drawings — 43
- Assembly Drawings — 30
- Schematic Drawings — 24
- Graphs — 16

WRITING
- Words/Phrases on Forms — 100
- Notes — 51
- Sentences on Forms — 46
- Internal Memos — 35
- Information Reports — 32
- Business Letters — 24
- Form Letters — 16
- Paragraphs on Forms — 19
- Single Paragraph Letters — 14
- Recommendation Reports — 14
- Technical Reports — 5

% 10 20 30 40 50 60 70 80 90

Plate 3. Percentage of 37 Occupations using Reading and Writing Skills

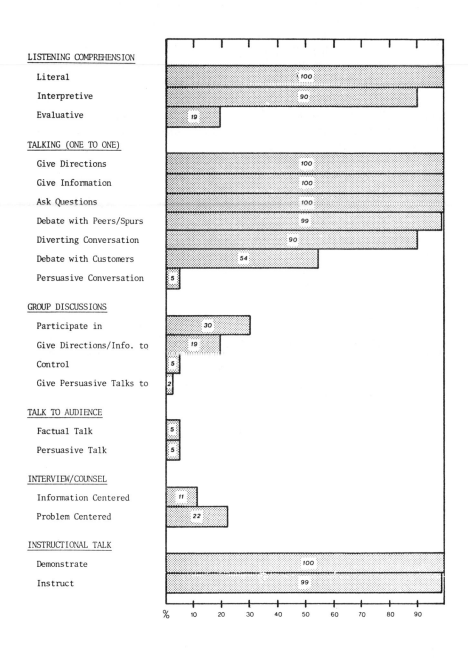

LISTENING COMPREHENSION
- Literal — 100
- Interpretive — 90
- Evaluative — 19

TALKING (ONE TO ONE)
- Give Directions — 100
- Give Information — 100
- Ask Questions — 100
- Debate with Peers/Spurs — 99
- Diverting Conversation — 90
- Debate with Customers — 54
- Persuasive Conversation — 5

GROUP DISCUSSIONS
- Participate in — 30
- Give Directions/Info. to — 19
- Control — 5
- Give Persuasive Talks to — 2

TALK TO AUDIENCE
- Factual Talk — 5
- Persuasive Talk — 5

INTERVIEW/COUNSEL
- Information Centered — 11
- Problem Centered — 22

INSTRUCTIONAL TALK
- Demonstrate — 100
- Instruct — 99

Plate 4. Percentage of 37 Occupations using Listening and Talking Skills

COMMUNICATIONS SKILLS USED BY SELECTED OCCUPATIONS

Data have been obtained in two surveys. In the first survey, which was carried out in urban and rural areas of the province of Saskatchewan, data were obtained from 340 workers, and, independently, from their 340 supervisors, in 27 different occupations. The occupations ranged from the aide or helper level up to technicians and covered a number of occupational families such as office workers, construction trades and transportation operators. The 27 occupations surveyed represent approximately 25 percent of Canada's labour force (excluding technical and professional).

The second survey was carried out in six of Canada's ten provinces. Data were obtained from 490 workers and 480 supervisors in 37 occupations (18 occupations repeated from the first survey). The first survey included 115 questions directly related to mathematics and communications skills. The second survey contained 226 questions related to mathematics, communications, interpersonal and reasoning skills.

The communications skills used, as indicated by the data obtained in the two surveys, are shown in Plates 1 and 2. There is appreciable agreement between the workers' and supervisors' responses. The questions were concrete rather than abstract and workmen's style of language was used to ensure a clear understanding of the intent of each question. This agreement clearly indicates that supervisors know what skills are actually used by their subordinates.

Despite the fact that the second survey included only 18 occupations in common with the first survey, there is marked agreement in skill usage between the two surveys. This indicates that the skills identified are generic to many occupations. As of the time of writing this paper, the results of the two surveys have not been integrated. However, the data from the second survey have been analyzed to determine the skills requirements by each occupation and the percentages (of the 37 occupations) who use each skill.

The graphs in Plates 3 and 4 show the percentages of occupations using various communications skills for task performance. The matrix in Chart 1 shows selected communications skills required by the 37 occupations.

OBSERVATIONS FROM PLATES 3 AND 4

The information derived in these studies should be considered in the context of a much larger array of skills than those which the author has called "communications" skills. If the study had been concentrated on only the skill areas discussed in this paper, then it is probable that more discrete treatment would have been made. No attempt, for example, was

CHART 1 — SELECTED COMMUNICATIONS SKILLS * - skill required 0 - skill optional		Policeman	Draftsman	Insurance Salesman	Farmer	Packaging Machine Mech.	Sheet Metal Worker	Radio & TV Serviceman	Lineman	Sales Representative	Electrician	Motor Vehicle Mech.	Hardware Sales Person	Nursing Assistant	Small Engine Mech.	Cook	Accountant Clerk	Sales Clerk	Painter	Nurse Aide	Bookkeeping Clerk	Bookkeeping, Clerical	Truck Driver	Carpenter	Machinist	Taxi Driver	Metal Assembler	Secretary	Janitor	Receiving Clerk	Construction Labourer	Cashier	Clerk Typist	Welder	Driver Salesman	Storeman	Heavy Equip. Operator	Waiter, Formal Service
READING	Literal Comprehension	*	*	*	*	*	*	*	*	*	*	*	*	*	*	*	*	*	*	*	*	*	*	*	*	*	*	*	*	*	*	*	*	*	*	*	*	*
	Interpretive Comprehension	*	*	*	*	*	*	*	0	*	*	*	*	*	*	0	*	*	*	*	*	0	0	*		*					0	0	*					
	Evaluative Comprehension				*	*					0	0					*	0	0		*				0			0										
	Forms	*	*	*	*	*	*	*	*	*	*	*	*	*	*	*	*	*	*	*	*	*	*	*	*	*	*	*	*	*	*	*	*	*	*	*	*	*
	Notes, Letters, Memos	*	*	*	*	*	*	*	*	*	*	*	*	*	*	*	*	*	*	*	*	*	*	*	*	*	*	*	*	*	*	*	*					
	Charts, Tables	*	*	*	*	*	*	*	*	*	*	*	0	*	*	0		*	*	0	*	*		*	0			*	0			*	*	0				
	Books, Manuals	*	*	*	*	*	*	*	*	*	*	*	*	*	*	*		*	*	*	*	*	*	*	*	*	*	*	*	*	*	*	*	*	*	*	*	
	Roman Numerals	*	*	*	0	*	*		*	*	0	0	*			*		0	*				0		*	0					0	0	*					
WRITING	Phrases on Forms	*	*	*	*	*	*	*	*	*	*	*	*	*	*	*	*	*	*	*	*	*	*	*	*	*	*	*	*	*	*	*	*	*	*	*	*	*
	Sentences on Forms	*	*	*	*	*	*	*		*	0	0	*	*		*			*		*	*	*		0	0			*				*		*			
	Paragraphs on Forms	*	*	*		*	0			*	0		0	*			*			*		0	0		0				0									
	Short Notes	*	*	*				*	*	*	0	0	0	*		*	*	*	*	*	*		*	*			*				*							
	Form Letters	*		*						*		0				*			*	*		0		*			*			0								
	Single Paragraph Letters								0					*	*	*		*	0		*			0			*		0									
	Internal Memos	*	*	*			*			0		*				*	0	0		*	*		0	*	0				*	0								
	Business Letters	*	*	*	*				*	0		0				*	0			*	*				*					0								
	Information Reports	*		*	*	*	0	*	*	*		0		*			0	0	0		*		*	0	0	0				0								
	Recommendation Reports	*		*		*	0		*	*		0						0																				
	Technical Reports	*		*			0			0								0																				
LISTENING	Literal Comprehension	*	*	*	*	*	*	*	*	*	*	*	*	*	*	*	*	*	*	*	*	*	*	*	*	*	*	*	*	*	*	*	*	*	*	*	*	*
	Interpretive Comprehension	*	*	*	*	*	*	*	*	*	*	*	*	*	*	*	*	*	*	*	*	*	*	*	*	*	*		*	*	*	*	*	*	*	*	*	*
	Evaluative Comprehension	*		*		*		0		*	0	*			0	*		0	0		0				*		0											
TALKING	Give Information/Directions	*	*	*	*	*	*	*	*	*	*	*	*	*	*	*	*	*	*	*	*	*	*	*	*	*	*	*	*	*	*	*	*	*	*	*	*	*
	Ask Questions	*	*	*	*	*	*	*	*	*	*	*	*	*	*	*	*	*	*	*	*	*	*	*	*	*	*	*	*	*	*	*	*	*	*	*	*	*
	Debate (Express Point of View)	*	*	*	*	*	*	*	*	*	*	*	*	*	*	*	*	*	*	*	*	*	*	*	*	*	*	*	*	*	*	*	*	*	*	*	*	*
	Diverting Conversation	*	*	*	*	*	*	*	*	*	*	*	*	*	*	*	*	*	*	*	*	0	*		*	0	*	*	*	*	0	*	*	*	*			
	Persuasive Conversation	*	*						0																													
GROUP TALKING	Participate In	*	0	*			0	*	*	0	*	0	*	0	*		*	0	0			*	0	0		0						0	*					
	Give Directions/Information to	*	0	*		*	0		*	*	0	0	0	*	0	0		0	0	0				*	0						0							
	Control Group	*	*					0																														
	Give Persuasive Talks to	0	*																																			
TALK TO AUDIENCE	Factual Talk	*	*						0																													
	Persuasive Talk	*	*						0																													
INTERVIEW/ COUNSEL	Information Centered	*	*	*					0			*													0													
	Problem Centered	*	*	*	*		*			*			*					0	*							0												
INSTRUCT	Demonstrate	*	*	*	*	*	*	*	*	*	*	*	*	*	*	*	*	*	*	*	*	*	*	*	*	*	*	*	*	*	*	*	*	*	*	*	*	*
	Instruct	*	*	*	*	*	*	*	*	*	*	*	*	*	*	*	*	*	*	*	*	*	*	*	*	*	*	*	*	*	*	*	*	0	*	*	*	*

made to prove or disprove the levels of reading comprehension suggested by Davis (2); Bloom, et al. (1); or Kingston (4). Instead, data were obtained on skills actually used by occupational workers rather than on the number and level of skills held by the workers in the occupations.

Certain core skill requirements for work performance appear evident. All occupations read and listen at the literal level of comprehension, read forms and write words/phrases on forms. Most of the skills of one-to-one conversation (giving job directions, giving job information, and obtaining information by asking questions) are common requirements. The requirement for all occupations to provide instructional communication (demonstrate and instruct) is intriguing, particularly in view of the fact that the survey included some rather unsophisticated occupations such as a Construction Labourer.

The evidence about the comprehension levels is most striking; 90 percent listen at the interpretive level and 54 percent read at that level; but only 19 percent and 11 percent respectively listen and read at the evaluation level of comprehension.

Only 30 percent of the occupations are required to participate in group discussions, 5 percent give formal talks, and only 11 to 22 percent use interviewing or counselling communications. (Data are now being reviewed from a third survey of first line foremen/supervisors and these latter skill requirements appear to be required at that level.)

The data on types of reading include skills which are, perhaps, traditionally considered mathematics skills. Whether these skills belong to one subject and/or another, the evidence should provide some indication of the types of reading performed and necessarily affect our instructional strategies.

IMPLICATIONS OF THE DERIVED READING SKILLS

Despite some lack of comprehensiveness, a wealth of information, which is appropriate to adult skill development in preemployment training, has been obtained. Fortunately, not everyone will agree on the further research and development that should be carried out as a result of this evidence.

The following conclusions appear pertinent and relevant to adult skill development:

1. The data on reading and listening suggest that increased emphasis should be given to a solid grounding in the basic literal and interpretive levels of comprehension and, perhaps, less attention to the writer's tone, style, mood, imagery, metric patterns, and other skills normally associated with evaluative comprehension.

2. It is neither relevant nor appropriate to teach rigorous sentence analysis, compound sentence structure, and elaborate paragraph structure to the 54 percent of the working force whose only writing consists of short notes and words/figures/phrases on forms, unless the adults wish to acquire these higher level skills for reasons other than preemployment development.

3. It would be appropriate to have adult students develop reading skills using business books and manuals instead of the literature commonly held in school libraries.

4. Adult students should systematically be taught effective questioning, listening, and task oriented conversational behaviors.

5. All adults taking preemployment training should receive instruction in the elementary techniques of instructional communications.

6. Reading tests should be devised which measure the ability to read business forms and manuals and should be used for preemployment training/testing in lieu of the various standard reading comprehension tests.

7. Writing and talking tests should also be developed which are criterion referenced to the communications skills used in carrying out occupational tasks.

FURTHER GENERIC SKILLS RESEARCH

These studies are being continued as follows:

1. Individualized skill packages are being developed for each of the identified generic skills. They will contain diagnostic and prescription tests to determine entry skills and to prescribe necessary learning activities and mastery tests to measure skill achievement. These packages will be criterion referenced to instructional objectives and to learning media.

2. Additional surveys will be carried out to identify a broader range of generic skills and to determine skills used in an expanded range of occupations.

3. Profiles of skill requirements for each occupation and clusters of skills (core skills, occupational families, and career ladders) are being developed to supplement the traditional grade levels used for preemployment and job employment practices.

OTHER NEEDED RESEARCH

The information obtained to date in the generic skills studies has possibly suggested more questions than conclusions. The following lines of research are offered as possible ways to obtain solid information needed by those who are involved in developing and teaching communication strategies:

1. Reading, writing, and talking standard tests, normatively derived, should be developed and criterion referenced to the communications skills actually used in carrying out occupational tasks. This seems particularly important, for both the emerging countries which have low literacy levels and for the disadvantaged populations of the more industrialized nations.

2. Studies should be carried out to examine the communications skills used outside the work environment. What skills are used by housewives? Do we know what communications skills are used in various community groups and associations? Perhaps the orientation in teaching strategies and in testing has been to "good" literature comprehension and appreciation and not enough to the more mundane requirements of reading newspapers, periodicals, and sales brochures which make up so much of the normal patterns of reading.

3. There appears to be an obvious need to carry out empirical studies to determine the relevance of the processes of skills thought to be involved in reading comprehension. Such a need was also identified by Davis (2).

REFERENCES
1. Bloom, B. S., et al. *Taxonomy of Educational Objectives, Handbook 1: Cognitive Domain*. New York: McKay, 1956.
2. Davis, F. B. Fundamental Factors of Comprehension in Reading," unpublished doctoral dissertation, Harvard University, 1971.
3. Davis, F. B. "Psychometric Research on Comprehension in Reading," *The Literature of Research in Reading with Emphasis on Models*. New Brunswick, New Jersey: Graduate School of Education, Rutgers University, 1971, 8-3 to 8-60.
4. Kingston, A. L. "A Conceptual Model of Reading Comprehension," in E. P. Bliesmer and A. J. Kingston (Eds.), *Phases of College and Other Reading Programs*. Milwaukee: National Reading Conference, 1961, 100-107.
5. Smith, A. De W. *Generic Skills*. Prince Albert, Saskatchewan: Information Canada, 1973.
6. Smith, A. De W. *Generic Skills Technical Supplement*. Prince Albert, Saskatchewan: Information Canada, 1973.
7. Smith, A. De W., et al. *Generic Skills in the Interpersonal and Reasoning Domains*. Prince Albert, Saskatchewan: Training Research and Development Station, 1974.

A Baker's Dozen of Personal Values in Children's Literature

Ruth Kearney Carlson
Cal-State University
Hayward, California
United States of America

Steinbeck described the special wonders and glories involved in reading a book when he said, "But Tom got into a book, crawled and groveled between the covers, tunneled like a mole among its thoughts, and came up with the book all over his face and hands" (4). One of the greatest values of reading literature is an engagement with life which children capture as they become engulfed in reading the words of a talented author. A short story, a novel, or a poem can often cause the reader to look at life differently to see a new slant that life is opening up to him.

Many boys have dreamed about owning a dog but the story of the overwhelming commitment which Billy Colman had to own two coon hounds is powerfully revealed in *Where the Red Fern Grows* by Wilson Rawls (24). Billy speaks of this yearning as a dog-wanting disease. Billy Colman certainly feels life and its problems deeply.

A second value of reading good literature is the way readers gain an appreciation of the glory and beauty of words. Some writers write in a rhythmical, poetic style. A child's ears become attuned to the loveliness of words and the appropriateness of the right word in the right place. When Rawls (24) writes his novel about Billy Colman and his hound dogs in *Where the Red Fern Grows*, he uses the colloquialisms of the people of the Ozarks. His metaphorical language reinforces the mood and setting of the story. As Billy attains maturity, he is proud to be old enough to go hunting. The reader reads the words:

> I cleaned my lantern and filled it full of oil. With hog lard I greased my boots until they were as soft as a humming bird's nest. I was grinding when Papa came around.

And when the mountain boy, Billy, goes to town and speaks of his experiences there, he says the town was *boiling* with people. The wagon yard was full of wagons and teams. Billy speaks of his sisters having "eyes as big as blue marbles," or as big as a guinea's egg. Children can learn to appreciate the beautiful in life and language when they read the words of Wilson Rawls who speaks of the first night when Billy is using his two hounds to go coon hunting. In the author's words:

> It was a beautiful night, still and frosty. A big grinning Ozark moon had the countryside bathed in a soft yellow glow. The starlit heaven reminded me of a large blue umbrella, outspread with the handle broken off.

Such writing as this should help readers to look at the world more freshly, to look at common things in an uncommon way, to appreciate the ways in which an author-artist spins his words together to weave a tapestry of truth and beauty.

One of the books which has created considerable interest recently in the United States is *Watership Down* by Richard Adams (1). This is a novel of many levels designed for adults, but some reviewers feel that it is an example of another book which gifted or precocious children may claim as their own. Mr. Adams writes enchantingly and magically of the fortunes of a band of rabbits, and the reader becomes engrossed in the events experienced by Hazel, Fiver, Bigwig, and other rabbits who behave as humans within their furry exteriors. The rabbits' thoughts, emotions, and actions are derived from their rabbit nature and the reader is drawn into sympathy and an identification with them. The novel is a struggle for survival, a journeying toward a new life, but it has many themes. The author successfully weaves poetry and original myths and legends into his novel and the rabbits are so humanized that one is captured by the oneness of nature. Imagine you are in a rabbit burrow. Listen to the flowing words of Silverweed who twitches his ears continually but whose voice has the movement of wind and light on the meadow:

> The wind is blowing, blowing over the grass.
> It shakes the willow-catkins; the leaves
> > shine silver.
> Where are you going, wind? Far, far away
> Over the hills, over the edge of the world.
> Take me with you wind, high over the sky.
> I will go with you, I will be rabbit-of-the-wind.
> Into the sky, the feathery sky and the rabbit.
> The stream is running, running over the gravel
> Through the brooklime, the king cups, the blue
> > and gold of spring.
> Where are you going stream? Far, far away
> Beyond the heather, sliding away all night.

It is impossible to lift a selection from the unified context of this novel and have it retain its full beauty and significance, but this poetic excerpt gives the listener an appreciation of the rhythmical loveliness of words woven together by the imaginative and gifted author, Richard Adams.

A third value of literature has been called "heart knowledge" by Rebecca Caudill who writes of her Appalachian heritage and of such writers as Jesse Stuart. She beautifully describes the mountains which are more to her than their mere physical shapes. In Caudill's words (9):

> They were the regal tulip poplars, the gay-blooming calico bush, and the fiery azaleas that grew on the mountainside. They were the wild huckleberries we picked in the summer and the paw-paws we gathered and ate in the autumn on our way to school. They were the black birch growing on the mountainside from whose inner bark we scraped sweet sap, drinking it as a ritual in celebration of the coming of spring.

These same mountains of Appalachia give a sense of independence. There is a feeling for families and an enjoyment of nature and the countryside. There is a joy of learning which is somewhat different from that in the usual traditional classroom. Rebecca Caudill learned to read at the age of three by studying the pages of the Louisville *Courier Journal*. This hunger for knowledge is a part of heart knowledge. Another kind of heart knowledge lies in a desire to walk uprightly and to care for one's neighbor.

It is seen in the writings of another Appalachian author, Billy Curtis Clark, who says (1):

> A novel, poem or short story, I believe, must be written from the heart. It is written from the love of creating. Do not be fooled. It requires a lot of work, determination and faith. Remember this word *faith*. It is very important. You must have faith in yourself and in the job you are to do.

In his autobiography, *A Long Row to Hoe*, one learns how Billy Clark had faith in himself to achieve an education at the University of Kentucky (7):

> In nineteen years of growing up here in the valley, hunger was my most vivid memory; and an education was my greatest desire. Recently the questions and doubts of the clique had added another feeder stream—a new desire. I wanted to prove them wrong and upset the pattern. They couldn't ration out desire and determination as they had the laws of the town. Instead, they were given freely to the poor as well as the prosperous by a Great Man whose hands could move a cloud aside and allow the sun to come through in the dead of winter, melting patches of snow to allow a common sparrow to find food.

In *Goodbye Kate*, Billy Clark writes about Isaac Warfield who was adopted by an aged and abandoned mule. In Clark's words:

> I saw her eyes, brown as butternuts, as hollow as the loneliness of a summer day.

Such a feeling for the old mule and Isaac developed that "she knew that me and her were as close as bark to a tree and you don't just go peeling that closeness off easy-like."

This same sort of heart knowledge is also seen in the ancient Nahuatl language. In their poetry the Nahuas Indians thought that a part of a teacher's duty was to "humanize people" or work "to make hearts strong with relation to things" (8). This is also beautifully illustrated in an adult novel, *The Chosen*, by Chaim Potak (23), when Reb Saunders tells Reuven that brilliance and genius is a hollow shell without a soul or a feeling of compassion:

> A *heart* I need for a son, a *soul* I need for a son, *compassion* I want for my son, righteousness, mercy, strength to suffer and carry pain, *that* I want for a son, not a mind without a soul.

So many of the great authors help endow a gift to the child reader, a personal feeling of heart knowledge or compassion.

Lloyd Alexander, the creator of fantasies for children and adults, offers a fourth personal value of children's literature, that of *hopeful dreaming*. In his address entitled "Wishful Thinking or Hopeful Dreaming," Alexander calls attention to hope which "comes very close to the heart and center of a human being."

Alexander (3) points out that hopeful dreaming is an active, not a passive process:

> Hope is one of the most precious human values fantasy can offer us—and offer us in abundance. Whatever the hardships of the journey, the days of despair, fantasy implicitly promises to lead us through them. Hope is an essential thread of all fantasies, an Ariadne's thread to guide us out of the labyrinth, the last treasure of Pandora's box. If we say, "while there's life, there's hope," we can also say, "while there's hope, there's life."

This valuing of hope instead of wishful thinking is seen in "The First Tale, The Foundling" which appears in *The Foundling and Other Tales of Prydain* (2). This is the story of Dallben who was found by three black-robed hags at the edge of the marshes of Morva. When Dallben is ready to venture forth into the world, he is offered three gifts: a sword studded with jewels and glittering with a thread of fire; a golden harp with golden strings which seem to play themselves; and the book, a heavy tome which "holds everything that was ever known" and wisdom, thick as oatmeal.

As Dallben takes his journey into the world, he is enchanted with the first part of his tome, for here is "knowledge he had never dreamed of: the pathways of the stars, the rounds of the planets, the ebb and flow of the tide and the book seems light and beautiful." Then, as Dallben continues on in his journey, the book grows heavy and dark and is "stained with blood and tears." For it is in this book that he reads of "cruelty, suffering, and death" and he learns of "greed, hatred, and war; of men striving against one another with fire and sword; of the blossoming earth trampled underfoot, of harvests lost and lives cut short," and each page which he read "pierced his heart" and "tears blinded his eyes" as he "stumbled to the ground." He is greatly disturbed by the destruction and suffering in the world until he discovers that "at the end of knowledge wisdom begins" and "at the end of wisdom there is not grief, but hope" (2).

Lloyd Alexander has created five Prydain Chronicles—The Book of Three, The Black Cauldron, The Castle of Llyr, Taran Wanderer, and The High King—and each of the novels leads to the final struggle between good and evil. It is hope which helps the heroes to combat the wicked forces of evil.

Another creator of fantasies, C. S. Lewis, has given children the magic land of Narnia. One can enter into this magical land in such imaginative books as The Lion, the Witch, and the Wardrobe; Prince Caspian; The Voyage of the "Dawn Treader"; The Silver Chair; The Horse and His Boy; and The Last Battle. In the land of Narnia, Aslan, the noble lion, leads his people to a wonderful new paradise. He and his people are frequently opposed by the wicked witch. The novel, The Magician's Nephew (20), also presents Aslan as a symbol of hope.

Such a fantasy as The Magician's Nephew leads the child reader into a fifth personal value of literature, the extension of the imagination. It is within the creative power of gifted children's authors to open the doors to new worlds through magical happenings, flying carpets, and golden-glinted orbs and spheres. Imagination offers new wings for the child's journey through life. Since the myth of Pegasus, the child reader has been enchanted with the miraculous flight of winged horses.

In The Magician's Nephew, the noble Aslan, the lion, is going to help Digory climb the cliffs to pluck an apple from the Tree of Life. Aslan turns to Horse and orders him in a roaring voice: "Be winged. Be the father of all flying horses." His name is Fledge.

Listen to the magical words of C. S. Lewis (20) and use your imaginative power to visualize Fledge in his shining glory:

> The horse shied, just as it might have shied in the old, miserable days when it pulled a hansom. Then it reared. It strained its neck back as if there were a fly biting its shoulders and it wanted to scratch them. And then, just as the beasts had burst out of the earth, there burst out from the shoulders of Fledge wings that spread and grew, larger than eagle's, larger than swan's, larger than angel's wings in church windows. The feathers shone chestnut colour and copper colour. He gave a great

sweep with them and leaped into the air. Twenty feet above Aslan and Digory he snorted, neighed, and curvetted. Then he dropped to the earth, all four hoofs together, looking awkward and surprised, but extremely pleased.

The extension of the imaginative vistas of the reader has been enlarged in recent years through the creation of stories in pictures in picture books. Visual literacy is being expanded through such books as *The Silver Pony* by Lynd Ward (35) and *April Fools* by Fernando Krahn (15). In *The Silver Pony* one meets a lonely boy who lives in two worlds, one of limited reality and one of the wider world of imagination where the unexpected is always happening. In eighty pictures and no words, Ward succeeds in transporting us to an imaginative world where a boy rides a silver pony to many imaginative places. Such pictures not only succeed in enlarging the imagination but also they invoke a poignant feeling of loneliness and compassion for those who suffer. It also reveals the gap between the everyday realities of farm life and commonplace lives of the boy's parents and the star-filled wonder in the boy's eyes as he glimpses the wider world of his imagination and dreams.

April Fools is a picture book of a different type—one of foolishness and humor. Two young boys attempt to make April Fools of foolish townspeople with a homemade monster.

Children can be entranced with fairy tales and fantasy land or engrossed in their feelings of compassion for human kind, so a sixth value of children's literature is one of learning to enjoy humor and laughter. We need humor in this world to combat the evils and hardships and eminent dangers of destruction and chaos. Child readers should learn that literature can make us chuckle quietly to ourselves, smile in gentle amusement at the antics of humorous characters, or occasionally laugh uproarishly at foolish numbskulls or simpletons. Reading should offer pleasure as well as a plucky determination to master the fundamentals of clues and cues which unlock words and their meanings.

In recent years, certain folklorists have been adding amusing anecdotes to the cultural traditions of American childhood. Alvin Schwartz has written *A Twister of Twists, A Tangler of Tongues* (25), *Tomfoolery: Trickery and Foolery With Words* (26), and *Witcracks: Jokes and Jests from American Folklore* (27). These books are full of ridiculous nonsense which tickles the funny bone of many readers.

Some examples of a rather subtle type of humor appear in *Would You Rather Be a Tiger?* by Robyn Supraner (33). In rather amusing lines, the author writes about different animals with such words as:

Would you rather be an elephant or a child?
A thumping, bumping elephant or a child?
Would an elephant's father grump
"Keep the noise down! Must you clump!"
Would you rather be an elephant or a child?

An older book which boys still find amusing is *Homer Price* by Robert McCloskey (22). This book includes Homer's amusing adventures in Centerburg under such chapters as "The Case of the Sensational Scent," the story of Aroma, the skunk, and the hilarious episode of the doughnut making machine which runs wild in "The Doughnuts."

Peter Hatcher doesn't think his life is funny in *Tales of Fourth Grade Nothing* by Judy Blume (5), but Peter's problems with his little brother, Fudge, are the sources for a hilariously funny book.

In addition to laughter, young readers learn to understand reasons for making moral and ethical choices. Lloyd Alexander (3) has said:

> We have machines to think for us; we have no machines to suffer for us, or to rejoice for us. Technology has not made us magicians, only sorcerer's apprentices. We can push a button and light a dozen cities. We can also push a button and make a dozen cities vanish. There is, unfortunately, no button we can push to relieve us of moral choices or give us the wisdom to understand morality as well as the choices.

This assistance in making moral choices through illuminating experiences in novels and stories is a seventh value in reading children's literature. A discussion of two different books might point out how this is accomplished by gifted authors. Lynn Hall demonstrates the gradual maturing of ethical values in *The Siege of Silent Henry* (13). Robert is a rather cold, calculating boy with an extraordinary mental ability and a desire to make his fortune by a get rich quick project such as chinchilla raising. He is a loner. He learns that another loner, an old man named Silent Henry Leffert, supports himself through gathering ginseng. He is determined to use his wiles to learn the source of the hidden ginseng supply. Robert pursues Silent Henry with a ruthless plan to rob him of the ginseng. Gradually, however, he becomes uneasy as Silent Henry's loneliness reaches out to him and they both seek companionship in each other. As Robert begins to have more and more qualms about his dishonest quest for the ginseng, he also ponders the dishonesty of selling one of his chinchillas which is worthless as it is a fur chewer. Robert is disturbed about his own father's moral values when he reminds him of the adage, "Let the buyer beware."

Another type of moral choice is involved in the plot, *About the B'nai Bagels*, by E. L. Konigsburg (14). The B'nai Bagels fight hard to win the Little League championship under the coaching of Mark's mother,

Bessie Setzer, and his older brother, Spencer. At the point of the greatest triumph for the team, Mark learns that twins Simon and Sylvester had shifted positions in the midst of the championship game. Mark worries about his mother's moral choice, but when she discovers the trickery of the twins, she unhesitantly forfeits the game even though the opponents on the Elks team were not protesting the use of an illegal pitcher. This moral dilemma helps Mark mature as a boy although he discovers at the Bar Mitzvah that "you don't become a man overnight because it is a becoming, becoming more yourself."

This process of becoming, this learning how to mature as a person, leads to an eighth personal value illustrated through literature. This is the process of growing up—the attainment of manhood or womanhood which is exemplified in many good novels for children. Each one of Joseph Krumgold's books about boys, such as *And Now Miguel* (16), *Onion John* (17), and *Henry Three* (18), is a quest for maturity. The classical novel *Caddie Woodlawn* by Carol Ryrie Brink (6), indicates the gradual growing-up process of Caddie who changes from her tomboy role to that of a beautiful young lady. In the words of the author, one reads Caddie's thoughts:

> When she awoke she knew that she need not be afraid of growing up. It was not just sewing and weaving and wearing stays. It was something more thrilling than that. It was a responsibility.

In recent years, relevance has been one of the characteristics of modern realistic fiction for children and relevance in literature is a ninth personal value which children cherish. Most of the books by Vera and Bill Cleaver are relevant to youth of today. *Where the Lilies Bloom* (11), a novel of a family of children struggling for survival in Appalachia without parents, seems relevant to many children who feel that they must face the problems of the world independent of adult guidance. Mary Call Luther turns to wildcrafting after her father's death. This provides a meager livelihood. *Grover* by the Cleavers (10) is also a book about death, but it includes the problems of developing an understanding relationship between Grover and his father, who is grief stricken over his mother's death from cancer. In *Me Too*, which is also by the Cleavers, Lydia Birdsong strives to change Lornie, her retarded twin. Lydia is not successful in helping her twin to be normal, but she gains a new understanding of the meaning of responsibility and love.

A tenth personal value of some novels and stories for young readers is the insight which novels give on ways to improve the self-image. Children can experience life vicariously and build better self-concepts when they read the right book at the right time. Many youngsters are fearful and lack courage to face obstacles. *Call It Courage* by Armstrong

Sperry (29) is the story of the Polynesian boy, Mafatu, who was known as "the Boy Who Was Afraid." However, Mafatu knew that the sea was ruled by the law of survival. In desperation over the taunts of the other islanders, Mafatu faces the sea alone. His frail craft is wrecked on a reef of an island and the boy commences a Robinson Crusoe type of existence as he gains confidence in his own power. In Ivan Southall's book *Josh* (28), one reads of a boy and a poet who appears to do everything wrong. His encounter with young people in Ryan Creek baffles him as he struggles to survive in a world which seems strange. He resents Aunt Clara, has many fights, and is almost drowned by the gang before he finds himself.

In *A Penny's Worth of Character* by Jesse Stuart (31), young Shan learns the value of honesty when his mother makes him walk back to Mr. Conley's store to supply another sack to replace the one with a hole in it which Shan had sold to Mr. Conley in hopes that he would not notice it. Young Shan had desperately needed that seventh sack so he would have enough money for a chocolate bar and a bottle of lemon soda pop.

An eleventh value of children's literature is the insight which it offers on sociological and cultural values. The October 1969 issue of *Elementary English* reviews research on five content analysis studies of sociological factors in children's literature (21).

At New York University, Aleuin C. Walker conducted a doctoral study entitled "Moral and Spiritual Values of Certain Basal Readers." Ten values which were studied in reading selections included 1) supreme importance of human personality, 2) moral responsibility, 3) institutions as the servants of men, 4) common consent, 5) devotion to truth, 6) respect for excellence, 7) moral equality, 8) brotherhood, 9) pursuit of happiness, and 10) spiritual enrichment. Walker concluded that value teaching could be fostered (21). A study conducted by Dewey Chambers at Wayne State University identified fifteen values appearing in Newbery books. These included: 1) civic and community responsibility, 2) cleanness and neatness, 3) importance of education, 4) freedom and liberty, 5) good manners, 6) honesty, 7) initiative and achievement, 8) justice and equality, 9) loyalty, 10) sacredness of marriage, 11) importance of religion, 12) responsibility to family, 13) self-reliance, 14) sexual morality, and 15) thrift and hard work (21).

A valuable guide to recent children's literature is *The Best in Children's Books: The University of Chicago Guide to Children's Literature 1966-1972* edited by Zena Sutherland (34). This reference volume has a developmental values index which is helpful in determining recent children's books which have thematic content based on such values as kindness to animals, aesthetic discrimination, consideration for others, cultural awareness, intergroup relations, intercultural understanding, and many others.

Helping youngsters to increase their *critical thinking* abilities is a twelfth personal value of children's literature. D'Angelo has discussed some ways of teaching critical thinking through literature in an *Elementary English* article (12). Critical thinking is defined as specific classroom behavior such as perceiving, analyzing, predicting, and judging. *Perceiving*, a stage of critical thinking, is when an awareness of a situation alters a person's perception of it. For example, "How did Johnny feel when he went out in the woods to hunt in the story, *The Biggest Bear?*" In *analyzing* a situation in a story, readers are asked whether complaints made by a neighbor are fair or unfair, and they must support their claims by citing passages from the book. In the *predicting* stage, child readers are urged to select alternative actions which could have been taken in the story. For example, in *A Penny's Worth of Character*, readers might be asked to predict what might have happened if Mr. Conley had looked at the seventh sack more carefully and discovered the boy's deception earlier.

The *judging* stage of critical thinking involves the development of criteria such as good language in dialogs or original plot and characterization. Then a good reader makes evaluations and conclusions based on these criteria.

The thirteenth personal value bestowed on readers is a realization that a careful reading of books should be the study of "literature of the human race" as expressed by Barbara Dodds Stanford (30). The author's creative talents and skills change the particular instance into the universal. Isaac Bashevis Singer has the gift of seeing "a little village [as] the whole of humanity" (32). In the words of Robert Lawson (19) the child needs literature for "the chuckles . . . the gooseflesh . . . the glimpses of glory" he loves. Let us hope that these glimpses of glory can become significant in the lives of child readers.

REFERENCES
1. Adams, Richard. *Watership Down*. New York: Macmillan, 1972, 91-92.
2. Alexander, Lloyd. *The Foundling and Other Tales of Prydain*. Pictures by Margot Zemach. New York: Holt, Rinehart and Winston, 1973, 9, 11, 13, 14.
3. Alexander, Lloyd. "Wishful Thinking or Hopeful Dreaming," *Horn Book Magazine*, 44 (August 1968), 384, 390.
4. Allen, Arthur T. "Literature for Children: An Engagement with Life," *Horn Book Magazine*, 43 (December 1967), 732.
5. Blume, Judy. *Tales of a Fourth Grade Nothing*. Illustrated by Roy Doty. New York: E. P. Dutton, 1972.
6. Brink, Carol Ryrie. *Caddie Woodlawn*. Illustrated by Kate Seredy. New York: Macmillan, 1935, 241.
7. Burns, Paul C. "Billy Curtis Clark—Appalachia's Young Novelist," *Elementary English*, 46 (October 1969), 723, 725, 728.
8. Carlson, Ruth Kearney. "To Humanize People or To Make the Hearts Strong," in Harold Tanyzer and Jean Karl (Eds.), *Reading, Children's Books, and Our Pluralistic Society*. Newark, Delaware: International Reading Association, 1972, 65.

9. Caudill, Rebecca. "Appalachian Heritage," *Horn Book Magazine*, 45 (April 1969), 144.
10. Cleaver, Vera, and Bill Cleaver. *Grover*. Illustrated by Frederic Marvin. Philadelphia: J. P. Lippincott, 1970.
11. Cleaver, Vera, and Bill Cleaver. *Where the Lilies Bloom*. Philadelphia: J. P. Lippincott, 1969.
12. D'Angelo, Edward. "The Teaching of Critical Thinking Through Literature," *Elementary English*, 47 (May 1970), 633-637.
13. Hall, Lynn. *The Siege of Silent Henry*. Chicago: Follett, 1972.
14. Konigsburg, E. L. *About the B'nai Bagels*. New York: Atheneum, 1969, 172.
15. Krahn, Fernando. *April Fools*. New York: E. P. Dutton, 1974.
16. Krumgold, Joseph. *And Now Miguel*. Illustrated by Jean Charlot. New York: Thomas Y. Crowell, 1953.
17. Krumgold, Joseph. *Onion John*. Illustrated by Symeon Shimin. New York: Thomas Y. Crowell, 1959, Apollo Edition.
18. Krumgold, Joseph. *Henry Three*. Illustrated by Alvin Smith. New York: Atheneum, 1967.
19. Lawson, Robert. *Horn Book Magazine*, 43 (December 1967), 737.
20. Lewis, C. S. *The Magician's Nephew*. Illustrated by Pauline Baynes. New York: Macmillan, 1955, 129.
21. Lowry, Heath W. "A Review of Five Recent Content Analyses of Related Sociological Factors in Children's Literature," *Elementary English*, 46 (October 1969), 736-740.
22. McCloskey, Robert. *Homer Price*. New York: Viking Press, 1943.
23. Potak, Chaim. *The Chosen*. Greenwich, Connecticut: Fawcett, 1967.
24. Rawls, Wilson. *Where the Red Fern Grows: The Story of Two Dogs and a Boy*. Garden City, New York: Doubleday, 1961, 24, 52, 67, 69.
25. Schwartz, Alvin. *A Twister of Twists, A Tangler of Tongues*. Illustrated by Glen Rounds. Philadelphia: J. P. Lippincott, 1972.
26. Schwartz, Alvin. *Tomfoolery: Trickery and Foolery with Words*, collected from American Folklore. Illustrated by Glen Rounds. Philadelphia: J. P. Lippincott, 1973.
27. Schwartz, Alvin. *Witcracks: Jokes and Jests from American Folklore*. Illustrated by Glen Rounds. Philadelphia: J. P. Lippincott, 1973.
28. Southall, Ivan. *Josh*. New York: Macmillan, 1971.
29. Sperry, Armstrong. *Call It Courage*. New York: Macmillan, 1940.
30. Stanford, Barbara Dodds. "Literature of the Human Race," *English Journal*, 62 (February 1972), 205-209.
31. Stuart, Jesse. *A Penny's Worth of Character*. Illustrated by Robert Henneberger. New York: McGraw-Hill, Whittlesey House, 1954.
32. Sullivan, Marjorie. "Reading for Relevance," *School Library Journal*, 15 (December 1968), 15.
33. Supraner, Robyn. *Would You Rather Be a Tiger?* Illustrated by Barbara Cooney. Boston: Houghton Mifflin, 1973, 18.
34. Sutherland, Zena. *The Best in Children's Books: The University of Chicago Guide to Children's Literature 1966-1972*. Chicago: University of Chicago Press, 1973.

Literature and Development in Reading

Richard Bamberger
International Institute for Children's Literature and Reading Research
Vienna, Austria

The place occupied by reading in our time is marked by a contrast between theory and practice. Through research in reading we have gained new insight into the nature, process, and importance of reading and drawn conclusions for education in reading. One would think, therefore, that reading might be taught with increasing success. In practice, however, it is evident that few people read and profit from reading. The main reasons for this are that there are several new media which perform a similar function in a much easier way.

It is just this recognition of the importance of reading as a thinking process and as intellectual training, affording the possibility for critical analysis and conversion of information to creative ends, which sets us the task of guaranteeing as many people as possible the right to read. This is all the more important as society, faced with a flood of manipulated information, needs more thinking and critical people than ever before.

We need effective education in reading which develops lifelong reading interests and reading habits. As a result of various Austrian research projects, we know that education in reading is only successful if the interest of the child can be secured.

We all know, of course, that a good teacher can work with any method for a limited period of time and achieve success. It is possible for him to teach systematically all the skills necessary for perfect reading: word recognition skills, comprehension evaluation of the message, and the ability to solve problems. He would no doubt concentrate especially on listening skills, language development and "knowledge structures" that facilitate reading.

As I began to work in depth with the American specialized literature following the Paris Congress of the International Reading Association, I really thought that a new worldwide era in reading education was under way. I was of the opinion that the reading teacher should know everything there was to know about the reading process and its effects and that he should apply this knowledge when using the appropriate texts—unbeknown to the children.

I must admit, however, that the exhibition of reading materials of every kind at IRA's convention in Denver made me stop to think. I asked myself how the teacher who worked through all this soundly based material for developing reading skills—the many readers with questions, tests, and workbooks—ever found time to get down to reading itself, to the genuine, powerful experience of reading.

In the light of these problems, the revival of education in reading—as it has come about during the past six years in Austria—and the various research projects connected with it seem to me to have some significance for international developments.

We attempted first of all to discover why some children read and many do not. The answer was paradoxical:

> Many children do not read books
> because they cannot read well enough.
> They cannot read well
> because they do not read books.

An examination of the reading situation showed clearly that the exceptional classes where the children read well and extensively were not those in which the teacher concentrated on reading skills, but rather those in which the main object was to develop joy in reading through acquaintance with books from the very beginning of instruction in reading.

The interpretation of the reading situation was confirmed by a sentence from the autobiography of the German dramatist Gerhart Hauptmann: "I didn't learn to read at school, but rather through *Robinson Crusoe* and Cooper's *Leatherstocking Tales.*

But these observations were not the end; we took them up again in a more rigorous research project, "The reading behaviour, reading interests, and reading attainment of ten-year-old children." The results of the study will be published in the near future. The investigation dealt mainly with the relationship between various factors which it was assumed would correlate with reading achievement.

Twenty-one variables were examined with regard to their correlations. The general impression that reading attainment depends mainly on socioeconomic factors was not confirmed nor was the preeminence of overall intellectual development (determined by the average grade at school).

Reading attainment, as measured by speed reading tests, was found to correlate with factors in the following order: 1) number of books read in the previous year, 2) number of books owned, 3) comprehension in the reading test, and 4) language quality of the composition.

These findings may be interpreted as follows:

1. The correlation between reading speed and the number of books read gives an insight into the effect of practice. One finding is certain: children who read a lot master a fluent reading technique which makes them capable of mastering the reading material in a much shorter time than unpracticed pupils.

2. The relatively high correlation between the number of books owned and the number of books read suggests that children with many books also read a great deal and/or borrow many books.

3. Results of the reading tests give no support to the view held by many teachers that the slow reader is the careful reader with high comprehension.

4. The relationship between mastery of language and reading speed is impressive. Better readers have better grades for their compositions and they use more unusual words.

Another interesting result is the comparison between schools or class groups. There was often a very large difference between school classes which were comparable in terms of other variables. This seems to be attributable to the number of books read.

Children need more than the mere opportunity to read, however, they must be lured into reading. This is only possible if the teacher supplies enough copies of the same text for each child to have one. Since many good children's books are now available in paperback, this should not present any problem.

ENCOURAGING THE READING HABIT

About six years ago we developed a programme with the motto *Lure into Reading*. The Austrian Children's Book Club provided interested teachers with a box containing thirty copies of a single book. Various methods of presenting the books to the pupils were tested. At first, the teacher simply distributed the books without comment and asked the pupils to return the books when they had finished reading them. Approximately 25 percent returned the books within a few days; 25 percent after a week or so; others took four to six weeks; and some forgot about it altogether.

In other cases, the teacher combined distribution with an "introduction." He told the children part of the story for about 10 minutes, then read to the class for another 5 or 10 minutes. The pupils were thus introduced to the plot (and the plot is the most interesting element for young people), and they got to know the characters and perhaps even identified with one or another of them. It is not difficult to imagine how happy the pupils were when the teacher then said, "I shall now distribute the books and you may read silently." But five minutes before the end of the lesson the teacher broke into the silent reading to ask the children how they thought the story would end. The pupils were delighted when told they could take the books home. They were asked to return the books after a week, however, so that the class could then discuss them. The result was that almost all the pupils read the book within the week.

This investigation posed the following problem: Should we concentate on individual reading skills or on maximizing the effects of practice through extensive reading? Anyone who has recognized the reading process to be a storage process wonders why so little attention has been given to the problem of the effect of practice in reading.

On the basis of the insight we gained into the reading situation in many of Austria's schools, we found that the effect of practice does not derive from systematic drilling of the various reading skills, and it certainly does not come from repeated reading of short texts from school readers. Rather it is most effective when the children have really been lured into reading, when education in reading stems from a literary source in the form of children's books. It is important to find texts which really awaken the child's interest and leave an impression strong enough to form permanent reading habits.

We believe that there is nothing comparable to the power that is derived from well written books. They not only link with the reading interests of the children; they can also heighten these interests. And how poverty stricken by contrast are the texts written with the goal of teaching various reading skills. Equally stricken are those texts which are written in the child's own language, using the language experience approach. This approach seems to be logical and convincing; the children are encouraged to read about what they have experienced themselves in language they normally use and can understand. Such an approach is all right upon occasion but by no means good enough to be used as the cornerstone for the teaching of reading. The life experience approach, which collects its vocabulary from practical life, is also most convincing. The children learn that reading is a help in real life, but in the long run, the sentences do not arouse their enthusiasm. The appeal here is to the intellect, not to the real interests of the children. These interests lie primarily in an exciting story.

Education in reading used to have the book as its goal; today the book is more than a goal; it is the means as well as the end.

The first experience is through listening. By beginning education in reading with storytelling and reading aloud, the joy of anticipation—the most important prerequisite for reading readiness—is awakened. By listening to exciting stories, children's vocabularies are greatly expanded and the plots offer a wealth of context clues.

Many reading methodologists, in every country, consider the use of literature in reading very important. Opportunities for reading are demanded, especially through classroom and school libraries and silent reading hours. The USSR method should be especially emphasized: Uninterrupted Sustained Silent Reading.

The opportunity to read, in itself, is enough for talented and interested children. They will certainly develop continuing reading habits by this method.

It might be objected that the Lure into Reading method directs children too strongly toward the excitement of the bare plot and that the special ability of content comprehension, critical reaction, recognition of the author's intentions, and recognition of problems are hardly taught. The objection would be justified if it were not for the concluding classroom discussion. If this can break out of the traditional schema of repeating the contents, there are many possibilities.

Since any attempt to deal with the book in detail and grasp all the characteristics means the death of reading interest, the teacher may emphasize only the most typical elements for each book. Now, it will be the construction of the plot; then, training the pupils to differentiate between various text structures; next, perhaps, critical opinion—for example, criticism of the behaviour of the characters. Then the teacher may ask about the author's intentions and about the solutions to problems. Without being aware of it, the children are trained to read creatively. I believe that this casual method has much more to commend it than the use of special exercises and reading programmes which are adjusted to special texts. Skills should be developed in such a way that the main objectives—the cultivation of reading interest and the reading habit—do not suffer.

GROUP AND INDIVIDUAL READING IN ADDITION TO CLASS READING

Class reading founded on the Lure into Reading method is not the only way to deal with literature. If class reading alone is employed there is a danger of manipulation; i.e., limiting the development of free thinking and literary taste. Reading as a class, which is used in many schools for the introduction of home reading of the book of the month, is therefore complemented by group and individual reading. Here the teacher can no longer lure into reading by introducing the story. With group reading it is only possible to mention the problems of the individual books. The main thing is to bring the right books and the right pupils together.

With free reading the delight of anticipation, the joy in reading, is decisive. Since this does not exist with every child, the entire school hour should not be devoted to silent reading, but rather no more than 20 minutes, letting the children read further in their free time.

The discussion in group reading can frequently take place as a kind of forum in which pupils present various viewpoints based on what they have read. They will report on how well they liked the books, so that the other children will be better able to decide which to choose for their free-time reading. In class, group, and individual reading the teacher's main task is the selection of or advice on reading material. This is not merely a question—as was thought in the past—of finding books worthy of being read at school. Books must be primarily interesting and stimulating. Moreover, it is important that content and form offer the possibilities for training in all the various types of reading and reading skills.

The best literature for the early reading years already has all the qualities which are found later in the best books for children and indeed in the great literature read by adults. Reading development is not so much a case of "reaching up" but of retaining all that young people should get from literature from the very outset. In every school grade, if children experience literature as children's books, nonfiction, and problem stories, they will develop interests and habits which they will retain in later life. By reading worthwhile books, children improve their reading accomplishment, and the effect of reading grows stronger and stronger.

It is important for the teacher to measure the growth of reading attainment by linking it closely to the volume and the quality of what is read. To this end, we in Austria have brought out a reader's passport which is something like the reading laboratory of the United States, except that often the children are not referred to the single sheets of text but to proper books, which are graded according to their degree of difficulty. The growth of attainment and the experience of pleasure in reading are linked closely together.

In conclusion, I should like to say this: just as we in Austria have taken over a great deal from the American Youth Book Clubs and adapted it for our own purposes, just as we have derived a wealth of incentives from the writings of the International Reading Association, so I could well imagine that in the age of the pocketbook many countries might take up the experiment of "luring into reading" and perhaps develop it further in their own way.

Children's Literature and Reading

Michio Namekawa
Tokyo Seitoku Junior College
Musashino, Tokyo, Japan

The meaning of *reading* should be considered on two levels, the comprehension level and the interpretation level. At the first level, a reader acquires the meaning of written symbols and comprehends the contents as they are written. At the second level, based on the first level, the reader finds the significance or the problems from what he reads and interprets them creatively in his own way. We should not overlook the importance of the second step. In real reading, a reader should be able to get his own creative opinion while he is accepting the contents which the writer wanted to tell, overlapping his thought with the writer's thought. Beginning reading or reading of preschool and early grade children must be discussed with this perspective to real reading.

It is essential that preschool and early grade children develop an interest in reading and form a reading habit. Japanese parents and teachers are active in arousing interest in reading by putting interesting books of children's literature within children's reach.

READING AND PUBLICATION OF JAPANESE
PRESCHOOL AND EARLY GRADE CHILDREN'S LITERATURE

Preschool education has "boomed" in Japan since around 1960. This is not only due to the fact that the importance of preschool-stage education has been recognized, but also is caused by the competition among young parents who want their child to achieve well in elementary school so that the child can enter good upper schools and, as a result, can obtain a good job.

Some of the Japanese educators are against the "preschool education boom" which sometimes pushes a child to learn letters or numbers before he is ready to learn. But in fact almost all Japanese children in urban areas can read and write Hiragana letters upon entering elementary school at age 6. They can read picture books or illustrated story books printed all in Hiragana, and they can also write anything that they wish using Hiragana only. This advantage is due to the Japanese orthography; that is, Hiragana is a set of phonetic symbols each of which has almost always only one sound.

The modern school system was established in 1872 and Japan has made progress in her compulsory education system for over a century. Japan is proud of her high level of enrollment in schools and her low rate of illiteracy.

It has been said that Japanese people like reading. In 1973, there were 30,429 different titles of books published in Japan, 16.1 percent of which were publications for children. About one-half of the publications for children were books for preschool and early grade children. In addition to those books, there were 9 different weekly magazines and 65 monthly magazines for children. Picture books have gradually improved in quality. Magazines are, however, often criticized by parents and teachers because commercialism is trying to please children with popular TV cartoon films and comic strips. Children are apt to be indulged in comics, actions, and thrillers which appear both in magazines and TV programs. It is an urgent problem to let those children know the pleasure of children's literature.

AROUSING INTEREST IN READING AT PRESCHOOL AND EARLY GRADE LEVEL

Many picture books, picture magazines, and illustrated story books can be seen on book shelves and library corners in kindergartens, nursery schools, and at home in Japan. We do not have the problem of book shortage, but we do have that of book selection. It is better to select "valuable books" and have them handy, rather than compete in terms of the quantity of books. In this way we can make children feel joy through reading and can stimulate their sound development as a whole. In addition, it is important that children be surrounded by adults who are avid readers and who will read stories to the children and answer questions the children ask.

Although picture books are no more than toys for babies, the children will learn to open the books and look at the pictures by the end of their first year. Mothers of two- and three-year-old children tell them folktales and read picture books and picture magazines to them. At this stage, children want their parents to read a favorite story again and again. About 70 percent of four- and five-year-old Japanese children attend one of the preschool institutes such as kindergartens, nursery schools, and day care centers. At this stage, Japanese children learn Hiragana letters while their mothers read picture books and picture magazines to them and show them the pictures and letters on each page.

Movements for parents-children reading, encouraging parents and children to read together, started in the 1940s in Japan. At present, there are several types of these movements going on. In "the twenty-minute mother-child reading movement," they sit together twenty minutes a day, the child reading a book to the mother. In another movement, reading hours are scheduled at home once a week, when everybody in the family reads a book according to his or her own choice, or sometimes all the family reads a certain book for children and talks about it after reading. Mothers in a community sometimes make a "reading circle" which studies children's books. This "parents-children reading" has spread nationwide, mainly among preschool and early grade children with their parents. The movements must have been supported by the wishes of Japanese mothers to arouse interest in reading and to form good reading habits among their children at the preschool and early grades stage. Parents prefer the influence of reading to that of TV, although their children prefer TV to reading.

According to a survey report, nonreading children have increased in number in the past ten years, and nonreading children are defined as those who did not read any books (excluding textbooks) in the month of May. This is the main problem of concern to both parents and teachers in Japan.

From the macroscopic point of view, now is a period of transition from letter-centered culture to image-centered culture. It can be said that now is the age of coexistence of letter media and image media. Coordination of pictures and sentences makes it possible to create a theme. To read a book, therefore, is not only to read letters but also to read pictures. Ability to read pictures as well as letters is necessary for modern people. Good picture books must help children develop abilities both in the appreciation of beauty and the interpretation of the theme presented by the pictures and sentences together. We must select good picture books for the sound development of our children.

CONCLUSION

Excellent works of children's literature from overseas have been translated and published in Japan since World War II. They have stimulated Japanese writers and helped to improve Japanese children's literature. They also have helped Japanese children broaden their view toward international understanding. These translations have helped Japanese children understand their own culture by comparing it to other cultures. Japanese children are happy because they can read both the Japanese and foreign works of children's literature printed in Hiragana.

An example of a book report written by a six-year-old Japanese girl is shown below. From this book report we can see how reading is related to the child's own inner thoughts and how she gained a deeper understanding of life as a young girl. Because of this function of reading, we must recognize the importance of reading at preschool and early grade stages. For the development of children as a whole, arousing interests in reading children's literature is more important than developing interests in science by nonfiction or knowledge books, although this is also necessary.

Three Little Pigs
Etsuko Matsumoto (First grade)

Three little pigs said that they would make a house for each. The first little pig said he would make a straw house because he could make it fast. The second little pig said he would make a wooden house. If I were him, I would make a wooden one. But later, the third little pig said he would make a brick house, which was strong enough to protect from a wolf. When I read this, I also thought that the third little pig's house was good. When three little pigs finished making each house, a wolf came over and blew off the straw house first. Then he blew off the second little pig's house, saying "just a blow." The brick house couldn't be blown off when the wolf tried to. The wolf got angry and tried it again. I was scared because I thought it would be blown off. The brick house was not broken. Then the wolf crashed the house with his body and fell down. I felt relieved because the wolf died. I thought the brick house was strong as I expected. I said "good for you! the third little pig." I was impressed by what the third little pig did. That is, he said, "Let's live together in my brick house from now on" to his brothers who laughed at him and said "Make haste, or you won't have a place to sleep tonight" when he was making his house. Sometimes I had a quarrel with my brother, but I think I should have been kind to him. I thought I would get on well with him, being kind to him like the third little pig.

Comparative Reading: State of the Art

John Downing
University of Victoria
Victoria, British Columbia
Canada

Comparisons of reading and learning to read in different nations, cultures, and languages were fairly rare, until recently. Now the interest in such comparative studies appears to be increasing. Therefore, it may already be appropriate to make a brief survey of what has been done to date; hence this article, "Comparative Reading: State of the Art."

WHAT IS "COMPARATIVE READING"?

The potential value of international studies and research in reading was recognized at an earlier date by some farsighted leaders in IRA. For example, IRA past president Nila Banton Smith (18) declared at the very first IRA World Congress in Paris, France, in 1966: "Eventually we shall have worldwide reading research. . . . This is truly one of the most significant promises which the future of reading holds out to us." Earlier still, IRA's first president, William S. Gray (12) had demonstrated the feasibility and the practical value of the worldwide study of reading in his classic book, The Teaching of Reading and Writing, published by Unesco in 1956. This practical application of international expertise in reading instruction through the collaboration between Unesco and IRA has borne further fruit recently in two undertakings by IRA's Executive Director, Ralph Staiger. He updated Gray's book with the contribution of an additional chapter (19) to the second edition published (after numerous reprintings of the first edition) in 1969. Staiger (20) also organized and edited the new Unesco source book on The Teaching of Reading which came out in 1973.

The phrase comparative reading itself appeared in the literature for the first time in one volume (5) of the proceedings of IRA's annual convention held in Boston in 1968. A paper presented there suggested that the term comparative reading should be coined to label a new area of research and study which was emerging in the field of reading. This new field encompassed the work mentioned in the preceding paragraph, but it was proposed that it should be widened in scope to include the following objectives:

1. The gathering together and application of practical teaching know-how from all countries of the world (as exemplified by Gray's classic work).

2. The compilation of the natural history of reading. In other words, descriptions of how reading is learned and used in different countries simply for the sake of that knowledge itself.

3. The development of a better theoretical understanding of the psycholinguistic processes of learning to read and reading, through the application of comparative, cross-cultural, and cross-language research methods from the sciences of psychology, anthropology, sociology, linguistics, and so on.

4. Improvements in the training of teachers and specialists in reading through new courses in comparative reading. Douglass (4) independently pointed out in the same year: "It is sometimes instructive to take a look at the ways of other people as they work with children; not because they warrant being copied, but rather for purposes of contrast so that one may be helped to entertain ideas that could lead to useful modifications in ways of helping children learn." Similarly, in linguistics, Whorf (22) recommended strongly the study of languages remarkably different to the student's own native tongue because, "in its study we are at long last pushed willy-nilly out of our ruts. Then we find that the exotic language is a mirror held up to our own".

Reaching these four objectives is clearly impossible through any one single traditional scholarly discipline. For example, the approaches conventionally employed in the study of comparative education would help with objective number 2, but they would not take us far toward the other three goals. Obviously this new area of investigation and study requires a multi and interdisciplinary approach as well as the cooperation of specialists from many nations of the world.

RECENT PROGRESS

Since that first paper on comparative reading was presented at the IRA convention in 1968, some progress has been made from a number of independent directions toward the four objectives listed previously. Staiger's contributions (19, 20) toward attaining objective number 1 have been mentioned already. The renewal of Gray's synthesis of worldwide knowledge of the superior pedagogical techniques of reading instruction and the new Unesco handbook should be of considerable practical help, especially to educators in less developed countries. In regard to objective number 2, each year has seen the publication of more and more articles which provide objective descriptions of reading and reading education in specific countries. The published proceedings of the IRA world congresses at Paris (1966), Copenhagen (1968), Sydney (1970), Buenos Aires (1972), and Vienna (1974) are rich sources of such information. The least progress has been made toward objective number 4. However, this need not be a discouraging sign for the development of college courses on comparative reading. Recent times have not been conducive to the growth of *any* new courses and programs. Nevertheless, interest in this potential for overcoming ethnic, linguistic, and pedagogical prejudice in reading is increasing and optimism seems appropriate for future progress toward this objective.

Most growth has been made in the area of objective number 3 and, therefore, the major part of the remainder of this article is devoted to reporting recent developments in that area.

FUNDAMENTAL RESEARCH

In every practical field, the chief stimulus for technical improvements is the outcome of fundamental research on theory. So also it must be in reading instruction. This was the declared objective of one of the comparative reading investigations completed recently by an international team which included specialists from the fields of reading education, psychology, psychiatry, and neuropsychiatry (7). The report states: "The proposition that is the basis of this book is that by making comparisons between the reading behaviors of people in different cultures and in varying languages we can understand better the fundamental psycholinguistic processes of reading and writing and the way in which these develop." Toward that objective various members of the team undertook the following tasks, each of which is reported in their book, *Comparative Reading:*

1. A consideration of the logic of research design and methodology in comparative reading investigations.

2. A review of previous research comparing the reading achievements of different nations.

3. An empirical analysis of the attitude contents in the reading primers of: England, France, India, Israel, Italy, Japan, Mexico, Norway, Soviet Union, South Korea, Turkey, United States, and West Germany.

4. An empirical cross-cultural and cross-language study of variables influencing the acquisition of reading and writing skills in: Argentina, Denmark, Finland, France, Germany, Great Britain, Hong Kong, India, Israel, Japan, Norway, Sweden, United States, and the U.S.S.R.

Comparative Reading:

This comparative reading report was the broadest in scope of all the investigations published in the past five years. Hence, it seems appropriate to use the main parts of that study as the framework for reviewing other recently published studies in addition. One other large scale project was the IEA survey of reading comprehension achievements, but since this topic was only one of the several themes of the comparative reading report, it too may reasonably be discussed under the relevant subheading (number 2, below).

1. *Research Design and Methodology.* The problems of devising valid and reliable designs and methods for comparative reading research are legion. The number of variables to be considered seems endless and there is a paucity of research information on some of them—for example, the effects of translation on tests of reading comprehension, attitude scales and even factual questionnaires. One particularly interesting contribution on this latter problem is McLeod's paper (16) presented at the 1974 International Congress of Applied Psychology. He notes that "Traditional multiple-choice tests of reading comprehension are even more suspect when used in cross-cultural studies"—as they were in the IEA investigation to be described in section 2 (below). McLeod tested the use of parallel cloze tests in Czech, English, French, German, and Polish. These were administered to samples of children in countries where these were native languages. Test performance was assessed on the basis of the child's contribution to overall language redundancy. McLeod's results indicate that his method is both reliable and valid. More of this kind of methodological research is sorely needed if objective measurement which is really valid for cross-national comparisons is to replace naive assumptions that existing techniques for one language or culture can be applied without any change, other than literal translation, in another.

Nevertheless, research on the basic psycholinguistic issues in comparative reading cannot wait indefinitely for such improvements in research methodology. The report concludes: "There is no time to sit back and wait for the development of better methodologies; mistakes may be made, but despite them the benefits will be immense" (3). Indeed, methodological progress will come partly as a result of learning from the errors made as research proceeds.

2. *Cross-National Surveys of Reading Achievements.* One rather popular way of thinking about comparing the achievements in reading of one country with those of another is to treat it rather like a sporting competition or, if a large number of nations are involved, as a sort of Olympic Games of reading. But in reality no gold medals for reading can be awarded for the two kinds of reasons noted in the comparative reading report:

a. International literacy statistics are of dubious validity because of concealed differences in the criteria being applied from country to country.
b. Variables influencing measurement from one nation to another are not adequately controlled.

This league table attitude toward international studies of reading achievements seems particularly prone to occur when the research has no clear theoretical or practical educational objectives, as was the case in the large-scale cross-national survey reported by Foshay, et al. (10) in 1962. This survey was one of three reports chosen for review in the comparative reading study as paradigms of cross-national comparisons of reading achievements. The results of all three in terms of basic knowledge are very disappointing. Lack of theoretical purpose was found to be their worst feature, though one of the three studies was better in this respect. The sterility of the results of the largest of these three surveys (Foshay, et al.) was further assured by the shallowness of the measure and the inappropriateness of the age level tested in the countries compared.

A few months after *Comparative Reading* came out, the results of the latest IEA survey of reading achievements were published in a monograph by Thorndike (21). Despite some improvements in sampling techniques and administrative planning, its results too were disappointing. A lack of theoretical purpose persisted and this aimlessness pervaded the design to such an extent that no theoretical or practical conclusions can be drawn from them (despite the author's claims to the contrary). This general weakness and more specific methodological errors have been noted in a recent review (6) and documented in detail in another article (8).

These attempts at cross-national measurement of reading achievements and the methodological discussions they have stimulated are important milestones in the growth of comparative reading research.

3. Attitude Contents of Reading Materials. In 1967 Klineberg (15) predicted that a comparison of reading materials from different countries would reveal important differences in their attitude contents. The comparative reading report of such a comparison supported Klineberg's hypothesis. Blom and Wiberg (2), the two psychiatrists in the team, reported: "The findings on thirteen countries resulted in twenty-eight statistically significant discriminative attitudes." The detailed differences between countries are provided in their chapter, which includes references to other studies in this area. A new addition to knowledge of this aspect of comparative reading is provided by Zimet's recently published monograph (23).

4. *Cultural and Linguistic Variables.* The fourth task of the comparative reading project resulted in a wealth of new data. Space in this article permits only the mention of a few examples of the way in which differences in culture and language influence the child's experiences in learning to read and write.

First, *Comparative Reading's* analysis of the individual reports on each nation's reading education found clear evidence that culture is indeed an important variable in learning to read. Nations vary in the importance given to literacy, and they vary in their relative educational priorities. For example, of the fourteen countries studied, the United States placed the greatest emphasis on learning to read. Another goal to which the same country seemed to give a lower priority in contrast to some other countries was the growth of a healthy personality and the maintenance of general mental health. Clearly the social pressures felt by a child in learning to read in the United States and Denmark, for instance, are likely to be very different.

Another outstanding example of cultural influences on reading acquisition discovered in this analysis is the sex role factor. In the United States, girls are consistently superior to boys in learning to read in the primary school years. In Britain, there is no significant difference between random samples of boys and girls. In Germany and India the boys are found to be superior. The report on India provided the key evidence that the cause is a social or cultural one. Evidence from another study, Abiri's large-scale reading research in Nigeria provided confirmation (1). Which sex is superior in reading depends primarily on social demands and cultural expectations in parents, teachers, and the general community. Empirical testing in the United States, England, and Nigeria reported recently by Johnson (13) confirms that sex differences in reading achievements vary from country to country, and another study confirms that reading is perceived as a feminine activity in North America (9).

Several language problems are revealed by the analysis of the data from the different countries in the comparative reading project. Most interesting is the way in which the child's development of reading and writing skills is retarded when there is a mismatch between the language of the child and the language of reading instruction used by the teacher or in the reading materials. If the child's language is completely different from the language of reading, gross retardation in learning literacy skills is the usual result. Even if the difference is only a matter of dialect, some retardation is likely to occur. Children are bound to become confused when the reading process is explained to them with reference to a language or dialect which they do not know. For example, they may not be able to pronounce or hear the phonemes of the language which their teacher is relating to written symbols. Often the child, whose language or dialect differs from that of the teacher, develops emotional problems as well as cognitive confusion, because he feels that the language of his home and community are being rejected by the teacher.

A number of other recent publications confirm this finding of the comparative reading project. One is the impressionistic description of an English teacher's frustrations in a secondary school in Tobago provided by Searle's book, *The Forsaken Lover* (17). He shows how children on this Caribbean island have been trained by their school experiences to despise their own dialect as a means of expression when the medium is written language.

The positive implications for reading education have been shown in Kaufman's study (14). Teaching reading skills in Spanish to Spanish speaking students in New York City resulted in improved performance *in reading English*. Here is one practical way of countering the confusion of mismatch between the pupil's language and the official one of the school.

Further evidence of the negative effect of the cognitive confusion caused by language mismatch was provided in the recent comparative study by Gloger (11). He found that in Switzerland children in the German speaking areas must learn to read in High German, a quite different dialect from their own. "Because of this conflict in the 'two' Germans there is a need for remedial classes," reports Gloger.

Perhaps the chief general theoretical contribution of these various comparative reading studies reviewed here is the way in which contrasts between different languages and cultures throw into relief the essential common predicament of the beginner's situation in learning to read in every nation and every culture. The common task of every beginner seems to be to try to make sense of the relationship between 1) what he knows about language from his past experience as a speaker and listener, and 2) what his teacher is telling him about the language he must use as a future reader. This problem solving task may be made more difficult in various ways; one hazard is that of mismatch between his language and that of the teacher. The chief practical implication seems to be that every feasible effort should be taken to clarify the relationship between speech and written language so that the danger of cognitive confusion may be minimized.

REFERENCES

1. Abiri, J.O.O. "World Initial Teaching Alphabet Versus Traditional Orthography," doctoral thesis, University of Ibadan, Nigeria, 1969.
2. Blom, Gaston E., and J. Lawrence Wiberg. "Attitude Contents in Reading Primers," in John Downing, et.al., *Comparative Reading.* New York: Macmillan, 1973.
3. Brimer, M. Alan. "Methodological Problems of Research," in John Downing, et al., *Comparative Reading.* New York: Macmillan, 1973.
4. Douglass, Malcolm P. "Beginning Reading in Norway," *Reading Teacher,* 23 (October 1969), 17-22.
5. Downing, John. "Comparative Reading," in J. Allen Figurel (Ed.), *Reading and Realism,* 1968 Proceedings, Volume 13, Part 1. Newark, Del.: International Reading Association, 1969.
6. Downing, John. "IEA Reading Study Design Poses More Questions Than It Answers," *Phi Delta Kappan,* 55 (May 1974), 639-640.
7. Downing, John, et al. *Comparative Reading.* New York: Macmillan, 1973.
8. Downing, John, and Ernest Dalrymple-Alford. "A Methodological Critique of the 1973 IEA Survey of Reading Comprehension Education in Fifteen Countries," *International Review of Applied Psychology,* in press.
9. Downing, John. "Sex Roles in Learning Literacy," paper presented at the 15 Interamerican Congress of Psychology, Bogota, Colombia, December 1974.
10. Foshay, Arthur W., et al. *Educational Achievements of Thirteen-year-olds in Twelve Countries.* Hamburg: Unesco Institute for Education, 1962.
11. Gloger, M. Ted. "Primary Reading Methods in 12 Countries," paper presented at the 19th Annual Convention of IRA, New Orleans, 1974.
12. Gray, William S. *The Teaching of Reading and Writing.* Paris: Unesco, 1956.
13. Johnson, Dale D. "Sex Differences in Reading Across Cultures," *Reading Research Quarterly,* 9 (1973-1974), 67-86.
14. Kaufman, Maurice. "Will Instruction in Reading Spanish Affect Ability in Reading English?" *Journal of Reading,* 11 (April 1968), 521-527.
15. Klineberg, Otto. "Life is Fun in a Smiling, Fair-Skinned World," in Joe L. Frost (Ed.), *Issues and Innovations in the Teaching of Reading.* Chicago: Scott, Foresman, 1967.
16. McLeod, John. "Comparative Assessment of Reading Comprehension: A Five Country Study," paper presented at the 18th International Congress of Applied Psychology, Montreal, Canada, 1974.
17. Searle, Chris. *The Forsaken Lover.* London: Routledge and Kegan Paul, 1972.
18. Smith, Nila B. "The Future of Reading," in Marion D. Jenkinson (Ed.), *Reading Instruction: An International Forum.* Newark, Delaware: International Reading Association, 1967.
19. Staiger, Ralph C. "Developments in Reading and Literacy Education 1956-1967," in William S. Gray (Ed.), *The Teaching of Reading and Writing* (2nd ed.). Paris: Unesco, 1969.
20. Staiger, Ralph C. (Ed.). *The Teaching of Reading,* Unesco source book. Paris: Unesco, 1973.
21. Thorndike, Robert L. *Reading Comprehension Education in Fifteen Countries.* Stockholm: Almqvist and Wiksell, 1973.
22. Whorf, Benjamin Lee. "The Relation of Habitual Thought and Behavior to Language," in Leslie Spier (Ed.), *Language, Culture, and Personality.* Menasha, Wisconsin: Sapir Memorial Publication Fund, 1941.
23. Zimet, Sara Goodman. *What Children Read in School.* New York: Grune and Stratton, 1972.

PART TWO

Some Implications
for the Reading Curriculum

Who Teaches the Child to Read?

Asher Cashdan
The Open University
Milton Keynes, England

The thesis that the child should be put at the centre of the learning situation is a recurrent one in education, although we often attribute it in particular to Thomas Dewey. In practice, however, we have often only gone halfway along the road. What we have done is to stress the need to consult the child's interests and motivation, to take into account his present intellectual level—in short to treat him as the person he now is, not as a miniature adult. Rarely has the teacher abdicated so far as to allow the child to dictate what he learns or how and when he does his learning. I propose to argue in this paper that there is plenty of evidence that we need to go much further.

THE CHILD AS LEARNER

The whole thrust of child development research has changed considerably in the past few years. The initial impetus came from the massive studies of Jean Piaget. But the thread has been taken up in a variety of approaches and methodologies, from the work of Thomas and Birch (12) in the United States to that of Bower and Trevarthen (21) in Scotland. These workers are beginning to demonstrate that right from birth the child's individual characteristics begin to manifest themselves and that variation between children is to some extent independent of life experience. And this applies not just to temperamental and social characteristics, but to the seeds of intellectual capabilities as well. The argument is not necessarily about inheritance and genes, but rather about congenital qualities (already affected by the first nine months or so of "prelife"). Perhaps the person who has most caught the popular imagination in this sphere is Chomsky with his espousal of the Language Acquisition Device. He argues powerfully that the child must be genetically programmed to acquire a highly complex and evolved language long before he has had any real exposure to one, hence the infant's ability to generate numerous sentences he has never actually heard.

I would not go the whole way with this analysis. For instance, a child who hears no language at all will not become a speaker, but it is true that the amount of exposure the child needs is small. The infant is a natural rule-maker; he is also a natural interacter with his environment. As Trevarthen has shown, small babies initiate conversations, rather than simply respond to what adults offer them.

THE LIMITATIONS OF TEACHING

There is no doubt that we now have to ask ourselves searching questions about the uses of a teacher. Certainly, there is enough here already to make us doubtful about the functions of direct didactic procedures. Cazden (4) found that attempts to improve children's language by "improving" what was offered were attended by less success than the offering of language models, in other words talking to the child in a much less specific way. In the same vein, J. S. Bruner (3) has argued that our ability to define effective teaching is so poor that much of what we do in that name is wasted. He has been experimenting with helping three-year-olds to solve problems. Discarding those situations where the task is either so difficult or so easy that the teacher's intervention is irrelevant, he is still having great difficulty in defining what constitutes an adequate intervention even when the task level is appropriately adjusted.

All of this makes me wonder how the highly structured compensatory education programme, such as that of Carl Bereiter (1), can possibly yield valuable results. One is well aware that the disadvantaged child has been argued to be in a rather special situation in which he has to learn faster and in a different way from the normal child. Yet, I am not convinced; in particular, I have doubts as to the generalisability of such externally imposed learning.

THE RIGHT BALANCE

If these remarks have served as an appropriate orientation to the argument of this paper, then we clearly must look again at how the child learns to read, who teaches him, and how this may be made more effective. Certainly, we cannot feel happy about the present position. In Britain (and we are not unique) it took twenty-five years for us to regain the ground lost in overall reading standards since before World War II; and a recent report (10) showed that this improvement has not continued. A major commission—Sir Alan Bullock's committee—is currently looking into the whole question of reading, English, and language arts work in schools. So there is no doubt that some reexamination is not out of place. Let us look at the child, the home, and the school.

There are two ways in which we can help the child to learn. One of them is by attempting to teach him, the other by facilitating his attempts to teach himself. Obviously, I am arguing for the second. There are a number of measures we can take to help achieve this goal; we need to consider the child's health, something which goes far beyond simple medical care into the fields of nutrition, housing, and ultimately money. There is also his personal adjustment and emotional security, both of which are again related to the social and economic setting in which he functions.

The positive side of what we are after is the giving to the child of the freedom to explore and to learn on his own. This is not a matter of providing optimal stimulation—if anything, the opposite of this. The point which I am continually wanting to make is that the child is self-stimulating and self-starting, provided conditions are right for him.

THE HOME

One of the most exciting recent researches is the one being carried out for the past few years at Harvard by Burton White and associates (14). Their main finding seems to be that the ideal parent is not the one who functions as a "stimulator," working constantly with the child, playing with him, talking, offering frequent help and advice. On the contrary, the best parents are turning out to be those who are not constantly helping the child, but who are constantly *available* to him as consultants. The ideal mother is there to answer questions when they are asked, to supply needed materials, to help solve problems that the child has encountered and is aware of, and to offer an occasional suggestion. She is usually too busy to do more than this (and this is probably irrespective of social class and education); but the child benefits from the fact that his mother does not create situations for him, but responds to them.

If a parent can fill a role such as this successfully, then the other most valuable thing he or she (or indeed any other adult in frequent contact with the child) can supply is a series of relevant models which have an orienting and motivating effect, rather than an intellectual effect. In the general social sphere, the parent can help the child to see the use of education and to have appropriate expectations of school and teacher. Such a child arrives at school expecting to use the school as a resource, not to suffer it as an imposition. The work of Hess and Shipman (7) with Negro mothers in the United States is highly relevant here. Much of their methodology has been criticised (notably by Ginsburg (6)), but I would accept it to the extent of suggesting that their studies probably do demonstrate that the way in which a parent talks to a child may not determine the child's intellectual capacities, or even his orientations, but that it is certainly likely to have a major role in his attitudes towards the teaching profession. There is plenty of other evidence (9) demonstrating a definite correlation between parents and children's views of the school situation.

When it comes to learning to read, the parental model is clearly highly relevant both to the child's motivation and to his appreciation of what the activity is about—its rationale. We are back to the old truism that if the parents do not read, the child will see no point in reading, or at any rate he will have to learn to value the skill himself.

THE TEACHER

It would be a great mistake, however, for the teacher to rush in to create this motivation. For what we have been leading up to is the suggestion that the teacher needs to be much nearer to Burton White's ideal parent. In other words, she must act as a facilitator or consultant, not as a didactic expert. The best of the British infant schools have long been admired for just this quality in their teachers. When the system is working well, the child is using the teacher as a resource, not being "taught" by his teacher. In the process, we hope to convince him (if he has not already started with this orientation) that school is a facility provided for his use, not an institution imposed upon him. At the same time, such a system avoids the danger of the teacher's assessing the pupil and deciding what he can do, rather than letting him make the decision for himself. We have heard enough of the self-fulfilling prophecy; we must constantly guard against premature judgments of a pupil's inadequacies—a much greater risk than that of overestimating him. Where the teacher's expertise really counts, as with the best consultants in other spheres, is in knowing what the client is going to want. So she will have appropriate resources available on offer, but she will not thrust them down the client's throat. These are bound to include systematic material for phonic learning—or better, for learning about the letter-code—such as Stott's Programmed Reading Kit (11), Words in Colour (5), or the Breakthrough to Literacy material (8), which does a great deal more. The significance of such material is twofold; not only does it give the child the tools he wants when he wants them (which I suspect is much earlier in the reading process than we have sometimes acknowledged), it also admits that letter-code work must be done at a very early stage if children are going to learn to write—something which is too easily forgotten. But if the child is teaching himself to read and write, he will not be the one to make artificial dissociations between the different skills.

I am not for a moment advocating that teachers should stop being educators. What I am saying is that the more they can allow themselves to hold back and allow the student to do his own learning, the more effective and better judged will be their interventions when they are really needed.

It could be added that the eternal-seeming controversy on methods and materials is largely due to the unwise attempt to fit the child to the system. A synthetic method may be best if one has to have one approach (and one sequence) for all children; but it will certainly be wrong for each one of them some of the time. On the other hand, the mature, experienced teacher who uses a wide mixture of methods may sound very convincing. If her judgment is uncertain, this may just mean that she gives every child the wrong treatment every time! If the child samples a rich menu himself he may make the fewest mistakes. As pediatricians never tire of saying, "babies normally know quite well what and how much they should eat."

CONCLUDING ARGUMENT

"What is it all for?" If we are expecting children to learn to read for recreative purposes, then are they getting joy out of the activity and is it contributing to their fulfillment? If we are concerned with helping them to access information, communicate with others, make sense of their environment, are they doing this because of a felt need—that is, to achieve their own purposes—or is the task an imposed one? These are not alternatives, simply questions that have to be asked differently according to the circumstances. Furthermore, for what purposes of society, for what occupational and personal goals do we feel reading to be necessary; and what is it we are doing when we try to persuade pupils to adopt our values? For, despite all that I have been saying, the element of indoctrination is not suddenly going to disappear from education. Nor would I wish it to; what I would wish to see is that we become much more explicit in our purposes and indoctrinations, so that we can look at our values and see where they need modification.

I do not doubt that the adult's eventual competency as a reader and his exercise of this competency has its roots in the circumstances in which he first learned to read. This gives us little comfort when we see, even in a highly industrialised and educated community such as the United Kingdom, the size of the adult literacy problem and begin to realise that we must do something about it. Of course this is a problem which has many contributory causes; I would suggest that one of them can be found in the child's first experience of school. For I would guess that the child whose learning is intrinsically motivated, and aimed at goals with which he genuinely identifies, will be unusually well protected against the storm ahead.

Who Teaches the Child

REFERENCES

1. Bereiter, C., and S. Engelmann. *Teaching Disadvantaged Children in the Preschool.* Englewood Cliffs, New Jersey, 1966.
2. Bower, T. "Competent Newborns," *New Scientist,* March 14, 1974.
3. Bruner, J. S. Unpublished lecture, 1973.
4. Cazden, C. . *Child Language and Education.* New York: Holt, Rinehart, 1972.
5. Gattegno, C. *Words in Colour.* Reading: Educational Explorers, 1962.
6. Ginsburg, H. *The Myth of the Deprived Child.* Englewood Cliffs, New Jersey: Prentice-Hall, 1971.
7. Hess, R. D., and V. C. Shipman. "Early Experience and the Socialization of Cognitive Modes in Children," *Child Development,* 36, (1975), 337-364.
8. Mackay, D., et al. *Breakthrough to Literacy.* London: Longman, 1970.
9. Robinson, W. P., and S. J. Rackstraw. *A Question of Answers.* London: Routledge, 1972.
10. Start, K. B., and B. K. Wells. *The Trend of Reading Standards.* Slough: NFER, 1972.
11. Stott, D. H. *Programmed Reading Kit.* Edinburgh: Holmes McDougall, 1962.
12. Thomas, A., et al. *Behavioral Individuality in Early Childhood.* New York: New York University Press, 1963.
13. Trevarthen, C. "Conversations with a Two-Month Old," *New Scientist,* May 5, 1974.
14. White, B. L., and J. C. Watts. *Experience and Environment, Volume 1: Major Influences on the Development of the Young Child.* Englewood Cliffs, New Jersey: Prentice-Hall, 1973.

Miscues, Errors, and Reading Comprehension

Yetta M. Goodman
University of Arizona
Tucson, Arizona
United States of America

Reading is a language process; miscue analysis shows that even young and beginning readers treat reading as if it were language (1, 4, 5).

Miscue analysis evaluates the unexpected responses produced in oral reading by asking questions about the substitutions, omissions, insertions, and reversals of clauses, phrases, words or word parts which readers produce. The questions evaluate:

1. The degree of graphic, phonemic, syntactic, and semantic similarity of word substitutions;
2. the degree to which miscues result in sentences which are semantically and syntactically acceptable;
3. the type of grammatical transformations which result from miscues; and
4. the degree to which miscues change the meaning and grammatical structure of a given text.

Evaluation of tens of thousands of miscues produced by hundreds of elementary and secondary school age children, as they orally read stories which they have never seen before of at least 500 words in length, permits the following conclusions.

TREATING READING LIKE LANGUAGE

Young readers make use of both the grammatical and semantic systems of language as they read. Early miscue research proved that when provided with written language context, young readers could read at least two-thirds of the words which they were unable to read if those same words were provided in isolated lists (2).

From the very beginning, readers substitute the same grammatical function for the text words.

Consider the following text sentence: *Penny rushed up the front steps and into the house.* One seven-year-old produced an English nonsense verb for *rushed* by saying *rooshed* as if the sound represented by the u was similar to the medial vowel in the word *boot.* When this child finished reading *up the front steps,* he reread enthusiastically saying "rushed, that word is rushed."

When I asked him how he knew what the word was, he replied "When I saw *up the front steps,* I knew that it had to be *rushed.*"

The child was able to explain that even though he had used sound-letter correspondence to produce a sound-alike word, it was the meaning of the phrase *up the front steps* which helped him make use of the semantic or meaning system of language in addition to the sound-letter and grammatical systems.

Another child reading the same sentence read: *Penny reached up the front steps and into the house.* Having produced a grammatically acceptable sentence, this child was satisfied and made no attempt to correct. There is a tendency for young readers to produce more syntactically acceptable sentences than semantically acceptable sentences. This is especially true when the concepts of the material are complex for the reader. The reader seems to be able to manipulate grammatical structure even when semantic meaning is not easily accessible.

Readers also indicate that they use their conceptual awareness in addition to sound-letter correspondence and their knowledge of language.

Frank was a child who was predicted to be a reading failure. At the end of his first year of reading instruction, Frank produced the following reading for the text. His substitutions are written over the original text which is set in type.

> Here is a little red toy. *train*
> Here is a big blue toy. *airplane*

In reading *train* for *toy,* Frank used initial consonants and picture clues. However, in the second sentence he changed from *train* to *airplane.* Frank may be suggesting that the same word cannot be used to indicate specific objects that are both *big* and *blue* as well as *little* and *red.*

Frank may be more concerned with concepts and meaning than the author of the text. The accompanying illustrations to the story supported Frank's view that there were no similar objects that were both *little* and *red* and *big* and *blue.* The author chose to use a superordinate or generalized term in order to repeat the word *toy* a certain required number of times. However, Frank seemed to know that in certain language environments a specific name is more appropriate than a generalized term. Frank knew the word *toy* in oral language. In fact, after the story, I asked him, "What were the children playing with?"

Frank responded, "With their toys."

In his response, a generalized term like *toys* is called for and he can use it appropriately. Miscue analysis has provided ample evidence that when the text provides inappropriate language cues, readers of all ages and even of various abilities can edit the author's writing and produce language more acceptable to the reader.

It is because miscues reveal how readers use language and experience as they read that we reject the term *error* which suggests incorrectness and randomness. All readers produce miscues (3). Whenever language is processed, both parties to the communication are actively involved. The minute one becomes actively involved in communication, translation or transformations begin to take place. This involvement causes mismatches among the parties in communication. The mismatches in reading are often indications of how well a reader is processing the language, as well as an indication of any difficulties a reader may be having. It is because the mismatch is caused by the language and experience cueing systems that such mismatches have been termed miscues.

EMPHASIS ON SKILLS

At any point where readers overuse any one of the language systems in reading to the exclusion of the others, there seems to be a breakdown in the reading process.

Usually, however, miscue analysis reveals that if readers overuse any one system, it is the graphophonic system—the relationship between sounds and letters. This may be due to an overemphasis on phonics and other word attack skills in early reading instruction.

At one point somewhat later than his earlier reading, Frank was provided with information which suggested that sounding out was the most important part of reading. At this point in his reading development he produced the following for the text passage. Substitutions are written over the text word and omissions are circled.

Bird   *dolls toy*
But the old toys (did) not
Monkey *newp*   *hair*
make the new doll happy.

The focus on isolated skills is not productive for early readers.

"Skills" fragment and isolate language into highly abstract units. Learning abstract units is a more complex task for young readers than learning to handle the same unit embedded in a familiar language context. Language in its whole and natural state is greater than the sum of its parts. Sounds change depending on linguistic environment, such as the word *can* in the sentence: *Can you put it in the trash can?* Words change sounds as well as grammatical function, depending on linguistic environment such as the word *police* in the sentences: *I will call the police* and *The police car will be coming soon.* Sentences change meaning from one language context to the other. For an example consider:

Mary whispered to her husband as she furtively pointed to the bride's ring, "Look at the size of that stone!"

"Look at the size of that stone." The highway construction foreman shouted loudly to all the men as he surveyed the huge boulder that the avalanche had placed in the path of his construction project.

Children learn to handle these differences in oral language because of all kinds of cues which exist in the oral language environment. Through miscue analysis, we are convinced that written language provides the same kinds of cues if reading instruction helps students focus on meaning and thus keeps all the cueing systems in proper relationship.

If children know from the beginning of their reading that reading is similar to listening, then they can use their language sense to predict, to reread and correct, or to continue reading and search for additional cues if their predictions don't work out. They can construct meaning as they read.

An emphasis on isolated skills makes readers believe that each letter, each word, each detail in written language is equally significant to every other letter, word, or detail. In language learning it is important to differentiate the significant from the insignificant. Readers in difficulty often exhibit through their miscues an inability to treat phenomena in a variable way. Rather than try an appropriate substitute like *pony* for *horse* or *house* for *home*, which proficient readers tend to do, less proficient readers will either omit the word or keep after the word, trying again and again unproductively to sound it out. Such readers sometimes believe that the only way to learn a word is to be given that word by the teacher. Such children will say, "I haven't had that word yet" or "We didn't learn that yet." These children tend not to trust their own sense of language and fall further behind as they continue to process each word and each letter as if each carries as much information as any other. Such students will even stop at proper nouns which would be difficult, if not impossible, for adult readers and try to sound them out. This takes so much energy that the reader will be discouraged at the end of a sentence containing one such name.

Even when readers focus on graphic information, the human need to produce language seems to emerge.

When focused on letter-sound correspondence or provided with minimal language context, beginning readers are known to confuse words which are similar in configuration or letter shape. Sometimes they even begin to reverse some letter-sound sequences, producing *on* for *no, spot* for *stop,* and *was* for *saw.* When these phenomena are examined in the reading of a whole story and evaluated in terms of what language phenomena are involved in such miscues, a complex picture emerges.

In context, *was* is substituted for *saw* occasionally but rarely if ever is *saw* substituted for *was*. In addition, the *was* for *saw* substitutions occur in subject-verb-object sentences like:

Text   I saw a monkey.

Reader   I was a monkey.

However, when *was* is a verb marker or when *was* is in a subject-verb-adjective sentence such as *I was happy*, a different set of constraints is involved and the same type of miscues are not produced. Also, if one considers that these sentences are embedded in long stories where both the semantic and syntactic constraints operate, then it becomes easier to understand why certain miscues do not occur in contextual material to the same degree as they occur in isolated word lists or unrelated sentences.

Another such reader confusion may add to the understanding of how grammar is involved in many miscues which were usually considered simple graphic confusions. Early readers often confuse *said* with *and*. Both words occur frequently at pivotal points in sentences. When readers make such miscues their oral intonation is usually produced appropriately.

Text   "I will call Father," said Mother.

Reader   "I will call Father and Mother."

Text   Mary and John and Sally do not go to school yet.

Reader   "Mary and John," said Sally, "Do not go to school yet."

It is interesting to note that, as reading material becomes more involved and such sentences are embedded in more complex story context, such miscues almost disappear.

IF NOT SKILLS, WHAT THEN?

We must treat written language as language and help students do the same. Early school experiences provide many opportunities for the teacher to help readers use written language in the same way as they learned oral language.

We need to saturate the environment with written language and involve the children in the process. Charts around the room can explain what is expected of the students and what the jobs are in the classroom. These should be written by the teacher as she and the student discuss the classroom operation. The charts can be reread at the beginning of each day to decide who is going to do what and at the end of the day to evaluate what has happened and to plan the next day's activities. Whatever activities are planned by the teacher, such as those involved with plants or fish tanks, can be explored with the children. These experiences can be written, in front of the children, by the teacher on large charts and become reading material for the children on future days when the experiences or experiments are reexamined or rediscussed. Materials can be sent out to the parents as newsletters and the children will be able to read them to their parents.

Not only should the room be saturated with materials that the children write and which become reading material for them, but all kinds of books, magazines, and newspapers written especially for children should be available. Children should be encouraged to read silently and independently as well as to small groups of other children. Learning to swim is done by swimming in pools, lakes, rivers, and oceans. Learning to drive is done by driving on mountain roads, highways, one-lane rural roads, and busy city streets. Learning to read is greatly enhanced by having much experience reading all kinds of written language.

In addition to doing a lot of reading, children should be read to often. With tape recorders and listening posts available, children have the opportunity to listen to all kinds of stories. Teachers should also read to children and rediscover the lost art of storytelling. Children exposed to a variety of linguistic styles and content through their ears are more likely to be able to predict such structures when they appear in their reading.

When students show a special enjoyment for certain kinds of written material, they should be encouraged to write their own stories using similar patterns. Songs and rhymes are good subjects for such experiences. Writing supports and enhances reading. Even when students learn certain patterns in their reading they seem to begin to predict the pattern in later reading settings. For example, one child after reading two sentences. "It is big." "It is blue." and read the sentence, "It is the big, blue airplane." as "It is little." then corrected to "big blue airplane." This reader picked up the subject-verb-adjective pattern from the first two sentences and predicted a similar pattern for the third sentence. He was able to correct part of the sentence when the additional language cues suggested that the pattern he had in mind was not what he expected.

Reading is a receptive process. That means that it is not necessary to be able to pronounce or produce every word as one reads. Readers should be encouraged to continue reading even when they come to unknown words and not to ask the teacher, a parent, or another student for such words. Teachers should help students realize that if they read through to the end of the reading material, they may be able to understand the meaning of an unfamiliar word even if they cannot pronounce it and that understanding is the most important aspect of reading—far more important than learning how to pronounce words.

Through miscue analysis, we have discovered that children are able to provide meanings for many concepts, such as *transom, typical, ewe, experiment, chemistry,* and *fawn,* even though they are unable to pronounce such words appropriately as they read them orally. We also learned that there are students who can pronounce such words appropriately, but they do not necessarily understand the concepts.

Through miscue analysis we have learned a great deal about what elementary school age children do when they read. We are convinced that the more children treat reading like language, the more easily they learn to read.

We are still not sure how children learn to read. Since the early 1900s, psycholinguists, psychologists, and linguists have been studying how children acquire oral language. They have done depth research of a small number of subjects. These children have been studied in their homes in natural settings and a great deal about child language development has been learned in this way. We have learned that language facility is a strength each child possesses. I would like to suggest that similar studies need to be done in written language acquisition. It is possible that in societies or communities where print is a natural part of the environment that written language acquisition may start as early as two or three years of age and may be acquired as easily and in a similar way to oral language.

I would urge additional diary studies like the Soderbergh study (6) done in Sweden. Soderbergh, however, taught her daughter directly. Oral language is learned more naturally. Is it possible that children develop rules about written language by being bombarded with television commercials, cans and cereal boxes at the supermarket, and the signs which pollute the environment?

Learning to read can be easy if children are permitted to learn in the natural direction of their own development. We need to find out what these natural directions are so that we can enhance children's learning to read.

REFERENCES

1. Clay, Marie M. "The Reading Behavior of Five-Year-Old Children: A Research Report," *New Zealand Journal of Educational Studies*, 2 (May 1967), 11-31.
2. Goodman, Kenneth. "A Linguistic Study of Cues and Miscues in Reading," *Elementary English*, October 1965, 641-643.
3. Goodman, Kenneth, and Carolyn Burke. *Theoretically Based Studies of Patterns of Oral Reading Performance*. U.S. Department of Health, Education and Welfare, Project No. 9-0375, April 1973.
4. Goodman, Yetta M. "A Psycholinguistic Description of Observed Oral Reading Phenomena in Selected Young Beginning Readers," unpublished dissertation, Wayne State University, 1967.
5. Goodman, Yetta M. *Longitudinal Study of Children's Oral Reading Behavior*, U.S. Department of Health, Education and Welfare, Project No. 9-E-062, September 1971.
6. Soderbergh, Ragnhild. *Reading in Early Childhood: A Linguistic Study of a Swedish Preschool Children's Gradual Acquisition of Reading Ability*. Stockholm: Boktryckeriet Kungl, P.A. Norstedt, and Soner, 1971.

Language and the Reader

Minnie Young Peaster
University of Mississippi
University, Mississippi
United States of America

The word *arts* as it is used with the word *language* aptly describes the skillful and creative blending of ideas about listening, speaking, writing, and reading. Through the selection and use of methods and materials, each facet of language arts comes to be considered a part of the whole. Children exposed to such an experience seem intuitively to know that listening is an integral portion of that which the British know as oracy. Learning to read and write holds no threat for them because they begin to feel somewhere in the developmental process a need to enlarge those skills they mastered in learning to listen and to speak. It is essential for this need to be felt.

Children who encounter such an educational experience are fortunate indeed. Teachers who have the know-how for the creation of a learning-favored environment are known as masters of the art. Hence, the term *language arts*.

LANGUAGE AND READING

Motivation for reading can therefore be said to come from an inspired search for meaning. This holds true for the arduous task of learning to read as well as for the seemingly less laborious one of perfecting and polishing reading skills. For some children there may be meaning enough in just being able to hold a book as they begin to read. At any given time, meaning may be one type of motivation for the beginner and quite another for the fluent reader. The magic key in either case is language. There are those, however, who feel that additional meaning lies in sound responses to symbols. The linguist, Leonard Bloomfield (2), advanced the idea that learning to read was so all-absorbing a task that to find meaning within the deep structure of material to be read was not a matter of great significance to the beginner. In translating this theory of Bloomfield's into action, an instructor takes from it according to his own personal theory of language only that which in turn can be transmitted in terms of learner capability. Probing farther into an understanding of language involves an investigation of meaning carried not only within definitions of words but in and between individual understandings of words. Syntax, or word order, carries a good share of meaning. Smith (5) demonstrates that he is moving closer to an understanding when he visualizes syntax as a bridge which allows meaning to go back and forth between the deep structure and the surface information carried by symbols. Yet he readily admits that he knows little about children or instructional procedures.

Strickland (17), through her deep awareness of child development combined with her knowledge of language development, saw a need to consider both in teaching children. Their natural love of language is a built-in motivation factor. In reporting her study of children's language she stressed the necessity for making children aware of meaning which is implicit in the suprasegmental phonemes of stress, pitch and juncture.

CHANGE IN VIEWPOINT

With the foregoing in mind, the question remains, what is behind the continued concern with reading? Are there some new and different implications remaining to be discovered and, if so, will changes in thinking precipitate changes in teaching techniques? Perhaps it is a persuasion that keeps professors professing, a persuasion born of the persistent feeling that it is possible for more teachers to become "masters of the art."

Impetus for change is seldom generated by teachers themselves. Not action but reaction to impingement of outside forces is expected and accepted as the general mode of procedure for people in the field of education.

WHY JOHNNY CAN'T READ

An outstanding exception to the accepted was demonstrated in response to the book *Why Johnny Can't Read*. The exceptions began with the furor caused when Flesch (6) published his book in 1955. Attention of such magnitude is rare for a book on educational matters. Running counter to expectations, the author was not from outside the field.

Teachers benefited from the controversy which raged between critics of school reading programs and experts in the field of reading. From the beginning, teachers were quite astute at picking up cues from their defenders. Pretested phrases and research results were assets to which they fell heir. They hastened to adopt techniques for helping parents and other concerned taxpayers understand the true status of reading instruction. Supported by the logic behind the reasoning, they helped people see that neither the sight word method nor the phonics method was usable in pure form for teaching reading.

One of the outcomes was that teachers discovered they could be more outspoken even in their own defense. For the first time teachers as a group began to see themselves as less subservient to authority figures. From issues which forced a meeting of minds between educators and the lay public grew the move to make working partners of parents. No longer were parents consciously made to feel that reading instruction was a mysterious process better left to the formal school setting.

The rash of enthusiasm for improving methods and materials was another increment for teachers of reading. Before this time the concerns of war and its aftermath had been so all-absorbing that little attention had been given to what was going on in the schools. Children in the classroom began to reap benefits from techniques which had been developed for the teaching of recruits for the army. Almost overnight there erupted a multitude of studies and research projects pertaining to reading.

CONTRIBUTIONS MADE BY OUTSIDERS

The evident need for improved methods and materials may have served as an attraction to some outside the field. Funds allocated for research in the area no doubt attracted others. Whatever the impetus, outstanding contributions have since been made by individuals engaged in activities not considered a part of primary education.

Sociologists have contributed greatly to the understanding of the needs of disadvantaged children. Neurologists have helped explain difficulties faced by learning disabled children. Medical specialists have demonstrated effects of dietary deficiencies on learning capabilities of children.

Contributions of a different ilk are those made by specialists who indiscriminately attach labels to human beings. A disquieting example of this are the optometrists and ophthalmologists who have developed remunerative practices through the diagnosis and treatment of that obscure malady, dyslexia. There is the possibility also that teachers have been offered a prepackaged escape from responsibility. Even parents have been lulled into a sense of security by having the services of a specialist for a child with reading problems.

There is a large and concurrently growing literature concerned with learning difficulties. Cohen (3) speaks to this point when he discusses the many labels used as smoke screens. He found them to be more of an obstruction than a help. In his attack on diagnostic abstractions, he cited studies of children with all the labels from *disadvantaged* through *dyslexia to minimal brain dysfunction* ". . . who suddenly read on grade level not because of neurological treatment, perceptual training, or mass psychotherapy, but because of a slight improvement in the quality of traditional classroom instruction."

These specialists and their critics are making a contribution in more than one way. They are spotlighting reading as an area for increased concern. In the literature on the subject there seems to be a noticeable trend toward making the teaching of reading one facet of a more comprehensive approach to language.

OTHER OUTSIDERS

It may be of interest to briefly document this emerging emphasis. Psychologists and linguists were among the first to show an interest in the reading process. B. F. Skinner (14), a distinguished Yale psychologist, is considered the initiator of the emphasis on programed reading. The talking typewriter is the work of another Yale psychologist (12). The work of both men promoted the use of teaching machines. Many teachers believe that instruction, thus envisioned, ignores the importance of language to human development.

Leonard Bloomfield (1) was one of the first linguists to apply his knowledge of language to reading, a process which he viewed as mechanical. He devised a "systematic methodology" for use in teaching his own child to read (2).

Charles Carpenter Fries, a distinguished authority on American English, was one of the first major linguists to develop methods and materials for classroom use (7). Using Bloomfield's work as a base, he added his own philosophy concerning meaning. He saw it as being more significant to the child's learning.

Carl Lefevre (11) stopped short of explaining total language development as it is slowly coming to be understood. He, however, went much further with meaning emphasis than Fries. It was Lefevre who advocated the use of the phrase, the clause, and even the whole sentence as units for instruction in reading.

Linguists are at this time turning their attention to clarification of the distinctions between decoding skills and the understanding of language (19). Smith (15) might well be speaking for the linguists when he says of himself: "I began by using reading as a way to study language, and ended by using language as one of the ways in which to understand reading."

The writings of Vygotsky (18) and Piaget (13) relating to their research on language and thought have had a tremendous impact on the thinking of teachers in the United States. This is evidenced by the steady flow of passports being issued to teachers on their way to take a look at British Primary Schools where they hope to see a practical application of the theories of these writers.

BRITISH PRIMARY SCHOOLS

Coming into their own, at last, Piaget's theories and research have been a determining force in the language arts approach to instruction in the British schools (4). His influence is seen in what Downing lists as the three important bases for the changes in methods and materials used for instruction: 1) In 1944, individualized teaching was proclaimed as the national goal of education; 2) teachers were accorded a genuine professional status; and 3) the particular needs of younger children were specially recognized.

One immediate effect of individualizing instruction was the abolition of *standards* or *grades*. When teachers were accorded professional status they were "given more and more independence and responsibility for the education of the children in their charge." Schools for children between the ages of five and seven were created to give educational treatment in accordance with the needs of this age group (4).

Reading research findings have joined hands with common sense to say again "it is the teacher who makes the difference." The educational jargon of today is filled with pungent truisms of the like. For example, we hear teachers explain their approach to instruction by using the worn phrase "take the child where he is and move him as far as his capabilities will allow." Hardly a teacher alive will admit to not making use of "the discovery method." No matter what the subject content, teachers profess to use "the child's interest" as a beginning point. The pet phrases spring easily to the tongue in casual conversation and in symposiums concerning education. But how widespread is practical application of the knowledge indicated by the use of such phrases? A combination of circumstances causes an awareness to be heard in the language which is not demonstrated in the classroom. In an effort to excuse this occurrence, teachers offer class size and lack of instructional space, equipment, or materials. The reason given most often for teachers not doing what they know full well would work in facilitating learning, is that freedom is denied them by a restrictive school administration.

If it is true that "the teacher makes the difference," then a teacher should have the authority to make educational decisions. In systems in which the faculty has been accorded professional status, the teacher is the one who chooses materials, makes the decision about content, and decides on the method by which it is to be taught. Then, and only then, can a teacher be creative enough to make a positive difference.

TEACHER PREPARATION

If *arts*, as it is used with *language*, is the key to more meaningful reading and the teacher is the answer, then what can be done to assist teachers in assuming their rightful prerogatives? Hopefully, more comprehensive preparation will enable them to automatically move in this direction. Instances of administrative failure in delegating responsibility should be met by significant demands from qualified and informed teachers.

In describing what is happening to training programs for teachers in the field of reading, Strickland (16) says, "More courses in reading in teacher education programs appear to make little difference in what is happening to children in the schools." She further laments, "Rarely is there any requirement that teachers understand language and its relationship to reading." From a language arts point of view, she has suggestions for meeting "obvious" needs in the field of reading:

> . . . give teachers a thorough knowledge of child development and of children's methods of learning and using language, thorough understanding of the psychology of learning, wide acquaintance with books and materials for children, and understanding of the many methods which can be adapted to the needs of children as they learn to read. They could then send teachers forth to study their own group of children and adapt all that they know to meet the needs of each one of them.

In teacher preparation at the undergraduate level and in programs for inservice training, the trend seems to be toward a study of language and what happens at each developmental stage. Interest in the relationship between language and reading is gradually expanding. More and more literature is appearing which steers thinking toward a study of language and its implication for learning, versus teaching.

Heilman, in his book, *Smuggling Language Into The Teaching of Reading* (9), writes "Language is the only magic available to the school; all the rest is routine, ritual and rote." The relationship between language and thought is a topic meriting space in the newer books on reading.

AN INNOVATIVE APPROACH TO TEACHER TRAINING

In preparing teachers to work with young children, Peggy Emerson (5) stimulates interest in new techniques as she probes even deeper into the study of language. She encourages investigation of the idea that "the educational system has overemphasized the discursive elements of language." She feels that language may not have developed solely as a means of communication. Her philosophy stems from the work of Langer (10). She feels intuitively and from her studies of young children that educators need to take into account the symbolizing process which is "unique to man." Her program is structured to "induce cognitive growth through the senses, by increasing the opportunity for presentational experience before and simultaneous with discursive experience." An approach of this kind is expected to contribute to both "thought" process and language development (5).

Herein, perhaps, lies the secret of success with language in methods and materials for primary students. Herein also is a rationale for incorporating reading into the total language arts program.

With all these things in mind—seeing reading as one facet of the language arts, seeing the teacher's responsibility grow to meet the demands of new knowledge and new school organization, and visualizing a more comprehensive teacher training program—the day will perhaps come when teachers have such an abiding respect for language that they will, as a matter of course, demonstrate their humanitarianism by leading children to a new feeling for their own. They may educate a new generation to feel about their language as Hammarskjold (8) expressed:

> Respect for the word is the first commandment in the discipline by which a man can be educated to maturity—intellectual, emotional, and moral. Respect for the word—to employ it with scrupulous care and an incorruptible heartfelt love of truth—is essential if there is to be any growth in a society or in the human race.
>
> To misuse the word is to show contempt for man. It undermines the bridges and poisons the wells. It causes Man to regress down the long path of his evolution.

Teachers will make a new declaration of independence in which they say: We hold these truths to be self-evident,

> . . . that when instruction becomes destructive
> to the joy of learning—
> that instruction should be abolished
> or modified
> in such a manner
> as to lead potential learners
> to experience
> > the power,
> > the beauty,
> > and the magic
> > of their language (8).

REFERENCES
1. Bloomfield, Leonard. *Language*. New York: Henry Holt, 1933.
2. Bloomfield, Leonard, and Clarence Barnhart. *Let's Read: A Linguistic Approach*. Detroit, Michigan: Wayne State University Press, 1961.
3. Cohen, S. Alan, and Thelma Cooper. "Seven Fallacies: Reading, Retardation, and the Urban Disadvantage of Beginning Readers," *Reading Teacher*, 26 (October 1972).
4. Downing, John. "Language Arts in the British Primary School Revolution," pamphlet reprinting of a paper presented at the NCTE Language Arts Conference, St. Louis, 1970.

5. Emerson, Peggy. "A Theory of Language as Expressive Form: An Approach to Teaching the Language Arts," unpublished dissertation, University of Mississippi, 1968.

6. Flesch, Rudolf. *Why Johnny Can't Read*. New York: Harper and Brothers, 1955.

7. Fries, Charles C. *Linguistics and Reading*. New York: Holt, Rinehart and Winston, 1963.

8. Hammarskjold, Dag. *Markings*. Translated by Leif Sjoberg and W. H. Auden. New York: Alfred A. Knopf, 1964.

9. Heilman, Arthur W., and Elizabeth Ann Holmes. *Smuggling Language into the Teaching of Reading*. Columbus, Ohio: Charles E. Merrill, 1972.

10. Langer, Susanne. *Philosophy in a New Key*. New York: New American Library, 1957.

11. Lefevre, Carl. *Linguistics and the Teaching of Reading*. New York: McGraw Hill, 1964.

12. Moore, Omar K., and Alan R. Anderson. *The Responsive Environments Project*. In R. Hess & R. M. Bear (Eds.) *The Challenge of Early Education*. Chicago: Aldine, 1967.

13. Piaget, Jean. *The Language and Thought of the Child*. Translated by Majorie Gabain. New York: Noonday Press, 1955.

14. Skinner, B. F. The Science of Learning and the Art of Teaching. Harvard Educational Review, 1954, 24 (2).

15. Smith, Frank. *Understanding Reading*. New York: Holt, Rinehart and Winston, 1971.

16. Strickland, Ruth G. "A Challenge to Teachers of Reading," *Bulletin of the School of Education*, Indiana University, 45 (March 1569).

17. Strickland, Ruth G. "The Language of Elementary School Children: Its Relationship to the Language of Reading Textbooks and the Quality of Reading of Selected Children," *Bulletin of the School of Education*, Indiana University, 38 (July 1962).

18. Vygotsky, L. S. *Thought and Language*. Translated by Eugenia Hanfmann and Gertrude Vakar. Cambridge, Massachusetts: M.I.T. Press, 1962.

19. Walcutt, Charles Child, Joan Lamport, and Glenn McCracken. *Teaching Reading*. New York: Macmillan, 1974.

Language Games and Literacy

Susan A. Wasserman
California State University
Northridge, California
United States of America

"Today, I'm going to learn to read!" This is the expectation of many youngsters as they enter school motivated to learn. It is also a fervent expectation of parents for their children, as well as being an area of deep concern. Will their children learn to read successfully?

"I can read! I can read!" So exclaims the young child with delight to the teacher, the parents, and all who will listen when realization dawns that the strange squiggles on the page can be deciphered and that the "secret code" can be broken. The fulfillment of this joyful expectation about reading occurs for children when they begin to understand the relationship between sound and symbol and are able to derive meaning from the printed page.

For some children, however, this understanding is not internalized readily. For these children, the motivation to read may begin quickly to dissipate; the joyful expectation of success may soon be buried beneath a proliferation of pencil and paper skill-type activities.

Andrew Wilkinson (9) coined the term *oracy* to refer to listening and speaking. He maintains that oracy must not only precede literacy (reading and writing) but must continue to be emphasized and expanded while literacy is being achieved. These arts of language, speaking, listening, reading, and writing must been seen by teachers as interrelated and interdependent if they are to help children succeed in them.

Although the close relationship of language proficiency and success in reading is well accepted, many well-meaning, conscientious teachers neglect oracy in their attempt to hurry young children into literacy. James Moffett (5) explains that many problems that teachers see as reading problems may in actuality be problems with language. As some children begin to experience such problems, motivation may be affected, self-concept may be diminished, and any further success in reading may be thwarted.

How then can teachers help young children succeed in reading? If children are to be successful, teachers must provide them a myriad of opportunities to "drink in" and use language in the classroom. Bill Martin (4), who has authored a series of reading books for children using fine literature, reinforces the importance of this idea of helping children "play" with language. He asserts that children must have joyous excursions into language and should not be confined only to tightly controlled drill-exercises that distort the wholeness of language. Martin further proposes that teachers help children analyze the language that is "firmly imprinted in their ears" so that they can better understand the structure of language and make it work for them in terms of their individual needs.

LANGUAGE GAMES FOR ORACY AND LITERACY

In his latest book, Ruddell (6) focuses on the idea that a reading program must, in actuality, be a reading-language program if it is to give children all of the activities necessary for success in reading. A number of teachers agreeing with this idea have found that the use of a variety of language games and selected related oral activities has served to heighten children's interest while providing essential experiences facilitating oracy which, in turn, lead to literacy.

The following language games represent only a few that can be an important part of a well-planned and implemented reading-language program. Although set in the context of the American-English language, these games could be adapted for use in other languages having syntactical differences, or be used to teach English as a second language.

The games are grouped here according to important concepts of language such as sentence structure, expanding and transforming sentences, and sequencing of sentences and events within stories.

SENTENCE STRUCTURE

Fish-A-Flash. This activity has as its objective the expansion of the child's syntactical resources.

   a. Fish shapes are cut out of colored paper and a metal clip is attached so that the fish can be "caught" by a magnet at the end of a fishing line attached to a small fishing pole.

   b. Nouns/noun phrases are printed on one color of paper (dogs, the chair).

   c. Verbs/verb phrases are printed on a second color (are running, played in the house).

   d. One child at a time fishes for two fish, one of each color.

   e. The child attempts to make a sentence, checking it orally with his fellow players.

   f. If the noun phrase and verb phrase don't combine to make sense, the child waits a turn to try again for two more fish.

Gradually, the children develop the idea that in the English language, syntax is based primarily on a binary structure of subject-predicate; they also grow in their awareness of what a sentence is.

Cut and Trade. The object of this activity is to help children generate sentences and develop flexibility and variety in sentence structure.

a. Children formulate orally a series of sentences, usually about objects or activities occurring in the room.

b. The teacher prints these on individual sentence strips (pieces of tag board). The teacher demonstrates the cutting of the sentences between the noun phrase and verb phrase (The boy/ran. The rabbit/is in the cage.)

c. The children are then given their sentence strips.

d. Working as partners, the children cut each sentence after the noun phrase and generate new sentences by substituting the noun phrases for other noun phrases and verb phrases for other verb phrases.

e. When each child has formulated as many sentences as possible that make good sentence sense, the child then trades noun and/or verb phrases with the partner. As the children work, they read each newly generated sentence aloud.

A later step is to help children understand that noun phrases can be divided between the determiner and noun (The/rabbit). At that time, the teacher can ask the children for words that describe the rabbit. These words can be written on cards and distributed to the children to expand sentences. Similarly, the verb phrase can be manipulated by the children.

EXPANDING AND TRANSFORMING SENTENCES

Surprise Basket (5). This activity provides for vocabulary development and opportunities for oral transformations and expansions of sentences by children.

a. Various items, commonly found around the home or at school, are placed in an attractively decorated straw purse or basket.

b. A child selects an object and identifies it in a sentence. (This is a key.)

c. The child then orally generates a series of sentences beginning the sentences with the name of the object. (The key is red. The key is small.)

d. The child can then be helped to formulate several different types of transformations. (The red key is small. The small key is not large. Is this a key?)

e.   Children expand sentences further by learning to use a variety of modifiers.

Children delight in this kind of activity and enjoy the idea of the variety of sentences they can generate. After much "play" with language in this way, children's sentences can be written so that they can see and read them in print.

Circle Look at Me. The purpose of this type of activity is to help children feel secure in manipulating sentences, resulting in more descriptive sentences.

a.   The teacher whispers to one child to perform a particular action.

b.   While the child is performing the action, the teacher asks the group, "What is Johnny doing?" After the children give an answer such as "John is walking," the teacher seeks other statements helping the children manipulate the noun phrase (He is walking. The boy is walking.) Descriptive words are also added by the children (The tall, smiling boy is walking.)

c.   The teacher continues to ask questions such as: "Where is John walking?" "How is John walking?" which elicit verb phrase changes. A variety of children's responses is always encouraged (John is walking around the teacher and children. The boy is walking very fast, but carefully.)

d.   Two children are asked to perform different actions (John is walking and Lynn is running around the circle. John is walking while Jill is running.)

SEQUENCE

Role Play and Show. The following activities develop and reinforce the concept of sequence:

a.   A story is read or told to the children. A small group of youngsters dramatizes the story after recalling the sequence of events.

b.   Using a camera, the teacher or a child snaps pictures of the dramatization. Later, these pictures are made into slides.

c.   The children's verbal presentation of the story is duplicated on a tape recorder.

d.   At a future time, the slides and tape are used at a listening post/viewing center (tape recorder, ear phones, slide projector and small viewing screen).

e.   After viewing and listening at the center, each child illustrates and then dictates or writes a series of sentences showing the sequence of events at the beginning, middle, and ending of the story. Later, these can be shared and discussed with the total group.

Around We Go. Children are helped in this activity to utilize the knowledge of sequencing gained from hearing stories so that they may generate a new story with attention to a logical sequence of events.

a. The teacher tells a group of children the beginning of a new story.
b. The children, sitting in a circle with the teacher, add the events for the middle and ending of the story.
c. The teacher, another adult, or older child prints the sentences on tag board strips as they are told orally by the children. After the story is completed, they review the story sequence by assembling the sentences in their appropriate order.
d. A variation of the activity is the changing of the sequence of some of the events by the children to see if the ending of the story is affected.
e. Another variation is the teacher recalling with the children a familiar motif of a story such as an animal's journey from home to confrontation with a monster. The children then decide on a story well known to them which utilizes the motif and they tell the story taking care to keep the appropriate sequence of events. Or, the children can decide to originate a new story with the appropriate motif developing a logical sequence for the story.

Sing a Story. This activity helps children decide on the sequence of events in a story and then use this sequence in a song format.

a. The teacher and children compose a song utilizing the elements of a story in sequence.
b. The sequence is reinforced by having different children sing each part of the sequence. An example is a song based on Marjorie Flack's book (2) *Ask Mr. Bear* (the story of a little boy searching for something to give his mother for her birthday).

Child A (singing Danny's part)	Mrs. Hen, Good day; Mrs. Hen, Good day, What do you have for my mother's birthday?
Child B (singing the hen's part)	Danny, Good day; Danny, Good day, I have an egg for your mother's birthday.

c. The song continues using the dialogue of each animal in the order that Danny meets them in the book.
d. Stanzas are charted separately so that children can reassemble them in sequence.

Constraints of time and space do not permit a presentation of many other language games such as *The Real Me, Stuff Me Box, Peek-a-Bag, The M & M Game, Hide and See,* and others which aid in the areas of vocabulary and descriptive language development and understanding of plot and character development.

LITERATURE AND RELATED ACTIVITIES

In addition to language games, there are other related activities that combine oracy and literacy. One of the best avenues for such language exploration is literature. Folktales, nursery rhymes, fanciful tales, fables, myths and poetry can be told or read orally so that children begin to connect the words, sentences, and connected discourse with which they are familiar in their spoken language with the printed symbols representing that language which they will later find in books. Using literature in this way, children are provided with the impetus to expand experiences, expand language facility, and expand abilities in most receptive and expressive communication skills.

Martin (4) affirms that by reading literature to and with children, they get a wholeness of reading from "ear to mouth to eye," soon enabling them to "hear" the language even on an unfamiliar page of print. Martin terms this "reading with one's ears."

As children build a repertoire of literary stories, they use these as models for original stories they dictate or write. After hearing *The Gingerbread Boy, The Pancake,* and similarly patterned stories from European countries, a group of five-, six-, and seven-year-old Mexican-American children dictated a story (1) which illustrates ethnic background and the children's ability to innovate on a theme or motif:

The Tortilla

Written by David, Ana Marie, Marta, Eddie, Isela, Lilian, and Raul

A woman made a big tortilla. She put it in the oven. She put it by the window to cool. The tortilla ran away!

The woman chased Mr. Tortilla. The farmer chased the tortilla.

"Don't chase me! I'll sing you a song."

"I ran away from the little woman.

I can run away from an old man.

I can run away from you, I can, I can."

The bear is in the forest. He saw the tortilla. "I can't hear, tortilla. Please come closer. Come even closer. I still don't hear."

So, the tortilla came closer. The bear said, "Come closer. I still can't hear. Come closer to my head."

The tortilla came closer. The bear opened his mouth and ate the tortilla all up.

Another group of children wrote a story entitled, *The Pizza Man* (1):

Run, run as fast as you can;
You can't catch me
I'm the flying Pizza Man.

Modeled stories, such as *The Tortilla* and *The Pizza Man*, are made into attractive booklets resembling those resulting from the language experience approach to reading. These booklets are reread by the child authors and illustrators, shared with other children in the classroom, placed at a learning center to stimulate other book writing and binding, or placed in a classroom or school library.

Literature also can be the basis for many other creative activities, including creative dramatics, improvisation, choral reading, puppetry, various types of oral and written composition, and the creation and utilization of tapes and films.

The reading-language teacher who selects lovely books for children, reads orally to them, and plans many creative language activities stemming from literature provides a program which realizes literary goals as well as oracy and literacy goals. This type of program allows children to delight in reading and to know how to read. After all, what good is a decoder who doesn't read? How much better is a reader who can decode!

A TIME TO READ FOR ENJOYMENT

For many children, reading at school is not an enjoyable experience, but it appears as a seemingly endless succession of workbooks to be completed and a myriad of teacher questions to be answered. Even the most successful child in reading, one who really loves to read, soon becomes disenchanted when busywork activities hang like a millstone everytime a book is to be opened and read.

Teachers must help children view reading as a pleasurable act. There must be ample time in the classroom to read for sheer enjoyment. A program including USSR$_2$R (Uninterrupted, Sustained, Silent, Right to Read) provides this time. USSR$_2$R represents time set aside within one classroom, or preferably all classrooms throughout the entire school, to provide children with the opportunity to read books based on their individual interests without requiring any follow-up activities. This period of time may range from 10 minutes to an hour or even more. When the USSR$_2$R is conducted throughout a school, all children, teachers, and other school personnel read for the sheer joy of reading. During the reading time, a modeling of reading by adults occurs and children begin to see reading as a pleasurable act that everyone engages in and enjoys.

SUMMARY

Young children can be successful readers when motivation is established through a reading-language program consisting of many language and reading games, much listening and responding to a carefully selected body of literature, and many uninterrupted opportunities to read for the sheer joy of reading.

A number of years ago, Audrey Linaberry (3) expressed poetically and symbolically many of the ideas set forth in this paper in this poem:

To My Teacher

Put learning in my way, then stand aside
To guide my footsteps,
But do not push—
Don't make me go too fast to see and hear
This lovely world.
Let joy keep pace with growing.

REFERENCES

1. Brockman, Martha, and Susan Wasserman. "The Right to Read," in Helen Fielstra (Ed.), *Reading Monograph*, San Fernando Valley State College, 13-14, 1970.
2. Flack, Marjorie. *Ask Mr. Bear*. New York: Macmillan, 1942.
3. Linaberry, Audrey M. "To My Teacher," quoted in Ruby H. Warner, *The Child and his Elementary School World*. New Jersey: Prentice-Hall, 1957.
4. Martin, Bill, Jr. "Let Them Read," *California English Journal*, Fall 1967, 5-10.
5. Moffett, James. *A Student-Centered Language Arts Curriculum, Grades K-6: A Handbook for Teachers*. Boston: Houghton-Mifflin, 1968.
6. Ruddell, Robert B. *Reading-Language Instruction: Innovative Practices*. Englewood Cliffs, New Jersey: Prentice-Hall, 1974.
7. Wasserman, Paul, and Susan Wasserman. "No Hablo Ingles," *Elementary English*, October 1972, 832-835.
8. Wasserman, Susan. "Raising the Language Proficiency of Mexican-American Children in the Primary Grades," *California English Journal*, April 1970, 22-27.
9. Wilkinson, Andrew. "Listening and the Discriminative Response," *California English Journal*, December 1969.

La Lecture à l'Ecole Maternelle

Madeline Brohon
Syndicat National des
Instituteurs, France

Lire implique savoir lire, c'est-à-dire non seulement acquérir des mécanismes, permettant de déchiffrer un code écrit établi selon des règles précises, mais aussi comprendre le sens attribué aux signes en fonction de leur assemblage par mots, phrases et textes, qui sont l'expression d'une pensée plus ou moins riche et nuancée. Il est évident que l'aisance dans la maîtrise des sons permet une interprétation plus sûre du message qui peut se révéler un mode de communication puissant.

Tout écrit, sous quelque forme qu'il se présente, lettre, revue, journal ou livre établit entre les hommes une relation qui se situe à des niveaux différents et tend vers des finalités diverses, à caractère éducatif ou propres à l'organisation des loisirs.

Il se définit comme un langage dont nous connaissons l'influence sur le comportement intellectuel et moral des individus. Il appartient aux éducateurs qui s'occupent plus particulièrement des adolescents de leur faire deviner les effets positifs de la lecture en tant que moyen d'information et de perfectionnement de la langue, de leur former le goût par une orientation judicieuse dans le choix de leurs ouvrages.

AUPARAVANT, QUAND APPRENDRE A LIRE ET COMMENT?

S'il est vrai que la lecture constitue un apport heureux à l'enrichissement culturel de l'homme, par des investigations dans le passé ou la vie contemporaine, à travers l'espace, apporte à l'adulte une documentation indispensable à sa tâche et le fruit de l'expérience des autres, éveille sa curiosité et son goût de la recherche, lui procure des satisfactions nobles ou une simple détente salutaire à sa santé, il semble bien naturel qu'on cherche à mettre l'enfant, le plus tôt possible, dans les conditions les meilleures pour l'acheminer vers un langage nouveau, tout en respectant sa personnalité et en évaluant ses possibilités.

Quelques réflexions nous sont suggérées par l'observation des enfants à l'école ou dans notre entourage.

Notons au passage quelques attitudes à propos de l'approche de la lecture:

- enfants qui font semblant de lire pour imiter les grands;
- enfants qui, face au livre, en regardant les images inventent l'histoire qu'elles lui inspirent;
- enfants curieux qui posent des questions.

L'Ecole Maternelle a le privilège d'être le plus souvent la première collectivité qui accueille les enfants à l'âge où ils sont les plus réceptifs; elle se trouve cependant devant des difficultés qui résultent de comportements très différents. Les sujets développés sur le plan intellectuel, au vocabulaire étendu, à l'esprit éveillé voisinent avec des apathiques, étrangers à toute sollicitation et qui s'obstinent dans leur mutisme, avec des instables fatigués de leur agitation stérile. De cette diversité, attribuée dans la majorité des cas à l'inégalité des milieux socio-culturels auxquels appartiennent les élèves, l'éducatrice doit tenir compte par l'installation de sa classe en groupes de travail.

Les institutrices d'Ecoles Maternelles sont bien placées pour connaître les enfants et savoir ce qu'elles peuvent attendre d'eux. Elles ne peuvent cependant que bénéficier d'une coopération amicale avec les parents, parfois susceptibles de les éclairer sur les causes de telle ou telle réaction des enfants devant les activités scolaires: perturbations de la vie familiale compromettant l'équilibre affectif, troubles de la physiologie, deficiences sensorielles, incidence héréditaire adaptation malaisée, facteurs multiples entravant un développement normal.

Ceci mis à part, *l'institutrice doit garder une certaine autonomie* à l'égard de l'opinion publique *lorsqu'il s'agit de son rôle éducatif.* Car, à propos de la lecture justement, circulent des rumeurs parfois contradictoires.

Pour certains, l'Ecole Maternelle est le lieu où l'on apprend à lire et la maîtresse est jugée en fonction de sa réussite dans cette discipline qu'elle inculque aux enfants; c'est encore bien souvent aujourd'hui l'avis de parents ambitieux ou de collègues mal informés des problèmes de notre enseignement.

Pour d'autres, l'apprentissage de la lecture doit tenir un rang de second ordre, l'Ecole Maternelle réclamant de ses éducatrices l'animation d'une multitude d'activités, plus utiles à l'épanouissement de l'enfant.

Une mise au point s'avère indispensable.

Il nous paraît en effet anormal d'accorder dans nos grandes sections une place trop importante à l'acquisition de la lecture, le cours préparatoire étant tout indiqué pour ce travail. Nous pensons également qu'une répartition ordonnée des disciplines, tant physiques qu'intellectuelles ou artistiques vise à un développement harmonieux de l'enfant. Nous nous opposons à un apprentissage forcé de la lecture préjudiciable à un déroulement régulier des travaux de la classe, nuisible aussi à la scolarité future de l'enfant par l'apparition de troubles dysléxiques et d'un comportement d'opposition aux études.

Par contre, il est regrettable de priver certains enfants dotés d'une maturité suffisante et attirés par la lecture, de moyens propres à faciliter les acquisitions.

Nous savons bien qu'il n'y a pas de règle absolue pour l'âge d'apprendre à lire. L'observation et l'expérience nous permettent seulement d'affirmer que les résultats les plus féconds s'obtiennent souvent dans le courant de la sixième année.

Dans l'idéal, l'Ecole Maternelle devrait être en mesure de donner à chaque enfant ce qui peut lui convenir. *Malheureusement, les effectifs pléthoriques de nos classes ne facilitent guère la tâche des éducatrices, lesquelles regrettent de n'avoir pas toujours, à l'égard des enfants défavorisés, la disponibilité que serait nécessaire.* L'Ecole Maternelle devrait accorder un soutien tout particulier aux enfants qui n'ont pas la chance d'être mis, dès le plus jeune âge, dans une ambiance familiale stimulante pour les premières découvertes.

L'Ecole Maternelle doit surtout être une initiatrice, c'est-à-dire celle qui met en route et trace la voie.

Comment jouer ce rôle à propos de la lecture?

En pratiquant une pédagogie attrayante, à l'esprit vivant et concret. Peu importe les méthodes; l'essentiel est de provoquer l'intérêt.

En se rappelant que cet enseignement est lié à toutes les autres activités, qu'il ne constitue pas un fait isolé et privilégié pour un éveil de l'intelligence. Au stade le plus élevé, avec des maîtresses averties, son insertion dans le thème de vie permet une concentration plus ferme de l'attention et s'étaie sur un langage oral plus riche. Bien avant que de savoir lire, l'enfant utilise les images, allant du simple objet qu'il nomme à la petite scène qu'il interprète à sa manière, avec un langage plus ou moins juste et cohérent. Nous pouvons utiliser cet attrait pour l'image, afin de l'amener progressivement vers le message écrit, dont il faut par ailleurs souligner l'utilité. Comment ne pas oublier l'histoire racontée à l'école, sinon en la fixant sur le papier, d'abord par le dessin, moyen d'expression courant chez les enfants, puis par les lettres dont l'assemblage réalise un graphisme plus rapide et plus précis.

L'assouplissement des relations entre l'image, l'expression orale et la trace écrite constitue la base de la pédagogie du français à l'Ecole Maternelle pour les acquisitions certes bien modestes de la lecture.

Le texte est au départ des premiers essais: il s'agit de bien pénétrer l'enfant de cette valeur de la langue écrite, en lui signifiant que le symbole est associé à l'idée et que lire sous-entend communiquer.

Ce qui paraît essentiel, c'est de donner avant tout aux jeunes le goût de la lecture, de leur en permettre une approche confiante et sereine, les engageant à poursuivre leurs efforts pour une assimilation plus parfaite.

Faut-il utiliser ou proscrire le manuel de lecture à l'Ecole Maternelle?

Il ne semble pas mauvais que l'enfant se familiarise avec lui, même s'il ne l'exploite pas d'une façon rationnelle; nous savons la fierté qu'il éprouve à recevoir son premier livret, synonyme pour lui de conquête et de progrès.

Pour conclure, quelques mots au sujet de l'Année Internationale du Livre (1972) qui a donné lieu en notre ville à des échanges d'idées ainsi qu'à une exposition d'ouvrages sélectionnés pour enfants, depuis les tout-petits jusqu'à l'adolescence.

Nous avons pu constater que les moyens modernes permettent l'édition de livres aux illustrations belles et riches en couleurs, aux textes simples, donnant aux enfants le désir d'en connaître le contenu.

L'Ecole Maternelle devrait pouvoir mettre à la portée de ses petits élèves une bibliothèque où ils pourraient en toute liberté regarder et se distraire. Quelle belle approche du livre qui serait préparatoire à des examens plus soutenus! Et quelle magnifique réussite que d'apporter à tous les promesses d'une future joie de lire!

A L'ECOLE MATERNELLE, PREPARER L'APPRENTISSAGE

JEUX ET EXERCICES PREPARATOIRES

La lecture demande une phase préparatoire qui se fait à l'Ecole Maternelle ou en section enfantine, et qui est d'une importance primordiale. Ce préapprentissage tend à développer les fonctions utiles à l'enfant lors des séances de lecture, en fin de Grande section d'école maternelle et à l'ècole primaire. L'enfant doit avoir une maturité suffisante pour aborder, dans les conditions les meilleures, le difficile et capital apprentissage de la lecture.

1. Observons les enfants.

L'observation des enfants dès la Section des Petits d'Ecole Maternelle peut permettre de déceler chez certains des troubles qui seront des handicaps lors de l'apprentissage de la lecture:

- handicaps sensoriels: enfant mal entendant;
- défauts de langage: mauvaise prononciation, bégaiement, zézaiement.
- difficultés dans la coordination des mouvements: mauvaise latéralisation; handicap moteur.
- instabilité: difficultés pour fixer l'attention.
- troubles affectifs.

Certaines de ces difficultés peuvent être signalées aux parents. D'autres seront à pallier à l'école même, avant de commencer la lecture.

2. Pourquoi le préapprentissage?

L'enfant ne peut bien apprendre à lire que si certaines conditions sont remplies:
- un niveau de langage suffisant;
- une représentation spatio-temporelle correcte;
- une bonne perception visuelle et auditive;
- des possibilités de mémorisation et une certaine capacité d'attention, d'analyse et de synthèse.

3. Comment peut se faire ce préapprentissage?

Langage: les enfants arrivent à l'Ecole Maternelle avec un certain niveau de langage.
- exploitation et enrichissement des apports;
- développement des fonctions d'expression et de communication;
- rectification des défauts d'articulation et de prononciation;
- exercices structuraux simples.

Représentation spatio-temporelle:
- schéma corporel: nommer et montrer les différentes parties du corps; reproduire des mouvements de plus en plus complexes;
- latéralisation;
- structuration de plan: acquisition d'un vocabulaire précis;
- notion de succession dans l'espace,
                    dans le temps;
- notion de chronologie.

Education de l'oreille: (exemples donnés dans le texte suivant).
- reconnaissance de sons;
- reconnaissance de rythmes simples,
                    de rythmes complexes;
- traduction par des symboles;
- codage et décodage progressifs de structures rythmiques.

Education visuelle:
- jeux de rapprochement d'images;
- jeux d'attention et jeux sensoriels;
- jeux qui tendent progressivement vers une certaine abstraction se rapprochant du symbolisme de la lecture.

Education de la main:

Tout ce qui est lu doit être écrit donc:

- nombreux exercices graphiques;
- "gymnastique" du bras, de la main, des doigts . . .

4. L'initiation à la lecture

La lecture n'intervient à l'Ecole Maternelle que sous forme d'initiation et n'est pas un apprentissage forcé et prématuré. Il faut que l'enfant aborde la lecture avec sérieux et goût, qu'il prenne pour cet apprentissage de bonnes habitudes mentales. Il faut qu'il sache fixer son attention sur les difficultés qui ne doivent pas être escamotées mais dominées.

Esprit de cette initiation:

- l'expression orale est liée intimement à l'expression écrite;
- importance de la motivation (correspondance, thème de vie en cours, cadeau . . .)
- pas de lecture sans compréhension. Dès le début, les enfants établissent un rapport entre les signes et la signification;
- le plaisir de lire est préservé et développé; lire doit être un plaisir et devenir un "besoin";
- toutes les phrases étudiées sont exploitées et non collectionnées;
- les moyens mis en oeuvre pour composer ou déchiffrer varient en cours d'année en fonction de l'acquis;
- importance fondamentale de la relation son-graphie (écoute-regarde).

Les étapes de cette initiation:

- présentation et étude globale de la phrase ou du texte;
- analyse de ce texte (décomposition en mots);
- fixation et utilisation des mots nouveaux;
- recomposition de la phrase-type et formation de nouvelles phrases;
- découvertes spontanées d'analogies et préparation à l'analyse des mots;
- l'apprentissage méthodique des lettres et des sons, les exercices de synthèse ne sont abordés que lorsque l'enfant est "prêt".

Il faut essayer de respecter le rythme naturel de l'enfant et ne pas le pousser trop tôt vers l'analyse. L'enfant d'Ecole Maternelle n'est souvent pas mûr pour ce processus intellectuel compliqué. Il faut lui laisser le temps nécessaire pour une lente compréhension des premiers symboles "bases essentielles des mécanismes".

5. Comment faire naître l'intérêt pour le livre?

Certains enfants influencés par le milieu familial manifestent dès leur arrivée à l'école le "besoin" du livre, d'autres n'y portent aucun intérêt.

L'un des buts de l'école est de favoriser la naissance de cet intérêt chez les enfants non préparés par le milieu familial, de le développer et de l'éduquer chez les autres enfants.

Par quels moyens y parvenir?

- l'amenagement dans la classe d'un "coin" bibliothèque permanent, confortable, agréable, livres renouvelés périodiquement.
- le respect de l'autonomie de l'enfant dans ce "coin":
    en le laissant s'installer à son gré;
    en lui donnant le temps de regarder les livres;
    en respectant éventuellement son isolement.
- le choix judicieux des livres:
    thèmes privilégiés: famille et maison, animaux . . .
    éviter les thèmes angoissants;
    illustration de bon goût.
- la valorisation de cet atelier:
    le proposer à l'enfant au même titre que les ateliers d'activités manuelles;
- intégration du livre à la vie de la classe à l'heure du conte:
    thème d'une séance de marionnettes ou d'une projection de diapositives ou de film;
    recherche de documents pour l'enrichissement du thème de vie.

Ainsi la présence constante du livre dans la classe, l'utilisation qui en est faite par la maîtresse, la liaison entre le livre et les diverses activités font naître et développent chez l'enfant le goût du livre, ce livre qui est toujours actuellement la base de toute culture.

AVANT LA LECTURE EXERCICES ET JEUX A L'ECOLE MATERNELLE

Les quelques notes qui suivent sont le résumé d'un essai de travail pratiqué à l'Ecole Maternelle et dont l'un des objectifs est la préparation à la communication en général, et à l'approche de la langue écrite (lecture/écriture) en particulier. Il s'appuie sur quelques hypothèses qui disent:

- que les premières années d'un individu sont les plus importantes pour son devenir;
- que l'enfant ne peut accéder à la connaissance qu'à partir de la prise de conscience d'un acte vécu par lui;

- qu'un apprentissage réussi de la lecture est une condition des plus importantes pour l'avenir scolaire de l'enfant et aussi pour son épanouissement d'adulte;
- que parmi les facteurs essentiels nécessaires à cet apprentissage, il faut que l'enfant ait acquis une représentation spatio-temporelle correcte et une discrimination auditive la plus fine possible (étant bien entendu que nous ne négligeons pas les autres conditions).

1. LOCALISATION DES SONS

1-1 *Jeu des instruments:* deux ou trois enfants, des instruments sonores identiques situés dans des coins différents de la pièce. Un enfant, yeux bandés, doit trouver celui qui a joué, ou se diriger vers celui qui a joué.

1-2 *Jeu de la taupe et de la sauterelle:* la taupe a les yeux bandés et la sauterelle les pieds attachés. La taupe doit attraper la sauterelle en écoutant le bruit des sauts.

1-3 *Beaucoup d'autres jeux sont des variantes de ceux-ci:* (la brebis, Roméo et Juliette . . .).

2. RECONNAISSANCE DE TIMBRES DIFFERENTS

2-1 *Matériel:* pipeau, tambourin, cloche.

2-2 *Déroulement:*

a) faire voir et entendre les instruments tour à tour plusieurs fois.

b) les enfants ferment les yeux (ou se retournent, ou la maîtresse se cache derrière un rideau).

c) les enfants doivent deviner l'instrument qui a joué (ils le nomment, ils le montrent, ils le traduisent corporellement, ils le traduisent dans un code dessiné mis au point individuellement, ils peuvent décoder le code d'un autre, passer à un code collectif.)

d) des notions de latéralisation, d'ordre et de mémorisation peuvent venir se greffer (aller dans le sens de notre écriture, de la gauche vers la droite, en symbolisant par des jetons ou des dessins les différents sous-entendus; se souvenir que l'on a d'abord entendu celui que l'on symbolise à gauche et ainsi de suite . . .).

2-3 *Variantes:* enregistrements au magnétophone (moto, camion, voiture de différentes marques), écouter des voix des personnes connues, jeux d'intonation différente, jeux de téléphone (plusieurs enfants sortent: qui a parlé?), reconnaître des bruits différents faits par un même objet tombant sur un tapis, sur un parquet, sur une vitre; jeu des plaques Martenot, jeu des bouteilles plus ou moins remplies d'eau colorée, reconnaissance d'instruments de musique beaucoup plus proches (cloche, clarine, chochette; ou tubes résonnants, etc. . .).

3. RECONNAISSANCE DE HAUTEURS DE SONS

3-1 *Matériel:* barres sonnantes.

3-2 *Déroulement:* 2 barres (1 aigüe, 1 grave) tenues chacune par 1 enfant.

- on écoute la musique faite par X,
- on écoute la musique faite par Y,
- on ferme les yeux,
- on se retourne, la maîtresse fait signe à F ou Z pour lui demander qui a joué,
- on change d'enfants, on change de barres aussi en raccourcissant de plus en plus l'intervalle.

TROP D'ENFANTS SORTENT ENCORE DE L'ECOLE PRIMAIRE SANS AVOIR DECOUVERT LE TRESOR QUI RECELE LE LIVRE

Comment peut-on espérer donner aux enfants de C.P. le désir de lire?

Donner aux jeunes enfants qui entrent à l'Ecole Elémentaire le désir de lire? C'est inutile: ils possèdent cette envie de lire, une des conséquences de cet élan qui les pousse à copier les adultes. Tous? Bien sûr, ils sont très différents les uns des autres. Mais qui n'a pas constaté avec quel intérêt, avec quelle ardeur ils suivent tous les premières leçons?

Reconnaissons que l'école contribue à développer ou . . . à ruiner cette motivation innée. Et il serait plus juste de se demander: "Comment, au cours préparatoire, peut-on conserver ce désir de lire?"

Par ailleurs, au moment de l'acquisition des mécanismes, la réussite encourage à persévérer, l'échec donne, de la lecture, l'image d'une activité pénible. A ce sujet, Monsieur le NY, professeur de Vincennes, constate: "Il s'agit d'un cercle vicieux. Plus l'enfant est satisfait, plus il s'entraînera et augmentera sa capacité de lecture. Au contraire, s'il subit un échec, il ne sera pas porter à l'améliorer."

D'où l'importance capitale des premiers contacts avec la lecture? Et comment ne décevoir aucun de nos petits élèves si différents les uns des autres, tant par leurs possibilités intellectuelles que par leur cadre de vie familiale? Une première réponse est donnée dans les instructions qui viennent de paraître:

"Il faut que le maître commence par observer ses élèves pour les répartir en groupes relativement homogènes auxquels seront demandées les tâches qui leur conviennent."

Au cours de classes-promenades:
- Regardons un homme au travail   ("Moi, mon père, il . . .")
- Admirons un parterre de fleurs   ("A ma maison, ma maman, elle aussi . . .")
- Arrêtons-nous devant une maison   ("Ma maison à moi, elle n'est pas pareille . . .")

Au cours de spectacles vus en commun:
- Une émission télévisée   ("Moi, je regarde souvent . . .")
- Une classe de "grands" au travail   ("Mon frère, il . . .")

Au cours d'exercices "plus scolaires":
- Une diapositive (bord de mer . . .)   ("J'ai été en vacances à la mer . . .")
- Un animal   ("Mon chien à moi s'appelle . . .")
- Une histoire racontée par le maître par l'image, ou tout autre moyen   (appréciation de la sensibilité des élèves).

Ainsi, la connaissance de chaque élève, peu à peu, se précise; les groupes se constituent. Et les nouvelles instructions précisent:

"Il ne faut pas s'attendre à voir tous les élèves apprendre à lire au même rythme. Ne pas sacrifier les plus lents, sans retarder personne, exige beaucoup de soin et d'attention. Au début du C.P., c'est une erreur que de vouloir emmener tous les élèves à la même allure."

Cernons mieux la nature de notre action: conserver le désir de lire; c'est "ne pas sacrifier les plus lents sans retarder personne." Difficile action qui peut paraître paradoxale. Mais n'est-elle pas vraie dans toutes les disciplines? N'est-elle pas la condition première qui définit notre efficacité?

Interroger davantage, "s'occuper le plus possible des élèves du groupe 'faible' ", ne suffit pas si le texte à reconnaître, le ou les mots à retrouver, l'expression à identifier sont les mêmes pour tous les groupes. D'où la nécessité de prévoir, au cours d'une leçon, à l'intention de chaque groupe de la classe, une progression très souple des diverses notions à acquérir. Nos élèves sont tous sur le même chemin. Certains apprennent à marcher mais ne retarderont pas ceux qui savent si ceux-ci, chemin faisant, sont amenés à découvrir le cadre qui les entoure: le temps de parcours de ce chemin, est-il une épreuve compétitive?

Un exemple (début de l'année: stade d'acquisitions globales): après la visite du jardin d'un élève et la mise au point des réponses obtenues (activité d'éveil), les phrases suivantes sont écrites au tableau par le maître:

Dans le jardin de Philippe, je vois des carottes. (dessin)
Bernard a des salades dans son jardin. (dessin)
Le jardin de Pascal est dans une caisse. (dessin)

Au cours d'une même leçon:

- En associant le dessin et le prénom des élèves (la connaissance de l'écriture de ces prénoms ayant été obtenue au préalable), certains élèves peuvent retrouver le sens de toutes les phrases écrites et mémoriser, en particulier, la lecture et l'écriture de l'expression "dans le jardin."
- Un autre groupe d'élèves peut se borner à identifier les prénoms et l'expression "dans le jardin."
- Un autre enfin, peut se limiter à retrouver les prénoms et à se familiariser avec le mot "dans."

Ainsi pensons-nous "ne pas sacrifier les plus lents dans retarder personne," et, en définitive, conserver le goût de lire chez tous nos élèves.

"Mais quand apprend-on à lire réellement?" dira mon collègue bilieux.

L'école décourage l'apprenti-lecteur en hâtant exagérément son apprentissage, en systématisant les leçons de lecture, leur objet, leur durée ("il faut deux jours pour étudier un son; on étudie deux sons par semaine; ma progression d'octobre prévoit l'acquisition de huit sons . . .")

Ce qui compte ce n'est pas le rythme des acquisitions: c'est le souci de garder chez tous les élèves le désir de lire et de lire encore.

"Et," ajoutera mon collègue ci-dessus nommé, "quelle méthode faut-il employer?"

Les discussions sur les MÉTHODES ont trop duré. Les nouvelles Instructions ont mis un point final à ces stériles controverses:

"Les enfants sont trop différents les uns des autres pour qu'une méthode soit la meilleure pour tous; mais pour tous, les pires méthodes sont celles qui découragent le désir de lire."

Mixte? Globale? Trois-quarts mixte? Questions secondaires si l'on considère l'importance de la motivation d'une leçon de lecture et de l'adaptation du contenu de cette leçon aux divers groupes de la classe.

Certains maîtres conçoivent leurs leçons quotidiennes de lecture d'après les activités d'éveil en cours: ils décloisonnent leur enseignement.

Pendant l'activité d'éveil, on relit occasionnellement tel ou tel mot de la lecture; pendant certaines leçons de lecture, on rappelle un des aspects de l'activité d'éveil esthétique ou éthique ou physique ou mathématique ou "scientifique". Tout en gardant son caractère propre, la "leçon de lecture" se fond avec les autres disciplines.

Et le désir de lire s'accroît avec le besoin de reconnaître, de savoir lire les courts textes écrits par le maître avec le concours des élèves pendant une activité d'éveil. Largement illustrés, les meilleurs textes sont copiés sur de petits livrets et constituent la base de départ d'une "bibliothèque" vivante, souvent consultée par les enfants ("auto-révision").

Ainsi, l'usage fréquent de ces petits livrets peut donner aux élèves l'habitude "d'aller chercher un livre."

Et si cette bibliothèque contient également l'excellent série du Père Castor par exemple, les enfants la consulteront naturellement. Ce geste symbolique: emprunter un livre, contracté dès le C.P., a toutes les chances de traduire une faim jamais assouvie et ne peut que favoriser le désir de lire.

Peut-on, par ailleurs, relier l'étude de tous les sons aux activités d'éveil? La àussi, gardons-nous d'ériger en système ce qui n'est qu'un des moyens d'obtenir le désir de lire.

Curieux naturellement, séduit par toutes nouveautés qui "cassent" le "ron-ron" quotidien, l'enfant peut être amené au désir de lire par bien d'autres motivations:

- Retrouver dans une histoire, les moments qui ont plu;
- Connaître la suite d'un récit;
- Exécuter une consigne écrite;
- Inventer la légende d'un dessin et la comparer avec celle qui existe déjà;
- Lire les bulles d'une bande dessinée;
- Lire dans une histoire racontée en trois images, le passage écrit après la 1 ère image;
- Lire la lettre des correspondants de la classe.

Et rappelons, pour finir, le conseil donné par les dernières Instructions:

"Il est capital de créer, dans la classe, un climat de sécurité et de confiance, d'éveiller et de soutenir l'appétit de lecture des élèves, de conduire les leçons avec entrain et vivacité, d'être attentif aux difficultés de chacun, sans trop s'y arrêter si elles ne paraissent pas essentielles."

"Soutenir l'appétit de lecture," conserver le désir de lire.

DE QUOI LUI SERVIRA LA LECTURE?

"De quoi lui servira la lecture quand on l'en aura rebuté pour jamais?" demandait déjà Rousseau.

Ne le rebute-t-on pas pourtant, cet enfant, dans certaines classes de C.P. ou de C.E. où les élèves ânonnent interminablement des suites de mots qu'ils ne comprennent pas? Ne le rebute-t-on pas, hélas, dans certaines classes de C.M. où, à tour de rôle, on répète machinalement et jusqu'à satiété un texte trop connu, que l'élève fait semblant de suivre et le maître semblant d'écouter?

Comment faire pour qu'à l'école, lire et s'ennuyer ne deviennent pas synomymes?

L'ennui, dit-on, naquit un jour de l'uniformité. La première condition consiste donc à éviter à tout prix la monotonie en recherchant la plus grande *variété:*

- *Dans les supports:* qu'on ne lise pas toujours dans le même livre, mais qu'on utilise des ouvrages divers, des publications, des articles, etc . . .
- *Dans les procédés de lecture:* à haute voix, silencieuse, dialoguée, dessinée . . .
- *Dans les différentes phases d'une séance:* faire alterner, par exemple, lectures et commentaires, ceux-ci motivant celles-là et vice-versa.

Le second moyen, essentiel, c'est de *lire vraiment.* Débiter mécaniquement des suites de sons, c'est traduire des signes graphiques en signaux sonores, c'est exercer la mémoire visuelle et auditive, mais non pas l'intelligence. Lire vraiment, ce n'est pas seulement déchiffrer c'est rendre la vie aux images, aux idées, aux émotions figées dans les signes, c'est *comprendre* les messages écrits: de même que l'écriture est l'instrument qui nous permet de communiquer notre pensée à des absents, la lecture est le moyen de prendre connaissance de la pensée de ceux qui ne sont pas là, et surtout de ceux qui ne sont plus. Elle ne peut trouver son objet, à l'école, que si l'on va, au-delà des signes et des sons, jusqu'à provoquer des représentations mentales: le maître y parviendra en se référant à l'illustration, en posant d'habiles questions sur le sens global du texte, et surtout en lisant lui-même de manière suffisamment évocatrice.

Mais le "grand mobile," le seul qui, selon Rousseau, "mène sûrement et loin," dans le domaine de la lecture comme en bien d'autres c'est l'intérêt. Or ce qui intéresse essentiellement nos élèves, c'est la vie. J'aimerais qu'à l'exception de certaines phases indispensables d'apprentissage, on ne fasse pas de la lecture un exercice gratuit, mais qu'on lise à *l'école comme dans la vie:*

1) Pour prendre connaissance d'un message dont l'auteur est éloigné dans l'espace (lettres de correspondants) ou dans le temps.

2) Pour s'informer et s'instruire: les journaux et les revues—qui pénètrent maintenant dans tous les foyers—et les ouvrages de documentation doivent être largement exploités à l'école, en liaison, notamment, avec l'actualité et les activités d'éveil. Ce seront d'ailleurs d'excellentes occasions d'exercer l'esprit critique.

3) Pour se divertir et pour rêver: chaque classe devrait disposer d'une bibliothèque abondamment pourvue en récits, contes et romans.

4) Dans le cas particulier de la lecture à haute voix pour communiquer aux autres ses propres découvertes ou créations. Quand un élève lit à ses camarades le texte qu'il vient d'écrire, quand il leur donne connaissance des documents ou des renseignements qu'il a trouvés, quand il désire leur faire partager l'intérêt qu'il a pris à un récit ou à un article, la lecture à haute voix n'est plus un exercice artificiel et gratuit, mais retrouve au contraire sa destination essentielle d'instrument de communication.

Ainsi les moyens ne nous manquent-ils pas de donner à nos élèves le sens et le goût de la lecture, ce sens et ce goût sans lesquels nos efforts seraient vains. Car il en est de la lecture comme de l'écriture, de la musique et du dessin: il ne sert à rien d'apprendre à se servir d'un instrument si on ne donne pas en même temps le goût de s'en servir.

OUVRAGES RECOMMANDES

1. *MATURITE POUR APPRENDRE A LIRE*. Auteur: A. LEROY - BOUSSION (Institut de Neuro-Physiologie de Marseille).

L'auteur a suivi pendant trois ans (5, 6, 7 ans) un groupe de 179 enfants, afin d'étudier leurs progrès en lecture, compte tenu de leur maturité mentale. Un enseignement systématique complet de la lecture a été donné dès la grande section de l'Ecole Maternelle.

De l'expérience, il ressort qu'entre 5 et 6 ans les enfants ne sont pas mûrs pour la lecture: ils parviennent tout juste, en moyenne, à déchiffrer quelques mots isolés, très faciles, à la fin de l'année scolaire. Seule une petite minorité peut assimiler tous les mécanismes de la lecture en un an (et sur le rythme moitié plus lent adopté en Maternelle pour cette recherche).

Entre 6 et 7 ans, une bonne partie des enfants sont parfaitement mûrs. Cependant une autre partie, majoritaire, a besoin d'un rythme plus lent, et même, pour un certain nombre, 3 à 6 mois d'enseignement de plus, voire d'un an.

Il semble donc que l'âge mental de la parfaite maturité pour la lecture soit aux alentours de 7 ans. L'apprentissage en une année, à 6 ans, est donc trop ambitieux pour la majorité des enfants. Le rythme doit être d'autant plus lent que les enfants sont moins mûrs.

L'auteur insiste sur le fait que son étude porte sur un petit nombre d'enfants et n'est pas suffisamment étayée par d'autres recherches pour qu'on puisse considérer ses résultats comme significatifs et généralisables à coup sûr. Il pense cependant qu'ils ont une validité suffisante pour qu'on en tienne compte.

2. *"VERS L'APPRENTISSAGE DU LANGAGE ECRIT."* Cahier de Pédagogie moderne n°45.

Ce cahier est réalisé, sous la direction de Mme J. Bandet, Inspectrice Générale, par une équipe comprenant des I.D.E.N., une Directrice et des Institutrices d'Ecole Maternelle.

Il rappelle les problèmes de l'apprentissage du langage écrit suggère une méthode qui met surtout l'accent sur la meilleure façon de préparer l'enfant à "Lire et Ecrire," deux moyens fondamentaux et irremplaçables d'accès à la culture.

Le langage étant défini comme "tout système de signes aptes à servir de moyen de communication," J. Bandet présente dans la première partie de l'ouvrage une idée essentielle qui oriente les suggestions pédagogiques ultérieures:

> "Avant de donner au langage écrit une place prédominante dans l'éducation des enfants, il sera bon, il sera nécessaire de leur donner, comme outils d'expression, d'autres systèmes de signes, naturellement ou conventionnellement en usage, parfois inventés par eux ou pour eux, qui leur donneront peu à peu les clefs d'autres messages . . . Il est nécessaire, si l'on veut éviter des difficultés ultérieures, de les habituer à des codes plus simples que celui de l'écriture alphabétique."

Il s'agit de donner à l'enfant des notions de "signe" et de "code" en lui en faisant utiliser ou inventer. (Langages gestuels ou langages graphiques). Ce qui est fondamental, c'est de faire comprendre aux enfants que *l'expression graphique correspond au langage parlé.* On propose ainsi, successivement, la liaison d'une expression orale:

- à des images d'abord figuratives puis abstraites;
- à des bandes dessinées qui introduisent l'idée d'une suite narrative et qui donnent l'habitude d'un déroulement linéaire de gauche à droite;
- à des bandes codées qui différent des précédentes en ce que les éléments sont déjà plus conventionnels; ils sont réduits à des traits (droites et courbes). On donne à l'ensemble le nom de "pictogrammes."

Comprehension and Teaching Strategies

David B. Doake
Christchurch Teachers College
Christchurch, New Zealand

In one sense, the term *reading comprehension* contains a redundancy. Any reading which takes place without some level of thoughtful interaction between author and reader must be labelled empty word-calling. When a person reads he must comprehend, otherwise he is not reading. Vygotsky (37) reminds us of this fact when he points out that it is in word meaning that thought and speech unite into verbal thought and that a word without meaning is an empty sound, no longer part of human speech. So the labellers have, in one sense, done us a disservice by implying that reading is one thing and that comprehension is something else. For the purpose of this paper, however, I will continue to use the term comprehension, although I believe we should begin to look for terms to describe the various kinds of reading we do for various purposes.

Later I will use the term *interactive reading,* which appears to me to be a more satisfactory way of describing the type of reading we would like our students to engage in when they open their textbooks to read for study purposes. This is reading in which the reader carries out a continuous, thoughtful dialogue with the information, ideas, opinions, or feelings expressed by the author. As he reads, the reader is constantly challenging, accepting, rejecting, weighing, and integrating the views expressed by the author. The reader consciously, constructively, and intuitively forms new meanings in the light of what he is reading. Interactive reading is characterised by steady, vigorous, and purposeful cognitive activity on the part of the reader.

We must look for reasons that so few students come from our schools willing and able to read in this manner. Unfortunately, most reasons lie with the present low level of skills of our teachers in teaching and understanding the processes involved in comprehension. Bormuth (3) states that comprehension is both one of the most important and one of the weakest areas of instruction in our schools. Hopefully, this paper will add a little to our knowledge and understanding of this critically important area of the school curriculum.

It is not possible to discuss teaching strategies and reading outcomes in comprehension without first examining some of the problems associated with reading comprehension and arriving at a mutual understanding of some of the more important processes involved in it. Three aspects will be briefly discussed: models of reading comprehension, the interrelation of language and reading, and the nature of reading comprehension.

MODELS OF READING COMPREHENSION

Our understanding of the complexity of the processes involved in reading has been widened through three publications: *The Literature of Research in Reading with Emphasis on Models* (7), *Theoretical Models and Processes of Reading* (30), and *Language Comprehension and the Acquisition of Knowledge* (5). Despite these valuable contributions to the literature on reading, it would appear that we still have not agreed on a comprehensive working model of the processes involved when a reader actively reads printed material.

Writers such as Wardeberg (38), Bormuth (3), and Anderson (2) are critical of the situation. Bormuth, for example, claimed that nearly all research and virtually all instruction is based upon a concept of comprehension which is faulty, subjective, and nebulous and, therefore, is misleading.

Armchair analysts frequently equate reading comprehension with learning skills which include remembering, organising, and outlining. While these skills may be desirable outcomes of reading activity, Wardeberg rightly asks whether they can be described as comprehension. Others have no difficulty in producing long lists of "comprehension skills" without any evidence to support them from the findings of basic research.

Finally, a number of writers define reading comprehension in terms of mental processes. Since these processes are not directly observable, Bormuth reminds us that attempts to describe them turn out to be vague and confusing to practically everyone except, perhaps, the person providing the description. This lack of a complete and consistent model of what a person has in his head when he has comprehended a communication creates serious questions for teachers, instructional-materials publishers, and test constructors. For example, the validity of most tests of reading comprehension must be seriously questioned since the tests have been constructed on false models of the processes involved. Both Anderson and Bormuth state categorically that this fact provides sufficient reason to reject as uninterpretable virtually all studies in reading comprehension.

THE INTERRELATEDNESS OF LANGUAGE AND READING

Over the years, researchers have tended to analyse artificially the processes involved in reading and have proceeded to study these separately. In failing to investigate, as Vygotsky (37) suggests, the interfunctional relationship between language and thought and by concentrating on this analytical approach, these researchers have ignored the unitary nature of the processes under study. By so doing they have encouraged teaching procedures which follow a compartmentalising approach to reading instruction where skills such as word recognition, vocabulary, comprehension, and study are "taught" as separate processes. The affective domain (22) has been largely ignored in this analytical approach despite the fact that the unit analysis procedures followed by Vygotsky and his coworkers clearly demonstrated the existence of a dynamic system of meaning in which the affective and the intellectual unite, where every idea contains a transmuted affective attitude toward the bit of reality to which it refers.

Fortunately for the field of reading, the work of the psycholinguists is finally being recognised and is making an impact on research and methods of teaching. The insights found in linguistics and psychology appear to be leading to a comprehensive examination of the traditional views concerning reading and how it is learned. The focus for the study and teaching of reading has shifted to an emphasis on a meaningful language-process where the child functions as a user of language. Goodman (14) states that it is becoming clear that reading is not a process of combining individual letters into words, and strings of words into sentences, from which meaning springs automatically. Rather, the evidence is that the deep-level process of identifying meaning either precedes or makes unnecessary the process of identifying words. Unfortunately, some commercially oriented psycholinguists are publishing "linguistically-based" materials and methods of teaching reading designed to appeal to the avaricious, panacea-seeking, educational market. Some of these materials tend to reduce the effectiveness of other professionally oriented contributions. Goodman reminds us that psycholinguistics provides insights into the reading process and the process of learning to read. A "psycholinguistic approach" to reading would be the very antithesis of a set of instructional materials.

THE NATURE OF READING COMPREHENSION

It is not difficult to find confident statements on the nature of comprehension by authors of textbooks on reading, as well as statements on what skills and subskills contribute to the whole area of the processes involved in interactive reading. These definitions and lists of hypothetical skills are usually supported by suggestions as to how teachers may promote the learning of these so-called comprehension skills. The suggestions usually take the form of procedures for asking various questions before and after the reading; and, from this test-oriented activity, pupils are supposed to "learn how to comprehend." It is now well past the time when reading methods textbook writers and authors of basal series distinguish between the processes involved in the act of comprehension and the processes involved in learning from printed material.

Two of the main sources of information concerning the processes involved in comprehension come from the field of psycholinguistics and from the field of verbal learning and memory.

From the studies made by psycholinguists concerning the response the learner makes, and should be able to make, to his language system, we find the process of semantic encoding being influenced by the reader's ability to handle systematically the various cues and signals imbedded in the material that he is reading. Such features as word meanings, the modification of word meanings by affixes, other words, phrases and various surface and deep structures in sentences, paragraphs and extended sections of the text, all have a role to play in how the reader arrives at a confirmation of his existing meanings, an understanding of the author's meanings, and the development of new meanings as a result of the interaction between his ideas and those of the author. Bormuth (3) suggests that the rules of the game are, to have the child learn to respond correctly to the signalling system of language without having conscious knowledge of even the existence of formal grammar and rhetoric.

The second source of information which contributes to our understanding of the processes involved in comprehending comes from recent developments in the research on verbal learning and memory. The area of interest of those investigating this aspect of comprehension lies in the manner by which information is processed in association with the contents of memory.

Nuthall (24) has provided us with a slightly simplified version of a model of the structure of learning and memory processes, published by Montague (23), which incorporates some features of the Shiffrin and Atkinson (29) model. Nuthall's description of the model states that during a process, such as reading, printed symbols are initially registered in the *sensory register* where their perceptual trace lasts just long enough for selective attention to operate. Selective attention results in some features of what is seen entering the short-term store and other features disappearing from consciousness. The short-term store is the conscious working memory where incoming material interacts with the contents of the long-term memory and is processed (encoded) for response construction or for return to the long-term store. Behind the operations of these processes lies a process monitor which exercises control over such functions as attention, memory-search and response evaluation.

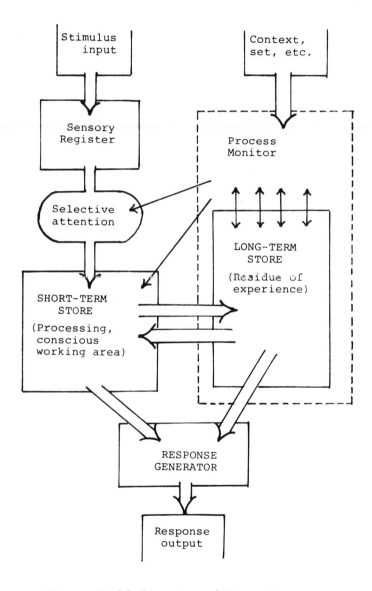

Figure 1. Model of Learning and Memory Processes

According to Samuels' review (27) of the research in this area, the effective life of visual and auditory stimuli in the sensory register is up to one second (the duration appears to be governed by the complexity of the stimuli), unless they are processed (10, 16).

Even more important is the finding that data put into short-term memory survives for no longer than 15 seconds if it is not encoded or rehearsed in some way (39). Data that enters long-term memory may survive for an extended period of time, depending on the amount and type of processing used and the attentional factors operating in the learner at the time.

The skilled reader, then, will have a wide base of meanings and experience which will assist him to begin to attend to and interact with the information and ideas on the printed page. As he reads, the reader will semantically encode, and/or rehearse the information and ideas that he sees as relevant to his purposes, so that these pass into long-term memory. As he proceeds through the material these new understandings will be available for him to interact even more effectively with the new material coming into his short-term memory.

The unskilled reader, on the other hand, has a limited base of available meanings and experience in his long-term memory. Because of this he may have difficulty in even beginning to attend to the material. He does not semantically encode and/or rehearse the new data effectively, but he tries to rely on his visual and auditory and short-term memory to interact with the material. By the time he has reached the bottom of the page, or even after he has read a few lines, he has already forgotten what he has read.

These investigations have raised some interesting problems for the reading researcher, especially in the area of comprehension. First, how are meanings stored? Are they stored as a network of associations for the words we have or are they stored as "vivid mental pictures"? There is some evidence to support the theory that the latter method results in a large increase in the effectiveness with which the material is stored (24). The other important question to be examined is how the incoming perceptual images are connected to the contents of the long-term memory store. What kinds of semantic or other cues facilitate this process and what kinds of teaching strategies develop these skills in the reader?

By constantly equating the teaching of comprehension with the practice of asking numerous terminal questions, reading teachers have done a grave disservice to generations of students. They have succeeded in convincing their students that they are inept and inefficient readers because they cannot read material and remember every important and unimportant detail, idea, and principle recorded on the pages. Teachers have generally failed in their responsibility to teach students the skills involved in semantic encoding. Teachers have not considered it necessary to explain the need for students to go through this process so that what is being read does enter long-term memory store. Teachers also have failed to teach students even the simplest skills involved in facilitating long term recall of material. Numerous students have exhibited poor self concepts of their reading abilities. They believe they should be able to remember virtually everything they read, usually as a result of one or two readings. On the basis of the evidence from the field of verbal learning and memory, it should be obvious that the ability to do this would rest with an extremely small percentage of the population.

Reading comprehension, then, is a process whereby the individual, through using confirmational, transformational and predictive strategies when attending to the syntactic and semantic clues of printed material, is able to encode the information and ideas expressed by the author. The reader may simply confirm his existing knowledge and ideas by comparison with those of the author; he may obtain new information and understanding from the author; or he may develop new insights, which go beyond those expressed by the author, as a result of the interaction between his own knowledge, ideas, and feelings and those of the author.

SOME OUTCOMES OF INADEQUATE INSTRUCTION IN COMPREHENSION

If we accept these ideas on reading comprehension and Bormuth's point of view (3) concerning the low state of comprehension teaching in our schools, it is obvious that there will have to be some radical changes in the teaching strategies used in this critically important area of the curriculum. The implications are very serious for any student who fails to develop his ability to read interactively. At the other end of the scale however, how many of the so-called successful students, who move into our various tertiary institutions, are unprepared or reluctant to read interactively? The evidence available from comprehensive, long-term studies and from experience demonstrates very clearly that far too many of these students are ill-equipped with higher-level processing skills in reading. They have a marked tendency to think that the book and their "information processing teachers" (1) can provide them with the answers. They all too frequently see their role as passive and fail to see the need for taking their meanings to the printed page and interacting with the author's ideas.

Too many teachers for too long have believed that they have been teaching their pupils how to comprehend by giving them a story or a passage to read, followed by a number of questions to answer. Teachers' manuals of many basal series and numerous books of comprehension exercises have unfortunately reinforced this belief. The practice is common in our schools and develops sloppy reading habits among readers. Children read the material knowing that they can reread to find answers to the questions; their first reading is not of the careful, processing kind. They know that at least 60 percent of the questions will be of the simple recall or recognition type (13, 15, 28) so that little thinking will be required of them. They also believe that the reasons for wrong answers will seldom be analysed and discussed and, therefore, it does not really matter whether their answers are right or wrong. Finally, and most important of all, they usually have been required to read some linguistically pasteurized, happy-ending adventure or family story, which was not selected on the basis of their interest. Interactive reading skills may be "caught but not taught" by this approach, but I do not believe that the acquisition of such important skills should be left to chance. What, then, are some of the strategies that teachers should employ to ensure that their pupils learn how to learn independently from printed materials?

EFFECTIVE TEACHING STRATEGIES AND READING OUTCOMES

The young child learns to attend to and use oral language primarily on the basis of need reduction. His need to communicate is the outcome of strong, intrinsically motivated, purposeful activity. He acquires new vocabulary and new language structures through a meaningful interaction with his environment. His communication makes sense and he usually obtains immediate and positive reinforcement.

If we accept that reading is a language-communication process, it would appear that these oral language learning principles should be applied to the process of learning to read. As Henderson (18) suggests, it would appear that comprehension, not word recognition, is the prerequisite for beginning reading. Kolers (21) reminds us that reading is only incidentally visual and children frequently have difficulty in learning a new word, not because of its sound but because of the concept to which it refers.

What are the implications of this principle of meaningfulness for the teacher? Any reading that the child does, especially in the beginning stages, has to come from a basis of direct or, in some cases, vicarious experience with the environment. These experiences should be provided by both home and school on an ever-widening basis. The book language and the child's language should be as congruent as possible, and the structures used should become increasingly complex as a result of the language interactions provided by home and school.

From an investigation conducted by Fasick (11) there is evidence which shows that the language used in children's television programmes contains only 34 percent of sentence structures which could be considered complex, whereas the language of trade books used for reading to children contains 66 percent of such sentences. It would appear, then, that children who have stories read to them would be more likely to develop ability to handle the more complex sentence structures of book language than those children who are exposed to a heavy diet of television viewing of children's programmes.

The child must have an intrinsic interest in what is being read and a desire to communicate with ideas recorded in print. This suggests that a self-directed learner requires a setting in which printed language is both a natural and purposeful communication, rather than, as Henderson (18) states, substandard language segments to be acquired on a conditioning basis. The language of reading should not be fragmented and teacher selected; it should be presented intact and in units that are meaningful to the child.

USE THE LANGUAGE OF THE LEARNER

An approach to beginning reading based on language experience techniques is implied. Here, the reading materials originate with child-based experiences and language. Here book and child language are exactly congruent, and here reading is a meaningful communication process resulting from child involvement. Reading teachers must abandon basal-type instructional materials and use experientially based ones until such time as the child can process chunks of material and utilise an ever increasing number of redundancies in his reading language. Once the child breaks this barrier, he will be able to give his undivided attention to the meaning aspect of reading rather than struggle with the processes of analytical word recognition skills. To expect him to do both is expecting the impossible. Readers who phonically grunt and groan their way through a story must disappear from our classrooms and be replaced by highly motivated readers who bring their experiences to the printed page; who anticipate words, phrases and sentences; and who read with obvious purpose and satisfaction.

CONCEPTS ABOUT PRINT AND READING

At the beginning stage of learning to read it is essential that children learn through experience the various concepts about print. Reading teachers for years have asked children to learn complex processing skills without understanding terminology. Research by Reid (25), Downing (9), Clay (6), and Francis (12), has amply demonstrated the difficulties children experience in acquiring such concepts as print, letter, sound, word, sentence, read, and left to right progression. Clay, in Reading: The Patterning of Complex Behaviour and Concepts About Print Test, has provided us with a comprehensive explanation, diagnostic tool, and description of children's learning needs in this important aspect of learning to read.

It is an educational truism that children learn better when they understand what it is that they are trying to learn. Through discussion, explanation, direct experience, and many opportunities to use words in a variety of situations, children learn to incorporate new words into their meaning vocabularies. Sensitively produced television programmes, informed parents, and kindergarten teachers all contribute to the child's understanding of important concepts.

READING SILENTLY FROM THE BEGINNING

Over the past fifty years, since Thorndike (36) conducted his classical experiment on reading comprehension, oral circle reading has been disappearing from our classrooms. Change comes slowly, however, and the practice of hearing children sight read material that is lacking in congruency with their oral language is still a common practice in beginning reading programmes in many New Zealand and Australian schools. Unless the material has been prepared silently first and unless it is the child's own experientially based story, this practice has the effect of producing nonthinking parrots and word-callers (33). From the results of interviews with five- and six-year-old children it is apparent that children have been conditioned to see reading as an oral process, where meaning is the last thing to be thought of, where to miss a word is a sin, and where reading is "reading to the teacher" or "something we do on the mat." Reading peers also are unable to think about meaning as they focus attention on detecting miscues made by their unfortunate companions. Holt (19), in his book on *How Children Fail*, presents an insightful and rather horrifying description of this practice, in a chapter entitled "Making Children Hate Reading." This material should be compulsory reading for all oral circle reading teachers.

During the period 1935-1945 Buswell (4) conducted a comprehensive long-term study in Chicago public schools on the non-oral method of teaching reading at Grade One and Two levels. He compared the progress of children taught to read where no oral reading was permitted with progress of children who were taught to read by the traditional oral circle methods. Although not all the differences were statistically significant, they were all in favour of the non-oral group. Buswell summed up the result of his exceptional study, by stating that non-oral reading is not a fad. It is a logical step in the evolution of teaching reading. That this logical step has not been taken by many of the teachers who exert the greatest influence on children's concept and skill development in reading is yet another example of the difficulty in bringing about a change in current classroom practice without extensive reeducation programmes for teachers.

The child must then be taught to read silently from the beginning as his concepts about reading develop. Teachers can help the child understand that reading is essentially a silent process by directing him to point to his own name and to other words he knows without saying them aloud. By reading silently in the child's presence and having him observe his parents and other children reading newspapers, books, and magazines silently, the teacher can promote an understanding of the private nature of reading. On every occasion that a reader is encouraged to engage in silent reading, purposeful, performance-free, interactive reading is made possible and self-evaluating techniques are facilitated. Whenever oral reading of new material in audience situations is required, the opposite conditions prevail. The reader is placed in an observed, test situation; and the emphasis on accurate word calling interferes with the processes of thinking about and predicting what meanings lie in the print.

COMPREHENDING AND TEACHING COMPREHENSION

But it is in the area of the active task of teaching comprehension that the greatest changes must occur in the strategies used by teachers. Teachers will need to understand and use the different procedures in teaching children the processes involved in comprehending while reading at increasingly higher levels of thinking. They also have to teach children how to learn the information and ideas obtained as the results of their reading.

Strategies to be employed for the processing aspects of reading will incorporate instruction which must be, as Bormuth (3) suggests, systematically designed to assume that children learn those systems by which language signals meaning. These signalling systems include at least:

1. the semantic meanings of words;
2. the ways word affixes influence the semantic meanings and syntactic functions of words;
3. the ways phrases and deep structures are assigned to sentences;
4. the ways the surface and deep structures of sentences govern the modification of word and phrase meaning;
5. the identification of antecedents of pronouns, proverbs, anaphora, and other prostructures; and
6. the ways structures are assigned to paragraphs and larger units of discourse and those structures used to modify sentence, paragraph, and section meanings.

Self monitoring techniques (17), the process by which the reader identifies ideas, processes them, and decides whether he is comprehending according to some specified criteria, must be developed fully in every reader. The question "Does it make sense according to what I know about language and my background experience?" must be present constantly when anyone reads.

The teacher must learn not only how to design and ask questions of increasing levels of difficulty, but must also know the problems involved for the child in answering them. As a result of an extensive review of the literature on the use of questions in teaching, Gall (13) concluded that in a half century there has been no essential change in the types of question which teachers emphasize in the classroom. Only 20 percent of teachers' questions require students to think, the remainder being of a factual recall or procedural kind. Unfortunately, practically all the research in this area has been on the kinds of questions teachers ask, not on the kinds of questions they should ask. As Hunkins (20) points out in his recent book *Questioning Strategies and Techniques*, effective materials and potentially stimulating situations will be of no value if the teacher lacks skills in formulating questions and using various questioning strategies.

Questioning strategies such as recommended by Taba (35), Suchman (34), and a combination of these outlined by Hunkins (20) are essential skills for every teacher of reading. Through the application of these questioning skills in the classroom, the teacher would be able to demonstrate the need for the reader to encode semantically as he reads and would make this kind of processing unavoidable. The availability of this new information in long-term memory, coupled with the reader's existing understandings would promote increasingly effective interaction as the reader proceeds through the material. Smith (32) reminds us that the qualities of the teacher's questions are undoubtedly strong determiners of the manner in which students read.

The technique of using adjunct questions (questions inserted in either pre or post positions in reading material adjacent to the section where the answers may be found) would appear to be a useful strategy for promoting interactive reading. The results obtained from my own research (8), on the use of adjunct questions to facilitate learning and remembering when reading textual materials, reveal that the facilitative effect is not simply the result of question type or question placement. A significant interaction effect was obtained between question type and question placement and this has important implications for the practice of inserting guiding questions throughout content materials. Postliteral adjunct questions were significantly superior to preliteral; and

Comprehension and Teaching Strategies

prereasoning adjunct questions were significantly superior to postreasoning.

If literal type questions are used, then the most effective position for them is in the postreading adjunct position. If reasoning type ("why" questions) are to be used, then the most effective position is in the prereading adjunct positions. The latter type of question in this position proved to be the strongest facilitator of learning on a long-term memory basis, even when the effects of the variable of time taken for the reading was extracted. The least effective ways to facilitate learning and remembering from reading textual materials were to use prereading literal questions or to instruct the students to read carefully.

Although there are dangers in generalising to the primary school level the results of research conducted at the college level, it seems reasonable to predict that well-framed and thoughtfully placed higher-order questions would cause the reader to interact with all the key ideas and information contained in the passage to arrive at the answer to the question. Through the semantic encoding required by this process, important data would be placed into long-term memory store. The important skills for teachers to develop lie in the area of question construction and the placement of these in specific adjunct positions throughout the material to be read.

LEARNING HOW TO LEARN

Having taught the child how to obtain information, ideas, and understandings from printed materials, the teacher still has the task of teaching the child how to learn for future retrieval purposes. Skills, such as outlining, classifying, analysing, and reorganising, are essential prerequisites for effective learning from reading and should be coupled with the application of the technique of overlearning. Retrieval cues, creating strong images for the material to be recalled and sequencing material to be learned are effective and necessary strategies for the teacher in the facilitation of pupils' verbal learning.

READING AS A DEVELOPMENTAL TASK

Read communication requires meaning, and Smith (31) makes the significant point that communication depends on some base of shared experience between sending and receiving parties. It appears to me that any reading programme which is dependent upon the teacher's constant selection of the materials for teaching purposes in reading, must exert a negative influence on student involvement in the most important aspect of learning to read. Reading must become, as soon as possible, a developmentally-based learning experience through which the child reads for the dual purpose of mastering the task and, as Roberts and

Lunzer (26) suggest, obtaining information or reducing uncertainty. Information has the effect of generating new uncertainty and, as a result, there is a cycle of uncertainty-information-new uncertainty. If reading can be accepted as an experience in itself, the Piaget principles of assimilation, accommodation, and equilibration would appear to be extremely important in explaining the child's intrinsic motivation to read. Unless the child is allowed considerable freedom to follow his particular interest on a self-selection basis, it seems unlikely that any preselected series of stories could by coincidence meet every child's particular needs in terms of interest. As Vygotsky (37) states, reading required of children in the instructional setting must meet the personal needs, interests, inclinations, and impulses of the thinker.

The teaching strategies required for this kind of programme are wide ranging indeed. To stimulate an ever increasing range of interests the teacher must employ a broadly based developmental-type programme where the child has constant opportunity to interact with his environment and to talk, listen, read, and write about these experiences, or have them written for him. It must be obvious that no single basal series can meet all learners' needs for this kind of programme, and so a wide range of books would be required with plenty of back-up materials. This does not mean that a basal series which has as its central aim the development of the interactive reading abilities of pupils should not be used, but basal series with this attribute appear to be extremely rare.

These, then, are some of the more important teaching strategies which could have as their outcome the development of readers who, from the beginning, understand clearly what it is they are learning— readers who constantly use their own knowledge of language and their experiential background to demand meaning from the material with which they are affectively involved, and who see reading as an intrinsic and essential part of living and learning. These strategies could have as their most significant outcome the development of readers who read interactively and who *want* to read for all the necessary and desirable purposes of life.

REFERENCES
1. Anderson, A. W. "Reading Instruction for Twelve to Eighteen Year-olds" in Dorothy Bracken and Eve Malmquist (Eds.), *Improving Reading Ability Around the World.* Newark, Delaware: International Reading Association, 1971.
2. Anderson, R. C. "How to Construct Achievement Tests to Assess Comprehension," *Review of Educational Research,* 42 (1972), 145-170.
3. Bormuth, J. R. "An Operational Definition of Comprehension Instruction," in K. S. Goodman and J. T. Fleming (Eds.), *Psycholinguistics and the Teaching of Reading.* Newark, Delaware: International Reading Association, 1969, 48-60.
4. Buswell, G. T. "An Appraisal of the Non-oral Method of Teaching Reading," *Supplementary Educational Monograph,* No. 61. Chicago: Chicago University Press, 1945, 51-57.

5. Carroll, J. B., and R. O. Freedle (Eds.). *Language Comprehension and the Acquisition of Knowledge.* Washington, D.C., V. H. Winston and Sons, 1972.
6. Clay, M. M. *Reading: The Patterning of Complex Behaviour.* Auckland: Heinemann Educational Books, 1972.
7. Davis, F. B. (Ed.). *The Literature of Research in Reading with Emphasis on Models.* New Brunswick, New Jersey: Graduate School of Education, Rutgers University, 1971.
8. Doake, D. B. "An Investigation into the Facilitative Effects of Two Kinds of Adjunct Questions on the Learning and Remembering of Teachers' College Students during the Reading of Textual Materials," unpublished thesis, University of Canterbury, 1972.
9. Downing, J. "Children's Concepts of Language in Learning to Read," *Educational Research,* 12 (1970), 106-112.
10. Eriksen, C. W., and H. J. Johnson. "Storage and Decay Characteristics of Nonattended Auditory Stimuli," *Journal of Experimental Psychology,* Vol. 68, 1964, 28-36.
11. Fasick, A. M. "Television Language and Book Language," *Elementary English,* 50 (January 1973), 125-131.
12. Francis, H. "Children's Experience of Reading and Notions of Units of Language," *British Journal of Educational Psychology,* 43 (1973), 17-23.
13. Gall, M. D. "The Use of Questions in Teaching," *Review of Educational Research,* 40 (1970), 707-720.
14. Goodman, K. S. "On the Psycholinguistic Method of Teaching Reading," in Frank Smith (Ed.), *Psycholinguistics and Reading.* New York: Holt, Rinehart and Winston, 1973, 177-182.
15. Guszak, F. J. "Teacher Questioning and Reading," *Reading Teacher,* 21 (1967), 227-234.
16. Guttman, N., and B. Julesz. "Lower Limits of Auditory Periodicity Analysis," *Journal of Acoustical Society of America,* 35 (1963), 610.
17. Hansen, D. N. "Information Processing Models for Skill Acquisition," in F. B. Davis (Ed.), *The Literature of Research on Reading with an Emphasis on Models.* New Brunswick, New Jersey: Graduate School of Education, Rutgers University, 1971.
18. Henderson, E. H. "Do We Apply What We Know about Comprehension," in Nila B. Smith (Ed.), *Current Issues in Reading,* 1968 Proceedings, Volume 13, Part 2. Newark, Delaware: International Reading Association, 1969, 84-96.
19. Holt, J. *How Children Fail.* London: Penguin, 1964.
20. Hunkins, F. P. *Questioning Strategies and Techniques.* Boston: Allyn & Bacon, 1972.
21. Kolers, P. A. "Reading is Only Incidentally Visual," in K. S. Goodman and J. T. Fleming (Eds.), *Psycholinguistics and the Teaching of Reading.* Newark, Delaware: International Reading Association, 1969, 8-16.
22. Krathwohl, D. R., B. S. Bloom, and B. B. Masia. *Taxonomy of Educational Objectives, Handbook II: Affective Domain.* New York: David McKay, 1964.
23. Montague, W. E. "Elaborative Strategies in Verbal Learning and Memory," in G. H. Bower (Ed.), *Psychology of Learning Motivation: Advances in Research and Theory.* New York: Academic Press, 1972, 225-302.
24. Nuthall, G. A. "Reading Comprehension and Verbal Interaction," paper presented at the Fifth New Zealand Conference on Reading, Christchurch, New Zealand, May 1974.
25. Reid, Jessie F. "Learning to Think About Reading," *Educational Research,* 9 (1966), 56-62.
26. Roberts, G. R., and E. A. Lunzer. "Reading and Learning to Read," in E. A. Lunzer and J. F. Morris (Eds.), *Development in Human Learning.* New York: American Elsevier, 1968.
27. Samuels, J. S. "Success and Failure in Learning to Read: A Critique of the Research," in F. B. Davis (Ed.), *The Literature of Research in Reading with an Emphasis on Models.* New Brunswick, New Jersey: Graduate School of Education, Rutgers University, 1971.

28. Schrieber, J. E. "Teacher's Question-Asking Techniques in Social Studies," unpublished doctoral dissertation. Ann Arbor, Michigan: University Microfilms, 1967, No. 67-9099.

29. Shiffrin, R. M., and R. C. Atkinson. "Storage and Retrieval Processes in Long Term Memory," *Psychological Review*, 76 (1969), 179-193.

30. Singer, H., and R. Ruddell (Eds.). *Theoretical Models and Processes of Reading.* Newark, Delaware: International Reading Association, 1970.

31. Smith, E. Brooks, K. S. Goodman, and R. Meredith. *Language and Thinking in the Elementary School.* New York: Holt, Rinehart and Winston, 1970.

32. Smith, H. K. "Responses for Good and Poor Readers When Asked to Read for Different Purposes," unpublished doctoral dissertation abstract, University of Chicago, 1965, 14.

33. Stauffer, R. G. "Reading as Cognitive Functioning," in H. Singer and R. Ruddell (Eds.), *Theoretical Models and Processes of Reading.* Newark, Delaware: International Reading Association, 1970, 124-134.

34. Suchman, J. R. *Developing Inquiry.* Chicago: Science Research Association, 1966.

35. Taba, H. *Teachers Handbook for Elementary Social Studies.* Reading, Massachusetts: Addison-Wesley, 1967.

36. Thorndike, F. J. "The Psychology of Thinking in the Case of Reading," *Psychological Review*, 24 (1917), 220-234.

37. Vygotsky, L. S. *Thought and Language.* Cambridge, Massachusetts: Massachusetts Institute of Technology Press, 1962, 1-8.

38. Wardeberg, H. L. Con-Challenger to: "Do We Apply What We Know About Comprehension?" in Nila B. Smith (Ed.), *Current Issues in Reading*, 1968 Proceedings, Volume 13, Part 2. Newark, Delaware: International Reading Association, 1969, 103-106.

39. Waugh, N. C., and D. A. Norman. "The Measurement of Interference in Primary Memory," *Journal of Verbal Learning and Verbal Behaviour*, 7 (1968), 617-626.

The Development of Comprehension:
A Curriculum for the Gifted Reader

J E Sparks
Beverly Hills Unified School District
Beverly Hills, California
United States of America

Seventeen years ago, in my first year at Beverly Hills High School in California, I became concerned about the need for giving more attention to advanced readers at the high school; so I approached the principal for permission to take a group of fifteen top seniors through an experimental set of eight experiences during the eight weeks prior to their graduation. I had complete freedom with those students in content and in scheduling, keeping them all day, if necessary, in the activity planned. In those eight weeks, the seniors had such experiences as a full day at the Hughes Aircraft Labs; an afternoon with a woman who wrote opera; an evening with Irving Stone, the author; and a session with Dr. Tom Dooley.

After those eight seminars, the students were so excited that they asked if they could continue meeting throughout the summer. And even though they had been graduated, they did meet for six summer sessions in various homes.

This set of experiences prompted the principal and me to establish a program the following September, to include about fifteen to twenty students from each of the four grade levels at the high school. These students met once a week as separate grade-level groups, with each of the four groups pursuing readings in philosophic thought. The sessions were patterned on the Great Books discussion program.

A year or so later there were about seventeen students, crossing all four grade levels, that we couldn't fit into their grade-level seminar. Rather than lose them, we found a time during the school day to get them all together. That group turned out to be the best of the year, and since then we have mixed together all of the grade levels. For a number of years now, the high school has had a special early-morning period from 7:30 to 8:15 for certain kinds of classes. Students choose the morning of the week they wish to attend; and as a result of that initial selection, each of the five morning seminars now includes some freshmen, sophomores, juniors, and seniors. I have found that, at an intellectual level, age makes no difference even though such students may not necessarily intermingle socially. What happens instead, at an intellectual level, is that the freshmen learn from contact with more mature seniors; and the sophisticated seniors are kept mentally alert by the eager freshmen.

Students are selected for seminar on the basis of an intelligence quotient over 132, a high reading achievement on a standardized reading test, an *A-B* grade average, and a teacher/counselor recommendation. Once selected at the end of their eighth-grade year, students may remain in seminar for the four years of high school; thus, they have the quite unique experience of four years of philosophic thought. In general, most of the students in seminar are the top leaders, the top athletes, the top scholars at the high school who usually gain admission to the colleges of their first choice.

CURRICULUM

The curriculum for seminar includes readings in philosophy, discussions of contemporary world affairs, and training in advanced language arts skills. In general, the groups start each September with Plato and Aristotle and progress throughout the centuries in chronological order with selected philosophers, reaching the twentieth century by June.

To illustrate the relevance of their study to contemporary events, the following is a summary of one program for a recent term:

Because it was in election year, students analyzed the Republican and Democratic platforms on education. Because I happened to be on the board of the Beverly Hills Modern Forum, a lecture series, these students had opportunities to hear and, in some instances, meet Governor McKeldin of Maryland on civil rights; Gerald Caplan on psychiatry; Joseph Kaplan on space; Ralph Bunche on Vietnam, the United Nations, and race problems; and Dr. and Mrs. Overstreet on extremism in America.

1973-1974

During the past school year the seminar focus was on a combination of the first-year Great Books Program of St. John's College in Annapolis, Maryland, and the first year of the Adult Great Books Program of the Great Books Foundation in Chicago.

For playwrights like Aeschylus and Sophocles, students pursued research through the Syntopicon of the Great Books. They took one of the 101 great ideas in the Great Books and studied it in relation to a group of authors. Herodotus has one of the most fascinating indices in print; these students selected some reference from his index and read about it in his *History*. Following a seminar discussion of the Hippocratic Oath, students interviewed a doctor for modern application and use of the oath. Aristotle's passage about the five forms of kingship led students to research history for examples of those forms. From Euclid, Archimedes, and Apollonius, students selected a mathematical proposition to present to the rest of the group.

Following the reading of Euripides' *Medea* and of Plutarch's biography of Pompey, students went to the *Reader's Guide* to discover modern versions of *Medea* being performed and to track down some contemporary references to Pompey.

Students took a page from John Locke to imitate the writing style. They could write on any subject of their choice, but they had to follow Locke's sentence patterning precisely. As would be expected, these students were quite clever in these imitations, which were aimed at making them more conscious of their own writing styles.

For the study of Adam Smith, students selected some current tax to analyze according to criteria read in Smith.

After their readings in Hamilton and the Federalist Papers, students wrote letters to governors or mayors to get their opinions regarding Hamilton's ideas about the unity of the executive. It was pathetic to receive so many responses from city and state leaders who didn't understand the students' questions.

Tocqueville, the Frenchman who visited America and then returned home to write so perceptively about Americans, was used as the basis for a letter to a United States Senator to request his opinion on the philosophic method Tocqueville described in one of his passages.

1974-1975

Every four years the seminar curriculum focuses upon Asian thought, so that students have exposure to Eastern philosophy once during their four years of high school. I personally believe that all students should learn something about the thoughts and lives of Asians; and during our most recent seminar on Asian philosophy, Richard Nixon quite conveniently made the year extra special for us by going to China.

I have found a Princeton University Press paperback, written by a Chinese professor, that traces in extensive detail, with translated original writings, the full history of Chinese thought from pre-Confucian times to Mao. Because this coming school term is to be devoted to Asian thought, I have decided to concentrate upon Chinese philosophy in particular. For the students I have excerpted for school district publication significant passages from all of the philosophers covered in the Princeton text, and students will also be given the Princeton book to keep and refer to for follow-up reading. The text divides Chinese philosophy into four major chronological divisions: Ancient, Medieval,

Contemporary, and Modern. The organization of the text fits well into the quarterly divisions of our school term.

WRITING

Because our seminar hopefully provides a total language arts experience for the students, there is periodic writing. During the past term, students wrote four philosophic papers, each of which necessitated the synthesis of readings and discussions for the quarter.

As part of the seminar, I give students some informal instruction in improving their language arts skills. Just a few brief lessons in how to express a main idea and support it with major and minor details are sufficient for gifted students in improving the expression of ideas on paper. In addition, I give students instruction in varying their sentence patterning in the twenty-three ways that are different from the usual subject-verb-predicate pattern. After four years of this kind of training, students are well prepared for college exposition.

In addition to my role as director of the seminars, I also teach reading skills classes at the high school. These classes are open to any student at the high school on an independent scheduling and highly individualized basis. I often encourage some of my gifted seminar students to come to the Reading Tower for some specialized need they may have in writing, vocabulary-building, or reading for flexibility.

PARENTAL INVOLVEMENT

In the Beverly Hills Unified School District we have a superintendent of schools who is very sensitive to public relations with his community. We never make any curriculum change in the school district without consulting parents; as a result, we have tremendous parental support for all of our programs.

In seminar, parents must sign the acceptance form that their children receive along with the invitation given to those eighth-graders selected by teachers and counselors for the high school seminar. Thus, parents have an understanding of the program from the beginning.

Each spring we hold an intellectual evening for all seminar students and their parents. When students and parents arrive at the high school cafeteria, they are seated in table groups of ten. Each table group has a different one-page philosophic excerpt to read and discuss. Table discussions are led by juniors and seniors while freshmen and sophomores serve as table hosts and hostesses. This experience enables parents to become involved in the same kind of discussions their children have during the school day. At the conclusion of about forty minutes of such discussion, the evening ends with all of the seniors at a head table giving their impressions of four years of seminar.

During the coming school term, with the emphasis upon Chinese thought, I will be adding another dimension to parent participation. Through the Beverly Hills Adult Education School I will be offering a seven-week course on Chinese philosophy for the parents of the seminar students. These parents will have philosophic excerpts to read and discuss in the same manner as their children have during the school day. Hopefully, this will enable parents and children to have some common experiences that will enrich family life.

FORMS

Over the years I have developed some special forms to be used for various purposes. And I have developed some special vocabulary for use with seminars.

For example, during the past term I did not want to call the students' writing by the usual terms of *composition* or *theme* or *paper*. So I went to the dictionary to discover the word *disquisition*, a formal discourse in which a subject is examined. During the coming term, student writings will be called *Scrolls*, in recognition of the focus upon Chinese thought.

I have a form known as Note and Quote Cards. Students use these to keep a record of extended reading they do beyond a seminar topic or discussion. These cards enable me to see the extent to which the seminar opens doors and to what extent students go through those doors.

Because the seminar session itself is an informal discussion group in which students sit around a table to share the reading of the week, I waste no time in asking concrete questions that focus upon the *who, what, when,* and *where* of the reading. These students have only forty minutes, once a week, together; and I want to make the fullest use of that time developing the critical and creative aspects of their thinking. I have a three by five card called *I Q*, for Interpretive Question. Each student gives me or the discussion leader, at the beginning of the hour, one of these cards on which he has written an Interpretive Question based on his reading. These questions then form the focus for the discussion. At any time, I can also give the leadership of the discussion to any student in the group who can start it going with his own *I Q* for the day. Thus, all students are prepared at all sessions to take over leadership; and I become chiefly the instigator who is there in a consultant capacity.

These students are never threatened by my presence nor my operation. There are no grades attached to seminar; it is part of the principal's honors program, and students do receive one credit per semester for it. Because I am not in a grading situation with these students, I am able to develop a completely different kind of relationship with them.

CONCLUSION

Students we now teach will become our leaders in the 21st century. The thought overwhelms me with its implication for the teacher's responsibility to those students who are classified as gifted.

Abraham Maslow wrote that man must be studied as an entity. Because the seminar at Beverly Hills High School focuses upon the philosophic aspects of man, it enables students to study man as an entity. Because of its positive approach, I have always been empathetic toward Maslow's concept of self-actualization. When attempting to develop self-actualization, we are trying to make full use of talents, capacities, and potentialities of people. Self-actualizing people seem to be fulfilling themselves and doing the best they are capable of doing.

In a world with so much uncertainty, violence, and antihumanhood, I believe we should give serious attention to that two percent of the population which may contain the self-actualizing person or persons who may make the 21st century the period when man asserts the power of his humanity.

Reading to Learn

Laurie F. Thomas and E. Sheila Augstein
Brunel University
Uxbridge, Middlesex, England

The effective reader is one who can vary his methods of reading to meet his varying needs from the whole range of written material. Thus the effective reader is self-aware and self-organised, able to relax and read for enjoyment as easily as he defines a specific purpose and pursues it. The basic skills of effective reading are, therefore, those of the self-organised learner.

In helping readers to become more autonomous and aware of their own processes, a generative model of reading and a number of new tools have been used. These tools include a flow diagram procedure for negotiating meaning and a method for recording reading behaviour. This reveals the tactics and strategies used in attributing meaning to a text. The "read records" enable the teacher to explore, with the learner, the thoughts and feelings underlying his (or her) interaction with the words on the page. By using the read record and the flow diagram as a basis for structured conversations about the process of reading, students become more effective: more precise, more flexible and more successful in their own terms. Three different methods of instruction are described. One method produced significant changes in academic performance. The others allowed the reader to define his own objectives. They were each designed to produce a different type of learning conversation with the reader, and to use this conversation as a basis for enabling him or her to achieve a greater degree of awareness and self-organisation.

THE PROCESS OF READING

In order to study how students "read-for-learning" a generative model of the process of reading was developed. The model relates to the theories of Bruner (3), Chomsky (4), and Miller (6), and is in some ways analagous to Goodman's view of reading as a psycholinguistic guessing game (5). This model structures our whole approach and serves as the basis for discussing the process of reading with students who wish to become more effective in their use of reading as a learning skill.

Meaning does not flow from the text into the reader's head. It originates in his head and is aligned, refined, and elaborated in his interaction with the words on the page. Most people are unconscious of these processes most of the time and cannot, therefore, bring them under review. An articulated model serves to mediate the conversational processes by which awareness may be achieved. The full model is elaborate, taking note of how beliefs, values, purposes, and prior knowledge along with the structure of the text itself, contribute to reading activity. In this presentation, *purpose*, *strategy*, and *outcome* are being used to indicate areas of primary interest.

Although simplified, the model must still include the concept of level, integrating word recognition, syntactic structure, and semantic organisation.

The structure of the words on the page provokes a search for stable meaning. The thoughts and feelings associated with this search take time. Therefore, the patterns of time revealed in detailed records of reading behaviour can be used to infer the sequence of feelings and thoughts that accompanied it.

THE READING RECORDER

How can such detailed records be obtained? A series of prototypes resulted in the development of a cheap, simple method for recording reading behaviour (7).

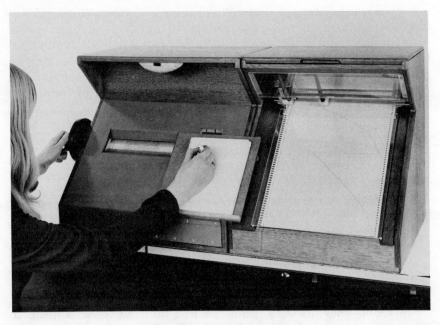

THE READING RECORDER

> The text is printed on continuous
> stationery and is reviewed through a
> window (represented by this rectangle).
> The size of the window can be varied
> to expose from 1 to 5 lines of text.

   The movement of the continuous stationery is under the direct control of the reader. He turns a handle on the side of the recorder to move the text past the window. The movement of this handle is transmitted directly to the pen of a chart recorder incorporated in the machine. This produces a graphical record that displays the hesitations, backtrackings, and forward skims that have occurred during the reading of the text. Figure 1 shows a simplified version of a record obtained on the Reading Recorder. This record shows the reading of a four-hundred line article in twenty minutes. We can see that the lines were not read at an even rate of $\frac{400}{20}$, i.e. twenty lines per minute. The first 100 lines were read in five minutes, i.e. at an average of twenty lines per minute, but

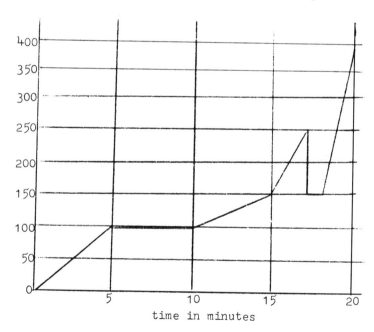

time in minutes

Figure 1. A simplified version of a record obtained on the Reader Recorder

then the reader spent five minutes not reading at all. Observation would have shown that he sat thinking for three minutes and then made some notes. From the tenth minute to the fifteenth, he read more slowly from line 100 to line 150, i.e. $\frac{150-100}{5} = \frac{50}{5} =$ ten lines per minute. Then the reader speeded up and read from lines 150 to 250 in two minutes, i.e. 100 lines in two minutes at fifty lines per minute. At line 250, he stopped and then turned quickly back to line 150 and spent one minute making notes, not reading. He then scanned evenly and very quickly from line 150 to line 400 in two minutes, i.e. at $\frac{250}{2}$ at 125 lines per minute.

AN EXPERIMENT

Two matched groups were asked to read a complex and unfamiliar text on the reading recorder. The first group had been through a series of reading events that led them to expect that they would be asked to do a multiple choice test to assess the effectiveness of their reading. They were also told that they would receive such a test after reading the text. The other group expected to be asked to write a summary and were asked to read in preparation for doing so. After the event, each group was asked to do both tasks. The results are shown in the illustration. Nineteen of those expecting to have to write a summary could successfully do so. But seven of those expecting to have to answer the multiple choice test could also do so. Twenty-five (19 + 6) of those reading to summarise were successful on the multiple choice test and so were twenty-one (7 + 14) of those who prepared themselves for it.

No one who was able to write an acceptable summary failed the multiple choice test. In both groups, only two-thirds (19 + 21) were able to reach the minimum standards on their intended task.

Before considering the reading records in relation to this experiment, it is useful to consider the general nature of the kind of behaviour that is recorded.

	TASK	
	Groups 1a and 1b learning for objective tests	Groups 2a and 2b learning for summary
Effective on summary and objective tests	7	19
Effective on summary only	0	0
Effective on objective tests only	14	6
Effective on neither	9	5
Total	30	30

$X^2 = 11.94$ $p = 0.01$

TYPES OF READ RECORD

It is useful to classify parts of the records of reading behaviour into the following five types of "read." These "reads" denote some of the basic skills of reading. They are an observable representation of the processes involved in attributing meaning to the text, i.e. comprehension. Any one complete record may be made up of a combination of such reads.

The *smooth read* seems to be associated with easy reading. The meaning generated in the reader's head maps immediately and

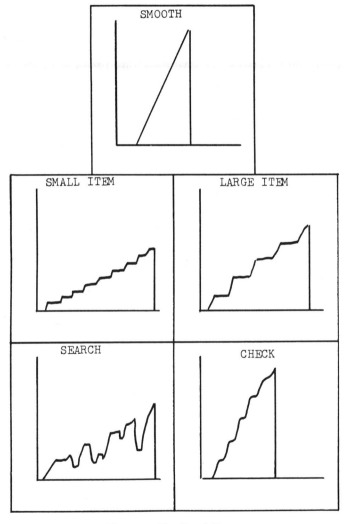

Figure 2. The Read Types

"correctly" onto the words on the page. The meaning may be simple or elaborate, and the criteria of "correctness" may be lax or stringent. Thus the sophistication and standards of the reader will determine what, for him, constitutes easy reading.

The *small item read* shows short sequences of reading, followed by hesitations. The reader needs time to work through the significance for him of each short section of text. This type of read seems to be associated with the remembering of small items of information.

The *large item read* is similar to the small item read, but the items remembered cover longer pieces of the text.

The *search read* seems to be associated with the active creation of meaning. The reader searches out the non-linear relationships that he finds to be compatible with the words in the text, jumping backwards and forwards and revising his meanings until they meet his criteria.

The *check read* is a rapid skim through the text with short pauses of intensive scanning at personally significant points.

These "reads" exist for various levels in the reading activity. In the processing of sentences, words are small items and phrases are large items; difficult syntax leads to searching and checking behaviour. In reading a paragraph, the sentence itself becomes the small item. For complete articles or chapters, these patterns can also be detected.

TACTICS AND STRATEGY IN READING

The reads described in the previous section may be thought of as identifying the tactics of reading. These basic skills require awareness and self-organisation if they are to be combined to form flexible strategies which are designed to achieve our needs and purposes.

In the experiment described earlier, the reading behaviour was recorded for each subject. The following combinations of "reads" could be identified (see Figure 3).

All of these strategy combinations were found among the members of both task groups. Specifying a purpose did not guarantee that an appropriate strategy was brought into play.

When the recordings are sorted according to the outcome achieved by the reader (rather than his purpose or intended outcome), a much clearer pattern emerges.

Type A strategy was associated with lack of success on both tasks. The text was particularly challenging to the subjects and no one among them could be expected to read it easily.

Type B strategy would be associated with success on the multiple choice task but with only partial success on the summary. Those who were successful on the summary took up to twice as long to compose it as those using C and D strategies.

Types C and D were associated with success on the summarising task. Subjects using Type D reports that the long pause (20 - 30 minutes) between the item read and the check read was used to sort things out (i.e. search) in their head.

Retested two weeks later, successful summarisers retained much more of their multiple choice knowledge than equivalent unsuccessful summarisers. This would support the view that the search activity is creating a schemata necessary for summarising and incidentally aiding longer term retention.

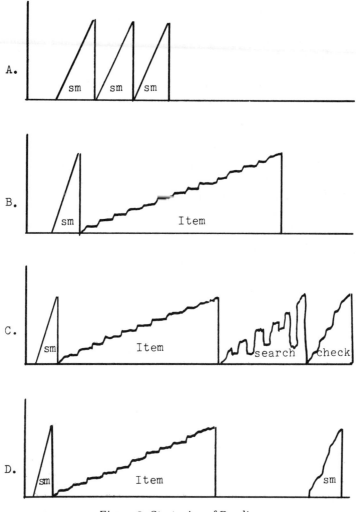

Figure 3. Strategies of Reading

PURPOSE, STRATEGY, AND OUTCOME

The results of this experiment raise a number of questions about self-organised activity. The reading outcomes were not always compatible with the assigned task. This may have been because the learner did not possess the basic skills out of which to generate the appropriate strategy; but it may also have been because the learner had misunderstood, or refused to accept, the assigned task as his personal purpose.

A reader progressively clarifies a specific purpose out of his general needs in relation to a text, and individuals vary in ability to do this with ease and precision. They also differ in ability to develop a strategy, hierarchical plan, or internal program which operates implicitly to organise their reading activity.

In addition to the results of the experiment here reported, the recorder has also revealed some interesting facts about the reading of words in a sentence. Sentences which are syntactically simple can be understood during one smooth read; but, as syntactic complexity increases, the smooth read becomes associated with incomplete understanding. An intuitive grasp of the generative rules of grammar is insufficient for one smooth processing of the linear sequence of words, to establish the complex pattern of meaning. Complete understanding becomes associated with item or search reads that allow time and/or activity to establish the required structure. Similarly, increasingly difficult tasks (or purposes) require more elaborate processing which eventually reveals itself as search activity. It would appear that the internal program becomes unable to handle the temporary storage and jump instructions required for the smooth read.

The purpose, as expressed through the strategy and tactics, results in an outcome. The immediate outcome is experiential; some reorganisation or addition has taken place in the contents of our personal understandings. Readers differ in their ability to appreciate the nature of these "learnings" realistically. Externalising the outcomes in the form of notes, spoken words, or changes in behaviour makes this appreciation of learning more public. But the aim of the efficient reader is to develop a proper appreciating system for continually monitoring the outcomes in his head.

Thus, purpose, strategy, and outcome are inevitably interrelated. Interim or lower level outcomes are used to revise and refine longer term or higher level purposes. This cycle continues until a personally acceptable degree of learning has been achieved.

CHANGING THE PROCESS OF READING

Reading habits are difficult to change. Having dropped into unawareness, they obstinately remain unavailable to review. A second experiment, not reported here (10), has established that a person's read record can be used to talk him through (i.e. into reconstructing) the original reading experience. This brings the process of reading back into awareness and, being visible, makes it available for revision.

In using the model to help a reader, a taxonomy of purposes based on Bloom (2) has been developed. Progressive exploration and elaboration of a personal taxonomy sharpens reader awareness of purpose in any given situation. This, plus awareness of strategy and tactics, focuses attention on the reading outcome. The flow diagram technique (8) and various forms of associative net provide a structured approach to the exploration of meaning. The Kelly repertory grid (1) is another technique for eliciting private meanings.

Having become aware of these three main aspects, the reader can now begin to experiment with the relationships between them. This awareness of the whole process of reading-for-learning is the basis for the achievement of self-organised improvement. These awareness-raising techniques enabled the authors to help seventeen-year-old grammar school students to considerably improve their reading performance.

ONE STRUCTURED COURSE

The reading recorder and the flow diagram technique were used as the basis for a course to assist students to improve their skills in reading-for-learning. The course consisted of ten, separate, tightly structured modules of instruction and practice. Each module represented one area within the taxonomy of purposes; and a self-assessment procedure, balancing speed and success, was built into each. Students were given individual attention, and they worked through the modules systematically.

Students in a College of Education (teacher training) spend an average of 35 hours each on this course. Significant changes in performance were recorded on the before and after tests associated with each module.

College assignments were used to test whether the improvement in reading-for-learning skill carried over into general academic performance. Results of a follow-up study six months after the end of the reading course are illustrated in Figure 4.

THREE TYPES OF COURSE

The second course was designed on the basis of group activity. Instruction in the reading recorder and flow diagram techniques was offered and, in discussion, the taxonomy of purposes was explored. Students were then left to practice with these techniques in their own way. Again, changes in performance were recorded but the weight given to various purposes varied from student to student.

The third course was much more student-centred. Much time was spent relating the needs of the student to the purposes of his reading. This led many students into reviewing their reasons for being in the college. A demand for counselling developed and, while many students changed their courses of study, attention was orientated away from reading and little or no change in this skill was observed.

CONTROL   EXPERIMENTAL

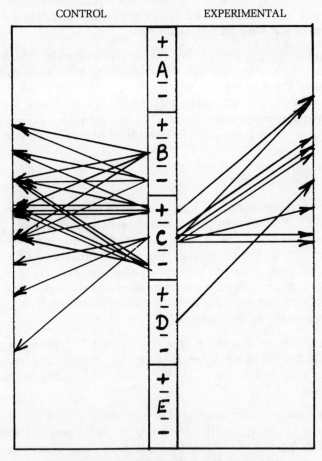

Figure 4. Change in Academic Performance

LEARNING CONVERSATIONS

To relate the model, the tools, and the methods of instruction, one to another, it is useful to introduce the idea of a learning conversation. The teacher and the learner engage in a structured negotiation, designed to assist the learner in becoming more skilled and self-organised. The model of the reading process offers an agreed language. Reference to purpose, strategy tactics, reads, outcomes, etc. takes on a precise meaning. The conversation can progress in normal verbal terms until problems of definition or unawareness require the use of more powerful tools. These offer the opportunity to raise the levels of consciousness and, hence, the capacity for self-organised learning. Each phase of the conversation can be carried out in any teaching mode, varying from styles based on Skinnerian behavioural modification to those approximating Rogerian client-centred therapy. The onus is on each teacher to develop a repertoire of teaching modes and to judge when and for what these are appropriate.

REFERENCES

1. Bannister, D., and J. M. M. Mair. *The Personal Constructs of Evaluation.* London: Academic Press, 1968.
2. Bloom, B. S. *"A Taxonomy of Educational Objectives,"* Vol. 1, The Cognitive Domain. London: Longmans, 1956.
3. Bruner, Jerome S. "The Course of Cognitive Growth," *American Psychologist,* 19 (1964).
4. Chomsky, Noam. "Language and Mind." New York: Harcourt, Brace and World, 1968.
5. Goodman, Kenneth. "Reading: A Psycholinguistic Guessing Game," *Journal of the Reading Specialist,* May 1967, 259-271.
6. Miller, George A. "Some Preliminaries to Psycholinguistics," *American Psychologist,* 20 (1965).
7. Thomas, Laurie F., and N. C. Farnes. "The Reading Recorder Handbook." London: Centre of the Study of Human Learning, Brunel University, 1970.
8. Thomas, Laurie F. "The Flow Diagram Technique." London: Centre for the Study of Human Learning, Brunel University, 1971.
9. Thomas, Laurie F., and E. Sheila Augstein. "An Experimental Approach to the Study of Reading as a Learning Skill," *Research in Education,* 8 (1972).
10. Thomas, Laurie F., and E. Sheila Augstein. *"Can Students Learn to Read for Learning?"* London: Centre for the Study of Human Learning, Brunel University, 1972.

139189

Techniques for Increasing Reading Rate

James I. Brown
University of Minnesota
St. Paul, Minnesota
United States of America

For teachers of reading, today's tremendous proliferation of printed material is a dramatic reminder of the need for increased reading rates. The veritable avalanche of print necessitates a closer examination of any and all techniques for meeting that need. My special concern in this paper is with teaching techniques especially useful with students at the senior high, college, and adult levels. Within this context, a strong pragmatic orientation seems indispensable.

FORMULATING AN OBJECTIVE

The first step in arriving at techniques for the improvement of rate is to formulate, carefully and thoughtfully, a specific objective. As a sample, consider the Efficient Reading course at the University of Minnesota.

Objective: To help each student develop the maximum rate possible, without significant loss of comprehension.

This statement of objective is intentionally open-ended so as to encourage maximum progress and provide desirable latitude for individual differences. After all, while a typical college class initially averages around 250 words-per-minute, with 60 percent comprehension, the range may be from 160 to 420 words-per-minute, with comprehension of from 20 to 90 percent.

CHECKING AVAILABLE AIDS

Once a reading rate objective has been phrased to your complete satisfaction, the next step is to examine all available resources of help in reaching that objective. Resources include films for use with regular motion picture projectors and films for use with special projectors. The latter include various kinds of *accelerators*, with shades, wires or lights to hasten the eyes down a printed page; and they include *tachistoscopes* for sharpening perceptual skills and increasing span. And not to be overlooked are *vocabulary-building aids* in film, TV, slide, card, or textbook form. The substrata-factor research by Holmes and Singer (1) indicates that vocabulary deserves predominant emphasis, since it contributes 51 percent to reading speed—far more than any other first-order factor.

With today's profusion of aids for increasing rate, how important are techniques? The first adult classes in reading taught at Minnesota in 1949 suggest an answer. At that time, we were using two aids, a tachistoscope and the Harvard Films, with accompanying readings. That very first class initially averaged 213 words-per-minute, with 79 percent comprehension. By the end of the course students had progressed to 519 words-per-minute, but they showed a disappointing drop to 55 percent comprehension.

For the very next class, the teacher of the first group used the same aids, materials, and tests. One change was made. Some new techniques were added. Initially, the second class averaged 283 words-per-minute, with 70 percent comprehension. Final results were 721 words-per-minute, with 66 percent comprehension.

In short, the first class read 2.4 times faster with a loss of 24 percent in comprehension. The following class read 2.5 times faster with only a 4 percent loss. Such evidence suggests that, while teaching aids are indeed important, the techniques we use with those aids are even more important.

IDENTIFYING ATTITUDES

Once a teacher sets an objective, surveys the available aids, and recognizes the vital importance of techniques, he should determine exactly what techniques are best. The teacher's success in determining techniques depends on knowing the students and himself well. To be effective, all techniques must be solidly grounded on an awareness of which student and teacher attitudes are helpful. Here, student feedback is crucial.

One student's performance will serve as an example. Initially, the student read at 170 words-per-minute, with 30 percent comprehension. In over a week he moved up only to 190 words-per-minute. When the instructor suggested he try a faster speed, the student shook his head. "I don't get much even when I read slowly and carefully. I wouldn't get anything if I went any faster." That remark revealed a personal roadblock. Until that block was removed, no teaching aid could be effective.

Only when attitudes, such as the one described, are identified and catalogued can one begin to develop specific techniques to circumvent deleterious effects. Building a checklist of such roadblocks, to be used at the beginning of the course to identify problems, provides invaluable help in selecting or devising appropriate techniques. Repeated at the end, the checklist serves equally well to evaluate success in meeting student needs.

At the University of Minnesota, we use a checklist of some thirteen possible reasons for rate difficulty. Students check the one which seems most apropos. During a recent quarter, "Fear of missing something" was checked most frequently by 53 percent initially and by only 22 percent at the end of the quarter. "Lack of confidence" was checked by 38 percent initially and by less than 1 percent at the end.

Student attitudes help or hinder in achieving objectives but so do teacher attitudes toward students and their capabilities.

Research by Rosenthal (2), first with mice and then with grade-school children, has led to the concept of "self-fulfilling prophecy." According to that research, teachers communicate very subtly their own attitudes and expectations toward individuals in their class, leading them to perform better or worse than they might have performed otherwise.

Consider the implications of that research for teachers of reading. For example, if a teacher is absolutely convinced that 800 words-per-minute is the top limit as a reading rate, class results would tend to reflect that limiting attitude. Or, consider a teacher who is skeptical about the effectiveness of a certain teaching aid. That skepticism will tend to permeate his efforts and be communicated to his students, vitiating the effectiveness of that aid.

Evidence bearing on this theory accidentally surfaced in our own program. A relatively new teacher taught a section of reading for the class hour devoted solely to the developing of scanning speed and accuracy. Fourteen scanning practice problems were planned, interspersed with suggested tips for increased efficiency. Normally, by the end of the hour, students are scanning at an average top rate of about 15,500 words-per-minute, with excellent accuracy. The new teacher was not told what to expect and was quite pleased with his results—an average of 2,161 words-per-minute on identical problems. Without realizing it, he had apparently conveyed to his students his belief that 2,000 words-per-minute was about all that could be expected.

If they are to bring maximum results, any techniques for increasing reading rate must be solidly based on insights drawn from careful evaluation of student and teacher attitudes. In one sense, this step may be more important than the actual techniques themselves. Once a proper foundation is laid, everything done during each class hour for the entire course will tend to fall into place. Separate technique minutiae will combine to make larger constellations.

MOTIVATIONAL TECHNIQUES

At this point, suppose we examine some sample or model constellations to suggest the many possibilities.

Active self-discoveries. Active self-discovery involves translating information normally conveyed by lecture into a heuristic or self-discovery form to generate heightened interest and more active student involvement. The difference between being told something and discovering it for ourselves is cardinal. Keats catches so well the excitement of discovery in his sonnet, "On First Looking into Chapman's Homer," a portion of those realms of gold making up the reading teacher's domain. Furthermore, so much of what goes on in a reading class can easily be translated or restructured into this general technique format.

For example, suppose you want to explain how, as a person now increases his rate, he soon reaches a top limit. Faster reading would result in skimming or skipping. With data from preceding classes, students can determine that the demarcation line would be, on the average, 336 words-per-minute.

Translate that information into an active self-discovery technique, however, and enjoy the quickened interest and enthusiasm. You raise the question. Your students discover the answer. Just give them these directions. "Read the directed selection at your absolute top reading rate. Don't skip. Don't skim. Read every single word, but read at your present top rate. The resulting figure will mark your exact upper reading limit, beyond which you must begin to skim or scan."

This one example should suggest how to restructure much of what is done in class into active self-discovery form.

Visual expeditors. The second general type of motivational technique might be labeled visual expeditors. These expeditors involve translating information into visual form, sometimes in combination with the heuristic. To time students as they read articles in class, teachers sometimes write on the blackboard or use a slide or transparency with reading time in minutes and seconds indicated.

It takes only a slight restructuring to translate that practice into a true visual expeditor. Instead of reading time in minutes and seconds, convert that information into a direct word-per-minute reading figure. When a student looks up after completing an article he immediately knows his word-per-minute rate. Take this a step further. If the figures go up only to 800 words-per-minute, students will be encouraged to consider that rate an upper limit. If the figures go up to 1,200 words-per-minute, a different expectancy is communicated. Such visual expeditors play an important role and students often raise their heads to check the figures.

1,000 Club. Perhaps the most useful visual expeditor for our adult classes has been the 1,000 Club card, a small card which fits nicely into a billfold. The club is described to the class a little past the halfway mark in the course, when interest may tend to lag. The club is unique in that it has no meetings, no dues, no officers, and no responsibilities—just honor. Any student who achieves at a certain level receives a signed card which reads as follows:

THE 1,000 CLUB
OFFICIAL MEMBERSHIP CARD

This is to certify that

_____

has achieved a reading speed of 1,000 words a minute or faster, with a comprehension of 80 percent or better, in the University of Minnesota's course in "Efficient Reading," Rhetoric 1147.

Date: _____

Attested: _____

(Instructor)

INSTRUCTIONAL TECHNIQUES

Next, let us turn from motivational techniques to an examination of sample instructional techniques.

Pacing. Perhaps the most common, and certainly one of the most useful, techniques for increasing rate is pacing. Pacing is predicated on the theory that we can do things under pressure that would be impossible otherwise. Pacing is the underlying principle at work in all reading films and accelerators. Furthermore, by using a stop watch and spoken commands, any teacher may pace any individual or entire class through any selection at a desired rate. Since pacing is so well-known, no further amplification is needed here.

Determining the best practice rate. This instructional assignment, the active self-discovery type, involves the reading of seven selections. Students graph their results, noting interrelationships between rate and comprehension. Students are told to read the first selection very slowly and then to read each of the remaining six from 75 to 125 words-per-minute faster than the preceding one, despite any adverse affect on comprehension. The resulting graph should reveal, among other things, students' present optimum practice rates. A secondary value is in removing the common attitudinal barrier summed up in the phrase, "the faster you read, the less you comprehend."

The best comprehension for about 70 percent of the students is not achieved at their slowest rate. The graph makes that point nicely, freeing them from undesirable stereotypes and attitudes which limit progress. The assignment also generates added reliance on the self-discovery technique.

It is relatively easy to get each student to circle his best comprehension score or scores and make the point that optimum results come from practicing beyond the rate at which he comprehended best. Practicing what you do well stops progress, just as additional hunt-and-peck typing keeps you from mastery of the touch system.

Using specialized reading-type skills. Still another technique involves the teaching of such specialized skills as surveying or overviewing, skimming, and scanning. These are important skills in their own right and deserve to be taught. Our concern here is to teach them in such a way that they make a major contribution to increasing reading rate.

Sequence is of particular importance. For example, when introducing skimming as a reading-type activity, have the class skim an article immediately *after* doing a timed reading. This insures meaningful comparisons. After providing complete directions as to how skimming is done, you raise the question, "Exactly how do reading and skimming rates differ and what about resulting differences in comprehension?" It is helpful to use a timing slide with suitably high rate figures to reinforce the expected rate advantage. Later, additional skimming practice is scheduled to fit immediately *before* a timed reading. Students will soon notice the accelerating effect of that juxtaposition and take advantage of it in better organizing their out-of-class reading.

Surveying and scanning can be treated in the same way and used as rate accelerators, as well as skills in their own right.

Individual progress sheet. One last technique involves a specially-designed, single-page record sheet with space for entering records of every reading activity. The sheet is organized so as to present a developing picture of progress, as well as to pinpoint difficulties. Each student picks up his sheet when he comes in, makes entries during class, and leaves it afterwards. The teacher has an accurate check of class progress as well as of individual problems needing attention.

RESULTS

In conclusion, a capsule look at results from three quite different structurings of efficient reading (Rhetoric 1147) provides added perspective for evaluating the kinds of techniques discussed.

1. *Regular version:* 3 credits. Meets for 30 45-minute periods (22½ hours of class time). This version involves direct student-teacher interaction, as described.

2. *Independent study cassette version:* 3 credits. No classroom time. Lectures, timing and pacing tapes, texts, and study guide provide instruction. Sixty-two students have enrolled since its recent inception. This version involves no face-to-face contact—only mail contact with the lessons.

3. *Independent study TV version:* 3 credits. Twelve 30-minute TV lessons—six hours of viewing. This version has had over 22,000 paid enrollments from open or closed circuit broadcasting. It provides a visual instructor but no live face-to-face relationship—only mail contact for the lessons.

<u>Results</u>

Version 1		Version 2		Version 3	
Initial	Final	Initial	Final	Initial	Final
rate comp	rate comp	rate comp	rate comp	rate comp	rate comp
252 - 63%	1548 - 62%	314 - 72%	889 - 74%	293 - 64%	903 - 66%
6.1 times faster		2.8 times faster		3.0 times faster	

For the visual TV medium, it was possible to multiply the use of visual expeditors, achieving unexpectedly good results considering the limited six-hour viewing time—results which point up the efficacy of such expeditors.

Finally, let me quote Hallock Hoffman—flier, sculptor, and photographer. He once divided mankind into the "quick and the dead." In his view the quick "are people who can hear questions" and the dead "are people who know answers." The quick are the pioneers, feeling the spell of unknown frontiers—the tug of discovery. The dead are settled stolidly into the comfort of a tidy, well-explained, questionless world.

Hopefully, you should consider this paper as not an answer but a question, leading you on to those further self-discoveries which make teaching the genuinely satisfying experience it is.

REFERENCES
1. Holmes, Jack A., and Harry Singer. "The Substrata Factor Theory: Substrata Factor Differences Underlying Reading Ability in Known Groups at the High School Level," Final Report Covering Contracts 538, SAE 8176 and 538A, SAE 8660. U. S. Office of Education, Department of Health, Education, and Welfare, 1961.
2. Rosenthal, Robert, and Leonore Jacobson. *Pygmalion in the Classroom.* New York: Holt, Rinehart and Winston, 1968.

Maturité pour la Lecture et son Evaluation par des Maîtres Préscolaires

Paul Dickes
Institute of Education
Walfardange, Luxemburg

1. INTRODUCTION

Pour le diagnostic de la maturité scolaire ou de la maturité pour l'apprentissage à la lecture, les échelles d'évaluation, malgré leurs inconvénients signalés par G. De Landsheere (1972, 68-75), sont à côté des tests psychologiques, des instruments complémentaires.

A. Jadoullee (1966) a mis au point un questionnaire concernant le comportement, l'attitude, l'autonomie et la disposition de l'enfant envers le travail. E. Leclercq-Boxus (1971) a montré la relation entre les réponses à ce questionnaire et la lecture en première année d'étude.

P. Dickes et E. Wagner (1974) ont trouvé que le jugement des institutrices sur leurs élèves est relativement bien différencié et que certaines dimensions s'avéraient très prédictives pour la lecture en première année d'étude.

M. Kohn et B. L. Rosman (1972a 1972b) ont dégagé avec leur échelle de compétence sociale deux facteurs stables qui réflètent les dimensions majeures du comportement adaptatif de l'enfant au préscolaire, à savoir: a) comment l'enfant utilise-t-il les opportunités pour l'apprentissage, pour le jeu et pour le contact avec les camarades? b) comment respecte-t-il les normes, les règles et les limites pour qu'une bonne adaptation au groupe soit possible? Les corrélations entre la première dimension et des tests de maturité scolaire, des tests de connaissance scolaire et des échelles d'évaluation scolaire sont significatives (entre .20 et .40).

Les buts poursuivis par ce travail sont: 1) mettre au point des échelles d'évaluation stables qui différencient bien les élèves et 2) étudier la valeur prédictive de ces échelles en ce qui concerne l'apprentissage de la lecture en première année d'étude.

Sur la base des études citées précédemment et après des essais préliminaires, un questionnaire a été élaboré qui entend mesurer les dimensions suivantes: a) le comportement de l'enfant au travail, b) le comportement verbal de l'enfant, c) son intérêt et sa participation et d) son respect des normes. Les deux dernières dimensions ont été postulées à partir des travaux de Kohn et Rosman (1972), les deux premières à partir de travaux préliminaires. L'apprentissage de la lecture est mesuré par les batteries LFT1 (Dickes et Wirtgen, 1973) et LFT2 (Dickes et Wagner, 1974).

2. METHODE

On a fait appel à la *méthode longitudinale*. Des enfants ont été évalués au jardin d'enfant par leurs institutrices au mois de février et lorsqu'ils étaient en première année d'étude on leur a fait passer des tests de lecture: 6 mois après, à la fin du premier trimestre (batterie LFT1) et 13 mois après, à la fin du second trimestre (batterie LFT2).

L'*échantillon* se compose de 126 enfants, représentatif de tous les enfants qui se trouvent en deuxième année du jardin d'enfant de la ville de Luxembourg. La représentativité est garantie par rapport à l'âge, au sexe et à l'origine sociale du père. On a utilisé la technique de l'échantillon stratifié pondéré. 21 classes furent choisies au hasard parmi les classes de la ville et à l'intérieur de ces classes, 6 enfants ont été sélectionnés suivant le hasard. L'âge moyen des enfants est de 67,52 mois avec un écart-type de 3,51 mois. L'échantillon se compose de 70 filles et de 56 garçons. 25 enfants ont une autre langue maternelle que le luxembourgeois.

En première année d'étude, certains enfants n'ont pas pu passer les tests de lecture (à cause de déménagements, maladies, etc.). L'échantillon pour le premier trimestre se compose de 110 sujets, pour le second trimestre il se compose de 109. La représentativité reste assurée.

Les *variables* utilisées dans cette étude sont les échelles d'évaluation et les batteries de la lecture LFT1 et LFT2. Chaque institutrice avait à apprécier 6 enfants. Les items sont présentés sous forme bipolaire et on a donné une courte description des extrêmités des échelles. La maîtresse dispose de 5 échelons par item et elle doit situer l'enfant sur un de ces repères. Les 6 enfants sont appréciés ensembles. L'ordre de présentation des items est déterminé par le hasard. Les réponses sont codées de 1 à 5 de telle façon que les polarités "positives" ou "favorables" reçoivent les chiffres les plus élevés.

Voici la liste des échelles d'évaluation. Pour chaque échelle on a mis entre parenthèses les chiffres attribués aux polarités extrêmes.

Liste des échelles d'évaluation

Comportement de l'enfant au travail

1. Lorsque l'enfant travaille à quelque chose il

   est généralement en retard par rapport aux autres (1)   —   a généralement fini dans les premiers (5)

2. L'enfant est-il indépendant dans ce qu'il fait à l'école?

   se débrouille tout seul (5)   —   ne sait rien faire tout seul (1)

3. Lorsqu'on a donné à l'enfant un travail à finir, il

   ne l'achève que   —   le continue jusqu'au bout
   rarement (1)   le continue jusqu'au (5)

4. Lorsque l'enfant fait un travail libre, il

   reste à son travail et ne   —   veut toujours faire autre
   demande pas à changer   chose (1)
   d'activité (5)

5. Lorsqu'on donne à l'enfant un travail qui contient quelques
   difficultés, il

   veut les surmonter (5)   —   abandonne facilement
                        devant celles-ci (1)

Respect des normes

6. En ce qui concerne l'observation des consignés de la vie quotidienne
   en classe, l'enfant

   n'en tient pas compte (1)   —   les accepte, sans difficultés (5)

7. En classe l'enfant

   laisse les autres   —   dérange facilement les autres
   enfants tranquilles (5)   enfants (1)

8. Lorsque l'enfant est fâché, il

   pique des crises de   —   parvient facilement à se
   colère (1)   contrôler (5)

9. Est-ce que l'enfant dérange la classe par son bavardage et sa turbulence?

   jamais (5)   —   souvent (1)

10. Envers les autres enfants de la classe, l'enfant se montre agressif

   (tape, pince, embête, etc.) (1)   —   ne se dispute jamais avec les
                        autres enfants (5)

Comportement verbal

11. Lorsque l'enfant s'exprime en luxembourgeois:

   ses phrases sont élaborées   —   il utilise de courtes phrases
   (emploi de conjonctions, de   peu structurées (1)
   subordonnées) (5)

12. Son vocabulaire luxembourgeois (connaissance de mots et expressions) est

   très pauvre (1)   —   étendu (5)

13. Lorsqu'on donne des consignes (en luxembourgeois) à
    l'enfant pour une nouvelle tâche, il

   comprend directement (5)   —   ne comprend pas; il faut
                        complèter la consigne par une
                        démonstration concrète (1)

14. La pronociation des mots luxembourgeois

   présente de nombreuses   —   est correcte, exempte de
   fautes (1)   fautes (5)

15. Les mots que l'enfant emploie en luxembourgeois sont

   utilisés de façon   —   précis et adéquats (5)
   approximative (1)

16. Pour les activités et les choses de son environnement,
    l'enfant manifeste
    très peu d'activité
    très peu d'intérêt (1)   —   beaucoup d'intérêt (5)

17. En récréation l'enfant joue d'habitude
    seul (1)   —   avec les autres enfants (5)

18. L'enfant
    accapare la maîtresse et   —   ne s'exprime jamais
    lui raconte les petits   spontanément (1)
    événements de sa vie (5)

19. Lorsque l'enfant exécute un travail qui l'intéresse, il
    ne communique pas avec   —   communique son intérêt aux
    les autres (1)   autres enfants (5)

Les acquisitions en lecture sont mesurées au moyen des batteries LFT1 et LFT2. Ces batteries sont destinées à mesurer les connaissances des élèves à la fin du premier, respectivement à la fin du second trimestre de la première année scolaire. Il ne s'agit pas de batteries parallèles, mais cumulatives, c'est-à-dire que les deux batteries sont construites au moyen des mêmes principes, contiennent le mêmes type de sous-tests, mais les items sont différents: les items du LFT1 sont représentatifs du manuel d'apprentissage de la lecture de la première moitié de l'année, alors que la représentativité des items du LFT2 se rapporte sur l'ensemble de l'abécédaire.

Voici la liste des sous-tests, avec une courte description et des indications quant à leur fidélité.

Liste des sous-tests de lecture

1. Copie d'un texte. L'enfant doit copier un texte dans un temps limité. Le score est constitué du nombre de mots correctement copiés (LFT1: $r_{tt} = 0,94$; LFT2: $r_{tt} = 0,99$).

2. Reconnaissance acoustique. Reconnaître visuellement un mot prononcé oralement par l'expérimentateur (LFT1: $r_{tt} = 0,83$; LFT2: $r_{tt} = 0,88$).

3. Compréhension d'images. L'enfant doit écrire le mot qui correspond à une image (LFT1: $r_{tt} = 0,82$; LFT2: $r_{tt} = 0,77$).

4. Reconnaissance de mots par l'image. L'enfant doit reconnaître le mot qui correspond à une image (LFT1: $r_{tt} = 0,72$; LFT2: $r_{tt} = 0,80$).

5. Reconnaissance de phrases par l'image. L'enfant doit reconnaître la phrase qui correspond à une image. (LFT1: r_{tt} = 0,63; LFT2: r_{tt} = 0,79).

6. Dictée de mots: Dictée de mots dans le contexte d'une phrase (LFT1: r_{tt} = 0,78; LFT2: r_{tt} = 0,87).

7. Closure de phrases (LFT1: r_{tt} = 0,75; LFT2: r_{tt} = 0,87).

8. Reconnaissance de phrases. L'enfant doit reconnaître une phrase qui lui est présentée visuellement (LFT1: r_{tt} = 0,85; LFT2: r_{tt} = 0,81).

9. Fusion visuelle de mots. L'enfant doit fusionner visuellement un mot présenté visuellement en reconnaissant le fragment qui correspond au mot sectionné (LFT1: r_{tt} = 0,68; LFT2: r_{tt} = 0,84).

3. RESULTATS

3.1 LES ECHELLES D'EVALUATION

Le tableau 1 montre la moyenne, l'écart-type, la médiane et le degré de biaisage des courbes de distribution. Les courbes sont nettement biaisées vers le côté favorable des échelles d'évaluation. Ceci est un phénomène courant des échelles d'évaluation qui s'explique par les excès d'indulgence des juges (G. de Landsheere, 1972, p. 73).

Variable no	Moyenne	Ecart-type	Médiane	skew
1	3,405	1,465	3,73	−2,095
2	4,024	1,156	4,40	−4,311
3	4,222	1,251	4,70	−7,049
4	3,905	1,223	4,21	−4,428
5	3,675	1,408	4,08	−3,272
6	4,032	1,131	4,32	−5,110
7	3,690	1,405	4,10	−3,196
8	3,794	1,286	4,10	−3,884
9	3,254	1,402	3,42	−1,442
10	3,444	1,190	3,67	−2,700
11	3,683	1,451	4,13	−3,298
12	3,857	1,257	4,16	−4,709
13	3,587	1,421	3,91	−2,894
14	3,802	1,431	4,30	−4,288
15	3,921	1,294	4,29	−5,075
16	3,968	1,265	4,38	−5,018
17	4,540	0,969	4,84	−10,471
18	3,405	1,529	3,72	−1,895
19	4,111	1,126	4,52	−5,275
20	3,381	1,419	3,70	−1,917

Tab. 1: Moyenne, écart-type, médiane et ''skewness'' des échelles d'appréciation (N = 126).

Le tableau suivant contient les intercorrélations entre les jugements:

Variables					Variables				
1	2	3	4	5	6	7	8	9	10
11	12	13	14	15	16	17	18	19	20

1	438	5·8	374	413	320	155	125	051	102
226	271	577	120	313	098	048	080	225	−002
2		561	472	467	336	167	186	080	062
424	476	673	356	499	148	253	099	361	077
3			479	518	458	240	138	195	234
281	437	592	297	401	217	098	145	334	−017
4				512	546	471	344	406	464
362	408	424	364	450	065	091	−009	281	−163
5					358	207	122	119	111
337	390	500	297	416	210	055	110	346	083
6						510	384	424	518
357	442	466	370	505	208	211	150	305	−152
7							593	714	700
081	147	164	184	259	−028	−058	−135	057	−229
8								469	625
033	021	054	125	192	−058	−025	−112	−050	−171
9									670
079	161	137	237	232	−095	−190	−194	−059	−411
10									
110	150	147	296	298	−086	−119	−051	−067	−404
11									
	721	603	670	663	182	254	163	257	−011
12									
		719	745	687	334	274	180	288	035
13									
			471	609	224	180	044	359	023
14									
				773	089	176	125	143	−085
15									
					116	143	154	319	−084
16									
						249	416	222	212
17									
							294	319	402
18									
								341	301
19									
									324
20									

Tab. 2: Matrice des corrélations Bravais-Pearson (x 1000) des échelles d'appréciation. N = 126

La matrice factorielle en composantes principales avant rotation et après rotation varimax se trouve au tableau 3. Nous voyons par le tableau 4 que nous expliquons 64,75% de la variance. L'analyse est arrêtée lorsque la valeur propre tombe en dessous de 1.0. La stabilité de la structure factorielle, mesurée au moyen du critère de Kaiser (Veldman, 1967) est à considérer comme satisfaisante (voir tableaux 5 et 6). Les variables 19, 18 et 20 sont moins stables. Ces variables saturent surtout le facteur III qui doit, dès lors être interprêté avec plus de prudence. La solution factorielle (tableau 3) après rotation varimax obéit au principe de la structure simple, sensu Thurstone.

L'interprétation des facteurs est aisée puisque les saturations élevées correspondent exactement au modèle théorique: le facteur I définit le comportement verbal, le facteur II le respect des normes, le facteur III l'intérêt, la participation et le facteur IV le comportement de l'enfant au travail. Le tableau 7 rend compte des relations entre le modèle théorique et l'analyse factorielle.

Variable	Avant rotation Facteurs				Variable	Après rotation Facteurs				
	I	II	III	IV		I	II	III	IV	h²
1	518	−091	−248	−477	1	054 .	057	006	−744	560
2	687	−226	−090	−305	2	342	046	−130	−699	625
3	688	−088	−261	−358	3	181	183	101	774	077
4	720	232	−165	−129	4	261	497	−012	−547	615
5	626	−143	−205	−336	5	198	105	−110	−711	568
6	726	209	−205	206	6	316	614	−248	−343	656
7	481	659	−261	179	7	030	859	052	−154	765
8	350	595	−273	191	8	−046	760	027	−082	587
9	407	722	−024	139	9	134	791	248	−038	707
10	463	720	−085	253	10	151	874	135	−018	805
11	678	−262	456	136	11	835	011	−136	−199	755
12	773	−275	362	136	12	829	070	−209	−294	823
13	778	−236	148	−221	13	591	038	−083	−611	731
14	691	−067	525	218	14	874	176	−038	−092	805
15	796	−078	344	091	15	784	222	−080	−310	766
16	262	−402	267	317	16	119	−002	−612	−112	402
17	242	−469	−200	433	17	193	−040	−683	−008	506
18	177	−469	−295	452	18	087	−034	−730	010	542
19	434	−419	−371	055	19	097	−003	−552	−436	504
20	−073	−623	−354	179	20	−144	−343	−638	−071	551

Tab. 3: Matrice factorielle des échelles d'appréciation, avant et après rotation (saturations multipliées par 1000). Les saturations supérieures à | .50 | dans la matrice factorielle après rotation sont soulignées. N = 126.

On a calculé pour chaque sujet ses quatre scores factoriels en se basant sur la matrice factorielle après rotation.

Facteurs	Avant rotation		Après rotation	
	Valeur propre	% variance expliquée	Valeur propre	% variance expliquée
I	6.504	32.52	3.605	18.02
II	3.388	16.94	3.587	17.94
III	1.616	8.08	2.348	11.74
IV	1.441	7.21	3.409	17.05
Total	12.949	64.75	12.949	64.75

Tab. 4: Valeur propre et % de variance expliquée de l'analyse factorielle des échelles d'appréciation, avant et après rotation.

Facteurs impairs	Facteurs pairs			
	1	2	3	4
1	0,9864	0,0390	0,0893	−0,1323
2	−0,0343	0,9989	−0,0125	0,0304
3	0,1302	−0,0252	0,0396	0,9904
4	−0,0942	0,0101	0,9951	−0,0271

Tab. 5: Cosinus entre les axes factoriels des échelles d'appréciation des sujets impairs et sujets pairs

Variable	Cosinus	Variable	Cosinus
1	0,906	11	0,967
2	0,983	12	0,973
3	0,964	13	0,961
4	0,992	14	0,979
5	0,985	15	0,904
6	0,978	16	0,932
7	0,964	17	0,969
8	0,963	18	0,826
9	0,938	19	0,672
10	0,985	20	0,879

Tab. 6: Cosinus entre les échelles d'appréciation des sujets impairs et sujets pairs

Modèle théorique	Facteurs			
	I	II	III	IV
comport. travail				1. rapidité travail 2. indépendance école 3. achève son travail 4. stabilité travail 5. surmonte difficultés
respect des normes		6. accepte consignes 7. laisse tranquille 8. non colérique 9. ne dérange pas 10. ne se dispute pas		
comport. verbal	11. élaboration phrases 12. richesse vocabulaire 13. compréhension consign 14. prononciation 15. utilisation mots			13. compréhension consign
intérêt partici-pation			16. intérêt entour. 17. jeux autres 18. contact institut. 19. intérêt milieu 20. communique	

Tab. 7: Répartition des échelles d'appréciation en fonction du modèle attendu et des facteurs obtenus. On a noté les items dort les saturations sont supérieures à | .50|. Les items dont les saturations sont supérieures à | .70 | sont soulignés.

Le tableau 8 contient la moyenne et l'écart-type des sous-tests de lecture pour la fin du premier (LFT1) et du second trimestre (LFT2).

Variable no.	LFT1: 1er trimestre N = 110		LFT2: 2ième trimestre N = 109	
	Moyenne	Ecart-type	Moyenne	Ecart-type
1	17,337	9,810	51,394	21,077
2	15,200	4,750	14,826	3,986
3	1,673	2,339	6,138	3,627
4	5,336	2,990	11,908	3,985
5	3,309	1,658	10,037	4,082
6	4,427	2,550	6,697	3,896
7	3,545	2,452	7,569	4,922
8	11,009	3,146	12,156	3,275
9	4,636	3,153	8,523	4,684

Tab. 8: Moyenne, écart-type des sous-tests de lecture (LFT1 pour la fin du premier trimestre, N = 110; LFT2 pour la fin du second trimestre, N = 109)

Les tableaux suivants contiennent les coefficients de corrélation Bravais-Pearson pour les sous-tests du LFT1 et du LFT2.

Sous-tests				Sous-tests					
	1	2	3	4	5	6	7	8	9
1		197	509	124	241	554	509	394	425
2			396	579	414	611	475	412	527
3				412	438	700	524	362	544
4					547	439	483	379	453
5						303	301	339	568
6							687	465	554
7								412	516
8									424
9									

Tab. 9: Matrice des corrélations Bravais-Pearson (x 1000) des sous-tests de la batterie LFT1 à la fin du premier trimestre N = 110.

Sous-tests					Sous-tests				
	1	2	3	4	5	6	7	8	9
1		347	416	267	300	443	418	364	427
2			637	477	630	706	641	542	584
3				716	676	770	802	456	693
4					704	544	680	446	649
5						576	732	619	684
6							810	474	602
7								543	719
8									489
9									

Tab. 10: Matrice des corrélations Bravais-Pearson (x 1000) des sous-tests de la batterie LFT1 à la fin du second trimestre, N = 109.

Au tableau 11 on peut voir les matrices factorielles en composantes principales avant et après rotation varimax du LFT1.

Sous-tests	Avant rotation		Sous-tests	Après rotation		
	I	II		I	II	h^2
1	609	−637	1	877	−058	772
2	722	333	2	306	734	632
3	768	−220	3	714	358	638
4	683	524	4	148	848	741
5	632	449	5	161	758	601
6	831	−255	6	784	375	751
7	762	−200	7	696	369	621
8	638	−046	8	501	398	409
9	783	086	9	518	593	621

Tab. 11: Matrice factorielle des sous-tests de lecture LFT1, avant et après rotation (les saturations sont multipliées par 1000). Les saturations supérieures à | .50 | dans la matrice factorielle après rotation sont souligneés.

Par l'analyse factorielle nous extrayons 64,34% de la variance (voir tableau suivant). L'analyse est arrêtée lorsque la valeur propre tombe en dessous de .80.

Facteur	Avant rotation		Après rotation	
	valeur propre	% variance expliquée	valeur propre	% variance expliquée
I	4,64	51,51	3,04	33,78
II	1,15	12,83	2,75	30,56
Total	5,79	64,34	5,79	64,34

Tab. 12: Valeur propre et pourcentage de variance expliquée de l'analyse factorielle des sous-tests LFT1, avant et après rotation.

La fidélité de la structure factorielle mesurée par la méthode de Kaiser sur les sujets pairs-impairs est satisfaisante. Le cosinus entre les tests des sujets impairs et pairs est le suivant:

Test	Cosinus
1	0,92
2	0,82
3	0,87
4	0,97
5	0,77
6	0,90
7	0,96
8	0,98
9	0,97

La stabilité est plus faible pour le test no 5, ce qui peut s'expliquer par sa faible fidélité.

Le premier facteur peut s'interpréter comme un facteur général de lecture qui est saturé par des tests aussi différents que copie d'un texte, reconnaissance de phrases, fusion de mots, compréhension d'images, dictée de mots et closure de phrases.

Le second facteur s'interprête comme un facteur de reconnaissance visuelle, puisque tous les tests à choix multiples (sauf reconnaissance de phrases) ont des saturations supérieures à .50. Le test reconnaissance de phrases n'est pas bien expliqué par cette analyse, car sa communauté = 0.409. La variance inexpliquée provient de facteurs spécifiques et de variance d'erreur.

Pour chaque sujet on a calculé les scores factoriels à partir de la matrice après rotation.

Le tableau suivant contient les matrices factorielles avant et après rotation varimax du LFT2.

Sous-Test	Avant rotation Facteurs		Sous-Test	Après rotation Facteur		
	I	II		I	II	h²
1	525	791	1	153	937	902
2	787	040	2	701	360	621
3	880	−067	3	829	301	779
4	782	−341	4	853	012	728
5	842	−247	5	869	121	771
6	842	119	6	718	455	723
7	905	−048	7	844	330	821
8	682	094	8	583	367	474
9	828	−040	9	771	305	689

Tab. 13: Matrice factorielle des sous-tests de lecture LFT2, avant et après rotation (les saturations sont multipliées par 1000). Les saturations supérieures à | .50 | dans la matrice factorielle après rotation sont soulignées.

Facteur	Avant rotation		Après rotation	
	Valeur propre	% variance expliquée	Valeur propre	% variance expliquée
I	5,67	62,99	4,85	53,87
II	0,84	9,29	1,66	18,41
Total	6,51	72,28	6,51	72,28

Tab. 14: Valeur propre et pourcentage de variance expliquée de l'analyse factorielle des sous-tests LFT2, avant et après rotation.

Si on examine le tableau 14, on voit que 72,28% de variance est expliquée par l'analyse factorielle. Après rotation l'importance du premier facteur reste relativement grande puisqu'il explique encore 53,87% de la variance. Le rôle du second facteur est plus secondaire (18,41% variance). La stabilité de la structure, calculée au moyen de la méthode de Kaiser entre sujets pairs-impairs est excellente et meilleure que pour le LFT1. Les cosinus entre les tests sont supérieurs ou égaux à 0,90 pour toutes variables.

Test	Cosinus
1	0,94
2	0,93
3	1,00
4	0,96
5	1,00
6	0,97
7	1,00
8	0,90
9	0,90

Ce phénomène peut s'expliquer par la meilleure fidélité des sous-tests du LFT2. Le premier facteur qui est le plus important est à nouveau un facteur global de lecture, puisqu'il sature fortement toutes les variables à l'exception du premier test: copie de texte. Le second facteur, moins important s'interprête comme un facteur écriture. Il est hautement saturé par le test: copie d'un texte (0,94) et demeure encore significatif pour le test: dictée de mots (0,46).

On a calculé pour chaque sujet les scores factoriels à partir de la matrice après rotation.

3.3 REGRESSION DES ECHELLES D'EVALUATION SUR LES TESTS DE LECTURE

Pour chaque sujet nous disposons de 4 scores factoriels, obtenus à partir des échelles d'évaluation et pour le premier, respectivement pour le second trimestre de deux scores factoriels obtenus à partir des tests de lecture.

Les corrélations simples entre les facteurs d'évaluation et les facteurs de lecture sont les suivantes:

Facteurs d'évaluation	Facteurs de lecture			
	LFT1 Facteurs		LFT2 Facteurs	
	1	2	1	2
1. comportement verbal	0,25xx	0,31xx	0,44xx	0,18x
2. respect des normes	0,11	0,14	0,17	0,08
3. intérêt, participation	−0,04	0,04	0,10	0,08
4. comportement travail	−0,13	−0,17	−0,21x	−0,16

Au moyen de l'analyse de régression multiple nous introduisons en régression, pas à pas les scores factoriels des échelles d'évaluation (Draper, N. R. & Smith, H. 1966) qui sont les variables indépendantes. Les variables dépendantes sont les scores factoriels, obtenus à partir des tests de lecture. Les résultats pour le LFT1 se trouvent reproduits au tableau 15 et pour le LFT2 au tableau 16.

Tests de Lecture LFT1

Echelles d'apprécia-tion	Facteur 1: Lecture			Facteur 2: Reconnaissance		
	somme carrés réduits (1)	% de la somme réduite (2)	% de la somme totale (3)	somme carrés réduits (1)	% de la somme réduite (2)	% de la somme totale (3)
Facteur 1: comport. verbal	7,06	60,82	6,4	10,71	63,71	9,7
Facteur 2: respect normes	1,30	11,20	1,2	1,92	11,40	1,7
Facteur 3: intérêt, particip.	0,84	7,24	0,80	0,05	0,30	0,0
Facteur 4: comport. travail	2,41	20,76	2,2	4,16	24,70	3,8
Total	11,60	100	10,6	16,842	100	15,3
R		0,325			0,391	

Tab. 15: Le coefficient de corrélation multiple (R), la somme des carrés réduits par les facteurs d'appréciation, les pourcentages des facteurs par rapport de la somme des carrés réduits et les pourcentages des facteurs par rapport à la somme des carrés totale pour les scores factoriels du LFT1 (N = 110).

Tests de lecture LFT2

Echelles d'apprécia-tion	Facteur 1: Lecture			Facteur 2: Ecriture		
	(1)	(2)	(3)	(1)	(2)	(3)
Facteur 1: comport. verbal	20,75	68,13	19,0	3,46	44,88	3,2
Facteur 2: respect normes	2,80	9,19	2,6	0,71	9,21	0,7
Facteur 3: intérêt, particip.	0,02	0,07	0,0	0,17	2,20	0,2
Facteur 4:	6,89	22,62	6,3	3,37	43,71	3,1
Total	30,46	100	27,9	7,71	100	7,1
R		0,509			0,266	

Tab. 16: Idem pour les scores factoriels du LFT2 (N = 109)

La meilleure prédiction est réalisée pour le facteur 1 du LFT2 puisque R = 0,509, ensuite elle reste très significative pour le facteur 2 du LFT1 (p < 0.01) et elle reste encore significative (p < 0.05) pour le facteur 1 du LFT1 et pour le facteur 2 du LFT2.

Le rôle du facteur verbal est important pour le premier trimestre, aussi bien au niveau de la lecture que pour la reconnaissance et reste prépondérant pour la lecture au second trimestre.

Au comportement de l'enfant au travail revient la seconde place surtout pour prédire la reconnaissance au premier trimestre et la lecture au second trimestre.

Le rôle des facteurs 2 et 3 des échelles d'évaluation est plus négligeable.

4. CONCLUSIONS

Les évaluations portées par les institutrices du jardin d'enfant sur les enfants ont été soumises à une analyse factorielle en composantes principales qui a dégagée une structure simple de 4 dimensions indépendantes: 1) comportement verbal, 2) respect des normes, 3) intérêt, participation et 4) comportement au travail. L'analyse factorielle des tests de lecture a donné à la fin du premier trimestre de la première année scolaire, deux facteurs indépendants qui sont: lecture et reconnaissance et à la fin du second trimestre: lecture et écriture.

La régression multiple des facteurs d'évaluation sur les facteurs de lecture a montré que la lecture au second trimestre est la plus prédictive. Le rôle du facteur verbal est le plus important dans la prédiction, suivi par le comportement au travail. Le rôle du facteur respect des normes et du facteur "intérêt, participation" est négligeable.

BIBLIOGRAPHIE
1. De Landsheere, G. *Introduction à la recherche en éducation*. Liège: Thone, 1972.
2. Dickes, P., et E. Wagner. Prédiction de l'apprentissage de la lecture à partir du jardin d'enfant. à paraître.
3. Dickes, P., et G. Wirtgen. "Itemanalyse und Eichung einer Testbatterie zur Erfassung der Lese- und Rechtschreibleistung (Für Erstklässer)," *Zeitschrift für Entwicklungspsychologie und Pädagogische Psychologie*, 3, (1973), 215-227.
4. Draper, N. R., and H. Smith. *Applied Regression Analysis*. New York: Wiley & Sons, 1966.
5. Jadoulle, A. "Questionnaire concernant la maturité de l'enfant de six ans," *XIIIe Colloque*, Genève, 2-5 (avril 1966).
6. Kohn, M., et B. L. Rosman, "A Social Competence Scale and Symptom Checklist for the Preschool Child," *Developmental Psychology*, 6 (1972), 430-444.
7. Kohn, M., et B. L. Rosman. "Relationship of Preschool Social-Emotional Functioning to Later Intellectual Achievement," *Developmental Psychology*, 6 (1972), 445-452.
8. Leclercq-Boxus, E. "Une méthode de prédiction en lecture en première année primaire," *Education Tribune Libre*, 127, (1971), 63-80.
9. Veldman, D. J. *Fortran Programming for the Behavioral Sciences*. New York: Holt, Rinehart and Winston, 1967.

Self-Evaluation and Reading Development

Don Holdaway
Auckland Teachers College
Auckland, New Zealand

It is necessary to define the limits, and some of the limitations, of this discussion. I would like to highlight a few special features of the subject, drawing almost exclusively on New Zealand experience and, at the same time, acknowledge a host of unstated relationships with the international culture of ideas.

READING AS ORCHESTRATION: AN ANALOGY

Listening in to the neat simplifications about learning to read produced by one methodology after another, we would hardly gain the impression that reading is among the most complex processes in creation—that it is almost as complex as man himself. Reading is an orchestration of disparate behaviours which, if they are to achieve their various and proper ends, must become an ordered and functioning unity.

Thinking for a moment of the human organism as an orchestra of many members provided with its own conductor, we may conjure up a suggestive analogy for our present purposes. We would not attempt to judge an orchestra simply by analysing the qualities of each instrument, nor by auditioning each player. We may approach the really significant aspects of evaluation only as the orchestra begins to function in performing from a particular score under the baton of a particular conductor.

Acknowledging the fact that our analogy fails to represent the complex relationships existing among individual human abilities, let us develop one or two suggestions from the model before dispensing with it.

First, the quality of an orchestra's performance from moment to moment depends in large measure on the sensitivity of each member to the performance of others as he hears them. In other words, channels of communication link each member in a feedback loop which influences the precise way in which that member carries out his own skilled function. Similarly, within the individual reader, different types of skills influence one another as they function; and the information loops which carry this influence are a vital part of the total activity.

Second, the governing influence of the conductor's presence and movement bring confidence and precision to the orchestration. Similarly, reading behaviour depends on some final, directing influence within the reader. A teacher, standing as he does outside the abilities to be controlled and cut off from the subtle messages of feedback which are being transmitted within the reader, cannot fulfill this function. He can only teach the reader to do so for himself. Reading is a self-governing process, a self-conducted performance.

THE DEVELOPMENTAL PERSPECTIVE IN EVALUATION

Any approach to evaluation which oversimplifies the content of reading behaviour, or fails to emphasize the central function of integrative and control processes, falls short of the reality. By approaching reading as a developmental process, and the learning of it as a series of complex developmental tasks similar to those involved in learning to speak, we avoid some of the most distorting simplifications of analysis. This point of view does justice to the kinds of priorities highlighted by the orchestration analogy, especially the emphasis it places on autonomous feedback and control, and on the need to evaluate parts as they function within an organic whole.

Let us consider two questions: 1) By what means may the teacher monitor the total array of behaviours which may reasonably be held to fall within the concept of reading competence? 2) How much of this monitoring should be undertaken by the pupil as an important part of his development as a self-organized learner?

The first interesting thing about these questions is their order. We take it for granted that evaluation is fundamentally a teacher task and only secondly a function of the learner. Now, in taking up the developmental perspective, we are forced to reorder these questions and look upon self-monitoring as the primary mode of evaluation influencing the learning process. Teacher evaluation, though still essential and powerful in shaping reading behaviour, takes the secondary role.

LEARNING TO READ AS A SELF-MONITORED PROCESS

The climate of thinking about learning to read in the past decade was greatly influenced by those who finally dispelled the myth that there was a perfect, best method of learning to read. How distracting that myth, and how deeply it distorted our view of evaluation. In the less cloudy climate that has prevailed since that time, research and development have been able to shift their emphasis to a proper focus on learning to read rather than on teaching reading.

A large proportion of children in all developed countries have learned to read successfully under very different regimes of method, and many recent research studies have been concerned with describing the actual behaviour of these children. Learning to read is beginning to be displayed as a series of natural, healthy progressions that look very similar in different instructional systems once the trappings of method have been taken away. Successful children are too busy forming their own destiny as literate individuals to take too much notice of what their teachers tell them to do. It is the really conscientious youngsters, who try to stick closely with the instruction instead of supplementing it liberally with common sense, who are really at risk as readers.

We have much to learn from closer observation of successful learners, and we are more likely to help the less confident children by inducing them to operate like the successful ones than by imposing the half-truths of some methodology which we must monitor closely ourselves because the child has no earthly chance of understanding what it's all about.

One of the most interesting things about successful readers is their comparative independence at all levels from extrinsic reinforcement and control. They approach reading with high motivation and self-confidence, aware from day to day of what print has to offer them, and they get from it that special sense of achievement which comes from the habit of self-monitoring. In learning to ride a bicycle, a child will drive his body to the point of exhaustion, skin his knees, and even risk life and limb as he wobbles down the footpath. So, at appropriate times, the child who comes to reading with the right developmental set chooses his own speed, his own threshold of frustration, his own tolerance for repetition and practice as he masters each new challenge of the task. True, he gains much from sensitive and interested adults around him—especially from his teachers—just as in his infancy, he took models for speech from his parents.

SELF-REGULATING SYSTEMS AND HUMAN SKILLS

Most human skills are self-regulating, even in their earliest stages of development, and a part of mastering skills at each stage is learning how to regulate them. As a technology has been developed for constructing such self-regulating mechanisms as computers, some researchers (9, 14) have taken up the significance of cybernetic theory. But we have a long way to go before we understand the feedback systems which control human skills and their acquisition.

In this decade, we have all seen the dramatic lift-off of the giant Apollo rocket, awesome in its power as well as its fingertip delicacy of self-regulating balance control. The giant rocket appears to defy all laws of experience as it hovers momentarily over the pad before accelerating upwards. Yet the electrogyroscopic balance feedback of the Apollo is like a crude mechano model in comparison with the organic computer and the neuron feedback loops guiding the reading behaviour of the ordinary child.

SELF-REGULATION IN LEARNING TO READ

Three important insights which arise from feedback theory are highly relevant to our subject. First, feedback and guidance systems are invariably more complex than the power systems they control; second, they can go wrong in a greater variety of ways than the power systems dependent upon them; and third, internal communication channels, responsive in miniseconds to changes in the power system, are vital to their function.

Now, if we see reading behaviour as a self-regulating system, we realize that self-evaluation of reading behaviour is at the same time more complex, more difficult to learn, more delicate and fragile, and more vital to success than is the response or performance side of the system. It would appear, furthermore, that in human learning, as distinct from contrived mechanisms, the feedback system fulfills a further function of reinforcing efficient behaviour and thereby implanting new levels of sophistication in the system as it is constructed. During the learning stages of a skill, this second function of human feedback may be even more important than the first.

A strong line of research pioneered by MacKinnon (10) in Canada, developed in depth by people such as Goodman (6), and represented locally by a decade of productive developmental research by Clay and her students at the University of Auckland (many later references), emphasizes the central importance of self-corrective behaviour in successful reading at all stages of development, but critically—and from a traditional standpoint, surprisingly—at the earliest stages.

Traditional methods and styles of teaching have tended to place the responsibility for performance on the learner, and have jealously preempted the roles of evaluation and reinforcement to the teacher. Such a misconception seriously distorts the natural learning of reading skills and threatens average and slow learners who tend to receive little reinforcement and a preponderance of negative feedback from a system in which the teacher and peer comparisons dominate evaluation. In such a system, successful readers beat the teacher to correction and are relatively independent of extrinsic reinforcement. Even so, it would appear that, at the early stage, many of these successful readers become increasingly hooked on the extrinsic rewards that are wastefully lavished on them at the expense of those who need the rewards. Their skill may then be misdirected toward performance for praise or

Self-Evaluation

competition on low level tasks, when they may have developed higher level skills had their reading been redirected toward self-satisfaction.

Whenever we correct a child who could correct himself, we subtly interfere with the growth of that system of reward and control on which he must rely to carry out the skill independently. To virtually take over a child's control system, as so often happens in well-intentioned remedial programmes, conceivably could cripple his ability to master any reading skill.

MONITORING AND TEACHING SELF-EVALUATION

If self-evaluation at all stages of development plays as vital a role in learning to read as research now tends to indicate, we must face many changes of emphasis in teaching and evaluating reading. We will favour patterns of organization and styles of teaching which foster the development of independence, and we will provide inducements for children to share more fully in the evaluation and control of their own learning.

Furthermore, since learning the strategies of self-regulation is necessary to mastery of any skill at any level, our own evaluation of children's progress must include an evaluation of their ability to evaluate. Techniques for recording and tallying self-monitoring behaviour should be an important part of our overall assessment procedures. New Zealand infant teachers have responded enthusiastically to the use of such procedures arising from Clay's research into early reading behaviour (2). When self-corrective behaviour is not evident, teachers are now seeking ways of inducing or teaching such behaviour, with manifestly positive results.

PROGRESS IN READING DURING THE FIRST FIVE YEARS OF SCHOOL

From the developmental point of view, we would expect to find a number of clearly defined stages in the development of literate children. We would expect to find some behaviours which appeared for a time and were then superceded, and we would expect to find appropriate forms of self-monitoring present in the behaviour at each level. Recent local research continues to fulfill these expectations, to the extent that it has directed our attention to the preschool experiences of high progress readers in order to observe the earliest stages of reading occurring under optimum conditions from infancy. Even in the reading-like behaviour of many preschoolers from the age of two years, we find clear evidence of self-corrective and self-regulating behaviour on the basis of syntax, meaning, sequence, picture cues, and memory for text.

It is possible to organize our observation of reading development over the first six years of schooling into five clear stages, beginning for some children as early as the second year preschool and only partially completed by some children as they complete the equivalent of Grade 6.

1. Emergent Reading Behaviour and the Development of a Set towards Literacy

A very sophisticated complex of attitudes, insights, and skills needs to be developed before the actual decoding of print symbols becomes meaningful or manageable. Included, for instance, are motivational factors, such as having high expectations of books as sources of special kinds of security-centred fulfillment; operational factors, such as the ability to use language without reference to presently available sensory experience; linguistic factors, such as gaining native language control over a wide range of written dialect forms; and orthographic factors, such as the awareness that the message is carried and preserved in every detail by the print rather than the picture.

This fascinating stage, which peaks for the majority of our children during the first year at school (5-6 years), encompasses many reading skills or their embryonic forms. To call this level *prereading, readiness for reading,* or even worse, *preliteracy,* is to underestimate or mis-construe the importance and nature of these emergent reading behaviours.

It could be said that the strength, content, and articulation of the set directing a child into literacy determine in no small measure the success or failure experienced at succeeding stages. In her Concepts About Print test, Clay (2) has developed a fine instrument for evaluating many important behaviours of this emergent stage.

2. The Early Reading Stage

In this crucial phase of learning, most young children acquire the range of skills set out in most beginning reading programmes—and much more. As the children begin to relate cues from different sources, carefully patterning a slow flow of language against a directionally oriented series of visual patterns, the miracle of true reading begins to occur. Cues are matched with deliberation. The finger or the voice points. Reruns and self-corrections often punctuate the performance. The active use of increasingly sophisticated strategies of self-correction and self-confirmation is of critical importance. These strategies help children to organize perceptions and to sustain attention on appropriate visual details for as long as is necessary.

Of special interest here is the high correlation between written language competence and success in reading as shown in the research of Robinson (13), in which writing vocabulary was the preeminent predictor of reading progress between the ages of 5½ and 6 years. This high correlation, which is suggestive of the need for better integrated literacy programmes, also offers the possibility of a simple, reliable instrument of evaluation at the early reading stage.

Further evidence of the importance of early success to later progress was demonstrated in another Auckland study by Munroe (12).

3. *Fluency and the Submergence of Overt Monitoring*

As children gain automatic control over perceptual skills, fluency develops and the operation of self-corrective strategies becomes covert. The child moves towards the stage where the orally verbalized crutch which has provided an eye-voice-ear link with the text is no longer needed. Silent reading gradually becomes a natural form of behaviour, but vocalization is only just below the surface and speed remains at or below the rate of speech. The efficient problem solving strategies built up at the previous stage and centred on the concrete sensory support of vocalizing and pointing, are still accessible whenever needed. As Clay puts it rather graphically, the child reading fluently is able to "drop to a lower gear" whenever difficulties in the text require it.

Williams (15), in a study of reading behaviour at the equivalent of grade 3 level, describes the strategies of successful and unsuccessful readers, the majority of whom were at this third stage of development. Again, self-confirming strategies were associated with success, especially if these strategies made strong use of syntactical and semantic feedback.

This stage is a time for widening horizons in reading as perceptual tasks come under largely automatic control and the energy previously drawn off for conscious matching operations becomes available for deeper reactions and higher level operations. Evaluation procedures should now be directed more clearly to appropriate emotional response, identification, creation of sensory imagery, and the whole range of comprehension skills from word meaning in context to critical and creative thinking.

4. *Consolidation: Tension between Oral and Silent Reading Skills*

As suppression of vocal responses allows rapid increase in the rate of silent reading, the child can no longer move with comfort back into the oral reading mode until he has learned a new battery of skills. When oral reading is forced on him he may bungle and stammer his way through the text, puzzled by the fact that he has no trouble when reading to himself; he cannot coordinate his responses when eye and voice are at different points in the text. Until he has received some instruction and purposeful practice in the special skills of audience reading, he is likely to report that he "hates reading aloud," and he has reason to.

At the same time, in the private security of efficient silent reading, he is likely to be gripped by a text and begin to adjust his style of attention, rate, and comprehension to suit the widening range of materials he is now able to process. On the other hand, this may not be a period of very active reading and his skills may remain at the previous level for several years before he makes a breakthrough to real ease and pleasure in silent reading. Even the new perceptual skills which he needs to master at this level, such as the increase in sight vocabulary to cover over 90 percent of word recognition, depend on the burgeoning of reading interests fed by the ease of comprehension of efficient silent reading.

Self-evaluation tends to be less apparent at this level and is certainly difficult to monitor. There is some evidence to suggest that the continuing emphasis of reading programmes on the evaluation of lower level skills may inhibit the natural drive toward wider interests and the desire to read. Carter (1), in another Auckland study, found that the equivalent of Grades 3 to 4, programmes emphasizing extrinsic evaluation of lower level skills tended to produce a narrow spectrum of progress favouring those skills, while programmes emphasizing intrinsic evaluation of higher order skills produced marked positive changes in attitude toward reading together with good skill development in vocabulary. Until better instruments are available to assess development of higher order skills, it is unlikely that schools will provide adequate opportunities or stimulus for development at this stage.

5. *Flexibility: Developing Styles of Reading for Different Purposes*

A competent minority of children at grade levels 5 and 6 display several mature styles of reading depending on motivation and purpose. These children tend to regard themselves as good readers and may display the same determination to master the difficult skills of audience reading as they displayed in mastering decoding skills at the second stage. In a challenging educational environment, they may develop astonishing flexibility in rate and in new perceptual strategies such as those involved in scanning, skimming, selecting, and sampling. A close study of the reading behaviour of these children may suggest ways in which we can assist the majority of children to diversify their skills at an earlier age but, currently, we cannot regard maturity at this level as characteristic of eleven- and twelve-year-old children.

WHAT IS GOOD READING FROM A DEVELOPMENTAL POINT OF VIEW?

Value judgements about the quality of performance at any of these five stages are likely to be valid only for the particular stage being observed. What we mean by *good reading* at one stage may be very different from what we regard as good reading at the next. For instance, if we take oral reading as a parameter for evaluation over these stages, the first, third, and fifth are likely to display fast, fluent, lively reading—although not equally accurate, of course—while in the intervening stages this is unlikely to be the case. Oral reading at the second stage is likely to be slow and meticulous, even laboured, while at the fourth stage it may be erratic, bumbling, and mannered. Each of these types of reading must be considered good reading for the stage at which it appears.

Evaluative judgements about different reading skills should be specific to the stage of development so that children may be reinforced for appropriate behaviour. In general, the children themselves seem to be able to make the necessary shifts of evaluation from stage to stage more easily than teachers or test developers—both of whom are tempted to run the same rule over reading behaviour at every stage.

EXTRINSIC MONITORING OF PROGRESS IN FUNCTIONAL READING

What are the implications of a developmental point of view for those who interact with children learning to read—the teacher who has the most profound influence as well as the department head, the principal, the inspector or supervisor or adviser, and the parents as they fall under the influence of the school? All these are included because together they constitute a powerful judicial force bearing down on the teacher, and hence on the children. It is often this third force which turns evaluation into a mockery of what it should be—an act of comparison or ranking rather than a sensitive measure of progress and need.

Assuming, then, that the teacher is permitted to evaluate the progress of each child in a sensitive way, what priorities stem from regarding reading as fundamentally a self-regulating task?

1. Nothing the teacher does should inhibit the use of self-monitoring procedures by the children. He should reinforce the most desirable behaviours and, for learning to read, that means preeminently reinforcing self-regulating behaviour. The teacher's highest praise must be reserved for that critical moment of self-awareness when the child's own feedback has informed him accurately of his own success.

2. Since self-regulation is more vital, more difficult to learn, and more open to malfunction than any other part of the reading process, the teacher has a responsibility to monitor the children's monitoring. The contributions of Clay (2) in this respect were mentioned earlier.

3. The full spectrum of reading attitudes, insights, and skills appropriate to the stage of development should be evaluated in a balanced and coherent way. Our standardised group tests set a bad example in this respect, since they measure only a portion of the spectrum. We need to be much more aggressive in demanding research-based procedures of evaluation covering the higher order cognitive and integrative skills of reading. The work of Taba in social studies, explored with considerable

success by McNaughton (11), holds promise for the objective evaluation of such skills.

However, even these studies omit many seldom-mentioned aspects of healthy reading behaviour which may be of first importance. Operations such as personal identification with characters or the ability to structure alternative plot possibilities, loom large in the experience of successful readers and may contribute significantly to their success.

Certainly, the affective area is of prime importance in sustaining healthy reading behaviour. In the study mentioned earlier, Carter (1) demonstrated marked changes in attitude toward reading, over comparatively short periods of time, associated with the use of particular materials and approaches at the equivalent of Grades 3 to 4. More ambitious longitudinal studies may show the possibility of bringing about changes in self-concept in relation to reading.

4. A balanced spectrum of reading behaviours may best be evaluated by observing functional reading rather than performance reading, especially under test conditions. The teacher needs techniques to assist him in observing and recording the progress of children in day-to-day reading under natural conditions. Types of organization, such as individualized reading, which readily display a wide range of reading behaviour or provide opportunities for personal interaction between teacher and pupil, may facilitate this day-to-day evaluation.

An informal prose inventory, sensitively applied, may be a most valuable instrument in monitoring progress in functional reading. A local attempt to extend and streamline these procedures (8) makes it possible to monitor and record a wide range of reading behaviours within a manageable framework.

5. Despite the cautions sounded previously, standardised tests are essential to certain proper functions of evaluation. However, since they need to be used no more than once or twice a year to fulfill these purposes, they should not be an obtrusive feature in the reading experience of children. The Progressive Achievement Tests, recently developed in New Zealand by Elley and Reid (5), have been provided with practical guidance and notes on interpretation of exemplary clarity, but a sampling of the use being made of the tests raises doubts as to the extent to which we can rely on advice communicated by a carefully designed manual. The potential for misapplication of standard measures seems to come from very deepseated assumptions about evaluation which persist despite being shown to be harmful. Assumptions which encourage the school to exercise a prophesy-fulfilling influence, limiting the progress of many children, seem to be among the most deeply entrenched prejudices of the school system. We need to know more about the actual uses and the real impact of standardised test

results before we can have a clear idea of their place and value in guiding the development of children who are learning to read.

6. Finally, diagnostic tests and procedures need to be used more widely to monitor normal development. Too often, careful diagnosis is not used to improve the efficiency of reading in a general sense, but is used for special purposes too late in the development of progressive disorders. A diagnostic approach to evaluation is desirable from the earliest stages if preventive intervention is to be effective. The diagnosis should be sufficiently functional to suggest the most appropriate forms of intervention. More often than not, the appropriate form will include restoring healthy self-regulating functions in the total operational strategy of the individual reader.

CONCLUSION

From the developmental perspective discussed in this paper, we are able to look critically at traditional assumptions about evaluating progress in functional reading. In particular, it is possible to see the inbuilt dangers in many of our accepted procedures of restricting the growth of vital, self-regulative skills in young readers, and of directing massive negative feedback into the learning endeavours of the children most in need of positive reinforcement.

We face a challenge to develop styles of teaching and procedures of evaluation which will encourage optimum development of self-monitoring strategies at every stage and over the whole spectrum of reading, and which will allow teachers to intervene more positively in the learning adventures of children who are struggling to master the skills of literacy.

Finally, we need to support classroom teachers in every possible way to make these changes, and remove the institutional and supervisory impediments which so often force teachers to adopt harmful procedures in evaluating the progress of children learning to read.

REFERENCES
1. Carter, Garry C. "The Effects of Reading Materials," unpublished thesis, University of Auckland Library, 1973.
2. Clay, Marie M. Reading: The Patterning of Complex Behaviour. Auckland, New Zealand: Heinemann Educational Books, 1972.
3. Clay, Marie M. The Early Detection of Reading Difficulties: A Diagnositc Survey. Auckland, New Zealand: Heinemann Educational Books, 1972.
4. Clay, Marie M. "Reading Errors and Self-Correction Behaviour," British Journal of Educational Psychology, 30 (1969).
5. Elley, W. B., and N. A. Reid. Progressive Achievement Tests: Reading Comprehension and Reading Vocabulary, Teacher's Manual. Wellington, New Zealand: New Zealand Council for Educational Research, 1969.
6. Goodman, Kenneth S. "Analysis of Oral Reading Miscues: Applied Psycholinguistics," Reading Research Quarterly, 5 (Fall), 1969.

7. Goodman, Kenneth S. "Reading: A Psycholinguistic Guessing Game," in H. Singer and R. Ruddell (Eds.), *Theoretical Models and Processes of Reading*. Newark, Delaware: International Reading Association, 1970.

8. Holdaway, Don. *Independence in Reading: A Handbook of Individualized Procedures*. Auckland, New Zealand: Ashton Educational, 1972.

9. Kirk, S. A., and J. J. McCarthy. "The Illinois Test of Psycholinguistic Abilities: An Approach to Differential Diagnosis," *American Journal of Mental Deficiency*, 66 (1961).

10. MacKinnon, A. R. *How Do Children Learn to Read?* Vancouver, British Columbia: Copp Clark, 1959.

11. McNaughton, Anthony H. "Research on Children's Written Language in Social Studies," in E. Malmquist and D. K. Bracken (Eds.), *Improving Reading Ability Around the World*, Proceedings of the Third IRA World Congress on Reading, Sydney, 1970. Newark, Delaware: International Reading Association, 1971.

12. Munroe, F. D. "The Prediction of Reading Performance: The Reading Achievement of Nine- and Ten-Year-Old Children in Relation to Their Performance in the First Year of Reading Instruction," unpublished thesis, University of Auckland Library, 1969.

13. Robinson, Susan. "Predicting Early Reading Progress," unpublished thesis, University of Auckland Library, 1973, 122.

14. Ruddell, Robert B. "Psycholinguistic Implications for a Systems of Communication Model," in H. Singer and R. Ruddell (Eds.), *Theoretical Models and Processes of Reading*. Newark, Delaware: International Reading Association, 1970.

15. Williams, Bryan. "The Oral Reading Behaviour of Standard One Children," unpublished thesis, University of Auckland Library, 1968.

Prediction en Lecture et Evaluation Formative

Elise Leclercq-Boxus
University of Liege
Liege, Belgium

L'égalité de réussite devant l'école, et non pas seulement l'égalité des chances, suppose une politique éducative globale et une attitude politique (P. Perrenoud, 1974).

Toute intervention à court terme ne peut que porter sur les mécanismes pédagogiques et institutionnels qui convertissent les différences culturelles en différences scolaires et donc, en échecs pédagogiques.

A l'école primaire, l'un de ces mécanismes patent est l'usage de l'évaluation normative qui "classe" les élèves... et sanctionne doublement les plus faibles: ils sont en bas de l'échelle et ils redoublent.

L'auteur a tenté de pallier à cette situation en travaillant, notamment au premier degré de l'école primaire.

Son objectif est d'aménager un vrai Mastery Learning, c'est-à-dire la maîtrise, par tous les élèves, d'objectifs opérationellement définis. Dans cette perspective, l'enseignement est réorganisé de telle sorte que chaque enfant progresse selon des modalités et à des vitesses différentes. Ce n'est plus la courbe de Gauss mais la courbe en J qui témoigne de l'acquis!

La position est donc clairement réaliste (c'est-à-dire consciente de ce que, dans nos sociétés occidentales, l'épanouissement des individus passe nécessairement par une maîtrise des acquisitions intellectuelles de base que sont la mathématique et la lecture) et interventionniste. En effet, loin de nier les valeurs apportées par la non directivité, il lui paraît que, dans un domaine où, même en incertitude, l'indécision n'est pas permise, plus d'arguments pèsent en faveur de l'option contraire. L'instruction générale et obligatoire, avec tous ses désavantages, lui paraît constituer un moyen non négligeable de rééquilibration des différences de départ.

Les techniques mises en oeuvre dans la perspective du Mastery Learning tel que l'auteur le conçoit reposent sur un certain nombre de principes qui seront brièvement décrits.

1. Une discrimination positive

Avec C. Chiland (1971), l'auteur pense que l'intervention pédagogique doit être "résolument inégale": il faut donner plus à certains enfants qu'à d'autres; c'est le principe même de la discrimination positive.

2. Une approche non pathologique

S'interroger sur la signification d'un dépistage précoce, c'est nécessairement chercher quelles conceptions de la prévention et de l'inadaptation scolaire le sous-entendent; c'est, en définitive, resoulever le problème fondamental de la norme et de la déviance.

Les enfants "inadaptés" (débiles mentaux, dyslexiques, dysorthographiques, dyscalculiques . . .) sont d'abord des enfants qui, à des degrés divers et selon des modalités variables, n'arrivent pas à suivre le rythme de la classe.

L'approche psychopathologique des échecs scolaires a peu à peu enlevé à l'école la responsabilité de ces problèmes.

3. Une alternance continue de l'enseignement et de son évaluation

Classiquement, après un apprentissage, on s'assure, au moyen d'une épreuve, de la maîtrise par chaque enfant du contenu enseigné. L'épreuve (ou test) est représentée ci-dessous par un losange, parce qu'elle constitue une source d'actions différentes conditionnelles aux résultats du test:

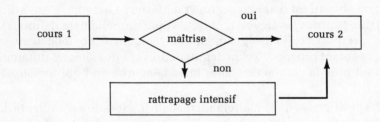

Le schéma dessiné ci-dessus est peut-être le schéma le plus simple que l'on puisse donner de *l'èvaluation formative.* Cette évaluation est d'autant plus au service de la maîtrise de la matière par l'élève qu'elle est diagnostique, c'est-à-dire qu'elle précise dans le détail les lacunes.

La pédagogie de la maîtrise répond au voeu de C. Chiland: ". . . comprendre les difficultés et y remédier au fur et à mesure qu'elles se présentent. Il vaut mieux les prévenir que les prédire."

4. Une politique de la maîtrise ou du dépassement selon les domaines

Si l'on peut concevoir que les élèves se diversifient (même très tôt) dans des options artistiques, scientifiques, sociales, etc., on peut moins accepter que certains ne dominent pas les acquisitions élémentaires qui constituent les bases indispensables de toute l'activité sociale et intellectuelle.

5. La prédiction, outil de mesure des actions

Ce rendement prédit représente la cote la plus probable qu'aurait atteint l'enfant si l'enseignant avait développé la même stratégie pédagogique que de coutume. Il est très intéressant pour l'enseignant de constater, chiffres à l'appui, l'ampleur du démenti (favorable) qu'a provoqué son action. Il serait regrettable en effet, de déployer une énergie considérable sans avoir un outil individuel de mesure de l'efficacité de cette énergie.

Cette procédure, qui consiste à mesurer les démentis de prédiction et à en rechercher les causes dans les actions entreprises (mesures administratives, familiales, et surtout scolaires), est évidemment très riche aussi sur le plan de la recherche. Elle permet notamment de comparer les effets d'actions différentes.

On le voit, la prédiction n'est pas utilisée dans une optique d'orientation vers l'enseignement spécial, mais, comme *évaluation formative*, dans une perspective de recherche et d'action.

6. Les prédictions sont probabilistes

Si les prédictions *à coup sûr* sont impossibles, cela ne constitue nullement une contre-indication aux prédictions. Les médecins le savent, qui formulent souvent leurs jugements de façon probabiliste: "Prenez ce médicament. Dans trois jours, vous devriez être guéri; sinon, rappelez-moi."

La *prédiction probabiliste* est acceptée en médecine, en circulation routière, en contraception, et elle guide utilement les décisions et l'action. Pourquoi, moyennant certaines modalités n'y aurions-nous pas recours en pédagogie?

7. Les prédictions doivent être communiquées

Reconnaître l'importance du préjugé du maître, c'est aussi admettre qu'il puisse jouer favorablement.

L'expression même de "réalisation *automatique* d'une prédiction" paraît malheureuse, car elle présente la réalisation de la prédiction comme *inéluctable, fatale*. Or, si la prédiction doit être probabiliste (voir ci-dessus), et présentée comme telle, elle doit aussi être conditionnelle.

8. Les prédictions sont conditionnelles

La prédiction ne peut être envisagée sans déterminer les modalités d'une action. Les valeurs prédites sont d'ailleurs liées à un certain nombre de conditions. Les modifications favorables introduites par l'enseignant devraient, en théorie, faire démentir (vers le mieux) ces prédictions.

LECLERCQ-BOXUS

C'est la raison pour laquelle, lorsque des prédictions peu favorables sont communiquées à l'enseignant, la consigne est, tout naturellement, d'agir de sorte à faire mentir les prédictions, vers le haut, bien entendu.

9. *La méthode importe plus que les instruments*

10. *Une méthode ouverte, combinant l'action et la recherche*

Actuellement, avec M. Detheux-Jehin, l'auteur met au point un système de codage des activités de l'enfant en classe (E.C.O.L.L.).

Le plan d'analyse E.C.O.L.L. est basé sur le modèle même qui sert à créer les questions des épreuves, intermédiaires et guides de l'éducation continue.

Le codage E.C.O.L.L. des comportements relève trois grandes dimensions:

1) le type de stimulus

2) le mode de réponse

3) l'objet de la réponse.

En outre, on note quatre caractères relatifs aux réponses:

1) la durée (en secondes)

2) la spontanéité ou non

3) l'adéquation ou non à la demande du professeur

4) l'exactitude.

Le but de l'ensemble du travail vise, la mise en relation des prédictions, des comportements manifestés en classe par l'élève comme par le professeur et du rendement de l'élève.

Les implications méthodologiques de cette entreprise de longue haleine pourraient être importantes. Le travail est loin d'être achevé: il nécessitera une collaboration de plus en plus étroite avec les enseignants et les chercheurs.

BIBLIOGRAPHIE

1. Bastin, G. *L'hécatombe scolaire*, Bruxelles: Dessart, 1966.
2. Bormuth, J. R. *On the Theory of Achievement Test Items*. Chicago: University of Chicago Press, 1970.
3. Carroll, J., et D. Spearitt. *Etude d'un "Modèle d'apprentissage scolaire."* Cambridge, Massachusetts: Center for Research and Development on Educational Differences, Harvard University, 1967.
4. Chiland, C. *L'enfant de six ans et son avenir*. Paris: P.U.F., 1971.
5. De Landsheere, G. *Les tests de connaissance*. Bruxelles: Editest, 1965.
6. De Landsheere, G. *Introduction à la recherche en Education*. Paris: A. Colin-Bourrelier; Liège: Thone, 1970.
7. De Landsheere, G. *Evaluation continue et examens, Précis de docimologie*. Paris: Nathan; Bruxelles: Labor, 1971.
8. De Landsheere, G. *Le test de closure*. Paris: Nathan; Bruxelles: Labor, 1973.
9. Detheux-Jehin, M., et E. Leclercq-Boxus. "Essai d'évaluation continue en éducation compensatoire par contrôles successifs du rendement de l'apprentissage de la lecture en première année primaire," *Recherche en Education*. Bruxelles: Ministère de l'Education Nationale, 1973.

10. Detheux-Jehin, M., E. Leclercq-Boxus, et J. Paquay-Beckers. *L'action en Première Année Primaire.*

11. Grisay, A. *Le déchiffrage de lettres et de syllabes en première année primaire, Analyse de quelques types d'erreurs.* Université de Liège, Laboratoire de Pédagogie expérimentale, 1972, document ronéotypé.

12. Henry, G. *Une technique de mesure de la lisibilité spécifique de la langue française.* Thèse de doctorat inédite, Université de Liège, 1973.

13. Henry, G., et A. Grisay. *Methodological Aspects of Reading Evaluation.* Université de Liège, Laboratoire de Pédagogie expérimentale, 1972, document ronéotypé.

14. Inizan, A. *Le temps d'apprendre à lire.* Paris: Bourrelier, 1963.

15. Inizan, A., et D. Bartout. *L'évaluation du "savoir lire" en cours préparatoire.* Paris: Bourrelier, 1972.

16. Jadoulle, A., *Apprentissage de la lecture et dyslexie* (2e éd.). Liège: Thone, 1967.

17. Leclercq, D. "Une banque de questions pour l'enseignement," *Education,* n°132 (novembre-décembre), 1971.

18. Leclercq-Boxus, E. "La maturité spécifique en lecture: une mise au point," *Education, Tribune Libre,* n°123 (mai 1970).

19. Leclerque-Boxus, E. "Une méthode de prédiction du rendement en lecture en première année primaire," *Education, Tribune Libre,* n°127 (janvier-février), 1971.

20. Leclercq-Boxus, E. "Etude différentielle de la prédiction du rendement en lecture en première année primaire," *Recherche en Education.* Bruxelles: Ministère de l'Education Nationale, 1973.

21. Lefavrais, M. P. "Epreuves combinées pour l'étude des connaissances en lecture et en orthographe," *Bulletin de la Société* Alfred Binet, n°447-448 (1959), 61 et suiv.

22. Limbosh, N., A. Luminet-Jasinski, et N. Dierkens-Dopchie. *La dyslexie à l'école primaire.* Bruxelles: Institut de Sociologie, 1968.

23. Noonan, R. *Images and Realities: Some Notes on the Use of Simple and Complex Models.* Rome: IEA/NTO Meeting, November 1970, document IEA IB/127.

24. Rosenthal, R., et L. Jacobson. *Pygmalion à l'école.* Paris: Casterman, 1971.

25. Rouanet, H., Ch. Barrey, et Regnier. "Note statistique sur la comparaison des moyennes à partir de données appareillées," *Bulletin du C.E.R.P.,* 18 (1968), 45-56.

26. Simon, J. "Les dyslexies et la psychopédagogie de la lecture," *Enfance,* n°5 (novembre-décembre), 1951.

27. Snyders, G. *Où vont les pédagogies non directives,* 1973.

28. Stambak, M., et M. Vial. *Problèmes posés par la déviance à l'école maternelle.* Cahiers du Cresas, 7, 1972.

29. Thirion, A. M., E. Leclercq-Boxus, et Detheux-Jehin. "Dépister est-ce dévoyer?" *Mosaïque,* n°18 (1973).

30. Thirion, A. M. *Education compensatoire et évaluation, Recherche d'une action.*

31. Thorndike, R. L. "Reviews," *American Educational Research Journal,* 5 (Novembre 1968), 708, 711.

32. Van Wayenberghe, A. *Test "6 ans."* Bruxelles: Presses Universitaires, 1962.

Evaluating Competence in Functional Reading

Hans U. Grundin
Teachers College of Linköping
Linköping, Sweden

The terms *functional reading,* and the closely related *functional literacy,* are beginning to be used fairly often in discussions of reading problems. There does not seem to exist, however, any generally accepted definition of functional reading. Obviously, the term must be related to the identification of three major stages defined by Malmquist (5): 1) the mechanics of reading; 2) the ability to read functionally; and 3) the ability to read critically and creatively, i.e. use the reading input as a basis for reflection, problem-solving, etc.

In accordance with this distinction, functional reading may be tentatively defined as the use of the mechanics of reading for different information purposes. Functional literacy may then be defined as that competence in functional reading which nearly all individuals in a society will need in their adult life. The level of competence and the range of skills included in functional literacy will, of course, vary from society to society. In a static, rural society functional literacy may need to include nothing but the bare mechanics of reading, while the standard must be much higher in a rapidly-developing, industrialized society. In the end, each society will have to determine what functional literacy should imply for its citizens.

FUNCTIONAL LITERACY IN THE FUTURE

As has been pointed out by Malmquist (3), most countries will need to "raise their sights about functional literacy" in the near future. In recent years some people have tried to make us believe that reading is rapidly becoming an old-fashioned means of information retrieval due to the media revolution. There is, however, little evidence to support such a hypothesis. On the contrary, several trends seem to contribute to the need for increasingly higher standards of functional literacy in most societies. Three of the most important of these trends are:

- The continuous increase in the production of reading materials in the form of books, newspapers, magazines, and computer output
- The growing need for education at the secondary and tertiary stages and for reeducation and permanent education of adults

- The efforts to engage a larger proportion of the adult population in the decision processes of the society and of its different organizations, involving a marked growth in information needs.

If a society has the aim of helping all its citizens reach a high level of functional literacy, systematic training of different reading skills must be pursued not only in the primary but also in the secondary school. As has been pointed out (2, 3), this is not generally realized in Sweden, nor in other parts of Europe (4). There is also reason to believe that many young students are ill-equipped in terms of reading skills (1).

A SWEDISH STUDY OF FUNCTIONAL READING

The development of certain basic reading, writing, and other communication skills throughout the primary and secondary schools has been the object of a rather extensive reading research project in Sweden (2). This research project was designed to permit an analysis of the extent of functional literacy at different age levels. The same test battery was administered to samples of students at grade levels 6-12. This battery included the following tests of reading skills:

- Comprehension of normal prose text measured by multiple-choice test
- Comprehension of normal prose text measured by cloze test
- Comprehension of tables (test using authentic tables concerning housing allowances)
- Comprehension of forms encountered in everyday life (test using authentic bank and health insurance forms)
- Comprehension of difficult prose text (test using authentic home insurance policy text)
- Rate of reading normal prose text

In all, about 2,600 students were tested in this project. The tests were administered twice with an interval of one year between test occasions to permit an evaluation of the increase in reading skills at different grade levels.

The reading tests included in this study do not pretend to cover the full range of skills needed for functional literacy in a modern industrial or postindustrial society. They are only intended to represent a sample of important skills, which will give a good indication of the competence in functional reading reached by different groups of students. The number of tests and the length of each test are the result of a compromise between the desire to cover several important areas of reading skill with sufficiently reliable tests and the need to restrict the total testing time to what was considered feasible for large scale testing within the school subject, Swedish Language and Literature. The total testing time for the combined reading and writing test battery, including 11 different tests, was 80 minutes.

Figure 1 presents an example of the reading test results obtained at the first test occasion in the research project discussed here. The figure shows the relationship between grade level (horizontal axis) and results on the multiple-choice reading comprehension test expressed as percentage of maximum score (vertical axis). The figure contains five percentile values (P_{90}, P_{70}, P_{50}, P_{30}, and P_{10}) for each of the seven grades (6-12). Each series of P-values for different grades form a percentile curve, which illustrates the development from grade to grade at that particular ability level. The tenth percentile curve (P_{10}), for instance, indicates the development of poor readers from grade 6 to grade 12. In Figure 1, the median for grade 6 and for grade 9 has been marked by broken horizontal lines. These lines will make it easier to see what proportion of the students in, say, grade 10 falls below the grade 6 median.

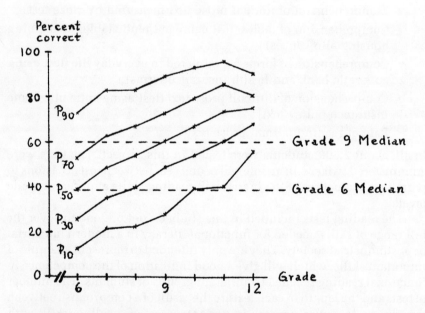

Figure 1. Normal prose reading: Multiple-choice comprehension test. Percentile curves for P_{90}, P_{70}, P_{50}, P_{30}, and P_{10}.

The figure shows an increase in reading comprehension from grade to grade at all percentile levels, with the exception of the highest percentiles in grades 11 and 12. This apparent stagnation in the development of the good readers may be due partly to a ceiling effect (a considerable number of students reach the maximum score). But it may also be due to lack of motivation among some of the oldest students. The different percentile curves are roughly parallel, at least up to grade 11. This means that the rate of reading skill development from grade to grade is about the same for the poor readers (P_{10}) as for the normal (P_{50}) and good readers (P_{90}).

For a correct interpretation of the data on reading skill development presented here it is necessary to take into account the degree of *retentivity* (the degree to which a school system retains the students taken in its lower grades throughout its higher grades) of the secondary school in Sweden. In comparison to many other countries, Sweden has a low degree of retentivity. Up to grade 9 an age group is kept practically intact in a compulsory comprehensive school (the exceptions are those in special schools, in institutions for mentally retarded, etc.). The upper secondary school (grades 10-12) recruits 85-90 percent of the age group in grades 10 and 11 and 45 percent in grade 12. The superiority of grades 10-12 compared to grade 9 may be due, at least partly, to the fact that a number of poor readers have left school. In turn, this may imply that the poor readers (at or below the P_{10} level) do not really improve their reading abilities after grade 9.

DIFFERENCES BETWEEN CLASSES IN READING COMPETENCE

Figure 2 gives the class means at all grade levels for the multiple-choice reading comprehension test. The average performance in the best grade 6 class is higher than that of the weaker classes in grades 10 and 11. In grades 10 and 11 the differences between classes at the same grade level may be due to streaming of students; there are theoretical, semi-theoretical, and vocational courses in these grades. (Grade 12 is not streamed, since only those in theoretical courses stay in the upper secondary school after grade 11.) In grades 6-9, however, there is no streaming. Except for the special classes, all classes are undifferentiated classes recruiting their students from a particular residential area.

It is not possible, at this stage, to tell to what extent differences between classes depend on differences in the student populations of different residential areas or on differences in the quality of instruction given in different classes. It is quite clear, though, that these differences between classes have important implications for the evaluation of reading competence.

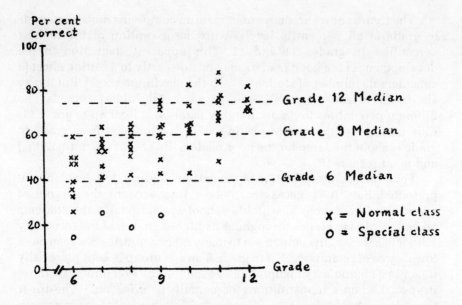

Figure 2. Normal prose reading: Multiple-choice comprehension test. Class means at each grade level.

At the classroom level, the most important implication seems to be that the individual teacher cannot evaluate reading competence unless he can refer his own observations or test results to some kind of national, regional, or local standard. Also, if the object of the evaluation is to determine whether the reading performance of a class of students is matching its potential reading ability, the teacher must relate data on reading performance to data regarding the students' capacities in terms of verbal intelligence, etc. If this is neglected, a teacher may feel satisfied with a class performing in accordance with a regional or local norm, although, if its potential was fully exploited, the class should be above the average.

AN ATTEMPT TO DETERMINE A MINIMAL SATISFACTORY
LEVEL OF READING COMPETENCE

Empirical studies of reading performance at different grade levels can never tell us whether the observed performances are satisfactory or acceptable or good. Such questions call for some kind of value judgment. Of course, value judgments are implied already in terms such as "poor readers" and "good readers." But these terms express some kind of relative value judgment—at least as they have been used by the present

Functional Reading

author. "Poor reader" means simply poorer than the average reader. When we ask if the reading ability or performance of a person is satisfactory, we want to know something quite different. We want a value judgment that is, if not absolute, at least related to some kind of external norm other than a group average.

One of the greatest problems with norm-referenced or criterion-referenced value judgments lies in the determination of the criterion. If we talk about satisfactory reading skill, we must decide for what purpose or to whom it should be satisfactory. And the judgment will be generally accepted only insofar as the criterion is recognized as valid. In Sweden, as in most countries, there is no generally accepted criterion of what is satisfactory reading ability in an adult citizen. To define such a criterion on the basis of an empirical study of the adult citizens' needs and interests seems possible, but such a study would be an extremely expensive and time-consuming project.

In the absence of an external, empirical basis for selecting a judgment criterion, there remains the possibility of soliciting the opinions of informed individuals. We tried to do this by mailing a questionnaire to some 950 head teachers of Swedish in the upper stage of the comprehensive school and in the upper secondary school. The questions put to these teachers were related to the tests employed in the project:

1. In your opinion, how many items in text X should a student of average intelligence, leaving the comprehensive school (or the upper secondary school), answer correctly before you consider his ability satisfactory?

2. In you opinion, how important is it that students leaving the comprehensive school (or the upper secondary school) have the skill or skills measured by text X?

More than 700 head teachers returned our questionnaire. This means that we got replies from more than 70 percent of the total population of head teachers in the subject Swedish in the comprehensive and upper secondary schools. These replies contained a great amount of information concerning the opinions of a group of fairly experienced teachers. To date only the more readily quantifiable part of this information has been analyzed. As an example of the results obtained, some of the data concerning the multiple-choice reading comprehension test are given in tables 1, 2, and 3.

Table 1 clearly shows the great variation in the teachers' opinion regarding what should be considered the minimal satisfactory level of reading ability. While some teachers believe that a score of 6 is satisfactory in a student leaving a three-year upper secondary course (USS III), others believe the average student leaving the comprehensive

Table 1 Teacher estimates of minimal satisfactory score in reading comprehension for average students leaving certain school forms. (The table gives response frequencies in percent of total number of responses.)

Minimal satisfactory score

School form	Final grade	4-5	6-7	8-9	10-11	12-13	14-15	Total
Comprehension	9	1	8	45	38	8	0	100
USS I	11	8	37	40	13	2	0	100
USS II	11	1	5	35	51	8	0	100
USS III	12	0	3	2	32	43	20	100

Note USS I = Upper secondary school: two-year vocational course with one year of Swedish

USS II = Ditto: two-year semitheoretical course with two years of Swedish

USS III= Ditto: three-year theoretical course with three years of Swedish

Table 2 Importance attached by head teachers to reading comprehension skill tested by conventional multiple-choice test. (The table gives response frequencies in percent of total number of respondees.)

School form	Final grade	Very great	Great	Some	Small	No	Total
				Degree of importance			
Comprehension	9	45	47	7	1	0	100
USS I	11	28	42	31	0	0	100
USS II	11	44	43	13	0	0	100
USS III	12	63	28	9	0	0	100

Note See note to Table 1

Table 3 Comparison between teacher estimates of minimal satisfactory scores and observed student scores on multiple-choice reading comprehension test.

School form	Final grade	Average min. satisfactory score	Average observed score	Difference
Comprehension	9	8.9	9.4	+ 6
USS I	11	7.3	7.4	+ 1
USS II	11	9.3	9.7	+ 4
USS III	12	11.5	10.9	+ 5

Observed score—minimal satisfactory score, expressed as percentage of minimal satisfactory score.

Note See note to Table 1.

school in grade 9 should reach a score of 12. Table 2 shows that a large majority of the head teachers find the kind of reading comprehension measured by this test very important. Only one teacher believes that it is of little importance. Table 3 presents a comparison between the mean values of the estimated minimal satisfactory levels of ability for different student categories on the one hand, and the observed test score means for those student categories on the other.

The most conspicuous thing about Table 3 is the high degree of similarity between the two series of mean values. In spite of the great variability in the teachers' opinions, the average minimal satisfactory level of performance is quite close to the actual performance level of the students tested in the project. This would, if interpreted literally, mean that about 50 percent of the students do not reach the minimal satisfactory level of performance defined by the teachers.

The results presented in Table 3 plus the gist of numerous commentaries to questionnaire replies have led us to believe, however, that a great part—perhaps a majority—of the respondees have tried primarily to make as informed guesses as possible concerning what results their students would reach, if they were given the test. If so, they have not really tried to make a norm-referenced value judgment. One may even argue that they have not made any value judgment at all. One obvious implication of this is that the correspondence between required and observed means in Table 3 reflects the ability of the teachers to make informed guesses about the reading skills of average students. The attempt to determine a minimal satisfactory level of reading competence by means of a teacher questionnaire has, consequently, not been very successful.

It must be emphasized, though, that the questionnaire presented here has been extremely valuable and informative, in spite of the fact that it has been of rather small help in determining a minimal satisfactory level of reading competence.

SUMMARY AND FUTURE PERSPECTIVES

The project presented in this paper originally grew out of research work in the field of primary reading and the consequent question: What happens to reading abilities later in school? This interest was then coupled with an interest in the whole issue of functional reading and functional literacy. The data gathered in the study will permit us tentatively to answer questions such as "To what extent has functional literacy (defined as a kind of minimal competence in functional reading) been reached at different grade levels in the comprehensive school and in different courses within the upper secondary school?"

The project also includes an attempt to arrive at a generally agreed upon operational definition of a minimal satisfactory level of reading ability for different student categories, i.e., essentially a definition of functional literacy. This attempt was not quite successful, since it seemed to indicate that many teachers can hardly be persuaded to make value judgments with reference to a personal, subjective norm and express them in terms of hard data such as scores on a given test. Instead of stating a personal opinion of what reading skill level a given group of students should reach, the teachers tend to make guesses about what skill level the students actually reach. Either the question of what is satisfactory is not touched or one must assume that their philosophy is: What is, is satisfactory!

Apparently, future progress in this field must be sought in other directions. The empirical study of the actual skills of students of different categories must certainly be pursued. Such descriptive work is vital to our understanding of the development of reading skills. But we must also constantly remember that description is not evaluation. To evaluate is to make value judgments on the basis of a combination of carefully defined criteria and objective empirical description of that part of reality which is to be evaluated. Consequently, as a complement to descriptive studies of reading skills, we need definitions of criteria or norms to which our observed data could be referenced.

The definition of such criteria or norms must always imply subjective opinion to some extent. In the end a concept such as functional literacy in a given country may have to be decided by means of a compromise between different opinions (perhaps opinions of different interest groups). Recognizing this, we should not go to the extreme of believing (or pretending to believe) that one opinion is as good as another. Opinions can be more or less informed, more or less rational, more or less biased, etc. It should be the task of reading research to present the facts on which such an opinion should be founded, to analyze different opinions in terms of their consistency and clarity, to criticize the opinions, and to make suggestions as to how they could be improved.

Unfortunately, the limits of space do not permit a more specific discussion of how to arrive at good criteria of functional literacy. I can only repeat that it must be done by means of gathering information about the opinions in the matter held by different groups and of analyzing, criticizing and synthesizing these opinions.

REFERENCES

1. Gardner, J. "The Student Reader," in A. Melnik and J. Merritt (Eds.), *Reading: Today and Tomorrow*. London: University of London Press, 1972, 365-369.
2. Grundin, H. U. "The Development of Reading, Writing, and Other Communication Skills During the Comprehensive and Upper Secondary School Years: Presentation of a Swedish Research Project," paper presented at the 1973 UKRA Conference at Totley-Thornbridge College of Education, England, in press.
3. Malmquist, E. "Reading: A Human Right and a Human Problem," in R. C. Staiger and O. Andresen (Eds.), *Reading: A Human Right and a Human Problem*, Proceedings of the Second IRA World Congress on Reading, Copenhagen, 1968. Newark, Delaware: International Reading Association, 1969, 1-8.
4. Malmquist, E. "A Decade of Reading Research in Europe, 1959-1969," *Journal of Educational Research*, 63 (1970), 309-329.
5. Malmquist, E. *Lasundervisning i grundskolan/Reading Instruction in the Comprehensive School*. Lund: CWK Gleerup, 1973.

Evaluating Progress in Recreational Reading

Helen K. Smith
University of Miami
Coral Gables, Florida
United States of America

One of the major goals of schools should be to help students become lifetime readers. Good reading programs provide for the development not only of reading skills but also of habits of reading for recreation and personal development, positive attitudes toward reading, and independence in reading among students.

The evaluation of progress in recreational reading is an important step in the fulfillment of the foregoing goal. This evaluation is concerned with unassigned reading, from both quantitative and qualitative points of view. Aspects usually evaluated include the extent of reading, as determined by the numbers of books, stories, or articles read; the breadth of the materials read or the different kinds of content or genres read; the depth or quality of the materials read; and the effects reading has on the reader.

Many stimulating ideas have been published concerning how to interest young people in reading, how to broaden their interests, how to determine their reading interests, and how to meet their interests with the right book. Little has been written concerning evaluation techniques useful for determining progress in recreational reading.

The dearth of satisfactory evaluation techniques may be due largely to the problems involved in this kind of evaluation. The task is an inexact and a qualitative one. Value judgments of both the student and the teacher become involved. No standardized tests are available to give exact scores indicating progress, nor is there agreement concerning which factors should be considered in the evaluation.

The second difficulty in this type of evaluation lies in the personal, individual nature of reading interests and recreational reading. Research studies have pointed out average group trends, but they are not reliable indicators for individuals. An indicator of progress in leisure reading for one student may be inappropriate for another. Recreational reading is the product of many interrelated factors such as general maturity, intelligence, home background, geographical location, cultural opportunities, physical environment, attitudes and customs of people with whom the student associates, and the school curriculum. Just as for the assessment of any other educational goal, evaluation must take into account the status of each student in relation to these factors, as well as to the availability of the materials he would most want to read.

A third problem is in the changing nature of reading interests and the resulting recreational reading. Interests are characterized by change, as well as by range.

Six guidelines are suggested here for the evaluation of recreational reading attainments. First, improvement in the status of recreational reading should be one of the goals or objectives of the school program. Schools must place emphasis on reading for enjoyment and provide a setting in which recreational reading can take place. Evaluation should obtain evidence on the extent to which both short and long range objectives have been accomplished.

Second, evaluation of recreational reading progress should be continuous rather than periodic. It should be continuous for any time period in which a teacher is instructing a student but also for the number of years the student spends in the school.

Third, various procedures, which will be discussed later, should be used in the evaluation, as no one will adequately give the desired information for all students. Each procedure has limitations as well as advantages; a combination of techniques will give more insight than any one alone.

Fourth, evaluation is more effective if it is carried on by a team of people rather than by one person alone. Teachers, parents, librarians, and students could be involved if time permits. Increasing emphasis should be placed upon student self-appraisal.

The fifth principle is that evaluators must start their appraisal at the individual's level of development. Since leisure reading is very personal, standards for recreational reading should be individual and not the same for all students. A student's reading should be compared with his past reading and not with that of the other members of the class.

Last, the evaluation techniques selected should not destroy the student's interest in and love of reading. The primary emphasis should be on the pleasure and personal development a student receives from reading. He should not be required to analyze in detail his reading nor feel that he must report formally upon everything he reads.

EVALUATION PROCEDURES

Few reports have been made of evaluation tools useful in determining progress in recreational reading. Although most of the techniques which will be described here have been used largely for determining interests in reading, they can be used also as evaluation instruments. Included are records of reading, inventories, question-naires, checklists, observations, conferences, incomplete sentence projective techniques, reading autobiographies, book withdrawals, book reports and substitutes for book reports, and hierarchical continuum plans.

The precision with which the evaluation can be done is dependent upon many factors, such as rapport teachers have with their students, the freedom students have or think they have in expressing themselves, the honesty they use in reporting, and the analysis made by the evaluators. The amount read and the range of the reading are considerably easier to evaluate than the quality of the reading or the effects of reading upon individual students.

Reading records. Some kind of record of reading done is often kept by schools and placed in the student's cumulative folder. The record may be a listing of books read with the name of the author and a statement about the book, a rating technique such as "excellent—one of the best books I have ever read," or "a good book," or "not very interesting," or "I didn't like it," or "I didn't finish it." Such ratings are more useful if students state their reasons for the ratings. At a later time, when reviewing the reading record, a student can choose the ones he would recommend to someone else and can determine what different books contributed to him in ideas, facts, insights, information, and personal satisfaction. Teachers can ascertain trends in the maturity of the student's free reading in regard to difficulty and taste. Reading records can also be used as the basis for conferences and for guidance in reading.

Records of outside reading or logs of recreational activities kept for a stated period of time, such as for one or two weeks, are used extensively in research and can be useful evaluation tools, especially if the activity is repeated at several times during the year. Such records help evaluators to discover the diversity, or lack of it, in reading done and to perceive developmental trends.

Interest inventories, questionnaires, checklists. Interest inventories, questionnaires, and checklists are probably the most popular techniques reported for determining the status of reading interests. Readministering parts of them at different times could be a means of checking progress. Published inventories (1, 2, 5, 6, 8, 10), or those prepared by a teacher or a school team, are easy to administer to large numbers of students and results are easy to tabulate.

Information usually obtained from these forms pertains to preferred leisure activities; newspapers, magazines, and books read; kinds of books enjoyed; the use of the school and public library; the amount of time spent in reading and in televiewing; methods of selecting books;

types of materials preferred in books; and lists or rank order of books enjoyed.

Inventories, questionnaires, and checklists may be somewhat difficult to interpret as check marks and some short answers can be analyzed in many different ways. Some students may answer or check items indiscriminately with little basis for their response or with the idea of gaining approval from the teacher. They may recall only the unique or recently read books and may project current interests into books read in the past, thus biasing results.

When checklists are used, additional questions can be asked of students: Why do you like or dislike the book? Which character do you like the best? The least? What do you like or dislike about him or her? Which character reminds you of yourself? Which parts interested you the most?

Observation and individual conferences. Observation is a basic technique employed every day by teachers and can be used in the informal evaluation of recreational reading. Some plan of recording observations should be prepared if they are to be remembered and used.

Informal evaluation can take place when the teacher observes what happens when the class browses in the library, what and how many books different students read, how students approach books, how they select books, and what books they pick from the table. Teachers can listen for references students make spontaneously to books and authors, to student conversations when they talk about reading, and to ways in which students share books with others. From these observations, insight can be gained concerning student attitudes toward reading, the uses they make of reading, student interest in reading for pleasure, and amount of reading done.

Although observations are continuous and provide insights that other means of evaluation cannot give, only tentative generalizations can be made. At best, a teacher can observe only a small part of a student's behavior and can make only inferences from observations. If they are recorded systematically from year to year, changes in recreational reading patterns can be revealed. Changes are not necessarily synonymous with growth.

Providing there is mutual trust between teachers and students, conferences or interviews with students may be the most natural way to obtain information concerning reading interests and habits of adolescents in relation to other aspects of their lives. Conferences may be used to augment or check other techniques, such as the questionnaire. Even though conferences are time-consuming, every wise teacher arranges to have purposeful conversations with pupils. If a mimeographed form for recording important information is prepared in advance, questions asked during interviews can be kept somewhat uniform.

Incomplete sentence projective technique. The incomplete sentence projective technique (Boning and Boning) has been used to obtain information concerning attitudes toward reading, effects of reading, or depth of reading. The students are asked to complete sentences concerned with reading interspersed with other incomplete statements. Examples of incomplete sentences are as follows: Reading is_____. I would rather read than_____. To me, books_____. I'd read more if_____. When I read, I feel_____. Recurring patterns of responses, if any, can be noted and may provide diagnostic information.

Students' free responses. Strang (9) suggested the use of free response in writing or in speaking as a means of evaluation of leisure reading. If students are encouraged to express their opinions freely, information can be gained concerning the effect reading has upon them, the depth of their reading, and their thinking about reading. Among the questions Strang suggested to provoke comment are "What kind of book or article would you choose to read above all others?" "Think of the books or articles you have read this year that you just could not stand. What was in them that made you dislike them so much?"

Reading autobiographies. Reading autobiographies contain information about an individual's reading development from his own point of view. Reading autobiographies can become a written developmental history of a student's reading experiences. From them, pupils (or teachers) can trace their reading interests and the influence reading has had on them.

From the reading autobiographies of approximately 600 adult readers, Carlson (4) reported finding an amazing uniformity in progress toward mature reading. The adults recalled the pleasure they had in juvenile series books, followed by better adolescent novels. Their first experiences with adult literature tended to be sentimental romances and adventure stories by authors their parents were reading. Late in high school, or early college, they began reading books recognized as real literature, with their first ventures often being twentieth century books. Almost no one indicated enthusiasm about books considered great literature until high school or college years; only then did they realize that previous reading was trivial.

Book reports and substitutes for book reports. Formal book reports have had a long history in the United States. They are used more often to check whether students have read the books than for estimating progress in leisure reading. Often they become a chore to students because the forms seem meaningless and unrelated to the curriculum. Yet students often wish to discuss the books they have read.

Recreational Reading

Instead of preparing a stereotype book report in coordination with their course work, students might write informal personal essays on topics related to reading, such as "Variety in Sports Stories" or some other classification, a monologue or diary of a major character, an episode from a book written in news story form, a critical review for the local or school paper, radio or television scripts, commercial book "blurbs" designed to motivate others to read the book, letters written to a present-day personality, in the style and character of the subject of the biography, or a description of what happened after the story ended. Students can write brief comments about books read on cards and file the cards in a box to be left in the classroom for the use of other students.

Hierarchical continuum plans. Different plans of hierarchical continuums have been used both in the classroom and in research in an effort to evaluate the maturity or depth of the students' reading. These plans have been variously called levels, planes, steps, scales, ladders, or sequences.

Teachers and students can develop their own book ladders which could include books on different themes or topics of interest at different levels of maturity, with the books on the lowest rung being of questionable or ineffective literary quality through different quality levels to the classics or other books of high quality on the highest rung. The ladders could also be concerned with easy to difficult reading or could be prepared in such areas as sports, sea, romance.

Gainsburg's criteria for steps of development toward a growing maturity of interest, as reported by Stiles (7), might aid a staff in the construction of ladders or in assessing the maturity of the students' reading. First, the author's dominant appeal to the reader's interest might be from stories of action, adventure, thrill, and humor followed by character stories, those having a clever or unusual development of plot, stories of mystery of problem solution whose appeal is in the unraveling of the problem, stories of background, and stories in which mood is predominant. Second, the nature of the conflict in the reading might progress from the thrill of physical conflict to conflict with nature or with a hostile environment, the struggle to overcome a personal weakness, a conflict with ideas, and a conflict with one's own inner nature. The third criterion is the plausibility of the treatment of the story; that is, one might consider steps from static characters and events which are dependent upon coincidence and catastrophe to plausible characters and events logically related to personalities or to previous events. The fourth criterion is the quality of writing—from obvious content requiring no thinking, followed by situations and characters presented more or less by inferential approach, to the use of figurative language.

The students' reading abilities should be considered as the foregoing criteria are applied.

Because of the lack of adequate evaluation instruments to assess recreational reading attainments, teachers have had to depend upon informal techniques. The interpretation of these techniques has been dependent upon the value judgments of both teachers and students. There is a definite need for more objective and sharper measuring instruments to be developed for this important area of reading. Criteria for the preparation of these instruments should be determined by groups of evaluators with varying opinions. Especially needed are evaluation tools to assess the quality or depth of reading and the effects of reading upon the reader. Until this is done, the techniques discussed here will continue in use.

REFERENCES
1. Austin, Mary C., C. L. Bush, and M. H. Huebner. *Reading Evaluation*. New York: Ronald Press, 1961, 85.
2. Beard, Richard L. "Reading Habits and Interests," *High School Journal*, 39 (January 1956), 210-211.
3. Boning, Thomas, and Richard Boning. "I'd Rather Read Than," *Reading Teacher*, 10 (April 1957), 197.
4. Carlson, C. Robert. "In Reading, Too, Experience Counts," *Chicago Tribune Books Today*, November 1, 1964, 4A.
5. Harris, Albert J. *How to Increase Reading Ability* (5th ed.). New York: David McKay, 1970, 462-466.
6. Karlin, Robert. *Teaching Reading in High School*. Indianapolis, Indiana: Bobbs-Merrill, 1964, 212-215.
7. Stiles, Helen L. "Report of Two Junior High School Programs," in Nancy Larrick (Ed.), *Reading in Action*, Proceedings of the International Reading Association, 2, 1957. New York: Scholastic Magazines, 34-35.
8. Strang, Ruth. *The Diagnostic Teaching of Reading* (2nd ed.). New York: McGraw-Hill, 1969, 110-117.
9. Strang, Ruth. "Reading Interests, 1946," *English Journal*, 35 (November 1946), 477-482.
10. Witty, Paul. *Reading in Modern Education*. Boston, Massachusetts: D.C. Heath, 1949, 335-339.

Evaluation of Progress in Spare-Time Reading

Lucia Binder
International Institute for Children's Literature and Reading Research
Vienna, Austria

Recreational reading is not important only because it helps to develop continuing reading interest and teaches children to regard reading as something natural, a part of daily routine. It is also important because it eases reading development and makes practice a pleasure, rather than a necessary evil.

A child's reading performance can be measured objectively by various tests and methods. Teachers have much greater difficulty, however, in evaluating a child's progress in free reading, for here the pupil's activity lies outside the school's direct sphere of influence.

One obvious way out of this problem is to assess the total amount of recreational reading that a child does. The importance of this measure has been demonstrated in studies undertaken by the International Institute for Children's Literature and Reading Research under the direction of Dr. Bamberger in Austria. These studies have demonstrated positive correlations among the number of books read in the course of a school year, reading speed, and degree of comprehension.

Experiments were carried out under the motto of "Intensive Therapy for Reading" across all grades in Austrian schools. A greatly increased quantity of reading matter was presented to children in the course of a year. This was done in such a way that the school merely gave the stimulus for reading, the actual reading being done at home. In this way, the pupils were not forced; they were enticed to read.

Cases containing books for each pupil in the class (for example, 30 to 35 copies of each title for class work, or 5 to 6 copies of each of 5 or 6 different titles for groups) were sent to the schools and then exchanged among the different classes. The teacher, or a pupil, would give a short and lively introduction and read a quotation or two. As soon as expectations and attention had been awakened, this procedure was stopped and pupils were left to read for themselves for the rest of the period. The pupils finished the books at home, usually in the course of a few days. Only then was there a general discussion in the classroom, focused not on the story but on personal reaction to the book.

Control groups were established in classes in which reading continued to be taught in the traditional form without the aid of additional material. Experi nental and control groups were tested at the beginning, in the middle, and at the end of the school year. The classes where intensive therapy had been applied showed approximately 25 percent better results than those of the control grades. The basic idea in this experiment was to have the teacher treat his pupils as individuals (not only as school children) and for the teacher to interest himself in their recreational reading outside of school as well as in class. Over and above this, it was intended as encouragement to the teacher to see his influence on recreational reading as an important task of reading education. The corollary of this is that he could then make use of recreational reading for school purposes.

These school purposes were defined as follows: the development of lifelong reading interests and reading habits, the development of judgment in selecting books to match reading intentions, and the development of enthusiasm for critical evaluation after reading.

Evaluation of individual progress in free reading must be based on the following formulations:

1. Is the child already interested in reading, even when not directly confronted with a certain book by the teacher?

2. How does the child react to the reading situation? Does he read daily or only sporadically; for example, when given a new book? Will he read during vacations without coercion?

3. How big is the share of reading within the total array of recreational activities?

Further points useful in clarification of a child's attitude toward reading may be whether he has already discovered that pure thriller and entertainment literature is to be read differently from a nonfiction book or poetry for children or whether he reads certain books or certain parts of a book more than once.

It is possible to see a connection with the capacity for literary judgment. Does the child make a choice or is his reading still ruled by chance? Does he know the names of some children's book authors who have written books for his age group? Is he able to distinguish among various categories (that things may happen in a fairy tale that would never occur in reality and that the fairy tale hero may be a true-blue hero, while in a realistic tale the characters will not be wholly good or wholly bad)? The child must learn that in a tale that purports to be realistic, the characters and events must be credible.

All of these questions must not be seen disjointedly, but must be seen as arising naturally in a particular context. Thus, the aim of an evaluation of recreational reading cannot be seen as one of exact progress measurement, but one of finding points of attack for promotion of the child's individuality. The crux is that the teacher should determine those areas in which he has been successful and those in which he has been less successful, so that he can adapt his methods accordingly.

An evaluation of recreational reading should, therefore, always be linked with measures to promote and advise reading. An important point of view that should not be overlooked is that pupils should never have the impression that recreational reading is a kind of school task, a piece of homework. It must remain something voluntary.

Within the general heading "Progress in Recreational Reading," I would first like to deal with the step from chance reading to fixed reading habits linked with predetermined intentions.

At the beginning of reading development, children usually read just what they are given. They are unable to make fine literary discriminations; they just enjoy getting to know something new. This first reading joy will soon end if the children are not guided to a higher phase of more conscious selection leading to the satisfaction of specialised interests. The teacher is able to note such progress when children begin to read selectively and look through the library for subjects dealing with specific fields of interest.

Assessment of reading interests and reading habits leads to an insight into the literary quality of recreational literature. This is the highest aim of reading education. In approaching this aim, we must be very much aware of the ages as well as the special interests of the children so that we can give effective advice on reading selection and provide step by step guidance toward an independent search and discovery of the relevant books.

It is important to advise children to record their reading. This can be done in different ways. Dr. Bamberger developed the Reader's Diary (diary-like notes concerning the books read)—a method better suited to the upper grades—and the Reader Passport. In the two years since its introduction, the Reader Passport has found great interest among teachers and pupils. It consists of several pages, allowing children to record their topical reading test results with regard to reading speed and comprehension. Further pages are reserved for the recording of recreational reading. A special column after each title allows the child to record his comment. In Austria, there are five credits and it has been suggested that pupils could record their comments in the same fashion: 1 = I liked this book very much. 5 = I didn't like it at all. The rear cover pages contain suggestions for the children as to the books or booklets suitable for their individual reading achievement.

Reader Passports are individually designed for various school grades. The children should keep them up to date independently. The teacher should review the Passports with the children from time to time and discuss the students' reading with them at that time.

The most important thing is to stimulate the children to come to grips with their reading material and to slowly move from chance reading to planned reading. By means of the Reader Passport, the teacher is able to obtain information as to the amount of reading, the choice of books, and the children's personal comments. In this way, the Reader Passport has become an important instrument in Austria, allowing the teacher to assess his pupils' progress in recreational reading and to link this with reading test results and reading achievement at school.

The Reader Passport is also helpful when the teacher is asked to give information to the parents. Pupils should be motivated to give their parents an opportunity to look at the Reader Passport to evaluate their child's progress. The Passport is also seen as a good base for the fulfillment of book requests.

Another basis for evaluation of recreational reading progress, and thereby of individual reading development, is the Reader Card in the school library and the public library. It is important to supplement such insights through other observations. Parallel to reading, how does the pupil's vocabulary develop and how far is he able to evaluate his own reading?

Many forms of discussion can be used:

1. Story hours offer opportunities to determine progress in reaction to the literary heritage and the development of literary taste.
2. Reading aloud. If we want to know a child's general attitude toward reading, we should ask him to read aloud from his favorite books. His choice of books tells as much as the style of reading; for example, does the child enunciate properly, does he try "to perform" in reading, or does he merely read mechanically?
3. Discussion about books read. A child's ability to find important passages and to comprehend basic moods helps us understand his attitude towards reading.
4. Individual reading periods. When the whole class silently reads books of their choice, the teacher can talk briefly with individual children to learn of their attitudes about books they have chosen.

Teachers should bear in mind that a child's recreational reading can slowly be brought to a higher level, but a child's personal characteristics must be considered. As an illustration, I would like to cite an example from the latest inquiry of the International Institute for Juvenile

Literature and Reading Research with regard to the reading interests of ten year olds: A great deal of space is taken up by so-called environment or children's stories—real stories about children who are the same age as the reader and have various experiences in common.

In the list of favorite books, curiously enough, there is a balance between the works of Enid Blyton and Erich Kästner or Marlen Haushofer. The reasons for favoring these books are rather similar: They make you laugh. It is easy to empathize with these stories because they are very lively and written in a very graphic manner. They concern children we would like to have as friends.

A great difference, however, is found in literary creativity. While the books of Blyton are altogether superficial and the acting characters are completely interchangeable, the books by Kästner and Haushofer say something. They are really humorous in the best way—they show human weakness and subject it to laughter, but it is warm, understanding, liberating laughter. Character design endeavors to be true to life and credible; the language is independent and original.

The predilection for humorous children's stories can thus be satisfied on entirely different levels: 1) by shallow, superficial books, the readers of which will probably end up one day with penny shockers; or 2) by easily read books of literary value, which offer food for thought, apart from entertainment, and prepare the way for more demanding stories and real reading development.

It seems important, therefore, that the teacher should know about and motivate his pupils' recreational reading, guiding them diplomatically to prevent stagnation at a primitive level and to help them on the way from "reading matter" to "literature."

Sequence and Structure in Reading Development

Donald Moyle
Edge Hill College of Education
Ormskirk, Lancashire, England

The search for a panacea for reading instruction is one of the great difficulties to have beset teachers and researchers over the years. Some years ago an experienced teacher approached me at the commencement of the last session of a 14 session course for remedial reading teachers and said "We have come faithfully to all the meetings; I hope that tonight you are going to tell us the secret of how it is really done."

In reading we have searched for the order in which to present the various facets of the process and to be sure that the sequence of learning was absolutely right. But when we talk about sequence and structure, what do we mean? Certainly in mathematics it would be difficult if not impossible to teach the concept of "twoness" before the child has established a concept of "oneness." Equally, multiplication would be an extraordinarily difficult process to master until the pupil had learned to add.

If there is a perfect linear order in which reading skills should be presented to the pupil, we do not now know what it is. Indeed, one might well question whether there will ever be the discovery of such an order. Two factors militate against such a possibility: first, reading is not a skill, but rather a mass of skills, techniques, and knowledge, various facets of each being brought into play according to the nature of the specific reading task undertaken; and second, the abilities, personality, and interests of the individual pupil seem to exercise a controlling factor on both the order and type of learning. This is not to say that there cannot be sequence or structure but rather that both child and task need to be considered in designing any reading programme.

Structure itself has often been used in terms of an order decreed by published materials or the teacher, but it could equally be interpreted as an overall plan or the main elements around which a programme could be built. Such a view would seem essential, for, although it is possible to devise activities specifically for the mastery of various comprehension, reference, and study skills, it is not possible to replicate all the varied reading situations in which these elements may be needed in the future. Indeed, the comprehension tests used in schools and research projects

are always unreal in comparison with the normal usage of comprehension skills in life. Authors do not write textbooks or novels in the
form of comprehension exercises and very often the pupil has to form the
questions for himself before he can think of looking for an answer.

Although reading undoubtedly has to be taught, the skill is used in
all areas of human activity and it is not employed for its own sake but
rather for its outcome in terms of information, ideas, or enjoyment. This
is only one of the problems which the teacher faces in trying to give
structure to the reading situation. When an architect designs a building,
he has a clear view of the finished product. Reading teachers have no
such clear view, yet efficiency in education depends upon the clarity
with which teachers can see the end objectives.

Gephart (1) writes,

> Many statements have been made which assert that our society has a
> reading problem. These assertions have been made with sufficient
> authority and frequency that they have been accepted as fact: a reading
> problem exists. What is the desirable level of reading competence to be
> achieved by the individual in our society? Even more basically, what
> level of reading competence is necessary to function in our culture?
> Neither of these questions has been answered on either an empirical or
> logical basis. Reading and reading achievement have been the target of
> measurement efforts over the years, but the data do not answer the two
> questions cited above.

In reviewing the literature as part of U.S. Project 0-9031 Adult
Functional Reading, Murphy (5) came to the conclusion, ". . . there
exists neither a good estimate of the reading ability necessary to function
satisfactorily in modern society nor a satisfactory estimate of the
absolute reading achievement of reasonably defined subgroups in the
United States." Though the quotation mentions the United States, the
problem is the same the world over.

Murphy tried to identify a number of tasks performed by adults in
carrying out their ordinary everyday activities. In a varied sample he
found that only 20 percent of the reading tasks could be completed by 90
percent or more of the adult population. A total of 20 percent of the adult
population could not complete 50 percent of the tasks satisfactorily,
even though the tasks themselves were judged to be simpler in nature
than the items in comprehension tests which might have been given.

Obviously, the transfer of reading skills to later adult reading activity
is not completely satisfactory. One sees the twelve-year-old child being
able to extract information from a reference book only by copying it out
word for word, the fifteen-year-old unable to cope with the use of the
passive mood in reporting an experiment in science, and the college
undergraduate wasting time because he is unable to decide which items

of printed matter are going to be of most help to him by any other method than reading them all.

It would seem clear that the test of the sequence and structure of reading instruction is not simply a matter of completing the learning activities correctly, nor reaching an expected level of attainment in a reading test, but rather the ability of the pupil to apply the skills learned to any reading situation in which he finds himself. I would suggest, therefore, that we need to think in terms of the reading curriculum rather than in the narrow terms of reading instruction.

The simplest definition of reading curriculum (4) is that it is the sum of all occasions in which a person has contact (or should have contact) with the written word. Immediately, you will note that the reading curriculum is wider than school experience; it covers all experience. Further, reading is considered a part of all school activity and not as something to be taught in isolation. Hence, reading instruction can take place when a need arises in a geography lesson, just as the skill can be used to seek out geographical information.

The reading curriculum also suggests preparation for the use of written language by adults in society and not only by students in school.

The reading curriculum has three aspects which need consideration in planning school work: 1) reading purposes, 2) reading media, and 3) reading skills and techniques.

Reading purposes. Purpose in reading is important for the following reasons:

- Motivates the child to read with some specific end in mind.
- Sets the type of reading behaviour which is most appropriate to the task.
- Sets the questions to which answers are to be found and helps the reader ensure that suitable materials are selected.
- Relates the work to living in general and enables the child to transfer skill learning from one task to similar tasks.

Reading media. Reading is too often thought of in terms of books. The child is not prepared for effective reading unless he has had experience with the whole range of media in terms of types of publication, types of writing, and types of author purpose.

Reading skills and techniques. These have been divided by Merritt (2) into the following:

- Goal setting skills—the organization of purposes and the setting of appropriate questions.
- Planning skills—accessing appropriate material, the survey and evaluation of materials, the selection of suitable reading strategies.

- Read skills—word attack skills, linguistic knowledge, and comprehension skills.
- Development skills—the evaluation of performance; the outcomes of reading; the storage, retrieval, and communication of the results of reading.

Structure and transfer are two interrelated problems which must receive careful attention when planning the reading curriculum.

STRUCTURE

There must be some structure in a reading programme if progress is to be made. However, there is little evidence to support the behaviourist claim that skills develop in a linear manner. There are generalised stages of development in reading but there does not seem to be any one perfect growth pattern with regard to the steps in the development of reading skills. Indeed, children at the same general level of reading ability display a wide variety of levels of development in the various subskills of reading. A single scheme of work in reading for all children to follow does not seem a realistic objective. A teacher should become knowledgeable concerning the skills of reading in order to analyse any task in terms of skill needs and know which type of help a child will need to successfully complete the task.

TRANSFER

A child can master a skill and still not apply it in other relevant situations. Most teachers observe this result in the use of phonics. It may be that the child has not learned how and where to apply the skill. The more numerous the various types of reading occasions set up for the use of a skill, the more likely the child is to recognize the occasion in which it is appropriate to use the skill. If skills are taught in devised situations in isolation from the areas where they could be used, it is obvious that transfer becomes difficult. It would seem, therefore, that the early association of skills with realistic purposes is most likely to result in effective usage later.

PLANNING THE READING CURRICULUM

No matter what situation the teacher is in there will be certain constraints which make an ideal reading curriculum unattainable. Nevertheless, the teacher must take a very close look at the situation to see what approaches are promising. There would seem to be two major directions: 1) commencing with the total curriculum and finding ways of ensuring that growth in reading skills progresses smoothly and 2) commencing with teaching of skills and then providing sufficient opportunities for their realistic application.

The following areas need to be considered: school building, materials and equipment available, how the staff is organised, how the children are grouped, what educational ideals are held, what type of behaviour is expected from the children in learning and teaching situations, and what contact is possible with other groups within and outside the school.

It is the writer's belief that the use of the total curriculum as the basis for reading instruction holds the greatest hope for a higher level of success in the future. This places a great burden upon teachers for they must carefully observe each child and the range of reading tasks he undertakes, using every opportunity offered to teach that which will extend skill development. The teacher needs to have some back-up services if this is to succeed. The following suggestions have been found to provide this type of teacher help but equally are usable by pupils at this stage of development. It will be appreciated that when children are involved in the planning of their own work, they become much more independent in the learning situation.

RANGE OF TYPES OF MEDIA

When helping a child to plan a piece of work it is useful to have some mnemonics which will help locate all the potential sources of helpful printed media. Frequently checklists of the type set out below can help the teacher find new dimensions to a well-worn subject area. A further use could be found in the development of resource systems within the school.

Fiction	Advertisements and Notices
Textbooks	Legal Documents
Reference Books	Reports and Minutes
Journals	Forms and Questionnaires
Magazines	Regulations
Newspapers	Instructions
Comics	Letters
Brochures	Children's Written Work
Pamphlets	Signs and Symbols
Fliers	

TYPES OF AUTHOR PURPOSE

The child should have contact with the full range of author purposes if he is to be able to set appropriate reading strategies and become an independent reader. It seems obvious that the intent of the author affects the presentation of the content and sets the scene for the type of responses the reader should make.

To entertain—novel or dramatic work
To inform—encyclopaedia, certain types of letters or brochures
To persuade—advertisement, political pamphlet
To elicit information—questionnaire, form, letter
To proscribe—legal documents, regulations
To prescribe—instructions

TYPES OF WRITING STYLE
Variations in writing style set limits on appropriate reading strategies as well as help in making decisions about suitability of a certain document to the purposes of the reader.

Descriptive—static—house specifications
Descriptive—dynamic—car production
Rhetorical—inductive—research paper
Rhetorical—deductive—philosophical paper
Imperative—legal document
Interogative—questionnaire
Exclamatory—religious tract

READING PURPOSES
Children must explore the range of human purposes if they are to use reading later as a major skill in adult life situations. The following are derived from the five basic divisions of human purpose proposed by Merritt (3): home and family, leisure, consumer, community, and employment.

ASSOCIATING PURPOSES AND MEDIA
It is useful to compile matrices combining two of the above lists or similar lists. Again, these could form the basis of resource units, but they are helpful in drawing up the possible range of printed material which could be of use for a given subject area or centre of interest. Further, keeping such matrices as records will tell the teacher whether the work undertaken is covering the whole range of purposes and media.

SKILLS
The teacher will find it helpful to list those skills which should be developed at certain stages of school life. The pupil must learn to read efficiently for any purpose for which a need arises and to plan his reading in the light of the purpose he has in mind.

The pupil must learn to locate the type of material which he needs to satisfy his purposes (library and survey skills) and find those sections of a text likely to be of most help (reference skills). The pupil must learn to select the most appropriate reading strategy for a particular task from three major types:

Study reading—a rather slow and careful approach involving all levels of comprehension, ability to make notes and precis, and to memorise.

Skimming—reading quickly to gain a general impression.

Scanning—reading quickly to find isolated pieces of information.

The pupil must learn to understand, process, and make good use of the results of his reading at a number of levels:

Literal comprehension. The ability to give answers to questions such as "What did the author say?" and follow simple directions.

Translation. No two people use the same vocabulary or sentence structures to express identical ideas. As we can only think effectually in our own vocabulary and structure, it is necessary to reexpress the author's work in our own language.

Reorganisation. The classification (and often reordering) of ideas into a form more easily handled by the reader.

Inference. Appreciation of main and supporting ideas, cause and effect relationships, and the prediction of outcomes.

Evaluation. Making judgments concerning relevance, reality, author purpose, and bias validity.

Appreciation. Emotional response to the material, style, characterisation, and plot.

Memorisation. Selection and memorisation of those elements considered to be worthy of the effort.

Action. Making use of the results of the processing. This could be immediate or long term and the action could be of a varying nature from imaginative thinking to the undertaking of some physical task.

PLANNING—STARTING WITH CONTENT

If a teacher tries to develop reading skills by taking opportunities for skill teaching which arise from the total curriculum, then some planning device is needed, as well as a thorough understanding of the nature of reading skills. I have found Merritt's G.P.I.D. sequence (3) of great value here, for the children can learn to operate it themselves over a period of time.

Goals. What should I do? What do I want to do and why? Which are most important to me and to others?

Plans. What might work? What information do I need? Which skills will I need?

Implementation. Am I exercising methods and techniques appropriately? Am I keeping my goals clearly in mind?

Development. Did I get what I wanted? How can I use my findings? How can I store my materials? What follow-up activities seem worthwhile?

On arrival at the planning stage, the following three possibilities might arise from the point of view of skill development.

1. All the skills needed to complete the activity have been learned so that the whole piece of work will be a consolidation of previous skill-learning.

2. Readiness for the development of skills not previously learned is such that, with support, the child will master the skills within the work to be carried out.

3. The child must have some specific instruction before he can proceed to the implementation of his plans. Transfer difficulties should not arise here as the need for the skill has already been realised and the mastered skill then will be used and consolidated in a realistic reading context.

PURPOSE—RESOURCE GRIDS

These grids form a simple but useful way of ensuring that reading for information is effectively carried out. One of the problems teachers find when young children are sent to books for information is that the children copy large chunks of text without processing it. The usual cause of this behaviour is that the questions to which answers are required have not broken down into sufficient detail and the child needs help.

Outline Example

Coal Mining

Purposes	Sources	Resources	Skills
How was coal formed?	1. Library 2. Museum	Text and reference books	Indexing, scanning, interpretation of diagrams, summarising, collecting information
What are miners like?	1. Miners 2. Union 3. Library	Interviews Union records Song books Sociological histories	Transposing spoken language into written language, reading between the lines, evaluating differing viewpoints
What is coal used for?	1. Library 2. Government ministries 3. Coal Board 4. Electricity Board 5. Gas Board	Charts Tables Description of processes	Interpreting and collating information, interpreting technical information

MOYLE

PLANNING—STARTING FROM SKILL-LEARNING

When one starts from a skill-learning base, it is important to legislate for the immediate wider usage of these skills. One might, for example, teach a particular phonic rule and find that the rule is forgotten before instances of that rule can be provided in classroom reading.

An interesting possibility arises in the case of reading laboratories. Basically, the child reads a short passage and then completes comprehension, word study, and phonic exercises based upon the passage. Left there, the skills could be associated only with the laboratory situation; however, the short passage must have some content and if the child is interested, there is the possibility of following the exercise with reading in the same topic area. This is facilitated when laboratories have a library of books matched for reading level and content and also a list of books from other publishers which cover similar subject matter.

Whichever approach is used, the goal of educators is to produce adults who *do* read, not merely those who *can* read. Murphy (5) suggests that the average American spends more than ninety minutes every day in some sort of reading activity; however, much of the reading activity appears to bring little satisfaction. Teachers, then, must add a further criterion for success—reading must be effective if it is to be worthwhile.

REFERENCES

1. Gephart, William J. *Application of the Convergence Technique to Basic Studies of the Reading Process.* U.S.O.E., 1970.
2. Merritt, John E. *Perspectives on Reading.* Milton Keynes: Open University, 1973.
3. Merritt, John E. *What Shall We Teach?* London: Ward Lock Educational, 1974.
4. Moyle, Donald. *The Reading Curriculum.* Milton Keynes: Open University, 1973.
5. Murphy, Richard T. *Adult Functional Reading Study.* Princeton, New Jersey: Educational Testing Service, 1973.
6. Strang, Ruth, Constance McCullough, and Arthur E. Traxler. *The Improvement of Reading* (4th ed.). New York: McGraw-Hill, 1967.

The Classroom Teacher's Responsibility to the Able Reader

Nila Banton Smith
Emeritus, University of Southern California
Los Angeles, California
United States of America

Every teacher needs to be a teacher of reading regardless of the grade level or subject he or she teaches. Wherever and whatever children study in school, they have to read. Learning to read basic reading materials in the primary grades doesn't equip children to read everything they need to read all through school. Hence, teachers beyond the usual reading instruction period should make it their business to know what the fundamental reading skills are and how to teach them so they can assist children who need help as they pass on to higher levels and increasingly more difficult and varied subject matter textbooks.

At present, reading is taught at various levels. Many schools teach reading only in grades one to three; others one to six; a few one to seven or eight; and a very few more, one to ten. In some cases, a reading specialist teaches remedial reading to all secondary students who need it.

If and when we have reading taught through the grades and in high schools all over the world, we probably shall have conspicuously fewer children suffering from reading disability. This is a worthy goal for classroom teachers to advocate.

TEACH SEVERAL WORD RECOGNITION SKILLS

Word recognition is the most basic of all reading skills. If a child can't recognize the names and meanings of word symbols, he or she just can't read. Very often, disabled readers are deficient in this area.

Once in a great while we find a child who has acquired the reading skills by himself or herself. Such a child, of course, is the extreme opposite to the disabled reader. It is refreshing, though, to hear about such a case and I would like to tell you about one.

An amusing description about a child who taught herself to read is given by the author of the Pulitzer prize winning novel,

To Kill a Mockingbird:

Jem said of his four-and-a-half-year-old sister, ". . . Scout there's been readin' since she was born, and she ain't even been to school yet." Then upon entrance in first grade, Scout, whose real name was Jean Louise, was asked to read something that Miss Caroline wrote on the chalkboard and she read it so well that Miss Caroline was visibly vexed. Miss Caroline then had her read most of the first reader and other readers and finally she asked her to read the stock market quotations in the *Mobile Register*. Jean Louise read beautifully in all of these situations. All of this time Miss Caroline's irritation was building up and she finally exploded: "Tell your father to stop teaching you. It will interfere with your learning to read in school." Jean Louise said that her father didn't teach her, and then she began soliloquizing to herself on how she did learn to read and she finally decided that it just came like learning to fasten the flap on the back of her union suit without looking around.

It is rare, indeed, that a teacher of beginning reading receives a pupil who has taught himself or herself to read so proficiently. In the majority of instances, the teacher has to teach reading from "the ground up" and word recognition is of great importance. Some people are still of the impression that the use of phonics is the only technique to be taught. While phonics is a valuable tool, there are several other very useful procedures for attacking new words. Every child should have all of these in his or her repertoire.

The use of *picture clues* is a word recognition process. This technique is most useful, of course, at beginning stages in which pictures are definitely designed to lead into what is said beneath them. Picture clues are useful, however, throughout the grades and I believe we should help children to employ these to a greater extent. All texts in all subjects are really beautiful picture books at this time and the pictures should be used fully both in word recognition and meaning activities.

Often teachers prepare and use picture-word cards and let children use them in games and various activities. Each card contains a picture with the appropriate word beneath it and the set of cards represents words children will soon need in their basic reading. These cards are very useful.

Then there are *sight words* to teach. The teaching of sight words has been the most abused of all the word attack skills. Developing a new reader lesson by having children memorize an isolated list of words on the chalkboard or drilling them day after day with words on flash cards are practices frowned upon by most authorities.

Durrell tells of an incident which illustrates the fallacy of depending upon the technique of flashing word cards. A certain boy who infallibly pronounced the word *children* when shown to him on a flash card couldn't read it in his reader. He declared that he had never seen the word before. He was then shown the word on the flash card which he pronounced correctly, as usual, and when asked how he knew the word was *children*, he replied "By the smudge over the corner."

Responsibility to the Able Reader

The point is that we can't always depend upon words learned from flash cards to be functional when the child is reading from text.

The nouns and verbs usually don't give much trouble. Such words as *where, this, she,* and *had* are difficult for many children. It is desirable to teach these in context. An example of one way of doing this is as follows: the teacher guides the children to give some sentences growing out of their experiences which contain certain sight words needing attention. The sentences are written on the board and various practice activities take place.

Now we come to the use of *context clues* which is an important word-getting process. Throughout the grades, the teacher should provide skillful comments and questions guiding children to make use of context clues. In this example Ted read the following:

"Fred and Uncle Bob were up early. Fred helped to wash the breakfast dishes."

Ted failed to recognize "breakfast." "Well, if they were up early, what meal would they have had at which dishes were used," asked Miss Lowe. "Breakfast," replied Ted and continued with his reading.

Thus, with guidance, children may become very skillful in deducing a word in context through reasoning about its meaning in a sentence, paragraph, or perhaps an entire selection.

Phonics is an important method of word attack which still is widely used. The way in which it is being taught in some places, however, is being criticized. I refer to that procedure in which children are taught to give exaggerated verbal sounds for separate letters as "buh" for *b*, or "cuh" for *c*. The critics say, rightly, that letters do not have the sounds of syllables when they are blended together in words.

The point is illustrated in an incident which I witnessed recently in a classroom. The teacher presumably was helping a boy to recognize *hat*, a word he had met in his reading. She wrote the word on the chalkboard and said, "Sound it." No response from the child. She then said, "Listen while I sound it," and proceeded to say "huh uh tu." "What is it?" The child said nothing. She repeated "huh uh tu. What have I?" A great light dawned on the little fellow's face as he answered "Hiccups."

One way to avoid presenting letter sounds as syllables is as follows, using initial consonant *h* as a sample: 1) develop visual discrimination by having the children find the letter several times in a mixed arrangement of chalkboard words beginning with different consonants; 2) develop auditory perception by pronouncing several of the chalkboard words beginning with *h*, and then have the pupils do the same thing; 3) give practice in blending by substituting *h* for the initial consonant in several known words, and have them pronounced; and

4) apply the practice in reading a selection in which some new words beginning with *h* appear.

There are many ways of teaching phonics. The procedure outlined is only one.

Structural analysis is another word attack technique entirely apart from phonics. In our changing world, there is an increasing frequency in the use of modified word forms. For this reason, it is very important to teach children to analyze and get meanings from structurally changed words. Unfortunately, this is given too little attention in large numbers of classrooms.

The elements of word structure with which children should be familiar are words in compound words; the stem word in a modified form; the inflectional forms *s, es, ed, ing, er, est*; prefixes; suffixes; possessives; contractions; and syllables. It is fairly easy for children to grasp these elements and ways in which they change meanings.

Use of the dictionary is perhaps the most complex of all the word attack processes. In beginning to use a formal dictionary, children must employ several previously acquired skills: knowledge of alphabetical arrangement, sounds of letters in words, and various word structure elements. In addition, they need to know diacritical marking and the effect of accent marks. They also must become skillful in selecting, from several meanings given, the most appropriate meaning for the particular situation in which it is to be applied.

This very complex dictionary skill as a whole usually is not mastered until the middle grades; however, foundations may be laid even in the first grade. Some teachers place on the chalkboard a miniature self-help dictionary consisting of pictures of needed nouns and verbs with the appropriate word under each. Some publishers are placing miniature dictionaries in the backs of their primers; and others are producing simple little paperback dictionaries for primary levels, including first grade.

In summing up this discussion on word recognition, I should like to emphasize that there are many important word attack skills in addition to phonics. These should be taught to the disabled reader so he will have several tools for use in recognizing words; if one tool doesn't work, perhaps another one will work. Poor readers especially need to have several word attack skills at their command.

GIVE MORE ATTENTION TO THINKING SKILLS IN GETTING MEANINGS

Disabled readers usually need help in getting meanings from what they read. Regardless of how well children learn to pronounce words, if they can't get the meanings when these words are strung together in sentences, they are destined for trouble ahead.

The word *comprehension* is a blanket term. There are different types of meaning-getting skills, just as there are different types of word-identification skills. Meaning-getting skills may be distinguished from one another in terms of the thought processes that are involved. For many years teachers made the mistake of laboring under the misconception that all they had to do to teach children to get meanings in reading was to give them some comprehension questions and exercises—the word *comprehension* connoting one big skill to be taught as a lump sum. Unfortunately, many classroom teachers still make this mistake, and this mistake may contribute to the inability of disabled readers to cope with reading materials.

On the other hand, the most proficient teachers are emphasizing thinking skills. The opinions of experts and results of experimental research and statistical analyses indicate that there are four major categories of processes which should be used in getting meanings, each of which in turn makes use of subordinate skills: *literal comprehension, interpretation, critical reading,* and *creative reading.*

The term *literal comprehension* is used widely for the process of getting the primary, direct, literal meaning of a word, idea, or sentence in context. Very little thinking is done in using this process. Children simply give back what is said in the book. Unfortunately, this is the only procedure used by many teachers.

The term *interpretation* of reading is used to include skills concerned with supplying or anticipating meanings not stated directly in the text: drawing inferences, making generalizations; reasoning cause and effect; speculating on what happened between events; anticipating what will happen next; detecting the significance of a statement, passage, or selection; identifying the purpose of the writer and the motive of characters; forming sensory images; and experiencing emotional reactions. Thus this category includes many thinking processes.

Critical reading is the third level in the hierarchy of reading for meaning skills. It includes literal comprehension and interpretation, but it goes further than either of these in that the reader evaluates or passes personal judgment on the quality, value, accuracy, and truthfulness of what is read.

Creative reading is involved to some extent in interpretation and in critical reading. In these cases, however, the child is working with the text and is thinking about what the author has said. In creative reading, the child goes beyond the text in seeking new insights and solving new problems.

Thinking, discriminating, decision-making individuals are what we need in this troubled world. Our students can best develop in these ways through participation in group thinking, where each one expresses his own thinking, checks others' thinking, and is checked by others—all of this guided by an astute teacher who will toss in a remark or question at the proper moment to stimulate deeper reflection.

In concluding my discussion on meanings, I can do no better than to quote from Samuel Coleridge, the distinguished English poet, journalist, and critic. In the early 1800s Coleridge wrote:

> There are four kinds of readers. The first is like the hour-glass; and their reading being as the sand, it runs in and runs out and leaves not a vestige behind. A second is like the sponge, which imbibes everything, and returns it in nearly the same state, only a little dirtier. A third is like a jelly bag, allowing all that is pure to pass away, and retaining only the refuse and dregs. And the fourth is like the slaves of Golconda, who casting aside all that is worthless, retain only pure gems.

Perhaps if classroom teachers teach the several thinking skills in reading more effectually, we shall avoid having so many disabled readers of the first three types that Coleridge mentions and produce those who "Casting aside all that is worthless, retain only pure gems."

TEACH STUDY SKILLS IN THE CONTENT AREAS

Sometime during the course of transmission of opinions, beliefs, and customs from one generation of teachers to another, there evolved a legend to the effect that reading should be taught during special periods set aside for the express purpose of giving the child control over the skills of reading. Likewise, legend dictated that science, geography, history, and mathematics should be taught at specific times in the daily program to develop distinctive skills or implant characteristic knowledge in each of these fields, usually with little or no consideration being given to reading development as one aspect of this specialized instruction.

As a matter of fact, in most schools, even children in the first grade have beginning books in science, mathematics, and social studies—social studies embracing both history and geography. These subjects are taught all through the grades and in high school. Children spend much more time reading in subject areas than they do in reading from readers and supplementary reading books, and they continue to read in subject areas long after general instruction in reading ceases.

It is in the third, fourth, and fifth grades that text in the subject textbooks becomes more substantial and it is also there that the disabled reader population begins to pile up.

Surely, the elementary classroom teacher, if he or she teaches science, social studies, and mathematics, or the special subject teacher if the school is so organized, has a major responsibility in teaching children how to read in these subject areas.

Specialized vocabulary is a consideration. Each subject carries its own vocabulary. For example, probably no one would doubt that *magnets, terrarium, velocity* are peculiar to the subject of science; *abolition, fortress, proclamation* belong particularly to the field of history; *hemisphere, continent,* and *equator* are special geography words; and *subtraction, cancellation,* and *divisor* are definitely mathematics words. Large numbers of children would profit from development and guided discussion of such words.

Studies have indicated that there are unique differences in skills used in different subject matter fields; and that while "general reading ability" is operative to a certain extent in all reading, there is also definite need for the development of specific skills to use in these different curricular areas. Research has shown that these specialized skills can be improved if singled out and given practice.

I analyzed 200 textbooks at different levels to find out what children had to do in *reading* when working with science, social studies, and mathematics texts. I discovered that these subjects made use of different patterns of writing, and the patterns called for different reading skills.

However, these study skills are common to all subjects: selection and evaluation, organization, recall, location of information, and following directions. Practice should be given on all these as needed.

Because of space limitations, I can only state the different patterns of writing and will be unable to describe them.

First, the specialized patterns in science are classification; explanation of a technical process; instructions for carrying out an experiment; the cause and effect pattern; detailed statement of facts pattern; problem-solving situations; and abbreviations, symbols, and equations.

In social studies we have maps, atlases, and globes; cause and effect which occurs with the highest frequency in this area; sequential events and their dates; and comparison and contrast. If students identify these patterns in science and social studies, and read in terms of each pattern, excellent results are obtained.

Mathematics content is very compact. It is usually composed of short paragraphs which, unlike other subjects, usually contain words mixed with numerals or mathematical symbols. In later grades, children need to recognize at a glance figures such as the triangle, pyramid, cube, and cylinder.

The chief characteristic of mathematics is that it predominantly contains problems to solve. This requires very careful thinking and reasoning. The differences between reading and mathematics should be discussed with children who should be urged to read problems carefully before working them on paper. The foregoing suggestions apply to mathematics as it is often taught in English speaking countries and not to the metric system now being used in many places.

At present, interest is high in teaching reading in the content areas. Studies, articles, and materials for children on this topic are appearing rapidly. This is good, for the classroom teacher or special subject teacher has a big job at hand in teaching children to read in the subject fields. Those who take this responsibility and perform it faithfully and well, will contribute tremendously to preventing the casualty of increasing numbers of disabled readers.

IMPROVE FLUENCY AND RATE

Reading fluently and rapidly is another basic skill development area and one which has become a topic of interest the world over.

There is an exaggerated emphasis on speed at this time. Many adults and teenagers consider that a high reading rate is the epitomy of being an excellent reader. They seem to think that a person should have one set, very high rate for reading everything.

I was director of the reading center at New York University for several years and among other offerings we scheduled evening classes in adult reading improvement. Sometimes I would pass through the hall while those who had come to take the course were registering. Invariably, they would ask me such questions as: "How many words per minute should I read?" or "How many words per minute will I be able to read when I finish this course?" I would often ask in return, "How many words per minute to read what? An easy popular article in the Reader's Digest? A scientific article packed with facts which you wish to fix in mind? A beautiful piece of literature in which you wish to pause for a bit to enjoy an intriguing expression or to reread a passage that has special charm or appeal for you?" Again I ask, "How many words per minute to read what?"

The registrants would look quite puzzled and confounded when I would answer them in this fashion. But they would come to realize what I meant as the course proceeded, for we taught them that there were many different kinds of material in reading and different purposes for reading, but with practice a person's various rates could be improved in pursuing all of the materials and purposes. Flexibility should be the watchword in speed improvement.

In the primary grades, fluency should be the major objective. Lipreading and fingerpointing must be broken up, and children urged to "read like they talk." Studies indicate that one of the best ways to promote rate at this level is to encourage wide reading of easy, interesting material. Having them read selections for specific purposes also serves as a spur to reading rate.

Practices used in the primary grades should be continued in the middle grades for any who need them. Purposeful reading and copious reading should be emphasized.

Studies indicate that systematic speed practice may best be initiated at fourth or fifth grade levels. It may be all right to give an informal check of reading rate in third grade, but systematic speed practice should be delayed until later.

There are published materials providing speed practice but these are not really necessary. Each teacher may prepare his or her own practice material based on the content of the classroom textbooks and used successively at intervals throughout the year.

DEVELOP INTEREST IN READING

Interest is the touchstone to reading achievement. Many disabled readers have no interest in reading. In fact, they dislike reading and seek their communication satisfactions in television and comic strips. Some teachers contribute to this lack of interest through their use of heavy drill work unaccompanied by interest-provoking activities.

Studies have shown that several factors and provisions may have favorable effects on interest.

Enthusiasm of the teacher. It appears that if the teacher is enthusiastic about books and reading, he or she somehow generates this enthusiasm in pupils.

Consulting with parents. Parents should know what to do and what not to do, they should be encouraged to have books in the home for their children and should be given advice concerning topics of interest and level of difficulty of the books they buy.

Recommending books to children. This practice has been found to be very effective. Of course, the teacher should not say "this is the book that is right for you." Rather, the recommendation should be indirect, as, "This is one of the most interesting books I have ever read. I'll place it on the book table for any of you who would like to read it." or "Joe, this is a book that answers some of the questions you were asking me about airplanes. I'll place it here if you wish to pick it up sometime."

Making books abundantly available. Books representing many topics and levels of difficulty should be at hand in the classroom for free reading. Be sure the supply includes easy books for the disabled readers. Often, one of the biggest problems, of course, is that of providing a large supply of books, since many schools have limited budgets. You may, however, borrow books from central school libraries, public libraries, and bookmobiles. These sources often loan teachers as many as twenty to thirty books a month. The children also may borrow from libraries and bring books from their own collections at home. Many parents are willing to buy one book to add to the classroom collection.

LOOK FORWARD TO TECHNOLOGICAL DEVELOPMENTS

We must face up to the use of technology in the future teaching of reading. We are undergoing a technological revolution all over the world. Technology has changed the patterns of progress in all major strands of civilization and it is beginning to change progress patterns in reading. The use of technological devices is appealing to disabled readers, and apparently effective with them.

In some places, films, filmstrips, slides, transparencies, and tapes are now commonly used in teaching reading. Television, computers, and even satellites are now entering the area of teaching methodology. Experiments are now being conducted with good results in the use of television to teach reading over large areas. Cable television and satellites are undergoing consideration and experimentation as teaching media.

The computer is, perhaps, the most spectacular technological device for reading instruction. One example of the use of the computer in reading is shown in this report which describes a procedure used in the Brentwood School, Palo Alto, California.

> The master computer that does the teaching has eighteen terminals. As the children come to the classroom, each one sits down before a screen at the end of his terminal. Various pictures, letters, or words begin to dance on this screen in front of him. Soon he is asked by the computer to make a response. This he does with a light-projecting pen. If the response is correct, the computer says "Good!" If it is wrong, the computer says "Nooooo." If there is a hesitation of more than 5 to 10 seconds, the computer says decisively, "Do it now!" If the child still sits and does nothing at all, the computer taps out a distress signal calling the teacher.

Computer experiments with disabled readers, as well as with normal readers, are mostly favorable.

It would be extremely hazardous to venture even a guess as to when computers, television, and satellites may be used for reading instruction the world over. This may happen during the lifetime of most of us, and we may as well be ready for it. In my opinion, however, machines will never take the place of teachers. There always will be moral, social, and educational values which cannot be developed solely through the use of machines, but which must be achieved through association of human beings with other human beings. Most definitely, teachers of reading still will be needed in the future.

Responsibility to the Able Reader

INTRODUCE GREATER FLEXIBILITY IN CLASSROOM ORGANIZATION

THE THREE-GROUP OR TWO-GROUP PLAN

For an undeterminable number of years the three-group or two-group form of classroom organization has prevailed in most places. Trends to loosen up this grouping plan are now taking place, much to the benefit of disabled readers.

In the traditional three-group plan, the teacher divides his or her class into groups according to reading ability: the fast-moving group, the average group, and the slow group. In the two-group plan there is the best group and a poorer group. In either case, each group is taught daily as a whole, working at a certain place in a basic reader.

This traditional plan is being criticized by many educators. As a result, adjustments are being made to supplement it. There may be times when pupils in the entire class meet to read for some purpose; temporary small groups may be formed to serve the skill needs; interest groups may be formed in terms of a topic of special interest of certain children. In these and other ways, the three-group or two-group plan may become much more flexible.

THE INDIVIDUALIZED APPROACH

In contrast to the three-group or two-group plan, many schools have adopted the individualized approach. Permanent groups in reading are done away with in the individualized classroom. Briefly, the procedure most generally used in individualized classrooms may be summarized as follows:

Each child selects a book that he or she wants to read. During the individual conference period the teacher sits in a particular spot in the room and each child comes and reads to him or her. During this period, the child's individual needs are noted and appropriate help is given. Finally, the teacher writes what the child is reading, his needs, and his strengths on a record card. Then another individual conference is held, and so on. If several children need help on the same skills, they may be called together for instruction and practice.

As in the more flexible three-group or two-group plans, sessions with the whole class may be held at times. Mutually prepared charts evolving from shared experiences, planned activities, or "how-to" directions call for whole-group participation and provide opportunities for whole-group reading. Notices placed on the chalkboard or bulletin board are read by the entire group.

The whole class may also be involved in planning activities, such as planning procedures for book selection or for individual conferences, planning what to do for independent work, and planning experiences in which one child or a group share reading with the class as a whole.

Sometimes a new reading skill is introduced to the complete group. Whenever there is a need or a reason for the entire class to work together, whole-class grouping may ensue. There is nothing in the philosophy of the individualized plan itself which precludes functional whole-group participation in a reading activity.

Small group arrangements take place often. Sometimes, children who are reading or have read the same book gather in a group to "talk it over." Such discussion may lead to plans for a sharing activity, such as a dramatization, a puppet show, or a mock radio or television program. At other times, children reading the same book may work as a group with the teacher during the usual individual conference period.

Now and then, two or three children who like to be together socially, gather in one spot when reading from their individual books. Usually there is considerable oral reading to each other and often the children help each other with unrecognized words.

Interest groups emerge at times. For example, four or five children may become interested in elephants. Regardless of their levels of ability, the children may work together and share information and interesting incidents from the books or stories being read at various levels of difficulty.

Skill groups are frequently formed to meet individual needs. If several children need help on the same skill, they meet as a group with the teacher for development of and practice on the skill. This group is disbanded one by one as children master the skill; and new groups, possibly composed of some of the original children plus new members, assemble to meet different skill needs. Thus, individualized instruction may also provide for some grouping to supplement the basic plan of having each child progress at his or her own rate.

This individualized plan is emerging rapidly in many countries. Because it provides opportunities for skill development, in terms of individual requirements and stages of growth, it should enable the classroom teacher to meet more effectually the needs of disabled readers.

CONCLUSION

Perhaps we may assume that we are now arriving at a philosophy in reading instruction which will enable us to apply a discovery made by Charles the Fifth.

Charles the Fifth was born in Vienna on April 16, 1643. He had a tremendous empire over which to rule—Austria, Spain, the Netherlands, Sicily, Naples, Germany, and Spain's colonies in the new world. The sway of Alexander, alone, is to be compared with that which was within the grasp of Charles.

He started his huge job at the age of sixteen. He stuck to it until he was quite old and then one day, becoming tired of the tinsel and show of a king, he handed over his empire to his two sons; loaded up a caravan of carts with all the clocks that he could buy, beg, or borrow; and hied himself off to a community of monks in a lost corner of Spain. There, between lauds and matins and vespers, he spent the remainder of his life trying to make the clocks keep time together. This he was never able to do.

"How foolish I have been," he said one day, "to make men think and do and move together, when I can't even make two clocks agree." And having gained this wisdom, he stopped striving to make either clocks or men work in unison, and spent the last days of his life in peace and happiness in the old monastery in a remote corner of Spain.

It has been over three centuries since Charles learned this lesson about men and clocks; it has been over two centuries since we began teaching children to read. Perhaps *we* are just beginning to realize how foolish *we* have been in thinking that children should "think and do and move together" in learning to read.

PART THREE

Writing Systems
and Early Reading:
Comparative Perspectives

Writing Systems in Japan

Takahiko Sakamoto
Noma Institute of Educational Research
Tokyo, Japan

There are four separate writing systems presently used in Japan: Hiragana, Katakana, Kanji, and Romaji. A consideration of Romaji is not included in this paper because it is merely the application of the Roman alphabet to Japanese rather than the Japanese orthography. It is used only to show the reading of the names of Japanese persons, places, and so forth in Roman alphabet for the sake of foreign people. Katakana is less frequently used than the other two systems (Kanji and Hiragana) because Katakana is now used only to write the foreign words that have entered the Japanese language, such as radios and television sets. It is not used to write a whole sentence at present. Thus, the Japanese orthography is the usage of Kanji with Hiragana or the combination of Kanji and Hiragana, plus some Katakana when necessary.

Hiragana, as well as Katakana, is a set of phonic symbols. In both systems, each symbol is monosyllabic and without meaning by itself. With few exceptions, each symbol has only one phonic pronunciation. Since the relationship between written symbols and spoken syllables is very regular, Hiragana and Katakana are easy to learn. The number of basic symbols in each system is 46. With the 46 symbols, plus other marks that give additional phonic values, all the 71 letters of either system can be written with any words or any sentences in the language which can be spelled out.

Kanji characters are ideographs that originally came from China. They are, therefore, often called Chinese characters from literal translation of the term into English. Kanji, however, are not completely Chinese but are very typically Japanese today. They are read differently and the significance of some characters in Japan is entirely different from that of the Chinese. Since each Kanji character has its own meaning, the number of characters is quite numerous. Since World War II, however, they have been officially limited to 1,850 characters for daily use. The learning of Kanji is more difficult than that of Hiragana or Katakana, not only because Kanji are more numerous but also because each Kanji usually has several alternative readings that range from monosyllabic to quadrisyllabic sounds.

Although Japanese can be written in Hiragana (or Katakana) only, as mentioned above, the Japanese orthography at present is a combination of Kanji and Hiragana which becomes a burden to children who must learn at least 1,850 Kanji characters in addition to 71 Hiragana and 71 Katakana letters. For more than a century, a group of people have campaigned for the *Abolishment of Kanji*. One group has been active in trying to abolish Kanji and to Romanize Japanese orthography. Another group has emphasized that all Japanese should be written in Katakana. This group has been successful in promoting in the business world the spread of Katakana typewriters with legible Katakana typefaces, which they developed by themselves. Presently, prints which are put out by computers are usually all in Katakana. In spite of these efforts, Japan is not going to change her orthography. Even in the case of computers, a new device which can print Kanji has been developed and will soon be used.

The main reason why Japan sticks to Kanji is practical rather than traditional. All of the experimental research has indicated that the Kanji-Hiragana combination is read faster than all Hiragana sentences with identical meanings. There are some reasons of efficacy in reading of Kanji-Hiragana combinations: 1) There are homonyms in Japanese which are hardly understood unless they are written in Kanji. When they are spoken or written in Hiragana, a reader must look for the cue of understanding in the context. 2) Key ideas or key words, which are usually nouns, roots of verbs, roots of adjectives, and adverbs, are usually written in Kanji, and the other parts of an average sentence are written in Hiragana. That is, roughly speaking, semantic elements of the sentence are written in Kanji and syntactic elements in Hiragana. This combination gives the reader a clue to rapid understanding. 3) In an average sentence, 25 to 35 percent of the total number of characters are written in Kanji and the rest in Hiragana. Since Kanji are complicated and square in shape, whereas Hiragana are simple and cursive, Kanji stand out visually from the main background of Hiragana and can be recognized easily. 4) When a Kanji is quadrisyllabic, for instance, it takes four letters to write the word in Hiragana, whereas it takes only one character in Kanji. In this way, Kanji-Hiragana combination makes a sentence short in terms of the number of characters, or in terms of line length.

Thus, the reader can quickly read the shorter sentence, picking up key ideas of Kanji that stand out against the Hiragana background and that convey the writer's exact meaning. This is true, of course, only if the reader learned enough of the 1,850 Kanji characters. The primary goal of Japanese reading instruction is, therefore, to teach children 71 Hiragana, 71 Katakana, and 1,850 Kanji characters.

HIRAGANA AND KATAKANA

Japanese children enter elementary school at six years of age, at which time the Ministry of Education requires that they start to learn Hiragana letters. But many children begin to learn Hiragana before school age without receiving any formal instructions; probably they learn in their daily life through books, magazines, toys, and TV programs.

According to the National Language Research Institute, Japanese children begin to learn Hiragana at the age of four and usually can read stories written entirely in Hiragana when they enter elementary schools. For the sake of these preschool children, many books and magazines are published using only Hiragana. The Publication Yearbook reported that about 400 new titles of books and 40 different magazines were published for preschool children in the year 1972. According to statistics, parents buy two or three of these books a month for their children. Preschool children also like monthly magazines and the most popular title sells more than one million copies a month.

Before children begin to read the books and magazines by themselves, parents read books to children. Sugiyama and others reported that 36 percent of parents, usually mothers, began to read books to children at one year of age, 31 percent of them began when the children were two-years-old, and 23 percent of them at the age of three. Only 7 percent of all the surveyed parents had not read to their children until four years of age. Sugiyama and others also pointed out that the earlier the parents began to read, the more fluently the children could read by themselves when they were five-years-old, and that when the mother's concern for the reading habits of her children was insufficient, reading development was slow.

No doubt, parents' concern for the reading of their children is one of the most important factors in this stage of reading development. Parents, however, do not actually teach children to read Hiragana letters. They usually arouse children's interest in reading by giving them picture books and Hiragana blocks, by reading books to them, and by answering their questions about letters. All of these are more important than teaching letters in a lesson-like situation. It is difficult to determine what teaching method Japanese parents use at the beginning stage of reading Hiragana. From the fact that almost all children play with Hiragana blocks (each of which has a Hiragana letter on one side and a word which begins with the letter on the other side with an illustration), we might say that they learn Hiragana by the word method.

Although about 60 percent of Japanese preschool children attend kindergarten (which is not compulsory), letters are not formally taught at these institutions. Many Hiragana letters can be seen in most kindergartens, however, and children's questions about them are answered by teachers. No readiness programs or beginning reading programs of teaching Hiragana have been developed. The Ministry of Education seems to leave the important job of beginning reading instruction to nontrained parents, without any good suggestions. A new beginning reading program will be needed for the sake of those parents who want to know the proper teaching method, who are not sufficiently concerned about beginning reading, and who have no time to take care of their child in the forthcoming period of woman liberation in Japan.

Teaching reading of Hiragana is not the main part of the first grade teacher's job. Although the Ministry of Education requires that teachers teach Hiragana, actually they merely have to review or reconfirm what most children already know. The teacher also identifies nonreaders. Those children who did not learn Hiragana before school age are taught in this grade to catch up with their classmates. They learn in normal classroom situations without any remedial programs or remedial teachers. Writing of Hiragana and reading of exceptional usages of Hiragana are taught to all children, so that all of them master both reading and writing of this system in the first grade.

Katakana is taught in the first and second grades. Since Katakana is also a set of phonetic symbols, there is no difficulty in reading instruction. The problem, rather, is in the writing or usage of the Katakana system. Children must learn which word should be written in Katakana; in other words, which word came from foreign languages.

KANJI

The Ministry of Education presently requires that 996 Kanji characters be learned during the six years of elementary school curriculum and 854 during the three years of junior high school, so that children complete the learning of all the 1,850 Kanji for daily use in the nine years of their compulsory education from ages 6 to 14. It is really a tremendous job to teach this number of characters to all children. In order to make reading instruction effective, several methods and systems have been developed.

One of the examples is what we in Japan call "the grade allotment of Kanji." Each one of the 996 Kanji characters, which is required learning in elementary schools, is allotted to a certain grade level according to its difficulty in usage. Although textbooks are published by private companies, all of them should be programmed to teach Kanji in accordance with the grade allotment. There are endless discussions on the allotment. Some will argue that this particular character should be taught before that or after that, and so forth. The allotment, however, has contributed to reading instruction in Kanji. In addition, it is noteworthy that the allotment has been a useful tool in editing commercial books and graded monthly magazines for children.

According to the allotment, even the first grade children must learn about 100 Kanji characters; the second graders must learn more. It can be said that a good number of characters are allotted to lower grades. The "radical method" and "deprivation method" are often used to motivate lower grade children. Kanji characters look complicated in shape, but they are not unsystematic constructions. A character can be divided into radicals which sometimes convey a certain submeaning related to the character. Through the radical method, children can classify Kanji characters in terms of common radicals and can find common implications. Since some Kanji characters are very pictographic, teaching of the deprivation of Kanji is used as another method to stimulate lower grade children. Although the deprivation method can be applied to a limited number of Kanji, pictorial explanations (such as the Kanji for moon was derived from the shape of the crescent moon) attract the children's interests.

Kanji characters are not taught separately but in the sentence. As mentioned previously, before children learn Kanji, they can read any sentence written in Hiragana. When the children learn a certain Kanji, they read a whole sentence in which a small group of Hiragana letters, representing a certain meaning, is replaced by the corresponding Kanji character with the same phonetic reading as well as the identical meaning. In this way, children become able to read Kanji with Hiragana sentences in which about 2 percent of total characters are written in Kanji by the end of the first grade. The percentage of Kanji to the total number of characters in the textbook increases as the grade goes up. That is, 7 percent for the second grade, 14 percent for the third, 18 percent for the fourth, 22 percent for the fifth, and 23 percent for the sixth grade. When children graduate from junior high schools, they are expected to read Japanese standard sentences in which 25-35 percent of the total characters are written in Kanji.

When children learn a certain Kanji, they must learn writing as well as reading. Writing Kanji is not easy for children; it is complicated in shape and has a stroke order which is strictly fixed and has to be learned. Practice in writing Kanji might be one of the main activities assigned to children all over Japan. Children pick out all the Kanji characters in a chapter and write them down; or, they write newly learned characters ten times each in a notebook. This kind of activity is usually assigned as homework every day; not only on school days, but also weekends, national holidays, and even during the summer vacations. Although children hate it, it is evident that the practice of writing reinforces their learning of reading. Here again, the role of parents is important. When parents sufficiently encourage their children to finish their homework every day, the children's achievements are high. Just as in the case of Hiragana, reading instruction of Kanji largely depends on the concern of parents.

Generally speaking, children learn easily those characters which appear frequently in the language. On the other hand, even when they are less complicated in shape, those characters which seldom appear in the language cannot be learned easily. Among the 1,850 Kanji characters for daily use, there are some which can hardly be learned until the end of compulsory education. Most of the characters are not often used now; obsolete words, very old words, military terms, special words related to the Emperor, and so forth. We cannot blame children, teachers, and parents for the failure in learning this kind of unfamiliar Kanji. The blame must be placed on the National Language Deliberation Council who is in charge of Japanese orthography. They selected the 1,850 Kanji nearly twenty years ago, and they have never revised them during the rapidly changing decades.

Reading Disability and the Writing System

Kiyoshi Makita
Keio University School of Medicine
Tokyo, Japan

While reading disability, reading difficulty, reading retardation, or whatever you prefer to call it, comprises a formidable portion of child psychiatric cases in the Western countries, its incidence in Japan is extremely rare, as was reported by this author in 1968 (8). No children were brought to the clinic for the said complaint in the past sixteen years, and the result of a questionnaire survey addressed to school teachers revealed that the alleged incidence of such reading difficulties was no more than 0.98 percent of the school population, which is only about one-tenth of the incidence reported in Western countries (1, 9, 10, 12). This author's report of these findings was critically opposed by Critchley (2). He wrote: "The alleged low incidence of reading disabilities in Japan deserves comment. Makita's suggestion that it is due to the inherent linguistic merits of the Japanese language is not plausible. The most probable explanation is that in Japan teachers, neurologists, and educational psychologists are not alive to the possible occurrence of dyslexia." They are alive! Moreover, they are searching diligently for dyslexic children. But the plain fact is that such Japanese specialists do not get any referrals.

There are various theories attempting to explain the aetiology of reading disability from hereditary, morphological, physiological, emotional, and other standpoints. Not one of the theories serves as a clear-cut explanation as yet, and not one indicates that the Japanese differ as an organism from other human beings in the causal situation of producing reading difficulty per se. What, then, can be the contributing factor which results in such a big discrepancy in the incidence of reading disability in Japan as compared with other countries?

It is hardly possible to assume that the Japanese are ten times better equipped in hereditogenetical terms, in morphological structure of the brain or in its development and in neurophysiological dexterity and are surviving in a ten times better emotional environment. In other words, a biological mechanism which is associated with reading difficulty is unlikely to differ at all from one ethnic group of human beings to another. It is notable that studies on reading difficulty conducted in

Western countries have been based on the alphabetical language as given, and that the nature of characteristics of the language and its script system—the very object of the reading behavior—have seldom been questioned. If the similarity of biological function of all races is taken into consideration, the discrepancy of the incidence may arise from the languages and their script systems, which are fundamentally different. The Comparative Reading project under the leadership of Downing (4) is really an ice-breaking and rewarding attempt in elucidating differences in the characteristics of languages and their script systems which doubtlessly will augment other valuable advances in our knowledge of reading capacity and disability. Hopefully, it may help to explain the discrepancies I found between the incidence of reading problems in Japan and in other countries.

JAPANESE SCRIPT SYSTEMS

Most Japanese writing consists of a combination of two decoding systems: morphemes called Kanji and syllables called Kana. The Kana system is comprised of 48 syllable characters, each of which represents the sound of either a consonant plus a vowel or of a single vowel only. Each character is always read in the same way without irregularity. The Japanese Kana script is similar to the alphabetic scripts in the sense that it represents phonological elements of language. The important difference is that Kana characters represent a different unit of sound—the syllable. The Kana script has two varieties called Hiragana and Katakana, which are more or less comparable to manuscript print and cursive writing, but the discussion need not go further into their differences since the mode of their cognition does not differ. In consequence, the script-phonetic relationship is quite stable in Japanese Kana, whereas it is often unstable in alphabets. Thus, the Kana system seems likely to cause less cognitive confusion in the initial learning stage.

On the other hand, each Kanji represents a morpheme. The Kanji system was derived from Chinese characters but it is read in different ways in Japan than it is in China. Many Kanji have hieroglyphic or pictographic origins and, in general, it could be said that a Kanji character is a logograph or an ideograph. Usually, one Kanji may be read two or more ways but it still conveys the meaning it represents. A Kanji may represent a monosyllabic or a multisyllabic pronunciation according to how it is used in combination with other Kanji or Kana, but the meaning it conveys is the same. In other words, at sight, a Kanji conveys the meaning it represents to the cerebral cortex without any sort of decoding or spelling out process and its reading comes out secondarily dependent on how it is used.

There are numerous varieties of Kanji characters which impress one as endless to memorize. In China, it has been said that a minimum of 3,000 characters have to be learned before one can be reasonably literate. It may require an even larger number of characters to reach the level of "full literate proficiency," according to Goody (5). The situation would be quite similar in Japanese pertinent to Kanji. In consideration of such an inconvenience, the minimum requirement in learning Kanji is limited to 1,850 characters for daily use at present, and difficult characters are supplemented by Kana. And yet, one may still receive the impression that it must be a heavy burden for Japanese children to have to memorize such a vast number of characters when compared to the learning of the 26 letters of the English alphabet. However, one must not overlook the fact that merely learning these 26 alphabetic letters does not accomplish literacy. Various redundant difficulties are involved in learning to read in alphabetical languages, and this is particularly so in English. As Leong (7) has noted, the difficulties in learning to read Kanji assumed by Western researchers can be challenged and the burden of memorizing Kanji can be much less than Goody (5) or Halle (6) suggest. Of course, there are confusing symbols in Kanji, in Kana, and also in alphabetical words. There are seemingly alike but different Kanji in their total figure or Gestalt. But most Kanji have some sort of regularity in their systematic parts. Kanji can be analyzed into smaller units or radicals that operate often systematically. Certain radicals imply metallic, vegetative, animal, or human nature. Many symbols are constructed from the combination of such units or radicals, which makes the learning of Kanji more or less systematic so that the memorization of Kanji cannot be compared to the rote memory of telephone numbers or of all the pictorial or abstract figures existing everywhere as claimed by such writers as Halle and Goody. Although the total figure of a Kanji is directly connected with the meaning it represents, the process includes a function of discriminating partial details. The discrimination of seemingly alike but ambiguous symbols is accomplished by the differentiation of partial details of each individual symbol. Misreading due to an erroneous total perception induced by the failure of discriminating partial details may be compared to such a misreading in English between *straight* and *steady* or *left* and *felt*. Misreading of Kanji differs from that of alphabetical words in that the former does not include the spelling factors.

THE DIFFERENCE OF MODE OF COGNITION BETWEEN READING ALPHABETICAL, KANA, AND KANJI SCRIPTS

Alphabets are phonemic codes and the reading of an alphabetical word is induced from the linkage of the phonemes which compound the word, which by way of the spoken word, finally leads to its comprehension. In other words, unless one perceives each visual symbol in terms of the correct phoneme, and unless one connects those visual code symbols one by one (the decoding process), one cannot realize the sounds of the word those code symbols represent and cannot arrive at the comprehension of the word represented. The mode of cognition in Kana reading is quite similar, but here the codes are not phonemic but syllabic, and therefore more consistent and stable in their sound to visual symbol coding relationship.

Being a morphemic code, the comprehension of Kanji is entirely different in its cognitive procedure. In reading Kanji, visual perception of a symbol can carry the meaning it represents at sight no matter how it is read. The visually perceived symbol is transmitted directly to the higher center of comprehension, not by way of the realization of a spoken word, and different readings of the perceived visual symbol emerge secondarily dependent on how it is used on the basis of the comprehension of the meaning it represents. In other words, the mode of perception, transmission, and comprehension is the other way around in the reading of Kanji compared to that of Kana or letters of an alphabet. It is generally agreed in Japan that the capacity for reading Kanji remains less affected than that of Kana in cases of acquired alexic/dyslexic disorders with a cerebral basis. This suggests that the cognitive process is very different in reading Kana and Kanji.

As was mentioned earlier in this paper, most Japanese writings employ a mixture of Kanji and Kana scripts, which it is claimed makes reading easier. The reason is said to be that the Kanji logographs play the roles of milestones in a sentence, facilitating an overall comprehensive orientation. This seems true on an empirical basis, for reading Japanese telegram messages is quite commonly recognized as being quite difficult and misleading and Japanese telegrams use Kana script only (for technical reasons). There has been a Kana script movement in Japan which aims at reforming Japanese writing in Kana script only for its technical simplicity. The unsuccessful development of this movement may be due to the above mentioned disadvantage and may serve to support the advantage of mixed Kana/Kanji writing.

COGNITIVE CONFUSION AND DYSLEXIA

In agreement with Downing (3) and Vernon (11), this author concludes that the fundamental and basic characteristic of reading disability appears to be dependent on cognitive confusion. The writing system seems to be an important variable in the learning to read process. The rarity of reading disability in Japanese children might be due to the Japanese writing system which, though superficially it may appear to be very complex, in reality, it is less confusing in its cognition. In particular, the different mode of perception of Kanji has to be taken into consideration. These points may serve as some clues in understanding reading difficulties in other languages. Although it is very difficult to prove that the Japanese writing system is less confusing compared to other writing systems, the discrepancy in the incidence of reading disability between Japan and many Western countries may imply that the Japanese writing system is less confusing in its cognition 1) because of the sound to visual symbol consistency of Kana and 2) because of the entirely different perceptual process of reading Kanji.

REFERENCES
1. Bach, W. "Über die angeborene bzw. frühkindlich-erworbene verbale Schreib-Leseschwäche (sogenannte kongenitale Wortblindheit)," *Allgemeine Zeitschrift der Psychiatrie,* 124 (1945), 25-69.
2. Critchley, M. *The Dyslexic Child.* London: W. Heinemann Medical Books, 1970.
3. Downing, J. "Cognitive Factors in Dyslexia," *Child Psychiatry and Human Development,* 4 (Winter 1973), 115-120.
4. Downing, J. *Comparative Reading.* New York: Macmillan, 1973.
5. Goody, J. *Literacy in Traditional Societies.* London: Cambridge University Press, 1968.
6. Halle, M. "Some Thoughts on Spelling," in K. S. Goodman and J. T. Fleming (Eds.), *Psycholinguistics and the Teaching of Reading.* Newark, Delaware: International Reading Association, 1969.
7. Leong, C. K. "Is Literacy Acquisition Easier in Some Languages Than Others?" *Visible Language,* 7 (Spring 1973), 145-154.
8. Makita, K. "The Rarity of Reading Disability in Japanese Children," *American Journal of Orthopsychiatry,* 38 (July 1968), 599-614.
9. Monroe, M. *Children Who Cannot Read.* Chicago: University of Chicago Press, 1932.
10. Schenk-Danzinger, L. "Probleme der Legasthenie," *Schweizer Zeitscrift für Psychologie,* 20 (1961), 29-48.
11. Vernon, M. D. *Backwardness in Reading.* London: Cambridge University Press, 1957.
12. Weinschenk, C. *Die Erbliche Lese-Rechtschreibeschwäche und ihre Sozialpsychiatrischen Auswirkungen.* Bern u. Stuttgart: H. Huber, 1965.

The Reading Ability of Preschool Children in Japan

Shozo Muraishi
National Language Research Institute
Tokyo, Japan

It is often supposed that due to cultural and social changes in modern society modern preschool children's language ability, literacy, and their methods of acquiring these are markedly different from those of earlier times. However, there has not been sufficient scientific data concerning this problem. Therefore, in 1967 Muraishi and Amano (4), working at the National Language Research Institute, investigated the reading and writing ability of preschool children in Japan. (See Supplementary Note *1.)

The report for this perspective contains most of the results of these studies and some new data as well. In this report we will discuss the ability of preschool children in Japan to read Japanese syllabic characters (the Hiragana letters) and the improvement in the rate of acquisition of characters for modern children over children of earlier times.

METHOD

Contents and construction of test. This test deals with the Hiragana letters, which we used to represent the seventy-one fundamental syllables of Japanese and the five kinds of special syllables (contracted sounds, assimilated sounds, prolonged sounds, contracted-prolonged sounds, and particles).*2 Children were tested on their ability to read the letters representing the fundamental syllables and words containing the special syllables.

Subjects. The parent population for this test was the approximately 500,000 children in the Tokyo, Tohoku, and Kinki areas in 1965. The sample consisted of 2,217 children (1,399 in the five-year-old class, 818 in the four-year-old class) from 122 kindergartens.

Operation and required time of test. Testing was done in the form of individual tests given by seventy-two investigators from universities and research institutes in the test areas. The test required ten to twenty minutes to complete.

Date of testing. Testing was carried out in November 1967.

Others. There were questionnaires for the kindergartens and the children's homes asking how much instruction had been given in the acquisition of Hiragana letters.

RESULTS

For the November 1967 test, the acquisition levels in reading of Hiragana letters are shown in Figure 1.

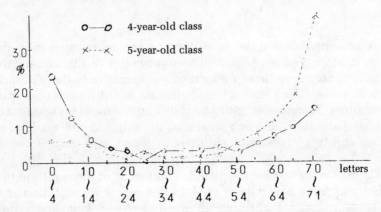

Figure 1.   Acquisition levels of Hiragana letters in preschool children.

This shows that 5.2 percent of the children in the five-year-old class and 23.2 percent in the four-year-old class could read fewer than four letters. On the other hand, 63.1 percent of the children in the five-year-old class and 33.1 percent in the four-year-old class could read sixty or more Hiragana letters. In a retest of children in large and middle-sized cities a month before entering primary school, 87.9 percent of the five-year-old class (176 subjects) could read sixty or more Hiragana letters. *3

From Figure 1 we can see that the distribution of the number of Hiragana letters the children can read is not a normal curve but J or a reverse-J type curve. This characteristic curve shows that they acquire most Hiragana letters for fundamental Japanese syllables rapidly, as soon as they have learned to read about twenty letters and have acquired some of the abilities required for learning to read. Amano (1) has shown that the most important of these is the ability to analyze and abstract syllabic structure of words.

The relationship between the acquisition level of Hiragana letters and ability to analyze the syllabic structure of words is shown in Figure 2. According to this figure, even in younger children who could not read any letters at all, relatively high percentages of correct responses are shown regarding the number of syllables. In the earlier stages, the act of identifying each syllable of a word is difficult, but it shows a tendency to improve rapidly at the first stage of acquiring the Hiragana letters. *4

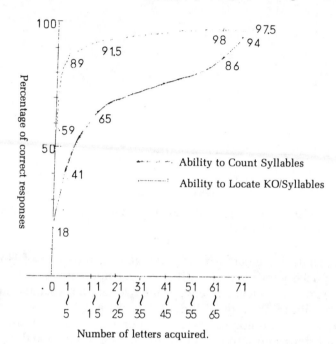

Figure 2. Relation between the acquisition level of letter learning and 1) the ability to count the number of syllables in words and 2) the ability to locate the syllable /ko/ in words

Children gradually acquired the ability to read the special Japanese syllables after they acquired sixty or more Hiragana letters representing the fundamental Japanese syllables. Figure 3 shows the relationship between the number of Hiragana letters acquired and the ability to read special syllables.

As shown in Figure 3, 15 percent of the children who have learned sixty to sixty-four Hiragana letters can read one or more kinds of special syllables. Moreover, of those children who have learned seventy-one Hiragana letters, 85 percent can read one or more kinds of special syllables and 18 percent have completely mastered five kinds of special syllables. In April of 1953 and 1954, investigations of reading and writing ability of Hiragana letters were conducted on first-year pupils in primary school by the National Language Research Institute. In Table 1 the results of these investigations are compared with the results of the recent investigations.

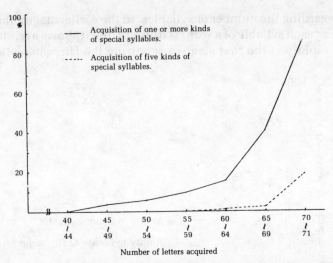

Figure 3. Relationship between the number of letters acquired and the ability to read special syllables

From Table 1 we can see that the age of acquisition of Hiragana letters, especially for reading ability, was considerably lowered during the thirteen or fourteen years between the two sets of investigations. The factors conditioning acquisition of Hiragana letters in preschool children were chronological age, sex, number of years of education, home conditions, and activities of children. It was found that the number of years of education in kindergarten was the most important factor. Figure 4 shows the percentage of children who can read sixty or more letters. One year of schooling means that the children entered kindergarten at age five years and got one year of schooling, and two or three of schooling means that they entered kindergarten at four years of age or younger and got two or three years of schooling.

Table 1. Hiragana reading and writing averages (for seventy-one letters) in three tests

Years	Subjects (Number)	Reading Average	Writing Average
April 1953	First-year pupils of private school (N = 650)	34.8	22.7
April 1954	First-year pupils of private school (N = 426)	42.9	29.3
November 1967	Kindergarten children		
	(4-year-old class N = 818)	33.5	13.7
	(5-year-old class N = 1,399)	53.0	33.5

Preschool Children in Japan

According to Figure 4, the two or three years of schooling group shows a higher rate of ability of reading letters than the one year of schooling group and in all classes of cities except first and second class (small towns) the difference is found to be significant ($p < 0.05$).

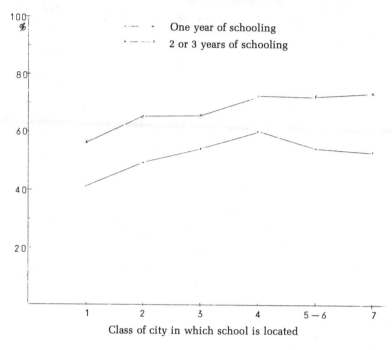

Figure 4.   Percentage of children who have acquired sixty or more letters according to class of city in which school is located

DISCUSSION

From the results, we find that most modern kindergarten children (87.9 percent) have acquired Hiragana letters from four years of age and have a high reading ability before entering primary school, and their acquisition of Hiragana letters is at a younger age than children in 1953 and 1954. However, we must consider the following four problems.

1. Does this improvement in the rate of acquisition of Hiragana letters by modern children mean that they have better word and sentence reading ability than children of the past? It is true that children who can read sixty or more letters can read simple sentences, but most of the children read the words merely letter by letter.

Figure 5 shows the relationship between children's acquisition level of reading ability and their reading skills.*5

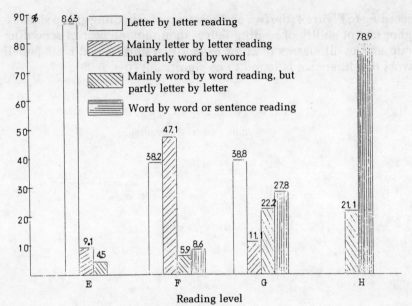

Figure 5.   Relationship between level of reading ability and reading skills

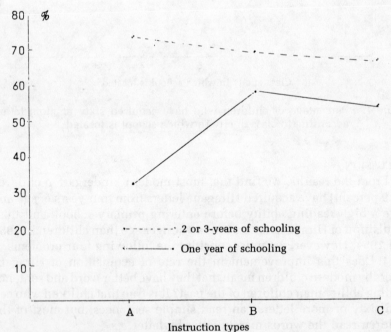

Figure 6.   Parents' instruction types concerning teaching of letter learning and reading (5-year-old class)

Preschool Children in Japan

According to Figure 5, at E level most of the children are at the stage of letter by letter reading, and as they come to master the reading of special syllables, they move up to the stages of word by word reading and sentence reading. Therefore, this indicates that just because a child can read Hiragana letters it does not mean that he can read sentences. This problem will have to be studied more in the future.

2. Why is the acquisition of reading Hiragana letters by modern children greater than that for earlier children? There is a tendency to assume that modern children acquire a knowledge of Hiragana letters at a young age because parents teach their children reading and writing at home, but the results of our investigation do not support this assumption.

Figure 6 shows the parents' instruction types concerning letters and percentage of children who can read sixty or more letters.*6 According to this figure, the type of instruction at home has no positive bearing on letter learning.

On the other hand, concerning instruction in letter learning in kindergarten, about 20 percent adopted a positive instructive attitude. Table 2 shows the levels of positive instructive attitude in each kindergarten and the percentage of children in them who could read sixty or more letters. *7

Table 2. Level of letter reading ability according to type of letter instruction in kindergarten

age	type	letter environment	letter presentation	reading and writing instruction
4 years old	high average low	37.09% $\chi_3^2 = 4.468$ 32.86 26.47 $p < 0.05$	27.70% 36.34 32.56	28.08% 35.75 34.29
5 years old	high average low	63.73 62.71 65.56	65.43 62.74 63.84	65.29 65.98 60.11

Percentage in table refers to percentage of children having acquired sixty or more letters

According to Table 2, a definite relationship between the level of letter instruction in kindergarten and the acquisition level of reading ability can be found only at the age of four. The other two factors do not act significantly on the acquisition of reading ability. Therefore, we can draw an inference that language development of children is hastened through preschool education (kindergarten, home) and then children acquire Hiragana letters by themselves in the modern sociocultural letter environment. So, the increased reading ability in modern children compared with that in earlier children is due to improvement of preschool education, especially the fact that children now enter kindergarten at a younger age and that a larger percentage of them attend kindergarten. *8

We must try to learn what fundamental reading abilities children acquire in preschool education. What are the fundamental abilities needed to learn to read letters? There seem to be three. The first is the ability to recognize letters. This is acquired through learning the roles of signals and signs in daily living. The second is the ability to decode written sentences. This is acquired by learning to respond to the meanings of written sentences in picture books, although the child is as yet illiterate. The third is the ability to discriminate syllables and different letter shapes. This is acquired through analyzing syllables and discriminating letter shapes in language games. In addition to these abilities, it is necessary that the children should have attained a certain level of intellectual and language development.

3. What is the difference between Hiragana letters and an alphabet? The Hiragana script is syllabic and it represents fundamental and special syllables. There are 71 letters representing the fundamental short syllables. Because these each correspond with a syllable, it is easy for children to acquire them. So, most children can read 60 or more letters before entering school.

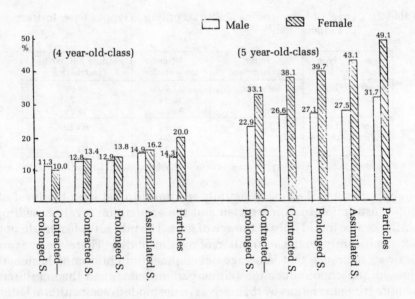

Figure 7.   Percentage of correct responses on special syllabic letters

There are five kinds of special sounds.*2 These syllables do not have their own letters, and are constructed in connection with two or three regular syllabic letters. Moreover, certain particles are read wa,e instead of ha,he in connection with the syntax. Figure 7 shows percentage of preschool children who are able to read correctly the special syllabic letters. The above figure shows that special syllabic letters are more difficult to read than fundamental ones. And until children learn them, they cannot read most sentences fluently.

4. There are two difficult features in letter learning for children in Japan. One is the fact that children cannot read sentences in newspapers unless they have learned the 71 Katakana letters, in addition to the Hiragana letters, at the lower grades of elementary school and have also learned the 881 or more Chinese letters taught in elementary school. We know from our case study that even preschool children, if they have learned 60 or more Hiragana letters, begin to read some Katakana letters and a few Chinese letters. However, it is also true that for Japanese children letter learning becomes the major burden in Japanese language learning.

The other difficult feature is the fact that children must write letters according to the rules of stroke order. But to children, the stroke order is so difficult that about 20 percent of letters with correct form written by children are written with incorrect stroke order.

Hiragana letters are written with between one and six strokes. The distribution of strokes per letter is shown in Table 3.*9

Table 3.   Stroke numbers of Japanese syllabic letters

Stroke numbers	1	2	3	4	5	6	Total
Frequency	10	19	20	11	7	4	71

Children in Japan have to learn the stroke order for each letter. In general, stroke orders can be described as follows: 1) the upper strokes precede the lower, 2) the left strokes precede the right, and 3) the horizontal strokes precede the vertical.

These rules don't depend on the features of lines but on the locations of lines. However, I verified that the rules of stroke order in copying depended on the visual features of lines to children who didn't know any letters (2). Thereafter, I undertook an experiment on the relation of stroke orders and the features of lines. In this experiment I had 179 nursery and kindergarten children copying 45 figures and letters.*10 According to the results of the experiment, the following were true for most of the children who could not read any letters (3):

1. Curved lines preceded dots and straight lines.

2. Longer straight lines preceded shorter ones.

3. Angular lines preceded nonangular ones.

Table 4 shows some samples of stroke orders distributed by children who could not read any letters.

Table 4. Some samples of stroke orders distributed by children who could not read any letters

Stroke order	(U)		(Yo)		(A)		(Figure)			
Correction	○	✕	○	✕	○	✕	○	✕	○	✕
%	7.1	50.0	3.6	50.0	50.0	7.1	80.4	3.6	17.9	67.9
x^2	10.472		13.868		6.920		24.872		8.924	
P	<.001		<.001		<.005		<.001		<.005		df = 1

As is evident from Table 4, it was confirmed that the rules of stroke order for children who could not read any letters depend on the visual features of lines. The standard stroke order rules were decided according to the writing facility for adults, but children who have little opportunity for writing can't understand these rules. The rules of stroke order based on the visual features are different from the ones based on the writing facilities produced by different stroke orders in the case of Hiragana letters. So, it is necessary either to change the standard stroke order rules or find a way to teach them to children.

Finally, we have to compare our results with findings in other countries to determine whether the acquisition of Hiragana letters before entering elementary school is due to the distinctiveness of Hiragana letters.

CONCLUSION

Most Japanese children acquire the ability to read Hiragana letters for fundamental Japanese syllables before entering elementary school. We can also show that acquisition of Hiragana letters occurs at a younger age than it did in 1953 and 1954, and the most important factor conditioning the acquisition of reading is the improvement of preschool education. In the future, we must study what effects the orthography of Japanese letters have had on the reading development of Japanese children.

SUPPLEMENTARY NOTES

* 1. S. Muraishi and K. Amano made the following studies over a three-year period of time.

On Reading and Writing Ability in Preschool Children (1967)
On Vocabulary Ability in Preschool Children (1968)
On Vocabulary and Communication Ability in Preschool Children (1969)

* 2. The letters representing fundamental Japanese syllables and the words containing the special Japanese syllables found in this test are as follows:

a. Voiceless sounds, Syllabic nasals, Voiced sounds, Semivoiced sounds

あ	a	い	i	う	u	え	e	お	o
か	ka	き	ki	く	ku	け	ke	こ	ko
さ	sa	し	shi	す	su	せ	se	そ	so
た	ta	ち	chi	つ	tu	て	te	と	to
な	na	に	ni	ぬ	nu	ね	ne	の	no
は	ha	ひ	hi	ふ	fu	へ	he	ほ	ho
ま	ma	み	mi	む	mu	め	me	も	mo
や	ya			ゆ	yu			よ	yo
ら	ra	り	ri	る	ru	れ	re	ろ	ro
わ	wa	を	wo	ん	n				
が	ga	ぎ	gi	ぐ	gu	げ	ge	ご	go
ざ	za	じ	zi	ず	zu	ぜ	ze	ぞ	zo
だ	da	ぢ	zi	づ	zu	で	de	ど	do
ば	ba	び	bi	ぶ	bu	べ	be	ぼ	bo
ぱ	pa	ぴ	pi	ぷ	pu	ぺ	pe	ぽ	po

b. Contracted sounds

ちゃ cha   しゅ shu   しょ sho
おもちゃ omocha   あくしゅ akushu   やくしょ yakusho
< Toy >   < Handshaking >   < Government>

c. Assimilated sounds

きって kitte   せっけん sekken   にっこり nikkori
< Stamp >   < Soap >   < Smile >

d. Prolonged sounds

おかあさん okasan   おねえさん onesan   おにいさん onisan
< Mother >   < Sister >   < Brother>
ふうせん fusen   おおかみ okami   けいさつ kesatu
< Balloon >   < Wolf >   < Police >
せいと seto
< Pupil >

e. Contracted-prolonged sounds

きゃあ kyā   しょう shō   ちゅう chū
やきゅう yakyū   すいしょう suishō   こんちゅう konchu
< Baseball >   < Crystal >   < Insect >

f. Particles

やまはたかい. Yama wa takai. The mountain is high.
うみはひろい. Umi wa hiroi. The sea is wide.
まちへいく. Machi e iku. I go to the town.
むらへいく. Mura e iku. I go to the village.

In the writing ability test the subjects were given only the letters they could read correctly, selected from 71 letters in all, including voiceless sounds, syllabic nasals, voiced sounds, and semivoiced sounds.

* 3. In the test carried out in November, 66.6 percent of the subjects showed the ability to read 60 or more Hiragana letters.

* 4. This experiment was conducted on 76 children in four- or five-year-old classes using 15 words from 3 to 5 syllables containing /こ/ (ko) such as く ねこ にしゅかけ >(cat, chair). The subjects were shown the pictures representing the given words and asked to analyze them by putting small wooden blocks into the squares drawn below the pictures one square for each syllable and by pointing to the location of /こ/ (ko).

* 5. This experiment was carried out by K. Amano. Children were asked to read aloud the sentence "There is a tiny bear in Hanako's house."

    はなこさんの うちには かわいい ちいけな くまが います。

The stage of their responses was analyzed according to each level. The levels are defined as follows, E means that children can read 60 or more letters but can't read any special syllables at all. F means that children can read 60 or more letters and have mastered 1 or 2 kinds of special syllables in addition. G means that children can read 60 or more letters and have mastered 3 or 4 kinds of special syllables in addition. H means that children can read 60 or more letters and have mastered all kinds of special syllables in addition.

* 6. Instruction types are divided as follows. Type A means the passive instruction type where parents give no special instruction and letter learning is entirely left up to the children themselves. Type B means the neutral instruction type where children are left learning letters spontaneously but parents give some materials such as wooden blocks or cards with letters written on them in order to facilitate the learning of letters. Type C means positive instruction where parents teach letters by giving blocks or cards with letters written on them to their children or make them workbooks. Of all the parents, 66.6 percent are included in type B.

* 7. Instruction in letter learning is divided into the following three factors: Letter environment, letter presentation, and reading and writing instruction. Letter environment means the arrangement of the environment; for example, teachers put the child's name on each of his things, or the class name plate is put above the entrance to the classroom. Letter presentation means the act of writing on the blackboard things such as the theme of a story during storytelling activities. Reading and writing instruction means systematic instruction in letter learning.

Preschool Children in Japan

* 8. Figure 8 shows the percentage of first grade children each year who had kindergarten experience.

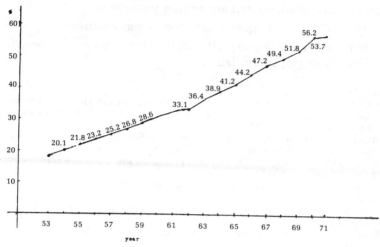

By statistical data of Educational Ministry

Figure 8. Percentage of first grade children each year with kindergarten experience

According to this, the percentage more than doubled between 1953 and 1967. But it must be noted that children with only nursery school experience are not included.

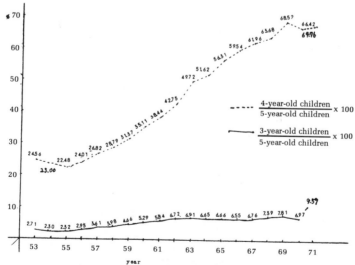

By statistical data of Education Ministry

Figure 9. Percentage of 3-year-old children and 4-year-old children in relation to 5-year-old children

As shown in Figure 9, the ratios of three- and four-year-old children to five-year-old children each year show that children's ages at the time of entrance into kindergarten are getting younger.

* 9. Many Chinese characters have ten or more strokes.

*10. In the design of this experiment, the arrangements and lengths of lines were not controlled.

REFERENCES

1. Amano, K. "Formation of the Act of Analyzing Syllabic Structure of Words and Its Relation to Learning Japanese Syllabic Characters (Kanamoji)," *Japanese Journal of Educational Psychology*, 18 (1970), 12-25.
2. Muraishi, S. "Acquisition of Reading Japanese Syllabic Characters in Preschool Children in Japan," 20th International Congress of Psychology, 1972.
3. Muraishi, S. "A Study of Educational Psychology on Children's Stroke Orders," *Study of Language*, 5 (1974), 242-262.
4. Muraishi, S., and K. Amano. *Reading and Writing Ability in Preschool Children*, 1972.
5. National Language Research Institute. *The Language Ability of Children in the Prereading Period*, 1954.
6. Results of investigations of the National Language Research Institute, unpublished data, 1954.

Sequence and Structure in a System with Consistent Sound-Symbol Correspondence

Dina Feitelson
University of Haifa
Mount Carmel, Haifa
Israel

In an impressive study on comparative reading, Downing (2) comments on the fact that some of the contributors who described the initial stages of reading acquisition in consistent systems like Finnish, Japanese, or Hebrew tended to assert that learning to decode in their respective language was easier than in a less consistent language such as English. Let us look for crucial differences between consistent and nonconsistent systems, which give rise to such assertions.

Learning to decode in a nonconsistent system means that the beginning reader has to acquire a staggering amount of information. Moreover, in a way the task is infinite. Even when the process is already well under way and a great deal of material has been covered, further contingencies remain for the learner to meet. Also, a very experienced reader might still come upon a word which he will not automatically know how to pronounce. This could never happen to an experienced reader in a consistent system. Sometimes the reader may not know the meaning of a word he has never met before, yet he will always be able to sound it out correctly.

Thus, one of the most pertinent qualities of a consistent system is that the number of contingencies is strictly limited. The body of knowledge to be acquired is always finite and, often, surprisingly small. In learning Hiragana—the syllable script with which reading instruction starts in Japan—all the child has to learn is forty-six symbol-sound relationships. Moreover, as each symbol represents a syllable, rather than a single letter like in alphabetic writing, blending is no problem. Small wonder that learning to decode is not considered very difficult in Japan, and that there is no illiteracy (9).

To sum up—the difference between learning to decode in consistent and nonconsistent systems is mainly that quantitatively, the learner in a consistent system has to learn infinitely less in acquiring the same competency—namely, the ability to pronounce correctly every word of one's mother tongue upon seeing that word in writing. Qualitatively, the little which has to be learned is less complex than in a nonconsistent system.

Someone who has had no first hand experience in teaching decoding in a consistent system may find it hard to accept such generalisations, especially in view of the lack of well-designed comparative studies to corroborate them. Therefore, it might be best at this stage to resort to a few examples.

The crucial point to remember is that, the more consistent a system

Figure 1.

is, the more often there will be a one-to-one correlation between grapheme and phoneme; in other words, between a letter and its sound value. Thus, in German, the grapheme *A* is always pronounced *ä*, and *M* always *m*. Figure 1 shows the first reading page of a Viennese primer.

The grapheme *I* is always pronounced *i* (see Figure 2).

Figure 2.

Hopefully, these examples help to provide an insight into the simplicity of the task faced by a beginning reader in a consistent system. Moreover, they may have conveyed an initial appreciation of the enormous power that careful sequencing can have under such circumstances.

The sound of the grapheme T is only and always t (see Figures 3 and 4).

TIM

MIMI __ MIT TIM .

MAMA __ MIT MIMI.
MAMI __ MIT MIMI.

Figure 3.

Sequence and Structure

SEQUENCE AND STRUCTURE IN CONSISTENT SYSTEMS

On the assumption that in any consistent system the amount of information which has been acquired by the beginning reader is indeed finite, it seems that it should be possible to experiment with different approaches to sequencing and structuring this information. Maybe it is not too ambitious to hope that in time it will be possible to discover general principles which could be applicable to initial learning

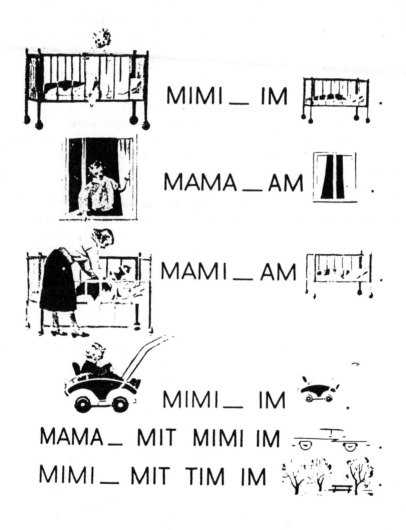

Figure 4.

sequences in more than a single language. Even the mere search for such principles could become an impetus for well-conducted comparative research efforts (3).

It is noticeable that initial learning approaches developed in different consistent systems sometimes show surprising similarities. They also seem to bear evidence of consistent efforts at developing efficient strategies. It may well be that the very success of several of these strategies precluded the next step; namely, fully controlled experimentation with different alternatives. With the latter aim in mind, we will describe the assumptions developed within the context of sequencing and structuring initial learning experiences in Hebrew.

REDUCING POTENTIAL SOURCES OF COGNITIVE
CONFUSION IN THE INITIAL STAGE

Evidence from a variety of writing systems seems to show that the more it is possible to reduce the amount of informational input the child is exposed to in his initial decoding experiences, the better he will be able to focus on the task at hand. Downing discusses one aspect of this assumption when he assumes that a concurrent introduction of capital and lowercase letters creates an unnecessary and, moreover, avoidable difficulty for the beginning reader (2). In i.t.a. this difficulty is dealt with by using one symbol, varying only slightly in size, for both capital and lowercase versions. The Viennese example we saw before, clearly indicates that their reading experts share the same view. Their solution was to use only capital letters in the initial stage. Lowercase letters are introduced only when the decoding of capital letters has already been achieved.

We shall return later to further implications of these practices and concentrate, meanwhile, on a second aspect of the Viennese material. Not only is informational input reduced by excluding temporarily the lowercase script, but meaningful initial decoding sequences are also achieved with the use of an absolute minimum of letters; in fact, only two. Introduction of further letter symbols proceeds slowly in strictly structured sequences. A glimpse of the table of contents of the Viennese primer shows that usually the pace is about two letter symbols a week. Letter combinations which have phonetic value of their own, for instance, *ei* or *sch,* are treated like single letters and allotted extra time.

Most modern Hebrew schemes proceed in exactly the same way. The first meaningful words are structured and decoded by combinations of one consonant with one vowel. Introduction of further letters is sequenced in such a way that each new letter contributes further word combinations (4).

Educators dealing with consistent systems in which the informational input which has to be acquired is much smaller than in nonconsistent systems, seem to feel that at the initial stage a further drastic reduction of information input is in order. In order to enable the student to apply his full potential to the main issue at hand—decoding—the act is simplified to the extent that it no longer constitutes a natural reading situation.

TRANSFER TO FURTHER CODES

An untested assumption, inherent in the practices just described, is that once the art of decoding is acquired, transferring the new skill to additional codes will be relatively easy. Thus, it is only in the initial stage that the complexities of a natural reading situation are simplified. A little later they are reintroduced gradually. In Vienna, lowercase letters used to be introduced in the second half of a child's first year at school. Cursive writing was also introduced the same year.

In Israel, the child normally meets three kinds of letters during his first year at school. A simplified alphabet is used in the initial stage, ordinary print follows after a few months, and then cursive writing is introduced (see Figure 5). During the next few years the child will

FIRST   GRADE

SIMPLIFIED   ALPHABET

בַּחַג   לִי

בַּחַג   לִי

REGULAR   PRINT

פִּתְאוֹם הוֹצִיא הַקּוֹף הַגָּדוֹל אֶת יָדוֹ מִבֵּין

הַסּוֹרְגִים וְתָפַס אֶת הַכּוֹבַע שֶׁל הַיֶּלֶד, קָפַץ

אֶל הָעֵץ וְהִתְחִיל לִקְרֹעַ אֶת הַכּוֹבַע.

CURSIVE   WRITING

הֶנֶּה בִּירָ-כְּנֶסֶת כְּנֶסֶת

Figure 5.

proceed to writing without vowels (the kind of shorthand used in everyday life) and to "Rashi," which is used in religious studies. Foreign alphabets follow a little later—English in Grade 5 and Arabic one to two years later (see Figure 6).

ENGLISH

The boys are sleeping.
They are playing football.
They are eating breakfast.

ARABIC

שעור ד

مُحَمَّد (د)

وَأَقَامَ مُحَمَّدٌ صلَّمَ فِي بَنِي سَعْدٍ إِلَى الْخَامِسَةِ مِنْ

عُمْرِهِ يَمْتَصُّ مِنْ جَوِّ ٱلْبَادِيَةِ ٱلطَّلِقِ رُوحَ الْمُرِّيَّةِ

Figure 6.

UNIT OF INSTRUCTION AND BLENDING

Recent work in English (6, 8, 10) confirms conclusions derived, by way of classroom experimentations in Hebrew, regarding the respective roles of letter names and letter sounds in initial decoding. According to both, the symbol-sound correspondences seem most efficient as basic units of instruction. On introduction, each new consonant is immediately blended with all vowels previously acquired to forestall future blending difficulties. New vowels are treated similarly (4). Once again, the Viennese material can serve as an effective illustration of this process.

Several further sequence-structure considerations such as concurrent or consecutive introduction of letters with identical or similar sound values, the catering to specific problem situations of a given script like the size and position of vowels in Hebrew, and many more have already been discussed elsewhere and need not be repeated here (3, 4, 5). Let us, therefore, proceed to one further point of interest.

THE PREDECODING STAGE

Once initial reading is seen as a tightly structured sequence, it becomes relevant to ask whether there is any one stage in a child's developmental cycle which is especially opportune to the introduction of this sequence, and also in what way the child should be prepared for this learning experience. MacGinitie's penetrating discussion of reading readiness research puts questions such as these in their proper perspective (7); however, few facts are available at present. Research by Calfee et al. (1) shows that visual discrimination of one letter from another is attained by a majority of children by kindergarten age. When one realises that in consistent systems the unit of instruction is indeed most often single letters, it becomes apparant that most children will not be in need of special visual discrimination exercises.

On the other hand, we need to pay serious heed to Thorndike's penetrating analysis and warning that "performance in reading, at least after the basic decoding skills are mastered, is primarily an indicator of the general level of the individual's thinking and reasoning processes" so that generally meager intellectual processes are apt to stand in the way of further development in reading and consequently "a wide range of further learning" (11). If this is so, it would seem that it is not specific subskills which should be taught in the predecoding stage. On the contrary, time and effort could be put to better use if they were invested in efforts aimed at promoting cognitive and emotional growth.

REFERENCES

1. Calfee, R. C., R. S. Chapman, and R. L. Venezky. "How a Child Needs to Think to Learn to Read," in Lee Gregg (Ed.), Cognition in Learning and Memory. New York: Wiley, 1972.
2. Downing, John. Comparative Reading. New York: Macmillan, 1973.
3. Feitelson, Dina. "Linguistic and Psychosocial Variables in Beginning Reading," paper presented at 20th International Congress on Psychology, Tokyo, 1972.
4. Feitelson, Dina. "Structuring the Teaching of Reading According to Major Features of the Language and Its Script," Elementary English, 42 (1965), 870-877.
5. Feitelson, Dina. "Teaching Reading to Culturally Disadvantaged Children," Reading Teacher, 22 (1968), 55-61. Also in E. E. Ekwall (Ed.), Factors in the Psychology of Reading. New York: Merrill, 1973.
6. Jenkins, J. R., R. B. Baufell, and L. M. Jenkins. "Comparisons of Letter Name and Letter Sound Training as Transfer Variables," American Educational Research Journal, 9 (January 1972), 75-86.
7. MacGinitie, Walter H. "Evaluating Readiness for Learning to Read: A Critical Review and Evaluation of Research," Reading Research Quarterly, 4 (Spring 1969), 396-410.
8. Rystrom, Richard. "Perception of Vowel Letter Sound Relationships by First Grade Children," Reading Research Quarterly, 9 (1973-1974), 170-185.
9. Sakamoto, Takahiko. "Japan," in John Downing (Ed.), Comparative Reading. New York: Macmillan, 1973.
10. Samuels, Jay. "The Effect of Letter Name Knowledge on Learning to Read," American Educational Research Journal, 9 (January 1972), 65-74.
11. Thorndike, Robert L. "Reading as Reasoning," Reading Research Quarterly, 9 (1973-1974), 135-147.

Sequence and Structure in a System with Problematic Sound-Symbol Correspondence

Joyce M. Morris
London, England

For historical, cultural, and commercial reasons, English is the most international of languages. It is the mother tongue or first language of approximately 250 million people, and authorities such as Quirk (7) estimate that a further 100 million have a working knowledge of English as a foreign language. In short, English is the most widely understood of all languages, although Chinese can claim a greater number of native speakers.

At the same time, English is recognized as a comparatively difficult language to master in its written form. This is so even for native speakers, as demonstrated by the considerable proportion who fail to achieve the lowest defined level of functional literacy in countries with well-established systems of compulsory education. For example, in Britain today there is reason to believe that at least 2 million adults are either unable to read and write, or cannot do so as well as the average nine-year old. Furthermore, this figure was not seriously challenged when recently published in a policy document called *A Right to Read: Action for a Literate Britain* (1). Indeed, the British government appears to have accepted it, and has already allocated a million pounds toward better provision for teaching adults to read and write.

A SOUND FOUNDATION FOR LITERACY

Even though it is essential to help adults who suffer from the crippling handicap of illiteracy, it is even more important to take preventative measures to ensure that all educable children build a sound foundation for literacy during their early schooling. There is a good deal of evidence from research (4), that children who fail to do this have a very poor prognosis. They rarely succeed in subsequent school life, and the majority inevitably join the ranks of illiterate adults who are unemployed or who are desperately clinging to a dwindling percentage of unskilled jobs.

THE NEED FOR SEQUENCE AND STRUCTURE

Building a sound foundation for literacy is not easy. For more than a decade, leading members of the United Kingdom Reading Association have stressed the need for sequence and structure in the teaching of reading, especially in primary schools. But so far, their well-intentioned counsel, though backed by reputable research, has not had the desired, widespread effect on classroom practice. There are many reasons for this, but perhaps the following three will suffice to illustrate the problem.

First, in Britain, notions of sequence and structure tend to be associated with rigid, curriculum centered education. Hence, they are unacceptable to many progressive teachers who, if successful, take just pride in their child-centered approach with its emphasis on discovery learning motivated by spontaneous interests.

Second, the professional training of British teachers has hitherto been oriented toward educational psychology and child development. Usually, training does not include a comprehensive course on reading which would cover such topics as the nature of the English language, linguistic processes, and skills. Accordingly, without explicit knowledge of what the learning task involves, it is understandable that inexperienced teachers often fail to appreciate the importance of a structured, sequential programme of instruction.

Third, by tradition, British teachers are free to decide their own methods, materials, and media. The best of them do so within a framework which ensures the progress of individual pupils. But sequence in learning is not guaranteed as children pass from class to class, because each successive teacher can exercise the traditional freedom of choice. Similarly, head teachers are not obliged to plan a school reading programme. although many do so in consultation with staff members.

It is unlikely that British teachers would ever work toward a government sponsored programme for reading instruction, or even one promoted by their local education authority. Yet, there are dangers in the present system as long as the need for sequence and structure is not universally recognized and teachers are trained accordingly.

THE LEARNING TASK

Against this background, let us consider the nature of the learning task for native English speakers during the first five or six years of their school lives.

NATURE OF THE ENGLISH LANGUAGE

Whatever their mother tongue, children find it relatively more difficult to master its written form than its spoken form. There are many obvious reasons for this, including the greater formality of written language and the less dramatic clues to meaning which it presents.

There is a wider gulf between speech and print in English than in other alphabetic writing systems. Twenty-six letters (graphemes) are used in various, not entirely consistent, ways to represent forty-four speech sounds (phonemes), depending on the dialect considered. This degree of mismatch is partly due to the fact that the prononciation of English has changed markedly over the centuries, while the orthography has remained relatively static. Moreover, English has many words borrowed from other languages.

In contrast, no other language possesses such a simple syntax and grammar.

1. There are no arbitrary genders, except, for example, in the rare instance of referring to a ship as she.
2. Nouns have no cases, except for the genitive, indicated by the possessive apostrophe.
3. Agreement between adjectives and nouns is unnecessary.
4. The definite article has only one written form.
5. Verbs have few inflexions and tend to be regular, with endings s, ing, and ed.
6. Most words in common use have fewer than four syllables.
7. English provides a wide choice of vocabulary to achieve precise expression of thought and to convey subtle overtones of association and feeling.

Thus, the nature of English is such that its major disadvantage is at the level of phoneme-grapheme correspondence, and this has to be tackled during the earliest stages of literacy acquisition and also has to be tackled systematically throughout children's schooling if they are to become not only effective readers but, as Peters (6) has shown, effective spellers as well.

LANGUAGE PROCESSES AND SKILLS

Let us turn to the language processes and skills involved in becoming literate. A detailed analysis reveals that they are intrinsically complex and interrelated in complicated ways. In short, like any other language, English consists of a number of linked systems, and structure can be seen in it at all levels from the phonological to the semantic.

Unfortunately, teachers of young children cannot concentrate solely on developing language at its most concrete, sound-symbol level; they must also develop it at its most abstract, semantic level. Otherwise, children will not grasp the fact that words have multiple meanings and the written language, in general, is a medium for intelligible communication.

Reading skills may be classified into two broad categories. First, there are the skills or abilities which belong to the repertoire of literacy, whatever the learner's language. These are too numerous to mention but they may be grouped under main headings such as word recognition, comprehension, interpretation, appreciation, critical evaluation, and study skills.

The second broad category of skills are those which are language-tied or specific to the acquisition of literacy in a particular language. For example, the ability to discriminate, name, and write the multigraphs or various letter forms of the English alphabet.

THE TEACHING TASK

Clearly, the nature of the learning task depends on the nature of the language involved and its orthography. This holds true with regard to the teaching task; although, such a seemingly obvious fact is not always recognized. For example, teachers who put their faith in whole-word methods and basal schemes with a predominantly look-say approach are virtually ignoring the fact that the English writing system is based on the phonemic principle, and is not logographic like Chinese. Similarly, those who do not accept the notion of sequence and structure are disregarding the fact that English itself is highly patterned and structured.

None of this would matter much if it were not a vital part of the teaching task to ensure that young children start, as soon as possible, to internalise a model of traditional orthography. As it is, youngsters are frequently left to sort out sound-symbol relationships for themselves with predictable consequences in terms of frustration, cognitive confusion, and failure. Not surprisingly, many children reject learning to read because it appears to them to be an illogical exercise which severely taxes the memory.

THE PRELITERACY STAGE OF DEVELOPMENT

When five-year-olds start school in Britain, their speech patterns naturally exhibit dialect and social class differences in language usage, style, and content. Their understanding of concepts such as reading and writing also varies. Accordingly, it is suggested that reception class teachers should use a language experience approach to literacy of the British kind as described by Goddard (2). Ideally, this should be of the purest form; that is, conducted through the medium of children's own oral compositions recorded by their teachers. But language experience approaches of a highly contrived type, such as Breakthrough to Literacy (3), are also recommended because, among other things, they give children an insight into some purposes of written language and its relationship to spoken language.

Needless to say, the preliteracy stage is a time to foster appropriate habits of handling books and a conscious awareness of certain conventions involved in their construction and use; for example, page-by-page, top-to-bottom, and left-to-right direction. It is also a time to develop a child's ability to "read" pictures per se, and as a prelude to using pictures as clues to verbal content.

INTRODUCTION TO BASIC MECHANICS

After children have been engaged successfully in the essential motivating, linguistic, and related skill-developing activities of the preliteracy stage, they are ready to learn precisely how to form alphabet letters, and to begin acquiring a knowledge of how speech sounds (phonemes) are represented by letters (graphemes).

Plenty of opportunities should be given to finger trace the letters, and to identify the phonemes they represent at the beginning of words. At the risk of being controversial, it is also recommended that the names of the letters be taught for, among other reasons, the identification of their graphic shapes and ease of communication in the teaching-learning situation.

SYSTEM OF PROGRESSION

Children who are ready for the next stage can identify the initial sounds in spoken words and relate them to corresponding graphemes. They can also write the capital and lowercase forms of the alphabet letters when engaged in language experience activities involving the copying of their own words, phrases, and sentences. In short, they have reached a stage when they must come to grips with the first basic spelling patterns of English if they are to make progress in reading and writing other than by simply memorising words in response to conditioning techniques.

At this point, because of the nature of the orthography, many children begin to experience failure. Moreover, if adequate measures are not taken, their chances are not good for growing up to be literate adults. Therefore, it would seem best to focus attention on a new system of spelling pattern progression designed to give maximum support to children struggling to internalise a model of traditional orthography. This does not mean that in the suggested programme all other aspects of reading would not be covered. It simply concentrates on a possible solution to the problems posed by what was earlier described as the "major disadvantage" of English.

The system is based on a detailed description of the English writing system, taking as its starting point the 24 consonant and 20 vowel phonemes of Received Pronunciation. It was devised with two observations in mind: 1) that monosyllables are a distinctive feature of English and they include among their number (about 10,000) some of the commonest words; and 2) that the correspondence between vowel phonemes and graphemes is a source of much greater difficulty for learners than that between consonant phonemes and graphemes.

Thus, the system begins with a division of monosyllables into major sets as follows.

Set A   Words in which the vowel letter corresponds to a so-called short vowel sound; e.g., *cat, hen, pig, dog, pup.*

Set B   Words in which marker, modifying, or magic e signals that the preceding vowel letter corresponds to a so-called long vowel sound; e.g., *lane, kite, robe.*

Set BB Words in which vowel diagraphs correspond to so-called long vowel sounds; e.g., *nail, eel, road.*

Set C   Words in which the rest of the vowel phonemes are represented in different ways; e.g., *hoop, cart.*

Within each of the above sets of spelling patterns, the system develops monosyllabic words with consonant clusters of various kinds. For example, the sequence in Set A is as follows:

(a) Double letters or their equivalent; *puff,* back.

(b) Consonant clusters which occur both at the beginning and at the ending of words; *skip, risk; spot, lisp; stop, lost.*

(c) Other consonant clusters of two or three letters which occur at the beginning or at the end of words; *club, crust, scrap, strap; steps, stands, blinks.*

(d) Consonant diagraphs which occur both at the beginning and the ending of words; *ship, fish; chop, latch; thin, moth; then, with.*

Next, within each of the major sets of spelling patterns, disyllabic words are introduced; for instance, present tense forms of verbs, such as *slipping* (Set A), *making* (Set B), *painting* (Set BB), and *shouting* (Set C).

The system also allows for the sequential introduction of words containing so-called silent letters, in addition to silent marker e words. Thus, words such as *knit* and *thumb* (Set A) are followed by *knave* and *comb* (Set B).

Hopefully, the system has been detailed (5) to indicate how it will help children build knowledge that there is pattern and order in written language. In consequence, the task of learning to read and spell will not be as daunting to them as it would at first seem to be from the confusing variety of printed words they see in and out of school. What is more, through this system, the teacher can provide the reader with a sequential, structured programme, despite the problematic sound-symbol correspondence of English. In doing so, the chances of a successful outcome for their joint endeavours will be greatly increased.

REFERENCES
1. B.A.S. *A Right to Read: Action for a Literate Britain*. London: British Association of Settlements, 1974.
2. Goddard, Nora. *Literacy: Language Experience Approaches*. London and Basingstoke: Macmillan, 1974.
3. Mackey, David, Brian Thompson, and Pamela Schaub. *Breakthrough to Literacy*. London: Longman, 1970.
4. Morris, Joyce M. *Standards and Progress in Reading*. Slough, Bucks: National Foundation for Educational Research in England and Wales, 1966.
5. Morris, Joyce M. *Language in Action Resource Book*. London and Basingstoke: Macmillan, 1974.
6. Peters, Margaret L. *Success in Spelling*. Cambridge: Cambridge Institute of Education, 1970.
7. Quirk, Randolph. *The Use of English*. London: Longman, 1968.

The Teaching of Spelling

Margaret L. Peters
Cambridge Institute of Education
Cambridge, England

In the 1967 *Review of Educational Research* it was noted that one limitation in spelling research has been neglect of the teacher variable. Little had been done to investigate the quality of the teacher as indexed by teaching grades or by survey of methods actually employed to teach spelling. One of the objectives of the writer's research (14) was to discover the attitudes of teachers toward spelling; how, if at all, they teach it; and whether what they do not do bears any relationship to children's progress. These research findings are distilled in this paper, supplemented by subsequent work on the nature of the spelling process.

SPELLING IS LANGUAGE SPECIFIC

It is a truism to say that spelling is language specific. Obviously, the orthography of each language is idiosyncratic. To say that one can spell in one language is not to say that one can spell in another. To be able to spell in a particular language, it is necessary to have internalised the serial probability of letters in that language. At an international seminar, Bruner (2) quotes an experiment he conducted with Harcourt on the ability to handle nonsense letter strings, in the style of different languages, revealing a real difference in ability favouring one's mother tongue, in reproducing nonsense in one's own language. For example, it is easy to place such words as mjolkkor, klook, épilement, fattaloni. Even to the naïve linguist, the words look as if they belong to a particular language. In other words, for a particular language, one knows what letter strings are likely to occur and which letter string will inevitably follow another. As Wallach (19) showed, good spellers have learned a coding system based on the probabilities of letters occurring in certain sequences—a coding system that, as Bruner says, "goes beyond words."

Code matters much more in spelling than it does in reading. Although in reading the reader is in fact decoding, he is doing so with the support of considerable redundancies through semantic and syntactic cues that help him to corroborate what he decodes. In spelling, the code alone matters. The child knows what he wants to say. To write this he must know the code and be able to encode; for example, he must know the only letter string possible which can be used at that point, a letter string determined by the preceding and succeeding letter strings.

THE NATURE OF THE CODE

Knowing the code entails the learning of letter strings that occur as a result of the conventions in the writing pattern of a particular language. Once internalised, these letter strings are more or less stable. When completely stable, the individual writes without hesitation. The pen flows as the individual thinks, and no spelling strategy is employed except when the individual is caught up by a word hitherto only present in his passive or orally active vocabulary.

At the other end of the continuum, spelling is not stable and the individual is faced at every letter string with decision making, often amounting to a conflict situation. Should it be *au* or *aw*? Should it be *c* or *s*? In such situations, and with some children, this decision making is often not at a conscious level and the child writes *au* or *aw*, *c* or *s* arbitrarily. In most languages, there is certainty that some letter sequences can occur and that some cannot. The good speller has learned, and uses habitually, those sequences that can and do occur. The poor speller has no knowledge of what can or cannot occur in his own particular language. In other words, he has not internalised the code. Obviously, the more regular a writing system, the easier it is for the individual to write acceptable letter strings, as in Danish or Spanish or Czech.

The English writing system is irregular but perhaps not as irregular as has been commonly supposed. It has been taken for granted, hitherto, that English contains 20-30 percent of graphophonemically irregular words that are completely unpredictable in their spelling. Albrow (1) has described the English system so finely that there is at least the theoretical possibility of knowing whether letter combinations can occur in English. But even if such a system were infallible, it is impossible for young children learning to spell to be expected to speculate on whether the spelling of a word is theoretically possible, since it demands an advanced cognitive level beyond that of the child at the age when he is normally learning to spell. This kind of speculation is more than the mere following of rules which have been shown to be of doubtful value in learning to spell (11).

THE SPELLING TASK

What, then, must the child do in order to spell correctly in a graphophonemically irregular writing system when he is faced with innumerable possibilities at every successive point in the spelling of a word? It is not enough to teach him lists of words, even if such words are selected from word counts (and many lists are remote from the words children want to use in their writing). As Fernald wrote a generation ago, such lists "will always fail to supply the particular word a person should learn at a particular time." A child who is writing needs a particular word at that moment and if the creative thought is to flow, he needs it without having to look it up in his word book or dictionary. What then is his strategy? As has been pointed out, he is too immature to speculate on the theoretical acceptability of the spelling of the word. Therefore, he must have the word or the letter strings of the word at his fingertips. The grapheme must flow as he subarticulates the word or part of the word. It is crucial that the child should be courageous in attacking these letter strings, for it is the confident speller that is the competent speller.

Spelling has been shown to be a skill very unlike reading (15). In spelling the child is, or is not, "on the way to becoming a good speller." In other words, he has either acquired the coding system and writes in a fairly close approximation to English, or he has not, and writes words randomly. Of course, the child who is on the way to becoming a good speller will present alternative spellings which are good errors since they are according to spelling precedent; for example, *saucer* might be written as *sawser* or *sorcer*. On the other hand, a child who is not on the way to becoming a good speller may offer, as some ten-year-olds wrote, *syer*, *sascaue*, and *saroer*. A child who has acquired the coding system is confident, even though he is not yet completely infallible, and as he becomes more and more accustomed to probable sequences in words, he will write with closer approximation to English.

The coding system then, is another way of saying there is a probability of certain letter sequences occurring. Internalisation of this coding system depends on a child's visual perception of word form, which can be acquired subconsciously (e.g., from advertisements), peripherally (subliminally or outside an immediate fixation), or by teacher direction. It depends on some form of imagery, in the sense that the shorter the exposure and the longer the sequence exposed, the more the individual must rely on some form of imagery to reconstitute the sequence. It is what Hebb termed "serial reconstruction." In 1968, Hebb (7) suggested that the difference between those who have little imagery and those who have much may not be a difference in the mechanism of thinking, but a difference in the retrievability of the image. In the case of spelling, it has been shown that training can help to retrieve the image. Given two weeks' training, Radaker (16) found that one year later the imagery trained groups scored significantly higher on spelling tests than did the control group, showing that the training of visual imagery is effective in improving spelling performance over long periods of time.

In analysing imagery, Hebb (7) emphasises the motor-component in imagery as much as in perception. What he calls part-perceptions are punctuated by motor excitations produced by peripheral stimulation. One of them becomes liminal and the result is eye-movement followed by another part-perception. That imagery is so analagous to perception, is highly relevant to spelling. In the first place, as Hebb says, the child cannot read backwards in imagery as quickly as he can from the printed word. "There is sequential left to right organization of the parts within the apparently unitary presentation corresponding to the order of presentation in perception as one reads English from left to right," and, of course, imaginal reading is basic to spelling. The incompleteness of such imagery is symptomatic of spelling difficulties. The individual can part-perceive a word and be held up when a new fixation does not produce a clear image. What one has to ask is why the new fixation does not produce an image. Is it because, in earlier perception of the word, attention was not directed to subsequent parts of the word—particularly to what has traditionally been known as "hard spots"; i.e., word sequences with possible and reasonable alternatives? The writer's own investigation would make this a plausible hypothesis, since rational correction technique which is entirely concerned with attention to hard spots is conducive to good spelling. Secondly, attention to serial probability of words, that is, to common sequences perceived peripherally in reading and daily life, facilitates imaging, and particularly what has earlier been termed reconstituting of a word or as Hebb put it, "sequential integration."

What Hebb says about perception is relevant in that there seems to be one aspect of the perceptual process that really does affect spelling. Hartmann (6) spoke of it as a particular form of looking which was quite distinct from any specific sensory ability or facility in integrating such sensory abilities. This increasing ability to perceive and reconstruct in imagery a word, or better still a sequence of words, is a vital step toward spelling competence. This ability depends on training the child to increase his span of apprehension; for example, not copying a letter at a time or even a word at a time, but taking in a whole phrase or line of text and storing it in the short term memory before reproduction in writing.

So far, the spelling task has been seen as the internalisation of a coding system particularly susceptible to visual learning with its dependence on imagery. There is a very close link between the visual and the motor aspects of spelling, if spelling is to be literally at the child's fingertips. Throughout the writer's research, the necessity for the teacher to teach handwriting is abundantly clear and a thorough understanding of sensory and motor organization with kinesthetic feedback is essential (20). A generation ago, Schonell (18) pointed out that the importance of the visual, auditory, and articulatory elements in spelling must be "firmly cemented in writing"; and Fernald (4) emphasizes this in her amalgam of sensory input. Teachers can avoid one area of conflict uncertainty by teaching formation of letters, and more important still, letter sequences in writing, and by encouraging swift writing—for the two are not incompatible. The careful writer tends to be the swift writer; and the good handwriter tends to be the good speller.

The competent speller, however, has a good spelling self-image and this is something Lecky (9) quoted as a paradigm example of human self-consistency. This good self-image is something to be cherished; for without it, an individual will write reluctantly, circumlocute, and, hence, write less precisely or not write at all.

THE TASK OF THE TEACHER

McKay and others (10) point out that "the traditional spelling lesson is an ad hoc approach to the task of internalisation and one which for lack of awareness of the working of the orthography falls back on random procedures and on rote learning." There is empirical evidence for this (14) in that greater progress in spelling is made where the teacher pursues a systematic, and not haphazard approach to the skill. Progress is made not only in quantitative terms of spellings that are right or wrong, but in the way children taught by a systematic teacher approximate more closely to spelling precedent in their own language. It is not too strong a statement to make that it is the policy and behaviour of the teacher of children in the middle years that determines whether children will spell badly or well in later years. This is not to say that the systematic teacher is uncreative. Indeed, the more linguistically divergent the teacher, and the greater the "play with words," the more experienced the children will become in writing letter sequences in different combinations and the more certain their spelling will become. It is, therefore, necessary to consider the responsibilities of the teacher when advocating a systematic rather than an ad hoc procedure in the teaching of spelling, and in the light of the foregoing arguments in this paper.

THE TEACHER'S RESPONSIBILITIES

Awareness of the working of the orthography. In order for teachers to be in a position to direct children's attention to likenesses and differences in word structure, it is obvious that they must, as McKay and others stress, be "made aware of the working of the orthography." One excellent way for teachers to become aware is presented in Morris' Resource Book (12). The fact that this taxonomy of spelling patterns is presented to children learning to read is of motivational value to teachers.

List learning. Teachers whose children learn to spell do teach lists; these lists are derived from children's writing needs, from words "asked for" in the course of children's own writing, and from lists prepared by the teacher in relation to words the children ask for—not from printed lists which would seem to have a detrimental effect on children's spelling progress. The teacher who uses printed lists probably believes her responsibility for teaching spelling ends there. The receptive teacher, who is attuned to the child's writing needs, delights in words and her awareness of word structure pervades her teaching.

Awareness of the importance of imagery. Teachers have to be aware of what children have to learn (the content of lists) and how they learn (the method). The importance of visual imagery in the reconstituting of seen words has been previously mentioned, and it is crucial that children should be trained to look at words with the intention to retain them and then to write them from memory.

The necessity to increase children's span of apprehension of letter sequences. The importance of training children to increase the span of letters, words, phrases, and sentences cannot be overemphasized. This is training and it is the duty of the teacher to help children gain this skill.

The necessity of teaching handwriting. Teachers must be aware of the interdependence of spelling and writing skills, for spelling ability is valueless unless one uses the ability in writing. The teaching of swift, certain formation of letters and sequences of letters is an essential duty of the teacher if her children are to write confidently and competently.

The self-image. Confident children have good self-images which are nurtured by the teacher and the parents. Hence, the teacher does not over-correct, but studies the children's spelling and uses the errors as miscues to guide his own teaching strategies (15).

CONCLUSION

Children will achieve spelling success 1) if the teacher is aware of essentials, consistent in her attitude, and sensitive in her response to children's requests for words; 2) if she finds the optimal study rate [not too much since limiting study time may well work to the advantage of the learner (5)]; 3) if she is rational in correction technique and encourages autonomy in the trying out of words; 4) if she teaches well-formed and swift handwriting; and 5) if she inspires a self-image as a good speller.

As Richmond (17), confirming Horn (8), points out, adequate research is available for spelling instruction. Marksheffel (12) adds, however, "The problem of how to get teachers to apply the findings of research to their classroom practices remains."

REFERENCES

1. Albrow, K. H. *The English Writing System: Notes Towards a Description.* Longman for the Schools Council, 1973.
2. Bruner, J. S., and R. A. F. Harcourt. "Going Beyond the Information Given," unpublished manuscript, 1953.
3. Bruner, J. S., et al. *Studies in Cognitive Growth.* New York: Wiley, 1966.
4. Fernald, G. M. *Remedial Techniques in Basic School Subjects.* New York: McGraw-Hill, 1943.
5. Gilbert, L. C., and D. W. Gilbert. "Training for Speed and Accuracy of Visual Perception in Learning to Spell," *California University Publications in Education,* 7 (1942), 351-426.
6. Hartmann, G. W. "The Relative Influence of Visual and Auditory Factors in Spelling Ability," *Journal of Educational Psychology,* 22 (1931), 691-699.
7. Hebb, D. O. "Concerning Imagery," *Psychological Review,* 75 (1968), 466-477.
8. Horn, E. *Teaching Spelling,* What Research Says to the Teacher, No. 3. Washington, D.C.: National Education Association, 1954.
9. Lecky, P. *Self-Consistency, A Theory of Personality.* New York: Island Press, 1945.
10. Mackay, D., and B. Thompson. "The Initial Teaching of Reading and Writing," *Progress in Linguistics and English Teaching.* New York: Longman, 1968.
11. McLeod, M. E. "Rules in the Teaching of Spelling," *Studies in Spelling.* London: University of London Press, 1961.
12. Marksheffel, N. D. "Composition, Handwriting, and Spelling," *Review of Educational Research,* 34 (1964), 182-183.
13. Morris, J. M. *Resource Book for Language Project: Language in Action.* New York: Macmillan, 1974.
14. Peters, M. L. *Success in Spelling.* Cambridge, England: Cambridge Institute of Education, 1970.
15. Peters, M. L. *Manual of Diagnostic and Remedial Spelling.* New York: Macmillan, 1974.
16. Radaker, L. D. "The Effect of Visual Imagery Upon Spelling Performance," *Journal of Educational Research,* 1963, 370-372.
17. Richmond, A. E. "Children's Spelling Needs and the Implications of Research," *Journal of Experimental Education,* 24 (1960), 3-21.
18. Schonell, F. J. *Backwardness in the Basic Subjects.* Oliver and Boyd, 1942.
19. Wallach, M. A. "Perceptual Recognition of Approximations to English in Relation to Spelling Achievement," *Journal of Educational Psychology,* 1963, 57-62.
20. Wedell, K. *Learning and Perceptuo-Motor Disabilities in Children.* New York: Wiley, 1973.

Early Reading: Some Unexplained Aspects

Phillip Williams
Open University
Milton Keynes, England

In 1918 Lewis Terman described the reading development of an otherwise unknown infant called Martha. Martha was taught to read at the age of 14 months by learning the names of the capital letters. Not surprisingly, she found this rather difficult at first, so difficult that after she had struggled to learn four letters, instruction ceased for five months. The rest obviously did Martha good, for when she was nineteen months of age she managed to learn all the capital letters in three weeks. She then learned all the small letters in a further three weeks and began to learn whole words. In the next four months she acquired a sight vocabulary of 200 words and her rate of acquisition of new words was so good that after being shown 51 new words one day she correctly recognised 38 of them the following day.

This illustration is interesting for a number of reasons. You may have metaphorically raised your eyebrows in surprise at the thought of beginning to read by learning the capital letters. You may also have been appalled by the thought of starting with a child as young as fourteen months. You may have noticed the great benefit which accrued from stopping instruction when Martha obviously was not learning. Personally, I was much more interested in the rapid rate at which Martha acquired a sight vocabulary when her reading really started: 38 new words retained from one day's learning! But we know very little about the rate at which reading development occurs. The little we do know is linked to anecdotes about the reading development of very young children, and usually these are the reading prodigies, whose progress is so unusual that it is reported in the literature.

Several of these prodigies were described by Lynn (1) some years ago. Norbert Wiener, the American mathematician, learned all the letters in two days at the age of eighteen months. Francis Galton could identify all the capitals at twelve months of age. One example that I particularly liked, though it does not in fact relate to rate of reading growth, is that of a German child, one Otto Pohler, who noticed his own first name in a newspaper at the age of fifteen months. I have a vision of this precocious fifteen-month-old child scanning the Frankfurter Zeitung over his morning milk and Farex. Of course, he had a slight built-in advantage, as some of you have already spotted, since Otto is one of the very few first names that are entirely reversible. But the purpose of these illustrations is to point out that people have logged the reading growth of the prodigies, but not the reading growth of ordinary children. Is this rapid rate of growth in word recognition, which Martha showed, characteristic of the reading development of all children? Or does reading development in most children proceed at a much more steady and gentle rate?

In this paper I want to focus on one narrow aspect of reading growth—the development of word recognition skills. The middle and higher order skills of reading for comprehension, for appreciation of literature, for precise work, for cataloging, and for referencing, all depend on the basic skill of being able to recognise words.

Many children have their word recognition skills measured. Remedial teachers, teachers in infant schools, and educational psychologists, all happily use tests of word recognition which tell us something about the reading age level of children. Who has not read a report which states that the reading age of Johnny or Sally is 7.3 years? Six months later we look with interest to see if Sally's reading age has reached the magic total of 7.8 years. And if she were a retarded reader initially we would hope for the rate of progress which was somewhat better than her chronological age.

What do these reading age differences mean? What is the difference between a word recognition age of six years and one of seven years? Does it mean the same as the difference between a word recognition age of nine years and one of ten years? Dozens of research results in remedial education assume so and average out the gains shown. So do reports of remedial work. Do the skills which our children acquire between the years of five and six represent the same kinds of word recognition skills they acquire between the reading ages of ten and eleven? These are the questions which deserve exploration, and which knowledge of the reading growth of ordinary children would illuminate. In this paper, I want to report some findings which have a bearing on this and which emerged as a spin-off from the Schools Council Project in Compensatory Education held at the University College of Swansea.

This project was largely concerned with constructing a screening device for identifying school entrants needing special help and producing a language programme for use in infant schools in deprived areas. But the development of these materials gave the opportunity of working with a population of young children with whom contact was maintained across the three-year period of their infant schooling. We used this opportunity to measure regularly, for a small subsample of the main group, the way the development of reading skills took place across the period when the children were five to eight years of age. But we did not measure their word recognition skills as a reading age. What we did do was to adapt a technique used by the pioneers in the studies of language and try to estimate the number of words which the children could recognise each time we saw them. We did this by using a word recognition test which gave us information about the proportion of the words in the Concise Oxford Dictionary that each child could read each time. The test was a sample of the words in the dictionary and the children were required to pronounce the words following a procedure similar to that of any one of the standard word recognition tests. The results were expressed, therefore, not as a reading age, but as percentages of dictionary vocabulary; for example, a child's word recognition score might be expressed as 30 percent or 41 percent of dictionary vocabulary recognised correctly.

Those who are familiar with child development theory realise that this kind of approach—regular measurement of the skills of individual children across a period of time—is a longitudinal study and as such does have a number of theoretical advantages, in particular the ability to reveal growth spurts which the normal cross-sectional kind of investigation does not possess. We hoped, that this approach would enable us to see more clearly the way in which the word recognition skills of individual children grow. The three points which I think characterise the enquiry are: 1) we concentrated on a narrow aspect of development (the growth of word-recognition skills); 2) we rejected norm based measures as we were not interested in average performances (we used a measure which was criterion based); and 3) it was a longitudinal study and we measured individual children over a period of three years.

The work was done with a total of 64 children: 32 boys and 32 girls, 32 from schools in advantaged areas and 32 from schools in disadvantaged areas. (This kind of breakdown was done in order to give us the opportunity to do another sort of analysis, not relevant to this particular enquiry.) One of the 64 children dropped out and the remaining 63 were examined each term at average intervals of about three to four months over a three-year period. Children who entered infant schools in the autumn term were tested seven times each and children entering school in the spring and summer terms were tested five times each. The average age of the group on the first assessment was five years, six months and on the last assessment, seven years, four months.

When we examined the reading growth curves in individual children, we found several characteristic points about them. The first point is that the growth of reading vocabulary usually began very slowly, and then proceeded through a stage of rapid growth. The rapidity of some of the growth spurts that were shown was astonishing. The growth tailed off, to complete an S-shaped curve.

Not all children showed precisely this development. One child's development was zero across the whole period of the exercise. A second child's reading standard was already very high at the time he started infant school in his sixth year. The first child was at the early part of the growth curve and the second child, although he was only in infant school, nevertheless was completing his reading growth spurt. Some children were half way along the curve of reading growth, pulling out into the beginning part of the growth spurt. Most of the children were either demonstrating the start of word recognition growth or showing the beginning of the growth spurt or just beginning to come out of the growth spurt.

We were very interested in those children (15 in all) who, by the end of the study, had already reached a word recognition skill of at least 30 percent of dictionary vocabulary, and who could therefore be expected to show evidence of the growth spurt in reading. In terms of reading age, this 30 percent facility level is approximately a reading age of eight years.

For these 15 children, we calculated the maximum velocity of growth. This was done by working out the velocity of growth between each of the pairs of points at which we saw the children. The growth rate formula may be expressed thus: Velocity $= \frac{T2 - T1}{\text{Time}}$ where T1 and T2 represent the facility levels reached at each point of testing and time the interval between testing. Thus, a child whose reading vocabulary was 45 percent of the dictionary sample on one occasion and 55 percent three months later could be said to be demonstrating a velocity of 10 percent growth in three months, or a velocity of 40 percent growth per year. The fascinating point revealed is that most children who reach this 30 percent level already show a growth spurt which, at its maximum velocity, proceeds at a very high rate. If this maximum rate (60-79 percent) were to be prolonged, it would result in between two-thirds and three-quarters of the total dictionary vocabulary being added to the word recognition performance of these children within a year. This rate is not sustained but it does indicate the enormous speed at which word recognition skills are developed for a short period of time.

Notice also the individual variation. For two children there was a period in which the rate of acquisition of word recognition skills was proceeding at a rate of over 120 percent of dictionary vocabulary a year. The growth of word recognition is not the steady process which norm-based word recognition tests imply. It is subject to rapid spurts, some of which are very steep. In some cases, in a period of a few short months, these children acquired a word recognition vocabulary which is quite adequate for supporting all the higher and middle order reading skills anyone would wish to teach. It may be that this word recognition performance improves gently over the next years in school, but the rate of improvement is marginal in comparison with the enormous earlier growth during the reading spurt.

The next question we must ask is, "When does this maximum rate of acquisition occur?" We looked at the figures for maximum growth and related them to the size of the word recognition vocabulary at the time. For most children, the peak of word recognition growth occurs when the word recognition vocabulary is between 20 and 29 percent or about a quarter of the dictionary vocabulary. So it is when a child had acquired about a quarter of the dictionary vocabulary that his rate of growth proceeds very rapidly. Within a space of perhaps a few months, however, the growth of his word recognition skills starts to tail off.

So far we have been describing the situation. We need to be able to chart reading growth before we can hope to attempt to explain it. But a more important question than "How?" is "Why?" Why is it that spurts of this sort suddenly occur and then tail off?

It is possible that the spurt in growth of word recognition skills may be associated with the kind of language experiences children enjoy, the kind of teaching in the infant school, or a development in the child's knowledge of patterns which underlie the regularity of pronunciation in the English language. The particular investigation we were concerned with allowed us to investigate this last question, since among the other measures we were using to assess the development of children was a measure of their phonic skills. For this purpose we had used an experimental instrument called the Swansea Test of Phonic Skills (2) which assesses the extent to which a child can attach the correct pronunciation to 65 of the most commonly used letter combinations or single letters in the early reading process.

This enabled us to examine the extent to which a child's growth in word recognition skills is linked to growth in a number of phonic skills which he successfully mastered. It would be surprising, though possible, that a child might manage to enter the growth spurt of word recognition skills without having mastered adequately a fair proportion of the phonic skills. It would be more reasonable to find that the growth spurt was either preceded or parallelled by a growth in the knowledge which a child showed of phonic skills as measured by this particular instrument. We proceeded to examine this hypothesis.

First, we restricted our analysis to children who had mastered at least 29 of the 65 phonic elements measured by the scale. The test manual indicates that a score below 29 is not particularly meaningful in relation to accurate assessment of a child's knowledge of phonics. Above 29, the score becomes relatively unaffected by guessing and gives a clear indication of the number of phonic skills which a child can reasonably be expected to have mastered.

There was no pattern of development of phonic skills which was as consistent as the kind of S shaped growth spurt mentioned in relation to the acquisition of word recognition skills. Some children showed little progress throughout the period of assessment; others had acquired a reasonable competence by the time they entered the infant school. Other children showed a dramatic increase in knowledge of phonic skills during a very short period of time. Perhaps this is a case of particularly skilled teaching, or of a child for whom the reading process suddenly clicked. This led us to examine the velocity at which children acquire phonic skills.

The rate of growth of phonic skills did not show quite the same peak as was the case in the rate of growth of word recognition skills. Thus, the maximum rate of growth of phonic skills measured as number of phonic elements per month was spread fairly evenly over the range. Although there was wide variation, at least 13 of the 33 children showed maximum velocities of over 70 phonic elements gained per year, a remarkably high rate of acquisition. One child showed a rate of acquisition of phonic skills of more than 140 per year. Had that rate continued for any length of time, that child's knowledge of the phonic elements would have been virtually complete in a matter of months. One child for example, acquired a knowledge of 37 phonic elements in two months.

Now let us turn to the question we asked earlier. How does this acquisition of phonic skills relate to the reading spurt? Let us examine those 15 advanced readers who, at the end of the study had acquired a minimum of 30 percent of dictionary vocabulary and in many cases significantly more. (These were readers whose reading age was approximately eight years or above on standardised word recognition tests.) Remember that the ability to read 30 percent of dictionary vocabulary is a standard which appears when a child is well into the early part of the growth spurt. Now let us consider the occasion on which the 15 children first reached a score of 30 percent or more on the word recognition test, when their average score was in fact 38.6 percent, or just over one-third of the dictionary sample. At that point, their average score on the test of phonic skills was 58; that is, they were scoring at a very high level on this test. They could recognise 58 of the 65 phonic elements. When children are launched on the reading spurt, their knowledge of the significant phonic elements in the reading process is virtually complete.

Another way of looking at the relationship between phonic skills and word recognition ability is to look at the maximum rate of growth on both tests. Are children showing maximum rate of growth of the phonic skills at the same time as they are showing maximum rate of growth of word recognition ability? After all, the maximum rate of growth on the word recognition test could occur at about the 30 percent performance level. The occasion of maximum rate of growth on both tests coincided for only 4 of the 15 children. The remaining 11 children reached their maximum rate of growth in phonic skills before their maximum rate of growth in word recognition skills. No child showed maximum growth of word recognition skills before maximum growth of phonic skills. It seems that a child needs considerable facility in phonic skills, a good grasp of the phoneme-grapheme relationship, before he can enter the word recognition growth spurt which is an essential process in achieving fluency in the fundamental reading skill, the ability to recognise words. What does all this mean in relation to the teaching of reading to children who have learning problems? I would like to raise two or three questions.

The first question relates to method of teaching. (But let me put in all those caveats that the researcher has to put in about the enquiry being based on a very small sample, as well as being a spin-off from another enquiry.) Nevertheless, it is interesting to note that not one of the 15 children we saw achieved success in word recognition without great facility in phonic skills. No matter how strongly the proponents of the Look and Say method feel and no matter how helpful it may be to introduce reading through a visual approach, it still seems that for our sample there are certain regularities in the English language which, after they have been grasped, enable a child's word recognition skills to shoot ahead at a remarkably rapid rate. These children were taken from a set of different schools; they came from different backgrounds; they were being taught in different parts of the country. Nevertheless, this point applied to each child, regardless of the range of teaching methods used.

What were these methods? There were a variety of teachers in the schools, and each stressed different approaches, but most schools introduced reading by a Look and Say approach, with teachers later introducing phonic skills at different points and with different emphases, depending on their own inclinations. The pattern of schools was not unrepresentative of what is acceptable practice in British infant schools, and I do not think we are considering an unusual set of teaching methods. In a school which stressed a visual approach, or in a school which stressed a phonic approach, a different result would have been obtained. But for these schools, phonics and phonic knowledge seem important before the word recognition spurt can occur. I think that might have implications for teaching reading.

The second point relates to measurement. Those persons who are concerned with children with reading problems are going to be involved in measurement. We all know the word recognition test and the reading age score which emerges. In view of the interesting reading spurts which occur at different stages, I am tempted to conclude that these could well be thrown out of the window. We would gain much more information if, instead of measuring children's reading performance on a test, we looked at children's reading in relation to considerations such as the size of their recognition vocabulary—how many words they have managed to acquire and how many phonic elements they have grasped. In this way, we do not compare child with child but we compare children's skills against the real backcloth that matters—that is, the extent to which they have acquired the defined pattern of skills required to master the ability to understand the printed English language.

To return to the question I asked at the start of this paper: a reading age improvement of one year between the reading ages of five and six is an entirely different matter from a reading age improvement of one year between the reading ages of ten and eleven. This is what the reading tests mask and it is because we have been wedded to measurement in this way for the past sixty years that we have failed to explore the fundamental principles underlying the development of reading skills—principles which matter so much in remedial education.

REFERENCES
1. Lynn, R. "Reading Readiness II: Reading Readiness and the Perceptual Abilities of Young Children," *Educational Research*, 6 (1963), 10-15.
2. Williams, P., et al. *Swansea Test of Phonic Skills*. Oxford: Blackwell, 1971.

PART FOUR

The Reader and the Media

Expressed Reading Interests of Young Children: An International Study

Dorothy I. Kirsch
Glen Cove Public Schools
Glen Cove, New York

Robert S. V. Pehrsson
East Meadow Public Schools
East Meadow, New York

H. Alan Robinson
Hofstra University
Hempstead, New York
United States of America

Many teachers appear to feel that students understand better when they are interested in what they are reading. As a result of this concern a number of investigators have naturally turned their attention to pursuing the interest factor in reading. More than 300 investigations of reading preferences were published prior to the 1960s, largely in the United States. Although the surge of studies has diminished to some extent, researchers still continue their pursuit of the interest factor. Only a limited amount of research has been focused upon the preferences of the beginning reader in the first and second years of school. To the investigators' knowledge, after a careful search of the literature, no investigators have previously explored the expressed reading interests of young children across a number of countries.

The purpose of the study was to survey and compare the expressed reading interests of children in the first and second years of formal schooling (not including kindergarten) in an attempt to determine similarities and differences among countries, within each of the school years, and from first to second year. The total sample consisted of 2,113 children. Three children would not or could not respond, leaving a final total of 2,110. Of these 2,110 children, 106 were from Austria, 105 from Canada, 196 from England, 103 from Israel, 88 from Italy, 99 from Japan, 80 from the Netherlands, 129 from The Republic of Panama, 126 from Sweden, and 1,078 from three geographic areas of the United States. The overall sample included 1,045 girls and 1,065 boys.

The study was originally designed by Dorothy Kirsch as an investigation of the expressed reading interests of children in grades one and two in three cities and suburban areas of the United States. This early part of the investigation was completed in partial fulfillment of the requirements for the degree of Doctor of Education at Hofstra University. Dr. Kirsch's study was then expanded and the results of her investigation were included in the investigation of children in ten countries. In most cases, classroom teachers conducted the interviews with the children. This phase of the investigation was completed under the direction of H. Alan Robinson who, in 1972, travelled to six of the ten countries to observe, answer questions, and assure parallelism, spending two or three days in each country.

PLAN OF THE STUDY

Information on expressed reading interests was collected from a total of 2,110 children by interviews on a one-to-one basis. The children's own drawings were used to elicit their expressed interests. Each child, interviewed alone, was asked to draw a picture showing what he would like to read or have read to him. The investigator confirmed the child's reading interest by means of a structured interview. When possible, the derivation of the interest was also elicited.

After the data had been collected, comparisons were made according to country, sex, intelligence, reading level, chronological age, and year in school.

1. The interests were expressed by the children at a single point in time. The feelings of the child about the reading interests that emerged were not probed psychologically or sociologically, nor were the interests then related to child development patterns.

2. The sample was limited to children in selected schools in the United States on the basis of urban and innercity locations in the metropolitan areas of New York, Detroit, and Los Angeles. The schools in the other nine countries were selected on the basis of convenience and cooperation. Since Robinson wrote to people he knew in various countries for their assistance in gathering the information, the samples were not randomized.

3. The technique used in collecting data—children's drawings in combination with an interview—was essentially subjective, even though the interview was structured. This interview was more detailed in the United States than in the other nine countries.

4. The designation of reading level was judgmental on the part of the teachers.

5. The designation of intelligence level as low, average, or high was obtained from the Goodenough Draw-A-Man Test.

6. There were differences in age, although the children were in the same grade. In Sweden, the children were generally one year older than

in other countries because, in Sweden, the children start school one year later. In England, the children were one year younger because they begin school roughly one year earlier. This variation has been taken into consideration in describing the results.

7. In the study of Alberta, Canada; Venice, Italy; and the Republic of Panama, data were collected by persons other than those immediately involved in the research project. The interpretations and carrying out of instructions were entrusted to persons who were residing and working in those areas at that time. In Japan, interviews were conducted by college students majoring in education. However, these students were well trained and followed the directions explicitly.

FINDINGS

In this section of the paper three main elements of the study are explored: 1) the topics about which children in the world sample expressed an interest in reading; 2) the classification of the topics into predetermined categories, which were then compared statistically to ascertain similarities and differences; and 3) an attempt to ascertain the derivation of the child's reading interest—whether it was fostered by books, television, or personal experiences. The data reveals striking similarities from country to country, along with unique differences.

THE TOPICS

Each child's reading interest, the subject drawn and talked about, was termed the *topic*. The topics were then allocated to seven prearranged categories: information-scientific, information-historic, information-1970s, realistic fiction, imaginative fiction, humor, and poetry. Generally, the child's drawing revealed the reading topic of interest; through the interview, the specific manner in which the topic was viewed. For example, if a child drew a dog, upon questioning he might reveal that he liked stories about real animals, which would be classified as *realistic fiction* in the categories. However, if he disclosed upon questioning that he wanted information on how to raise dogs, it would then be allocated to *information-scientific*. Or, perhaps, he stated that he liked stories about make-believe dogs, in which case his interest would be classified as *imaginative fiction*.

The 1,062 children in the first year of school who participated in the study made 1,095 choices, which are classified as 24 appropriate topics. The number of choices exceeded the number of children by 33; some children made more than one choice. Fictional topics numbered 851, or 78 percent of the choices; nonfiction topics numbered 244, or 22 percent of the total. The first 10 topics reflected more than 89 percent of the reading interests of children in the first year of school. These topic choices are shown in Table 1.

Table 1.   Topics Chosen by Children in the First Year of School

Topic	Total	Percent	Rank
Fairy tales and fantasies	297	27.12	1
Stories about children	173	15.80	2
Stories about real animals	146	13.33	3
Information about animals	110	10.04	4
Stories about people	80	7.31	5
Monster stories—superhuman personalities	53	4.84	6
Real-life adventure stories	40	3.65	7
Funny stories	31	2.83	8
How to make and/or operate mechanical vehicles	29	2.65	9
Information on vocations	23	2.10	10
TV cartoons	17	1.55	11
How things grow	15	1.37	12
Mystery and ghost stories	13	1.19	13
Prehistoric life	12	1.10	14
Historic events and famous people	11	1.00	15
Information on sports	10	.91	16
Chemical and biological information	8	.73	17
"How to . . ." information, other than mechanical	6	.55	18
Famous contemporary people	6	.55	18
Current events	5	.46	19
Religious themes	4	.37	20
Information on space	4	.37	20
Ecology	1	.09	21
Science fiction	1	.09	21

Titles mentioned as favorite fairy tales or fantasies by 297 (27.12 percent) of the children in the first year of school across the ten countries included both classic fairy tales and modern fantasies. Named by some subjects in 50 percent or more of the countries surveyed were the time-honored favorites: Cinderella, Little Red Riding Hood, Snow White, The Three Bears, and Jack and the Beanstalk. Frequently mentioned was the Swedish modern-day fantasy, Pippi Longstocking. Children also named as favorites tales which were apparently indigenous to their country. Thus, children in the Netherlands spoke of a story about Santa Claus arriving in the Netherlands on a steamer; Austrian children appeared to favor Hansel and Gretel; and Japanese subjects named A Small House.

Requests by 173 children (15.80 percent) for "stories about children" appeared to mirror the everyday pursuits of the subjects. Thus, there were requests for stories about children playing, children at school, children getting lost, and children going on trips. Among the titles specifically mentioned were *Tom Sawyer*, *Heidi*, and from Israeli children, *Hanna's Shabqt Dress*.

One hundred forty-six (13.33 percent) of the first year children apparently desired to read about all kinds of animals—pets, circus animals, and wild animals. Books in the *Lassie* series were frequently mentioned; others included *Fury* and *Black Beauty*. Information was requested about a tremendously varied group of living creatures: dogs, horses, and cats were the favorites; but there was also interest in birds, lions, pigs, guinea pigs, elephants, tigers, whales, reindeer, ants, and grasshoppers.

Interest in real-life adventure stories included requests by 40 (3.65 percent) children for stories about cowboys and cowgirls, soldiers, sailors, knights, boys and girls in different lands, and a desire to see other places through books, arriving there by car and plane. Among the titles were *The Desert Fox* and *The Sardinian Drummer Boy*.

Stories about people seemed to reflect the everyday life of 80 (7.31 percent) of the subjects; requests frequently were made for stories about family members, particularly siblings.

Among the characters mentioned in monster stories were witches, devils, and robots. *Dracula* and *Zorro* were among the specific titles; Japanese children mentioned a number of monster stories which were apparently unique to their country. Stories which appealed to children because of humor included such titles as *Willie Wonka and the Chocolate Factory*, *Rolling Rice Ball*, and *A Man with a Yellow Hat*. "How to . . ." information included interest in how to make cars, operate submarines and trains, make marionettes and dolls, collect butterflies, and learn to bake. Information about sports included interests in gymnastics and football; information on vocations included requests for reading material on how to be an astronaut, a policeman, a doctor, and a teacher. Religious themes mentioned characters from both the Old and New Testaments. Choices listed under TV cartoons included *Donald Duck*, *Mickey Mouse*, *Tom and Jerry*, *Top Cat*, *Bugs Bunny*, and *Woody Woodpecker*.

Table 2, which lists the first three choices of the children in the first year of school of each country in the survey, shows the similarities and differences in the choices made by children throughout the sample.

Fairy tales and fantasies, which was the first choice of the sample, received the greatest degree of interest in eight of the ten countries, with Japan and Canada giving it the second highest frequency. *Stories about children*, the second choice of the sample, received the second highest frequency of interest from four countries, the third highest from two. *Stories about real animals*, the third choice of the sample, was chosen first by Canada, second by the Republic of Panama, and third by Israel; *information about animals*, the fourth choice of the sample as a whole, was the second choice of Italy and Sweden, and the third choice of the United States. *Stories about people*, sixth choice of the sample, was Japan's first choice and the Netherlands' third; and *real-life adventure stories*, the seventh choice of the sample, was the third choice of both England and Japan.

Table 2. First Three Rankings of Topics by Countries: First Year
(Roman numerals represent topic rankings over the entire sample; parenthetical numbers represent ranking within a particular country for that topic.)

I.   Fairy tales and fantasies
    Austria (1)
    Canada (2)
    England (1)
    Israel (1)
    Italy (1)
    Japan (2)
    the Netherlands (1)
    Republic of Panama (1)
    Sweden (1)
    United States (1)

II. Stories about children
    Austria (2)
    Canada (3)
    Israel (2)
    Italy (3)
    the Netherlands (2)
    Republic of Panama (3)
    United States (2)

III. Stories about real animals
    Canada (1)
    Israel (3)
    Republic of Panama (2)

IV. Information about animals
    Italy (2)
    Sweden (2)
    United States (3)

V.   Stories about people
    Austria (3)
    England (2)

VI. Monster stories
    Italy (3)*
    Japan (1)
    the Netherlands (3)

VII. Real-life adventure stories
    England (3)
    Japan (3)

VIII. Funny stories
    Italy (3)*
    Sweden (3)

XVII. Chemical and biological information
    Italy (3)*

XVIII. "How to" information, other than mechanical
    Italy (3)*

*Same degree of preference

KIRSCH, PEHRSSON & ROBINSON

Whether the differences in choices between the countries are culturally based, are a result of a curriculum-directed experience, or can be traced to the affective domain of the child, is conjectural. There are differences among the interests of children in the countries represented in the sample, but obviously there are similarities—*fairy tales and fantasies* are of great interest to many children in the first year of school across the ten countries.

An analysis of the choices of children in the second year of school reveals that the 1,048 children in the survey made 1,130 choices, which are classified as 25 topics; the additional interest was the dictionary which accounted for two choices. The number of choices exceeded the number of children by 82; apparently, more children in the second year of school than in the first had multiple reading interests. Fictional topics numbered 721, or 64 percent of the second year choices; nonfiction topics numbered 409, or 36 percent of the total. Thus, although fiction was still the major reading interest of children in the second year of school, there was a marked increase in requests for factual reading material. The first 10 topics reflected 79 percent of the expressed interest rather than the 89 percent evidenced by those in the first year of school, which appeared to indicate that interests were widening with a portion of the children.

Second year topic choices are shown in Table 3.

As a comparison of Tables 1 and 3 indicates, topics chosen by first and second year children were similar. There were, however, differences in the degree of interest shown in the topics, and in the second year, *fairy tales and fantasies* was again the topic which received the greatest frequency of interest. However, *stories about children*, which was the second most popular topic in the first year, ranked third in the second year. *Information about animals*, which ranked fourth in the first year, was the second most popular topic in the second year. *Stories about animals*, ranked third in the first year, was ranked fourth in the second year.

There was greater interest in *TV cartoons* and *how things grow* among children in the first year. There was considerably more interest in *information on space* in the second year, where it was ranked tenth as compared to a ranking of twentieth in the first year. There was also a greater interest in *information on sports*.

As in the first year, analysis of the first three choices of each country reveals both similarities and differences, as shown in Table 4. *Fairy tales and fantasies*, which ranked first with the second year sample also ranked first with eight countries, and second with Sweden and the United States. *Information about animals*, which ranked second with the second year sample, was the first choice of Sweden and the United

Table 3. Topics Chosen by Children in the Second Year of School

Topic	Total	Percent	Rank
Fairy tales and fantasies	266	23.54	1
Information about animals	145	12.83	2
Stories about children	116	10.27	3
Stories about real animals	85	7.52	4
Real-life adventure stories	65	5.75	5
Monster stories—superhuman personalities	57	5.04	6
Stories about people	44	3.89	7
How to make and/or operate mechanical vehicles	42	3.72	8
Funny stories	39	3.45	9
Information on space	36	3.19	10
Information on vocations	30	2.65	11
Information on sports	28	2.48	12
Historic events and famous people	26	2.30	13
TV cartoons	24	2.12	14
Prehistoric life	22	1.95	15
Chemical and biological information	21	1.86	16
Mystery and ghost stories	20	1.77	17
"How to . . ." information, other than mechanical	16	1.42	18
How things grow	14	1.24	19
Religious themes	10	.88	20
Famous contemporary people	9	.80	21
Current events	6	.53	22
Science fiction	5	.44	23
Dictionaries	2	.18	24
Ecology	2	.18	24

States, second choice of Japan, and third choice of the Republic of Panama. *Stories about children*, the topic ranked third, ranked third with Austria, Canada, England, Japan, Sweden, and the United States, but second with the Republic of Panama and Israel. The topic ranked fourth, *stories about real animals*, was the second choice of Canada and the Republic of Panama; but it was the third choice of Israel and Italy. The topic ranked fifth, *real life adventure stories*, was the second choice of Austria, England, and the Netherlands; the topic ranked ninth by the total second year sample, *funny stories*, was ranked second by the second year children of Italy; *information on space*, which was ranked tenth by the entire sample was ranked second by Austria; and the topic ranked sixteenth by the total second year sample, *chemical or biological information*, was ranked third by the second year children of the Netherlands.

Table 4.   First Three Rankings of Topics by Countries: Second Year
(Roman numerals represent rankings of entire sample; parenthetical numbers represent rankings of country.)

I.   Fairy tales and fantasies
    Austria (1)
    Canada (1)
    England (1)
    Israel (1)
    Italy (1)
    Japan (1)
    the Netherlands (1)
    Republic of Panama (1)
    Sweden (2)
    United States (2)

II.   Information about animals
    Japan (2)
    Republic of Panama (3)
    Sweden (1)
    United States (1)

III.   Stories about children
    Austria (3)
    Canada (3)
    England (3)
    Israel (2)
    Japan (3)
    Republic of Panama (2)*
    Sweden (3)
    United States (3)

IV.   Stories about real animals
    Canada (2)
    Israel (3)
    Italy (3)
    Republic of Panama (2)*

V.   Real life adventure stories
    Austria (2)*
    England (2)
    the Netherlands (2)

IX.   Funny stories
    Italy (2)

X.   Information on space
    Austria (2)*

XVI.   Chemical or biological information
    the Netherlands (3)

*Same degree of preference

THE CATEGORIES

The topics children chose were then allocated to seven prearranged categories (as discussed previously): information-scientific, information-historic, information-1970s, realistic fiction, imaginative fiction, humor, and poetry. As has been noted, *poetry* was probably too abstract a designation for this age group and was not chosen by any child.

The statistic chi-square, used to compare a set of observed frequencies with a hypothetical set of expected frequencies, was employed to determine statistical significance. In this study, the *observed frequencies* expressed (within each group) the frequency with which a category was selected, while the *expected frequencies* were the frequencies that would have been expected if no differences existed in the preferences of the groups being compared. The greater the variation, as shown by a numerically larger chi-square, the greater is the certainty that the difference is not due to chance variation. Chi-square tested the differences in the proportion of the responses that fell within each category for the different groups, rather than differences between groups in the ranking of the categories. The category choices of the 2,110 children who took part in the survey could be ranked 1) imaginative fiction, with 742.5 choices; 2) realistic fiction, with 633.5 choices; 3) information-scientific, with 406.4 choices; 4) information 1970s, with 224.5 choices; 5) information-historic, with 57 choices; and 6) humor, with 46 choices. However, the proportion of choices falling in each category varied from group to group.

The study in the United States was completed in advance of the study in the other nine countries and with a far larger sample. Thus, some of the data had to be statistically examined without including the United States in the table as the numerical weight of the U.S. sample would have skewed the compilations.

Nine questions formed the framework for the statistical analysis:

1. Are there significant differences in the expressed reading interests of children in the first year of school among the ten countries surveyed in the study? Chi-square analysis showed significant differences at the .01 level. The proportion of responses to *information-scientific* was greater in Italy, Sweden, and the United States; responses to *realistic fiction* were greater in England and Israel and markedly fewer in Italy; responses to *imaginative fiction* were greater in the Netherlands and Italy.

2. Are there significant differences in the expressed reading interests of children in the second year of school among the ten countries surveyed in the study? Chi-square analysis showed significant differences at the .01 level. The proportion of responses to *information-scientific* were markedly fewer in England and Israel than in the rest of the sample; responses to *information-1970s* were greater in the United States; responses to *realistic fiction* were greater in England and Israel, and markedly fewer in Italy; and responses to *imaginative fiction* were fewer in Sweden and the United States.

3. Are there significant differences between the expressed reading interests of first and second year children in the ten countries surveyed in the study? Chi-square analysis revealed significant differences at the .01 level. The proportion of responses were greater in the second year than in the first year to *information-scientific, information-historic,* and

information-1970s. The proportion of responses were greater in the first year to *realistic fiction* and to *imaginative fiction.*

4. Are there significant differences in the expressed reading interests of first year boys and first year girls? (The United States was treated separately because of the size of the sample.) Chi-square showed no significant differences in the proportion of responses of first year boys and girls. However, for the United States sample alone, there were significant differences at the .01 level in the expressed reading interests of first year boys and girls, with boys showing a far greater proportion of interest for *information 1970s.*

5. Are there significant differences in the expressed reading interests of second year boys and second year girls? (The United States, because of the size of the sample, was treated separately.) Chi-square showed no significant differences in the proportion of responses of second year boys and girls. The United States sample alone, however, did show significant differences at the .01 level between second year boys and girls, with girls showing a far greater preference for *realistic fiction* and *imaginative fiction* and boys exhibiting greater interest in *information 1970s.*

The pronounced differences in expressed reading interests between young boys and girls in the United States presents a puzzling contrast to the similarity of reading interests shown between boys and girls in the other nine countries surveyed. Additional research appears needed.

6. Are there significant differences in the expressed reading interests of first year children of high, average, and low intelligence? (The United States, because of the size of the sample, was treated separately.) Chi-square showed no significant differences in the proportion of the responses of first year children of high, average, or low intelligence. The United States sample alone, however, showed significant differences at the .05 level, with children of high intelligence expressing a greater interest in *information-scientific* and *information-1970s,* and children of low intelligence showing a greater interest in the category *realistic fiction.*

7. Are there significant differences in the expressed reading interests of second year children of high, average, and low intelligence? (Again, the United States was omitted from the overall compilation.) Chi-square analysis showed significant differences at the .05 level, with children of high intelligence showing a higher proportion of interest in *information-scientific* and *imaginative fiction* than did children in the other categories. Conversely, the United States sample showed no

significant differences in the expressed reading interests of second year children according to intelligence.

8. Are there significant differences in the expressed reading interests of first year children of high, average, and low reading level? (The overall compilation did not include the United States.) Chi-square analysis showed significant differences at the .01 level between first year children of high, average, and low reading level. Children of high and average level showed a greater proportion of interest in the category *information-scientific* than did children of low reading level; children of low reading level showed a greater interest in *realistic fiction*, and children of high and average reading level showed more interest in *imaginative fiction*. The United States sample showed a similar pattern: significant differences at the .01 level, with children at the low reading level showing a greater proportion of interest in *realistic fiction*.

9. Are there significant differences in the expressed reading interests of second year children of high, average, and low reading level? Chi-square analysis showed no significant differences in the proportion of responses of children of high, average, and low reading level in any of the countries including the United States sample. See Table 4 for listing of significant differences.

In addition, the variation of age in each year were scanned in relation to category choice (5.1 to 7.2 in the first year; 6.2 to 8.4 in the second year), but no consistent age-choice pattern could be discerned.

To sum up this portion of the study: There are some significant differences in reading interests in both first and second year children among the 10 countries of the survey. There are some significant differences in reading interests between first and second year children in the ten countries.

In compilations which did not include the United States, there were no significant differences in reading interests between boys and girls of either first or second year; significant differences in reading interests were shown in second year children, according to intelligence, but not first year children; significant differences in reading interests were shown in first year according to reading level, but not in second year.

The United States sample showed significant differences in reading interests between boys and girls in both first and second year; significant differences were evident in reading interests in first year children, according to intelligence, but not among second year children; and, as in the nine countries, significant differences in the reading interests of children in the first year of school were demonstrated, according to reading level, but this was not true of children in the second year of school.

Table 5. Significant Differences in Reading Interests

Grouping	Grade Level	Significance Level
Between ten countries	1, 2	.01
Between first and second years; ten countries	1, 2	.01
Boys and girls—without U.S.	1, 2	none
Boys and girls—U.S.	1, 2	.01
Intelligence—without U.S.	1	none
Intelligence—U.S.	1	.05
Intelligence—without U.S.	2	.05
Intelligence—U.S.	2	none
Reading level—without U.S.	1	.01
Reading level—U.S.	1	.01
Reading level—without U.S.	2	none
Reading level—U.S.	2	none

EXPRESSED DERIVATION OF INTEREST

In the final section of this report on findings are the data related to the ascertaining of the source of the expressed reading interest. This was determined through a probing question which concluded each child's personal interview. Some children gave several sources, so that the replies exceeded the number of children in the study.

The replies of first and second year children were similar. Twenty percent of the first year children and almost 18 percent of the second year children could not designate the interest source. Trade books accounted for more than 30 percent of the expressed derivation in both years (slightly higher in second than in first); television accounted for more than 16 percent of the derivation of the interest source (slightly higher in first than in second); and personal experiences, such as trips, having a pet, family events and family background, accounted for approximately 23 percent in each year. The designation *other*, which accounted for slightly less than 5 percent of the expressed derivation in each year, included such items as model kits, phonograph records, Sunday school, movies (other than TV), and comic books.

Analyzing the sources for each category in percentages reveals great similarities between years one and two (Tables 6 and 7). In the category *information-scientific*, both trade books and TV show slight increases as interest sources in the second year. For *information-1970s*, there is an increase in trade books as a source, a decrease in television. *Realistic fiction*, in the second year, shows less involvement with personal experience than was evident in the first year; *imaginative fiction* shows somewhat greater use of books as a source in the second year.

Difficult to tabulate but ever-present in the comments of the children were the influences of both home and school. "My Mommy told me I'd like this book; my teacher said it was a good program, my Dad read that book to me, the whole family went on a trip to the seashore."

Table 6. Expressed Derivation of Interest
World Sample, First Year: Percentages

| | Books | | | Personal | | | |
	Trade	Basals	TV	Experience	Other	Unknown	Totals
Information Scientific	25.56	1.98	10.43	31.27	4.46	26.30	100
Information Historic	21.74	—	21.74	4.36	26.08	26.08	100
Information 1970s	12.18	—	32.69	29.49	5.13	20.51	100
Realistic Fiction	27.90	2.98	10.21	36.62	3.48	18.81	100
Imaginative Fiction	42.21	1.16	25.18	7.22	4.89	19.34	100
Humor	44.83	31.04	20.69	—	—	3.44	100
Poetry	—	—	—	—	—	—	—

Table 7. Expressed Derivation of Interest
World Sample, Second Year: Percentages

| | Books | | | Personal | | | |
	Trade	Basals	TV	Experience	Other	Unknown	Totals
Information Scientific	31.99	.34	12.95	31.29	3.15	20.28	100
Information Historic	50.00	—	16.67	14.59	9.37	9.37	100
Information 1970s	20.83	—	24.61	32.81	5.67	16.08	100
Realistic Fiction	29.06	2.36	8.28	30.24	4.39	25.67	—
Imaginative Fiction	46.49	3.74	20.38	12.18	4.21	13.00	100
Humor	50.00	—	23.33	10.00	6.67	10.00	100
Poetry	—	—	—	—	—	—	—

CONCLUSIONS, IMPLICATIONS, AND SUGGESTIONS

There is little question that this study is limited by several factors; broad generalizations cannot and must not be made. The study can only stand for what it is: an expression by children in the first and second formal years of school (excluding kindergarten) to their momentary interest in a topic to read or have read to them.

These children did not seem to be handicapped by being asked to draw a response except in London, England, where a number of the first year children in the sample were not used to drawing and were younger than most of the subjects in the sample. On the other hand, children of the same ages in Manchester, England, did not appear to have the same problem.

Also, it could be that a different group of interests might be elicited at other times or in other settings. This remains for future investigators to determine. (Our hunch is that most of the same topics would appear and that the rankings would be unchanged.) Our only evidence at this point is the pilot work being conducted by Kirsch who finds interest quite constant after repeated interviews. We have not tried other situations outside of the school or with other interviewers, such as peers or parents.

However, based on the findings of this study and for this sample and keeping in mind the limitation of the study, the following conclusions are drawn:

1. Although there are some significant differences, there appear to be more similarities than differences among the expressed reading interests of first and second year children in ten countries.

2. Fairy tales and fantasies are the most preferred expressed reading interests of first and second year children in the ten countries.

3. Fairy tales and fantasies, stories about children, plus stories and information about real animals were the top choices of over two-thirds of the children in the first year of school for the entire sample. The same choices in a slightly different ranking order were the top choices of 54 percent of all the children in the second year of school. More of the second year children expressed a greater diversity of interests.

4. Reading interests of second year children demonstrated more preferences for nonfictional topics than the interests of first year children.

5. Reading interests among children in the first year of school for the ten countries differed significantly in relation to reading levels as judged roughly by classroom teachers. Other differences were inconsistent in terms of statistical significance.

6. Derivations of interests were similar for both years with trade books as the most popular source, personal experiences next, and television third.

IMPLICATIONS

It must be reemphasized that the implications grow out of a study limited in design and scope. Nevertheless, some speculation about what meaning the findings might have seems warranted in the light of even this limited evidence.

1. Anyone involved with planning for young children's reading should be aware of the variety of topics children appear to be interested in.

2. If the significant difference between interests and reading levels in both years is reliable (and this may be demonstrated by additional

experimentation), planning for instructional experiences should consider such differences. It appears that children in the second year of school, reading at a lower reading level than placement in school, will not have their interests met through the use of materials meant for the first year of school.

In analyzing the content of readers intended for the first year of school, Blom and others (1) found their content too bland and "happy family centered" for first year children. The content would appear to be even more inappropriate for second year children who are reading at levels more closely related to first year performance. Second year children of low reading ability might profit from instruction using easy-to-read books with a focus upon factually related topics and imaginative fiction.

3. Young children throughout the world (at least as viewed through the samples in these ten countries) appear to have many similar interests. This conclusion would seem to point toward the implication that more universal, structured, educational activities could be planned as early as school years one and two involving interrelationships among children in these ten countries. Art work, photography, and pantomime are possible ways of using common interests to build mutual understandings at early ages.

SUGGESTED RESEARCH

Obviously, replications of this study are needed in other countries and at other times of the year to ascertain the validity of these expressed interests as more than momentary choices. Also, the same children should be asked to draw and explain their interests a number of times within a month to determine the reliability of the expressed interests. Once the expressed interests appear to be valid and reliable over a number of studies, the interests should be compared to the curricula in the first two years of school. Although educators wish to expand children's interests, early experiences in school ought to relate to the interests of the learners if they are to conceive of learning as interesting and relevant. The children in this study did not demonstrate any great desire to read about family life but appeared to want to expand their worlds to a multitude of areas beyond their everyday living.

REFERENCE
1.   Blom, Gaston L., and others. "What the Story World is Like," in Sara G. Zimet (Ed.), *What Children Read in School*. New York: Grune and Stratton, 1972, 1-18.

Selecting Textbooks: Some Preliminary Thoughts

George R. Klare
Ohio University
Athens, Ohio
United States of America

Michael Macdonald-Ross
Institute of Educational Technology
The Open University
Milton Keynes, England

Teachers and administrators look to research workers for practical help with an important recurring task: the selection of textbooks for the classroom. A great deal of money is spent on textbooks; apart from the teacher, they are the main, and sometimes the only, source of information. So it is natural for those who select books to look for guidance; to seek ways of making better decisions for the benefit of the students and of the taxpayers.

Research workers, on the other hand, tend to avoid facing such a complex and confusing practical matter. Knowledge about textbooks and their use is patchy (4), and background research relevant to printed materials is scattered unevenly through many disciplines (21). We must also recognise that research knowledge by itself may never be sufficient to solve practical problems. After all, to resolve a particular problem you must take account of the specific situation at hand. There is a limit to the usefulness of theoretical knowledge; circumstances will alter cases.

Despite these reservations, we are persuaded that the task of selecting textbooks is so interesting and important that we should offer these thoughts for your consideration. In no sense does this paper present a complete survey of all the considerations involved in selecting textbooks. We have chosen a few topics for discussion, and we accept without reservation that other topics may be equally important. Indeed, we intend to return to this subject from time to time, so that eventually our treatment will become more comprehensive.

SOME REASONS FOR THE LACK OF RESEARCH

Research workers have a natural bias towards soluble problems; moreover, they tend to avoid the problem of making decisions in the real world:

> The usual textbook does not control the behaviour of the learner in a way which makes it highly predictable as a vehicle of instruction or amenable to experimental research. It does not in itself generate a describable and predictable process of learner behaviour, and this may be the reason why there has been very little experimental research on the textbook (20).

Reinforced as they are by the behaviour of funding agencies, there is little incentive for researchers to revise their ideas. Actually, it seems that the situation gets worse as time goes on. The second handbook of research on teaching (34) appears to contain less than one paragraph out of 1,400 pages directly concerned with textbooks. Does this accurately reflect the work being done by researchers?

Publishers are also partly responsible for the lack of textbook research. Publishing is a commercial business, and there is nothing wrong with that: those countries with state control of publishing never produce the wide variety and the fast response of the commercial enterprises. However, unlike most industries, publishers do not have in-house R&D (Research and Development) capabilities, and generally do not fund special-purpose research in universities. Therefore, it seems fair to say that publishers have not yet shouldered the responsibility of making sure their product is effective. It is most unusual for a publisher to know how his books work in practice: he is interested in how well they sell. It follows that in-house editing is kept down to an absolute minimum, and simple controls (for example, readability measures) are not used unless large purchasers insist on certain minimum standards.

STANDARDS AND JUDGMENTS

In principle, there are two ways to operate a selection system. One way stresses preset rules, and is summarised by the word *standards*. The second way stresses individual situations and the need to compare one alternative with another. This is the way of human judgment. The crux of our argument is that neither way is sufficient by itself: any system for selecting textbooks will need both well-defined standards and sensitive judgment.

The word *standard* deserves some attention. We use it here in the sense of "an authoritative or recognised exemplar of correctness, perfection, or some definite degree of any quality" (shorter O.E.D.). Yet, clearly, this sense will cover several different uses. At one extreme is the absolute standard or criterion. For example, a book may be so illegible or unreadable that it should be rejected no matter what other features it may have. Or, the book may exhibit such political bias or moral turpitude as to be unacceptable to society. It may be rejected for that reason, provided the criteria for such a decision are known and agreed publicly.

Usually, however, the standards are relative to particular situations. A practical choice must be made, based on the alternatives available. A book will have these advantages but those disadvantages; seldom does a book score on all counts. Moreover, a book may be best for some purposes, but not for others. For example, a book which works well when used for reference may be poor for self-instruction. And, of course, a book suitable for one age group or type of student may not suit others.

If most standards are relative, it follows that teachers and administrators must continue to use their judgment. In other words, you cannot replace judgment by hard-and-fast rules, except in a few extreme cases. This is a blow to those who hope to eliminate the frailties of human judgment; but we feel our opinion does justice to the real complexities of educational situations. We offer this consolation: it is possible to improve one's judgment. By systematic attention we can develop textbook standards which, however fluid or relative they may be, can inform judgment and so help to improve the decisions taken by teachers and administrators.

A PROCESS MODEL

Our simple model of the way textbooks should be chosen includes these stages:

1. *The target population.* Most of the research aids we suggest cannot be used for action unless a good deal is known about the potential user. For example:

- Reading skill. Reading test information is desirable, and can be modified by the teacher's informed opinion. Records of teacher's opinions can be kept and checked against various external criteria. Such a learning system is necessary whenever personal opinions are used for decision making.

- Entry knowledge. A specific entry test for a textbook usually isn't available, but one could be constructed in special cases. Otherwise, general achievement tests covering the content area are needed and past educational history should also be recorded. Teacher's opinions can be collected, though once again this means a longer-term evaluation of those opinions must also be set up.

- Level of motivation. No simple tests are available here, but there are some useful signposts. For example, will the book be a free choice of the reader or will it be assigned? Will it be required reading in a subject often disliked by the student? The less motivated the student is, the more we should demand good legibility, easy readability, and good quality explanations and exercises.

2. *Collecting alternatives*. Obviously, it's important to make sure all candidates are lined up for the selection process. Therefore, at this stage no criterion is needed except face validity. In other words, all textbooks in the language covering the subject area, at roughly the right level, should be placed together. In general, it pays to suspend judgment during the collection stage, otherwise, half-baked opinions may preempt the more sophisticated judgments we hope to foster.

3. *Screening*. The purpose of this stage is to eliminate those books which are clearly unsuitable according to well-specified criteria. Examples of such criteria might be:

- Cost. A book might be rejected if its cost exceeds some official limit.
- Bias. Political, religious, or moral bias might be a cause for rejection provided a proper procedure of content analysis was used, and the standard for rejection was known and agreed in that particular society. Of course, the question of whether a society should set up such criteria is quite beyond the bounds of this paper; we simply want criteria to be public and systematic as far as is possible.
- Production quality. Books may be rejected if they are illegible, if they fall to bits during use, or are otherwise impractical.
- Readability. Books may be rejected if there is a clear mismatch between the reading skills of the students and the readability level of the material.

It is important for officials to make the criteria public and to tell the publishers why certain books were rejected. By such means publishers can be influenced; the criteria will gradually force them to institute in-house standards. Also, the publishers would have the chance to counterargue; such a debate might well improve the detailed wording and application of standards.

4. *Judgment*. Since the process of judgment can't be avoided, we suggest that it be built into a more organised practice. By using critics' and teachers' accounts a picture can be built for the decision making stage.

5. *Decision*. Some countries dictate choice of textbooks from the centre; others allow individual teachers to choose. We realise that, to some extent, selecting a textbook is a political act. We suggest that the act of choice should take place in two stages.

Stage 1: *Reduction*. The judgments are used to remove candidates until a small number remain (never more than six nor less than one). This may be done centrally by the Ministry or by the local district. In England, the autonomy of teachers can be respected by making available to the teacher the information which in other countries would have been used directly by central officials.

Stage 2: *Selection*. This is the actual choice of textbooks to be used in a particular class. We suggest that this be done as far down the chain as local circumstances allow. The point is that local situations will differ, and if there is a genuine choice between good alternatives, the teacher will be best able to see what suits his situation. Preliminary weeding-out protects children against the worst random choices, and yet leaves the teacher with a professional responsibility. Much could be learned by collecting the reasons given for this final choice, and we suggest these expressed reasons be collected and analysed systematically.

6. *Evaluation*. Every detail of the first four stages is capable of systematic improvement. If careful records are kept, the process is bound to become more effective as time passes. Frankly, it does not matter if some mistakes are made first time around; the important thing is to make sure that lessons are learned and procedures revised.

Another possibility is to experiment directly on the way student performance is affected by alternative texts. Lumsdaine has spelled out the difficulty of this approach but it may well be worth funding some research to tackle the problem head-on. The results of such research could, if interpreted with sophistication and caution, be added to the process of judgment (stage 3).

In the following sections of this paper we consider some ideas that could be useful for the screening and judgment stages.

Typography. A number of reviews summarise the research on legibility of type: Burt (6) and Spencer (30) are good starting points; Tinker (33) is the standard reference work and Hartley, Fraser, and Burnhill (14) have a useful recent bibliography. There are some studies on our particular topic, the relation of typographic research to textbooks; Blackhurst (1), Buckingham (3), Burt (7), and Tinker (32). Burnhill and Hartley (5) summarise work relevant to the design of instructional materials. However, it is difficult to apply these results to the practical problem of choosing textbooks. One reason is that a textbook embodies a complete set of design decisions, whereas research workers usually test each variable separately. Another reason is that changes in design fashions have outdated much of the older research. For example, almost all the work reviewed by Tinker used justified type, a traditional (serif) typeface, and paragraphs denoted by indention. Nowadays, unjustified type, sans serif faces, and spacing between paragraphs is quite common.

Often these variables interact; for example, consider the tests of optimal line-lengths. If you use justified type with shorter lines, the spacing between words becomes visibly stretched or compressed; a longer line allows a more natural adjustment. We can predict, therefore, that tests with unjustified type would favour shorter line lengths than tests with justified type. Therefore, the results of earlier work cannot be taken at face value and used directly for decision making. The results need reinterpretation by skilled researchers and designers, and research is needed on modern design fashions and on overall page design. These problems are spelled out in more detail by Macdonald-Ross and Waller (23), who put forward a conceptual framework for improving research and practice in typography.

For practical purposes, the single most important lesson is that combinations of nonoptimal or marginal typographic arrangements can diminish legibility to a striking degree (26). With a world shortage of paper, publishers will no doubt try to cut corners by reducing distance between lines, reducing type size, and increasing line length. This must be watched very closely; officials should use expert researchers and designers as consultants and empirical research funded in especially important cases.

Note, also, that there is almost no typographic research for alphabets other than the Roman. Since many countries are now rejecting the English they once used as their chief educational language, they are depriving themselves of an important stock of research results. We clearly need some international research centres to provide, for other scripts, the basic legibility data we now have for the Roman alphabet.

Readability. Readability formulas provide the simplest way to get a reliable prediction of the style difficulty of text ("how something is said," as opposed to "what is said"). Typically, these formulas use counts of word and sentence variables which can be made easily by hand or by computer. The word counts most often use some index of familiarity, such as frequency of occurrence or length (in syllables). These two measures are strongly related and give a good indication of whether readers will be able to handle the vocabulary. The usual measure of sentence difficulty is average sentence length (in words), which is strongly related to syntactic complexity. Thus, the formulas combine these two simple vocabulary (semantic) and sentence (syntactic) counts into one score predictive of reading difficulty. The two formulas most widely used on English language text over the years, those of Dale and Chall (11) and Flesch (13) are good examples and remain excellent choices for most readability users. Many other formulas have been developed for various reasons. Some have used more variables and claimed greater predictive power. But careful examination and long experience have shown that such substitutions usually add little to the accuracy of prediction for what is often a great deal of extra effort in application. The apparent increase in power, furthermore, is often more a matter of the kind of criterion used than the discovery of superior variables and/or procedures. Miller (25) illustrated this in a comparison of the Dale-Chall, Flesch, Bormuth (2), and Coleman (10) formulas. In contrast, some formulas, especially those intended for a special body of text, have only one variable rather than two for ease of use. This limits applicability of the formula, and may even result in significant loss of predictive power for other samples of what appears to be the same body of text (8). In many cases, computer programs and aids designed for manual use can accomplish the same savings in time with no loss in power. The literature of readability is quite extensive; those who are interested should consult the earlier reviews of Chall (9) or Klare (16, 17).

At their best, readability scores can be an ideal management device because (unlike legibility) you can often use a simple figure as a rough screen or filter. This single figure is the difference between the reading skill of the students and the readability level of the material. (In the United States this would usually be expressed in school grade levels; Europeans tend to use age levels.) Since the reading level of the student is "given" (that is, can't be changed easily), the control problem becomes one of deciding where to draw the line. What degree of mismatch is acceptable? Four kinds of information are needed to answer this.

- The predictive accuracy of the formula you are using. A standard error of estimate of one grade level means that you could expect errors of prediction of less than one grade level 68 percent of the time, or less than two grade levels 95 percent of the time. The standard errors of published formulas range from .38 to 2.37 at least. The former is unusually small and the latter unusually large. A reasonable generalization is to assume that formula scores are probably not statistically accurate within about one grade level. If you know the standard error of estimate for the formula you are using, you can refine this judgment.

- The range of reading ability in the target population. The greater the variation among the readers you are selecting books for, the less likely it is that one readability score will be accurate for all. You should keep in mind that, as you go from grade 1 to grade 12 (or age 6 to age 17), the range of reading ability within each grade will increase. The poorer readers will tend to fall behind the average, and the better ones to pull ahead. If you know that your population is highly variable, you may wish to select two or three screening scores for the different groups, perhaps one each for good, average, and poor readers.

- The degree of background knowledge in the target population. Put briefly, this says that the more a reader knows about a particular subject-matter, the more readable new material on this subject is likely to seem to him. This problem of prior knowledge is least noticeable at the lower grade levels, since special bodies of knowledge have not yet been built. At college level, the degree of background knowledge becomes a more important consideration.
- The levels of motivation of the target population. Almost everyone readily agrees that motivation is critical to nearly every aspect of human behavior—then promptly ignores this when interpreting data. Some effects are fairly obvious. A highly motivated reader may struggle through a very difficult book, at one extreme, while at the other extreme a poorly motivated reader may ignore the best-seller on the table in front of him. But other effects are more subtle. Klare and Smart (19) found a very high relationship (rank-order correlation of .87) between the readability level of United States Armed Forces Institute printed correspondence materials and the probability that students would send in all of their lessons. The clear-cut effect found in this field study would probably seldom, if ever, be found in an experimental study, since this setting tends to raise the learners' motivation and also circumscribe his behavior. On the other hand, in the above field setting, the motivational level of the learners was lower, which was typical, and the effect was, therefore, more markedly shown. Denbow (12) provided another interesting example. He measured the amount of information gained from more versus less readable versions of each of two different passages. One passage, because of its topic (gun control in Great Britain) was preferred by readers to the other (cotton prices in the United States). As expected, the more readable versions, compared to the less readable, increased the amount of information gained from both passages. The amount of gain was, however, significantly greater for the nonpreferred passage! Motivation is an important consideration, whether it arises from intrinsic (interest) or extrinsic (reward) bases. A good rule is that a readability score overestimates difficulty for strongly motivated students and underestimates difficulty for weakly motivated students.

Bearing all this in mind, we must again ask what degree of mismatch is acceptable between the reader's skill and the readability level of reading material. We suggest that for the typical textbook reader (one with average motivation, reading skill, and prior knowledge of the subject matter), this relationship can be expected; if the readability level of a book is more than two grades beyond his level, his reading is likely to be inefficient. This will affect his ability to learn from the book, and will probably also affect his attitude toward the subject matter. Thus, a mismatch of two grades puts a book on the borderline, while a mismatch of as many as three grades could justify outright rejection.

We wish there were better research evidence for our generalization. Many studies have been made, but most of them simply deplore a mismatch when it exists, without looking carefully at its effect upon reader behavior. One of the best available indications of what happens comes from a study by Sticht, et al. (31). They found that military jobholders who need information increasingly turn away from printed sources as the mismatch increases, and rely more upon what they can gain by listening to others. For the job of cook, the readability level of the printed source materials ranged from approximately the same as the average skill level of the men to two grades above. These men indicated that they used their printed source materials 80 to 90 percent of the time when they needed information. For the jobs of repairman and supply specialist, the readability level of the printed materials was about five or six grades above the average skill level of the men. These men indicated that they used their printed information sources only from about 30 to 60 percent of the time (depending upon their skill level).

Formulas have long been available for helping to avoid mismatches of English language materials and their potential readers. Recently, formulas have also become available for Chinese, Dutch, French, German, Hebrew, Russian, and Spanish materials. In addition, English language formulas have been applied to Hindi materials. Other formulas could, and should, be developed for other languages. The procedure for doing so is now well understood; all that remains is the necessary research. An international research center, perhaps under Unesco sponsorship, would provide the best assurance of needed development. Such a center could also run computer analyses of readability, since a number of good programs are now available (17). The time, effort, and/or tedium of large scale manual applications, which prevent widespread use even where formulas themselves are easily available (as in the United States), could thereby be avoided.

For language materials where formulas are not yet available, an interim solution is possible through use of the cloze procedure. Cloze scores are produced thus: every fifth word is deleted and replaced with a standard-sized blank, which the reader attempts to fill in. All words replaced exactly are scored correct. The score produced is related to the usual readability scores, though precisely how is still under investigation (27). It is safe to say that of several texts, the most readable is the one where the most blanks can be filled. Cloze has been used successfully on a number of non-European languages, including Japanese, Korean, Thai, and Vietnamese. Cloze has also been used with English as a foreign language. Klare, Sinaiko, and Stolurow (18) have reviewed the literature on the cloze procedure.

One final word of warning. Though readability scores do show reliably when a text should be rewritten, they do not show how it should be rewritten. In other words, the scores can be used for prediction, not production, of readable writing. Writing readably is a complex, high-order skill which cannot be done by formula. A formula gives you a score after the event, and can in that way be an aid in rewriting; but it should, even then, be used only as a screening device. The value of readability formulas for that purpose is now firmly established.

THE PROCESS OF JUDGMENT

After the screening process, we are still left with the reasonable candidates: those textbooks that do not violate some preset criterion. From now on, the decisions become more difficult. We assume that, generally speaking, no book will combine all the possible virtues. If it did, it would probably have swept the market already. But actually, no book can combine all the virtues since some are incompatible with others. A book designed for self-instruction will never be completely adequate for reference; and a reference book will always be somewhat defective when used for self-instruction (the self-instructional book needs to impose some sequence which a reference book must avoid). A book that goes into the detail needed for advanced students can't have room for elementary explanations, and thus can't be used for beginners. And a book which holds to a particular style of teaching may rule itself out for other styles. This is all very obvious. It leads us to admit the need for human judgment to weigh the balance, the pros and cons of the candidates.

Rothkopf (29) found experts to be poor judges of the effectiveness of educational materials, but his experiments are not sufficient to cause us to remove human judgment from the scene. Rather, it causes us to think about how best to use judges so that their opinions become more reliable and more useful for the decision maker. If you think about the role of the critic in the humanities you will surely agree that the art of judgment is thoroughly respectable and of longstanding. This is what Richards (28) meant when he said: "what we want is the further development of what is already an advanced art, the art of intellectual discernment." Scientists made extensive use of expert judges to referee papers and grant proposals. All in all, there is no reason to be defensive just because the process of judgment cannot be reduced to a precise formula.

We have the start we need: the widespread habit of journals using critics to provide reviews for textbooks and other academic works. The critic does not make the decision for you; he illuminates the scene, provides insights, and judges the work according to various ill-defined but, nevertheless, valuable intellectual standards. This puts you in a better position to see the strengths and weaknesses of the book, and to see whether it suits your circumstance.

We suggest that critics should be used in a more organised manner to provide the basis for decision making. The procedure is simple in principle. Between two to six experts are chosen to provide detailed criticisms of the book in question. Experts should be paid enough to show that their effort is valued and deserves serious attention on their part. They should be chosen to counterbalance each others' weaknesses, but all should be experts in a relevant area. For example, at least one critic should be a research expert; one should be expert in teaching the subject-matter; if there are different schools of thought on the subject, both or all should be represented. But, above all, one should look for critics of outstanding intellectual calibre. Criticism is not an exercise in democracy; one man's criticism is not as good as another's.

A file should be kept on every book criticised and on every individual critic. After a time, the consequences of decisions become known and it is possible to go back to the original criticisms to see to what extent they identified key features of the books, and to what extent they turned out correct. This means building a track record for critics. Those who prove most useful should be used more and paid more. Those who say nothing, or who show poor judgment, can simply be replaced. Thus, it does not matter whether the first choices are perfect as long as records are kept and lessons are learned.

Moreover, it is possible for the activity of textbook criticism to develop its own methodology, and to identify problems that need research. Very likely, such research would be quite different in character from much of what passes today as research on teaching, since it will need to face the problem of judgments about quality. An example of what we might hope for is given by Metcalf (24) in his interesting discussion of the study and teaching of explanation.

The final decision in our scheme is made by administrators and teachers. By our process we put them in the best position possible, and we set up the system so that it improves as time goes on. This then is our advice: make the best use of research and the best use of human judgment. Others have taken quite a different approach to the problem; they have said "let us see what the objectives are and whether the book achieves those objectives." The most extreme example of this approach was provided by the Joint Committee on Programmed Instruction and Teaching Machines (15). Their criteria for assessing programmed instruction materials were so demanding that (so it is said) no program ever published satisfied their requirements. We have some reservations on the use of objectives in education (21), and really do not feel that they will prove more than minor aids in the decision making system. The truth is that human expertise and critical judgment are always necessary; if these skills are not used formally then they get used surreptitiously. By accepting critical skills as a formal part of the process we allow teachers and administrators to improve the quality of their decisions in a practical manner.

REFERENCES

1. Blackhurst, J. H. *Investigations in the Hygiene of Reading*. Baltimore: Warwick and York, 1927.
2. Bormuth, J. R. *Development of Readability Analyses*. Final Report, Project No. 7-0052, Contract No. OEC-3-070052-0326. Washington: USOE, Bureau of Research, U.S. Department of Health, Education, and Welfare, 1969.
3. Buckingham, B. R. *New Data on the Typography of Textbooks*, 30th Yearbook of National Society for the Study of Education, 93-125, 1931.
4. Buckingham, B. R. "Textbooks," in C. W. Harris (Ed.), *Encyclopedia of Educational Research* (3rd ed.). New York: Macmillan, 1960.
5. Burnhill, P., and J. Hartley. "Psychology and Textbook Design: A Research Critique," *Aspects of Educational Technology VIII*. Pitman, 1974.
6. Burt, C. *The Psychological Study of Typography*. Cambridge University Press, 1959.
7. Burt, C. "The Typography of Children's Books: A Record of Research in the UK," *Yearbook of Education*, 242-256, 1960.
8. Carver, R. P. *Improving Comprehension: Measuring Readability*. Final Report, Contract No. N00014-72-C-0240, Office of Naval Research. Silver Spring, Maryland: American Institute for Research, 1974.
9. Chall, J. S. *Readability: An Appraisal of Research and Application*. Columbus, Ohio: Bureau of Educational Research, 1958.
10. *On Understanding Prose: Some Determiners of its Complexity*. NSF Final Report GB-2604. Washington, D.C.: National Science Foundation, 1965.
11. Dale, E., and J. S. Chall. "A Formula for Predicting Readability," *Educational Research Bulletin*, 27 (1948), 11-20, 37-54.
12. Denbow, C. J. "An Experimental Study of the Effect of a Repetition Factor on the Relationship between Readability and Listenability," unpublished doctoral dissertation, Ohio University, 1973.
13. Flesch, R. J. "A New Readability Yardstick," *Journal of Applied Psychology*, 32 (1948), 221-233.
14. Hartley, J., P. Burnhill, and S. Fraser. *A Selected Bibliography of Typographical Research Relevant to the Production of Instructional Materials*. University of Keele, Department of Psychology, 1973.
15. Joint Committee on Programmed Instruction and Teaching Machines. *Recommendations for Reporting the Effectiveness of Programmed Instruction Materials*. Division of Audiovisual Instructional Service, National Education Association, 1966.
16. Klare, G. R. *The Measurement of Readability*. Ames, Iowa: Iowa State University Press, 1963.
17. Klare, G. R. "Assessing Readability," *Reading Research Quarterly*, 10 (1974).
18. Klare, G. R., H. W. Sinaiko, and L. M. Stolurow. "The Cloze Procedure: A Convenient Readability Test for Training Materials and Translations," *International Review of Applied Psychology*, 21 (1972), 77-106.
19. Klare, G. R., and K. Smart. "Analysis of the Readability Level of Selected United States Armed Forces Institute Printed Instructional Materials," *Journal of Educational Research*, 67 (1973), 176.

20. Lumsdaine, A. A. "Instruments and Media of Instruction," in N. L. Gage (Ed.), *Handbook of Research on Teaching*. Chicago: Rand McNally, 1963.
21. Macdonald-Ross, M. "Behavioural Objectives: A Critical Review," *Instructional Science*, 2 (1973), 1-52.
22. Macdonald-Ross, M., and E. B. Smith. *Bibliography for Textual Communication*, Monograph No. 3, Institute of Educational Technology, The Open University, 1973.
23. Macdonald-Ross, M., and R. Waller. "Criticism, Alternatives, and Tests: A Conceptual Framework for Improving Typography," *Journal of Programmed Learning and Educational Technology*, 1975, in press.
24. Metcalf, L. E. "Research on Teaching the Social Studies," in N. L. Gage (Ed.), *Handbook of Research on Teaching*. Chicago: Rand McNally, 1963.
25. Miller, L. R. "A Comparative Anlysis of the Predictive Validities of Four Readability Formulas," unpublished doctoral dissertation, Ohio University, 1971.
26. Paterson, D. G., and M. A. Tinker. *How to Make Type Readable*. New York: Harper & Row, 1940.
27. Peterson, J., E. Paradis, and N. Peters. "Revalidation of the Cloze Procedure as a Measure of the Instructional Level of High School Students," *Diversity in Mature Reading: Theory and Research*, 22nd Yearbook of the National Reading Conference, 1. Boone, North Carolina: National Reading Conference, 1973.
28. Richards, I. A. *Interpretation in Teaching*. Boston, Massachusetts: Routledge and Kegan Paul, 1938.
29. Rothkopf, E. Z. "Some Observations on Predicting Instructional Effectiveness by Simple Inspection," *Journal of Programmed Instruction*, 2 (1963), 19-20.
30. Spencer, H. *The Visible Word*. Lund Humphries, 1968.
31. Sticht, T. G., et al. "Determination of Literacy Skill Requirements in Four Military Occupational Specialties," *HumRRO Technical Report*, 71-23. Alexandria, Virginia: Human Resources Research Organization, 1971.
32. Tinker, M. A. "Print for Children's Textbooks," *Education*, 80 (1959), 37-40.
33. Tinker, M. A. *Legibility of Print*. Ames, Iowa: Iowa State University Press, 1963.
34. Travers, R. *Second Handbook of Research on Teaching: A Project of the American Educational Research Association*. Chicago: Rand McNally, 1973.
35. Watts, L., and J. Nisbet. *Legibility in Children's Books: A Review of Research*. National Foundation for Educational Research, 1974.

Some New Developments on Readability

Albert J. Harris, Emeritus
City University of New York
New York, New York
United States of America

One of the major tasks for the teacher of reading is to provide the student reader with material that he can read and understand. The term *readability* refers to the qualities of reading material which determine how easy it is to understand, how fluently it can be read, and how much interest it generates. This paper, however, is concerned with readability only in the sense of ease or difficulty of comprehension.

The term *new development* needs to be made more explicit. Two fairly recent publications provide a starting point: *Readability and Reading* (27) which provides good coverage of research published between 1965 and 1970, and Gilliland's *Readability* (12) published in 1972. The present paper emphasizes developments too recent to have been covered in those two very helpful sources. Some earlier work will also be discussed.

On first thought it may seem that the logical way to determine the readability of a selection is to give it to someone to read and to check his comprehension. Such a procedure, sometimes called "trying the book on for size," can establish how well that person has been able to read the book. But usually we want to predict how a selection, or a whole book, will fit an individual or group's ability to understand before deciding if they should be asked to read it.

THE MEASUREMENT OF READABILITY

To get away from the need to try a book with each potential user, it is necessary to obtain a score which can express the book's readability on an easily interpreted scale. This is done by measuring the book's scores on characteristics which can predict where it would belong on a scale of reading selections whose readability scores have already been established.

The scale of reading selections that has been used most widely in readability research is a collection called *Standard Test Lessons in Reading* (24), originally published in the 1920s and revised in 1961. There are five booklets, each containing about 70 one-page test lessons. For each lesson there is a short selection, followed by about ten multiple-choice questions. At the bottom is a table giving the grade score corresponding to each possible number of right answers. These grade scores were originally established by giving the test lessons and a standardized reading test to several thousand pupils. The readability formulas developed by Lorge (21), Flesch (10), and Dale and Chall (8) all used the McCall-Crabbs test lessons as a criterion.

Another way to set up a readability scale is to use the cloze technique to determine the comprehension difficulty of a number of selections. In the cloze procedure, usually every fifth word is deleted in a regular pattern and the reader's task is to write in each missing word. The average number of correct cloze answers for a group can be used to rank selections in readability, setting up a scale against which other selections can be compared. The cloze technique has been used in much recent readability research, particularly by Bormuth (2, 3) and by Coleman (5, 6, 7).

A third procedure is to take several series of carefully graded books and use their average characteristics to establish a graded scale. In the United States, widely used basal reader series have been used as criteria for the development of readability formulas by Spache (28) and in the new Harris-Jacobson formulas which will be described a little later in this paper.

A fourth procedure is to have the selections rated by a group of judges, using the average rating to establish a scale. However, the ratings of judges on the same book can vary widely. Jongsma (19) had 12 Newbery Award winning books rated by 44 school and public librarians. One book was rated in difficulty all the way from third grade to twelfth grade.

ELEMENTS OF READABILITY

Numerous studies have shown that the two main elements of the difficulty of reading material are the difficulty of the vocabulary used (semantic difficulty) and the difficulty of the sentence structure (syntactical or grammatical complexity). Of these two factors, vocabulary difficulty has consistently shown somewhat greater importance. Klare (20) wrote: "Frequency of occurrence of words . . . clearly plays an all pervasive role in language usage. Not only do humans tend to use some words much more often than others, they recognize more frequent words more rapidly than less frequent, prefer them, and understand and learn them more readily. It is not surprising, therefore, that this variable has such a central role in the measurement of readability."

Measurement of the difficulty of words has been done in a variety of ways. The procedure most often used is to determine what percent of words in a sample are not found in a particular list of common words. Two lists compiled by Edgar Dale—a short list of 769 words and a list of about 3,000 words known to fourth grade children—have been used in several readability formulas including those by Lorge (21), Dale and Chall (8), and Spache (28). Recently there have been efforts to update these lists. Spache (29) expanded the original short Dale list to 1,041 words, adding words from the Harris-Jacobson Core List (14) and from library books of first and second grade levels, and revised his readability formula accordingly.

The publication in 1972 of the Harris-Jacobson *Basic Elementary Reading Vocabularies* (14) provided a possible improvement in the measurement of vocabulary difficulty. The Harris-Jacobson word lists are based on a computerized analysis of about 4,500,000 running words found in 14 series of elementary school textbooks, from beginning first grade through sixth grade. A first grade list; a combined first and second grade list; and a combined first, second, and third grade list were tried out, and the combined first and second grade list proved to have the highest correlation with reading level from grade one through grade six. This combined list contains 912 root words and 1,880 inflected forms, such as plurals and regular verb endings (-ed and -ing), totalling 2,796 words. Since all allowable variants of a common root word are in the list, one does not have to remember a variety of rules or repeatedly consult the list of rules to see what constitutes an unfamiliar word. If a word is not in the list, and is not a proper noun, it counts as unfamiliar. The percent of unfamiliar words has the highest correlation with basal reader level of a large number of measures of vocabulary and sentence difficulty tried.

Several other measures of vocabulary difficulty have been used in the more than fifty different readability formulas that have been published to date. Average number of letters per word, average number of syllables, average number of vowel letters, number of prefixes and suffixes, percent of one-syllable words, percent of words having three or more syllables, and percent of words having more than five letters have been tried. Studies have also shown that the proportion of certain parts of speech is related to readability. Coleman (7), for example, used the number of pronouns and number of prepositions per 100 words as minor elements in his readability formulas.

All of these different ways of getting at vocabulary difficulty have substantial to high intercorrelations, but not all are of equal value in measuring readability. Unpublished results by Harris and Jacobson show that over the range from beginning first grade through sixth grade, percent of unfamiliar words had the highest correlation, .87; percent of words with more than five letters, .80; and average number of letters per word, .74. The percent of unfamiliar words was 21 percent more accurate in measuring readability than average number of letters per word. In recent years, ways have developed for scoring many of these variables by computer. A computer can easily determine whether a word is in a given list, count its letters, and so on, but it is much harder to write a program which will accurately identify syllables or prefixes. In the future, only variables which can be scored by computer are likely to be retained in readability research.

In 1973, Harris and Jacobson (15) reported that the percent of words beginning with the letter e has a substantial correlation with difficulty in primary reading material, and Jacobson followed this by identifying more than 1,000 spelling patterns in English words and correlating them with difficulty. In a 1974 paper, Jacobson (18) reported that 37 spelling patterns, when combined in a multiple regression equation, correlated .92 with primary reading difficulty. In further work not yet published, Jacobson has found that when one group of 12 spelling patterns is used for primary material and another group of 12 is used for middle-grade material, a combined multiple correlation of .965 is obtained. Using these spelling patterns is possible only with a computer and a very complicated computer program. Spelling patterns are probably related to readability in two different ways. One is that certain spelling patterns have greatly variable sound-symbol relationships. Initial e, for example, can represent at least seven different phonemes, as in each, ear, early, elephant, English, eight and eyesight. This obviously increases the difficulty of decoding words beginning with e. The other way is that some spelling patterns tend to occur mainly in long words which are also uncommon and difficult, while other patterns appear predominantly in short, common, easy words. Spelling patterns present a new and promising approach to the measurement of vocabulary difficulty, but are usable only by those who have appropriate computer resources.

SENTENCE DIFFICULTY

From the beginning of readability study, it has been recognized that the difficulty of a sentence involves elements beyond the difficulties of the words in it. The average number of words per sentence has been used in many readability formulas and provides a reasonably satisfactory measure of those sentence characteristics that influence readability. In general, long sentences tend to have more modifiers and qualifiers, more embedded phrases and clauses, and complex rather than simple structure.

Since 1960 a number of efforts have been made to measure the linguistic or syntactic difficulty of sentences. Hunt (17) developed a measure called the T-unit, which is one main clause and its related words, phrases, and clauses; in most cases, these amount to the number of words in the sentence. Golub (13) developed a Syntactic Density Score which uses the T-unit and also takes account of such items as complex verb expansions and prepositional phrases. Since then, Golub has developed a program (unpublished) which can obtain his Syntactic Density Score by computer. Bormuth (3) included measures of right depth of sentences and left depth of sentences among the variables used in some of his readability formulas. Botel and Granowsky (4) developed a formula for measuring the syntactic density of individual sentences; the average score for the sentences in a selection should correlate with readability.

Such methods of sentence analysis obviously help to show why one sentence may be harder to understand than another of similar length. But there is no evidence as yet that they can give a better indication of the difficulty of a whole selection than average sentence length does. MacGinitie and Tretiak (23) compared the sentence depth measures devised by Yngve (31) and by Allen (1) with average sentence length and found that average sentence length gave the best prediction of readability when each was combined with a measure of word difficulty. Similar research is needed for the other measures of sentence complexity. Since scoring sentences for these variables is slow and laborious, future research in this area is likely to emphasize variables that can be scored by computer.

To summarize this discussion on the elements of comprehensibility or readability, the most important element in the difficulty of reading material is the difficulty of the vocabulary employed. This is measurable in a variety of ways, among which the percent of words not found in a list of common, easy words seems to be the most satisfactory as well as the one most commonly used. The other main variable affecting readability is sentence complexity, which is well represented by average sentence length.

NEW READABILITY FORMULAS

The increasing use of computers in readability research has made it easy to develop readability formulas for special purposes. However, most users of readability measures do not have computers available, and ease and speed of scoring and computation are important factors in choosing which formula to use. This discussion will be confined to new formulas that are applicable by hand to children's materials for the elementary grades.

At IRA's 1973 Denver Convention, Harris and Jacobson presented some data on new readability formulas (15). Since then, the formulas have been further revised and a large number of new formulas have been tested. Many different combinations of variables provide measures of about equal accuracy. Two formulas, one for grades one through three, and one which works from grades one through six but is mainly for use above third grade, have been selected as providing the best combination of ease and rapidity of application and high correlations with difficulty. Both formulas have correlations of .90 with reader level. The primary formula has a standard error of estimate of .38 of a year; the other formula has a standard error of .71 of a year. Complete directions for using these formulas appear in a book by Harris and Sipay (16), published in 1975.

Spache (29) published a revision of his formula for primary grade material. The new formula is based on 100 samples of about 100 words each, or a total of about 10,000 words, in comparison to the Harris-Jacobson formulas which are based on 661 samples totaling about 135,000 words. Spache reports the very high correlation of .95 with book grade level.

SPECIFIC FEATURES OF DIFFICULT PROSE

The kinds of conjunctions used by writers seem to influence the difficulty of their material. Stoodt (30) reported on the comparative difficulty of commonly used conjunctions for fourth grade children. The ones that were best understood were *and, for, as*; comparatively difficult were *when, so, but, or, where, while, that, if*. Robertson (25) found that clauses introduced by *however, thus, which, although*, and *yet* were difficult for children in grades four through six, and success in understanding such clauses was closely related to general reading comprehension.

Rosenshine (26) used long passages which were equivalent in difficulty according to readability formulas but on which college students showed varying degrees of comprehension. He found five factors that tended to influence the readability of the passages. Difficulty was increased by vagueness and ambiguity, which is shown by the excessive use of indeterminate qualifiers such as *rather, any number of*, and *quite a bit*, and also by excessive use of probability words such as *might, possibly*, and *sometimes*. A factor aiding comprehension is frequent use of explaining links like *because, in order to, if . . . then*, and so forth, which call attention to a cause, a result, or a means. A third factor was frequent use of examples, which seemed more important in difficult material than in easy material. The fourth factor was use of a rule example-rule pattern, in which a generalization would be stated, followed by one or more examples, and then by a restatement of the generalization or rule. This seemed more beneficial than either an inductive or deductive pattern of presentation. The fifth factor was irrelevancy, which increased the difficulty of the material. Digressions and unnecessary restatements seem to lower the amount of information gain. These five factors are worth noting by those who write and lecture.

We have only a beginning of research on the specific features of prose writing that make material easy or difficult to read. We need to distinguish between inherent difficulty that results from the necessary use of concepts and relationships that are hard to explain and hard to understand, and unnecessary difficulty which is created by distinctive features of an author's style. When the subject matter is inherently difficult, one can lower a readability formula score artificially by chopping long sentences into short ones and by substituting more common for less common synonyms. Geyer and Carey (11) rewrote American History materials to reduce the Dale-Chall readability scores by about two grades. However, the comprehension scores of students were no higher on the easier than on the harder original versions. Apparently, the kind of rewriting that was guided by the formula did not reduce the inherent difficulty of the content.

All too often, an author creates unnecessary difficulty for his readers. In addition to the factors of vagueness and irrelevancy discussed by Rosenshine, we have to guard against excessive use of the passive voice and the subjunctive mood. We have to check to see if modifying phrases and clauses are placed close to the items they modify. We have to note whether the antecedents of pronouns are easily identified. We have to observe whether sentences follow in a logical sequence, whether each paragraph actually has a main idea, and whether appropriate emphasis is given to the most important statements. These factors are not measured by readability formulas, but they do affect the ease or difficulty with which one can grasp the thought content of written material.

READABILITY OF LANGUAGES OTHER THAN ENGLISH

This paper has considered only readability research on English prose. Readability studies have been conducted on quite a number of other languages, including French, German, Dutch, Spanish, Hebrew, Hindi, Chinese, Korean, Japanese, and Vietnamese. The limitations of this paper do not permit going into detail on these studies, most of which were done before 1970. Professor G. De Landsheere of the University of Liege has been a leader in European research on readability. Very briefly, it seems safe to generalize that the two variables of vocabulary difficulty and sentence length are useful indicators of comprehensibility in any language. The features of specific written languages may encourage use of such variables as syllable counts or measures of the visual complexity of Chinese characters.

SUMMARY

One can measure the readability of any piece of material for an individual or a group by having the selection read and then testing for comprehension. Increasingly, the cloze procedure has come to be used in preference to multiple-choice questions. A scale of selections can be arranged based on the average comprehension scores of a group. Other readability scales have been based on previously scaled passages, on carefully graded books, and on the combined judgments of a group of experts. Once a scale has been constructed, many different characteristics of the material can be measured, and each set of measurements can be correlated with the scale. Using the technique of multiple correlation, the best combination of variables and the best ways to weight them so as to get a maximum correlation can be discovered. Computer procedures which can score the selections for many variables, as well as compute multiple correlations almost instantly, have greatly simplified and speeded readability research in recent years.

Consistently, two variables have stood out as providing the best combination in the measurement of readability. The first, and most important variable, is the difficulty of the vocabulary used. This is usually measured by finding the percent of words that do not appear in a specific list of common, easy words. Spelling patterns as indices of vocabulary difficulty have just begun to be explored and seem promising. The second widely used variable is average sentence length, which seems to represent the many specific reasons why long sentences are usually harder to understand than short sentences. Now that beginnings have been made in the automatic computer scoring of complicated linguistic variables such as syntactic depth and density, more refined measures of sentence difficulty may appear in future readability formulas. Recent formulas that use the two variables of percent of unfamiliar words and average number of words per sentence have multiple correlations of .90 or better with difficulty, seeming to indicate that not much further improvement is possible.

The specific factors that make some reading material hard to understand have begun to be analyzed. Vagueness, ambiguity, and lack of explicitness concerning important relationships are among the factors noted thus far. Much more research is needed in this area.

Most readability research has been conducted on English prose. Some work has been done in a number of other languages, both European and non-European, which lie outside the scope of this paper.

Progress in the measurement and understanding of readability will improve the ability of authors and teachers to achieve a better fit between the abilities of readers to understand and the materials they are expected to read.

REFERENCES

1. Allen, Robert L. *The Structure of the English Sentence.* New York: Noble and Noble, 1968.
2. Bormuth, John R. (Ed.). *Readability in 1968,* a research bulletin prepared by a committee of the National Conference on Research in English. Urbana, Illinois: National Council of Teachers of English, 1968.
3. Bormuth, John R. *Development of Readability Analyses.* Washington, D.C.: Project No. 7-0052, Final Report, United States Office of Education, 1969.
4. Botel, Morton, and Alvin Granowsky. "A Formula for Measuring Syntactic Complexity: A Directional Effort," *Elementary English,* 49 (1972), 513-516.
5. Coleman, E. B. "Experimental Studies of Readability, Part I: Stimulus Dimensions that Affect Readability," *Elementary English,* 45 (February 1968), 166-178.
6. Coleman, E. B. "Experimental Studies of Readability, Part II: Measures of Readability and Relevant Populations," *Elementary English,* 45 (March 1968), 316-323, 333.
7. Coleman, E. B. "Developing a Technology of Written Instruction: Some Determinants of the Complexity of Prose," in E. Z. Rothkopf and P. E. Johnson (Eds.), *Verbal Learning and the Technology of Written Instruction.* New York: Teachers College Press, Columbia University, 1971.
8. Dale, Edgar, and Jeanne S. Chall. "A Formula for Predicting Readability," *Educational Research Bulletin,* 27 (January 21 and February 17, 1968), 11-20, 37-54.
9. De Landsheere, G., G. Henry, and J. Donnay. "Etude sur la Compréhension des Messages Contenus dans les Journaux Parlés et les Journaux Télévisés," *Scientia Paedagogica Experimentalis,* 7 (1970), 23-64.
10. Flesch, Rudolph. *Marks of a Readable Style.* New York: Teachers College Press, Columbia University, 1943.
11. Geyer, James R., and Albert R. Carey. "Predicting and Improving Comprehensibility of Social Studies Materials: The Role of Cloze Procedure and Readability Adjustment," *Reading World,* 12 (December 1972), 85-93.
12. Gilliland, John. *Readability.* London: University of London Press, 1972.
13. Golub, Lester S. "Linguistic Structures in Students' Oral and Written Discourse," *Research in the Teaching of English,* 3 (Spring 1969), 70-85.
14. Harris, Albert J., and Milton D. Jacobson. *Basic Elementary Reading Vocabularies.* New York: Macmillan, 1972.
15. Harris, Albert J., and Milton D. Jacobson. "The Harris-Jacobson Primary Readability Formulas," paper presented at the Annual Convention of the International Reading Association, Denver, Colorado, May 1973.
16. Harris, Albert J., and Edward R. Sipay. *How to Increase Reading Ability* (6th ed. rev.). New York: David McKay, 1975.
17. Hunt, Kellog. *Grammatical Structures Written at Three Grade Levels,* NCTE Research Report No. 3. Urbana, Illinois: National Council of Teachers of English, 1965.
18. Jacobson, Milton D. "Predicting Reading Difficulty from Spelling," *Spelling Progress Bulletin,* 14 (Spring 1974), 8-10.
19. Jongsma, Eugene A. "The Difficulty of Children's Books: Librarians' Judgments vs Formula Estimates," *Elementary English,* 49 (January 1972), 20-26.
20. Klare, George R. "The Role of Word Frequency in Readability," *Elementary English,* 45 (January 1968), 12-22.
21. Lorge, Irving. "Predicting Readability," *Teachers College Record,* 45 (March 1944), 404-419.
22. Lorge, Irving. "Readability Formulas—An Evaluation," *Elementary English,* 26 (February 1949), 85-95.
23. MacGinitie, Walter H., and Richard Tretiak. "Sentence Depth Measures as Predictors of Reading Difficulty," *Reading Research Quarterly,* 6 (Spring 1971), 364-377.
24. McCall, William A., and Leila M. Crabbs. *Standard Test Lessons in Reading* (rev.). New York: Teachers College Press, Columbia University, 1961.
25. Robertson, Jean E. "Pupil Understanding of Connectives in Reading," *Reading Research Quarterly,* 3 (Spring 1968), 387-417.
26. Rosenshine, Barak. "New Correlates of Readability and Listenability," in J. Allen Figurel (Ed.), *Reading and Realism,* 1968 Proceedings, Volume 13, Part 1. Newark,

Delaware: International Reading Association, 1969, 710-716.

27. Seels, Barbara, and Edgar Dale. *Readability and Reading* (rev. ed.). Newark, Delaware: International Reading Association, 1971.

28. Spache, George D. "A New Readability Formula for Primary Grade Reading Materials," *Elementary School Journal*, 53 (March 1953), 410-413.

29. Spache, George D. *Good Reading for Poor Readers* (rev. ed.). Champaign, Illinois: Garrard, 1974, 195-207.

30. Stoodt, Barbara D. "The Relationship between Understanding Grammatical Conjunctions and Reading Comprehension," *Elementary English*, 49 (April 1972), 502-504.

31. Yngve, V. H. "A Model and an Hypothesis for Language Structure," *Proceedings of the American Philosophical Society*, 1960, 444-466.

Content Bias in Adult Reading Materials

Michael R. Molloy
St. Joseph's College of Education
Belfast, Northern Ireland

BIAS IN THE READER AND BIAS IN PRINTED MEDIA

The phenomenon of bias is complex to analyse. The psychological or sociological concept to which it is closely related is prejudice. From the various definitions proposed for prejudice, the following by Klineberg (14) may be taken as typical:

> Prejudice may be described as unsubstantiated prejudgement of an individual or group, favourable or unfavourable in character, tending to action in a consonant direction.

For the purpose of examining bias in the printed media, this definition requires to be extended to include ideas, descriptions, accounts, and opinions. Two key characteristics of bias are 1) its unsubstantiated nature, although Alport (2) has pointed out that a prejudiced person will almost certainly claim he has sufficient warrant for his view; and 2) the predisposition of a biased person to react to certain ideas in a predetermined manner. Bias can, therefore, be considered as an attitude.

In the reading experience we can expect to find bias in two interacting elements: the reader and the printed media. As far as the reader is concerned his biases are part of what he brings with him to the reading experience; they represent his conception of the topic to be discussed by the author. Predisposed to cling to his conceptual structure, he will probably select those media which are likely to reinforce his present point of view. Where the author's ideas are congruent with his own, his conceptual map will be strengthened and he will feel pleased at seeing "his" point of view in print. If the author's ideas are not congruent with his own, his conceptual map may be threatened with possible undesirable consequences in feeling and action.

An illustration of the concept of selecting congruent and ignoring noncongruent material is the situation in Northern Ireland vis-a-vis

Catholic and Protestant newspaper readership. A survey (6) in two adjoining ghetto areas in Belfast showed that the Catholic newspaper was taken by 83 percent of the sample in the Catholic area but by only 3 percent in the Protestant area. The Catholic loyalty to this paper is not surprising because the paper supports the political aspirations of most Catholics and gives substantial coverage to the affairs of Catholics (games, schools and church). A similar situation existed in the Protestant area. How is it possible to gain insight into the concepts, perspectives, and opinions of others if there are no opportunities for exposure to the "other" point of view? The Belfast situation is not unique. Parallel instances occur in the United States in relation to race and in England in relation to social class. What is alarming about these situations is the near hopelessness of being able to counter the biased attitude. When conflicting groups refuse to read each other's newspapers they are like people with their ears "tied to no tongue but their own" (Shakespeare: Henry IV, Part I). The situation says little for the level of the reading competency of the population.

It is difficult to explain how bias and prejudice are so ingrained in people. Klineberg (14) argues that prejudice is not a normal phenomenon of human social life and that, since it is not present in young children, the individual learns the biases of his culture in the process of socialization from childhood. Individuals seem to find security in identifying with the prevalent attitudes of the groups to which they belong. Exposure to alternative points of view is perceived as a threat to this identity and security. Perhaps through lack of courage the biased person refuses to swim against the tide, succumbs to the pressure of the group, and accepts without substantiation the major concepts and perceptions of the group.

Is there any escape from the cycle of continuous reinforcement of biased opinions? Is there a case for banning the publication of biased views? Such censorship does not seem to be effective. Has education a role to play? What part can reading play in breaking the vicious circle?

As an optimist, I believe that the only way out of this dilemma is to provide an effective education for children and adults with emphasis on the development of informed, imaginative minds and on critical reading. In this way, it may be possible for future adult readers to be in a position to challenge their own points of view as well as the views of others. The arguments that go on between nations, communities, institutions, groups, and individuals are waged in pages of print day after day and week after week—in newspapers, magazines, journals, books, and pamphlets. Arguing involves reasoning, thinking, and the precise use of language. Arguing requires skill in taking in and thinking through a variety of points of view; it demands differentiating between logical and emotional reasoning, between facts, allegations, and opinions; and it requires honesty, integrity, and accuracy in interpreting and expressing a point of view. To investigate an issue adequately (be it a report, a rumour, an offer, or a threat) requires open-mindedness, objectivity, detachment, sensitivity, and feeling.

Am I being excessively idealistic in expecting all readers to come to the reading experience armed with such qualities? Isn't this the responsibility of education?

The printed media are not apart from society. They mirror the society which produces them. Like the ideas and institutions of society, not all that goes into print is of equal value. It is unusual for those responsible for the printed media to forewarn their readers of the quality of what they offer. The onus rests with the reader who must bring with him to the reading experience a competency which will enable him to discriminate what he should read from what he could read, to select carefully what he will read, and to evaluate thoughtfully what he does read.

Reading is a risky business. When we expose ourselves to the ideas and viewpoints of others, there is a latent, if not manifest, possibility of conflict within ourselves and with our family, friends, or colleagues. As a human being, the reader needs courage to challenge an author's interpretation of a situation. He requires even more courage to challenge his own conception of a situation. To resolve any conflict, the reader must be capable of evaluating and judging his own and the author's ideas. These kinds of competencies have been described as critical reading.

The complexity of the interaction between the reader and print is summarized by Smith (17) in the following terms:

> In critical reading we need to read with an attitude of inquiry, a desire to seek the truth and a will to search further if necessary. We need to evaluate, challenge, decide upon truthfulness, bias, authenticity. In critical reading, the individual needs to react personally in agreeing or disagreeing with the author as a result of personal judgement based upon experience, facts gleaned from various sources or possibly as a result of clear-cut reasoning.

Critical reading is a necessary process in and product of education and learning at all levels. Harris (12) has pointed out that one of the most important aspects of critical reading is the ability to detect and resist the influence of propaganda. The chief purpose of propaganda is to spread a particular message or to give information. The techniques used include name calling, glittering generalizations, testimonials from well-known people, the bandwagon approach, and distortion (8). However, these techniques are sometimes used by writers of allegedly informational texts. Among the distorting devices used in the printed media we may include: ignoring important facts, giving undue prominence to some facts, mixing facts and opinion, omitting alternative points of view, and failing to provide evidence to support opinions and conclusions. All of these devices can lead to bias in the context of the printed media, though such bias is not always intentional. For example, the writer may not have sufficient space to present a range of facts or opinions, he may not have had adequate time or facilities to acquire alternative perspectives or facts, or the facts may not have been available at the time of writing. In these cases, some degree of bias or distortion is inevitable. Again, the onus is on the reader to identify the origin of the bias.

Evaluative comprehension is the most crucial reading skill required to deal with bias in the printed media. Barrett (3) claims that evaluation requires the reader to compare the author's ideas with external criteria provided by other authorities or other written sources, and with internal criteria provided by the reader's experiences, knowledge, or values. In the higher levels of his taxonomy of the dimensions of reading comprehension, Barrett identifies a number of key questions which readers need to apply to the content presented by the author in order to detect what bias it may contain.

After reading, what? Following the encounter with the printed material, interaction with and reaction to the author's ideas, what is the reader left with? If the encounter has involved the kind of inquiring critical attitudes suggested by Smith (17) and Barrett, the reader will be in a position to accept or reject the author's ideas as he understands them. In addition, what Gray (10) identifies as assimilation can take place. This involves the fusion of previous ideas, prejudices, attitudes with the facts, descriptions, explanations, and opinions presented in the text. Integrating novel ideas into an established conceptual structure requires the reader to reorganise his structures to accommodate new points of view. The results of such rethinking are seen in revised concepts, new understandings, and changes in attitudes and behaviour.

EXAMPLES OF POSSIBLE BIAS IN THE PRINTED MEDIA

In this section, a number of instances of bias in a variety of printed media will be presented and analysed. The examples may be summarized as follows:

- conceptions of the Northern Ireland problem
- analysis of newspaper coverage of events in Northern Ireland
- a *Reader's Digest* view of the KGB
- conceptions of the population problem

The situation in Northern Ireland is known internationally, so the following examples of its analysis should be understandable to an international audience. The first is a political commentary from an independent review published in Northern Ireland.

MR. WHITELAW'S PACKAGE
Before the Civil Rights campaign Northern Ireland was, like many other countries, an unjust but relatively stable state. The injustice was of a sectarian rather than a class nature, but for a long period it was mutually acceptable to both sides. Catholics preferred to keep themselves apart, even at the cost of fewer opportunities and less prosperity.

Fortnight, June 7, 1974

The second is from an article by an economist published in a community relations journal (9).

THE NORTHERN IRELAND PROBLEM:
RELIGIOUS, ECONOMIC, OR WHAT?
Social conflict in the sense of class conflict would not seem to be a major aspect of the Northern problem. However, we do have our ghettos, predominantly working class, and distinguishable as Protestant or Catholic. But the ghettos are more a consequence than a cause of community conflict, and to ameliorate the religious and political conflicts would be to lessen the significance of the ghettos.

Community Forum, Spring 1971

The third is from a newspaper published by militant Protestants.

WHO IS OUR ENEMY?
There are those who mistakenly analyse the Ulster situation in terms of social and economic factors, in terms of politics, or philosophies. These theories and analyses collapse because they ignore, deliberately or otherwise, the main key, and to us the most obvious factor: Protestantism versus popery. Whether it is subverting morality or governments, organising murder or revolution, the Church of Rome is expert.

The Protestant Telegraph, June 15, 1974

Three assessments—which of them is biased? The political journalist does not prove his generalizations any more than the *Protestant Telegraph* substantiates its assertions. How, therefore, do they differ? Each seems to have a different function. To use Britton's terminology (7), the first is an "analogic low-level generalization." The third comes into his "conative-persuasive" category where the writer is trying to support a course of action he recommends, or put forward an opinion, attitude, or belief. Britton points out that one of the strategies of persuasive language is to work on the reader's feelings. The first is not looking for an affective or action response whereas the language, tone, and title of the third is designed to persuade its readers that Catholics must be their enemies. Perhaps we can accept such a biased viewpoint on the grounds of free speech. However, where we would expect the contents of a Protestant newspaper to include news of the affairs of the particular Protestant church which it represents, it is not easy to accept as unbiased its contents as revealed in such headlines as "Blaspheming Bishop," or "Priest Linked with Mafia Murder." It is hard to imagine how information of this nature could provide insight into the Northern Ireland problem.

The second example is typical of the theories and analyses described as distortion in the third. Here we find a serious attempt by an academic to unravel the complex issues and agents involved. The situation is conceptualized from different angles. The terms used are neutral and descriptive, not prescriptive (11) or normative. Where the *Protestant Telegraph* is looking for an enemy, the academic is searching for understanding.

These instances, while interesting in themselves, raise the general theoretical problem of content analysis. The type of analysis used in examining the preceeding paragraphs is purely impressionistic, lacking an adequate theoretical framework. The key question in conducting an analysis of bias of this kind is: "How far is it possible to compare alleged bias in one text with alleged bias in another?" Such comparisons may be accurate only if we first categorize texts in some systematic way. The categories suggested by Britton (see appendix), derived in part from Moffett (15), seem to provide a worthwhile starting point in any attempted classification. It should then be possible to devise criteria that are appropriate for each category. Having identified the function of the writing, we are in a better position to evaluate the nature and extent of the bias it may contain. Difficulties will almost certainly arise in cases where the text has more than one function. In general, however, it should be possible for the reader to identify the function of the writing from the purposes set by the author in the titles he uses, the questions he poses, and his statements at the beginning or end of the text. Within this framework, the detection of bias involves establishing the author's purpose and evaluating how far his writing achieved that purpose using acceptable criteria (such as truthfulness), offering a balanced range of viewpoints, and providing supporting evidence and adequate instances to sustain generalizations and conclusions.

In 1969, Huczynski (13) made a survey of the coverage given in newspapers to events in Northern Ireland during one week of abnormal activity. The content of the newspapers was analysed to determine: 1) the absolute amount of attention paid to the conflict, 2) the attention paid to particular groups and agents, and 3) how far the content was "directed" in favour of any particular group. Six newspapers were selected: two published in England, two in Northern Ireland, and two in the South of Ireland. The first purpose was achieved by counting column inches of space; the second, by comparing the number of text references and photograph appearances in the six publications; and the third, by categorizing headlines and photographs according to whether they were considered by the researcher as "neutral" or "directed." The categories, derived from Berelson (5), were: 1) neutral, 2) pro-Catholic and anti-Protestant or police, 3) pro-Protestant and police and anti-Catholic.

A number of significant points emerge from an analysis of the results (see Tables 1, 2, and 3). On the average, half of the photographs and headlines of all newspapers were neutral, the other half almost equally favouring Catholics and Protestants (Table 1). Both English newspapers fell below the 50 percent neutrality level (45 percent), and were more directed in favour of Protestants (35 percent) than Catholics (20 percent). The South of Ireland newspapers, while exceeding the 50 percent neutrality level, were more directed in favour of Catholics (26 percent) than Protestants (20 percent), though the difference was less than that of the English newspapers.

Table I. Percentage of content in the three categories for various newspaper groupings.

Newspaper Groupings		Neutral	Direction of Content	
			Pro-Catholic, and anti-Protestant and Police	Pro-Protestant and Police, and anti-Catholic
Northern Ireland newspapers		52%	23%	25%
South of Ireland newspapers		54%	26%	20%
English newspapers		45%	20%	35%
All six newspapers		45%	20%	35%
Conservative English newspapers		42%	13%	45%
Northern Ireland newspapers	E	50%	30%	14%
	F	47%	17%	36%

Table 2. Total word/appearance count for selected agents/items in each of the six newspapers.

| | NEWSPAPERS | | | | | |
| | English | | South of Ireland | Northern Ireland | | |
Agents/items referred to in photographs/text	Popular daily A	Conservative B	C	Pro Catholic D	E	F
Catholics	23	45	51	48	82	65
Protestants	22	21	36	28	46	45
Police	5	16	75	47	59	58
B-Specials (a reserve police force)	12	16	51	49	49	27
Petrol Bombs	30	19	29	15	28	10
Bernadette Devlin (Civil Rights Leader)	6	6	7	1	1	29

Table 3. The percentage of neutral, specified, and unfavourable terms used by each of the six newspapers.

Categories of terms used to describe individuals or groups in action						
Neutral	4%	3%	11%	6%	11%	9%
Specified	4%	4%	6%	7%	5%	5%
Unfavourable	6%	2%	4%	3%	3%	9%

Taken together, both Northern Ireland newspapers come very close to the average for all newspapers but there were considerable differences between them. The admittedly Catholic newspaper (E) reached a higher neutrality level (56 percent) than the other newspaper (F) with 47 percent. However 30 percent of the remaining content of the Catholic newspaper favoured Catholics, with only 14 percent favouring Protestants. In the second Northern Ireland newspaper the opposite was the case; 17 percent of the content in favour of Catholics, 36 percent in favour of Protestants and police. Is this newspaper pro-Protestant? Certainly while it continues to be read by as big a proportion of Catholics as Protestants (6), its editors would not agree.

As a whole, a reader of both Northern Ireland newspapers would gain insights into what would appear to have been reality during those six days. Either one gave a somewhat biased coverage. The English newspapers seem to have been more biased in favour of Protestants than the South of Ireland papers, which were biased in favour of Catholics.

But it is important to remember that over the six days one-half of all headlines and photographs were not biased either way.

A deeper analysis of the content was attempted by employing a word and photograph count of the agents and items involved in the conflict (Table 2). The picture which emerges provides an interesting parallel to the analysis of headlines and photographs. The use of the term "Catholic" ranged from 23 in one of the English newspapers to 82 by the pro-Catholic Northern Ireland newspaper which also used the term "Protestant" 46 times, twice as often as the English newspapers. This would appear to be a rather doubtful measure of bias, at least in these instances. However, there would seem to be some significance in the relatively few references to the police in the English newspapers and the considerable number of references to them in both the Northern Ireland and South of Ireland newspapers. Similarly, while the English newspapers seemed to play down the role of the B-Specials, both the Northern Ireland newspapers gave them a considerable share of attention. The other Northern Ireland newspaper behaved more closely to the English papers in this instance. It would seem reasonable to conclude that all papers were pressing particular perceptions of this force and as the force was later abolished, it is possible to argue that, while all papers were biased at the time, the pro-Catholic papers (C, D, and E) were closer to reality than the others. However, this is pure conjecture. As is usual in such cases, it is difficult to assess which newspaper is walking successfully the tightrope of truth.

This was the first week of petrol bombs in Northern Ireland. The visual impact of the violence proved especially newsworthy in the English popular daily (A), one of the South of Ireland newspapers (C), and in the pro-Catholic Northern Ireland newspaper (E). The other Northern Ireland newspaper played down the petrol bombs while, at the same time, emphasising the role of Bernadette Devlin, the militant Civil Rights leader who was the most photographed person of the week.

The final analytical measure used was a classification of the terms used to describe individuals and groups in action in the conflict. Descriptions were categorised as "neutral" (people, crowd, participant), "specified" (Catholic, civil rights march) and "unfavourable" (attacker, extremist, rioter). Over all newspapers, the figures which emerge are 44 percent, 31 percent and 27 percent for the three categories. The Northern and South of Ireland newspapers used a significantly higher proportion of neutral descriptions than the English newspapers. The highest number of unfavourable descriptors were used in one Northern Ireland newspaper (F), and in the popular English daily (A). However the second English newspaper (B) had the least number of instances in the unfavourable category. While there is some pattern in these results, perhaps the only valid generalization is that all newspapers used all three categories.

How far it is possible to quantify instances of bias, using word counts or other measures, remains a complex problem in analysing reports. It may be quite misleading to isolate headlines, photographs, and descriptive terms from their total context. However, the total picture of the results from this survey seems to be sufficiently consistent to be suggestive of an overall pattern of bias. A total survey of all English, Northern Ireland, and South of Ireland newspapers would have been even more enlightening. We must also ask whether the analytical system employed here is any more reliable than the impressionistic system used earlier. Perhaps both systems are valuable. For the next two examples we will return to impressionistic evaluation.

A READER'S DIGEST VIEW OF THE KGB

It is not only in newspapers and magazines that bias appears. A recent book (4) on the secret agents of Soviet Russia listed the names of 1,400 Soviet Citizens engaged in clandestine activities. This would appear to be one of those books which should be put into circulation only if accompanied by a competent review. The nature and extent of its bias can be gauged by the following quotation in a review published in a newspaper:

> Unfortunately the evidence against those on the list is, in most cases, not shared with the reader, and he is left to take Mr. Barron's word for it. This is true for much of the book, a racey, anecdotal, spy thriller, with all the essential ingredients of such, including a fair suspension of belief required from the reader.
>
> Irish Times June 18, 1974

This reviewer comes right to the heart of the question of bias and the skills required of the competent reader in coping with propaganda: where the writer's statements are not substantiated by relevant sources and acceptable evidence, the writer's competence and integrity must be seriously questioned. While this onus of assessment rests with the reader, writers and publishers have a responsibility to their readers to write to some kind of criterion of truth and to demonstrate in some appropriate way that they have done so.

THE POPULATION PROBLEM

At higher levels of writing, one might expect to find less bias. Yet, an examination of statements on such issues as pollution, crime, abortion, race, and religion presented in books and journals reveals such a wide spectrum of opinion and belief that it is difficult to decide when differences of interpretation end and bias begins. One example of this type is the range of assessments of the world population problem (1):

> It is widely recognised that the growth and control of human populations is the major biological problem overshadowing the second half of the twentieth century.

Here again, the reader is being asked to believe the writer's unsubstantiated assertions which not only give a misleading picture of the situation by ignoring its social dimensions but infer that its solution lies in developing birth control techniques. The dimensions of problems cannot be selectively ignored by writers and readers.

CONCLUSIONS AND IMPLICATIONS

This paper has presented a brief view of the nature and extent of bias in the reader and in the printed media, and has offered a small range of instances of potential bias in various kinds of writing. From the comments at each stage in the presentation, a limited number of conclusions can be drawn and a series of questions raised.

It seems appropriate to ask writers to state clearly their purposes, using evidence and examples to support generalizations and conclusions, and to present a balanced range of perspectives of a problem or situation. Where evidence is conflicting or not available it should be admitted. The route through a text should be properly marked so that the reader knows where the writer is leading him and what is being offered as fact, inference, conclusion, evaluation, generalization, or opinion. The language and terminology employed should be appropriate to the function the writing is to serve. Trying to meet these criteria raises problems of readability as Turner and Gilliland (18) have shown in examining humanities materials.

The clear message for the reader is that he must bring to the reading experience a range of competencies and attitudes which will enable him to evaluate the author's statements and to challenge his own conceptions. As so much of our culture is primarily accessible through the printed media, it would seem justifiable to urge that everyone should be sufficiently competent to read to learn from the printed media.

Since most of what is learned in school is out of date by the time children become adults, the business of school and adult education should be to produce people who know how to find out and evaluate what they find. Despite advances in the technology of communication, there is evidence that, at least in advanced industrial countries, adults do a considerable amount of reading to meet a variety of needs. Sharon (16) has reported that reading is an ubiquitous activity of American adults which takes up a substantial proportion of their waking hours. Most of the average adult's reading time is spent on newspapers, magazines, books, and work related material. If it is possible to generalize from the examples quoted earlier, adults need to be very alert to the problem of bias in the reports and descriptions in the printed media to which they are constantly exposed.

To continue with the educational implications, I would like to offer a set of specific proposals which I feel might be of some value in schools, youth clubs, and adult education centres in Northern Ireland. Though I am aware of the tremendous difficulties of penetrating deeply rooted prejudices, I believe that communities would learn a lot about each other from reading each other's newspapers with open minds and a sensitive attitude. Possibly, this would have some effect on the attitudes and behaviour of one community toward another. I am assuming that, by learning to cope with bias in the printed media, people will learn to cope with bias in their social situations.

1. Groups could carry out a survey of the number, titles, and origin of the newspapers sold in Protestant, Catholic, and mixed areas in Northern Ireland.

2. Twin groups in schools in different communities could write a newspaper for each other every week. This could carry news, interviews, cartoons, and letters. Time should be set aside for reading the other group's newspaper. Reaction may be communicated in letters, articles, and editorials in the next issue.

3. School time should be spent reading and analysing the three major newspapers in Northern Ireland. Only in school will people be exposed to the newspaper of the other group. Pupils can compare accounts of the same incident or speech, the size of headlines, and use of neutral or unfavourable language.

Finally, it seems to me that we face four major problems in examining content bias in reading materials for adults.

1. Who decides when bias exists and on what grounds?

2. How do we classify instances of bias?

3. How do we ensure that people are capable of coping with bias?

4. How do we persuade writers and publishers to employ higher standards of conduct in relation to what they write and publish?

What's the use? A schematic account of language functions (7).

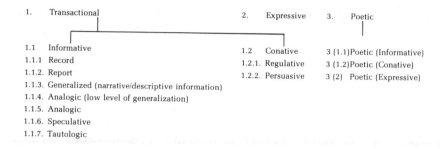

| 1. | Transactional | | 2. | Expressive | 3. | Poetic |

1.1 Informative
1.1.1 Record
1.1.2. Report
1.1.3. Generalized (narrative/descriptive information)
1.1.4. Analogic (low level of generalization)
1.1.5. Analogic
1.1.6. Speculative
1.1.7. Tautologic

1.2 Conative
1.2.1. Regulative
1.2.2. Persuasive

3 (1.1)Poetic (Informative)
3 (1.2)Poetic (Conative)
3 (2) Poetic (Expressive)

REFERENCES
1. Allison, A. (Ed.). *Population Control*. Penguin Books, 1970.
2. Allport, G. W. *The Nature of Prejudice*. London: Addison-Wesley, 1954.
3. Barrett, T. C. "Taxonomy of Cognitive and Affective Dimensions of Reading Comprehension," quoted in T. Clymer "What is Reading? Some Current Concepts," in H. M. Robinson (Ed.), *Innovation and Change in Reading Instruction*, 67th Yearbook of the N.S.S.E. Chicago: University of Chicago Press, 1968.
4. Barron, J. *The KGB: The Secret Works of Soviet Secret Agents*. London: Hodder and Stroughton, 1974.
5. Berelson, B. *Content Analysis in Communication Research*. Hafner, 1971.
6. Boal, F. W. "Territoriality on the Shankill-Falls Divide, Belfast," *Community Forum*, 1 (Spring 1971).
7. Britton, J. "What's the Use? A Schematic Account of Language Functions," *Language and Education: A Source Book*. London: Routledge and Kegan Paul/The Open University Press, 1972.
8. Cheyney, A. B. *Teaching Reading Skills through the Newspaper*. Newark, Delaware: International Reading Association, 1971.
9. *Community Forum*, published quarterly by the Northern Ireland Community Relations Commission, Bedford Street, Belfast.
10. Gray, W. S."The Major Aspects of Reading," in H. M. Robinson (Ed.), *Sequential Development of Reading Abilities*. Chicago: University of Chicago Press, 1960.
11. Hare, R. M. *Freedom and Reason*. London: Oxford University Press, 1963.
12. Harris, A. J. *How to Increase Reading Ability*. New York: Longmans, Green, 1956.
13. Huczynski, A. "A Content Analysis of English, Eire, and Ulster Newspapers between 11-16 August 1969," unpublished paper on inspection in the Northern Ireland Community Relations Commission, Belfast, Northern Ireland.
14. Klineberg, O. "Prejudice: The Concept," *International Encyclopedia of the Social Sciences*, Volume 12. New York: Macmillan, 1968.
15. Moffett, J. *Teaching the Universe of Discourse*. Boston: Houghton Mifflin, 1968.
16. Sharon, A. T. "What Do Adults Read?" *Reading Research Quarterly*, 9 (1973-1974).
17. Smith, N. B. *Reading Instruction for Today's Children*. Englewood Cliffs, New Jersey: Prentice-Hall, 1963.
18. Turner, B., and Gilliland. "The Use of Cloze Procedure in the Measurement of the Readability of Schools Council Humanities Project Materials," *Reading*, 6 (June 1972).

Techniques for Teaching Teachers About Readability

Alton L. Raygor
Ronald Kirsch
University of Minnesota
Minneapolis, Minnesota
United States of America

Since the beginning of formal instruction in reading, one of the major problems to face reading teachers has been that of providing reading material at the appropriate level of difficulty. In some cases, teachers have been able to ignore the problem to some extent by using materials furnished by writers of basal readers, who assume that a normal progression through their materials will assure that the reader will get the right book at the right time. That such an assumption is unwarranted is clear from the many research studies comparing grade level materials on various readability formulas.

It seems clear that teachers are going to have to know enough about readability to make their own judgments in order to provide each child with the right material.

At the secondary and adult levels, such knowledge on the part of the teacher is even more important, since little is done in the preparation of materials to deal with the problem. The reading teacher often serves in the role of materials expert when it becomes apparent that other teachers do not know enough to select materials of appropriate difficulty.

One of the most useful services that can be rendered by a high school or college reading teacher is consultation with other teachers on the books and materials assigned to the students. In fact, the reading teacher can sometimes make a significant impact on the quality of instruction by increasing the other teachers' awareness of the importance of readable instructional material.

The purpose of this paper is to describe the development and informal tryout of an instructional module designed to teach enough about readability so that teachers will be qualified to determine the readability of materials.

The instructional goals of the module are to ensure that the student will: 1) use each of four readability formulas and the cloze procedure; 2) determine the independent and instructional levels of reading materials through the use of the cloze procedure as explained by Bormuth (2); 3) compare the results obtained from the use of the four formulas in a follow-up exercise, and examine the expectations of the use of readability formulas; 4) develop a cloze exercise to be used with other members of the class (material used for the development of this exercise to be of the student's own choosing); and 5) apply the information gained from readability and cloze procedures to reading instruction.

The teaching module contains a pre-test to determine the initial level of familiarity with technique for selecting materials and for predicting the readability of materials.

After the pretest is taken and scored, the learner consults with the instructor. Any learner who is proficient in the use of a particular formula is not required to complete the relevant part of the module.

The actual teaching part of the module begins with a reading selection on the general topic of selecting books. It requires access to *Reading Instruction in Classroom and Clinic* by Edward Fry (4). This text provides a discussion of such topics as difficulty, interest levels, type sizes and styles, sources of book lists, and other areas relevant to book selection.

After the initial introductory section, the module continues with a subset of readings and exercises on each of four readability formulas. In each, the learner reads the original introductory article in which the formula was introduced by its author or inventor. The next step is to apply the formula to a reading selection, using materials and worksheets furnished in the module. The results are compared with answers given in the module. The learner proceeds in the above manner, reading about and computing the Dale-Chall (3), Gunning-Fog (5), Spache (9), and Fry (4) formulas. The next step is to read aloud and apply the cloze procedure in a practice exercise. The approach used is that of John R. Bormuth.

After the formulas and the cloze procedure have been studied, each on a different selection, the learner has an opportunity to put it all together by calculating the readability of a single selection using all of the formulas, and comparing the results obtained. This gives an overview and comparison that puts the formulas, their differences, similarities, convenience, accuracy, and use into better perspective.

In order to increase that perspective, the module concludes with an article by Sylvia-Lee Tibbets (10) on "How Much Should We Expect Readability Formulas to Do?"

The instructional module has been used now on two groups of students. The first group consisted of graduate and undergraduate students at the University of Minnesota in a course in Reading in the Secondary School. Systematic comments and criticisms were collected from the group. They indicated that learners spent an average of about three and one-half hours of working time on the module. Comments were generally favorable, except for some students who obviously would have preferred to spend less time and learn only one or two approaches.

The second group using the module were members of an International Reading Institute in Leysin, Switzerland; all experienced teachers in secondary schools and junior colleges. While their responses were not gathered as systematically as were those of the first group, many useful comments and criticisms were obtained.

In general, the module has been well received, and experience with it has led to the following generalizations about teaching teachers about readability:

1. Teachers want to feel that they can really understand and use readability formulas.

2. A variety of formulas gives teachers a respect for both the advantages and disadvantages of formulas.

3. Using the formula authors' own introduction seems to stimulate interest in the development of approaches to readability.

4. Most important of all, after actually applying the formulas, teachers have a strong feeling of confidence in their own ability to use readability formulas. One typical comment written by a teacher summarizes it well. She wrote, "This was an interesting exercise about a topic entirely new to me. Note that my lack of confidence led me to do all three procedures in pencil but now I have a 'can-do' feeling about it. I'd say that's the sign of a good lesson!"

REFERENCES
1. Bamman, A., and R. J. Whitehead. *Wheels*. San Francisco: Field Publications, 1967.
2. Bormuth, John. "The Cloze Readability Procedure," *Elementary English*, 45 (April 1968), 429-436.
3. Dale, E. and J. S. Chall. "A Formula for Predicting Readability: Instructions," *Educational Research Bulletin*, 27 (February 18, 1948), 37-54.
4. Fry, Edward. *Reading Instruction for Classroom and Clinic*. New York: McGraw-Hill, 1952.
5. Gunning, R. *The Technique of Clear Writing*. New York: McGraw-Hill, 1952.
6. Graf, Richard. "Speed Reading: Remember the Tortoise," *Psychology Today*, December 1973.
7. Morris, Desmond. *The Naked Ape*. New York: Dell Publishing, 1969.
8. Raygor, A., and G. Schick. *Reading at Efficient Rates*. New York: McGraw-Hill, 1970.
9. Spache, George. "A New Readability Formula for Primary Grade Reading Materials," *Elementary School Journal*, 53 (March 1953), 410-413.
10. Tibbetts, Sylvia Lee. "How Much Should We Expect Readability Formulas to Do?" *Elementary English*, 50 (January 1973), 75-76.

Une Technique de Mesure de la Lisibilité Spécifique de la Langue Française

Georges Henry
University of Liege
Liege, Belgium

Le but général des recherches de lisibilité est d'apprendre à prédire et à contrôler la difficulté du langage écrit. Elles devraient permettre l'amélioration voire l'optimisation de l'efficacité de la communication écrite (sans préjuger de l'application de techniques similaires aux tests de lisibilité à d'autres formes de communication).

La premier aspect de la lisibilité auquel les chercheurs se sont attachés est celui de la "legibility." Les études entreprises mesurèrent l'influence de facteurs matériels (présentation des textes, aspects typographiques, sous-titrages, etc.).

Le second aspect est celui de la *readability*. Carter V. Good la définit comme suit: "Quality of a piece of reading matter that makes it interesting and understandable to those for whom it is written, at whatever level of educational experience."[*]

Etalonnage pour la langue française

-	Livre de lecture - 2e primaire	80
•	TV enfantine (niveau pré-scolaire)	65
-	Bandes dessinées: Tintin - Spirou	60
-	Livre de lecture - 5e et 8e primaire	50
-	Documents historiques - 1re année de l'enseignement secondaire	40
•	TV scolaire - enseignement secondaire inférieur	35
-	Leçons d'histoire - 1re année de l'enseignement secondaire ⎫	
-	Textes de Saint-Exupéry ⎭	30
•	TV scolaire - enseignement secondaire supérieur	25
•	Journaux parlés ⎫ Journaux télévisés ⎭ R.T.B. R.T.L. Europe 1	15-25
-	Journaux écrits Le Monde ⎫ Information internationale La Meuse ⎬ basée sur dépêches d'agences La Lanterne ⎭	15
•	Emission radio très difficile (sociologie)	0
-	Texte difficile de Proust	-10

---

[*] Lorsque, par la suite, nous parlerons de lisibilité, ce sera au sens restraint de *readability*.

Si les travaux sont extrêmement nombreux pour la langue anglaise, peu de formules existent, en revanche, qui permettent de prédire la niveau de difficulté d'un texte français. Les seules recherches effectuées jusqu'à ce jour ont été réalisées à partir d'adaptations de la formule de Flesch (5) à la langue française. De Landsheere (4) utilise la formule de Flesch* en conservant les variables ainsi que les coefficients de pondération, mais en apportant des changements importants aux méthodes de comptage, en raison des différences linguistiques entre l'anglais et le français.

Un nombre important de textes extraits de sources diverses ont été analysés par cet auteur et par ses élèves et un étalonnage a été établi.

Ces recherches restaient cependant gravées d'une hypothèque: elles se référaient à une formule conçue spécifiquement pour la langue anglaise. Il importait donc de mettre au point une formule de lisibilité propre au français et présentant, si possible, un niveau de validité plus élevé que la formule de Flesch.

Dans une recherche récente, une série de formules répondant à ces critères ont été mises au point.

Pour obtenir ces formules, il a fallu analyser une soixantaine de textes, dans lesquels ont été étudiées un certain nombre de variables susceptibles de prédire la difficulté. Ces variables appartiennent à différents groupes:

LES VARIABLES FORMELLES

Elles prédisent bien la difficulté des textes, mais sont dépourvues de tout pouvoir explicatif. Exemple: le longueur des phrases.

LES VARIABLES LEXICALES

Ce sont surtout des variables de fréquence. Depuis le début des recherches sur la lisibilité, on a associé deux concepts: celui de la facilité du vocabulaire utilisé dans un texte et celui de la fréquence de l'emploi des mots dans la langue parlées ou écrite. Cette association s'est très souvent révélée fructueuse, car, quelle que soit la liste de fréquences utilisée, on a toujours trouvé une relation importante entre le poids du vocabulaire mesuré en termes de fréquence et la difficulté du texte évalué, quel que soit le critère qui a présidé à l'évaluation de la difficulté.

LES VARIABLES CATEGORIELLES

Depuis Gray et Leary (7), ces variables ont été utilisées par tous les chercheurs, mais d'une façon non systématique. Tout texte se compose

---

*Score Flesch: 206,835 - 0,846 sm - 1,015 mp.
sm = nombre de syllabes pour 100 mots.
mp = nombre de mots par phrase.

d'une succession d'unités qui appartiennent à des classes et à des sous-classes grammaticales. Ces classes et ces sous-classes se définissent par leurs propriétés syntaxiques. On suppose que la fréquence relative d'apparition de certaines classes ou sous-classes est liée à la difficulté des textes: d'où l'intérêt de construire des variables catégorielles et de mesurer leur valeur prédictive.

LES VARIABLES SYNTAXIQUES

La plus ou moins grande complexité syntaxique d'un texte est liée à la difficulté de compréhension. On peut s'attendre à ce que la plupart des transformations qui ont pour effet de déplacer les constituents soient corrélées avec la difficulté de compréhension. Inversément, on peut aussi émettre l'hypothèse que certaines transformations allégeant la structure superficielle peuvent être liées à la facilité. On comprend donc l'intérêt d'une liste des structures susceptibles de prédire la difficulté de compréhension.

LES VARIABLES DE POIDS STRUCTURAL

Elles se calculent au départ d'une description de la structure superficielle des phrases représentées sous la forme d'un arbre. En effet, le message écrit est appréhendé par le sujet de façon linéaire. Le compréhension du message est donc conditionnée à tout moment, par le poids de la partie du passage stockée en mémoire et par les contraintes syntagmatiques que la partie de la séquence déjà lue impose au reste de l'énoncé. Pour quantifier l'importance de ces contraintes, on calcule deux poids pour chaque phrase. Le premier, poids à gauche, rend compte de la complexité des contraintes que les structures déjà rencontrées imposent, à chaque instant, à la partie de la phrase non encore abordée.

LES VARIABLES DE DIALOGUE

Les manuels scolaires étudiés se composent de textes didactiques, narratifs ou dialogués. On peut supposer que ces derniers, plus familiers, sont plus faciles à comprendre. Parmi les variables retenues dans ce chapitre, notons les pronoms personnels de dialogue, première et deuxième personnes, les points d'exclamation, les guillemets de dialogue, etc.

UNE VARIABLE DE REDONDANCE LEXICALE: LA TYPE TOKEN RATIO

On peut émettre l'hypothèse qu'il existe une corrélation entre la degré de redondance d'un texte et son niveau de difficulté. En principe, une redondance élevée facilite la compréhension. La type = token ratio employée récemment par Coleman (2), est déjà ancienne. Elle a déjà été utilisée avec succès en 1928 par Vogel et Washburne (*11*), et consiste à calculer le rapport entre le nombre de mots différents et le nombre total de mots d'un texte.

Pour construire ses formules, l'auteur a employé une méthode statistique dérivée de l'analyse de régression multiple. Il a pris comme critère de validation la difficulté des textes estimée à l'aide du test de closure. Trois groupes de formules (voir tableau 1) ont ainsi été obtenus.

Les formules du premier groupe sont construites à partir de huit variables. Le coefficient de corrélation multiple rend compte de la validité maximale obtenue à partir des variables considérées.

Les formules du second groupe ont été construites à partir d'un sous-échantillon de variables pouvant être calculées directement par ordinateur à partir du texte perforé sur cartes et moyennant une préparation peu importante effectuée par une personne non qualifiée.

Les formules du troisième groupe, courtes et utilisables sans l'appui d'un ordinateur, ont été construites à partir de variables aisées à repérer sans un appareillage complexe.

Les formules du premier groupe sont d'un maniement lourd et constituent essentiellement un instrument de recherche. Les formules du deuxième groupe complètement automatisables paraissent être appelées à devenir un outil d'une grande utilité dans tous les secteurs intéressés par l'évaluation de la lisibilité, spécialement en pédagogie. Les formules du troisième groupe, utilisables sans appareillage, sont susceptibles de rendre des services, tant au premier stade d'une évaluation où l'on désire procéder à quelques sondages préliminaires que dans des cas d'usage restreint, par exemple pour calculer le score d'un texte bref et isolé.

Ces trois groupes de formules sont spécifiques de la langue française. Pour la première fois, il ne s'agit plus d'une adaptation de formules américaines.

Tableau 1
G. Henry   1973

Trois groupes de formules

A. Toutes variables   **Validités**

  - Type = token ratio (TTR)   Grades 5-6   .93

  - Absents de la liste de Gougenheim (AG)   Grades 8-9   .90

  - Mots concrets/abstraits (C/ACD)   Grades 11-12   .83

  - Pronoms personnels dialogue (PPD)

  - Conjonction de coordination (CC)

  - Transformations passives (TP)

  - Transformations déplacement (TD)

  - Transformations relatives et de subordination (TRS)

Logit (cloze 5 - 6)

= (1,37326 x TTR) - (1,91816 x logit AG)
+ (0,56149 x eC/ACD) - (0,12642 x log PPD)
+ (0,01301 x CC) + (0,02508 x log TP)
- (0,01801 x TD) - (0,30962 x log TRS)
- 3,74742

Logit (cloze 8 - 9)

= - (0,60436 x TTR) - (1,02452 x logit AG)
+ (0,42826 x eC/ACD) - (0,12642 x log PPD)
- (0,00623 x CC) - (0,05015 x log TP)
- (0,01801 x TD) - (0,11431 x log TRS)
- 0,82619

Logit (cloze 11 - 12)

= - (0,76887 x TTR) - (0,96673 x logit AC)
+ (0,28507 x eC/ACD) - (0,12642 x log AG)
- (0,00678 x CC) + (0,02508 x log TP)
- (0,01801 x TD) - (0,07650 x log TRS)
- 0,17184

B. Ordinateur   **Validité**

- Nombre de mots par phrase (MP)
- Type token ratio (TTR)   Grades 5-6   .86
- Absents de la liste de Gougenheim (AC)   Grades 8-9   .83
- Pronoms personnel de dialogue (PPD)   Grades 11-12 .77
- Prénoms employées seuls + points d'exclamation
  + guillemets de dialogue (DEXGU)

Logit (cloze 5 - 6)

= - (1,22331 x log MP) - (0,55498 x TTR)
- (0,87521 x logit AG) - (0,10538 x log PPD)
+ (0,28257 x log DEXGU) + 0,29130

Logit (cloze 8 - 9)

= - (0,98665 x log MP) - (2,19456 x TTR)
- (0,54567 x logit AG) - (0,10538 x log PPD)
+ (0,16847 x log DEXGU) + 2,07061

Logit (cloze 11 - 12)

= - (0,74999 x log MP) - (2,06408 x TTR)
- (0,87521 x logit AG) - (0,10538 x log PPD)
+ (0,05436 x log DEXGU) + 1.85507

C. Manuelle

	Validités	
- Nombre de mots par phrase (MP)		
- Absents de la liste de Gougenheim (AG)	Grades 5-6	.84
- Prénoms employés seuls + points d'exclamation	Grades 8-9	.78
+ guillemets de dialogue (DEXGU)	Grades 11-12	.70

Logit (cloze 5 - 6)

$= - (1,39590 \times \log MP) - (1,17831 \times logit AG)$
$+ (0,11731 \times \log DEXGU) - 0,00846$

Logit (cloze 8 - 9)

$= - (1,17961 \times \log MP) - (0,90158 \times logit AG)$
$+ 0,81974$

Logit (cloze 11 - 12)

$= - (0,96331 \times \log MP) - (1,17831 \times logit AG)$
$- (0,11731 \times \log DEXGU) + 0,73738$

Jusqu'à présent, les formules de lisibilité les plus utilisées aux Etats-Unis, celles de Lorge, Dale-Chall ou Flesch, prédisaient la lisibilité des textes de manière uniforme pour les divers niveaux scolaires. De même, les formules présentées ici utilisent les mêmes variables pour prédire la difficulté d'un texte à divers niveaux scolaires. Par contre, les coefficients de pondération affectant ces variables diffèrent selon les niveaux, ce qui permet de prendre en considération l'importance différentielle des facteurs de causalité dont les variables ne sont que l'indice.

Par ailleurs, les formules de lisibilité qui viennent d'être décrites ne deviendront opérationnelles que lorsque trois conditions seront remplies:

- construction des programmes d'ordinateur permettant le relevé automatique des variables utilisées,

- étalonnage d'un nombre important de textes,

- construction d'abaques pour le calcul rapide des scores de lisibilité au moyen de la formule courte.

Ces travaux sont actuellement en cours au Laboratoire de Pédagogie expérimentale de l'Université de Liège.

BIBLIOGRAPHIE

1. Bormuth, J. R. "Readability: A New Approach," *Reading Research Quarterly*, 1 (Spring 1966), 79-132. *Development of Readability Analyses*, U. S. Department of Health, Education and Welfare, Final Report, 1969, Project 7-0052, Contract OEC-3-7-070052-0326.
2. Coleman, E. B. "Developing a Technology of Written Instruction: Some Determiners of the Complexity of Prose," in E. Z. Rothkopf (Ed.), *Symposium on Verbal Learning Research and the Technology of Written Instruction*. New York: Rand McNally, 1968.
3. Dale, E., and J. Chall. "A Formula for Predicting Readability," *Educational Research Bulletin*, 27 (1948), 11-20, 37-53.
4. DeLandsheere, G. "Pour une Application des Tests de Lisibilité de Flesch à la Langue Française, *Le Travail Humain*, 26 (1963), 141-154.
5. Flesch, R. *Marks of Readable Style*. New York: Columbia, 1943. "A Readability Formula in Practice, *Elementary English*, 25 (1948), 344-351. "A New Readability Yardstick," *Journal of Applied Psychology*, 32 (1948), 221-233.
6. Good, C. V. *Dictionary in Education* (2nd ed.). New York: McGraw-Hill, 1959.
7. Gray, W. S., and A. B. Leary. *What Makes a Book Readable?* Chicago, 1935.
8. Henry, G. "Une Technique de Mesure de la Lisibilité Spécifique de la Langue Française," thèse de doctorat, mai 1973.
9. Lorge, I. "Predicting Difficulty of Selections for Children," *Elementary English Review*, 16 (1939), 231-232.
10. Smith, N. B. "Reading: An International Challenge," in D. K. Bracken and Eve Malmquist (Eds.), *Improving Reading Ability Around the World*, Proceedings of the Third IRA World Congress on Reading, Sydney, 1970. Newark, Delaware: International Reading Association, 1971.
11. Washburne, C. W., and M. Vogel. *Winnetka Grade Book List*. Chicago, 1926.

Technology of Film and Teaching Reading: Present and Future

Leo Ruth
Deborah Ruth
University of California
Berkeley, California
United States of America

Film, as a means for developing language and meaning, is basic to reading at all instructional levels. There is, or should be, a place for film study and film-making in both elementary and secondary curricula, independent of any other purposes film may serve in teaching reading or other subjects. Film, as the art of the 20th century—eclectic, technological, universal, and accessible—deserves serious study in schools, and should not be used exclusively for enrichment or as a supplementary aid.

Because we define technology simply as "a process for handling specific technical problems," we consider film to be an important and versatile technological process for advancing instruction in all school curricula. But, for reasons to be explained, film lends itself especially well to instructional processes for developing language and meaning, and the cognitive and emotional growth fundamental to reading. We hope to demonstrate how film offers a primary source of experience for expanding the personal cognitive structures which give shape and meaning to print.

We are not referring to the more common use of film as an audiovisual aid to provide background or motivation for particular reading assignments. Neither are we considering film as a way to "turn literature into life" by translating print into moving pictures with sound and color. Too often when we think of film as a component in reading instruction, we allow its most obvious features to dominate and limit its true potential. Film does offer clever ways to illustrate or animate a language or reading concept. Film also offers lively means of presenting ideas and of attracting and holding attention. And it is within film's capacities to perform such varied but repetitive stimulous functions that are capitalized upon so imaginatively in our internationally famous children's television programs, *Sesame Street* and *The Electric Company*. Doubtless, this instrumental use of film in television provides a powerful vehicle for conceptual learning and cognitive growth, though I am not certain that we know exactly what kind of interaction may be occurring between the child and the program content. (That is another matter which bears exploration elsewhere.) What we are interested in here is the unique capacity of film to promote before a live audience and under management of a skilled teacher, active mental and emotional processes that foster particular features of cognitive growth. We are proposing the bases for what we think is an unexplored philosophical-theoretical direction in the use of film in reading instruction.

Before outlining the theoretical base to our film teaching method in reading, we must provide our definition of reading. First, we note that speech precedes its printed forms. We think of reading as a process of internalized recall of spoken language evoked by a written text. We think of getting meaning, or more accurately, of making sense of the speech/reading event as requiring interpretive procedures to process the message content in its oral or written form. It is at this point that the message receiver's lack of vocabulary, limited cognitive processes, or restricted experience shows up and breaks the live circuit necessary to establish a true connection between reader and writer, listener, and speaker. A cognitive gap appears between the text of the writer or speaker and the mind of the reader or listener. Film offers a unique resource for closing this gap by offering controlled means of enlarging the underlying store of cognitive skill and referential knowledge a reader/listener brings to performance in reading and listening. Now, let us explore some ways film may enlarge cognition.

Films provide information content, something for the mind to work on. Even as films provide materials for practicing acts of cognition, they also convey social and cultural information. They make accessible to potential readers means of forming concepts and of entering varied worlds of information and ideas. Film, as content with a range of auditory and visual cues unavailable in the reduced cuing system of print, is a vehicle with the accessibility and the power to expand cognitive and emotional background and all those internal structures the students must bring to the reading event.

Film content is organized and, in a sense, that organization is uniquely visible. Thus, film as patterned experience contributes to the growth of logical thinking in cognitive development. Various patterns of order—chronological, cause and effect sequences, classification and definition, comparison and contrast—are logical relations observable in the types of films we use. In film, there is a content of logic and organization available to the mind's eye that students may combine with their own associations and inferences in making meanings for discussion, writing, and reading.

Film content provides material for linguistic manipulation. It is an obvious source of vocabulary, of categorizations, and of category criteria. Film also provides material for question framing, manipulating and reordering data, extrapolating from data, and making associations. Film offers materials for making inferences, generalizing, summarizing, and synthesizing. Film gives students multiple routes to refinement of their symbolic capacities and to development of abstracting capacities crucial to formal education and to much of the reading that comprises formal education.

Film serves to develop social sensitivities important to reading and helps students to assimilate social reality and to achieve reciprocity in their views of one another. Film also helps the individual organize and develop the self in ways important to reading: it contributes to the growth of imagery and imagination; it changes structures of thinking; it increases understanding of the nature of objectivity and the persistence of subjectivity in making meanings. Further, film aids cognitive development in movement from intuitive to concrete thought, from absolute judgments to relative, conditional ones.

Film as an information source also helps overcome the uneven social distribution of knowledge and experience and the difficulties associated with the restricted language experience of different households. Sociologist Aaron Cicourel (1) speaks of the "limited oral dictionaries" possessed by different households. It is these limited oral dictionaries which students bring to reading. Film, and talk associated with it, can enlarge these limited oral dictionaries, providing a base for generating active language production in speech and writing, which, in turn serves recall, recognition, and interpretive functions required in making sense of reading.

These features of cognitive development are not intrinsic or exclusive properties of film or any other instructional medium. They are born in interactive teaching approaches and grow from talk about and around films and other media. Discussion of film, or other focal points of talk, affords students needed opportunity for activating their self-organizing social, emotional, and intellectual capacities. As students participate in the unfolding interaction of discussion about a film, the discussion helps participants to develop strategies for ordering and processing experience. Discussion points up information failures arising out of loss or distortion of data, provides the reflexive interchange that helps students develop and practice practical reasoning, and helps students learn descriptive vocabularies for handling bodies of information and associated activities and concepts. In discussions, utterances get expanded as participants practice code-switching, sentence transformations, and all manner and variety of linguistic choice. It is in the midst of talk about a shared experience, such as one a film provides, that social and personal meanings are constructed. The kind of external dialogue that discussing a film brings into play constitutes a rehearsal of the silent dialogue that enables the active reader to make sense of written texts.

We are especially fond of animated films because, as abstractions of social reality, they can depict social relationships and processes without rooting them in specific, identifiable objects or people. In our viewing and discussing of many hundreds of such short films, we have devised a three-level discussion technique—a pattern of questioning—intended to enhance the student's "visual literacy" as well as his ability to use language precisely to discover, examine, and create meaning. This technique also aims to open the student's cognitive and emotional response to film and, by extension, to literature and other art forms.

The discussion technique is as follows: level 1, "What did you see?"—questions on the literal level; level 2, "What did it mean to you?"—questions on the interpretive level; level 3, "How well did you like it?"—questions on the judgmental level. On all three levels, we emphasize the individual viewer's responses to the film.

Our level 1 questions, "What did you see?" or "What do you remember seeing on the screen?" call for a literal narrative or retelling of what the student saw, told in straight, objective, noninterpretive, nonjudgmental language. This approach emphasizes the role of perception in remembering and reporting; it acknowledges the fact that although we may all look at the same film, we all actually see different films. We may all share a common visual happening, but we all bring to a film our own experiences from different contexts, different sets of personal expectations, and different cultural experiences and backgrounds.

This first level of discussion is intended to enable us to recall the actual objective data on the screen. Inevitably, during this discussion, students will hear each other recount incidents in the film that they themselves didn't remember or that they may not have seen—or consciously registered. Thus, at the end of this first level of discussion, the class has moved toward constructing a unified, shared experience. Ideally, at this point, we would show the film a second time, to check out the accuracy of our perception and memory. This is the only point where a student can be said to be right or wrong in accounting for objective data.

We begin at this objective level for two reasons: first, many students and teachers want to begin immediately to look for the message, the meaning, and seek to find a correct interpretation before they're even fully aware of all the data available to their senses. Second, many students' first response to what they don't fully grasp in a film or a book is "That's dumb," or "That's stupid." We consider this response a level three—or a judgmental—response, appropriate only when based on a foundation of knowledge gained through observation and interpretation, which are the first two levels.

When we come to level 2, we ask "What did it mean to you?" "What else might the film be saying besides what it showed?" "What meaning might there be for you in the film beyond what was discussed in level 1?" The discussion opens to interpretation, construction of possible symbolic meanings, messages, morals, etc. Any construction of meaning is acceptable as long as it is linked to the film's available stock of information, as developed on level 1. This interpretive level encourages exploration into the subjective nature of meaning and of the selection of language necessary to communicate these discovered meanings. Students should be free to make their own decisions of relevance and applicability in selecting descriptive labels, in assigning motives, and in establishing causal sequences. The procedure of allowing meaning to unfold through interaction of personal interpretations discourages the "one right answer" syndrome too often observed in the behavior of teachers and students. In this approach, there is the implication that no one person—teacher, student, or the filmmaker himself—can assign a single correct meaning to a given work. Each viewer and each reader constructs personal meanings, but he needs to understand the sources of these meanings: the objective data on the screen interacts with the subjective nature of the viewer's own predispositions to produce meaning.

When we reach level 3, we ask, "How well did you like it?" "What did you think of it as a film?" "Based on what you thought the film meant (your level 2 discoveries), how well did you think the film communicated this meaning?" "Was it worth communicating?" This is the judgment level, the criticism level, the "I liked it!" or "That was a stupid movie!" level, followed by the reasons for these personal reactions. When discussion begins on this level, most students aren't able to articulate the reasons for their feelings; but by the time they've gone through levels 1 and 2, they not only are more in touch with the reasons, but their initial response may actually have changed. This level of discussion helps students develop genuine critical faculties which can contribute to their self-confidence and self-esteem. Knowledge of the foundations of their opinions, of the processes of judging and criticizing, can place them in an intellectually valid position to challenge the teacher, the filmmaker, or anyone else who poses a "right" answer. This level helps the student understand that a film (or a story or a poem) brought into the classroom can be liked or disliked for valid reasons.

This discussion technique is useful with stories and poems too, and it is easily adaptable to writing exercises. This way of discussing a film is intended to evoke the same kinds of responses and the same kinds of development of language and meaning that should, but often don't, follow a reading experience. If you have ever felt lost while viewing an abstract or complex film, that feeling is comparable to the lost feeling a student experiences upon encountering a story he can't make meaningful. The reading experience in which the reader perceives words, feels, understands, and makes meaning is much the same as the film experience in which the viewer perceives images (and sounds), feels, understands, and makes meaning. Both experiences have the power to involve, to enlarge perception, provide insights, and build the stock of cognitive skills and experiences the viewer or reader takes to the next viewing or reading experience.

For the reluctant reader, the slow reader, the uninterested reader, or anyone having difficulty making meaning out of written works, the film (especially the short, nonnarrated film) provides a resource for developing language skills, increasing interest and involvement, and building self-confidence while still maintaining the basic integrity of film as an art form. Successful encounters with films and the accompanying linguistic development through discussion can motivate and prepare students to try for the same kinds of rewarding experiences through reading. Film needn't replace reading, but it can enhance the reading experience for students of all ages.

The future development of film use for teaching reading does not depend on the development of more elaborate machinery or on the production of more audiovisual aids, but on more sophisticated selection and use of the equipment and films presently available. We already have the products; we need to make better use of them.

REFERENCE
1.   Cicourel, Aaron V. *Cognitive Sociology: Language and Meaning in Social Interaction.* New York: Free Press, 1974.

Reading and Television in the United States

Pose Lamb
Purdue University
West Lafayette, Indiana
United States of America

In *Television and the Classroom Reading Program*, Becker (4) writes:

> Did you know that today's student spends about three hours a day watching television? This means that during a regular school week he spends almost as much time watching television as he does in the classroom. And when you take into account holidays, vacations, and time lost from school because of illness, you realize that today's student actually spends more time in the course of a year watching television than he spends in the classroom . . . . Television offers an ideal bridge between the school world and the other world of outside activity which students often find so much more exciting and stimluating. Two currently popular educational injunctions are relevant in this regard. The first of these injunctions is: Start where the child is. For the many children who watch television this represents an ideal starting place. The second injunction is: Proceed from the known to the unknown. For the average student of today, television obviously represents a very well-known commodity.

Becker, then, would have the teacher of reading look carefully at and use to full advantage the cognitive, linguistic, and affective influences of the out-of-school television viewing of his pupils. In view of the presence, or omnipresence, of a television set in nearly every home in North America, teachers can hardly ignore this medium, whether or not it is directly and specifically used for instructional purposes. One of the significant factors to be reviewed in this paper is the influence of out-of-school viewing on children's reading.

Instructional television is another factor of great significance to those interested in reading. Teachers are making increasing use of videotape, closed circuit instructional programs, and lessons procured from national tape distribution centers. In one midwestern city in the United States, a television series was used to intervene with and, hopefully, prevent the typical decline in reading achievement which occurs during the summer between the first and second grades. A second purpose of this paper is to review the data regarding instructional television used in the classroom.

Sesame Street and *The Electric Company* have received international attention—both favorable and unfavorable. Since approximately 9 million children, in school and out, watch *Sesame Street* and an estimated 7 million view *The Electric Company*, these influential programs will receive some attention in this paper.

Finally, some questions will be raised regarding the unrealized potential of television as a medium to be used for more effective reading instruction. There are reading objectives which television programs are achieving; there are broader educational objectives which are not being met.

OUT OF SCHOOL TELEVISION VIEWING

Savage (17) reports that "virtually every individual in this country has access to a home television set and statistics show that we watch television an average of 45 hours a week. The average viewing time for preschoolers is 28½ hours per week. Children in the six to eleven age range watch almost 24 hours of television a week and teenagers about 20 hours." With specific reference to reading, Savage comments: "Through television the child acquires some simple and basic knowledge about his world. Television can be the jumping off point for books, magazines, and other sources of learning through print. While in one sense, television segregates us from reality, in another sense it brings us a little closer to reality by providing vicarious experiences that can only be brought through television."

In a study reported at a meeting of the American Educational Research Association 90 children, two to four years of age, were randomly selected from a group of 500 whose parents expressed interest in the project. Dunn (8) states her hypotheses as follows:

1. Systematic instruction by television will result in significant gains among children two through four years of age on the following reading skills: the alphabet, alphabet sounds, and basic vocabulary.

2. A variation in gains in selected reading skills will occur and will have a significant relationship to age, verbal IQ, socioeconomic level, and time spent on follow-up activities.

For twelve weeks, parents and their preschool children attended videotaped, closed circuit presentations designed to teach specific reading skills. Parents were given a manual of activities and were asked to work with their child at least ten minutes each day. Pre-post comparisons were made of performance on the Peabody Picture Vocabulary Test, matching a group of randomly selected letters with related sounds, recognition of letters of the alphabet and what Dunn termed "alphabet sounds," and, finally, children were asked to supply definitions of the words on a 22 item vocabulary list.

Dunn found that the gains made by the experimental group were greater than those made by the control group, at the .001 level of significance. Further, she found that time spent in follow-up activity varied in a positive ratio to the gains measured, and that socioeconomic level had a significant relationship to gains, with the greatest gains made by children from homes classified as lower socioeconomic level. Age and verbal IQ were not significantly related to the gains. Dunn concludes:

> In summary, the findings that children two through four years of age can be effectively taught these reading skills by the use of the television medium is of major importance. Learning problems may be reduced or at least better assessed at an age when the child responds more quickly to remediation. Gifted children may be found at an age more advantageous for their continued guidance. The availability of this type of skill to more children may help to achieve proper utilization of the period most sensitive to language which will lead us close to optimal development of man's learning potential.

Two of Dunn's findings deserve emphasis and are typical of the evidence gathered by most researchers in this area: television, as an instructional medium, is of special benefit to children who aren't in the cultural mainstream and the greatest benefits accrue when the television lesson is somehow supplemented by work with parents, teachers, or aides. Television *by itself* is of less value than television plus discussion; completion of worksheets, puzzles, or workbook exercises; and reinforcement activities of some sort.

Another example of an effort to teach preschoolers to read at home, and to aid beginning readers as well, is reported in a recent issue of *Educational and Industrial Television* (14). Caleb Gattegno's Words in Color program was interpreted in terms of 50 second pop-ups—talking letters and words—which NBC telecast on Saturday mornings. A review of the literature, however, failed to disclose any evaluative data, nor is it clear how extensively these 18 "lessons" were viewed.

On the basis of reviews of several studies of the relationship between television viewing and children's reading, Feeley (11) notes that out-of-school reading occupies about one-third as much time as is spent viewing television. She concludes: "Television looms large in the lives of children; it is the first of the mass media to which most children react, and the 'set' against which they judge all other media, including print. Age, sex, intelligence, emotional needs, and sometimes socioeconomic status affect the uses children make of television. Generally, they look to TV for fantasy and entertainment; the above factors influence their choices of programs at various ages and stages." The extent of this influence is a matter of some controversy. Feeley continues:

There is divided opinion about the effect television has on reading tastes. While both British and American researchers agree that viewing can stimulate reading interests, although only fleetingly, they differ concerning the role played by TV in taste formation. The British see an underlying pattern of taste running through all media selection; they feel that television has broadened, raised, and matured the reading tastes of most children. The American team poses the hypothesis that since television has been introduced to children as a means of satisfying fantasy needs, it functions mainly on this level. Books are used to answer reality needs and, therefore, are usually thought of as separate from TV.

Feeley raises some very important questions, questions deserving serious attention by researchers in media, language acquisition, and reading:

1. What is the relationship, expressed in terms of quality as well as quantity, between children's preferences in television programs and in trade books?

2. Is it feasible to attempt to broaden, or deepen, children's tastes in print materials by exposing them to certain types of television programs? If so, how will the most desirable directions for this development be determined?

The current controversy, in the United States, over the Newbery and Caldecott Award procedures and the selections themselves suggest that there is no board of literary experts whose qualifications entitle and empower them to shape children's tastes in literature. Further, as Feeley suggests, the two media may satisfy quite different needs; their roles may be supplementary rather than complementary. In any case, there are significant questions to answer and issues to be resolved. As will be noted later, the contribution of television to the field of reading has, to this point, been very narrowly prescribed, concentrating almost entirely at the decoding level. Its qualified success in achieving certain goals in word perception suggests that broader, more significant goals may be susceptible of attainment. Literacy, at fundamental levels, is a worthwhile goal; the Right to Read program in the United States is based upon the premise that children are not achieving what they can and should be achieving in the area of growth in the acquisition of such skills; these skills are necessary but hardly sufficient. Knowing how to read is of little value if one doesn't read, or reads at a level which might at best be termed marginally literate (tax forms, employment records). Instructional television, if not commercial television, may make its most significant contribution in the area of developing higher level cognitive skills, critical/creative thinking, and in exposing children to a wide variety of literary genre, authors, and selections with which they are not yet familiar.

In concluding this brief review of the data and expressed opinions regarding out-of-school television and its impact on reading, Fasick's work should be noted. She writes (10):

> During the past twenty years, the verbal environment in which preschool children live has been changed dramatically by the introduction of television. Television now reaches almost every home in North America, and it reaches across class levels. Disadvantaged children apparently watch as many hours of television as do middle-class children.
>
> Since the visual image on television is almost always accompanied by verbal dialogue or commentary, by the time a child reaches first grade, he is likely to have heard thousands of hours of television language. It would seem likely that the exposure to this quantity of language would have some influence on a child's developing verbal skills.
>
> Yet the flood of standard English on television, which is now part of the language heard by preschool children from the most impoverished background, does not seem to have lessened the gap in language development between middle-class and lower-class children.

Fasick then cites Carol Chomsky's most recent study related to the acquisition of syntax. Chomsky's most pertinent findings relate to the strong positive correlations between children's performance on tests of syntactic maturity, their scores on a test of literary understanding, and parents' reports of the amount and quality of reading to children. In other words, the quality and quantity of material read by and to children has a direct relationship to their acquisition of more mature syntactic forms at the competence and performance levels. Fasick monitored three television programs and subjected five books to syntactic analysis. She writes: "The objective is to determine whether the apparently different effects of children's books and children's television programs might not be the result of a difference in the language used in these two media. The comparison involves two factors which are indicative of language maturity: the proportion of complex sentences used and the amount of subordination in these sentences."

As might be expected, Fasick found that the language of the books she analyzed exhibited far more subordination and a wider range of subordination than the television programs she monitored. She concludes that television language has less impact than book language because linguistic forms which might add to the child's syntactic maturation and growth are not repeated.

Fasick concludes: "A study of the differences in language used in children's television shows and in children's books indicates that a far wider range of syntactic patterns is used in the books. Books thus make possible a closer match between the language of the book and the language-readiness of the child in a way that television does not."

The major conclusions from this review of data related to out of school television viewing and reading might be summarized as follows:

1. The influence of television is pervasive. Nearly every preschool and school age child has available to him one or more television sets.

2. The so-called culturally different, diverse, divergent, or disadvantaged view about as much television as their more economically privileged neighbors. Television may prove to be a useful means of involving preschool children in activities deemed essential for success in reading.

3. Television presentations are most beneficial when they are supplemented with activities designed to reinforce and augment. Simply watching a television lesson "brought to you by the letter H" is not as productive, as productivity is typically measured, as television viewing followed by completing worksheets or some other related and obviously significant activity.

4. Print apparently has more influence on children's language development than television programs. The informality of the language used on television (sentence fragments, nonstandard dialects) may not provide the model needed by speakers of nonstandard English (however, this is defined), if they are to become bidialectical.

5. The goals of most television programs may be too narrowly prescribed, in terms of teaching reading. The potential of the television medium for teaching higher level cognitive skills, and developing broader and more eclectic tastes in literature, has yet to be explored.

INSTRUCTIONAL TELEVISION

Some personal reflections on classroom instructional television might be appropriate at this point. For a number of years an airplane circled over five states in the midwestern United States telecasting a complete range of lessons—math; social studies; foreign language; and related to reading, an i/t/a course, Freedom to Read and a phonics course, Listen and Say.

The lessons were taped, many of them at the university where the author teaches, and the school systems were charged a fee based on number of viewers. The program was denied continued federal funding and was unable to maintain itself economically, with fees as the only income. Criticisms of the i/t/a and phonics series related to the high degree of structure, the redundancy of concepts, the lack of recognition of problems created by regional and social dialect differences, and the low level of involvement of viewers. Obviously, there was a massive vote of no-confidence registered by nonsubscribers in spite of an extensive publicity campaign. Children were not enthusiastic when the time came for lessons, and the teacher resented the need to plan the day around an inflexible television program schedule. The value of follow-up activities has already been mentioned. This was obvious to all who used the programs. The manuals, suggesting appropriate activities, were provided by the sponsoring agency, the Midwest Program on Airborne Television Instruction (MPATI). Nevertheless, many teachers retreated to the lounge once the set was turned on and did not return until the lesson was nearly over. Classroom teachers may be instructional television's most potent foes.

Humphrey (13), reports an interesting study of the use of instructional television as a summer supplement to the classroom reading program. He compared the loss in reading achievement, as measured by a standardized test, of children who did and did not participate in a television reading program, *Ride the Reading Rocket*, telecast in the summers of 1965 and 1966. The hypotheses are stated as follows:

1. To determine the reading loss or gain of first grade children (analyzed for sex and intelligence differences).
2. To develop and present a summer reading program by television.
3. To test the null hypothesis that there is no difference between the means of reading achievement tests taken by children who did and who did not participate in a summer television program.

The research design involved a pre-post test procedure. Humphrey summarizes the results as follows:

> In the post-summer tests, the differences between the two groups was wider than in the pre-summer tests. The control group has losses over the summer in all areas except the comprehension test for girls. The biggest loss was in the vocabulary test where there was much larger loss than in the comprehension test. The girls outscored the boys in all areas of the post-summer control group reading tests. Girls had less loss over the summer than boys . . . . All areas of the post-summer experimental group tests were higher than the control group post-summer tests. Boys made higher gains in the experimental group in vocabulary, comprehension, and total reading than girls, but girls still had higher scores in all areas on the post-summer scores.

Humphrey underscores the need for close cooperation between home and school, and recommends the wider use of television as a means of alleviating the typical summer loss in reading achievement (13).

Ayers (1) conducted a survey of the attitudes of elementary school pupils toward instructional television. In reviewing the findings of other studies of attitudes, he reports: "Recent studies have concluded that elementary school children think they learn more from television than do high school and college students. In the lower grades, attitudes are either quite favorable or unfavorable toward the entire range of programing with indifference not being frequently expressed. As one goes up the grade scale, attitudes become specific to individual programs." Ayers asked 1,862 pupils, grades four to six, to respond to a set of open-ended statements (e.g., Television in school is . . .). His findings can be summarized as follows:

1. There were few sex differences.
2. Long-time viewers of instructional television tended to be more criticial and their enthusiasm dropped.
3. Programs in science and social science were the most popular; 22 to 30 percent of the pupils listed reading programs as most preferred.
4. There is a need for more preparation prior to viewing and more follow-up activities following instructional television programs. Teachers appeared to be negligent in these areas.

The major conclusions from this review of data related to instructional television and reading might be summarized as follows:

1. Teachers need to involve pupils in more activities prior to and following television instruction than is typically the case.
2. Instructional television can be used effectively to minimize the typical loss of reading skills which occurs during the summer vacation.
3. Pupils tend to become more critical of instructional television as they use more of it and their enthusiasm wanes. This trend may not be irreversible, however.

SESAME STREET AND THE ELECTRIC COMPANY

Tierney (20) writes: "Sesame Street has been hailed as one of the most significant contributions of public television. As a result of a joint public-private venture involving the Carnegie and Ford Foundations and the United States Office of Education, an award of $8,000,000 was given to Children's Television Workshop, the corporation set up to research and produce Sesame Street. The series is designed to appeal to preschool children from low income innercity families. Extensive pretesting and observation of viewer responses resulted in several changes in the proposed format.

Songs, rhythms, stories, puppetry, and direct instruction are used to teach vocabulary, letter names, and beginning sounds. Robeck (15) comments, "The discriminations on television are made easier by presenting them explicitly, by repeating them endlessly, and by making them attractive aesthetically." She reviews the results of the evaluation program under the auspices of the Educational Testing Service as follows: "The children who watched the most learned the most, and skills that received the most attention in the program were the best learned by the children. The goals of the program directly related to reading included recognizing, naming and matching capital and lowercase letters, recognizing and matching letters in words, recognizing initial sounds and reading words . . . . The results from *Sesame Street* point up the importance of being specific about educational goals and directing the educational program toward these goals."

Blanton (6) lists the specific prereading objectives for the program, which is viewed in classrooms as well as in homes all over the United States. The following are excerped from this list:

PREREADING OBJECTIVES

Letters

1. *Matching.* Given a printed letter, the child can select the identical letter from a set of printed letters.
2. *Recognition.* Given the verbal label for a letter, the child can select the appropriate letter from a set of printed letters.
3. *Labeling.* Given a printed letter the child can provide the verbal label.
4. *Letter Sounds.*
   a. For sustaining consonants (f, l, m, n, r, s, v), given the printed letter the child can produce the letter's corresponding sound.
   b. Given a set of words presented orally, all beginning with the same letter sound, the child can select from a set of words another word with the same initial letter sound.
5. *Recitation of the Alphabet.* The child can recite the alphabet.

Words

1. *Matching.* Given a printed word, the child can select an identical word from a set of printed words.
2. *Boundaries of a Word.* Given a printed sentence, the child can correctly point to each word in the sentence.
3. *Temporal-Sequence/Spatial-Sequence Correspondence.* (Words and sentences are read from left to right.)
   a. Given a printed word, the child can point to the first and last letter.
   b. Given a printed sentence the child can point to the first and last word.

4. *Decoding.* Given the first five words on the reading vocabulary list (ran, set, big, mop, fun), the child can decode other related words generated by substitutions of a new initial consonant. (Example, given the word *ran* the child can decode *man* and *can*.)

5. *Word Recognition.* For any of the words on the *Sesame Street* word list, the child can recognize the given word when it is presented in a variety of contexts.

6. *Reading.* The child can read each of the 20 words on the *Sesame Street* word list.

Sprigle (18) reports some negative results for pupils who viewed *Sesame Street.* He compared Metropolitan Readiness Test Scores of kindergarten pupils who had not viewed *Sesame Street* but had had a prereading program similar to that offered on the program with those children who had viewed the program on a regular basis. He writes: "The year before *Sesame Street* we selected a group of kindergarten children using the identical selection procedures as were used to select the *Sesame Street* children. In other words, the children of the year before would be paired with the *Sesame Street* children." They went to the same kindergarten and had the same teachers as the *Sesame Street* children." Clearly, such a research design has many flaws. However, Sprigle reports: "The disadvantaged children who viewed *Sesame Street* are no better prepared for first grade than a matched control group in the same kindergarten with the same teacher the year before the program went on television. Actually, the scores of the *Sesame Street* graduates tend to be lower."

One must conclude, with Blanton (6), ". . . the *Sesame Street* series has been accepted by the public and by many educators with some enthusiasm. The effectiveness of the series has been questioned, sometimes with more passion than objectivity. The educational community would be well advised to withhold judgment on the effectiveness of the series until additional evidence is offered."

Another popular production of Children's Television Workshop is *The Electric Company*, designed to supplement the teaching of reading to seven to ten-year-olds. Approximately half of the six or seven million viewers watch it in school. Roser (16) notes that the show is designed to emphasize these curricular items:

1. The left to right sequence of print corresponds to the temporal sequence of speech.

2. Written symbols stand for speech sounds. They "track" the stream of speech.

3. The relationship between written symbols and speech sounds is sufficiently reliable to produce successful decoding most of the time.

4. Reading is facilitated by learning a set of strategies for figuring out sound-symbol relationships.

5. The goal of decoding is to extract meaning from the written message.

Those who have watched *The Electric Company* with any consistency might question the degree to which programs appear to be designed to reach these goals. In practice, *The Electric Company* seems to operate within a much narrower frame of reference.

Ball and Bogatz (3) report a study of the effectiveness of *The Electric Company*. Again, a matched-pairs-of-classes design was used, with gains from pre- to posttest being compared. One hundred classes participated, first through fourth grades. Fifty classes watched the programs in school, while the teachers of the other fifty encouraged children to watch at home. Findings suggest that "viewing classes had significantly larger adjusted gain scores on the grand total than the nonviewing classes . . . . For the lower grades, the differences were larger than those obtained in the higher grades." Teachers were generally favorably disposed toward the program, but the attitudes of pupils toward reading or toward school were not affected by viewing or not viewing.

This writer's view, based on reviewing the research and on several exposures to the program, is well stated by Roser. "What *The Electric Company* seems to have turned on is the *Laugh In* fans who love the fast-paced slapstick, the parodies, and even the puns of a set of tuned-in writers and actors. What it has missed, in the opinion of this critic, is the opportunity to illustrate the reading process in its fullest sense—as a communication process. No love of reading can evolve from a "sounder," a student so conscious of getting the sounds in order he misses the meaning. Cannot all the pizazz of *The Electric Company*, which has made decoding come alive for children across the country, be directed more specifically toward developing in its viewers an appreciation for reading as a part of a total communication process? Perhaps *The Electric Company* needs an added charge."

SUMMARY

This comment leads naturally to the most significant summary point. Both *Sesame Street* and *The Electric Company* have been moderately successful in achieving some rather narrowly conceived goals. In the future, one would hope that those responsible for the programs would make more concerted efforts to help viewers think about the material presented and to work toward increased literary appreciation, in the broadest, most eclectic sense in which this term can be used.

CONCLUDING QUESTIONS

On the basis of this brief review of data and commentary related to television and reading, the following questions are raised. They appear to be of sufficient significance to warrant serious attention for concerned educators, media specialists, and researchers.

1. What can be done to increase the positive influence of educational television, in school and out, on children typically classified as culturally disadvantaged?

2. What can be done to broaden the objectives of programs such as *Sesame Street* and *The Electric Company*? Given the evidence that they are successfully achieving a rather narrow set of objectives, might viewers not anticipate help toward larger goals (e.g., use of more sophisticated linguistic structures, critical thinking and reading, and literary appreciation)?

3. How can the goals of television reading programs and the goals of those who plan reading programs for schools be made more consistent so their content becomes complementary as well as supplementary? This must be done, if at all possible, without violating the professional integrity of either group.

Television has tremendous potential. It is pervasive and its impact is great. Although those who are interested in reading are typically concerned with *print* and specifically print between book, booklet, or magazine covers, we must not ignore television's influential, readily accessible resource. Children can learn much from television which will make it possible for them to benefit by responding to print more efficiently and with greater understanding.

REFERENCES
1. Ayers, Jerry B. "Elementary School Children's Attitudes Toward Instructional Television," *Elementary English*, 50 (January 1973), 137-140.
2. Ball, Samuel, and Gerry Bogatz. *The First Year of Sesame Street: An Evaluation.* Princeton, New Jersey: Educational Testing Service, 173.
3. Ball, Samuel, and Gerry Bogatz. *Reading with Television: An Evaluation of the Electric Company.* Princeton, New Jersey: Educational Testing Service, 1973.
4. Becker, George J. *Television and the Classroom Reading Program*, Reading Aids Series. Newark, Delaware: International Reading Association, 1973, 5-6.
5. Best, Tony. "On the Other Side of *Sesame Street*," *American Education*, 10 (May 1974), 6-10.
6. Blanton, Bill. "Preschool and Junior College Reading," *Reading World*, May 1972, 6, 328-334.
7. Congreve, Willard J. "Implementing and Evaluating the Use of Innovations," *Innovation and Change in Reading Instruction*, 67th Yearbook of the National Society for the Study of Education. Chicago: University of Chicago Press, 1968, 291-319.
8. Dunn, Barbara J. "The Effectiveness of Teaching Selected Reading Skills to Children Two through Four Years of Age by Television," paper presented at the American Educational Research Association Conference, 1970.
9. *Electric Company Guide*, 13 (April 8, 1974).

10. Fasick, Adelle M. "Television Language and Book Language," *Elementary English*, 50 (January 1973), 125-131.
11. Feeley, Joan. "Television and Children's Reading," *Elementary English*, 50 (January 1973), 141-148.
12. Feeley, Joan T. "Television and Reading in the Seventies," paper presented at the International Reading Association convention, 1974.
13. Humphrey, Jack W. *The Effect of a Summer Television Reading Program on the Reading Achievement of Children*. Washington, D.C.: United States Department of Health, Education, and Welfare, 1967, 52, 57.
14. "Pop-Ups Teach Reading," *Educational and Industrial Television*, March 1973, 22.
15. Robeck, Mildred C., and John A. R. Wilson. *Psychology of Reading: Foundations of Instruction*. New York: John Wiley and Sons, 1974, 8, 434.
16. Roser, Nancy L. "*Electric Company* Critique: Can Great Be Good Enough?" *Reading Teacher*, 27 (April 1974), 681-684.
17. Savage, John F. "Jack, Janet, or Simon Barsinister?" *Elementary English*, 50 (January 1970), 133-136.
18. Sprigle, Herbert A. "Can Poverty Children Live on *Sesame Street*?" *Young Children*, 26 (March 1971), 206-217.
19. "Television's Values for Primary Students," *Educational and Industrial Television*, September 24, 1973.
20. Tierney, Joan D. "The Miracle on *Sesame Street*," *Phi Delta Kappan*, 52 (January 1971), 296-298.

Reading and Television in the United Kingdom

W. Keith Gardner
University of Nottingham
Nottingham, England

Television output in the United Kingdom is limited to three main channels. Two of these are controlled by a public corporation, the BBC; one is operated by a number of commercial companies under the Independent Broadcasting Authority (IBA). For broadcasts to schools, there is liaison between the BBC and IBA, and it is unlikely that there would be direct competition for a viewing audience at any specific time. That is to say, a televised reading programme would not be transmitted simultaneously on two channels. Indeed, up to this time, there has been such a level of agreement in programme planning that it has been rare for a school series to have any direct competition. In the United Kingdom, about 91 percent of secondary schools, 96 percent of junior schools (pupils seven-to-eleven-years-old), and 64 percent of infant schools (pupils five-to-seven-years-old) are equipped with television. Normally, junior and infant schools have one television receiver to serve the entire school.

THE GENERAL DEVELOPMENT OF BROADCASTS TO SCHOOLS

Both the BBC and IBA have expanded their educational output in recent years. Programme planning has to balance the needs of a wide age range of pupils over most aspects of the curriculum. In the general area of language, the emphasis has been on English, rather than on learning to read. Nevertheless, over the past ten years one or the other of the broadcasting companies has provided a weekly series, extending over a school year, which deals specifically with learning to read. Programmes with a general language content, designed for seven-to-nine-year-old children, have captured the largest audiences. Typical figures for such programmes are: five-to-seven-year-olds, 47 percent of schools; seven-to-nine-year-olds, 70 percent of schools.

In contrast, reading programmes have recorded the following audience figures: five-to-seven-year-olds, 42 percent of schools; seven-to-nine-year-olds, 35 percent of schools. These figures should not be taken to indicate a smaller interest in reading programmes than in programmes with a wider language content; rather, they show how it is easier to design general language programmes with a wider application than is possible when one constructs material for learning to read.

THE STRUCTURE OF READING PROGRAMMES

The earliest programmes used a central figure in the role of teacher, and the program shape and form followed closely a normal classroom lesson. In brief, the television screen was used to gain an audience for an expert teacher who used his tried and tested classroom techniques supplemented by the added sophistication of professional graphic work, animated charts and diagrams, and dramatisation. The broadcasting companies produced good backup materials for teachers, and the opinion has been expressed that these were more valuable than the programmes.

In 1970, the present writer wrote a series which broke new ground in two directions: 1) an attempt was made to bridge the gap between prereading and reading, taking in a preschool as well as a starting school audience; and 2) the human teacher disappeared from sight, and the series was written around the phantasy world of animated puppets.

The nature of the larger population demanded a link between the general language programme and the learning to read programme so the technical resources of television were used to illustrate the relationship between spoken and written language. Three broad objects were isolated 1) to provide a motivated situation in which children listened to sophisticated language and were introduced to simple and complex language structures, 2) to show how the graphic form of language used a unique directional sequence and also used space as boundaries between words, and 3) to indicate that letters and sequences of letters are cues to interpreting graphic language.

The programmes essentially served as a stimulus. The puppets and a magic box created a phantasy world in which letters and words had an integral part in events. The teaching was left to the classroom teacher who was provided with a copy of the script, a description of the author's intentions, and some suggestions for activities. Because the home and the classroom were considered from the outset, simplicity and nontechnical language was the keynote of the backup materials. It is interesting to note the fundamental similarity between this kind of thinking and the much more ambitious *Sesame Street* developed in the United States. One should add that the total budget for the United Kingdom project was in the region of $50,000.

Another recent development has been the production of a series for slow learners based on the thinking of a research team, rather than one particular author. This pooling of resources (testing of ideas before production, and the involvement of groups of teachers in evolving programmes) is likely to become an important aspect of programme design.

PROBLEMS

Over the past twenty-five years, there has been a definite moving away from the prescribed syllabus and prescriptive teaching in British primary education. As a result, the formal reading lesson has become almost extinct and individualised tutoring more common. In these circumstances, it is difficult to foresee a future for television as a means of mass instruction.

Clearly, there will be a wide range of abilities and needs in any group of twenty to forty children. The chance is very slight that all, or even the majority of the children, will benefit from a small segment of specific teaching. Hence, the future of the television programme, with special reference to the teaching of reading, has to be envisaged in two ways: Ideally, the teacher requires a library of taped materials which can be used with small groups of pupils at the appropriate time. It is asking too much to assume that an audience is ready for teaching at the time selected by the programme planners of a broadcasting company.

With the spread of television facilities, such materials might be produced in units attached to colleges and universities rather than by the television companies. This is already happening in the United Kingdom, and some of the first results are encouraging. We can even envisage children in schools producing viable materials. The main obstacle, especially in primary schools, is the comparative scarcity of videotape equipment and the prohibitive cost of providing it.

It is interesting to note that, if this kind of development does find favour with teachers, the provision of a number of small television sets in school will be more important than the installation of one large set. At the present time, television in school is most often seen in terms of mass, rather than group or individual, viewing.

Television is part of a child's environment in the United Kingdom; its potency as a means of gaining attention is unquestioned. The role television can play in education, however, needs to be determined. The writer feels that, through television, an author can create the ideal world for his purposes and children can experience sights, sounds, and events beyond the range of their normal living. It is the teacher, however, who must bring form and shape to experience through personal contact with the children. Television can be a vital aid but it cannot replace the teacher and it cannot make bad teaching good.

Contributions of Technology to Reading Success

Joan M. Irwin
Copp Clark Limited
Calgary, Alberta
Canada

The early years of the twentieth century witnessed the introduction of new pedagogic devices in education. The magic lantern and slides, the phonograph and cylinder records, the camera and photographs, duplicating equipment, and the radio were viewed as supplementary aids to the basic media of instruction: the teacher and the book (6). In the 1920s technological innovations directly related to reading instruction appeared. These machines were mainly of a tachistoscopic nature, designed to improve the reader's eye movements, and, consequently, the rate of silent reading. Today, the array of technological devices available for use in the reading programme is impressive. The innovations vary in form and complexity: radio, television, videotape recorder, computer, film loop, cassette, tape recorder, and microform are but a few of the materials. It is apparent that technology is very much a part of reading instruction and of education generally.

Despite the number and variety of technological devices available for use in the teaching of reading, there is some disagreement about the use of nonprint materials to develop a process that requires responses to printed matter. The controversy has been heightened in recent years.

Publishers of reading series have added technological components such as filmstrips and tape recordings to their basic materials for reading instruction. The extent to which such supplementary materials are used, and the effectiveness of these materials in improving children's reading performance, are areas needing investigation.

Some writers predict the demise of the printed word. Marshall McLuhan (9), for example, maintains that literacy has outlived its usefulness. Electronic media is the stimulus which provokes our senses to active participation in the learning process. It is also projected that with more sophisticated and less expensive mechanical means of information storage and retrieval, an individual may no longer require the ability to read. At the present time, however, we do not know whether printed forms of information will eventually disappear. Observation of the current proliferation of books, both hard and soft cover, magazines, newspapers, and pamphlets would seem to indicate that the demise of print is not imminent.

It is quite evident that the school tends to perpetuate the use of print. Many educators indicate that children spend at least 80 percent of their instructional time involved with printed materials. This figure compares inversely with the amount of time children spend with electronic media outside of school.

In both advanced and developing countries, reading is often the basis of the educational system. It is a skill that is necessary to survival in the programme of studies. Furthermore, in many countries there are societal expectations that at a certain age children will enter school and learn how to read.

There are many arguments which could be presented both for and against the use of nonprint material in the reading programme. Perhaps, because print is an "old technology" (14) we find certain "familiar and comforting images" (9) in it. Being familiar with the conventions of print, we do not have to develop new patterns of behaviour to deal with it. Instead of debating whether print will be superseded by other communication forms and in what ways other communication forms are more effective than print, we need to explore the ways in which educational technology can make greater contributions to success in reading.

The term *educational technology* needs clarifying. In popular usage, the term is often equated with audiovisual media such as films, tape recordings, overhead projectors, and reading machines. Proponents of technology in education disagree with this limited definition. Instructional media is a more appropriate term for the aforementioned materials. On the other hand, educational technology embraces all the newer media used for instructional purposes as well as instructional modifications necessary to incorporate the media into the curricular framework (2, 3, 6). In the view of these writers, educational technology provides a systematic way of approaching the teaching/learning situation through the application of experience and knowledge of resources and materials to the problems of education. Through the implementation of instructional media in the context of the total programme, a better arrangement of the learning situation should be achieved.

For administrators and teachers contemplating the inclusion of instructional media in the reading programme, there are a number of questions which should be considered:

1. What are the essential features of the present reading programme?
2. What are the main deficiencies in the present programme?

3. In what ways will the inclusion of instructional media help overcome the present programme deficiencies?
4. What kinds of instructional media materials are available? Can the media be classified according to purposes in reading instruction, methods of use, and kinds of pupils who would profit from such materials?
5. What changes in teacher and pupil behaviour will be required by the inclusion of instructional media?
6. What changes in the physical arrangements of classrooms will be required by the inclusion of instructional media?
7. In what ways has a more balanced reading programme resulted from the inclusion of nonprint materials?

Such questions should serve as a guide for programme planners in working toward a better arrangement of the learning situation.

The teacher is instrumental in effecting change within the reading programme, for the teacher controls the social setting into which educational technology and instructional media may be introduced. The extent to which benefits will be derived from technology is greatly influenced by the social setting (10).

How well are teachers prepared to cope with instructional media in their reading programmes? There are frequent references in the literature to the need for preservice and inservice teacher training courses on the application of technology in the classroom (13). In a survey conducted by the Canadian Teachers Federation in 1969 and 1970, an effort was made to determine trends toward teacher education in technology. While twenty-five of the thirty-five institutions surveyed offered courses in instructional media, the courses were not compulsory. It is apparent that, in Canada, many teachers are entering the classroom without any background in educational technology (4). Considering this information, along with the fact that many Canadian teachers have minimal training in reading methods, we may seriously question the extent to which instructional media will be incorporated effectively into the reading programme (7).

Educational technology could also be used in teacher training courses in reading methods. Films, television productions, or videotape recordings could be developed to demonstrate the practical application of different theoretical approaches to reading (1, 16).

Although teacher education institutions in Canada do not appear to place much emphasis on preparation for the use of educational technology, this does not mean to imply that Canadian schools are without instructional media. A 1967 survey indicated that most Canadian schools had a rather extensive stock of technological materials, including computers (used in large urban school systems for pupil records and library cataloguing), reading machines (tachistoscopes, controlled readers), language laboratories, and the usual audiovisual materials (8). In addition, schools have easy access to many materials which would accompany the hardware of instructional media (15).

In a more general way, technology has made many contributions to the teacher's professional development in reading instruction. Many of the complex research investigations completed in the past ten years could not have been done without the computer and various recording devices. As a result, our background of information related to the reading process, to children's language development, and to characteristics of the written form of the language has been greatly enhanced. The availability of research studies and professional papers on microforms has made it much easier for teachers to examine the professional literature. Presumably, opportunities to study the professional literature will result in improved reading instruction.

Earlier in this discussion it was mentioned that many publishers of reading series are including instructional media as supplements to the traditional reader and workbook. The availability of such a variety of materials provides the teacher with many opportunities to modify instruction to meet the needs of various pupils. A specific concept may be approached through print, pictures, filmstrips, or tapes in some of the published programmes. What flexibility is offered a teacher in developing a more vital reading programme! Many other materials are available for use independently or in conjunction with series of readers (12, 13, 15).

Television is another means which can facilitate progress in reading. It provides an effective way of influencing children's attitudes toward the learning task as well as making the task easier for them. Animations and filmed stories can provide a highly motivating situation for children who have encountered reading problems (11).

It may be noted, however, that the use of television in an instructional setting may require a reorganization of the child's previously acquired viewing habits. In the home environment, television viewing may be part of an intimate, personal situation over which the child has some degree of control. In school, television viewing is naturally formalized as a group activity which requires attentiveness and some degree of conformity. While the child may have to make some behavioural adjustments for television viewing in the school setting, the benefits gained from successful reading experiences cannot be overlooked or underrated. Perhaps television should permeate the schools in much the same way that reading does.

Although many researchers seem to be opposed to the use of reading machines, current research literature does not offer sufficient evidence to substantiate such a point of view. On the positive side, the motivational aspects of reading machines are usually considered of utmost significance, particularly in situations where teachers are working with pupils who have encountered difficulties in reading. On the other hand, reading machines featuring behaviourally designed programmes which require one right answer obtained by the following one right route should be critically appraised. Not all facets of the reading process can be developed effectively through such procedures (13).

Instructional media and the concept of educational technology are still in their infancy. Many devices and plans are presently available for use within the reading programme; many devices and plans are in the developmental stages; others are just sparks in some creative imagination. It is not so much the media that contributes to success in reading—rather it is the teacher's effective use of the technological aids that determines success in reading.

REFERENCES

1. Affleck, Muriel. "Videotapes in Preservice Education: Do's and Don't's," in Jane H. Catterson (Ed.), *Reading Education in Canada, 1970.* Vancouver: Kellee Educational Publishing, 1972, 1-5.
2. *APLET Yearbook of Educational and Instructional Technology 1972/3.* London: Kogan Page Limited, 1973.
3. Apter, Michael J. *The New Technology of Education.* London: Macmillan, 1968.
4. Channon, Geraldine. *Innovations in Teacher Education in Canada.* Ottawa: Canadian Teachers' Federation, 1971.
5. George, Frank H. *Science and the Crisis in Society.* London: Wiley-Interscience, 1970.
6. Gillette, Margaret. *Educational Technology: Toward Demystification.* Scarborough: Prentice-Hall of Canada, 1973.
7. Hooper, Richard. "Educational Technology: Strategy for Success," *Educational Television International,* 4 (June 1970), 128-133.
8. Lucow, W. H. "A Survey of Automated Teaching and Learning Devices in Canadian Schools," *Education and the New Technology,* Canadian Council for Research in Education Symposium, 1967, 26-29.
9. McLuhan, Marshall, and Quentin Fiore. *War and Peace in the Global Village.* Toronto: McGraw-Hill, 1968.
10. Mesthene, Emmanuel G. *Technological Change: Its Impact on Man and Society.* Cambridge: Harvard University Press, 1970.
11. Morris, Joyce M. "Television and Reading," in John Merritt (Ed.), *Reading and the Curriculum,* Proceedings of Seventh Annual Study Conference, UKRA, Durham, 1970. London: Ward Lock Educational, 1971, 125-134.
12. Moyle, Donald, and Louise M. Moyle. *Modern Innovations in the Teaching of Reading.* London: University of London Press, 1971.
13. Palmatier, Robert A. "The Role of Machines in the Reading Program," in Howard A. Klein (Ed.), *The Quest for Competency in Teaching Reading.* Newark, Delaware: International Reading Association, 1972.
14. Postman, Neil. "The Politics of Reading," in Sr. Rosemary Winkeljohann (Ed.), *The Politics of Reading: Point-Counterpoint.* Newark, Delaware: International Reading Association, 1973, 1-11.
15. Snow, Kathleen M., and Philomena Hauck. *Canadian Materials for Schools.* Toronto: McClelland and Stewart, 1970.
16. Westermark, Tory, Kenneth Slade, and Kenneth Ahrendt. "The Development and Use of Film in the Lanuage Experience Approach to Reading," in Jane H. Catterson (Ed.), *Reading Education in Canada, 1970.* Vancouver: Kellee Educational Publishing, 1972, 6-10.

PART FIVE

Special Problems

Promoting the Reading Habit: Cultural Problems

M. Jean Greenlaw
University of Georgia
Athens, Georgia
United States of America

Cultural problems. Many teachers erroneously and automatically assume that this is synonymous with cultural deprivation and is a major determinant in reading failure. By assigning the cause to the culture of the child, we relieve the teacher and the educational system of the burden of guilt. After all, we cannot be held responsible for the home environment of the child!

The term *cultural deprivation* has been used by some educators to refer to those students who did not hold the same values as the majority of their teachers. Because these students did not function in the same patterns as their teachers and did not profess the same standards, they were labeled "deprived." These children are not culturally deprived. They may be culturally different from the accepted standards of the school system, but they are not culturally deprived.

Culture is the learned behavior of a human being. It reflects the values, traditions, and conventions of a group and includes the social and political structures and its modes of procedure. No one is deprived of culture; there merely exist different cultures. It is highly presumptuous of us to place value judgments on the relative worth of these different cultures. Furthermore, a child cannot easily renounce his culture, and any attempt by the teacher to force this renunciation meets with great resistance. Verbal and nonverbal behavior, on the part of the teacher, that exhibits contempt for another culture is not likely to encourage students to perform well in school.

CULTURE AS IT AFFECTS BEHAVIOR IN SCHOOL

It is not the culture but teacher attitudes toward and inadequate knowledge of various cultures that are the causes of many of the problems in multiethnic schools. Often, the school is seen as an alien and hostile environment by both students and parents. Parenthetically, when a teacher enters a situation where the dominant culture is different from his own, he, too, exhibits hostile behavior.

A few examples of cultural differences will suffice to show the problems that can exist:

American Indian. Many Indian cultures value silence and are highly skilled in nonverbal communication. English used by Indian adults is often composed of short and simple patterns, so the child comes to school with oral patterns that are not acceptable by school standards. His highly developed abilities of nonverbal communication are ignored because schools place value on verbal communication.

Another area of conflict arises in the competitiveness that exists in many schools. In some Indian cultures, it is considered bad manners to do better than your friends. This lack of willingness to compete is often misinterpreted as laziness.

Cuban American. Right to Read is a federally funded program which is designed to eradicate illiteracy in the United States by 1980. An extensive project entitled "The Right to Read Through Sports" proved to have variable results in a Miami, Florida, school. The school is composed of 58 percent Cuban children and 42 percent black children. Black boys and girls and Cuban boys participated with much enthusiasm; Cuban girls were extremely reluctant to be more than passive observers. Examination of these behaviors revealed that Cuban culture views sports as a masculine pastime, while blacks view it as a possible way to improve their status.

Mexican American. Essentially the same belief in the proper role of females and males is reflected in a study to determine the effects of stereotyping on the self-concepts of Mexican Americans reported by Palomares (9). Girls were expected to exhibit behavior that was passive in nature while boys were expected to be active. Both extremes of behavior can cause negative reactions by teachers who lack knowledge and understanding of Mexican American culture.

Urban, Low Socioeconomic Groups. There are numerous reasons for the afflictions of our city schools. Added to ethnic differences, there are conditions of poverty, variable family structures, and dialect differences. Most teachers commute to their jobs and have little understanding of the nonschool life of their students. For those who think that their children deliberately choose to fail as an act of defiance or out of sheer apathy, this quote from the work of a sixteen-year-old (11) provides a different perspective:

what i dont like school—No A

what i dont like school is that I come evey day thanking I will get a A.
But I never git a A. Just wonst I want to git a A. Ever sins I remember I go
to school a thousand day a year or more I git no A. No A

> JUST WONST
> I WANT AN
> A ONE BIG FAT
> A

All I git is a big bunch of F
A hundred F. A thowsand F
A lowsy bunch of F

Rural, Low Socioeconomic Groups. Problems present in innercity living are also faced by the rural poor. In our recent endeavors to create materials that reflect the cultures in the United States, we have tended to neglect the existence of rural areas. Thus, these students now choose from materials with suburban or urban settings which reflect little that is familiar to their rural experience.

INFLUENCE OF TEXTBOOKS

Research has shown that there are many kinds of bias in textbooks and that these books do have an effect on children's attitudes. In one such study, Litcher and Johnson (6) investigated attitude change toward blacks following the use of multiethnic reading texts. They found that white students developed markedly more favorable attitudes toward blacks after use of the multiethnic version of a basal reading text for four months. The control group used the nonethnic version of the reader and showed little or no change in attitude. One would hope that similar results might be obtained in the case of other ethnic groups.

Recognizing the influence that texts can have on students, it is to be hoped that minorities will exert more influence on textbook selection and production than was shown in a research study by Greenlaw (4). This study was based on a random sampling of 75 school systems in the United States, and it was found that in the majority of these systems minority representation in the texts was not specifically considered as a criterion for selection. Where minority groups were considered, the influence came mainly from school personnel. Five representative publishers reported that they had received few requests from school systems for changes of reading materials.

Recent news stories do give us hope that this trend is changing. Demands from organized groups, such as those advocating broader women's rights, are leading to greater responsiveness by publishers to the needs of cultural minorities.

PROMOTING THE READING HABIT

Acknowledging the abundance of problems related to culture that we have in school, how can we promote the reading habit in children? We need to begin with something that is basic to facilitating all education, not just reading. That basic ingredient is an atmosphere conducive to learning in the classroom. There are specific actions that will enable more students to feel that they belong in school.

Teacher education. Teachers often are unprepared to teach in our public schools, and they are trained to cope with the average child in a nonthreatening situation. Institutions of higher learning have a responsibility to design teacher training programs that expose future teachers to a variety of challenging situations and to introduce methods of teaching effectively in those situations.

Another aspect of teacher education is inservice education. Inservice programs, designed by individual schools, are often planned to provide teachers with greater content knowledge. Our first priority should be self-knowledge and knowledge of the children we serve. Every teacher in a school should be apprised of the cultures of the community served by the school. More information is needed, however, than population statistics. Opportunities for exploring cultural attitudes and behaviors are essential if teachers are to interact effectively with students and parents.

Development of awareness sessions will also reinforce positive attitudes toward cultural differences on the part of more established teachers and administrators. Several of the federally funded Right to Read projects spent a considerable portion of their funds on sessions of this type. As Southeast Director of Right to Read, I believe that observations show that the reward is high in attitude changes of both teachers and students.

Teacher integration. We often speak of school integration, but we are generally referring to the pupils. All schools should endeavor to become integrated on the teacher level as well. Cultures represented in the pupil population should be reflected in the teacher population—not for the purpose of establishing arbitrary hiring or placement policies by percentage of minority group, but of presenting children with a model of effective interaction among peoples of various cultures. Merely hiring an integrated faculty is insufficient. Programs designed to increase teacher interaction should become part of the school inservice planning.

Language acceptance. Artificial barriers are often erected between teacher and child because the teacher believes that it is his duty to "educate" the child and interprets this belief as requiring the child to speak standard English. Some teachers do not realize that attacking the language of a child, is attacking the child himself. It is more reasonable to establish the idea of alternative languages and not place value judgments on the worth of the various alternatives. Children eventually come to understand the appropriate times for using the languages they possess.

By developing an appreciation of language, the child is more willing to learn of the diversity of language; on the other hand, attempts to correct dialect may defeat some children.

An effective device to show appreciation for the language of other cultures is to have a planned program of instruction in those languages. A Right to Read school in Miami, Florida, holds classes to teach Spanish to English speakers as well as the reverse. The result of this activity led to better communication among the students and greater empathy for the difficulty of learning a new language.

Language experience. The language experience approach is one method of promoting the reading habit. A child dictates a story to the teacher or aide who records it exactly as spoken by the child. The student then uses his own words as the basis for reading and language study. Motivation certainly is increased when a child reads his own writing or when he shares a friend's creation.

Sharing the reading experience. Positive feelings toward reading are engendered through the warmth of sharing books aloud. Teachers of all levels should read aloud to their classes consistently from a wide selection of books. The teacher should share books that he knows and enjoys and he should strive to perfect a reading style which is attractive to children.

Additional value is gained by having a variety of readers visit the class. The principal, other teachers, children from other classes, and the pupil's family members can all serve as a resource pool for readers. Tape recorders can be sent home to record reading or storytelling by family members who cannot come to school.

Community involvement. A child is a representative of his culture so it behooves the school to involve the community in the education of the child. School volunteer programs should not be limited to parents but should encourage participation of all segments of the community.

A Right to Read school in Miami, Florida, designed a volunteer plan which included members of a retired Cuban businessmen's association (one member arrived at school at 8 a.m. each morning and was the last to leave each evening), local high school students, students enrolled in education classes at a nearby junior college, and relatives of many of the children. Cubans, blacks, and whites ranging in age from 14 to 79 participated. All took their roles seriously and the students of that school benefited from a marvelous mixture of these additional aides who functioned in many capacities. An added advantage was afforded through improved community relations and less physical damage to the school.

A school in Athens, Georgia, conducts a similar volunteer program and even provides transportation to evening parent-teacher meetings. Thus, obstacles can be overcome through effective planning and reasonable effort.

USE OF TRADE BOOKS

When a comfortable and supportive atmosphere has been generated, we can concentrate on the selection and use of good literature with children. Trade books can be used in numerous ways to develop cultural appreciation.

Recognition of stereotyping. Teachers who use books with cultural settings should be alert to the existence of stereotyping in children's literature. Gast's study (3) showed that although recent children's books incorporated favorable stereotyping, the result, nevertheless, *was* stereotyping. Teachers should make an effort to locate books that reduce stereotyping to a minimum.

Book selection aids are available to support teachers in their search for fine literature. *Reading Ladders for Human Relations (10)* is an annotated bibliography of books carefully selected to reflect many aspects of human affairs of social and cultural significance. The committee responsible for producing this volume represented a diverse cultural population.

Interracial Books for Children provides another aid to book selection. It is published as a periodical, in tabloid format, by the Council on Interracial Books for Children. Editors of this provocative publication review books which are judged as fair cultural representations; and they attack, in depth, those books believed to be racist. Recently, the reviewers have begun to evaluate films and textbooks which contain derogatory or harmful references to minority populations. Although one does not agree with the viewpoints expressed, the material provokes thought and is valuable as a source of minority expression.

Strengthening personal identity. Numerous studies have shown that children like to read stories about characters with whom they can identify. In my opinion, it is vitally important that books representing minority cultures present strong, positive models for children. It is equally important that realistic situations be represented honestly.

Authors are beginning to produce books that would have been taboo a short time ago. *Black Is Brown Is Tan* by Arnold Adoff (1) is a story about the author's family. He is white, his wife is black, and their children are shades of brown. Think of the number of children who now have a wholesome book that depicts this family situation. And consider the American Indian who is written about as if he exists only in the past. Miles' *Annie and the Old One* (8) is a beautiful book with a modern setting that explores Annie's refusal to face the impending death of her grandmother. This book presents a realistic and acceptable explanation of death, another topic long avoided by authors of children's books.

Broadening cultural appreciation. No child should read only one restricted form of literature, just as no child should read only books about one culture. One tremendous value of books is that they allow us to experience new situations.

Books can be used to explore many cultures. Hawkins (5) reported that a study of nursery rhymes shows that they reflect the language, food, standards of behavior, and attitudes of the people and the time. An excellent study of social beliefs could be developed in upper grades through comparison of traditional European nursery rhymes as discussed in *The Annotated Mother Goose* (2) with modern American rhymes as depicted in *The Inner City Mother Goose* (7). Fiction and folklore should also be a strong part of a curriculum that strives to represent cultural diversity. Children should be exposed to many cultural patterns even though they have no direct contact with those cultures.

An aid to language development. Children learn language by imitating models presented to them. Books can be used as an aid to language development by providing new vocabulary gleaned from the context of the story. This is of particular help to the child who is learning a distinctly different language or dialect. Children possessing only standard English should also be exposed to different language patterns through books. At no time, however, should literature be dissected for vocabulary study or be employed in training sessions on the use of the glossary and dictionary. Aid should come in informal manner, through story discussion and sharing of new ideas.

Availability. Children will read more if books are readily available and they do not have to exert great effort to obtain them. Book collections should be present in every classroom. The source of these collections can be the school library, public library, parental and community donations, paperback book clubs, and second-hand book stores.

The recent trend to open school libraries is excellent. The relaxation of stringent rules, such as limiting students to borrowing only one book during a designated period, is overdue. Some children enjoy reading more than one book at a time and may even prefer alternating their reading selections from one book to another.

Paperback book clubs have been of tremendous value in providing a wide variety of good children's literature at reasonable prices. Many publishers have also cooperated with Reading is Fundamental (RIF), a national program designed to give free books to children in the United States. Schools and sponsoring organizations can purchase books at greatly reduced rates to distribute free to children. This project has stimulated much interest in reading, and some children now have a book of their own for the first time.

CONCLUSION

An attempt has been made to delineate some problems of cultural origin in promoting reading habits and to suggest a number of remedies. These can be summarized in terms of two essentials: create a good atmosphere for reading and provide good books. How have we failed?

REFERENCES
1. Adoff, Arnold. *Black Is Brown Is Tan*. New York: Harper and Row, 1973.
2. Baring-Gould, Williams S., and Ceil Baring-Gould. *The Annotated Mother Goose*. New York: Bramhall House, 1962.
3. Gast, David K. "Minority Americans in Children's Literature," *Elementary English*, 44 (1967), 12-23.
4. Greenlaw, Jean. "A Study of the Influence of Minority Groups in the Selection and Development of Basal Reading Programs," in William Joyce and James Banks (Eds.), *Teaching the Language Arts to Culturally Different Children*. Reading, Massachusetts: Addison-Wesley, 1971.
5. Hawkins, Roberta. "Nursery Rhymes: Mirrors of a Culture," *Elementary English*, 48 (October 1971), 617-621.
6. Litcher, John H., and David W. Johnson. "Changes in Attitude toward Negroes on White Elementary School Students after Use of Multiethnic Readers," *Journal of Educational Psychology*, 60 (1969), 148-152.
7. Merriam, Eve. *The Inner City Mother Goose*. New York: Simon and Schuster, 1969.
8. Miles, Miska. *Annie and the Old One*. Boston: Little, Brown, 1971.
9. Palomares, Geraldine Dunne. *The Effects of Stereotyping on the Self-Concepts of Mexican Americans*. Albuquerque, New Mexico: Southwest Cooperative Educational Laboratory, 1970.
10. Reid, Virginia (Ed.). *Reading Ladders for Human Relations*. Washington, D.C.: American Council on Education, 1972.
11. Summers, Andrew. *Me the Flunkie*. Greenwich, Connecticut: Fawcett, 1970, 19.

Problématique du Lire dans une Société en Voie de Développement

Abdelkader Ben Cheikh
Tunesian Institute for Educational Sciences
Tunis, Tunisia

PRELIMINAIRES

1.1 CADRE GLOBAL

Les études entreprises en Tunisie dans le domaine de la lecture sont relativement récentes (1). Centrées sur les méthodes d'apprentissage, orientées vers l'élaboration des supports didactiques destinés à l'institution scolaire (2) elles prirent progressivement une plus grande importance aussi bien en extension qu'en profondeur.

Le développement de la scolarisation et principalement au niveau de l'enseignement primaire, l'évaluation du premier plan decennal de scolarisation (3) ont favorisé une prise de conscience de l'importance du phénomène éducatif, de sa complexité ainsi que des rapports qu'il entretient avec d'autres phénomènes: sociaux économiques et culturels.

En effet la population élèves qui était en 1956-57 de 226-919 atteignait en 1971-72, 934-827 enfants scolarsés seulement dans le cycle primaire (4). Ce phénomène de massification pose le double problème de la fonctionalité du système éducatif et de sa rentabilité; c'est que l'entreprise est perçue, comme finalité et moyen dans une société ou le processus de décolonisation (5); s'est amorcé avec la volonté de récupérer la nature et la culture; la lutte contre le sous-développement qui demeure l'objectif du "moi national" se pose en termes de combat "muqàwamatu at-takhalluf", de décollage "al intilàqà."

La référence à la modernité et à ses modèles multiples est une quête permanente mais elle est en même temps référence et recherche d'une certain authenticité (6); c'est-à-dire que le passé n'est que rarement absent dans la construction du projet national.

C'est à partir de ces données que peuvent être saisies l'importance et les limites des travaux consacrés au fait éducatif. L'approche du lire ne peut être isolé de ce cadre global car la problématique du lire est inscrite au coeur même de la problématique du développement.

2.2 OBJECTIFS ET HYPOTHESES

L'étude des conditions de motivation de l'enfant à la lecture en milieu éducationnel tunisien nous conduit à formuler nos objectifs dans les termes suivants:

1. Le désir de lire apparait bien avant l'aptitude à la lecture déchiffrement (7) c'est-à-dire avant l'introduction de l'enfant en milieu scolaire (8); il constitue le premier niveau du pouvoir être lecteur. Introduit à un âge précoce le support de lecture prépare le sujet à vivre l'expérience prévilégié de la communication avec des êtres autres que ceux appartenant au groupe familial; d'où cette perspective de préparation du moi à s'affirmer (3 ans), à différencier (au cours de la 4e année) à se fixer un modèle (entre 5 et 6 ans) (9). Cette intégration de l'imprimé est par ailleurs du meilleur effet sur les relations entre parents et enfants, relation d'une extrême importance dans la phase d'apprentissage (10).

La prise en considération de ce principe appelle l'interrogation 1 qui constitue un niveau important de notre approche de la problématique du lire.

L'acte de lire préoccupe-t-il la famille tunisienne en tant que structure de base ayant pour charge l'éducation de l'enfant, éducation qui implique une préparation adéquate à son intégration dans une société où les mutations touchent certes à des degrés divers; les références, les modèles, les attitudes et les structures, en d'autres termes tous les paliers de la société globale.

Notre hypothèse est que dans la phase actuelle du développement de la société tunisienne, des conditions objectives socioéconomiques et culturelles déterminent un rôle plutôt marginal de la famille dans le processus de motivation de l'enfant à la lecture.

Des causes de la marginalité de la famille dans le processus de motivation de l'enfant à la lecture (11) marginalité (12) nous entendons l'absence partielle ou totale des membres agissants du groupe familial dans le circuit de la consommation des supports de lecture. Cette absence traduit l'indifférence du sujet à l'égard du pouvoir formateur et, ou, délassant de l'objet: le kitâb en l'occurence. Quels sont les facteurs qui contribuent à expliquer l'absence du lire et de la communication par la lecture en milieu familial? Trois niveaux d'analyse sont à prendre en considération (13).

Le premier nous renvoie à l'examen de la conception des loisirs; le second implique que l'on tienne compte des conditions économiques et intellectuelles d'accès au lire. Le troisième fait appel aux données qui relèvent du degré de participation de la famille à la consommation culturelle.

2.1 CONCEPTION DES LOISIRS

L'approche du concept loisir est une tentative qui dépasse le cadre de cette contribution; nous évitons donc d'intervenir dans le débat relatif au rapport de la sociologie du loisir, de la sociologie du travail et de la sociologie de la famille. En Tunisie, l'expression 'awqàt al Faragh (14) est d'usage très récent.

Est ce à dire que ce phénomène socio-culturel est étranger à une société en voie de développement dont les préoccupations se posent en termes de besoins vitaux (15)? Espace à plusieurs dimensions, le loisir est toutefois inscrit au coeur de la culture vêcue (16). La conception que les sujets se font du loisir est certes fonction de leur degré d'intégration dans le circuit de la culture imprimée (y compris les mass-média) "de la distantiation vis à vis des modèles traditionnels et l'adhésion enthousiaste à la modernité" (17).

Le temps en milieu rural, par exemple, est du type linéaire: c'est ce que le sujet accomplit en réalisant, mais essentiellement par le travail, la tâche. Au delà c'est l'interruption qui prépare la reprise du contact avec la terre et les hommes. A cet égard l'attitude de la famille est significative: Le jeu relève du temps gaspillé; c'est l'activité que l'enfant réalise par lui-même ne se référant qu'a son pouvoir d'imagination, et celui du groupe auquel il appartient dans l'espace de la rue; au niveau du groupe familial, jouer est rarement inscrit dans le temps éducatif il n'est ni construit ni animé, c'est à dire perçu comme un moyen de formation où l'intérêt et l'attrait se confondent.

Cette conception linéaire du temps se manifeste au niveau de la signification qu'accorde le milieu familial à l'acte de lecture. "Vas lire ton livre?" est une invitation impérative d'usage courant qui en refusant à l'enfant la rupture par le jeu ou une autre forme de délassement, l'engage dans la tâche contraignante qui n'est pas sans rappeler l'exercice d'autant plus que le ktab (le livre) est perçu par rapport à sa fonction essentiellement scolaire.

Jouer et lire ne sont que très rarement envisagés comme un acte gratuit, inscrit librement dans le temps-loisir que l'enfant apprend progressivement à vivre en famille. Il y a là une forme de rigidité culturelle qui ne favorise nullement la communication entre les parents et les enfants. Certes par leurs fréquents contacts avec le monde extérieur et plus particulièrement leur appartenance à l'école et la rue, les enfants (18) cessent de se référer exclusivement aux seules valeurs de la cellule familiale.

2.2 LE POUVOIR MATERIEL ET LE POUVOIR DE DECHIFFREMENT

Mais la tradition de lire en milieu familial Tunisien n'est pas tributaire—de la seule conception du loisir et de l'attitude de la USRA (Famille) à l'égard du ktab (livre); Elle est aussi et essentiellement fonction des conditions socio-économiques qui déterminent le pouvoir d'accés matériel et intellectuel au lire. En d'autres termes, l'intérêt qu'accorde la famille est dicté dans une large mesure par le degré de son appartenance au travail. Or d'après le recencement de la population de (1966) 19% seulement des sujets participent réellement—par le travail continu—à la vie active (19). Au niveau de la répartition des revenus la persistance des désiquilibres est importante dans la mesure où une proportion assez élevée de la population—plus de 40% dispose d'un revenu inférieur à ce que le premier Ministre actuel appelle le seuil de la pauvreté (20).

L'institution du salaire minimum inter-professionnel garanti fixe l'heure de travail dans les entreprises à 130 millimes et à 27 dinars le salaire mensuel pour une semaine de 48 heures (21). En ce qui concerne la population agricole qui représente 41% (22). L'ensemble de la population active, le salaire journalier est de 0D800 (23) millimes par jour ouvrable. Or l'effectif des salairiés appelés à bénéficier de ce relèvement des salaires minimums agricole est estimé pour l'année 1974 "à environ 101.000 travailleurs permanents et 191.000 de salariés saisonniers ou occasionnels" c'est-à-dire un total de 292.000 salariés soit moins de "50% de la force de travail estimée à 654.000 personnes en 1972" (24).

L'examen de la distribution des ménages et des personnes suivant les classes des dépenses par personne et pour l'ensemble de la Tunisie montre "qu'environ 43% des ménages n'ont pas atteint le niveau optimum de 50 dinars par personne" et par an (25). Ce pourcentage est plus important lorsqu'on tient compte des ménages appartenant aux zones fortement ruralisées (26).

L'analyse des dépenses en milieu familial nous permet de constater que l'essentiel des besoins dans la phase actuelle est orienté vers les dépenses alimentaires qui absorbent 50,3% (27) la part des dépenses réservées à la culture, à l'enseignement et aux divertissements y compris le tabac, ne dépasse pas la moyenne de 7D236 par an, c'est-à-dire le $^1/_{10}$ du budget total et le $^1/_5$ du budget non alimentaire. Cette somme est à répartir comme suit pour l'ensemble de la Tunisie:

- 3,3% pour le tabac
- 2,7% *seulement pour la culture et l'enseignement*
- 1,7% pour le divertissement
- 2,4% sont consacrés à des dépenses diverses (argent de poche, achat de bijoux, fêtes et mariages)

Ainsi sur les 6 grands groupes de dépenses que le ménage peut réaliser, la part de dépenses reservées à la culture se situe au 4e rang après l'alimentation, l'habitation et l'habillement.

2.3 DE LA PARTICIPATION A LA CONSOMMATION DU LIVRE ET DES SUPPORTS DE LECTURE

Le troisième niveau du pouvoir lire en milieu familial tunisien concerne le degré de participation à la consommation du livre et des supports de lecture, participation qui constitue nous semble-t-il un critère important dans l'étude des conditions de motivation de l'enfant à la lecture.

La tradition de lire est—avons nous souligné précédemment—liée à la conception du temps libre, à la qualité de l'appartenance du groupe familial au monde du travail; mais elle est aussi fonction du degré d'intégration dans la circuit de la culture imprimée.

Or cette intégration n'a guère été vécue avec le même pouvoir de disponibilité et d'intensité aussi bien en milieu fortement urbanisé où sont concentrés les supports de formation et de loisirs qu'en milieu rural dont la population représente 49% de la population tunisienne. Ce pourcentage est en fait inférieur à la réalité surtout si l'on tient compte du critère socio-culturel qui détermine le degré d'urbanité ou de ruralité en matière de consommation de la culture (29) le développement d'un réseau d'animation culturelle comportant 75 maisons du peuple, 10 maisons de culture (30) et 187 bibliothèques, y compris les centres de prêts municipaux et les bibliocars (31) a certes contribué à élargir les zones d'influence et d'interaction en matière de consommation culturelle.

Ces foyers demeurent toutefois insuffisants et inégalement répartis d'autant plus qu'ils sont pour la plupart concentrés soit à Tunis, ou dans les grandes villes et chef-lieu de gouvernorat.

Un autre obstacle—et non des moindres—participe à l'affaiblissement de la tradition de lire en milieu familial: il s'agit de l'importance de la masse des analphabètes.

Population analphabète

Population déclarée	
Hommes	Femmes
805.704	1.209.500
TOTAL: 2.025.204	

Population analphabète en milieu urbain et rural

Population Urbaine	Population Rurale
650.805	1.374.399

Source: Institut National des statistiques (Recensement 1966).

En effet, parmi la population âgée de 10 et plus, 2 millions (32) de personnes environ sont analphabètes le nombre des femmes qui traditionnement assument un rôle déterminant dans l'éducation de l'enfant atteint 82% de l'ensemble des analphabètes. La population rurale ne compte pas moins d'1.374.339 personnes ne sachant ni lire ni écrire (33).

Mais l'absence ou le faible pouvoir de consommation du lire et des autres supports de lecture n'est pas spécifique aux populations analphabètes et socio-économiquement défavorisées. L'examen de la place qu'occupe la lecture dans les loisirs de l'adulte constitue le dernier palier de notre approche du pouvoir de consommation culturelle. Une investigation relative à la place qu'occupe la lecture loisir auprès d'une population appartenant aux cités et aux quartiers environnants de la ville de Tunis a permis de constater que 35% seulement de l'échantillon préféraient meubler une soirée par la lecture; 22% exprimaient le désir d'utiliser une après-midi ou une journée libre à lire (34). La lecture en tant qu'activité réelle n'occupe par contre qu'une position très marginale, la 6eme place pour les adultes de sexe masculin et la 7ème pour les adultes de sexe féminin; elle se situe après la promenade, les visites, le spectacle sportif, le tricotage, la radio et la TV. Cette marginalité de la lecture est confirmée par le degré de fréquentation des bibliothèques publiques pour adultes.

En effet le nombre de lecteurs abonnés qui était en 1971 de l'ordre de 20225 diminuait de 50% pour une tranche d'âge passant de la trentaine à la quarantaine: le nombre d'abonnés dont l'âge se situe entre 30 et 40 ans est 8 fois inférieur à celui des abonnés dont la tranche d'âge se situe entre 19 et 25 ans. Une chute extrèmement importante concerne la tranche d'âge dépassant la quarantaine.

La fréquentation des bibliothèques—clef du développement— diminue de 7 fois en l'espace de 20 ans. Quant à la lecture des journaux dont le tirage se situe autour de 107.000 exemplaires, elle ne préoccupe que 16% seulement des tunisiens. Ce sont là les symptômes d'une vieillesse intellectuelle avant terme et les signes d'une nouvelle forme d'analphabétisme. De notre approche du rôle de la famille dans le processus de motivation à la lecture se confirme notre hypothèse de départ.

Dans la phase socio-historique actuelle, la USRA (ou cellule familiale) ne peut assumer qu'un rôle très marginal. La tradition de lire en milieu familial tunisien et principalement dans les ménages socio-économiquement et culturellement défavorisés est objectivement inéxistante. La préparation de l'enfant est donc limitée au milieu fortement acquis à l'importance du lire dans le développement de la personnalité de l'enfant en général, dans la préparation à l'apprentissage efficace au pouvoir et savoir lire, conditions d'une scolarité sans entraves.

Car lire est l'acte quotidien qui intervient d'une manière continue à chacun des moments de l'apprentissage de l'enfant; les taux de redoublements et de déperditions (35) scolaires sont certes dûs à des causes profondes qui relèvent des conditions socio-économiques et culturelles du milieu familial et de la qualité de l'environnement immédiat; mais il est probable et c'est une hypothèse que nous formulons, qu'il relève de ce faible pouvoir d'accès matériel au livre et aux supports de lecture, l'acte de naissance du lecteur n'est pas encore délivré par le père et la mère; il dépend en Tunisie d'une autre structure institutionnalisée: L'école.

3. PROLONGEMENT

L'acte de naissance de l'enfant lecteur dépend donc en grande partie de l'institution scolaire qui est perçue dans la phase actuelle comme le cadre priviligié pour la prise en charge de l'apprentissage et du développement du pouvoir lire.

Ce caractère priviligié s'explique par:

1. Le pouvoir d'attraction de l'école est pleinement senti comme étant le lieu où se prépare la société. En scolarisant l'enfant, la famille vise un double investissement: la promotion du scolarisé et de la sienne.

2. Par l'importance de l'infrastructure et des effectifs scolaires; le recencement des bâtiments scolaires pour l'année 1972-73 permet de dénombrer 2.238 écoles primaires pour une population atteignant 883.734 élèves (36).

3. Par l'importance du coût considéré comme le signe d'une disponibilité en vue de produire les cadres du développement.

4. Par le rôle de médiateur que joue cette institution en tant que structure favorisant—en interaction avec d'autres apports extérieurs (37). La réalisation des conditions de dépassement de certains modèles culturels traditionnels (38).

Ce statut renforcé de l'école tunisienne. Conséquence de la marginalité de l'environnement familial et des limites du troisième milieu—a-t-il permis à l'institution scolaire d'assurer pleinement son rôle dans le processus de motivation de l'enfant à la lecture?

Les méthodes préconisées, les moyens utilisés ont-ils favorisé la réalisation des conditions du pouvoir lire spontanément et sans contrainte, conditions inscrites dans les objectifs de départ de la plus importante des entreprises tunisiennes? Notre seconde hypothèse est que malgré l'importance de l'investissement, l'absence de structures pré-scolaires le contact tardif avec le support de lecture, l'insuffisance de l'impact des méthodes et des techniques d'apprentissage, participent à la remise en question de l'efficacité du système éducationnel actuel, principalement quant au développement du pouvoir lire que beaucoup considèrent à juste titre comme l'une des clés du développement.

Trois expériences sont actuellement en cours: la première concerne la *préparation* de l'enfant aux *apprentissages instrumentaux* (lecture, écriture, calcul) au niveau pré-scolaire (41) l'activation de l'apprentissage de la langue arabe et française en 1ère et 2ème année de l'enseignement primaire par la *méthode orale "technique du conte"* (42). La 3ème expérience dite motivation à la lecture (43) vise à développer le *désir de lire* et la *communication* par la lecture: ainsi que l'apprentissage progressif de la *production* des supports de lecture. Ces expérience (44) dont certaines en cours d'extension (méthode orale et motivation à la lecture) participent en milieu scolaire et au niveau des bibliothèques publiques pour enfants à creer les conditions d'une promotion de la lecture en Tunisie, d'autant plus que la production nationale des supports de lecture prend de plus en plus d'importance (600 titres) sont actuellement en diffusion.

Recherches et programmes d'action se poursuivent. La prise de conscience de l'importance du lire est inscrite dans les champs des préoccupations à l'échelle nationale et régionale. La conscience internationale en a été saisie (1972). Notre débat (certes de courte durée en est une contribution fort importante.

Annexe

Publications relatives à l'approche des problèmes de la lecture et des supports de lecture en milieu éducationnel Tunisien réalisées à l'Institut National des Sciences de l'Education.

ORIENTATIONS: Ces publications peuvent être demandées à L'Institut National des Sciences de l'Education, 17 Rue Fénelon, Tunis, Tunisie.

1. Psycho-sociologie de la lecture
   Approche des phénomènes de comportement de la lecture en milieu éducationnel tunisien: famille école foyer socio-culturel.
2. Socio-pédagogie de la lecture en milieu éducationnel
   Méthodes techniques moyens
   Motivation à la lecture: conception et expérimentation
   Formation et intervention scolaire
   Motivation à la lecture et attitude des élèves et des enseignants
   Production expérimentale des supports de lecture
3. Sociologie des supports de lecture
   Approche quantitative et qualitative de la production intellectuelle et matérielle des supports de lecture et de communication: Ecrivain-édition impression diffusion

4. Approche bibliothéconomique: organisation-gestion
   Bibliothèque scolaire
   Bibliothèque publique

5. Approche socio-littéraire
   Problèmes théoriques et méthodologiques
   Lectures
   Autobiographie ou itinéraire d'écriture
   Anthologies: textes théoriques et textes littéraires

6. Production audiovisuelle
   Dossiers audiovisuel de motivation à la lecture
   Film
   Télévision scolaire

ORIENTATIONS	TITRE	PRODUCTEUR(S)	ANNEE	LANGUE	TRADUCTEUR
Psycho-sociologie de la lecture: approche des phénomènes de comportement de lecture	Situation de lecture en milieu scolaire semi-urbain: Grombalia	M. Belajouza S. Kortas A. Ben Cheikh A. Larabi	1971	Fr.* Ar.	B. Ben Salem
	De la lecture publique en Tunisie: Problèmes et perspectives	Direction des Bibliothèques Publiques	1971	Fr.	
	Lecture et bilinguisme dans les bibliothèques enfantines en Tunisie	S. Ben Rejeb	1971	Fr.	
	Situation de la lecture en 6e année de l'enseignement primaire Tunisien	M. Belajouza S. Kortas A. Ben Cheikh T. Lazhar	1972	Fr. Ar.	A. Lahmar
	Situation du livre et de la lecture: Bibliothèque Charles DeGaulle. Mission Culturelle Française	F. Anne	1972	Fr.	
	Situation de la lecture dans les écoles de Tunisie	M. Belajouza A. Ben Cheikh T. Lazhar	1974	Fr. Ar.	M. Bachouche M. Hajji A. Lahmar
Psychologique et Socio-Pédagogique	Enquête sur le degré de maturité pour l'apprentissage de la lecture d'enfants de 5 ans	Mme Lousaief	1973	Fr.	
1 - Le milieu Pré-Scolaire	Enquête sur le niveau de développement opératoire d'un groupe d'enfants de 5-7 ans	Mmes Kortas Belajouza	1973	Fr.	
	Une expérience de prévention du retard scolaire (communication faite au séminaire sur l'éducation préscolaire 10-11 Mai 1974)	A. Maaquia M. Belajouza H. Hamzaoui S. Kortas A. Loussaief T. Lazhar	1974	Fr.	
	Une expérience de prévention du retard scolaire (objectifs-méthodes-résultats)	A. Maaquia Mastouri M. Belajouza H. Hamzaoui S. Kortas A. Loussaief T. Lazhar	1974	Fr.	

*Ar. signifie que le texte est disponible en langue arabe.
 Fr. signifie français.

ORIENTATIONS	TITRE	PRODUCTEUR (S)	ANNEE	LANGUE	TRADUCTEUR
2. Apprentissage de la lecture en en Arabe et en Français	Contribution de l'arabe fondamental à la production du livre	A. El Aied	1972	Ar. Fr.	
	Nouvelle approche de l'apprentissage de la lecture	M. Corcos M. Chouchane	1972	Fr. Ar.	
	Evaluation de la méthode orale: Technique du conte	M. Belajouza S. Kortas			
	Pédagogie de l'expression: La méthode orale	U.E.R. Pédagogie du Primaire	1974	Fr.	
	Motivation à la lecture et points de vue des éducateurs: Colloque El Omrane (Mai 1971): Itinéraire et transpositions possibles	F. Ben Osmane	1971	Fr.	
	Expérience de Motivation à la Lecture au lycée de J. F. Bab Djedid	Z. Bellil Z. Hannablia M. Hajji	1971	Fr.	
	Une expérience pour améliorer le niveau d'expression des élèves: le projet T.W.L.	Ch. Fitouri	1971	Fr.	
	La lecture productive ou prolongement de lecture	Travaux d'élèves	1969 1974	Fr. Ar.	
	Analyse de contenu d'un conte pour enfant ''Illissa''	M. Bachouche	1971	Ar.	
	De la motivation à la Lecture	A. Ben Cheikh avec la collaboration de l'U.E.R. Motivation à la lecture.	1972	Ar. Fr.	B. Ben Salem M. Hajji A. Lahmar
	Itinéraire pratique d'une séance de Motivation à la Lecture	A. Ben Cheikh avec la collaboration: M. Saied A. Sfar S. Fekih	1972	Ar. Fr.	
	Vers une évaluation de la difficulté des textes	Matériel d'information recueilli et analysé par J. Soyez	1972	Ar. Fr.	
	Insérer dans notre enseignement la lecture à part entière	A. Abdemmebi	1972	Fr. Ar.	
	Les valeurs éducatives dans les contes tunisiens pour enfants	S. Mahfoundh M. Bachouche M. Hajji	1974	Fr.	
Sociologie des supports de lecture	Séminaire: Le manuel scolaire, le livre littéraire et scientifique pour enfant	Rapport de synthèse	1972	Ar. Fr.	
	Contribution à l'étude des problèmes du livre et de la lecture: Notes et documents: réunion d'experts sur la promotion du livre dans les pays arabes (le Caire)	A. Ben Cheikh	1972	Ar.	

ORIENTATIONS	TITRE	PRODUCTEUR (S)	ANNEE	LANGUE	TRADUCTEUR
	Une approche des problèmes du livre et de la lecture (séance d'ouverture du Colloque Maghrébin d'Hammamet)	M. Mzali	1972	Ar. Fr.	
	De quelques aspects des problèmes de la diffusion: (intervention au colloque)	L. Kabadou	1972	Fr. Ar.	
	La coopération du service bibliographique à la diffusion du livre	M. Harran	1972	Ar. Fr.	
	Méthode d'approche d'une texte: L'analyse de contenu, un approche théorique et méthodologique	S. Mahfoudh	1972	Fr. Ar.	
Approche bibliothéconomique: Organisation, gestion	La restructuration d'une bibliothèque scolaire critères et conditions pédagogiques et matérielles	D. Masmoudi	1972	Fr. Ar.	
	Les bibliothèques Scolaires	Z. Bellil	1972	Fr. Ar.	
	La bibliothèque scolaire foyer d'animation et de production	M. Bachouche M. Hajji	1974	Ar.	
	La lecture à l'université	B. Fani	1971	Fr.	
	De la lecture en Tunisie: problèmes et perspectives	Direction des bibliothèques publiques	1972	Fr.	
Approche socio-littéraire Texte théorique	Concepts et contenus: lecture et supports de lecture: Recueil de texte théorique: 1ère édition 2ème édition	A. Ben Cheikh S. Mahfoudh	1971 1972	Fr.	
Lecture	Nizar Kabbani Muntakhabat	M. Hachicha	1972	Ar.	
	El Farsi: Al Quantara hya-al-hayat	A. Zoueri	1972	Ar.	
	A. Attia: Al Munbat	A. Zoueri	1972	Ar.	
Ecrivains de chez nous	A. M. El Wazir	Conception A. Ben Cheikh	1972	Ar.	
Production de dossier de Motivation	Dossiers audiovisuel de Motivation à la Lecture	Production Collective	1969 1974	Ar. Fr.	

A. Paraître

TITRE	AUTEUR	LANGUE	DATE PREVUE
Une approche des problèmes du livre et de la lecture			
*Cahier 3 Les bibliothèques scolaires et publiques en Tunisie	Colloque Maghrébin	Edition Bilingue	4e trimestre 1974
*Cahier 4 Quelques aspects des problèmes de l'édition et de la diffusion	Colloque Maghrébin	Edition Bilingue	4e trimestre 1974
Attitudes des jeunes vis à vis de la culture traditionnelle et leurs aspiration en matière de loisirs	M. Belajouza A. Ben Cheikh T. Lazhar	Français	4e trimestre 1974
Les enseignants et la lecture	H. S. Ammar A. Ben Cheich	Français	Juin 1974
Annachra at-tarbawiya (bulletin pédagogique)	Production Collective	Numéro spécial consacré à la lecture en langue arabe	Edition du Centre National Pédagogique Septembre 1974
Situation de la lecture en milieu familial Tunisien	M. S. Ammar	Français	Octobre 1974
Document filmique: Texte en mouvement 1er problèmatique du lire dans un pays en voie de développement 2e de la motivation à la lecture productive	A. Ben Cheikh A. Belcadi	Bilingue	Octobre 1974

NOTES ET REFERENCES

1. Nous faisons figurer en annexe et à titre indicatif une bibliographie relative à l'étude des problèmes que posent la lecture en milieu éducationnel Tunisien.
2. Cette orientation caractérisait par ailleurs l'essentiel des recherches sur le fait éducatif c.f. A. Ben Cheikh, N. Dhahri, A. Dhib. L'expérience tunisienne en matière de recherche en éducation in l'avenir de la recherche en éducation en Tunisie journées d'études I.N.S.E. Tunis 1974, 4-27.
3. Il s'agit du premier plan de scolarisation de la période post. indépendance (1958-1968) considéré comme étant le premier acte de décolonisation de l'enseignement en Tunisie.
4. Ministère de l'Education Nationale Direction de statistiques et de la planification. Etude sur l'Education Nationale et bilan. Tunis 1972, 38.
5. Voir à propos de ce concept J. Berque: dépossession du Monde Le seuil Paris 1964. A Boudhiba A la recherche des normes perdus M.T.E. Tunis 1973.
6. A propos d'authenticité et de modernité nous renvoyons le lecteur à A. Laroui. L'idéologie arabe contemporaine. Maspéro Paris 1967.
7. Au sens traditionnel du terme.
8. En Tunisie l'enfant est scolarisé à partir de l'âge de 6 ans.
9. J. Wittwer. Un régulateur de la vie de l'enfant le livre 13e Congrés International des livres pour la Jeunesse Nice Mai 1972, 31.
10. A. Dehaut A. Gomme mettent l'accent sur la mauvaise relation de base entre l'enfant et les parents; ils la considérent comme un niveau d'obstacle à l'apprentissage de la lecture. In votre enfant apprend à lire Castermann Poche. 1972, 111.
11. Deux verbes sont couramment utilisés pour signifier l'acte de lire: qàraa et tàla'a.

12. Le caractère partiel de cette marginalité se traduit par ce qui est convenu d'appeler. La fragolité de la lecture.
13. S'agissant, à notre connaissance, de la première approche des problèmes de la famille et de la lecture, notre analyse ne peut avoir qu'un caractère global.
14. Des recherches relatives aux loisirs en milieu tunisien, nous citerons. Municipalité de Tunis, étude sur les loisirs des jeunes tunisois Tunis Mai 1968. B. Bchir problèmatique des loisirs en Tunisie Ministère de la jeunesse et du sport doc. Ronéo Tunis 1973.
15. Ce qui ne signifie pas qie nous considérons le loisir culturel comme un besoin vital secondaire.
16. J. Dummazdier: Réalités du loisir et idéologie. Revue Esprit n°6 Juin 1959, 874.
17. B. Bchir, op. cit., 2.
18. Les garçons plus que les filles.
19. Ministère de l'Economie Nationale Direction de l'Aménagement du territoire. Groupe 8: Villes et développement Tunis 1973, 13.
20. H. Nouira Discours de présentation du budget 1974 devant l'assemblée Nationale. Journal la Presse n°11. 742 du 18-12 1973, 5.
21. Recencement de la population de 1966.
22. Il s'agit d'une loi recente (1974) réglementant le salaire en milieu agricol.
23. M. Seklani. le champ d'intervention du salaire minimum s'élargit dans l'agriculture. Revue conjoncture. Ministère de l'Economie Nationale n°4 Juillet Août 1974, 25.
24. Institut National des statistiques: la consommation et les dépenses des ménages en Tunisie. Tunis 1968, 23.
25. Institut National des statistiques: la consommation et les dépenses des ménages en Tunisie. Tunis 1968, 23.
26. Institut National des statistiques, op. cit., 261.
27. L'habitation absorbe 19,3% et l'habillement 13,2%.
28. La population tunisienne atteignait en 1971 5,1 millions d'habitants.
29. Les 49% relèvent d'une population dispersée; vu regroupée dans un espace socio-géographique de—2,000 habitants.
30. Ministère des Affaires Culturelles Retrospectives décennales 1962, 1971. Tunis 1972, 95, 97.
31. Ministère des Affaires Culturelles Direction des Bibliothèques publiques Tunis Juin 1974. Doc. Ronéo, p. 2. Ronéo p. 2. Ce chiffre comprend les bibliothèques pour adultes, pour jeunes et pour enfants.
32. Institut National des statistiques. Annuaire statistique de la Tunisie 17e vol Tunis 1967, 22.
33. D'après le recensement de Mai 1966. Mais il est important de tenir compte de l'apport de la scolarisation et de la lutte contre l'analphabétisme.
34. Municipalité de Tunis. Service des études générales. Etude sur les loisirs de jeunes tunisois. Rapport préliminaires Mai 1968, 35, 48.
35. Le taux d'inadaptation en 1ère année du primaire est de l'ordre de 30%, 20% seulement des effectifs accomplissent une scolarité primaire normale c.f. A. Baffoun Contribution à l'étude des pertes d'effectif scolaires dans les pays du tiers-monde: l'exemple de la Tunisie. Thèse de 3e Cycle 1969 doc. Ronéo.
36. Ministère de l'Education Nationale Direction des statistiques, op. cit., 59, 65.
37. Nous faisons allusion surtout à l'impact des mass-média et des contenus culturels véhiculés en langue française.
38. La réalisation des conditions de dépassement passe habituellement par des situations conflictuelles entre parents et enfants.
39. Le nombre des jardins d'enfants alimentés en cadres et en programmes de formation adéquate et très limités.
40. Le premier contact avec le livre passe par le manuel scolaire et à l'âge de 6 ans.
41. C.f. en annexe, 3-4.
42. C.f. en annexe, 4-5.
43. C.f. en annexe, 3-7.
44. La 1ere et la 2éme ont été objet d'évaluation.

Class Size and Reading Development

Richard D. Arnold
Purdue University
Lafayette, Indiana
United States of America

When one is concerned with slow learning children, and particularly with children who are having reading problems, the concept of class size takes on new dimensions. Not only must the evidence on class size in general be considered, but certain important related factors must also be taken into account. Among these are such variables as additional teaching personnel, materials and facilities, discipline problems, and teacher morale and training. Thus, the issue of the relationship between class size and reading development is quite complex. To facilitate organization, in this discussion, the problems will be examined in terms of the following topics: 1) class size and general achievement, 2) class size and achievement in reading, 3) the achievement of reading disabled children and class size, and 4) other important educational factors related to class size and reading achievement.

CLASS SIZE AND GENERAL ACHIEVEMENT

A comprehensive study of class size was conducted by Blake (8) in the United States in 1954. After reviewing many published studies up to that time, he eliminated those that did not meet his criteria for "good research." Of the 85 studies meeting his criteria, he found that, for achievement in general, the results of 35 studies favored small classes, the results of 18 studies favored large classes, and the results of 32 studies were inconclusive.

In 1964, Holland and Galfo (31) reviewed the results of many research studies concerning class size. The following are some of their major conclusions:

1. The research indicates there is no optimum class size, nor is there a perfect pupil-teacher ratio.

2. Teacher ability and flexibility may be more important than pupil-teacher ratio per se.

3. The overall pupil-staff ratio is more important than pupil-teacher ratio.

Of the many studies that relate to class size and achievement, the Blake and the Holland/Galfo reviews are considered among the most comprehensive. Based on these data only, it would seem reasonable to conclude that class size is not an important consideration. But it is suggested that judgment be deferred until further data are considered.

CLASS SIZE AND READING ACHIEVEMENT

Several important studies have been reported recently that relate directly to class size and reading achievement. The contributors to Downing's book (17) report the average class sizes for the following countries.

Country	Average Class Size
Britain	40
Denmark	28
France (Paris)	50
Germany	38
Norway	30
Sweden	18
United States	25

It can be seen that there is considerable variation of class size. Although it is dangerous to generalize data from one study to another, it is felt that the class sizes listed may be representative of those in the countries studied by Thorndike (50) in 1973. In Thorndike's study of reading comprehension, it was found that considerations of family background and whether the country was developing or already developed were more important than school related factors, such as class size, teacher training, and availability of special teachers. Thorndike warns that the correlational data presented in the study cannot be considered causative. Nevertheless, important relationships are revealed from the study.

After conducting a rigorous study in England, Morris (41) reported in 1959 that relatively large classes did not seem to harm reading achievement. Several studies (19, 30, 37, 47) report findings similar to those of Thorndike and Morris.

Two important longitudinal studies, however, have implications for the study of class size and reading achievement. Furno and Collins (23) conducted a five year investigation concerned with class size and reading achievement as these factors relate to pupils who are typical, culturally deprived, or of limited mental ability. Students in smaller classes (1-25) made greater gains in reading than those in larger classes (over 25). It should be noted that students in smaller classes made significant gains despite the fact that pupils in larger classes received instruction from teachers who were supposedly more knowledgeable and had had more teaching experience. Small class size was more effective for nonwhite students than for their white peers. Students in special education made greater gains in small classes than those in large classes.

In 1967, Balow (7) reported the findings of a three year experimental reading program in the primary grades. A 50 percent reduction of reading class size was accomplished by having half of each class come to school an hour early in the morning. The other half of the class received its reading instruction the last hour after the first group had gone home. Class size for reading was reduced from 30 to 15. Balow concluded from this study that significant gains were made by the children who began the program in first grade. The results suggest a positive effect, with first grade being the critical year. Findings also suggest that by the middle of third grade, achievement patterns are pretty well stabilized and class size alone is not enough to change these patterns. Boys seemed to benefit most from the program. And, perhaps most important, at three of the four levels specified by the readiness test, children in the experimental groups achieved more than children in the control groups. Results from this study suggest that class size reduction is beneficial to the child who learns easily as well as the child who finds reading difficult. Frymier's study (22) in 1964 also indicates that the effects of class size are most critical at the first grade level.

From the studies sampled in this section regarding class size and reading achievement, it can be said that the data are equivocal. The Thorndike and Morris studies were nonsupportive of small classes but the Furno and Collins and the Balow longitudinal studies suggested possible positive effects of small classes. It is the author's opinion that, from the studies stated thus far, it would be difficult either to support or refute the notion that small classes are beneficial to the overall improvement of reading instruction.

CLASS SIZE AND THE READING DISABLED CHILD

The effect of class size for reading disabled children is of major consideration in this paper. If a case for small class size is to be made, it must be demonstrated that small group instruction, individualized instruction, tutoring, and/or clinic instruction is of value to children having special problems with reading.

Harrison and Brimley (29) reported a study in 1971 that investigated a highly individualized reading program for low achieving six-year-old children featuring one-to-one tutoring. After six weeks of special help only 5 of the 33 children originally ranked in the lower third of the class were still in the lower group. Many studies support individualized approaches to teaching reading at all grade levels (1, 2, 3, 5, 12, 16, 32, 35, 48).

In 1972 Franco (21) found that slow-learning junior high students profited from daily two hour sessions of tutoring in groups of five students. He found the students made gains in reading, language arts, study skills, mathemtics, and social science.

In 1965, Balow reported five earlier studies which support the belief that remedial reading instruction produces substantial gains in reading during the time students receive treatment (6, 9, 11, 34, 38, 42). However, the study also indicates that after returning to the regular classroom, pupil growth begins to diminish in proportion to the amount of special help offered. Those who received some special help continued to grow but not as rapidly as during the special remedial program, while those who received no extra help, did not continue to grow. Balow concluded that long term remediation is needed for seriously disabled readers. Several studies support the Balow findings (18, 19, 20, 21, 36, 49).

At the international level, it is evident that small classes are considered important. According to Malmquist (39) in Sweden and Jansen (33) in Denmark, classes are divided in half for a few hours per week in the first three grades to aid in individualized instruction. Such division of classes has proven very satisfying. Malmquist and Jansen also report success with clinical and corrective programs which provide instruction individually and in small groups. Ruthman (45) reports similiar corrective procedures in France. Finally, Downing (17) says, "there seems to be worldwide agreement that classes should be smaller."

In summary, the evidence reported in this section of the paper strongly supports the idea that individual, small group tutoring and remediation is highly beneficial to slow learning children and to students who have serious reading problems. Not reported here, but to be considered, are the hundreds of case studies that have, over the years, continued to demonstrate that special remedial help is highly beneficial to individual children. Remediation, based on careful diagnosis, may produce improvement two to four times greater than the rate attained without remediation (51).

OTHER FACTORS RELEVANT TO CLASS SIZE

It seems appropriate to identify briefly several other factors which may have implications when one considers class size and teaching disabled readers: classroom practices, facilities, use of staff other than teachers, behavior or discipline of the children, and teacher morale and training.

While many studies suggest large classes do not adversely affect achievement, several of these studies involve high school and college students (28). In 1955 Richman (44) as well as McKenna (40), found that in classrooms of 25 students or less, certain teaching practices improved. Their findings suggest that, in smaller classes, teachers are better able to know and guide the students in terms of teaching content as well as dealing with noncognitive aspects such as discipline and emotional factors. In other words, when a teacher has fewer children, he has more time to devote to them individually and in small groups, not only in terms of guiding learning, but also in guiding other, more humanistic behaviors.

In a study by Hammill et al. (26), reported in 1972, 22 educable mentally retarded children were integrated into regular classes but were provided with extra supportive teaching in a resource room. The instruction was offered individually and in small groups. Gains in reading scores suggested that the progress of these children was accelerated during the time they participated in the program. Sabatino (46), and Quay and Glavin (43) have also demonstrated that learning disabled children (and most of these children are also reading disabled) can be successfully integrated into regular classes, if ancillary services are available.

Cook and Blessing (15) found in their study that teacher aides helped to increase reading achievement in the primary grades. The Right to Read program in the United States has been supporting many projects of this nature, where the aim is to increase instructional time available for individual children.

In 1970, Cook (14) found a direct relationship among noise level, achievement, and class size. The results suggest that smaller classes are not as noisy and achievement is higher. Cannon (13), and Cook and Blessing (15) found that there was less disruptive behavior in smaller classes.

Collectively, the results of the studies just mentioned tend to suggest that small classes are beneficial to children because the teacher and other staff members in the school can aid in the improvement of reading instruction as well as influence other nonreading behaviors typically dealt with in the school.

One final factor will be considered in this paper—the teacher. The writer has never talked with a teacher who has not endorsed the concept of small class size. Teachers have a greater task set for them if they are asked to manage a class of 40 in comparison to a class of 25. From my own personal experience, I found my class of 38 third graders far more taxing in every way than the 28 fourth graders I had taught the previous year. A dedicated, conscientious teacher will be under considerable pressure in trying to provide the best for each child when the class size is unduly large. If the mental health and morale of teachers is an important consideration in the teaching profession, then classes should not be allowed to become too large.

In 1956, Gray (24) pointed out in his international survey that the teacher variable is an important consideration. Holland and Galfo concluded that teacher training and motivation are very important; well-trained, dedicated teachers can work effectively with large classes, even though they may prefer small classes. Harris and Morrison (27), reporting on the findings of the CRAFT project in 1972, suggest that procedures such as reducing class size and adding auxiliary personnel may continue to give disappointing results if teaching skills are not improved. Griffiths, Gillen, and Dankel (25) support this view; and their evidence suggests that after teachers are given inservice education to improve reading instruction, the children who have been doing poorly earlier begin to make normal progress.

Austin (4) points out that teachers and teacher training are more important to improve reading instruction than are method, material, and organizational plan. Findings of the well-known Cooperative Research Program, as reported by Bond and Dykstra (10), support the importance of the teacher variable. It seems that teachers do, indeed, make a difference.

CONCLUSIONS

Data have been examined concerning the relationship between class size and reading achievement. Some of the data are contradictory. In the final analysis, a synthesis of such data must be a highly individual matter. In summarizing my own views, I would emphasize that I am merely stating an opinion, and the reader must accept or reject the various points as he wishes.

First, I would like to acknowledge that the data are inconclusive and it is not possible to state that small classes are, in general, highly desirable. I find the results of the Thorndike study most enlightening in that they suggest that factors related to family and background may be far more fundamental and powerful than class size. This is probably truer in developing countries. However, I suspect that there may be other situation-specific instances where factors other than class size alone may be far more influential and powerful.

Second, given a certain level of school functioning similar to that described by Thorndike as characteristic of so-called developed countries, class size may be a significant factor. However, even at this level of school development, class size alone does not appear to be the most important factor affecting reading achievement. Many children learn to read regardless of whether they are in small or large classes. It is also clear that some children fail to learn to read, and reading problems persist, regardless of class size.

Third, there is abundant evidence that individual and small group reading instruction has proven beneficial to many disabled readers and many other types of children including those who learn easily. Corrective and remedial programs in which teachers work with from one to six children are not uncommon, and the expense of such programs seems justified.

Fourth, small classes seem most important in the early grades, where reading instruction is initiated. It seems reasonable that, when children are beginning to learn to read, carefully monitored attention by the teacher is crucial. And diagnostic teaching is time consuming.

Fifth, other factors being equal, teacher training and morale are important. It may be that children are better off in a large class than in a small class when the teacher is poorly trained, unmotivated, or just plain lazy. But if the teacher is well trained and dedicated to providing the best instruction possible for each child in his class, it seems logical to expect that he will be able to accomplish more if he has fewer children with whom to work. With a reasonable class size, a professional teacher should be able to create an atmosphere where growth in reading and learning in general are facilitated.

REFERENCES

1. Acinapuro, P. J. "A Comparative Study of Two Instructional Reading Programs—An Individualized Pattern and a Three Ability Group Pattern," doctoral dissertation, Columbia University, 1959.
2. Aronow, M. S. "A Study of the Effect of Individualized Reading on Children's Reading Test Scores," *Reading Teacher*, 15 (1961), 86-91.
3. Askov, Eunice N. "A Case History Approach to Study the Effects of Individualized Reading Instruction," in Joseph Nemeth (Ed.), *Reading Rx: Better Teachers, Better Supervisors, Better Programs.* Newark, Delaware: International Reading Association, 1975.
4. Austin, Mary. "United States," in John Downing (Ed.), *Comparative Reading.* New York: Macmillan, 1973.
5. Ayres, A. J. "Improving Academic Scores through Sensory Integration," *Journal of Learning Disabilities*, 5 (June 1972), 338-343.
6. Balow, Bruce, "The Long-Term Effect of Remedial Reading Instruction," *Reading Teacher*, 18 (April 1965), 581-586.
7. Balow, Irving H. "A Longitudinal Evaluation of Reading Achievement in Small Classes," University of California, 1967.
8. Blake, Howard. "Class Size: A Summary of Selected Studies in Elementary and Secondary Schools," unpublished paper, Teachers College, Columbia University, 1954.
9. Bliesmer, E. T. "Evaluating Progress in Remedial Reading Programs," *Reading Teacher*, 15 (March 1962), 344-350.
10. Bond, Gay, and Robert Dykstra. "The Cooperative Research Program in First Grade Reading," *Reading Research Quarterly*, 2 (Summer 1967), 5-142.
11. Bond, Guy L., and Leo C. Fay. "A Report of the University of Minnesota Reading Clinic," *Journal of Educational Research*, 43 (January 1950), 385-390.

12. Camper, V. T. "A Comparison of Two Methods of Teaching Reading, Individual and Group, in the Teaching of Reading Skills in Combined Classrooms of Selected Fourth, Fifth, and Sixth Grade Children in the Public Schools of Howard County, Maryland," doctoral dissertation, New York University, 1966.

13. Cannon, Gwendolyn. "Kindergarten Class Size: A Study," *Childhood Education*, 43 (September 1966), 9.

14. Cook, J. "Noise Levels in the Classroom," *Exceptional Children Abstracts*, February 1970.

15. Cook, J. J., and K. R. Blessing. *Class Size and Teacher Aides as Factors in the Achievement of the Educable Mentally Retarded*, Final Report. Wisconsin State Department of Public Instruction. ED 047 484.

16. Cyrog, Frances V. "A Longitudinal Study of an Individualized Program in Reading," master's thesis, Claremont Graduate School, 1964.

17. Downing, John. *Comparative Reading: Cross-National Studies of Behavior and Processes in Reading and Writing*. New York: Macmillan, 1973, 119.

18. Eubanks, L. L. "Study of Slow Learning Children in Regular and Specially Designed Classes," doctoral dissertation, 1969-1970.

19. Faunce, R. W. *Evaluation of a Reading Program for Severely Retarded Readers*. Minneapolis, Minnesota, Public Schools, October 1971.

20. Fiedler, M. "Did the Clinic Help?" *Journal of Reading*, 16 (October 1972), 25-29.

21. Franco, E. J. "Operation Upgrade," *Journal of Reading*, 16 (November 1972), 120-123.

22. Frymier, J. R. "The Effect of Class Size Upon Reading Achievement in First Grade," *Reading Teacher*, 18 (November 1964), 90-93.

23. Furno, O. F., and G. J. Collins. *Class Size and Pupil Learning*. Baltimore, Maryland, Public Schools, October 1967.

24. Gray, William S. *The Teaching of Reading and Writing*. Paris: Unesco, 1956.

25. Griffiths, A. N., J. F. Gillen, and R. Dankel. "Leave Dyslexics in the Classroom," *Academic Therapy*, 8 (Fall 1972), 57-65.

26. Hammill, D., et al. "Retardates' Reading Achievement in the Resource Room Model: The First Year," *Training School Bulletin*, 63 (November 1972), 104-107.

27. Harris, A. J., and C. Morrison. "The CRAFT Project: A Final Report," *Reading Teacher*, 22 (January 1969), 335-340.

28. Harris, Chester W. (Ed.). "Classroom Organization," *Encyclopedia of Educational Research: A Project of the American Educational Research Association* (3rd ed.). New York: Macmillan, 1960.

29. Harrison, Grant V., and Vern Brimley. "The Use of Structured Tutoring Techniques in Teaching Low Achieving Six-Year-Olds to Read," paper presented at the meeting of the American Educational Research Association, New York, February 1971.

30. Hawkins, M. L. "Mobility of Students in Reading Groups," *Reading Teacher*, 20 (November 1966).

31. Holland, Howard K., and Armand J. Galfo. *An Analysis of Research Concerning Class Size*. Richmond, Virginia: Division of Educational Research, State Department of Education, 1964.

32. Jackson, W. J. "A Study of the Relationship Between a Small Group Discussion Activity, the Self-Concept and Reading Achievement of Selected Fourth Grade Boys and Girls," doctoral dissertation, Oregon State University, 1973.

33. Jansen, Mogens. "Denmark," in John Downing (Ed.), *Comparative Reading*. New York: Macmillan, 1973.

34. Johnson, L. R., and D. Platts. "A Summary of a Study of the Reading Ages of Children Who Had Been Given Remedial Teaching," *British Journal of Educational Psychology*, 32 (February 1962).

35. Judson, Arlene. *An Individualized Audiovisual Instructional Program for Primary Grade Students with Reading Problems*, Final Report. Washington, D.C.: National Center for Educational Research and Development (DHEW/OE), Regional Research Program, June 1973.

36. *Lakeshore Curriculum Study Council: A Three Year Longitudinal Study Comparing Individualized and Basal Reading Progress At the Primary Level, An Interim Report*. Milwaukee, Wisconsin, Department of Education, University of Wisconsin, 1965.

37. Little, A., C. Mabey, and J. Russell. "Class Size, Pupil Characteristics, and Reading Attainment," in Jessie F. Reid (Ed.), *Reading: Problems and Practices,* London: Ward Lock, 1972, 86-93.
38. Lovell, K., C. Byrne, and B. Richardson. "A Further Study of the Educational Progress of Children Who Had Received Remedial Instruction," *British Journal of Educational Psychology,* 33 (February 1963), 3-9.
39. Malmquist, Eve. "Sweden," in John Downing (Ed.), *Comparative Reading.* New York: Macmillan, 1973.
40. McKenna, Bernard H. "Measures of Class Size and Numerical Staff Adequacy Related to a Measure of School Quality," unpublished doctoral project. New York: Teachers College, Columbia University, 1955.
41. Morris, Joyce M. *Reading in the Primary School.* London: Newnes, 1959.
42. Mouly, G. J., and V. Grant. "A Study of Growth to be Expected of Retarded Readers," *Journal of Educational Research,* 49 (February 1956), 461-465.
43. Quay, H. C., and J. P. Glavin. *The Education of Behaviorally Disordered Children in the Public School Setting,* Final Report, Project No. 48227. Washington, D.C.: Bureau of Education for the Handicapped, 1970.
44. Richman, Harold. "Instructional Practices as Affected by Class Size," unpublished doctoral project. New York: Teachers College, Columbia University, 1955.
45. Ruthman, Paul. "France," in John Downing (Ed.), *Comparative Reading.* New York: Macmillan, 1973.
46. Sabatino, D. "An Evaluation of Resource Rooms for Children with Learning Disabilities," *Journal of Learning Disabilities,* 4 (1971), 84-93.
47. Sartain, H. W. "The Roseville Experiment with Individualized Reading," *Reading Teacher,* 13 (April 1960), 277-281.
48. Seeber, F. M. "An Evaluation of Two Methods of Meeting Individual Differences in Teaching First Grade Reading," master's thesis, University of Kansas at Lawrence, 1965.
49. Taylor, Derek B., and Margaret Fleming. *More Effective Schools Program, Disadvantaged Pupil Program Fund, Fund Number 97-16, 1971-1972 Evaluation (Year 3).* Cleveland, Ohio: Public Schools, Division of Research and Development, November 1972.
50. Thorndike, Robert L. *Reading Comprehension Education in Fifteen Countries.* New York: John Wiley and Sons, 1973.
51. Tinker, Miles A., and Guy L. Bond. *Reading Difficulties: Their Diagnosis and Correction.* New York: Appleton, 1973.

A Nonsegregation Policy in Remedial Education

Jesper Florander
Gladsaxe School
Bagsvaerd, Denmark

THE TRADITION OF SEGREGATION AND SOME CRITICAL COMMENTS
In Denmark there has been a strong tradition of segregation of pupils for various specialized forms of teaching. During the past few decades remedial instruction, to a still greater extent, has been given in segregated groups, segregated classes, and special schools. The idea behind this educational policy is that pupils who cannot cope with the normal teaching situation have a right to effective support from specially trained teachers and that such support should be given in small, separate groups.

This segregation policy has shown certain disadvantages. First, both the pupils and their parents may develop a feeling of defeat. Second, the segregation of slow learners tends to affect normal teaching. Because there is no challenge to the teacher to try new ways of teaching with the slow learners, instruction may go on in the same way that it has for years.

Criticism of the segregation policy began in the 1960s and has grown since then. It was first directed against school readiness testing and the provision of special classes for so-called immature pupils. Eventually, some of the critics submitted proposals for a nonsegregation policy. One such proposal and its implementation was the New Way of Starting School at Gladsaxe (Denmark, 1968). Another was the introduction in 1971 of support centres, instead of special classes, for slow learners.

THE NEW WAY OF STARTING SCHOOL
A growing awareness of the great range of individual differences among pupils in any class leads to a demand for individualized instruction. This was regarded as a fundamental principle. A second principle that gained general acceptance was that special instruction should begin in the normal class situation and should continue there as far as possible.

The first stages. The following plan for starting school was set up in 1968:

1. All children enrolled in the school are automatically accepted.

2. The first six weeks in class one are an observation period. This is carried out by the classroom teacher and a specially trained support

teacher whose subsequent role is to give remedial instruction to those who need it. The school specialists (school psychologist, medical officer, and others) also take part in the observation.

3. At the end of the observation period a conference is held at which all persons involved discuss each pupil and set up a programme for his instruction.

4. Special support, both educational and emotional, is arranged for those who need it. This support can be provided in a special group, as individual help in the classroom, or as a combination of both.

Individual classroom help and the combination of individual and group help are most frequently used. The support comprises five lessons per week for each class one, and it continues with four to three lessons per week during classes two to four. The support continues until, at a case conference, the teachers decide that it may be discontinued. This allows for great flexibility in the nonsegregation policy.

This approach poses certain questions:

- How many slow learners are there?
- Who are they?
- How much support will they need and for how long?
- Are the teachers able to find the slow learners?
- Can the slow learners stay in the normal class?

To help answer these questions, during 1968-1971 the first group of pupils needing support was observed through classes one to four. In class one, 160 pupils were selected for support. A control group (matched in terms of school, sex, age, and social status), was set up so that a comparison could be made between the 160 selected pupils and the children who were not selected for support. Table 1 shows that this number is equal to 14 percent of the year's intake. Twice as many boys as girls were selected. The two groups differed significantly in terms of the social status of their parents, the selected pupils having a much higher proportion from the lower social groups and from one parent families (see Table 2). The observers recorded their judgments on observation sheets in terms of certain behavioural characteristics.

Table 3 shows that the behavioural traits described are noted four to five times more frequently among the 160 pupils than among pupils in the control group. However, the table also shows that the difference must be quantitative, not qualitative. For example, "lack of concentration," "restless," and "talkative" account for 44 percent of the boys in the remedial education group and 51 percent of the boys in the control group. This difference is not due to age nor to social background. Objective test results have confirmed the teachers' observations.

Table 1. Pupils in remedial education group, class one 1968/1969.

Remedial education				No. of pupils in class one		
Boys	Girls	Total	Percentage of pupils in class one	Boys	Girls	Total
107	53	160	14%	576	583	1.159
67%	33%	100%		50%	50%	100%

Table 2. Distribution of class one pupils by social group.

Social group	All class one pupils	Remedial education group pupils
I	4%	2%
II	8%	3%
III	20%	7%
IV	41%	44%
V	16%	22%
VI	10%	22%

I = academic   V = unskilled   VI = one parent only

Table 3. Distribution of behavioural traits. Observation Sheet 1.

	Boys (94 pairs)		Girls (47 pairs)	
	Remedial education group	Control group	Remedial education group	Control group
Lack of concentration	17	20	16	11
Restless	15	17	8	9
Talkative	12	14	8	6
Lack of independence	10	8	15	20
Easily tired	10	9	10	9
Slow	9	1	12	9
Passive	9	8	13	6
Agressive	5	0	0	0
Nervous traits	4	8	5	0
Fearsome of making contact	3	1	1	0
Timid	2	5	5	9
Shy	2	8	7	23
Total	98%	99%	100%	102%
Number	362	76	136	35

A follow-up study was conducted eighteen months later. Table 4 shows how many pupils were still receiving special support in the middle of class two. More than half of the pupils in the support group still received special support. The table shows that once a pupil has started receiving support he very often will continue to do so. A total of thirty-eight pupils in the support group stopped receiving remedial education because it proved superfluous.

Twenty-three pupils were transferred to kindergarten classes or other institutional aid or they were dismissed from school. These pupils, comprising about 2 percent of the year's intake, could not be kept in the normal class. All pupils in the control group had remained in their normal class.

Further follow up was undertaken when the pupils moved to class four. The results showed much the same picture.

To summarize, a nonsegregation arrangement for the first school years has shown that teachers are able to identify slow learners at an early stage and can teach them in the normal class when these pupils are given special educational and emotional support. Only 2 percent of pupils need other forms of support. In most cases, support is given for an extended period of time. The teachers' impressions are that this arrangement creates a more beneficial context for personal development.

Table 4. Remedial education in classes one and two.

	Remedial education group	Control group
Number	143	145
Have received remedial education	100%	26%
Still receiving remedial education	57%	22%

SUPPORT CENTRES: SOME ADDITIONAL DETAILS

Location. The support centre is placed centrally in the school.

Equipment. The centre is well equipped with teaching materials for individualized instruction—books, audiovisual and audiolingual aids, and learning programmes. There is also material for leisure activities.

Access. The support centre is open to classes two to ten and remains open during the entire school day. A pupil may go to the support centre if and when he wants to.

Functions. The support centre gives both instructional and emotional support.

Selection. The teachers may send a pupil to the support centre.

Staff. There are always two teachers present at the support centre. The support teachers may go into the classrooms and give support there as well.

THE FIRST SUPPORT CENTRE: SOME ADDITIONAL OBSERVATIONS

The first support centre to be established was in contact with 32 percent of the pupils d ring the school year. Two groups of pupils presently go to the support centre: long-time pupils who attend regularly three to four lessons per week, and short-time pupils who attend only a few lessons.

Long-time pupils. Nearly half of the 94 pupils have come because of reading difficulties. A rather large group is supported because of social-emotional difficulties. It is characteristic that nearly all pupils have both emotional and instructional handicaps.

Half of the pupils get support for at least one year, but 25 percent of them need support for about three months only. Twice as many boys as girls get support. The long-time pupils are rather evenly distributed over classes two to eight (see Table 5). There is, however, a sharp drop in members in classes nine and ten. A systematic recording of pupil progress shows that most pupils make satisfactory progress both in learning and in emotional stability.

Short-time pupils. Two-thirds of the short-time pupils visit the support centre for only one lesson during the whole school year (see Table 6). More than half of these come from classes five and six. More pupils come for the late lessons than for the other lessons. Characteristically, they come because of conflicts with schoolmates or teachers. Curiously, they do not tend to come from lessons in reading or mathematics but from other lessons: e.g., music or science. The number of pupils coming because of conflicts increases during the school day.

As a result of experience with this pilot project, developmental work has been followed up quickly by other schools. Since 1972, every school has had a support centre.

The nonsegregation policy. The nonsegregation policy has become characteristic of the Gladsaxe school system. Nevertheless, we still have special schools for backward children and for emotionally disturbed children. In addition, we still have a few special classes for retarded readers. But the principle of nonsegregation is now in force in every school. The new way of starting school and the support centres provide a flexible mixture of reading clinic, clinic for children with conflicts, and relief centre.

Mixing age groups is one great advantage. This allows for development of mutual concern among the pupils. Another advantage is that conflicts are dealt with at once, before they become serious. A third advantage is overall pupil acceptance of the support. And not least is the integration at the teacher level as the teachers at the support centres go into the classrooms and give support.

Socially, both the new way of starting school and the support centres have proved to be a success. The slow learner has been allowed to learn slowly and has no feeling of being frustrated. His parents share in this feeling. The teachers are highly satisfied with the nonsegregation policy, as was shown by a survey in 1973, and they want it to continue.

In terms of educational achievement, we do not yet know how much we have gained. We suppose that the slow learners learn the same as usual, but we feel confident that they learn in a healthier way.

Table 5.   Distribution over the classes of 94 long-time pupils at support centre.

Class	Percentage of pupils
2	14
3	11
4	14
5	17
6	11
7	11
8	18
9	4
10	1

Table 6.   Number of lessons at support centre for 95 short-time pupils.

Lessons	Percentage of pupils
1	67
2	16
3	8
4	3
5	-
6	2
7	-
8	1
>8	3

Split-Half Classes

Flemming Lundahl
Farum, Denmark

Split-half classes are organised in order to give the teacher more opportunities to attend to the needs of the individual child. For this purpose, classes are divided into groups of equal size and each group is instructed separately. The splitting is random, takes no account of such factors as sex, and there is no differential treatment of pupils.

In Denmark, we have had experience with split-half classes in mathematics (during the first two grades) and in the native language (grades one to four), as well as in foreign languages and in various other subjects at different grade levels. This paper is concerned with our experiences with split-half classes during the first two grades in the native language and in mathematics.

The split-half classes comprise about 5 percent of the total number of periods on the curriculum for the public school in Denmark. The allocation of split-half classes corresponds to 50 percent of the total number of special education lessons provided by the public school. The principle of integration started with the introduction of split-half classes for children starting school. This enabled many slow learners to benefit from instruction while remaining in their own classes, instead of immediately being segregated for special educational treatment.

ECONOMIC ASPECTS

The size of the class is of interest to the teachers and to the community at large. How many pupils should there be in a class or in a group if they are to obtain the maximum educational value from public investment in this sector? The very small class or group, considered by many people to be educationally ideal, means a heavy drain on resources. Larger classes constitute a saving in financial terms but may, at the same time, reduce the educational potential. The problem, therefore, is how to assess the relationships between size of class expenditure and educational gain in order to provide a rational basis for the determination of optimum size. The financial aspects of split-half classes are easily estimated. In Denmark, the average class has about 20 pupils. If you increase the average number of periods from 28 per week to

30 per week, with two periods being allocated to split-half classes, this would involve an increase in salaries to teachers aggregating Dkr. 116 mill. (Salaries to teachers represent approximately 62 percent of the public school's annual working expenses.)

The educational aspects are far more difficult to assess. For example, how will size of class affect a child's ability to work independently on a problem area? And how can we obtain a valid measure of educational benefit? Such problems have for many years been of concern to teachers, administrators, and politicians. For this reason, they have been the subject of a very large number of educational experiments throughout the world. In this paper, I shall indicate how we have approached these problems with students in split-half classes and how these classes have affected the teaching of children starting school in Denmark.

THE INTRODUCTION OF SPLIT-HALF CLASSES

With the enactment of the Danish Educational Act of 1958, split-half classes came as an innovation. Instead of a general reduction of the number of pupils in a class, the municipal authorities were allowed to introduce split-half classes in the first four grades for teaching Danish and mathematics. The purpose of this was to facilitate the transition from home to school and provide for better and more personal contact between the teacher and his pupils. By means of split-half classes, the teacher would have a better chance of becoming well acquainted with each child, thus getting to know his special strengths and weaknesses. At the same time, a better background could be created for individualization and innovation of the teaching which would otherwise be obstructed by the large number of children in the class.

During the 1960s, split-half classes were introduced by the great majority of large municipalities. The teachers seem to have accepted these classes as an educationally rational way of meeting the desire for smaller classes.

RESEARCH INTO THE FUNCTIONING OF SPLIT-HALF CLASSES

The above arrangements within the public school system in Denmark have provided a unique chance of supplementing the international research on the influence of class size on teaching. A comparison between split-half classes and full classes offers an experimentally ideal situation, as a number of factors are held constant which otherwise are difficult to keep track of:

The teacher is the same in both cases.

The pupils have the same basic qualifications.

The availability of educational materials is the same.

However, it is not only the size of the groups that varies when comparing the two classes; it is also the teaching tradition developing in connection with split-half classes. It is necessary, therefore, in a study of split-half and full classes to ascertain whether the teaching is adapted to variations in the size of the group involved and, if so, the quality and extent of such adaptation. These problems were investigated in a study conducted by Poul Erik Jensen, of the Danish Institute for Educational Research.

The split-half system has been functioning for about 15 years and there are many indications that it will be adopted to an increasing extent within the public school in coming years, particularly in the teaching of foreign languages. In the subject of Danish, it has been followed with methodical instruction and, in this subject, the split-half classes have gradually settled in a certain form. This makes it possible to study those adaptations to variation in class size which have been found to be most advantageous. The more general aspect of the study has been an evaluation to determine whether changes in size of class do, in fact, result in a significant variation in teaching methods and in curriculum activities, given a certain amount of inservice training and a sufficient period for teachers to adapt to the new situation. Eighteen grade three classes, from suburban municipalities in the Copenhagen metropolitan area, were involved in the study.

The method adopted for assessing the teaching of full, as well as split-half, classes was systematic classroom observation based on an observation schedule. The observations covered three aspects of teaching: organizational form of the class, degree of differentiation expressed in the teaching, and pupil activities in the term of subject area skills. The independent variables were the basic qualifications of the pupils, the teacher, the external framework, and the time element.

CONTENT OF INSTRUCTION

Pupil/teacher communication in the full classes was of the instructive, one-way type. Pupils were corrected more frequently than in the split-half classes where more individual guidance was given. There are indications, therefore, that in the split-half classes, communication was marked by greater concern for the individual pupil.

Hardly any instruction was given in oral rendition in either class. In respect of written assignments, the training was practically the same in full as in split-half classes, and there were no signs of increased differentiation in the teaching in this field. In the full classes, the reading lessons mainly took the form of oral reading by individual pupils while the rest of the class looked at the text. In this situation, all pupils are taught together and there is no differentiation in the teaching.

In the split-half classes, the predominant activity was independent reading. This situation provides a possibility for traditional ways of working and for differentiation in the teaching, as it is possible to adapt assignments and materials to the individual pupil's reading skills, interests, and working capacity. There are signs of such adaptation in that the pupils in the split-half classes are frequently observed to be working with different materials, on different activities.

FORM OF INSTRUCTION

Periods which at no time made differentiated teaching possible were far more frequent in full than in split-half classes. Periods where one organizational form was followed throughout constituted approximately 40 percent of the total number of periods for full, as well as for split-half, classes. There was a marked difference in choice between these periods, however. In the full classes, 81 percent of the time was devoted to teamwork against the split-half classes, with 69 percent of the time being devoted to individual activities with differentiated teaching.

Periods starting with teamwork represented a large percentage of the total number of periods. In these periods, the teamwork generally continued for a greater length of time in the full classes than in the split-half classes. In the latter classes, moreover, individual work was more often allowed to proceed throughout the entire period than in the full classes where it was interrupted by teamwork.

These results show that in the split-half classes the forms of organization and time structures chosen made for an increase in the individual work and differentiation in the teaching in terms of frequency and duration.

INTERPLAY OF SEVERAL FACTORS

A number of conditions may have a bearing on the educational effect of any change of class size. The following factors are particularly important: 1) a recognition on the part of the teacher of the necessity of the intended changes; 2) the teacher's knowledge of different forms of teaching (methods); 3) the availability of educational materials for varied use; and 4) the size of the class. These four factors may contribute to changes in the teaching in the direction of increased differentiation and this will be reflected in more individual work, different concurrent class activities, and adaptation of activities to the basic qualifications of the pupils. The factors are interrelated so that the effect of one factor depends on the other three.

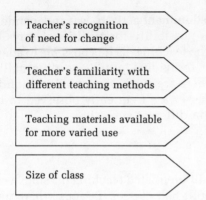

Teacher's recognition of need for change	Changes in teaching aimed at increased differentiation, e.g., effected through
Teacher's familiarity with different teaching methods	more individual work
Teaching materials available for more varied use	various concurrent activities
Size of class	Adaptation of activities to basic qualifications of pupils

The introduction of split-half classes in the subject of Danish represents a conscious effort to influence all of these factors with a view to achieving a generally increased differentiation of the teaching. The number of pupils in a class was changed and at the same time, an effort was made to make the teacher more conscious of the need for increased differentiation of teaching and for improved knowledge of different applicable forms of teaching. This is to be seen from the educational guide and teachers' manuals.

Concurrently, a development has taken place in educational materials, organized particularly with a view to this form of teaching. The study on split-half classes may be seen as a demonstration of the fact that a simultaneous effort at influencing the mentioned four factors may result in increased differentiation in teaching.

That this was not found to be the case in oral rendition and written presentation may be explained by the fact that no educational material has been published on oral rendition, and comparatively little on written presentation, that would make possible increased differentiation in teaching. Moreover, it seems likely that a large number of teachers are unfamiliar with procedures of a more systematic nature for training pupils in oral rendition. The literature available on educational methods tends to support this impression. Quite probably, the majority of teachers do not acknowledge oral rendition as an educational goal for their pupils. The fact that activities in oral rendition occupied only 4 percent of the time devoted to the teaching of Danish confirms this suspicion.

A COORDINATED EFFORT IS NECESSARY

A concerted effort to overcome these factors is difficult, as it requires extensive coordination. Changes in the size of the class are made at political and administrative levels. The supplying of classes with educational materials and the development of such materials with a definite aim are also decided elsewhere. These different agencies generally do not inform the teacher of their intended educational goals, assuming that any such goals have been clearly defined. Finally, the preservice and inservice training of the teacher in the application of different teaching methods comes under still other authorities. A number of efforts, therefore, must be coordinated if an educational development is to be achieved without great waste of resources.

In conclusion, it can be said that for any value to accrue to the slow learner, any change in class size should be accompanied by information on and discussion of the goals of any such change. Moreover, it should be followed by a systematic effort aimed at the development of teaching methods and educational materials adapted to such methods. It should also be established that all special education must start in the ordinary class. The relationship between the slow learner and split-half classes should be viewed in this light.

An Experimental Investigation into the Effects of Counselling Retarded Readers

Denis Lawrence
Somerset Education Department Psychological Service
Taunton, Somerset
England

"At a time when we all pay lip service to the emotional concomitants of backwardness, it seems odd that our efforts should so often take the form of a direct attack on the presenting symptoms" (2). Although Bradshaw made this comment over twenty years ago, the same sentiments apply today. It is probably true to say that unless a retarded child is showing overt symptoms of emotional disturbance or unless his behaviour impinges unpleasantly on adults, then his emotional needs will receive scant attention. There is rarely a consideration that he may have underlying conflicts or unsatisfied emotional needs which prevent his learning. The possibility is generally acknowledged that he may have developed poor self-esteem through repeated failure; but apart from an encouraging attitude on the part of the teacher, no systematic attempt is made to try to help the child.

The neglect of this area is even more surprising when one considers the voluminous research available which confirms a relationship between reading failure and emotional maladjustment. Morris (4) shows clearly how retarded readers become anxious and depressed and show general symptoms of emotional maladjustment. Malmquist (3) shows a significant difference between good and poor readers on tests of emotional instability and the relationship between school achievement and self-concept has been highlighted by Punkey (5). It is not possible to review all the literature in this paper, but it is evident that there is a recognition of the emotional concomitants referred to by Bradshaw, even if there is no direct attack on them.

The studies reported in this paper accept Vera Southgate's view that "the essence of good teaching is a structured situation in which the child remains curious and enthusiastic." These studies set out to investigate a possible method of restoring the lost curiosity and enthusiasm of the retarded reader by using a system of individual personal counselling.

HYPOTHESIS

Reading is a skill which is highly valued in our literate society and failure in this area for the child means failing to please adults. The child who continually fails to please the adults around him (parents and teachers) will soon begin to feel unworthy and unloved. Eventually he begins to see himself not only as an inferior reader but as an inferior person and he develops poor self-esteem. The child's self-concept is formed by his experiences, and this concept often determines his future experiences. Since self-concept is a powerful motivator, the child who has developed a poor self-concept and failed in reading will not be easily motivated toward reading situations, as he does not see himself (self-image) as a reader.

EXPERIMENT I

Four schools in a Somerset rural community were selected as being typical village schools. The headteacher in each of these schools was asked to submit a list of children who, in his opinion, were retarded in reading. All the children were then given the following tests:

1. Schonell Word Recognition Test. This was the simplest available reading test.
2. The Sleight Nonverbal Intelligence Group Test. Although a more recent standardized test would have been desirable, economic considerations prevented it.
3. The Porter and Cattell Children's Personality Questionnaire (CPQ). This was administered orally by the experimenter as the children could not easily read the questionnaire themselves. The CPQ was also given to a random sample of good readers in the school containing the counselled group.

From this information, it was possible to match four groups on chronological age, sex, mental age, and reading attainment. Each group contained eight boys and four girls; each group received different treatments. Group 1 received remedial teaching from a specialist teacher. Group 2 received remedial reading and counselling. Group 3 received counselling only. Group 4 received no treatment.

The experiment ran for two terms (twenty weeks). At the end of this time, all the children were retested on the Schonell Word Recognition Test. The children in the counselled group were retested on the Porter and Cattell Personality Questionnaire.

CONCLUSIONS

At the end of a six-month period, the children in the counselled group showed a greater improvement in reading attainment than all other groups, together with improved self-images as measured on the Children's Personality Questionnaire.

Although this experiment showed that individual personal counselling was effective, the regular use of professional psychological staff in this way would be impracticable. It was felt, however, that the sort of counselling programme described in Part 1 could have been implemented by any untrained person. Expert psychological knowledge was not required. Part 2 of the study was then planned to test the hypothesis that untrained personnel would obtain equally successful results.

Before embarking on Part 2, a pilot study was carried out on two selected schools where children were already receiving remedial reading.

Table 1.   Mean reading ages and reading gains in Experiment 1.

Group 1 RT + Coun.			Group 2 Coun.			Group 3 RT			Group 4 Control		
Before	After	Gains	Before	After	Gains	Before	After	Gains	Before	After	Gains
5.1	5.9	0.3	5.3	6.1	0.3	7.2	8.1	0.4	6.6	6.9	-0.2
5.7	7.2	1.0	7.0	8.2	0.7	5.7	7.5	1.3	5.8	6.5	0.2
7.7	8.3	0.1	7.7	8.7	0.5	5.8	5.9	-0.4	6.7	7.2	0.
7.7	8.6	0.4	6.6	8.1	1.0	5.5	6.0	0.	8.7	8.6	-0.6
8.1	9.1	0.5	6.5	8.0	1.0	7.4	8.1	0.2	5.2	5.2	-0.5
7.9	9.0	0.6	5.1	7.3	1.7	7.6	8.2	0.1	5.4	5.4	-0.5
5.6	6.4	0.3	7.3	8.0	0.2	8.9	9.1	-0.3	5.5	6.3	0.3
8.1	8.5	-0.1	8.6	9.7	0.6	8.2	8.1	-0.6	6.7	7.4	0.2
8.3	9.2	0.4	6.6	7.9	0.8	5.4	7.3	1.4	5.6	5.5	-0.6
7.9	Left	-	7.5	8.1	0.1	7.3	7.7	-0.1	8.2	9.0	0.3
6.0	7.3	0.8	7.7	8.4	0.2	6.4	Left	-	5.4	5.6	-0.3
5.4	6.0	0.1	5.5	6.8	0.3	5.1	5.5	0.1	8.7	9.0	-0.2
	X Gain 0.40			X Gain 0.62			X Gain 0.17			X Gain -0.16	

NB   0.5 was subtracted in each case to allow for the fact that the children were six months older at the end of the experiment.

PILOT STUDY

Two schools were selected on the basis of their particular interest in the project. The headteachers in each case submitted lists of children retarded in reading. These children were then given the Sleight Nonverbal Intelligence Test, the Schonell Graded Word Recognition Test, and the Porter and Cattell Personality Questionnaire.

From the results of these tests, it was possible to match seven children in each school with a control group in each school on the following characteristics: chronological age, mental age, reading age, and sex. Each group contained five boys and two girls.

The system of counselling was the same as that used in Part 1 of this study. It extended over two terms (eighteen weeks).

Table 2.   Comparison of average differences in reading gains in Experiment 1

| | | Mann-Whitney 'U' Test | |
	Group	'U'	Significance level
1 V 3	RT + Coun. V RT	34	NS
2 V 4	Coun. V Control	12	0.001
2 V 3	Coun. V RT	30	0.01
1 V 2	RT + Coun. V Coun.	50	NS

Selection of the counsellor in School A was made by the headteacher on the grounds that she was known to the school as an intelligent parent who was eager to help. Selection of the counsellor for School B was made by the psychologist and approved by the headteacher on the grounds that she was intelligent, eager to help, and also sympathetic to children with difficulties.

Both counsellors met together with the psychologist on three occasions before the experiment, during which time the counselling principles were explained. Suggestions for background reading were made but limited to *Client-Centred Therapy* (6) and *Counselling in Schools* (Schools Council 1967). Instruction was also given in the administration of the CAT and CPQ. Both counsellors were asked to make notes after each session to help compile an indvidiual summary record and to complete the Cattell 16PF Questionnaire.

Except for three more meetings during the project, no further help was given. A general discussion on children's emotional needs took place at these meetings.

In this small pilot experiment, the experimental group was significantly superior to the control group at the end of the period. The statistical findings, together with informal observation, led to certain tentative conclusions:

1. It would appear to be possible for nonprofessional personnel, with a minimum of training, to carry out successfully individual counselling of retarded readers.
2. In addition to the more obvious personal qualities of interest and intelligence, the selection of a suitable personality for counselling may be important.

3. The physical conditions provided for the counselling seem to be significant.
4. Children must be able to rely on utmost confidentiality.

It was decided to check these conclusions by means of a similar experiment conducted on a larger scale.

EXPERIMENT II

To investigate the effects on an individual personal counselling programme carried out by nonprofessionals on primary school children retarded in reading, four schools were selected by the headteachers and staff on the basis of interest in the project shown. Each school submitted a list of children considered to be retarded in reading and the following tests were administered: the Sleight Nonverbal Intelligence Test; Porter and Cattell Children's Personality Questionnaire (the CPQ was also given to a random sample of thirty good readers and compared with thirty poor readers); and the Schonell Word Recognition Test. From this information it was possible to match six children in each school with a control group in the same school. They were matched on sex, mental age, chronological age, and reading age.

The headteacher of each school contacted a woman in the area whom he considered to be a suitable person for the experiment, and a preliminary meeting was arranged at which the psychologist approved the selection. The suitability of one of the counsellors, however, gave rise to a little concern in the light of the experience obtained in the pilot study. (The group subsequently counselled by this person later proved to be the only group which did not show a significant rise in reading attainment.)

The method of counselling was explained to the counsellors and suitable background reading was suggested. Once again, the system of counselling was identical to that used in Part 1 and each counsellor was interviewed three times during the programme which again extended over two terms.

Table 3. Mean reading ages and reading gains in Experiment 2.

		RA before	RA after	Gains
School M	Counselled	7.1	8.0	0.45
	Control	6.9	7.1	-0.5
School N	Counselled	7.2	8.7	1.18
	Control	6.9	7.6	0.46
School P	Counselled	5.8	6.7	0.65
	Control	5.8	6.0	-0.03
School Y	Counselled	7.5	8.4	0.41
	Control	7.6	8.1	0.31

Table 4. Comparison of average differences in reading gains in each school in Experiment 2.

School	(Mann-Whitney 'U' Test) 'U'	Significance level
M	1	.002
N	6	.032
P	5	.021
Y	13	.2

BRIEFING THE COUNSELLORS

The word *briefing* has been chosen carefully to distinguish from *training* as the success of this method depends to a great extent on using people unsophisticated in formal counselling techniques. This is not to detract in any way from the valuable function of a highly trained skilled therapist or counsellor involved in personal counselling of persons showing symptoms of emotional disorder. They perform a different function in a different context. The sort of counselling envisaged here is, in many ways, a replication of a normal, happy, instinctive, spontaneous, mother-child relationship.

This method is wholly experiential and in no way a cognitive system of treatment. There is no interpretation of the material produced in the discussions. Treatment is centred on the emotional attitude generated. The aim must be to establish as natural and sincere a relationship with the child as can be achieved through the natural human qualities of the counsellor, and this relationship is dependent on the degree of empathy which the counsellor can provide. She will attempt to achieve this through working with the child's best means of expression, which is likely to be verbal. Some children may communicate best through the use of dolls or other models; others, through plasticine modelling. Media other than verbal, however, should only be used where the child is obviously not communicating verbally. Much communication will take place unconsciously, on a nonverbal level, through smiles, nods, gestures, and voice tone.

The following is a summary of the main principles:

THERE SHOULD BE TOTAL ACCEPTANCE OF THE CHILD'S PERSONALITY

Through this kind of relationship, the counsellor communicates to the child that she understands his views and also understands what it feels like to be him. This is the unique nature of the counselling method; it is completely noncritical and wholly supportive.

RESPECT FOR INDIVIDUALITY

Our retarded reader is aware of his reading failure and used to being treated as "retarded." The kind of relationship established in the counselling sessions should be aimed primarily at changing the child's view of himself as an inferior person. Where there is genuine concern for a person in distress, there is always the danger of too much compassion and sympathy which may be interpreted as being patronising. If a patronising attitude creeps in, this will only serve to increase the child's feelings of inferiority. He then becomes rooted in his inadequate role. It is well to be aware of this danger and to recognise that, even though the counsellor is superior in many ways to the child, there are many ways in which the child who is retarded in reading may be superior to the adult.

RESPECT FOR PRIVACY

Judging from the material elicited from the children in the experiments, most of their worries and fears were centred on family relationships. Sooner or later, the child will bring up these areas in the counselling sessions; should he fail to do so, it would be unwise for the counsellor to investigate this aspect by direct questioning. There may be good reasons why the child does not wish to discuss certain areas of his life and one should respect his need for some degree of privacy.

ENJOYING THE CHILD'S COMPANY

What does "valuing the child" mean in practice? First and foremost, it means communicating to him that he is an interesting person. It can be quite a revelation for some people to suddenly become aware that they have thoughts and ideas which are of interest to others besides themselves. This goes for both children and adults, but in the case of the retarded child it is likely that this happens for the first time in his life. Early in the programme, the counsellor should aim to communicate to the child that he enjoys his company. This is not a difficult task by any means, as those who have listened to the young child at play will fully appreciate. The young child's attitudes toward life can be very illuminating, as they tend to simplify so much of what the adult makes complex.

Nonverbal communication, particularly through smiles and voice tones, is important. We do not smile enough at our children.

COUNSELLOR STATUS

The question of counsellor status is important. This does not mean that the counsellor should set herself up as an expert or superior being. On the other hand, the very fact that the headteacher allows this stranger to use the counselling room, and the courtesy with which the head treats the counsellor, add up in the child's eyes to an image of the counsellor as somebody who must be very important indeed. Research evidence from studies on the powers of suggestion indicate that people are more susceptible when the person doing the suggesting possesses status. This influence is even greater when there is also a warm, affectionate relationship (1).

CONCLUSIONS

1. Children retarded in reading may have unsatisfied emotional needs which must be taken into account in planning a remedial programme.

2. These children can be helped in school by individual personal counselling carried out by suitable ancillary helpers.

3. The organization and selection of children suitable for counselling should be made in association with the educational psychologist, to eliminate children who may need a different kind of help.

REFERENCES
1. Argyle, M. *The Psychology of Interpersonal Behaviour.* Harmondsworth, Middlesex: Penguin Books, 1967.
2. Bradshaw, F. R. "Remedial Work in Schools," in Buhler (Ed.), *Childhood Problems and the Teacher.* 1953.
3. Malmquist, E. *Factors Related to Reading Disabilities in the First Grade of Elementary School.* Stockholm: Almqvist and Wiksell, 1958.
4. Morris, J. *Standards and Progress in Reading.* Slough: NFER, 1966.
5. Punkey, W. *The Self and Academic Achievement.* 1967.
6. Rogers, C. *Client-Centred Therapy.* Boston: Houghton Mifflin, 1965.

Reading Deficiencies in the German and English Languages

Horst G. Taschow
University of Regina
Regina, Saskatchewan
Canada

Numerous studies in the world literature on reading have reported on reading difficulties and disabilities. Other studies have voiced concern about reading deficiencies encountered by bilinguals who are compelled to read and learn in the language of monocultural and monolingual school systems. We must ask: How do bilingual students think when they are required to read for understanding in the weaker language of the unilingual textbooks? How do bilinguals handle the stronger versus the weaker language? This study addresses itself to these problems with a view to the formulation of practical recommendations for teacher education to assist bilinguals.

ORIGIN OF THE STUDY

This study began with the question, "How can the monolingual classroom teacher in a multicultural setting help German-English bilinguals to understand better what they have to read in the English language?" Twenty-three German-English bilingual boys and girls, ranging from grades three to six in Saskatchewan's public and separate schools, worked with the investigator for one year.

INTRODUCTORY DIAGNOSTIC TREATMENT

Biometric eye measurements in reading 100-word sample target cards in English did not reveal unusual discrepancies from the Reading-Eye Reading Performance Profile (11). Reading comprehension, however, measured by ten yes/no answers, fell below the 70 percent minimum performance. The 100-word English passages on the target cards were then translated into German passages of equal length and ten words per line. The results showed increases in comprehension after silent reading with scores ranging from 60 to 100 percent. It seems unlikely that these improvements were due entirely to the effects of practice.

Following this, an Individual Reading Inventory (IRI) (1, 5, 10) was constructed in English and then translated into German. Both tests were administered to the subjects. Again, it became apparent that comprehension after oral and silent reading in English was significantly lower than in German. To analyze the English meaning gap in greater detail, all the words contained in the oral and silent reading passages in the IRI were arranged in order of frequency and then checked against the Thorndike-Lorge List to ascertain difficulty ratings. From word recognition performances, it was apparent that the subjects knew most of the words, although pronunciation time was longer than when compared with native English speakers. Nevertheless, results indicated that subjects could recognize and pronounce the words in the English oral and silent reading passages.

WORD MATCHING

Next, the question was asked, "'How successful are bilinguals in responding to the meanings of printed words?" Subjects were given the list of words they had recognized and pronounced earlier and were asked to say each word and then demonstrate its meaning by using the word in a sentence. Responses were tape recorded. An examination of these responses led to the conclusion that there were no significant differences when compared with those of the English monoglots.

Next, words like *run*, *heavy*, and *broke* were used in sentences where each of the three words had more than one connotation. The sentences were arranged in order from concrete to abstract. For example:

> The man carries a *heavy* load on his back.
> The man carries a *heavy* load through life.
> John and Paul *run* to the store.
> It was the usual *run* of the mill.
> Lena *broke* the glass.
> Bill *broke* the rule.

How did the subjects arrive at the English meaning? Subjects translated the English sentences in direct word cluster relationships into the German language, applied German meaning from their stronger background experiences, and transferred the German understanding back to match the words in the English sentence. Translation in cluster relationship in form of word matching is demonstrated in the following example:

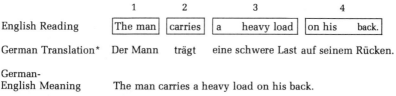

	1	2	3	4
English Reading	The man	carries	a heavy load	on his back.
German Translation*	Der Mann	trägt	eine schwere Last auf seinem Rücken.	
German- English Meaning	The man carries a heavy load on his back.			

Figure 1.   Word Cluster Relationships

*Although the German word order is incorrect, the German translation conveys adequate understanding.

The subjects seemed to assume that when the sentence means something in German, it must also mean the same in English. They generally agreed that it could not mean anything else. Could it be that the stronger language controls thinking? When asked why they had translated the English words *The man* together, subjects replied that it is *Der Mann* and not "die" or "das" Mann. The German language makes a grammatical distinction, rather than a natural distinction, for the genders. Similar comments were made for cluster relationships 3 and 4.

WORDS THAT DO NOT MATCH

While the English to German to English translations had worked successfully with the concrete samples, the same procedures did not work when applied to sentences with abstract connotations. In "The man carries a heavy load through life," the subjects were obviously dissatisfied with the outcome of their efforts and said: "It doesn't sound right," "Das sagt man nicht so" (one doesn't say this in German), "that is what I don't know in school." Some asked, "Why would a man always carry a heavy load through life? What would he carry? He is not the man in the moon—or is he?" These questions indicated that concrete rather than abstract connotations were applied. Similar attempts were observed in *the run of the mill*, which in German is not *das Rennen der Mühle*. Perhaps, it is at this point where the transfer of meaning from the stronger into the weaker language ends. The mill in German does not run but *clatters* (that is *klappern*), and in English, the mill does not *clatter* but *run*.

In an effort to match word for word, sentences with concrete connotations were correctly translated via German back to English because the German background was identical to the English message conveyed in the sentences. But in sentences with abstract connotations, verbatim translations did not produce understanding of the English sentences.

WORD MANIPULATION

When further sentences with abstract connotations were examined, students resorted to manipulating words in order to attain meaning.

In the examples, *The voters registered a heavy vote, Joe broke the bank at Monte Carlo, Old Mr. Brown was a man who often flew off the handle (3), and Susi turned the tables on her sisters*, the English words were translated one by one only to find that, when put together, the sentences lacked German meaning. In their given order, German word matching did not produce understanding by saying, *Die Wähler verzeichneten eine schwere Wahlstimme, Joseph brach die Bank von Monte Carlo, Ein alter Herr Braun war ein Mann der oft wegward den Stiel*, and *Susi drehte die Tische um ihre Schwestern*.

When the subjects were questioned about the meaning they had given to the English words and how they make sense within the whole sentences, subjects manipulated words to make sense. Thus, *Susi places the tables at the side where the sisters are sitting*, or *places the tables closer to the sisters*. The German translation of *on* as *um* may hint at word manipulation to establish meaning forcefully by moving the tables *around* the sisters. When questioned about the phrase, "flew off the handle," explanations were offered that *handle* in English means *Henkel* or *Stiel* in German and *flew* is *flog* which, so it was agreed, did not make sense in German and therefore was changed to *wegwarf* which in English is *threw away*. Then, so it was argued, the English sentence makes sense after all: "Herr Braun warf oft die Stiele weg." For justification, an additional explanation was offered that, perhaps, old Mr. Brown did not like handles or, maybe particular kinds of handles. The understanding of the English phrase, *broke the bank*, was thought to mean that Joseph apparently *brach ein in die Bank*, that is, *entered the bank* with the added explanation that he wanted to take or steal the money or to rob the bank. But one subject volunteered that Joseph did not hold up the bank.

How did the bilinguals arrive at comprehension of the English language? When the same language operations as described in Figure 1 were applied to the above sentences, the subjects hesitated, sometimes abandoned cluster translation, examined single words, and reexamined German meanings. As a result of this, German words were manipulated to accommodate better German understanding, which was then transferred to fit the English sentence. Figure 2 tries to demonstrate the English-German-English language word meaning manipulation.

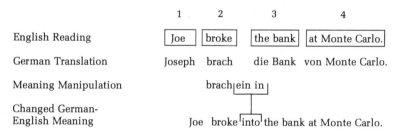

Figure 2. Word Cluster Relationships

In the completed manipulation, the rootword *brach* (German), and *broke* (English) has been maintained in both languages to which, in German, the separable prefix *ein* and the preposition *in* have been added, resulting in the new English word *into*. Relating the new meaning structured through German language manipulations to the given English sentence, the sentence would convey Joe's intent to rob the bank which differed markedly from the original English sentence.

It can be concluded, from the results of these samples, that the subjects translated a word or word cluster from English into German, then associated German meaning experiences and, lacking sufficient English language experience, accepted the German version instead. Did they actually try to tailor the weaker language background through meaning manipulation derived from the stronger language background? How were these students able to get into higher grades? Perhaps the requirements in the lower grades were within their limited English language power and maybe they had benefitted from frequent and repetitious seat work. However, when the subjects reached the upper elementary grades, the traditional textbooks written for monoglots of the Anglo-Canadian and Anglo-American cultures became too difficult; even too difficult, perhaps, for some of the German speaking parents to help their children. As for the teachers, they were unilingual and had little or no awareness of the multilingual mixture in the classrooms in which traditional lesson plans were taught "as if all the students were profiting from the lesson" (12).

THERAPY RECOMMENDATIONS

Instead of making teachers the disseminators of interminable unilingual monologues, which bilinguals may not always be able to follow and understand, teacher education should train teachers to learn to listen to the bilingual student, talk with him, and observe how he learns (4). In such learning-centered situations, the bilingual is given the fullest opportunity to act upon the materials to be assimilated and accommodated for learning and, when supported by independent questioning, this will strengthen the weaker language background experiences. It is hoped that teachers will then begin to understand how bilinguals learn and how to broaden and deepen the intellectual horizons of bilinguals beyond the limits of their own language and culture by seeking and making available many and varied purposeful opportunities for them to grow into the national language, until this language becomes their own (9). This process may be managed more effectively if the teacher organises each activity in terms of: 1) preparation, 2) direction, 3) discussion, and 4) application.

IMPLEMENTING THE STEPS

Preparation. The bilingual is exposed to the main ideas of the new reading-learning experience. A question like, "What do you know about it?" will start exploration of background experiences as well as of meaning resources in the weaker language. Auditory discrimination is activated by clear enunciation leading to imitation of the correct soundgestalt of words.

During background explorations, new words are introduced orally and written on the chalkboard for visual inspection. Meaning is established from context, through listening and discussing with other monoglots, or, as a last resort, through explanation by the teacher. The time allowed for thinking must be generous. Bilinguals should be encouraged to make comparisons with the stronger language as long and as often as they feel the need. This sets the purpose for reading. It is difficult even for monoglots to develop the habit of setting a clearly defined purpose and efficient teacher questioning is a necessary prerequisite in accomplishing this goal (8). This is particularly important for the bilingual because it helps him to build syntactical and grammatical facilities in the weaker language.

Direction. Through the learner-centered activities in preparation, the bilingual's weaker language has been directed toward the assigned silent reading task. Silent reading receives encouragement from within the reader because he has reached equilibrium through assimilation of meanings already known and learned. In addition, teacher observation during silent reading will give the student assurance that help will be available should unforeseen comprehension uncertainties arise. Individual help at such times provides opportunities for the teacher to spot obstructing and distracting reading symptoms.

Discussion. The bilingual is challenged to use the weaker language to its fullest extent by discussing orally what he has read silently. To encourage vocal expression, fact, vocabulary, and inference questions are recommended. For example: "What did Joe do?" (fact question); "What is the meaning of the phrase 'run of the mill' as used in this sentence?" (vocabulary question); and "What would you have done if you had been in Bill's place?" (inference question). This kind of questioning guides the reader from literal to critical reading. In seeking answers to questions when correct recall fails, oral rereading for specific purposes is employed. Purposeful oral rereading serves to reinforce the weaker language. It provides an opportunity for verifying doubtful or incorrect answers and recovering forgotten or overlooked words, phrases, idiomatic expressions, and other information. At this point, unilingual teachers should restrain themselves from simply supplying answers and rushing the students. Instead, the teachers need to learn that the bilinguals depend upon their support to grow in the weaker language through their own efforts rather than being forced from without.

Application. Any difficulties that have been experienced in the foregoing steps should be explored further with help from the teacher or from a competent unilingual student tutor. Help should be directed primarily toward widening background experiences in the weaker language. Expanding and refining the weaker language must be regarded as the primary activity. Word recognition and comprehension skills become secondary; nevertheless, they must supplement the primary activities. However, secondary activities must not be taught in isolated drill fashion, for this may not only hinder and interfere with, but also positively destroy healthy inner growth of the weaker language.

CONCLUSION

This study suggests that bilinguals may be unjustifiably hindered in their reading progress by monocultural and monolinguistic oriented school systems. Other bilingual studies have expressed similar concerns (6, 7). It is proposed that bilinguals should not only be helped to survive among monoglots but encouraged to grow in the weaker language and make it their own. To assist in reaching this goal, the study recommended basic reading-learning principles, outlined in four steps, for the use of unilingual teachers in unilingual classroom instruction. It is hoped that this study will stimulate further research on how to improve reading instruction for bilinguals in monocultural and monolingual societies.

REFERENCES

1. Betts, E. A. *Foundations of Reading Instruction.* New York: American Book, 1957, 438-485.
2. Fisher, J. A. "Dialect, Bilinguals, and Reading," in Robert Karlin (Ed.), *Reading for All*, Proceedings of the Fourth IRA World Congress on Reading, Buenos Aires, 1972. Newark, Delaware: International Reading Association, 1973, 86-95.
3. Heilman, A. W. *Principles and Practices of Teaching Reading* (3rd ed.). Columbus, Ohio: Charles E. Merrill, 1972.
4. Inhelder, B., and J. Piaget. *The Growth of Logical Thinking from Childhood to Adolescence.* New York: Basic Books, 1958.
5. Johnson, M. S., and R. A. Kress. *Informal Reading Inventories*, Reading Aids Series. Newark, Delaware: International Reading Association, 1965.
6. Kellaghan, T., and J. Macnamara. "Reading in a Second Language in Ireland," in Marion Jenkinson (Ed.), *Reading Instruction: An International Forum*, Proceedings of the First IRA World Congress on Reading, Paris, 1966. Newark, Delaware: International Reading Association, 1967.
7. Macnamara, J. *Bilingualism and Primary Education.* Edinburgh: University Press, 1966.
8. Sanders, N. M. *Classroom Questions, What Kinds?* New York: Harper and Row, 1966.
9. Swinford, E. J. "Das Kinderdorf Pestalozzi: A Swiss School that Educates for Peace," *Phi Delta Kappan*, 55 (June 1974), 659.
10. Taschow, H. G. "Uber Ursachen, Diagnose und Behandlung der sekundären Lese-Schwächen von Kindern. Aus der Lese-Heilpädagogen-Ausbildung in Kanada," *Heilpädagogische Forschung*, Band 4, Heft 3 (1973), 372-392.
11. Taylor, S. E., et al. *Bulletin No. 3.* Huntington, New York: EDL, 1960.
12. Zintz, M. V. *The Reading Process, the Teacher, and the Learner.* Dubuque, Iowa: W. C. Brown, 1970, 336.

Outcomes of Visual Perceptual Training

George D. Spache
Spache Educational Consultants
Sarasota, Florida
United States of America

Since this is to be a brief presentation of a complex area, perhaps it would be wise to begin with definitions. Classically, in some textbooks, *visual perception* is defined as the stimulation of the sensory organ plus the resulting action. Others consider perception the interpretation of sensory data from past experiences. Those who construct tests in this area apparently have their own definitions drawn from the labels on the tests they create. For example, in the United States there are now available 83 tests of a single visual perceptual type of behavior and 21 multiple test batteries. If we take the labels of the various tests at face value, there are apparently dozens of components of visual perception.

Another approach to defining visual perception is present in the use of factor analysis. In this technique, a large number of tests are administered and the results intercorrelated. In this fashion, tests which have common elements, and presumably the basic components of visual perception, can be identified. One such factor analysis of some 35 tests identified in the mind of the author what she considered to be 5 major components. These were motor planning and eye hand relations, form constancy and space relations, hyperactivity and distractibility, lateral awareness of sides of the body, and figure ground discrimination. It is apparent that this study included not only what might be considered measures of visual perception but also interferences with visual perception. Thus, the results are a little clouded.

Another factor analysis identified 6 major elements of visual perception as organization of movements in space, ocular control, dynamic balance, rhythmic writing and postural stability, form percepetion, and motor planning and control. Interestingly enough, this factor analysis of a popular multiple test battery grouped and labeled the test differently than the original author. The problem in interpreting these factor analyses is that they can yield no more information than is put into the computer. In other words, we cannot assume that because a large number of tests are studied in this fashion, the entire area of visual perception is necessarily included. Therefore, the results do not really tell us what visual perception is, but merely indicate what relationships there are among the few tests the authors chose to analyze.

Another way of attempting to define visual perception is to look at the major types of tests which are now being sold under this label. One such major type may be called the Part-Whole Test. This usually includes matching parts to a whole or recognizing that pictured parts of an object belong to a whole. The test may take the form of simply manipulating cutouts or of attempting to draw the missing parts when an incomplete drawing is present. A second very popular type of visual perception test is that in visual memory for designs. As its name implies, this test usually requires the child to reproduce a geometric shape or form. Among the tests which use this approach are Bender Gestalt, Benton Visual Retention, Graham-Kendall Memory for Designs, Beery, Minnesota Percepto-Diagnostic, and Winter Haven Perceptual Achievement Forms. All of these tests are in wide use in the United States. However, the measurement of visual memory for design in this fashion raises doubts in some minds. Most of these tests were originally built to detect brain damage in persons much older than the school children to which the tests are now being applied. Most of the tests are seriously influenced by intelligence, short term memory, and various methods of administration. Yet, for the most part, the authors of these tests ignore these possible influences and consider their tests adequate measures of visual perception in toto. A third type of test, figure ground, is one in which the individual attempts to recognize a drawing or a picture which is embedded in a confusing background. There are at least eight different ways of measuring figure ground discrimination employing marbles, intersecting figures, simple geometric forms, and pictures embedded in a highly structured background. No one has tried to find out which one of these is the best measure and few of the tests have really been validated as highly predictive of reading success. A fourth type is that of form discrimination, perhaps second only to the visual memory for designs in its popularity. This approach usually involves tasks of matching various geometric shapes either visually or by cutouts. In some quarters, it is widely and uncritically accepted that performance in this type of test is highly related to early success in reading.

Another type of visual perception test is labeled *form constancy*. Here the task is that of recognizing a form or a shape despite rotations or reversals of the form.

These are only the five major types of visual perception tests and there are many others available. Critics of these approaches to the measurement of visual perception have pointed out that many of the tests have low predictive value, are unclear in their intercorrelations and overlap with other tests, and are almost irrelevant to an attempt to diagnose a beginning reader's needs. Other critics point out that the tests are often based on a *post hoc ergo propter hoc* reasoning. That is, if a child is poor in one of these tests in visual perception in the third grade, it explains his reading failures in first and second grades. There is also a strong tendency toward loose interpretation of correlations of the tests with reading achievement. Authors often accept statistically significant but minute correlations with reading as indications of validity of the test. For example, Thurstone's Identical Forms Test was used in the first grade studies and yielded correlations from .27 to .40 with paragraph meaning at the end of the first grade. While these correlations are probably statistically significant, they mean that the ability to match forms as it is measured in this test accounted for between 7 and 16 percent of the variance in reading success. In other words, 84 to 93 percent of what determines reading success in the first grade has nothing to do with this kind of measurement. But many of the test makers use data of this quality to justify their peculiar definitions of visual perception.

By this time, perhaps some readers are expecting a definition of visual perception. I do not believe we are ready to define it in terms of the available data. We do not know what all the components or elements of visual perception are as a result of the test labels, factor analyses, or the claims of the test authors. If this discussion leaves you confused as to exactly what visual perception is, this was my intention. It is not certain that we know what visual perception is as it functions in early reading nor whether it is worth our time to use the various tests and other instruments which are being offered.

To reinforce this impression of confusion in the field, let us cite some of the results of the studies of the significance of various well-known perception tests for early reading. The author has collected 38 correlations of the Frostig battery with measures of reading achievement. Of these 38 correlations, 15 are statistically insignificant and, thus, useless for prediction. Only 7 of these 38 correlations achieve a level indicating a moderate relationship that is .40 to .60, and none reach the marked relationship level, above .60. As for the total score on the Frostig of the 8 correlations with reading only one reaches the upper range of usefulness. To interpret these correlations from another view, the total scores in this battery claiming to measure five aspects of visual perception account for from 10 to 38 percent of the variance in reading scores, while any of the subtests account for anywhere from 0 to 30 percent in the variance in reading. In other words, neither the subtests of this very popular battery nor the total score are very useful in predicting early reading success.

The author has made a similar collection of the predictive studies using the Bender Gestalt. In predicting readiness for reading of 11 correlations of the Bender with such a test, 3 are very low, 4 are moderate, and 4 are relatively high correlations. In predicting reading achievement of 22 correlations, 10 are very low, 8 are moderate, and only 4 are high. In other words, this very popular tool of American and European psychologists tends to show very weak relationships with reading achievement, and only slightly better relationships with readiness. Moreover, the interpretation of the relevance of this test to reading achievement is clouded by the fact that the Bender is considered by some to be a measure of intelligence, by others, a measure of personality adjustment, an instrument for detecting probably brain damage, and a measure of ego strength. When a test has this many meanings for its various users, how do we interpret its relevance to visual perception and early reading success? We could go on citing other collections of data on the remaining popular tests of visual perception, but the implications would be very similar. Those that have desirable reliabilities often have apparently no relationship to reading or readiness success, as in the case of the Benton Visual Retention. Some tests, such as the de Hirsch Predictive Index, were constructed under peculiar circumstances in very small groups and their results generalized elsewhere without ample statistical support. Many make no attempt to control the influence of intelligence, of the speed of the child's reaction or the effects of the timing in the test, or the memory factor in trying to recall the matter of the test.

TRAINING PROGRAMS

But the title of this discussion is "Outcomes of Visual Perception Training"—not really a discussion of what visual perception is or what is wrong with the tests in this area. I have deliberately delayed in beginning a discussion of training programs to give a set toward interpreting their results. When the field is so poorly defined, and when the instruments used in the field are of such dubious quality, we can well imagine that the follow-up training programs would be difficult to interpret.

However, let us describe the various types of visual perceptual training programs now current in both America and Europe. As you will note, there is a very loose use of terms to describe the training, with every trainer seeming to have his own concepts and his own labels for the activities he describes. Another interesting aspect of many of these training programs is that we find 8 or 9 types of activities prescribed on the basis of a solitary measure of visual perception such as form discrimination. In other words, it is not easy to understand exactly how these complex training programs are related to the diagnosis obtainable from many of the current tests in visual perception. But we will proceed with describing them in any event. Basically, the activities offered in such training programs fall into five major types:

BODY SCHEMA

Body schema implies knowledge of the body and its parts and control of its functions. It is also called training in self-concept, motor planning, mobilization, and body image. Among the variety of activities usually offered are jointed dolls, rhythmic movements to music, movement games, rope skipping, and limitation of movements of another person.

BALANCE

This type of program is concerned with the control of the body and its parts. It is often called training in laterality, directionality, postural flexibility, or movement training. Usually the program includes such items as the walking beam, a walking obstacle course, stepping games, the balance disc, and the trampoline.

HAND EYE COORDINATION

This program implies the integration of visual information with the motoric responses of the hand. It is sometimes called perceptual-motor match or organization of movements in space. Training in this particular type of program usually involves templates, chalkboard exercises, coloring, cutting, pasting, bean bags, ball throwing, ring toss, rhythm bands, bead stringing, and paper and pencil activities in tracing and dot patterns.

OCULAR CONTROL

The purpose of this training is to enable the child to develop controlled effective movements of the eye. It is also called training in distance, size, and shape in space. The techniques usually include the Marsden Swinging Ball, fingerplay, straight line and rotary pursuit tasks with flashlights, and use of walking beam while fixating on a wall target.

FORM PERCEPTION

This program obviously stresses the recognition of visual shapes and symbols. Training may be conducted on a three dimensional or a two dimensional level. It may include such three dimensional activities as those involving puzzles, peg boards, parquetry, mosaic tiles, and block designs. The two dimensional level may include paper and pencil tasks in tracing, reproducing, matching forms, desk plates, or drawing.

A few program directors include activities in the area of visual memory, visual rhythm and sequencing, and temporal and auditory sequencing. In fact, the breadth of activities may well expand to include dealing with the learning modalities of the child; i.e., the training is focused on the proposed channel appropriate for the child's learning, whether this be visual, auditory, tactile, or kinesthetic. The breadth of activities in visual perception training, often followed after a single test of form discrimination or memory for design, are certainly a testimony to the creativity or imagination of program directors. It is difficult for some of us to see how the diagnosis really indicates this multiplicity of needs for children who are presumably handicapped in the area of visual perception.

To guide us in such programs, there has been a flood of guides, syllabi, and commercial kits available in the general market. These are being contributed by physical educators, psychologists, optometrists, kindergarten-nursery groups, and many others. These types of specialists have their own concepts of visual perception and desirable training programs and it is quite interesting to make comparisons among them. In addition, there are a number of esoteric programs which are not as widely known or used as those that are so readily available through the commercial market. For example, there is the Delacato program based on an irrelevant theory of cerebral dominance. The Delacato training is an attempt to produce complete sidedness in an individual by creeping, crawling, walking, and sleep posture training. According to its author, this program is a definite cure for most language and reading difficulties, particularly those in the perceptual area.

Another approach is the Orthomolecular treatment program which consists of massive doses of vitamins and minerals and a high protein, low carbohydrate diet. Presumably, this medication (if you can call it such) will produce the desired results of success in early reading with children who have "perceptual problems." Those who promote this medical approach, however, do not use the amphetamines or the tranquilizers that so many medical people are offering for these same reasons. Perhaps, because of the diversity of training activities available, we also see many combinations of programs involving visual coordination, gross and fine motor skills, plus various types of auditory training.

The American optometrists also have entered the field in offering their visual training program to improve binocular coordination, the accomodation convergence function, the accuracy of fixation, and other such visual functions.

In a field as diverse as this, we might well expect that results from training programs would show extreme variations from completely negative to various degrees of positiveness. Many of those conducting visual perception training programs really have not attempted to determine the effects upon reading but are satisfied if they produce gains in a retest of visual perception. We have reviewed some 28 programs of this type. Of these, 15 produced gains in the perceptual test as they had hoped to; 7 did not. The remainder did not even retest to determine whether there were gains in visual perception. Of these that evaluated the effects on readiness, 9 were negative and only 1 was positive. Of the 14 programs testing for effects on reading, all were negative. Most of these 28 programs emphasized the visual motor training or form perception types of activities, including those we have previously described under the rubrics of body schema, ocular control, eye-hand coordination, and balance.

Another group of seven studies emphasizing the visual discrimination of forms, letters, and words were reasonably successful. Some would generalize from this particular group of studies that it is more profitable to employ training materials which closely resemble the matter ordinarily obtained in the act of reading. Another group of 11 studies also stressing the visual motor programs, however, were largely successful in improving readiness or reading achievement. Another reviewer cites 11 studies selected from the literature because of the quality of the research and finds 5 of these positive in effects upon reading, 5 negative, and 1 completely inconclusive. It might be noted that his 5 studies resulting in negative results dealt with children of normal reading ability of middle-class socioeconomic status, while 3 of the 5 positive studies dealt with children of low socioeconomic status or retarded readers. Perhaps these results are telling us that perceptual training is related to reading improvement only among those children whose preschool experiences have been very limited or those children likely to have difficulty in early reading programs. It may be that such training is relatively pointless for the brighter, middle-class children or those who would normally succeed in our beginning reading programs.

In addition to these studies which emphasize the visual motor type of program, we have collected 18 studies on the Frostig program. This is a commercial program emphasizing training in the five areas sampled in the subtests of the Frostig battery. In 6 out of 8 of these studies in which a retest was made on the Frostig battery, there were gains in that performance. But in readiness, 7 out of the 10 programs employing the Frostig materials achieved no improvements and in 9 out of 19 studies, there were no effects upon reading achievement. There is additional evidence, however, that in those studies which were seemingly successful in producing gains on a retest in perception, the gains were only temporary and no greater than would normally have occurred as a matter of maturation.

We have no explanation for the fact that the visual motor programs, as they may be called, produce success in about one out of every two studies. There are hints in the data that perhaps the effect of the visual motor type program is greatest among lower-class, lower socioeconomic children and it is relatively irrelevant for readiness or reading achievement among middle-class children. There is also strong evidence here that the use of commercial programs that have not had careful field studies and validation seems quite pointless.

My own experiences have been successful in using chalkboard and seat work exercises, in place of reading instruction, for hand-eye coordination among low socioeconomic children. In this study, the children were given from two to six months of such training, without that same amount of reading instruction. The 34 experimental classes equalled the reading achievement of the controls who were directly introduced to the basal reading program. Obviously, the substitution of this specific kind of training did not prevent normal reading achievement. In contrast, the experimental children in the lowest quarter of intelligence for the entire group and the black children in these classes exceeded the reading achievement of comparable low ability control pupils or the white experimental pupils. In other words, the training was decidedly profitable for low ability, low socioeconomic, and black children. It was not as profitable for low socioeconomic white children, and of little value for middle-class children, white or black.

There are those who would question whether visual perception, as it is currently being identified, really has anything to do with early reading achievement to any appreciable degree. The contradictory results in many studies certainly would give rise to such a question. Let us return then to the major types of training currently being offered, presumably to improve visual perception and reading achievement. Can we see any obvious relationships between these types of activities and the child's efforts in learning to read? We might say that the body schema and the balance exercises would be profitable in terms of teaching the child directionality, orienting him to the parts of his body and, in a sense, giving him orientation to objects in space. Whether this is related to reading achievement is still highly questionable.

The third type of major activity, hand-eye coordination, has obvious relationships to handwriting, to letter formation, and to letter and word discrimination or recognition. Unless children can form letters consistently, we can hardly expect them to recognize letters and words consistently. It is true that some children with very poor hand-eye coordination do learn to read quite well. But, in general, children who are handicapped in hand-eye coordination show these difficulties in handwriting, letter formation, and letter and word recognition. Thus, there may be some direct relevance to reading achievement in this type of training.

Ocular control or the ability to maintain fixation, or to put it more simply, to direct one's eyes where one wishes, is certainly related to the mechanical aspects of reading. For example, one study showed that over 50 percent of kindergarten children could not sufficiently control their eyes to look at a series of dots successively and repeatedly. In other words, they could not coordinate well enough to perform the basic act of fixating on a line making the sweep to the next fixation, and so on, and repeating the return sweep to the next line. Ocular control activities do tend to promote development of this mechanical control and probably will show direct relationship to reading achievement for those children who need such training.

The last of the five types of training programs, emphasizing form perception, is perhaps the most popular of all. This usually takes the form of matching, reproducing, and arranging geometric forms. The research, however, seems to indicate that if this form discrimination were practiced with letters and words the results might be more closely related to reading achievement. Hence, in the present form, most programs emphasizing form perception are not very relevant to reading success. In some reports, several of these types of activities are given to a group of children in the expectation that this sort of shotgun treatment will result in greater scores on a readiness test or better performances on a reading test. If our deduction about the relevance of these various types of training are correct, it is not surprising that the results in these multitype training programs vary considerably from one study to the next.

La Prédiction de l'Apprentissage de la Lecture et Sensible à l'Action Pédagogique

Andre Inizan
Centre National de Pédagogie Spéciale
Beaumont, France

Les travaux relatifs à l'apprentissage de la lecture, à sa préparation et à ses avatars ait tour à tour mis l'accent sur les particularités psychologiques des enfants et sur les institutions caractérisées dans leur ensemble (les méthodes, les familles, les sociétés). Fidèle au cadre scolaire, nous nous appliquons depuis une décennie à saisir les faits en direct et en gros-plan, observant individuellement des écoliers à leur poste de travail.

Presentons quelques résultats:

1. *Le premier sera relatif à la notion de validité des tests prédictifs*

Auteur du premier instrument français de cette sorte, la Batterie Prédictive de l'apprentissage de la lecture, j'ai eu évidemment, à me préoccuper de cas pour lesquels la prédiction ne se réalisait pas. Bien qu'ils réduisaient de la validité du test, ces cas n'étaient pas pour me déplaire car ils accréditaient notre conception de l'aptitude à apprendre à lire dont nous ne faisons pas une donné congénitale et organique. Quand nous cherchons à évaluer chez un enfant de sans son aptitude à apprendre à lire nous nous limitons à caractériser à un certain moment, un ensemble d'habiletés psychologiques répertoriées non pas avec exhaustivité mais avec clarté et qui, chez cet enfant candidat à l'apprentissage de la lecture fera que la tâche sera plus ou moins facile.

Nous considérons donc surtout l'aptitude comme un effet du vécu de l'enfant or, un enfant de 5 ans a déjà beaucoup vécu et s'est trouvé selon une variabilité inouïe plus ou moins heureusement sollicité par son entourage, plus ou moins bénéficiaire d'expériences éducatives. Dans cette perspective il est facile d'admettre qu'une variation soudaine et importante des conditions de vie de cet enfant pourra invalider la prédiction.

Bien entendu cette conception est source de liberté et valorise l'action pédagogique: puisque la prédiction peut mentir, tâchons de faire mentir les mauvaises prédictions. Faut-il ajouter que lorsque notre Batterie Prédictive ne sert qu'à déterminer l'orientation d'un enfant, par exemple on maintien en grande section de Maternelle ou, tout au contraire son passage précole en première année (CP) ou encore son admission dans une classe spéciale, l'instrument et la méthode des tests dont il se réclame, sont trahis. Si un test aide à définir et à comprendre une situation personnelle d'écolier, il vaut finalement par les suggestions favorables à son évolution qu'il apporte.

Aussi, la nécessité de mieux saisir l'action pédagogique vécue par l'écolier jour après jour s'est imposée à nous. Cela nous a conduit dans les classes de première année, pendant leur fonctionement banal, afin d'observer tel et tel écoliers en train d'apprendre à lire.

Par chance nous avons dégagé un facteur puisamment explicatif du devenir des prédictions et que nous désignais par le sigle ALPECLE, en français: activité laborieuse personnelle de l'écolier en contact visuel avec la langue écrite. Plusieurs relations ont été solidement établies:

1—l'ALPECLE varie entre les élèves d'une même classe, mais bien davantage d'une classe à l'autre, d'un maître à l'autre, tant et si bien qu'on peut faire de cette ALPECLE une estimation, un indice caractéristique de toute action pédagogique.

2—une forte corrélation s'est révélée entre l'ALPECLE moyenne de chaque classe et la rentabilité de cette classe évaluée en fonction des acquisitions des élèves rapportées à leurs possibilités de déparer.

3—enfin l'ALPECLE rend compte de la plus ou moins grande validité des prédictions. Si on oppose les classes en deux groupes selon leur rentabilité, on constate que la validité des prédictions est beaucoup plus élévée dans les classes à forte rentabilité (qui sont aussi, rappelons-le, les classes a forte ALPECLE moyenne). Ainsi il y a des classes ou practiquement toutes les prédictions se réalisent sauf les mauvaises et d'autres où seules les mauvaises prédictions se réalisent, toute prédiction étant démeurée ignorée des maîtres.

Parce que trop souvent maintenue dans la pénurie, l'action scolaire est loin d'avoir révélé à tous ses possibilités de réduction des carences psychologiques constituées par les manques de stimulation éducative familiale. Ne retenais que l'optimisme qui se dégage de cette démonstration de la puissance potentielle de l'école fondamentale.

2. *Notre deuxième résultat porte atteinte à la notion courante de dyslexie*

De notre population d'expérience forte de 300 enfants de première année, nous avons dégagé les cas de contradiction les plus flagrants entre la prédiction de l'apprentissage de la lecture et sa réalisation.

—un groupe de 14 écoliers était constitué par ceux qui avaient tout pour réussir et pourtant n'ont pas réussi c'étaient tous ceux et exclusivement ceux qui au départ présentaient à la fois un âge mental supérieur de plus de trois mois à l'âge réel ainsi que le degré de prédiction de l'apprentissage de la lecture le plus favorable, et qui cependant en fin d'année n'atteignaient pas à notre épreuve de contrôle (Batterie de Lecture) le score de 38 pts critère du "savoir tout juste lire." Déjà, la plupart de ces enfants passaient alas pour dyslexiques.

—à l'opposé, ceux qui n'avaient rien pour réussir et qui pourtant atteignaient les fameux 38 pts en fin d'année, au nombre de 13, ils présentaient au départ un âge mental inférieur à l'âge réel de plus de trois mois et leur score à la Batterie Prédictive laissait prévoir l'échec de l'apprentissage de la lecture.

Eh bien! Les élèves du premier groupe d'une part, et ceux du deuxième groupe d'autre part n'appartenaient pas aux mêmes classes les premiers étaient élèves de classes à faible ALPECLE moyenne et les seconds élèves de classes a forte ALPECLE moyenne. Ajoutons que nous n'avions dépisté chez les premiers aucun déficit électif commun à partir de leurs résultats partiels à la Batterie Prédictive, aucun "germe de dyslexie" en quelque sorte.

Ainsi, l'appartenance à la classe fréquentée—effet du hasard—avait grandement décidé des acquisitions de chaque élève et permettait d'expliquer la réussite imprévue des uns comme l'échec inattendu des autres. Par contre l'explication habituelle par l'hérédité, dédaigneuse de l'exploration fine de l'action pédagogique vécue par l'enfant, et qui projette dans son lointain passé devenu inaccessible la cause de son échec présent apparaît plus aventureuse que jamais.

On a trop dit que l'école, de toute façon, ne peut qu'arriver trop tard. C'est encore une conclusion optimiste.

3. *Le dernier résultat que nous présenterons intéresse la didactique de l'apprentissage de la lecture.*
Puisque l'ALPECLE constitue une estimation de la rentabilité à venir de la classe, tout accroissement de cette ALPECLE pourra être considéré comme traduisant un meilleur investissement pédagogique. Cela revient à chercher ce qui détermine l'ALPECLE.

Pour y parvenir nous avons tenté de dégager les faits didactiques communs aux classes à forte ALPECLE, opposés aux classes à faible ALPECLE. Ainsi ont été élaborées les recommandations suivantes dont l'objectif lointain n'est autre que de faire mentir les mauvaises prédictions:

* la querelle des méthodes, opposés traditionnellement au nom de leur adéquation aux processus psychologiques qui seraient devenus fonctionnels chez les élèves, est tout à fait vaine: nos classes extrêmement opposés du point de vue de la rentabilité se réclament de la même méthode. La même étiquette cautionne le meilleur et le pire.

* toute rencontre prématurée avec l'écrit présente des risques. De nombreux élèves de première année remarquables par leur faible

ALPECLE présentent des séquelles des tentatives de pédagogisme de plus en plus répandues dans nos grandes sections de maternelle au seul profit des quelques enfants favorises d'avance, et dont le principe est de faire acquérir n'importe quoi à n'importe qui, n'importe quand. La langue écrite y jouit d'une tel préstige que l'entraînement des enfants à l'imitation, aux discrimination perceptives, aux activités rythmiques et graphiques, à la compréhension à la pratique et à l'analyse du langage oral, à la représentation montale et au passage gradue du figuratif à l'abstrait et de l'indice au sigue, tout cela pour les autres, pour la plupart des élèves est escamoté. C'est que l'analyse de donnés familières par exemple d'énoncés verbaux (oraux) et l'analyse de la transcription abstraite (écrite) de ces énoncés correspondent à des niveaux de développement psychologique très nettement distincts. L'entraînement au premier type d'analyse peut sans doute développer l'habileté à exercer le second, mais de fort loin, au cours d'activités antérieurs d'un an de plusieurs années et non de quelques minutes.

Développer l'aptitude à apprendre à lire n'est pas apprendre à lire. Les contenus des activités appropriés ne se confondent pas et un risque grave réside dans l'introduction prématurée de fragments d'écrit dans les matériels d'observation correspondant aux activités préparatives à l'apprentissage de la lecture.

* Même si on a su préparer le moment de proposer l'observation de fragments d'écrit, une autre practique se révèle redoutable: la profusion. Considérons les clefs de l'apprentissage de la lecture. Ce ne sont pas les lettres mais les relations (beaucoup plus nombreuses que les lettres) entre phonèmes et graphèmes. L'importance de la parfaite connaissance de ces clefs est évidente tant pour la maîtrise de l'orthographe phonétique que pour le déchiffrage en lecture. Avec la méthode dite "naturelle" de plus en plus pratiquée en France, on ne peut concevoir processus plus intelligent pour assurer l'acquisition de ces clefs que celui par lequel les élèves les dégagent, tels des "invariants," à partir de la confrontation et de l'analyse de fragments significants de langue écrite. Elles sont ce qui est "pareil" à la fois pour l'œil et pour l'oreille, malgré les contextes différents, visuel, sonore, voire affectif.

Cependant, cette façon de définir les clefs implique que se résolve vite le flou initial qui caractérise toute perception enfantine, car il faut craindre d'installer les enfants dans le flou. Or, c'est souvent ce qui se passe: les accumulations quelconques et approximatives de proposition provoquent dans l'esprit des élèves une superposition d'images syncrétiques de mots d'où aucune connaissance nette ne peut surgir. Tant qu'un enfant ne sait pas écrire sans modèle les mots qu'il cherche à comparer et à analyser, il peut manipuler des étiquettes mais il ne peut opérer, faute d'intériorisation de représentation mentale des donnés.

L'analyse est une activité mentale et ne saurait se réduire à l'usage des ciseaux.

Plus le monde réel est riche et complexe (TV comprise) plus il importe que l'école aide les enfants à filtrer, à structurer les informations chaotiques et informelles qui les assaillent.

Le plus nécessaire des filtrages (le corpus de langue écrite destiné à l'apprentissage de la lecture ne peut être que de volume très réduit) contredit la mode en faveur de l'occasionnel, de l'imprégnation de la profusion. La plupart des manuels le montrent bien: on profite de l'apprentissage de la lecture pour envisager toutes sortes d'acquisitions et en particulier pour enrichir le vocabulaire et la syntaxe, comme si l'apprentissage de la lecture n'était pas en soi assez difficile et comme si l'acquisition de l'écrit ne devait pas se fonder sur la pratique de l'oral.

En fait, seules certaines expressions des élèves les moins avances peuvent sans risque servir à apprendre à lire à tous.

Sans doute quelques dizaines de mots ne sauraient suffire à la définition de toutes les relations phonèmes-graphèmes, mais exiger que chaque combinaison soit extraite par analyse et chaque syllabe étudiée pour elle-même, c'est négliger les possibilités d'extension que les enfants présentent et les effets éducatifs de leurs découvertes.

* La brièveté des mots de référence et leur sobriété d'écriture et de groupement tout comme leur ensemble réduit et leur origine très familière pour tous, conditionnement l'appropriation et l'exploitation du capital acquis en commun pour les élèves du même collectif. Reste à savoir si ce collectif se confond avec la classe entière on correspond à l'un des groupes au sein de la classe.

* La personnalisation de l'action pédagogique, qui jouit partout d'un préjugé favorable, demeure une illusion ou une espérance. Alas que les maîtres, comme tous les travailleurs, recherchent de meilleures conditions de travail et répugnent à affronter la stratégie de la conduite simultanée de plusieurs groupes, l'homogénéité des âges réels constitue la base du groupement des élèves par classe plus responsable de l'accentuation des différences que de l'égalisation des chances. Ce sont les élèves d'avance le plus évolués qui présentent les durés et les vaux à l'ALPECLE les plus élevés. Les "faibles" végètent à leur ombre. Ce processus conservateur à pour effet d'accroitre la validité des prédictions, ce n'est pas une raison pour ne pas le dénoncer.

Enfin, alas que les séquences d'ALPECLE ne dépassent qu'exceptionnellement 2mn, et que la durée moyenne d'une séquence n'est que de 305, il importe de préférer aux séances de travail qui s'étalent de façon monotone et homogène souvent sur plus d'une demie-heure une pluralité d'activités coordainés et poursuivant le même objectif, mais cependant très variées: orales manipules ou graphiques, collectives ou individuelles, incitant à l'immobilité ou au mouvement.

La préparation psychologique à l'apprentissage, les filtrages des corpus d'écrit digues de servir à apprendre à lire, la solide mémorisation des mots, qui les constituent, l'organisation de leur traîtement en vue de la définition des clefs de la lecture par les enfants eux-mêmes, la garanté du plein emploi des possibilités dynamiques de chacun, ces réalités sont autant de déterminants de l'ALPECLE ainsi que des facteurs de rentabilité de l'action pédagogique scolaire. Elles soulignent l'anachronisme de la querelle des méthodes encore fondée sur l'opposition des processus analytique et synthétique.

Je voudrais terminer par un appel: il revient à notre Association Internationale de constituer une commission qui serait chargée d'élaborer une fiche signalétique dont les rubriques pourraient s'inspirer des critères que nous venons d'évoquer. Les auteurs et les éditeurs de méthodes seraient tenus de s'en servir pour définir après expérimentation, leurs produits didactiques, chiffres contrôlés à l'appui. Les usagers pourraient alors mieux ajuster leur action aux besoins changeants des élèves dont ils ont la charge, à leur goûts et à leur compétences.

Alas que dans les sciences dites exactes, fécondes comme on sait, les définitions sont depuis longtemps opératoires, objectives, précises et coordonnés dans le domaine de l'éducation, elles demeurent descriptives, subjectives, floues, et isolées. Nous savons combien les premières tentatives, relatives à l'aptitude à apprendre à lire et aux degrés successifs du "savoir lire" rencontrent de résistances farouches. Ne nous décourageons pas; proclamons notre besoin de produits pédagogiques et de moyens d'approche de l'action pédagogique qui soient de véritable outils de communication et de recherche.

Effects of Early Intervention Programs

Doris Roettger
Drake University
Des Moines, Iowa
United States of America

During the past decade, we have seen increased emphasis on early childhood education in the United States. It has become axiomatic that the early years in a child's life are a critical period of growth that determines the potential for future development. According to Hunt (9), children's encounters with their environment during this period should be regulated to achieve a faster rate of intellectual development and a higher level of intellectual capacity. Bloom (3) has suggested that 50 percent of the intelligence measured at the age of seventeen was developed by the age of four and another 30 percent by the age of eight. This emphasis on the critical role of early experiences has contributed significantly to the movement toward early intervention.

Since the early 1960s, much concern has been directed toward the educational performance of minority and lower-class children. Coleman (4) found that, as early as first grade, children from low socioeconomic backgrounds scored significantly lower on most measures of school achievement than children from higher socioeconomic backgrounds. He observed that this gap widened as children moved through the grades. There is a concensus that failure is almost inevitable for the many children who come to school poorly prepared because of their impoverished environment.

Much attention has been focused on language deprivation. Deutsch (5) observed that children of low socioeconomic groups lack the knowledge of context and of syntactical regularities which lead to comprehension of language sequences. Bereiter and Engelman (1) concluded that disadvantaged children master language which is adequate for maintaining social relationships and which are satisfactory for meeting their social and material needs; however, they do not master the cognitive uses of language. What is lacking is use of language used in school to explain, to describe, to inquire, to analyze, and to compare. One of the special weaknesses in language development of lower-class children is the tendency to treat sentences as a "giant word" which cannot be taken apart and recombined. A second weakness, which may be an outgrowth of the first, is the lack of use of structure words. The prevalence of this so-called language deficiency has become one of the bases for large scale intervention programs.

In this discussion of the effects of early intervention programs, the central question is: "Can early intervention counteract the effects of deprivation?" In answering this question, other questions must be asked. "Is incidental learning or direct instruction more effective?" "Should emphasis be on cognitive learning or should attention be given to the development of the whole child?" "Should parents be involved in early intervention programs?" Early intervention programs have become varied and sometimes confusing. It's almost like Alice's response when the caterpiller asked, "Who are you?" Said Alice, "I hardly know sir, just at present. At least I know who I was when I got up this morning, but I think I must have been changed several times since then."

In this paper I will describe various curriculum models for early intervention programs, identify the critical variations among them, and assess their effectiveness. Most preschools can be placed into one of the following categories: structured cognitive, programed or academic skills model, structured environment, and child-centered.

STRUCTURED COGNITIVE PROGRAMS

In the structured cognitive programs, the structure is derived from the programs' clearly stated goals for specific cognitive and language development (17). The curriculum focuses on the underlying processes of thinking and emphasizes that learning results from direct experience and action by the child. The teacher has clear guidelines of how the program is to be organized. Teacher planned situations or activities focus on improving oral language abilities, memory, concept formation, and problem solving.

One of the earliest structured cognitive programs was the Early Training Project conducted by Gray and Klaus (6, 7). They attempted to offset progressive retardation of black children living in deprived circumstances. Their intention was to make the intervention developmental rather than remedial. The criteria for judging the effectiveness of the program were performance scores on intelligence tests and reading achievement tests. The experimenters set up four groups of children: two experimental groups and one control group. One experimental group had three summers of preschool and a second group had two summers of preschool. The summer activities were planned around two categories of variables: *attitudes* relating to achievement (achievement motivation, persistence, interest in school-type activities) and *aptitudes* relating to achievement (perceptual development and the development of concepts and language). Between the summer sessions, a project teacher visited weekly the homes of both groups. One of the purposes of the visits was to involve mother and child in activities similar to those of the summer. The control groups consisted of a local group and a group in a nearby community. Both groups took all the tests but had no intervention program.

Three years after the end of intervention, the two experimental groups remained significantly superior to the two control groups in their performance on the Stanford Binet intelligence test. At the end of first grade, the experimental children scored significantly higher than the control children on the three reading subtests of the Metropolitan Achievement Test, and at the end of second grade they were significantly superior on the word knowledge and reading subtests. While there was no significant difference between the experimental and control groups at the end of fourth grade, there was a suggestion of residual effect, since in six of seven comparisons the experimental group was superior. It is a remarkable achievement to have maintained an impact on the intellectual development through the seventh year of a study and four years after formal intervention.

In the Ypsilanti Early Education Project, three- and four-year-old children attended a Piagetian cognitively oriented preschool for two years (11, 17). Verbal stimulation and interaction, sociodramatic play, and the learning of concepts were considered more important than social behavior and other concerns of traditional nursery school programs. The families of these children received weekly home visits. Parents were encouraged to participate in the instruction of their children and to attend group meetings. A control group received no special educational services. At the beginning of the program there was no significant difference on the Stanford Binet between the experimental and control groups. When retested at the end of kindergarten, the experimental group scored significantly higher, but by the end of first grade the scores of the two groups were essentially the same. However, the experimental group scored higher than the control group on the California Achievement Test at the end of the second and third grades. In addition, elementary teachers rated the experimental group higher than the control group in academic, social, and emotional development.

PROGRAMED ACADEMIC SKILLS PROGRAMS

A more rigidly structured type of program is the programed or the academic skills model. The most widely used program of this type is that developed by Bereiter and Engleman (1), which is based on the premise that culturally deprived children need direct training to overcome their backwardness in skills necessary for later academic success. The area of greatest deficiency is their use of formal language. The teacher directs all activities and the children participate in highly structured, prescribed activities.

STRUCTURED ENVIRONMENT PROGRAMS

A third approach to intervention is a structured environment best exemplified by a Montessori curriculum. The program stresses that "children must be in touch with reality through manual activity" (15). It provides the children with self-directed and self-selected cognitive activities. Control comes from the organization of the environment rather than from the teacher as in a structured cognitive approach. The teacher is a moderator between children and materials. Kohlberg (13) found a significant increase in IQ scores in a year-long intervention program using a Montessori curriculum.

CHILD CENTERED PROGRAMS

The bulk of traditional preschool programs found on college campuses and in Headstart projects are child centered. These curricula tend to focus on the development of the whole child. The hallmark of a child centered curriculum is an open classroom where children are encouraged to express their interests and help create their own environments. The teacher capitalizes on informal experiences for learning. Considerable attention is given to social adjustment and emotional development through imitation of adult roles (17).

Evaluation studies of preschool intervention programs have primarily compared a single program with a control group which has not been involved in the program. Such studies, even when they are adequately designed, allow only the most tenuous comparisons between programs because each program is evaluated by a different experiment and conducted in a different location with a different population and with different examiners. There have been a few long ranged studies which compared different types of preschool programs using experimental procedures designed to maximize comparability of results.

COMPARISONS OF DIFFERENT KINDS OF PROGRAMS

The Ypsilanti Preschool Curriculum Demonstration Project was established to study the effectiveness of three different kinds of programs (17). The programs selected were a cognitively oriented Piagetian program, a language training program following the Bereiter and Engelman Curriculum, and a unit based curriculum which emphasized social-emotional goals. After the first year, the initial findings indicated no significant differences among the three curricula on almost all measures. These measures included the Stanford Binet, classroom observations, and ratings of children by teachers and independent examiners. At the end of the second year, the results were almost the same. By the third year of the study, while there were no significant differences, the unit-based program was not matching the record it had established during the first year. This was especially true on the Stanford-Binet, which was the cognitive measure.

Karnes (12) compared the Karnes' Ameliorative program, which was a structured cognitive program, with a Bereiter-Engelman program and a traditional program with an emphasis on language development. The participants were all lower-class children. In addition, a traditional program with emphasis on psychosocial development was compared with a traditional Montessori program. The performance of the children in the Ameliorative and in the Bereiter-Engleman program was significantly better than the performance of the children in the two traditional programs and the Montessori group on the Stanford-Binet, ITPA, and Metropolitan Readiness Test. A more recent review by Bissell (2) of cognitive structured, academic skills and child-centered curricula reaches the same conclusion. Preschool programs with specific emphasis on language development and with teacher-directed strategies that provide structured activities fostering cognitive growth are more effective in producing cognitive gains for disadvantaged children than are programs lacking these characteristics.

Now let us turn our attention to Project Head Start, a major government effort to provide comprehensive intervention for preschool children. Head Start sought to bring about "greater social competence" in disadvantaged children (18). Parents and community members have been involved in planning and evaluation, and they are used as aides and volunteers. Focusing on the development of the whole child, Head Start has attempted to enhance a child's physical well being, his self-concept, his motivation, and his emotional and intellectual development.

Within federal guidelines, each Head Start site has established its own program. Many projects have adopted a traditional nursery school approach, emphasizing positive self-concept and social interaction. However, many reflect considerable preoccupation with school readiness, emphasizing that a child be able to speak in sentences, name colors, know his address, and sort shapes.

Standardized measures of performance such as IQ scores, achievement tests, and checklists of skills have been widely used by local sites for assessing the effectiveness of Head Start programs. However, evaluating the effect of the total program nationally has been difficult because of the wide variance in objectives, program delineation, and evaluation procedures.

Currently, the Educational Testing Service is conducting a longitudinal evaluation of Head Start children (16). The study is attempting to answer two questions: What are the components of early education that are associated with cognitive, personal, and social development of disadvantaged children? and What are the environmental and background variables that moderate these associations? The population was identified prior to the collection of data and is drawn nationally from four dispersed geographic regions. Information is being gathered on the family, teacher, classroom, community, and child. The emphasis is on the parent/child and teacher/child interactions, modes of information processing, influence techniques, and reinforcement strategies. The ETS study will follow the same children for five years to determine the degree to which primary grade curricula are congruent with, and capitalize on, what the child has learned in Head Start. The first group of children were in Head Start in 1969-1970. The final testing should have been completed in the spring of 1974.

The preliminary findings are that 75 percent of the children eligible for Head Start attended. It was also determined that these children performed significantly less well on a variety of cognitive tasks than those children who attended other preschools or no known preschool prior to their enrollment in Head Start. The findings also indicated that at the age of four the affective domain may not be highly differentiated. There is, however, strong evidence for differentiated personal-social characteristics. An important finding was that there was a range of variation in performance. Children from low income families exhibited a wide range of cognitive, personal-social, and perceptual functioning.

In summarizing the studies, questions must be asked in assessing early intervention programs: Does intervention contribute to success in school? How lasting are the results?

The studies discussed indicate that it is essential that goals and objectives by specifically defined for intervention programs and that day-to-day activities be centered on objectives. Evidence cited suggests that structured programs (as opposed to a traditional environmental approach) can produce significant gains through the third grade.

Within specific programs, instructional procedures must be adapted to the needs of individual children. Programs must recognize the differences between children who make progress and those who do not. Attention should be directed to specific characteristics of programs, to the children participating in them, and the interaction of the two. Hunt (10) describes this as a proper match between a child's cognitive development level and specific learning tasks.

All too often, early intervention programs have been inadequately evaluated. Although they are part of a major federal effort, many Head Start programs have been poorly evaluated at the local level. Evaluation frequently has had a low priority at local sites, and the instruments used have had low predictive validity (8). While each year's group is evaluated, few long term studies have followed children through the grades as a basis for making necessary modifications in the programs.

IQ scores have been used frequently as a criterion for assessing the effectiveness of intervention. This appears to be inadequate. Lucco (14) suggests that upward shifts in IQ performance do not necessarily reflect the cognitive development required for abstract thinking.

Other aspects of early intervention programs may be questioned. Programs seem to be designed to prepare children for success in schools as they now exist. It seems unrealistic to expect gains to be maintained unless necessary adjustments are made in the curricula of elementary schools.

In addition, children from birth through five years of age will spend a relatively small amount of time in intervention programs. Thus, these programs in themselves cannot totally offset the results of deprivation. Parents must become involved to change the home environment of the child.

The past decade has been the emergence of early intervention programs on a wide scale. The challenge of the coming decade is the refinement of these programs on the basis of the results of evaluation.

REFERENCES
1. Bereiter, Carl, and Siegfried Engelman. *Teaching Disadvantaged Children in the Preschool.* Englewood Cliffs, New Jersey: Prentice-Hall, 1966.
2. Bissell, Joan. "Effects of Preschool Programs for Disadvantaged Children," in Joe Frost (Ed.), *Revisiting Early Childhood Education.* New York: Holt, Rinehart and Winston, 1973, 223-239.
3. Bloom, B. S. *Stability and Change in Human Characteristics.* New York: Wiley, 1964.
4. Coleman, J. S. *Equality of Educational Opportunity.* Washington, D.C.: Office of Education, 1966.
5. Deutsch, Martin, et al. *The Disadvantaged Child.* New York: Basic Books, 1967.
6. Gray, S. W., and R. A. Klaus. "An Experimental Preschool Program for Culturally Deprived Children," *Child Development,* 36 (December 1965), 887-898.
7. Gray, S. W., and R. A. Klaus. "The Early Training Project: A Seventh Year Report," *Child Development,* 41 (December 1970), 909-924.
8. Hoepfner, Ralph, Carolyn Stern, and Susan Nummedal. *CSE-ECRC Preschool/Kindergarten Test Evaluations.* Los Angeles, California: UCLA Graduate School of Education, 1971.

9. Hunt, J. McV. *Intelligence and Experience*. New York: Ronald Press, 1961.
10. Hunt, J. McV. "The Psychological Basis for Using Preschool Enrichment as an Antidote for Cultural Deprivation," *Merrill-Palmer Quarterly*, 10 (July 1964), 209-248.
11. Kamii, Constance. "A Sketch of the Piaget Deprived Preschool Curriculum Developed by the Ypsilanti Early Education Program," in Joe Frost (Ed.), *Revisiting Early Childhood Education*. New York: Holt, Rinehart and Winston, 1973, 150-165.
12. Karnes, M. B., A. S. Hodgins, and J. A. Teska. "An Evaluation of Two Preschool Programs for Disadvantaged Children: A Traditional and Highly Structured Experimental Preschool," *Exceptional Children*, 34 (May 1968), 667-676.
13. Kohlberg, L. "Montessori with the Culturally Disadvantaged," in R. D. Hess and R. M. Bear (Eds.), *Current Theory, Research, and Action*. Chicago: Aldine, 1968, 105-118.
14. Lucco, Alfred A. "Cognitive Development After Age Five: A Future Factor in the Failure of Early Intervention with the Urban Child," *American Journal of Orthopsychiatry*, 42 (October 1972), 847-856.
15. Orem, R. (Ed.). *A Montessori Handbook*. New York: Capricorn Books, 1966.
16. Shipman, Virginia. "Disadvantaged Children and Their First School Experiences," in Julian Stanley (Ed.), *Compensatory Education for Children, Ages 2 to 8*. Baltimore, Maryland: John Hopkins University Press, 1972, 22-66.
17. Weikart, David. "Relationship of Curriculum, Teaching, and Learning in Preschool Education," in J. C. Stanley (Ed.), *Preschool Programs for the Disadvantaged*.
18. Zigler, Edward F. "Project Headstart: Success or Failure?" *Children Today*, 2 (November-December 1972), 2-7, 36.

Adult Illiteracy in England and Wales

Margaret Bentovim
Adult Literacy Project
Liverpool University Settlement
Liverpool, England
and
Jenny Stevens
Literacy Project
Cambridge House
London, England

Illiteracy has traditionally been regarded as a problem which solely concerns the underdeveloped countries. Unesco estimated that in 1970, 783 million or 34.2 percent of the world's population aged fifteen and over were totally illiterate. In fact, Unesco (10) stated in 1966 that "The developed countries eliminated illiteracy during the second half of the nineteenth and early twentieth century." Compared to underdeveloped countries, the problem of illiteracy in the developed countries may seem insignificant, but it is, in fact, extremely alarming. Although the percentage of the population who are functionally illiterate is much smaller, the actual numbers concerned still run into millions. The very existence of illiteracy in highly developed, industrialised countries presents a challenge to the traditional assumption that illiteracy will disappear with the economic advance of Asia, Africa, and South and Latin America, and with the establishment of free, compulsory education.

The existence of illiteracy in developed countries is particularly evident in the United States where the Office of Education estimated in July 1973 that almost 19 million adult Americans were totally or functionally illiterate and another 7 million elementary and secondary school students had severe reading problems. The recognition of this problem resulted in the launching of a national Right to Read programme with the goal of eliminating adult illiteracy by 1980.

Only in the past year, has illiteracy become recognised as a major problem in Britain. It is now accepted that there are at least 2 million illiterate adults in England and Wales (22). This means that approximately 6 percent of the adult population is either unable to read or write at all or has a literacy level below that of an average nine-year-old child. This figure is not based on direct research since there has not been a national survey of reading attainment. It is based on the best related evidence of six surveys into reading standards carried out between 1948 and 1964 by the National Foundation for Educational Research (13, 23, 29), and on informed opinions of such authorities as Joyce Morris (22) and Peter Clyne (7). [For further information see *A Right to Read* (1).] It must be pointed out that these figures do not include those people who, although possessing reasonable competence in reading, cannot write and spell adequately. Nor do they include adults with a reading age of over nine years, since they are at present regarded as functionally literate by the NFER and the Department of Education and Science (DES). Yet, Unesco assesses functional literacy as equivalent to a reading age of thirteen years.

One good working definition of functional literacy is provided by the U.S. National Reading Centre: "A person is functionally literate when he has command of reading skills that permit him to go about his daily activities successfully, or to move about society normally, with comprehension of the usual printed expressions and messages he encounters."

In fact, in its analysis of readability levels, the British Association of Settlements found that labels and instructions on household products and various daily newspapers required a reading age of between fourteen and sixteen and one-half years. Government forms, including those for application for welfare benefits, required a reading age of between fourteen and a half and seventeen years. These are not esoteric documents but are examples of written material which people are required to deal with every day. Each one of these examples requires a reading age higher than the Unesco level of functional literacy. If the number of people who do not have a reading age of even thirteen years were added to the estimated 2 million adult illiterates, the figure would become more realistic and even more horrifying.

The English Right to Read campaign has been particularly concerned with the political ramifications of illiteracy. The British Association of Settlements (BAS), which has pioneered the Adult Literacy campaign, believes that literacy is a right. No one who is capable of learning to read should be denied the opportunity of doing so. Without this right, people are denied even the possibility of participating in decisions which affect them and their community. The right to and the acquisition of literacy are seen by BAS as part of the struggle to enable people to control their own lives. As such, it is compatible with the Unesco definition of literacy and is closely related to the Freire approach.

ILLITERACY AND THE INDIVIDUAL IN THE URBAN CONTEXT

The recognition of the economic importance of literacy as a productive factor for development in industry, commerce, and agriculture, is largely responsible for the present impetus to promote literacy programmes in underdeveloped countries. To this end, literacy programmes are increasingly being related to the occupational requirements of the countries concerned. The British situation is quite different, partly because of the comparatively smaller degree of illiteracy, and partly because the scope of the problem and its implications have not yet been fully appreciated by relevant agencies such as the Department of Employment. However, there is undoubtedly a growing awareness of the effect that the declining number of semi- and unskilled jobs is likely to have on the illiterate population.

An illiterate in a developed country feels a deep sense of shame about his inability to read. He is so acutely embarrassed about his illiteracy, that he may go to inordinate lengths to conceal his difficulty. Most illiterates do not confide in their own friends, in members of their immediate family, and in some cases (13 percent in one sample) not even in their own spouses. It is vital that literacy programmes seek to erase this sense of shame and embarrassment which stems from a concept of personal failure and inadequacy. Until the illiterate can place his illiteracy in a social and political context, and can accept that the failure is also that of the educational and social systems, he will not be able to come forward and demand a solution.

Those involved in English literacy schemes have become increasingly aware of the need to understand and draw upon the motivations of students (5). The student's own perception of the limitations that his illiteracy places upon him is a key factor. Undoubtedly, the work situation presents some of the most awkward and often insurmountable obstacles for the nonreading worker. Few illiterates have access to professional and intermediate occupations (Class 1 and 2—Registrar Generals' classification), but many (46 percent of one sample) are heavily involved in skilled occupations (Class 3), which involve varying amounts of reading and writing. Many (39 percent of one sample) are reliant on a spouse, friend, or colleague to help them with their reading and writing work commitments, and live in constant fear of ridicule or redundancy because of the possibility of discovery of their disability by employer or workmates (30).

In some cases, illiteracy may be not only a disability but also dangerous. One factory in Britain, which manufactures high explosives, has just realised the implications of illiteracy among its workers who are unable to read safety instructions.

Many illiterates seek tuition because of their wish to change jobs, or to seek or accept promotion to positions requiring literacy skills. Employment prospects are therefore limited for illiterates. For those who are unemployed or disabled, the situation is even more serious. Not only is their choice of jobs severely restricted, but British Employment

Exchanges now operate a system whereby vacancies are listed on cards to be read by prospective employees. Government Industrial Rehabilitation Units, which attempt to make workers employable by providing training in new skills, do not as yet provide tuition in reading and writing (3).

Apart from the work environment, there are many other areas of life which are difficult for the adult illiterate. Being illiterate means being continually reliant on someone else to read and write letters, to fill in forms, make a hire purchase agreement, or even write a cheque. The problems are even more severe for those who have spouses who are also illiterate. Most illiterates are especially conscious of their inability to read to their own children and to help them in their school work.

Almost every aspect of life in Britain involves literacy—from distinguishing which toilet to enter to reading the oath when serving on a jury. Francois (10) describes illiteracy as a bottleneck to development. In a developed society it is the individual's development, as well as that of his society, which is retarded by illiteracy.

SOME CAUSES OF ADULT ILLITERACY IN ENGLAND

Why then, since universal compulsory education is well established in Britain, does the problem of adult illiteracy exist? Although there has never been large scale research into adult illiteracy in Britain, there is an abundance of well-documented sociological and educational research whose findings confirm those of the writers. Illiteracy in England is basically a working-class problem and is untimately connected with socioeconomic background and the so-called cycle of deprivation. Illiterates tend to come from large families with a poor level of educational attainment. Their parents tend to have been unaware of their children's reading difficulties and most parents (60 percent of one sample) never approached the school about it.

Some illiterates have had specific difficulties, such as auditory, visual, or emotional problems which have militated against the easy acquisition of literacy skills. In the writers' experience, adult illiterates are often of average or above average intelligence. This is confirmed by the experience of the Army School of Preliminary Education. This is not to say that there are not sizeable numbers of illiterates, not included in the 6 percent statistic, who are in fact educationally or severely subnormal (27).

Although individual disabilities and home circumstances play an important part, adverse school conditions are at least equally responsible in preventing an individual from realising his full reading potential. Research indicates that while many children in junior schools are having serious difficulties with reading and may be several years behind, an alarming number of junior teachers have received no training in the teaching of reading (13). This fact, coupled with large classes, high teacher turnover, inadequate remedial facilities, and the traditional alienation of working-class parents from the schools (11), contributes to a situation in which an illiterate who has attended school regularly will fall behind and may never catch up.

THE STATE OF CURRENT LITERACY PROVISION IN ENGLAND

Until the past year there has been a marked unwillingness on the part of some local education authorities to recognise the existence and extent of adult illiteracy in Britain. Clyne (7) in his research for the Russell Committee of Enquiry into Adult Education, found that only about one-half of the local education authorities in England and Wales were making any kind of provision. More often than not, the provision available has been quite inappropriate. For example, it has been known for adult institutes to ask a student joining a literacy class to fill in an enrollment form.

At present, literacy provision is made in a variety of ways:

1. By local education authorities as part of their adult education provision or, occasionally, as part of the work of social service departments;

2. by independent bodies in partnership with local education authorities or financed by them either in part or in whole;

3. by entirely independent bodies;

4. by the education department of the home office in prisons or other penal institutions;

5. by the department of employment and a few rehabilitation units; and

6. by the armed forces.

It is estimated by Haviland (15) that, taking into account all these various forms of provision, not more than 10,000 and perhaps as few as 5,000 are receiving some kind of tuition. These estimates imply that, at best, one-half of 1 percent of adult illiterates and, at worst, no more than one-quarter of 1 percent, are being taught to read and write.

The English Right to Read campaign, initiated by BAS, maintains that in the final analysis it is the responsibility of statutory authorities to provide the facilities which will ensure that the chance for acquiring literacy skills is available to everyone. The situation is slowly beginning to improve since the inception of the English Right to Read campaign, but, as yet, provision is quite inadequate to meet the needs of the illiterate adult population.

THE ENGLISH RIGHT TO READ CAMPAIGN

The English Right to Read campaign began when individual Settlements (Settlements are independent action centres), some of which had been involved in operating literacy projects since 1963, came together in 1973 under the auspices of BAS in order to ensure that their work was reflected in social reform. To this end, a national conference "Status Illiterate—Prospects Zero" was held in November 1973. The aim of this conference was to draw attention to the extent of the problem, illustrate some of the root causes, and point out some of the individual and social effects. It was also intended to provide a forum for discussion and debate on the most efficient and effective provision for adult illiterates. The enormous interest in this, and in the transcript of proceedings subsequently published, indicated that many organisations and local education authorities had no conception of the problem of adult illiteracy. Having recognised this, the demand for more information and for guidance increased dramatically.

The BAS Literacy Steering Group decided to approach the problem in two ways. First, it plunged deeper into the campaign for the extension and improvement of provision. It did this by consulting with other national groups and, with their support, publishing a policy document, *A Right to Read* (1). It also convened a public meeting to establish a committee to press for the formation of a National Council for Literacy and for the readication of the problem of adult illiteracy by a target date of 1985. Second, the steering group took steps to enable those providing or contemplating the provision of tuition for adult illiterates with the opportunity to develop their own knowledge and expertise. To this end, a folder containing a blueprint for setting up a literacy scheme was prepared to meet immediate needs and two workshops, which were attended by 200 delegates from all over the country, were held in March and June 1974 (2).

The most recent development has been the support of the Department of Education and Science for the proposal to employ a BAS Literacy Organiser. This appointment is intended to work toward the adequate provision of flexible and effective tuition for adult illiterates and to ensure that the government assumes responsibility for national literacy development after a given period.

Although the campaign is relatively new, it has already been largely successful in achieving the minimal objectives it set for itself. However, the problem of adult illiteracy in Britain is unsolved and every effort must now be made to intensify the campaign in order to realise its long term objective of eradicating adult illiteracy in Britain by 1985.

REFERENCES

1. BAS Adult Literacy Group. *A Right to Read*, J. Harrison (Ed.). London: BAS, 1974.
2. BAS Adult Literacy Group. *Extent of Adult Illiteracy in England and Wales*. London: BAS, 1973.
3. Belbin, E., and R. M. Belbin. *Problems in Adult Retraining*. London: Heinemann, 1972.
4. Bentovim, M., and J. Stevens. *Policy Pointers*. London: BAS, 1973.
5. Bentovim, M., and R. J. Kedney (Eds.). *Aspects of Adult Illiteracy*. Liverpool: Merseyside Institute for Adult Education, 1974.
6. Clark, M. M. *Reading Difficulties in Schools*. Harmondsworth: Penguin, 1970.
7. Clyne, P. *The Disadvantaged Adult*. London: Longman, 1972.
8. Davids, R., N. Butler, and H. Goldstein. *From Birth to Seven*. London: Longman, 1972.
9. Douglas, J. W. B., J. M. Ross, and H. R. Simpson. *All Our Future*. London: Panther, 1971.
10. Francois, L. *The Right to Education*. Paris: Unesco, 1968.
11. Fraser, E. *Home Environment and the School*. London: ULP, 1959.
12. Gardner, K. "The State of Reading" in N. Smart (Ed.), *Crisis in the Classroom*. London: LPC, 1968.
13. Goodacre, E. J. *Reading in Infant Classes*. Slough: NFER, 1967.
14. Harman, D. "Illiteracy: An Overview," in A. Melnik and J. Merritt (Eds.), *Reading Today and Tomorrow*. London: ULP, 1972.
15. Haviland, R. M. *Provision for Adult Illiteracy in England*. Reading: University of Reading, 1973.
16. ILEA. *Evidence to Bullock Commission*. London: 1972.
17. Kellmer Pringle, M. L., N. R. Butler, and R. Davie. *11,000 Seven Year Olds*. London: Longman, 1966.
18. Kellmer Pringle, M. L. "Language Development and Reading Attainment of Deprived Children," in J. F. Reid (Ed.), *Reading Problems and Practices*. London: Ward Lock Educational, 1972.
19. Lovell, K., and M. E. Woosey. "Reading Disability, Nonverbal Reasoning, and Social Class," *Educational Research*, 6 (1964).
20. Malmquist, E. *Factors Related to Reading Disabilities in the First Grade of the Elementary School*. Stockholm: Malmquist and Wiksell, 1958.
21. Malmquist, E. "Reading: A Human Right and a Human Problem," in A. Melnik and J. Merritt (Eds.), *Reading Today and Tomorrow*. London: ULP, 1972.
22. Morris, J. "The Nature and Extent of Adult Illiteracy," *Transcript of BAS Status Illiterate Conference*. London: BAS, 1974.
23. Morris, J. *Standards and Progress in Reading*. Slough: NFER, 1966.
24. Morris, J. M. *Reading in the Primary School*. London: Newnes, 1959.
25. Plowden Report. *Children and Their Primary Schools*. London: HMSO, 1967.
26. *Reading Ability*. London: HMSO, 1950.
27. School of Preliminary Education. "The Army's Approach to the Problems of Soldiers with Reading Disabilities," evidence submitted to the Bullock Commission, 1972.
28. Southgate, V. "Reading and the Language Arts," submission to James Committee's inquiry into teacher training, 1971.
29. Start, K. B., and B. K. Wells. *The Trend of Reading Standards*. Windsor: NFER.
30. Stevens, J. "A Study of Certain Characteristics of a Sample of Illiterate Adults Approaching Cambridge House Literacy Scheme," unpublished dissertation. London: 1974.
31. Vernon, M. D. "The Effect of Emotional Factors on Learning to Read," in Jessie F. Reid (Ed.), *Reading Problems and Practices*. London: Ward Lock Educational, 1972.

A Cross National Study of Factors Related to Reading Achievement and Reading Disability

Gaston Blom
University of Colorado Medical Center
Denver, Colorado
United States of America

Mogens Jansen and Peter Allerup
Danish Institute of Educational Research
Copenhagen, Denmark

This cross national study emerged from two long standing interests of the senior author: One is content analyses of primer stories from various countries (2, 3, 25); the other is sex differences in reading behaviors (1).

In the United States, boys exceed girls in the extent and severity of reading disability; girls also have consistently higher reading achievement throughout the elementary grades. In 1972, an opportunity developed to find out if the same or different phenomena existed in other countries and what might be offered in explanation. This is a special advantage of comparative study, as pointed out by Bruner (6), Downing (8), Leong (17), Malmquist (18), and Thorndike (22). The senior author personally visited 32 reading specialists in 14 European countries to inquire about a series of questions that related to sex differences— prevalence and incidence of illiteracy, school dropouts, reading retardation, dyslexia, reading achievement, and other school issues. Limited objective data on these questions existed in some countries, but mostly impressions were gained in some of the countries. Yet, these were sophisticated impressions from professionals knowledgeable in the fields of reading and elementary education.

From the start, the professional visits involved discussions of issues broader than sex differences which were associated with reading. These issues could be grouped according to cultural, school, language, teacher, family, personality, biological, and political factors. Again, one was impressed by the sophisticated opinions of these reading specialists— opinions that were not available in publications and reports. Published and unpublished objective data, about reading in various countries, were obtained whenever possible (24, 16, 21). In addition, a review of published comparative studies was done which will be subsequently reported (5, 7, 8, 9, 10, 11, 12, 13, 15, 19, 20, 23, 24).

On the basis of the experiences and study, the authors formulated an opinion questionnaire on factors related to reading achievement and reading disability; and they were distributed to three reading professionals in each of 14 countries: Denmark, England, Finland, France, Greece, Iceland, Ireland, Italy, Norway, Scotland, Sweden, United States, USSR, and West Germany. All of the items on the questionnaire were in the English language. The authors tried to use words and thinking that were in common practice by reading specialists.

The questionnaire contained 162 scorable items that involved ratings, estimates, opinions, and objective data. The items were grouped according to the eight factors previously indicated. In this paper, the authors present some preliminary findings from these data. The results are based on a cluster analysis, a technique that made it possible to greatly reduce the data. The authors suggest some heuristic possibilities that were developed to look at countries which were found, by the use of this statistical method, to be similar to and different from each other.

There are, of course, many methodological questions that are posed by this type of study. One can wonder about reliability and validity issues in such data. Reliability will be discussed later in the paper. There are questions about definitions of terms, the use in questions of the English language only, the translation of responses into English, assumptions of common language and ways of thinking, and many others. The authors do not defend their work against these and other criticisms. It was our hope that a systematic collection of this information from qualified people would be helpful to those interested in comparative and national studies of reading. Such information could become the basis for developing and testing hypotheses. The data, it is hoped, may indicate trends within and across countries which could serve a useful purpose.

Preliminary findings are reported from 24 respondents in 12 countries (Denmark, England, Finland, France, Greece, Iceland, Ireland, Norway, Scotland, Sweden, United States, and West Germany), representing a reply rate of 67 percent. There were 21 male and 3 female respondents. They consisted of 2 educators, 4 school psychologists, 17 university professors, and 1 government administrator. In 3 of the 12 countries there were replies from only 1 respondent (France, Greece, and Scotland). Therefore, there were no reliability measures for these countries. The findings on respondents are indicated in Table I.

The data analyses and findings are presented in three sequential steps. The results from cluster analysis will be reported first. This led to ordering the 12 countries along a bipolar dimension of similarity to dissimilarity. Then, findings relative to sex differences will be presented using the similarity-dissimilarity dimension. Finally, some findings of special interest to the authors will be given in country-by-country comparison. The authors plan to relate these and other findings to published and unpublished national and comparative studies.

CLUSTER ANALYSIS

The data from the questionnaire could be viewed as consisting of twelve vectors, each vector representing a country with its elements being the answers to the 162 questionnaire items. The dimension of the vectors was 162, consisting of 71 main items and many subitems. Many ability tests result in the same kind of vector information; only in this instance, countries represented persons. However, the resemblance stops at this point since, in ability tests, the answers from a single person are customarily added to obtain a sum score as an apparent measure of the ability. In our case, with the questionnaire data from 12 countries similar data reduction was not possible.

In order to reduce the data, all of the 162 questionnaire items were assigned to 6 homogeneous groups named factors: 1) language, 2) country, 3) school, 4) teacher, 5) pupil, and 6) family. A number of the questionnaire items were assigned to more than one factor. The results were as follows: 72 - 1 factor items, 74 - 2 factor items, 14 - 3 factor items, 1 - 4 factor item and 1 open question item which could not be assigned to a factor. Of the 162 items, 24 had to be eliminated because of insufficient information. Very specific content had been requested in 18 of these 24 items. This left 138 items consisting of 60 - 1 factor items, 67 - 2 factor items, and 11 - 3 factor items. These procedures are indicated in Table 2.

Instead of 162 dimensions on each country vector, smaller dimensions were developed with items related to 1 of 6 factors: language, country, school, teacher, pupil, or family. Response patterns to the items for each factor for each country could then be interpreted. The response patterns were called profiles and the group of items on which a profile was constructed was the profile base. The identification of a single country and comparisons among the countries were carried out by means of profiles.

Profiles were developed for each country within each of the 6 factor areas. Cluster analysis was used to determine if a group of countries could be identified with very similar profiles; i.e., they were positioned closely and formed a group. The distance function used was the ordinary metric on two dimensions generalized to more dimensions. In addition, profiles from other countries were estimated as well connected to the group, far away from the group, or in no particular relationship to the group. The group does not represent a mean value, a center of gravity, or the most important group of countries. It defines a starting point for contrasting profiles. Through this clustering method, it was possible to plot relevant profiles in a simple graph, draw conclusions about the characteristics of a country, and evaluate differences between countries.

The original data from the questionnaire were translated to a set of new values to make the scoring more uniform and easier to read and to understand its content. Since different numbers of respondents from each country answered the questionnaire, disagreements and no answers existed on a number of items. In giving a score of a country to an item, some disagreement was indicated with an asterisk (e.g., two respondents agreed and a third scored the item quite differently). Complete disagreement and no answers were indicated with a bracket and a cautious interpolated score was calculated so that the country did not get an extreme weighting from one of its scores. A measure of reliability in relation to items was obtained in terms of reliability within a profile base. This was called the error index. It was also possible to evaluate the contribution to this index from each item in the profile base and in relation to countries in a group versus the other countries.

In Table 3 the number of items included in profiles for each country on each factor are indicated as well as error index information. While the error index was quite high for pupil (.201) and family (.237) factor items, it can be seen that the hard error (interpolated—indicating no answers and total disagreement) represented a small percentage in all factors. There are also items within factors which accounted for a large amount of the error.

LANGUAGE FACTOR

The procedure of analysis and interpretation will be illustrated by discussing the language factor. The cluster analysis for the language factor based on 17 items revealed a group consisting of England, Germany, Scotland, and the United States which were close to each other. Six of the 17 items contributed very little to the variation, such as irregular sound-symbol relations (items 31.1 and 31.2), number of letters in the alphabet (item 32), Roman alphabet (item 33), children write in print in the first grade (item 34) and script writing is introduced at a later grade (item 35.1). The exception was Greece which had a highly phonetic language, few sound-symbol irregularities, and a Greek alphabet with 24 letters.

The gestalt for the group included: 1) a somewhat high importance given to the language factor in reading retardation; 2) while mother tongue dialects existed to a considerable extent, they effected reading instruction to a low extent; 3) minority groups had more reading difficulty than the majority and binguality existed to some extent; 4) languages were considered relatively low phonetically; 5) there were relatively few hours given to language instruction in the first grade (mean of 1.13 hours per day); 6) script writing had a relatively low influence on reading achievement; 7) teaching other languages in the

Achievement and Disability

elementary grades had a relatively favorable effect on mother tongue instruction; and 8) language exposure in the home was related to a high extent to reading achievement.

Table 4 indicates the profile base and profiles of the group countries, Greece (far away country) and Denmark (well connected country). The well connected with the group countries were Denmark, Norway, and Sweden. At great distance from the group were France, Greece, and Ireland (far away countries). No relationship could be established for Finland and Iceland.

France had 4 discrepancies from the group out of 17 items, Greece 9 discrepancies and Ireland 5 discrepancies. As mentioned previously, the Greek language has 24 different symbols, sound-symbol regularities, and is considered highly phonetic. In addition, a large number of hours per day (2) and per week (12) are devoted to language instruction in the first grade. School attendance is 6 days a week for 32-34 weeks of the year. Teaching other languages in the elementary school affects mother tongue language unfavorably, perhaps because of quite different alphabets and sounds. Language as a factor in reading retardation is considered to be relatively low in importance.

OTHER FACTORS

Cluster analyses of the other 5 factors were also completed. These included family with 17 items, teacher with 16 items, country (nation) with 67 items, school with 52 items, and pupil with 44 items. All of these factors had a group with similar profiles, countries well connected to the group and countries far away from the group. In the school factor there were 2 distinct groups.

Some representative items in these 5 factors will be briefly mentioned to indicate their composition:

1. family factor—SES and minority status, average number of children, family mobility
2. teacher factor—class origin, salary and status in country, teacher training
3. country factor—sex role, amount of television, importance of preschool
4. school factor—starting school age, instructional methods, duration of school year
5. pupil factor—sex differences, personality, biological and genetic influences.

ALL FACTORS

It is possible to summarize these data on groups, well connected countries, and far away countries in relation to the six factors: language, country, school, teacher, family, and pupil. This is demonstrated in Table 5. Finland belonged to the group on 5 of the 6 factors with language being the exception. On the language factor it was neither well connected nor far away from the group. France was far away from the group on 5 of the 6 factors with family being the exception, while France was neither one of the group nor well connected.

A rank ordering of countries was done on the basis of group membership, well connected, and far away on all 6 factors. This is illustrated in Table 6. These data were plotted along a linear axis line representing similarity-dissimilarity. The results are demonstrated in Figure 7. These findings suggested that 7 of the 12 countries were more similar to each other, possibly sharing a Nordic similarity except for Greece, which was close to the others except for language. On the right side of the 0 in Figure 7, one can observe 4 countries that were quite dissimilar. Scotland was positioned between the groups on the similarity side of the axis.

These results from cluster analysis offer some possible new ways of looking at data about reading across nations. From a large number of items (137) assigned to 6 factors, groupings developed which could be rank ordered on a dimension of similarity-dissimilarity. When this dimension was related to incidence figures of illiteracy and reading retardation, some interesting findings emerged. The data are shown in Tables 8 and 9 where lower mean percentages existed for all illiteracy and retardation estimates in the 7 countries of the similar group. The 5 dissimilar group countries (Scotland, England, Ireland, United States, and France) had higher percentages. There were some exceptions to these trends.

AN EXAMINATION OF SEX DIFFERENCES

There were 18 items on the questionnaire which dealt with sex differences. The findings on these items have been grouped in a number of tables. Where countries are listed, they are placed in the order of similarity to dissimilarity previously mentioned.

Table 10 shows sex difference in relation to incidence and prevalence data on reading and dropouts. Nine countries had higher dropout rates for boys except for Scotland, the United States, and France where they were equal for boys and girls. There seems to be a trend in the entire group of countries for girls to exceed boys in reading achievement through the elementary grades. Boys start equalizing in late elementary grades so that by secondary school the overall picture of achievement becomes more equal.

Tables 11 and 12 illustrate findings on sex difference in relation to school, teacher, pupil, and country factors which may influence reading.

Table 11 shows that teacher attitudes were unfavorable toward boys in Sweden, Denmark, the United States, and France; the percentage of male teachers of the mother tongue was highest in Denmark, Greece, Ireland, and France and lowest in Finland, Sweden, Scotland, England, and the United States. Table 12 demonstrates that sex role orientation was rated traditional in Ireland; modern in Sweden, Denmark, and Scotland; and transitional in the other countries.

Table 12 relates 5 indices of reading achievement in children as to sex with 8 measures of factors that influence reading according to sex. Indices of reading achievement included illiteracy in children (item 2.2) and reading achievement at 4 points in time from the start of school to secondary school (items 4.1, 4.2, 4.3, 4.4). The number of times these indices favored boys>girls, girls>boys and both boys and girls were counted for each country. The results are shown at the top of Table 13 with Greece, Scotland, Ireland, the United States, and France showing different patterns from the other countries. France, Ireland, and the United States favored girls while Greece and Scotland favored both. Eight measures of school, country, teacher, and pupil factors in which sex differences are present included: percentage of male teachers (item 43), teacher attitudes towards boys and girls (items 49.5 and 49.6), biological factors (item 66), sex role orientation of the country (item 6), sex of authors of primers (item 18.4), and primer content appropriate to boy and girl interests (items 18.9 and 18.10). It was assumed that these measures would influence achievement (outcome) measures relative to the sexes. The results of counting the factor items favoring boys, girls and both are shown at the bottom of Table 13. The patterns of results may be interpreted as follows: countries favoring boys were Denmark, France, Germany, and Ireland; countries favoring girls were Finland, Norway, Sweden, and the United States; countries favoring boys and girls equally were England, Greece, Iceland, and Scotland. Somewhat direct relationships between influencing factors and indices of reading achievement were present in four countries. Greece and Scotland favored boys and girls equally in factors and indices. France and the United States favored girls more than boys in factors and indices. An exception was Ireland which favored boys in factors and girls in indices of reading achievement.

SOME SCHOOL AND COUNTRY FACTORS

Five questionnaire items on school and country factors are included in Table 14. The findings indicate a range in classroom size (i.e., number of children/class, item 19) from lowest in Denmark, Finland, Iceland, Norway, and Sweden to highest in Germany, Greece, and Ireland with England, France, Scotland, and the United States between. The lowest group corresponded to low population size countries (item 12.1) although small countries were represented in highest class size and between the extremes. Large population countries were between the extremes for the most part.

Another item (18.1) in Table 14 is whether reading textbooks are given to children or borrowed from school. Most of the countries gave children primers, the two exceptions being England and the United States. This was a small but interesting finding which may have important implications as to a country's attitudes toward literacy and children and the country's political-economic system. In England and the United States, textbook publishing is a profit making industry and school districts which purchase books largely from local funding, try to economize. What borrowing, rather than giving, books means to children can be conjectured. A book that is owned should have greater emotional significance and the chances are that a child under these circumstances will tend to read the book more often, and, therefore, get more practice.

In Table 15 there are 5 questionnaire items that relate to instructional stability: family moves (55), percentage of first grade children who change schools during a year (56), number of years a child has the same mother tongue language teacher (48), extent of central educational control (67), and degree of uniformity in primary education (68). The findings show greatest stability in Germany, Norway, Iceland, and Sweden and the least stability in England and the United States. Table 16 summarizes these data by totalling the number of items which reflect stability, relative stability and instability.

SUMMARY

The authors have presented some preliminary findings from a cross national questionnaire study of factors related to reading achievement and reading disability. Data have been presented from 12 countries represented by 24 respondents sophisticated in primary reading. Given the limitations of reliability and validity in the research method used and the resulting information, some results have been reported which are provocative of further study. The authors particularly call attention to the use of cluster analysis which makes it possible to indicate which countries do and do not resemble each other according to certain characteristics. This would appear to have considerable heuristic value. It has advantages over a country by country comparison in relation to specific items of information or a group of items.

Table 1.   Characteristics of Respondents to Questionnaire

Countries	Number of Respondents	Male Respondents	Female Respondents	Educators	School Psychol.	Univ. Profs.	Govt. Adm.
Finland	2	2	0	0	0	2	0
Germany	3	3	0	0	0	3	0
Norway	2	2	0	0	1	1	0
Iceland	2	2	0	0	1	1	0
Sweden	3	3	0	1	1	1	0
Denmark	3	2	1	1	1	1	0
Greece	1	1	0	0	0	0	1
Scotland	1	1	0	0	0	1	0
England	2	1	1	0	0	2	0
Ireland	2	2	0	0	0	2	0
United States of America	2	1	1	0	0	2	0
France	1	1	0	0	0	1	0
TOTALS 12	**24**	**21**	**3**	**2**	**4**	**17**	**1**

Table 2.   Procedures in Cluster Analysis

Assigned Factors	Number of Original Factor Items	Number of Final Factor Items
Language	72-1 factor	60-1 factor
Country	74-2 factors	67-2 factors
School	14-3 factors	11-3 factors
Teacher	1-4 factors	
Pupil	1- not assigned to factor	
Family	162 items	138 items

Table 3.   Reliability Measures on the Six Factors

Factors	Number of profile items	Error index	Asterisk % some disagree	Inter-polated % Blank & total disagree	Total errors	Number items contribute to errors
Teacher	16	.114	10%	1%	22	2 items with 7 errors
Language	17	.123	6%	7%	26	3 items with 10 errors
School	41	.163	11%	5%	79	5 items with 22 errors
Country	59	.177	13%	3%	126	7 items with 46 errors
Pupil	40	.201	12%	6%	89	5 items with 42 errors
Family	17	.237	16%	8%	48	3 items with 33 errors

Table 4. Profile Base—Language Factor

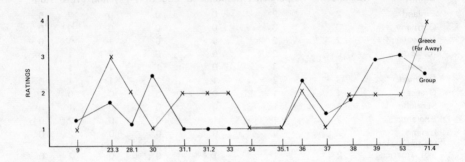

Profile Items

Group	1.3	1.8	1.1	2.6	1	1	1	1	1	2.3	1.4	1.9	2.9	3	2.5
Denmark	1	2	2	3	1	1	1	1	1	2	2	2	3	3	2
Greece	1	3	2	1	2	2	2	1	1	2	1	2	2	2	4

Table 5. Constellations of Countries in Relation to Factors

Factors	Group	Well Connected	Far Away
Language	England, Germany, Scotland, United States of America	Denmark, Norway, Sweden	France, Greece, Ireland
Country	Denmark, Finland, Norway, Sweden	Germany, Greece, Iceland	England, France, United States of America
School	I: Denmark, Finland, Iceland, Norway, Sweden	Scotland	England, France, United States of America
	II: Germany, Greece, Ireland		
Teacher	Finland, Germany, Scotland, Sweden	England, Greece, Norway	Denmark, France, Ireland
Family	Finland, Greece, Iceland	Denmark, Germany, Norway	Ireland, Scotland, Sweden, United States of America
Pupils	Finland, Germany, Iceland, Norway	Denmark, Sweden	France, Scotland, United States of America

Achievement and Disability

Table 6. Number of Times Each Country Present in Group and Other Positions—All Six Factors

Rank Order	Group	Well Connected	Far Away
1. Finland	5	0	0
2. West Germany	4	2	0
3. Norway	3	3	0
4. Iceland	3	1 (country)	0
5. Sweden	3	2	1 (family)
6. Denmark	2	3	1 (teacher)
7. Greece	2	2	1 (language)
8. Scotland	2	1 (school)	2 (family & pupils)
9. England	1 (language)	1 (teacher)	2 (country & school)
10. Ireland	1 (school)	0	3
11. United States of America	1 (language)	0	4
12. France	0	0	5

Table 7. Linear Relationship of Countries Along Similarity—Dissimilarity Axis

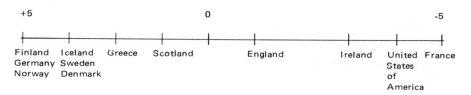

Table 8. Illiteracy and Retardation Rates in Relation to Similar and Dissimilar Countries

Country	Illiteracy Adults	Illiteracy Children	Reading Retardation Overall	Reading Retardation Children	Reading Retardation Adults
Finland	1%	<1%	5-10% (7.5%)	5-10% (7.5%)	5-10% (7.5%)
Germany	4%	2%	10-15% (12.5%)	5-10% (7.5%)	10-15% (12.5%)
Norway	<1%	<1%	5-10% (7.5%)	10-15% (12.5%)	5-10% (7.5%)
Iceland	3%	6%	5-10% (7.5%)	10% (10%)	5% (5%)
Sweden	1%	0%	5-10% (7.5%)	5-10% (7.5%)	5-10% (7.5%)
Denmark	1%	4%	5-10% (7.5%)	10-15% (12.5%)	5-10% (7.5%)
Greece	14%	1.4%	[10-15%] (12.5%)	<5% (5%)	10-15% (12.5%)
mean%	3.6%	2.2%	(8.9%)	(8.9%)	(8.6%)
Scotland	2%	2%	10-15% (12.5%)	10-15% (12.5%)	10-15% (12.5%)
England	5%	6%	15-20% (17.5%)	20-25% (22.5%)	20-25% (22.5%)
Ireland	7%	8%	5-10% (7.5%)	5-10% (7.5%)	5-10% (7.5%)
United States of America	20%	15%	20% (20%)	15% (15%)	20% (20%)
France	1%	1%	10-15% (12.5%)	5-10% (7.5%)	10-15% (12.5%)
mean%	7%	6.4%	(14%)	(13%)	(15%)

Table 9. Illiteracy and Reading Retardation Rates

	Illiteracy		Reading Retardation		
Similar Countries	Adults	Children	Overall	Children	Adults
Finland, Germany, Norway, Iceland, Sweden, Denmark, Greece					
mean %	3.6%	2.2%	8.9%	8.9%	8.6%
range	1-14%	0-6%	5-15%	5-15%	5-15%
Dissimilar Countries					
Scotland, England, Ireland, United States of America, France					
mean %	7%	6.4%	14%	13%	15%
range	1-20%	1-15%	5-20%	5-25%	5-25%

Table 10. Sex Differences in Relation to Incidence and Prevalence Data on Reading

Item		Fin	Ger	Nor	Ice	Swe	Den	Gre	Sco	Eng	Ire	USA	Fra
2.1	Illiteracy in adults	=	=	=	=	>M	>F	>F	>M	>M	>M	>M	=
2.2	Illiteracy in children	=	=	>F	=	>M	=	=	>M	>M	>M	>M	>M
4.1	Reading achievement start school	>F	=	>F	>F	>F	>F	=	>F	=	>F	>F	=
4.2	Reading achievement and first grade	>F	=	>F	>F	>F	>F	=	>F	>F	>F	>F	>F
4.3	Reading achievement late elementary	=	>F	>F	>F	=	>F	=	>M	=	=	>F	>F
4.4	Reading achievement secondary school	=	>F	=	=	=	=	=	>M	>F	>M	=	>F
5	School dropouts	>M	>M	>M	>M	>M	>M	>M	=	>M	>M	=	=

Code: >M more frequent or higher in males
= same frequency or equal in males and females
>F more frequent or higher in females

Table 11. Sex Differences in Relation to Teacher and Pupil Factors

Item		Fin	Ger	Nor	Ice	Swe	Den	Gre	Sco	Eng	Ire	USA	Fra
43	% male teacher teach reading first grade	3%	7%	5%	7%	1%	35%	42%	1%	1%	25%	3%	32%
49.5	First grade teacher attitudes towards boys	Fav	Fav	F-U	Fav	Un	Un	Fav	F-U	F-U	Fav	Un	Un
49.6	First grade teacher attitudes towards girls	Fav	F-U	Fav	Fav	Fav	F-U	Fav	F-U	F-U	Fav	Fav	Fav
66	Biological factors effect boys more	Yes	No	Y-N	Yes	Yes	No	No	No	No	Yes	Yes	No
71.1	Relative importance of sex difference as a factor in reading retardation	Lo	Lo	Hi	Lo	Hi	Lo	Hi	Lo	M	Lo	M	Lo

Codes: Yes, No, Yes-No (Y-N)
Hi - high, Lo - Low, M - medium
Fav - favorable, Un - unfavorable, F-U - mixed

Table 12. Sex Differences in Relation to Country Factors

Items		Fin	Ger	Nor	Ice	Swe	Den	Gre	Sco	Eng	Ire	USA	Fra
							Countries						
6	Sex role orientation in country	Tras	Tras	Tras	Tras	Mod	Mod	Tras	Mod	Tras	Trad	Tras	Tras
18.4	Sex of authors of primers	>F	>M	>F	>M	=	=	=	=	>F	>M	>M	=
18.9	Primers appropriate to girl interest	Yes	No	No	No	Yes	Yes	Yes	Yes	No	No	Yes	No
18.10	Primers appropriate to boy interest	Yes	Yes	Yes	Yes	Yes	Yes	Yes	Yes	No	Yes	No	No

Codes: Tras - transitional
     Trad - traditional
     Mod - modern

M - more males
= - males and females equal
F - more females

Table 13. Sex Differences
Current Indices of Reading Achievement X Current Factors that Influence Reading

Indices of Reading Achievement – 5 items	Fin	Ger	Nor	Ice	Swe	Den	Gre	Sco	Eng	Ire	USA	Fra
						Countries						
Favor boys > girls	0	0	0	0	0	0	0	2	0	1	0	0
Favor girls > boys	2	2	3	3	3	3	0	3	3	3	4	4
Favor both equally	3	3	2	2	2	2	5	0	2	1	1	1

X

Factors that influence Reading – 8 Items	Fin	Ger	Nor	Ice	Swe	Den	Gre	Sco	Eng	Ire	USA	Fra
Favor boys > girls	1	5	1	3	0	3	2	2	1	5	1	3
Favor girls > boys	3	1	4	2	4	1	1	1	2	2	4	1
Favor both equally	4	2	3	3	4	4	5	5	5	1	3	4

Table 14. Some School and Country Factors

Item		Fin	Ger	Nor	Ice	Swe	Den	Gre	Sco	Eng	Ire	ISA	Fra
							Countries						
12.1	Total population in millions	4.6	60	3.5	.21	8	5	8.7	5	55	2.9	250	50
19	Average first grade class size	20-25	>35	20-25	20-25	20-25	20-25	30-35	25-30	25-30	>35	25-30	25-30
13.1	Age officially start school	7	6	6	7	7	7	6	5	5	6	6	7
13.2	Should it be earlier, same, later	E	E	?	E	E	S	S	S	S	E	E	?
18.1	Reading textbooks given to children or borrowed from school	Giv	Giv	Giv	Giv	Giv	G/B	Giv	Giv	Bor	Giv	Bor	Giv

Codes: Giv - given
     G/B - given and borrowed
     Bor - borrowed

E - earlier
S - same
? - uncertain

Table 15. Instructional Stability in Relation to Family, School, and Country Factors

Items		Countries											
		Fin	Ger	Nor	Ice	Swe	Den	Gre	Sco	Eng	Ire	USA	Fra
55	Family mobility (mores)	+++	+	+	+++	++	++	++	+	+++	++	+++	++
56	First grade children change schools	10%	5-10%	10%	5-10%	5-10%	10-15%	.5%	5%	10-30%	5%	25-30%	15-20%
48	Years child has same teacher in mother tongue language	1-2	2-3	2-3	2-3	2-3	2-3	1-2	1-2	1	1	1	1
67	Extent primary education under central control	Cont	Cont	Cont	Cont	Cont	Cont	Cont	Some Cont	Adv	Cont	Adv	Cont
68	Degree of uniformity in primary education throughout country	Unif	Unif	Unif	Unif	Unif	Unif	Unif	Unif	Not Unif	Unif	Not Unif	Unif

Codes: + little   Cont - central control   Unif - uniform
        ++ some   Some C - some central control   Not Un - not uniform
        +++ much   Adv - central advice

Table 16. Instructional Stability in Relation to Family, School, and Country Factors (5 items)

	Countries											
	Fin	Ger	Nor	Ice	Swe	Den	Gre	Sco	Eng	Ire	USA	Fra
X Number of items that reflect:												
Stability	2	5	5	5	4	3	3	3	0	3	0	2
Relative Stability	2	0	0	0	1	2	2	2	0	1	0	0
Instability	1	0	0	0	0	0	0	0	5	1	5	3

REFERENCES

1. Blom, G. E. "Sex Differences in Reading Disability in NINDS," *Reading Forum*, Monograph #1. Washington, D.C.: U.S. Government Printing Office, 1971, 31-46.
2. Blom, G. E. "An Examination of the Content of Introductory Reading Textbook Materials in Six Countries," paper presented at the International Reading Association Convention, Detroit, Michigan, May 1972.
3. Blom, G. E., and J. L. Wiberg. "Attitude Contents in Reading Primers," in J. Downing (Ed.), *Comparative Reading*. New York: Macmillan, 1973, 85-104.
4. Brimer, M. A. "Methodological Problems of Research," in J. Downing (Ed.), *Comparative Reading*. New York: Macmillan, 1973, 13-31.
5. Bronfenbrenner, U. "The Three Worlds of Childhood (Mainland China)," presentation at the University of Colorado Medical Center, 1974.
6. Bruner, J. "Patterns of Growth," an inaugural lecture delivered before the University of Oxford. Oxford: Clarendon Press, 1973.
7. Burnet, M. *ABC of Literacy*. Paris: Unesco, 1965.
8. Downing, J. (Ed.). *Comparative Reading*. New York: Macmillan, 1973.
9. Foshay, A. W., et al. *Educational Achievement of Thirteen-Year-Olds in Twelve Countries*. Hamburg: Unesco Institute for Education, 1962.
10. Gray, W. S. *The Teaching of Reading and Writing*. Switzerland: Unesco, 1956.
11. Harman, D. "Illiteracy: An Overview," *Harvard Educational Review*, 40 (1970), 226-244.
12. Husen, T. (Ed.). *International Study of Achievement in Mathematics*. Stockholm: Almquist and Wiksell. New York: Wiley, 1967.
13. International Bureau of Education. *The Teaching of Reading*. Paris: Unesco, 1949.
14. Jansen, M., B. Jacobsen, and P. E. Jensen. *The Teaching of Reading without Really Any Method*. Copenhagen: Munksgaard, 1974.
15. Laubach, F. C., and R. Laubach. *Toward World Literacy: The Each One Teach One Way*. Syracuse, New York: University of Syracuse Press, 1960.
16. Lee, W. R. *Spelling Irregularity and Reading Difficulty in English*. London: NFER, 1960.
17. Leong, C. K. "Language Differences and Reading Disabilities," paper presented at the International Reading Association Convention, Detroit, Michigan, May 1972.
18. Malmquist, E. "Primary Reading in Various Countries," paper presented at the International Reading Association Convention, New Orleans, Louisiana, May 1974.
19. Staiger, R. C. "The Geology of Reading," in Downing and Brown (Eds.), *The Second International Reading Symposium*. London: Cassell, 1967.
20. Staiger, R. C. "Developments in Reading and Literacy Education, 1956-1967," in W. S. Gray (Ed.), *The Teaching of Reading and Writing* (2nd ed.). Paris: Unesco, 1969.
21. Swan, T. D. "The First R in Ireland," paper presented at the International Reading Association Convention, New Orleans, Louisiana, May 1974.
22. Thorndike, R. L. "Major Findings of the IEA Research," paper presented at the International Reading Association Convention, New Orleans, Louisiana, May 1974.
23. Wall, W. D., F. J. Schonell, and W. C. Olson. *Failure in School*. Hamburg: Unesco Institute for Education, 1962.
24. *World Illiteracy at Mid Century*. Switzerland: Unesco, 1957.
25. Zimet, S. G. (Ed.). *What Children Read in School*. New York: Grune and Stratton, 1972.

Recent Studies of Reading Standards in the United Kingdom

Elizabeth J. Goodacre
University of Reading
Reading, England

The United Kingdom is usually understood to include the countries of England, Wales, Scotland, and Northern Ireland and is not an educationally unitary state. There are separate services, and different methods and criteria for measuring reading attainment have developed in each of the four countries.

The Department of Education and Science (DES) has carried out a series of reading surveys at four yearly intervals since the war for England, and more recently also for Wales and Northern Ireland, providing data on national standards. There are also within England and Wales local education authorities (LEAs) which administer education at the local level, but only recently (1970) was information obtained about the use of reading tests and attainment surveys by the local authorities (2).

NATIONAL SURVEYS

The last of the DES surveys of the reading ability of samples of eleven- and fifteen-year-old pupils was conducted in 1970-1971, and results have now been published for England (9), Wales (4), and Northern Ireland (12). The following problems emerge from a study of these reports.

Type of test used. Tests of oral reading must be given individually, and are usually too time-consuming for large scale surveys. The type of test used has been one of reading comprehension of sentences, as shown by the ability to fill in missing words or answer questions on content. One of the assumptions in assessing changes in reading comprehension standards over time (continuing to use the same test from the time of establishing a base line) is that the language one is expected to comprehend remains constant.

> If, in our rapidly changing society there is a commensurate change in language, a particular test can only be expected at most to serve as a valid method of assessment over a moderately short period of time. Over a period of years a test may change appreciably in difficulty because of a shift in the type and scope of language that an "educated reader" is expected to comprehend rather than because of any real change in the reader's ability (9).

Standards in the United Kingdom

An important issue, therefore, is the aging of an established and tried test over time and the obvious need for a "rolling" technique of testing which facilitates continuous updating as well as valid comparisons with the past.

Level of cooperation. Some of the randomly selected English schools declined to take part in the latest survey because they had recently taken part in an international study. There was also an unforeseen event in a postal strike, which affected the organisation of the testing programme. This raises the question of whether school cooperation may be related in some way to reading ability, and how much refusal can be tolerated before affecting the validity of the results. The stage beyond this is pupil cooperation in the sense of the importance of absenteeism at the time of testing. Absenteeism was a particular problem with the fifteen-year-olds, many of whom were within a few months of leaving school. If the figures for this age group are unreliable, it may well be that the incidence of reading backwardness is underestimated at this stage of the educational system, and this in turn would affect estimates of the incidence of adult illiteracy in society.

Extrapolating findings from one age group to another. Bookbinder (1) criticised national surveys for the practice of extrapolating the findings at eleven down to seven years, suggesting the only valid figures for the latter group would be obtained by actually giving the particular test to seven-year-olds. The idea that the same rate of progress obtained between eleven and fifteen also applies between seven and eleven may be an unjustified conclusion, ignoring the possibility of learning plateaus in the early stages of acquiring the skill, and spurious findings may be passed on from one survey to another, making comparisons of standards between one period and another hazardous.

LOCAL SURVEYS

The national surveys used standardised tests; but, at the local level, children in need of remedial help may be chosen on the basis of their teacher's assessment and nomination, their progress through a reading scheme or primer, and their score on a group or individual reading test. There appears to be an increasing use of standardised group tests for survey purposes by LEAs, apparently as a more effective way of allocating scarce remedial provision than relying on the subjective estimates of individual teachers. A small number of LEAs are now carrying out testing programmes at regular intervals, and from such local or regional data, results are emerging which suggest certain trends. Factors considered in such surveys are size and type of school, urban/rural location, and socioeconomic status of catchment area. Pupil characteristics such as preschool experience, length of infant schooling, sex, immigrant status, home background, and number of schools attended are also considered.

LEAs USE OF READING TESTS

A survey of LEAs in 1970 (80 percent return) by the writer (2) found that half the authorities left the assessment of reading standards to the head teachers of schools, who decided when testing should take place in the pupil's schooling, what form of assessment should be used, and how often testing and recording of progress should take place. While LEAs were changing over from a selective procedure for secondary education (11+ system), some head teachers were using continuous assessment records and including reading tests as part of this procedure.

A number of heads used word recognition tests (Schonell, Vernon, and Burt) to assess pupil ability to pronounce words and read them without contextual help. It could be argued that such tests are more in tune with the criteria of reading progress used in English schools some thirty years ago (when the tests were originally designed), rather than the present day reading goals which stress reading for meaning from the beginning and encouraging children to use their language knowledge to anticipate and work out unknown words.

VARYING CRITERIA OF READING BACKWARDNESS

This same survey indicated that many of LEAs were making use of a difference criterion, usually that of a two year difference between reading and chronological age. It was usually the LEAs using screening surveys (to discover early those children with difficulties before these were exacerbated by anxiety and emotional problems) who selected pupils more than one standard deviation below the norm as being "backward readers."

In using the findings of local reading surveys, comparisons are sometimes difficult because of the use of different criteria of reading backwardness, different types of tests, different levels of school and pupil cooperation, and random or complete population sampling for particular age groups.

SOME FINDINGS FROM RECENT SURVEYS

Sex differences. The Inner London Education Authority (ILEA) 1972 follow-up survey of pupils transferring to secondary schools (first surveyed as seven-year-olds) reported virtually no change in standards (6). It was noted, however, that the girls' performance deteriorated over the period. The Northern Ireland survey also reported deterioration in girls' attainment between ages eleven and fifteen. This is of particular interest because, in the majority of past surveys, girls' attainment has been superior, with usually five backward boy readers to one backward girl reader. If national standards of reading comprehension have not risen during the past ten years, it may well be because girls, as well as boys, are failing to maintain their initial progress, losing the skill through lack of use for enjoyment and relaxation. There is some evidence (10) in the leisure reading of secondary pupils which suggests that, as they grow older, secondary girls read teenage girls' comics, giving up hardback reading for entertainment. The most popular writer with girls was Enid Blyton; with boys, Ian Flemming. It may well be that, from early in their schooling, boys are less willing to read uninteresting reading materials, but teenaged boys and girls have a range of leisure pursuits to choose from, and school reading materials must compete against the competition of television, pop culture magazines, paperbacks, and "soft porn" reading material.

Social class differences. The ILEA figures also showed that, although there continued to be good readers within each social class group, there tended to be an increase in the number of poor readers in the semi- and unskilled groups during the years spent in the primary school (years seven to eleven). A Scottish local survey (8) also noted the sharp decline in the standards at age ten of children from the lower working classes in comparison with those from professional homes who improved or maintained their progress during the primary years. This trend had become more marked in this particular area during the past decade. Halsey and his colleagues (3) also drew attention to the problem of deteriorating standards in the EPAs (Education Priority Areas, i.e., schools with a high proportion of socially and economically disadvantaged pupils). For instance, the percentage of nonimmigrant readers (R.A. two years less than C.A.) was 19 percent for London, 18 percent for West Riding, 22 percent for Liverpool, and 36 percent for Birmingham for EPAs in these cities and regions. (The national figure was approximately 15 percent at this stage of the educational system.) Halsey did not consider that this was a problem of individual nonachievers in these schools, but rather a much more general and independent pattern of low achievement. In an international study (11) it was shown that, as in the local authority surveys, reading progress in Britain was closely related to socioeconomic factors, with reading comprehension at age ten being influenced three and one-half times more by the home than the school. The difference persisted at age fourteen, but beyond this age disappeared, when pupils at school were there because they wished to be and not by reason of compulsory schooling.

Length of infant schooling. The usual procedure in the United Kingdom is to admit children to infant schools at intervals of four months; that is, termly intakes. (In many parts of Scotland, however, children are taken on a yearly basis.) In contrast to most countries which have one school entry point, in England and Wales there are generally three: September, January, and after Easter. However, children are promoted to junior school or department only at intervals of twelve months; that is, on a yearly basis. Children must go to school at the beginning of the term after their fifth birthday and they are promoted to the junior school or class in the September following their seventh birthday. This means that the groups of children transferring annually to the junior school or class differ considerably in age and in length of infant schooling. Also, the number of pupils in the infant school varies greatly from term to term, and this affects learning conditions, particularly for the summer born children.

In another local survey (5), it was possible to examine the relationship between month of birth, age, and reading attainment for the first year junior pupils, and although there was roughly the same proportion of backward readers among the younger and older pupils in the age group, the reading scores of the older children were significantly higher than the younger children, who had had two terms less in the infant school. The ILEA survey also reported that the later the age of entry, the poorer average reading score, even six years after the children had first started school.

Lunn (7) examined the effects of infant schooling on academic performance when season of birth was held constant. She found that the number of terms in the infant school affected performance of summer born children, with those children having only six terms performing at a lower level than those having a longer period of infant schooling. Analysis of social class and school type (streamed or unstreamed) showed the same tendency. Lunn also reported that 40 percent of pupils in remedial classes had had only six terms in the infant school: i.e., a whole year less of this type of schooling.

In view of these findings, it would seem important for research studies of the effectiveness of remedial techniques to use standardised reading tests which are likely to compensate not merely for age, but also for differences in length of infant schooling associated with age. Also, in remedial studies, the research design should take into consideration the variable length of infant schooling. This factor seems to be of particular importance in England and Wales because there is a tradition that the task of learning to read is mainly the responsibility of the infant school, and as the ILEA survey discovered, few first year Junior teachers are experienced and competent teachers of reading from the beginning. Some LEAs are changing to an organisation of schools in which pupils aged four to eight years are in first schools and eight- to twelve-year-olds, in middle schools. This will give first school teachers a longer time to establish the skill, but will not completely solve the problem of a staggered entry to school followed by a fixed transfer date to junior or middle school with its emphasis upon using a fully developed skill rather than continuing with its firm establishment and development.

REFERENCES

1. Bookbinder, G. E. "Should We Believe What the Reading Survey Tells Us?" *Reading,* 7 (1973), 14-20.
2. Goodacre, E. J. *Provision for Reading.* University of Reading, 1971.
3. Halsey, A. H., et al. "Reading Standards in Educational Priority Areas," *Remedial Education,* 8 (1973), 16-24.
4. Horton, T. R. *The Reading Standards of Children in Wales.* Windsor, Berks: NFER, 1973.
5. Hurn, H. S. *Reading Standards Survey 1973.* Slough, Berks: Education Department Schools Psychological Service, 1973.
6. Inner London Education Authority. *Literacy Survey: 1971 Follow-up Preliminary Report.* ILEA, 1973.
7. Lunn, J. B. "Length of Infant Schooling and Academic Performance," *Educational Research,* 14 (1972), 120-127.
8. Nisbet, et al. *Reading Standards in Aberdeen 1962-1972.* Aberdeen: Department of Education, 1973.
9. Start, K. B., and B. K. Wells. *The Trend of Reading Standards.* Windsor, Berks: Slough, 1972.
10. Taylor, J. "The Voluntary Reading Habits of Secondary School Pupils," *Reading,* 7 (1973), 11-18.
11. Thorndike, R. L. *Reading Comprehension Education in Fifteen Countries.* New York: John Wiley, 1973.
12. Wilson, J. A. *Reading Standards in Northern Ireland.* Belfast: Northern Ireland Council for Education, 1973.

Reading Comprehension in Fifteen Countries

Robert L. Thorndike
Teachers College, Columbia University
New York, New York
United States of America

The purpose of this paper is to report some of the results of various cross national studies of reading. The primary emphasis was on reading comprehension. The youngsters in the study were aged 10, 14, and 18. The reading study was part of a larger enterprise involving testing in science, civic education, and other areas in which testing before the age of 10 did not seem to make a great deal of sense. IEA has hopes of carrying out a longitudinal study of the beginning stages of reading on a cross national basis, providing funding problems for such a study can be resolved.

What I shall present here is at most a very limited sampling of the mass of data we accumulated. The data are reported more fully in the volume, *Reading Comprehension Education in Fifteen Countries*, which represents one of the first three of the series of eight or nine volumes based on our most recent cross national research. However, even this volume includes only a fraction of the material available on computer printout and in the data bank which is being established at the University of Stockholm in Sweden. Readers who are interested can eventually address the data file at Stockholm and carry out further analyses in relation to their own special interests.

Our material is capable of analysis at the level of the single individual, the level of the school, and the level of the country as a complete unit. These levels of analysis appropriately address themselves to somewhat different questions, and I will provide a small sampling of the kinds of information that emerged at each of the levels of analytic study.

Except when looking at the country as the unit of analysis, my tendency has been to think of the several countries as replications and to look primarily for uniformities and consistencies of relationship that extend across national boundaries. Possibly, more attention should have been paid to the variations from country to country in the factors that are associated with individual achievement or with school effects, but the patterns are often quite consistent so that I have tended to emphasize the consistencies rather than the variations. However, I will point to a few instances of differences between countries in either individual or school factors and leave them as queries so that the reader can decide whether they make sense as representing differences in the national culture or the national curriculum.

INDIVIDUAL DIFFERENCES

Let us start with factors associated with individual differences in reading ability, and ask what kinds of information we were able to obtain from the individuals in these fifteen countries that tended to differentiate the good reader from the poor reader. Available information about individuals was limited to that which could be gathered through questionnaire methods. Thus, what I report here are relationships between facts reported by the youngsters and the reading test scores. The accuracy of the reports is somewhat suspect, but we did a certain amount of preliminary work to verify that the information provided by the youngsters was reasonably consistent with information that could have been obtained from their parents.

In general, we identified two kinds of background factors that seemed to be moderately predictive of the achievement of individual pupils within a country. One was a cluster of family socioeconomic variables, for example, parental occupation and parental education; the other was a cluster of variables that might be roughly characterized as reading resources in the home. This second cluster was based on the child's report of the number of books in the home, the number of magazines subscribed to, the availability of a daily newspaper, and the availability of a dictionary. These two clusters were of relatively equal importance, varying from country to country as to which carried the greater weight in predicting reading comprehension scores of the youngsters. In the United States, the balance was slightly in favor of socioeconomic variables.

Two other family factors that might be mentioned, since they added a little to the prediction of achievement, are family size and the child's report that his parents helped him with his homework. These are both negative indicators. That is, the child from a larger family tends to be a poorer reader, even when the family socioeconomic situation is taken into consideration. The poorer readers are the ones who report that their parents help them with their school work. Apparently parental help is more an indicator of educational difficulty than of parental commitment and support.

PREDICTABILITY OF ACHIEVEMENT

For the group of Western and developed countries that represented twelve of our fifteen, the patterns were generally consistent though the relationships were stronger in some countries than in others. Israel, with its heterogeneous immigrant population stemming partly from European and partly from Asiatic sources, was the country that showed the strongest relationship between individual background factors and achievement. The United States also tended to be quite high in the predictability of achievement, perhaps reflecting the diversity of its ethnic and socioeconomic backgrounds. By contrast, the three developing countries—Chile, India, and Iran—showed modest relationships between the background factors and reading achievement of youngsters in the schools. We are not entirely able to interpret these results. As I shall point out later, reading achievement was very low in these countries and it is possible that the reading burden that was represented by the questionnaire was so heavy that the responses to it are not dependable. It is also possible that the kinds of indicators that are rather consistently associated with academic performance in Western cultures do not have the same significance in the developing countries.

READING PREFERENCES

A fair number of the items of information obtained from individuals provided information on what might be called concomitants rather than predictors or antecedents of reading achievement. In contrast to father's education, which is clearly antecedent to the child's performance, the amount and type of reading done by the child is a concomitant variable and his reading preferences, his educational plans, his occupational aspirations, his attitudes toward school and academic matters are all concomitants which interact in complex ways, influencing and being influenced by his effectiveness as a reader. A number of these concomitants show appreciable, though not extremely dramatic, relationships with reading score. Thus, not surprisingly, the better readers aspire to larger amounts of further education and to occupations higher in the occupational hierarchy. They tend to read more and go to the movies less. Especially in the younger groups, the better readers are more likely to like school and to be motivated to achieve. At the older ages they tend to be interested in science and in literature, to value science, and to see their school as structured and content centered.

Some of the concomitants are not entirely what one might expect. For example, we asked the youngsters to indicate their liking for different kinds of reading materials and we are able to associate the expressed liking with the reading ability displayed by the youngsters. Thus, we can see what kinds of reading preferences tend to differentiate the better reader from the poorer. The most differentiating type of reading material for fourteen-year-olds is humor, with sports and love stories showing a reversed relationship. The part of the newspaper that most differentiates the able reader from the less able is a preference for reading the comics.

SEX DIFFERENCES

One item that may be of interest is the relative reading achievement of boys and girls. This is one respect in which one does find differences between countries, although sex differences in the reading achievement scores were not marked or dramatic in any of the countries. In the United States we are quite accustomed to thinking of girls as being the better of the two sexes as far as reading and similar verbal competencies are concerned; and United Sates girls do, in fact, perform slightly better on reading tests than do boys. This is also true for the majority of the countries in our study. However, there is a minority of countries in which the boys read better than the girls: this holds for 3 out of 14 countries for children at age 10; 5 out of 15 countries at age 14; and 5 out of 15 countries at the end of secondary school. Thus, it looks as though the differential between the sexes is to a considerable extent cultural rather than organic by the time one reaches the ages of 10 and above; and the way the culture treats the two sexes, or the extent to which it educates them and emphasizes educational goals for them, makes an appreciable difference in how the sexes compare in something as basic as reading comprehension. Girls were better on the literature tests in every one of the countries in which the matter was studied but did less well on the science tests in every one of the countries. The differentials in these subjects were universal and rather substantial. However, one suspects that this result represents more nearly a uniformity of culture across the range of countries in which we operated than something which is inherently and biologically fixed.

BETWEEN-COUNTRY DIFFERENCES

Let us turn our attention now to the differences between countries. As far as the IEA project was concerned, we have tended to play down the International Olympics aspect of the study and have not made a great deal of the differences from country to country in average score on our tests. Generally speaking, the differences between the European-oriented Western developed countries were relatively modest in size. In our study the dramatic between-countries differences were those between the developing countries, whose past status both in economic development and in general level of education has been relatively low, and those countries that have both an industrial plant and a tradition, for several generations at least, of widely available education.

For the reading study there were three countries that we considered to be developing countries. These were Iran, Chile, and the Hindi-speaking part of India. In all of the tests, not merely those in reading, these countries fell well at the bottom of the heap. In reading comprehension, the differences were such that the top performer in a class in one of these countries would be no more than barely average in one of the Western developed countries. The difference was so large that in these countries the tests that we had developed, and which had unfortunately been tried out mostly in developed countries, were clearly too hard, with the result that numbers of youngsters were getting essentially chance scores. We had an easy reading speed test consisting of paragraphs such as the following:

> "Peter has a little dog. The dog is black with a white spot on his back and one white leg." The color of Peter's dog is mostly
>
>   black   brown   grey.

Even this test turned out to be a power test in the developing countries, with 10-year-olds averaging over 50 percent errors in one country, and even 14-year-olds averaging 30 percent errors.

The deficit in reading in the developing countries is not surprising when you consider the circumstances under which the schools and the children operate. We may take the Hindi-speaking area in India as an example. Although the tests were given in Hindi, for many children in the areas in India where Hindi is the official language, Hindi is actually a second language. It is not the language of the home or of the immediate peer group with whom the child associates and is as much a new language to these youngsters as English is to some of the Hispanic youngsters in the United States. In addition 1) many of the parents have had little or no education and there is no support of literacy within the home itself; 2) in most cases, the homes are meagerly equipped with reading matter; 3) radio and television are rare sources of language stimulation; and 4) schools are not well equipped with reading materials and children have no single book continuously available to them to read. In some ways, the difficulties that plague a country like India, so far as developing literacy in youngsters is concerned, are very similar to the problems that plague the innercity communities and ethnic ghettos in this country, where a number of the factors that I have described are characteristic of these subcommunities within the United States.

Readers are interested in United States' standing among the countries participating in the reading study. At the ten-year-old level, the United States was ninth out of fourteen; at the fourteen-year-old level, third out of fifteen; and at the end of secondary education, twelfth out of fifteen. The poor showing of the United States at the end of secondary education is explainable in considerable measure by the fact that the United States retains a much higher proportion of children through to the end of secondary schooling, including the less academically inclined, and consequently the average performance is relatively low. We estimated that the United States retains about 75 percent of the age group through to the end of secondary school, and as compared to a range of 10-25 percent in many of the other countries in the study.

One might want to try to determine which characteristics of a country are associated with the overall reading achievement by youngsters in that country. Our study included only fifteen countries, however, and these countries differed in linguistic, educational, cultural, and economic dimensions, making fruitless the task of identifying the particular determiners responsible for between-country differences. By including the three developing countries, almost any index of economic development will show a rather strong relationship with the reading score, when considered across the whole set of countries. The simple variable, "average hours of watching television," gives a correlation of 0.92 for the set of fifteen countries. However, if one excludes the three developing countries and looks at the remaining twelve, the relationships shift markedly and any attempt to identify significant national concomitants of reading achievement becomes very difficult.

The country that showed the best reading at age 10 was Sweden, while the top country at age 14 was New Zealand. These are small countries that are culturally and economically homogeneous and it is not surprising that they show rather good achievement. New Zealand, in particular, has long placed high emphasis on literacy and upon making books available throughout the country, even in remote and inaccessible areas, and the evidence indicates that these emphases have paid off.

BETWEEN-SCHOOL DIFFERENCES

The final analysis concerns differences between schools and attempts at learning what there is about a particular school that leads to good results in reading comprehension for its students. In this case, the one obvious determiner of achievement is the input of youngsters into the school. In the United States, for example, there is a correlation of 0.75 between an index of average economic and cultural background of the entering children and the average reading achievement for the school. This economic and cultural background index is one that takes account of the factors referred to earlier as relating to achievement of individual youngsters within a school. Thus, to a considerable extent, the outcome in reading comprehension from a school is determined by the input in terms of the variety of youngsters who attend. Anything about a school that is correlated with this measure of input will tend to be correlated with output; however, even with this substantial correlation, it would still be possible for various types of school factors to have a further impact on reading achievement and we made a determined attempt to identify such factors.

At this point, our results were most disappointing. It is my impression that so far as the reading comprehension test is concerned, we found substantially no variables of school background that could be counted on to be consistently related to reading achievement from country to country. Factors of class size, teacher training, resources of materials and specialists in the school, and techniques of presentation or instruction were all relatively fruitless as predictors. Why was this?

In the first place, it must be recognized that our information about the schools was limited to what could be obtained by questionnaire methods. Our resources did not permit us to visit the schools and see what went on. Furthermore, we were dealing with youngsters at age levels where whatever reading instruction had operated on them had operated largely in the past—sometimes in the remote past. That is, one would hardly expect to find anything in the current instructional setting of fourteen-year-olds that would differentiate the reading comprehension of different groups. The most important reading instruction they would have had would have been at ages 6, 7, and 8, with lessening emphasis as the years went by. Whatever the reasons, we have to confess that our effort to identify organizational or instructional factors that contributed to reading achievement was a disappointing and unproductive enterprise.

In some of the other curricular areas in which our IEA has worked, the situation has been rather different. The one that shows the sharpest contrast, is the area of foreign language. Here it is fairly clear that whatever the American child learns of the French language he learns in school. Community factors have little or no direct impact, the difference between good and poor instruction appears to be substantial, and some of the determiners of good instruction seem to be identifiable. This is in sharp contrast to the domain of reading which is supported by a wide range of out-of-school experiences where, at least at the levels where we were working, we could find nothing about what the school did that seemed to make a difference.

This failure to find significant school effects emphasizes again the desirability of starting reading at a considerably earlier age level, and the prospect of making a cross national study of beginning reading is a very appealing one. Such a study would have to be very different from the one we have carried out. Because of the need for the study to be more detailed and intensive, we would visualize it as being longitudinal, involving classroom observation and individual testing, and using a substantially smaller number of children. Many of us hope that such a study can be carried out in the not too distant future.

I have tried to give you some sense of our findings and our frustrations. Massive cross national surveys provide plenty of both. The practical limitations of time and resources and the limitations in our own foresight and wisdom, have limited the questions that we have been able to answer. But we do now have some basis for viewing both our common educational *achievements* and our common educational *problems*.

PART SIX

Raising Teaching Standards

The Development of Competency Based Teacher Education in Reading

Robert Karlin
Queens College of the
City University of New York
New York, New York
United States of America

In an article published in an educational journal in 1958, I proposed that persons who were offering reading services to children with reading problems should be licensed by the state. Just as physicians and dentists, electricians and plumbers, beauticians and barbers, and other craftsmen are required to demonstrate ability in their chosen fields before being allowed to practice their skills, so should reading "specialists" be required to demonstrate their proficiency before being permitted to serve the public. This proposal seemed so radical in 1958 that the editor of the publication, fearing adverse reactions from readers, printed the article in the form of a letter to the editor. The editor's fears were not confirmed, and although the proposal did evoke some response among people in the profession, to my knowledge the proposal has not been adopted in the United States. Of course, some individual states have certified (licensed) reading teachers, reading clinicians, and reading consultants who work in the public schools. But such certification, as other certifications, is based upon the satisfactory completion of specified courses and not upon demonstration that applicants possess the required abilities to perform their tasks.

PROS AND CONS

Today, as a result of demands by state legislative bodies and citizen groups who say that they want greater returns from their tax dollars as demonstrated by increased pupil learning (the assumption being that the only way to measure teacher effectiveness is to demonstrate whether pupils have learned), we seek to change the way in which all teachers are certified. Essentially, current plans for certification call for a unified effort by university, school, and professional groups to jointly assess teaching competencies through performance in school settings. Thus, no teacher would be able to obtain or retain a position unless he or she could demonstrate initial and continuing competence, however it is defined.

Although teacher groups have long recognized the inadequacies of some members, certain groups have advocated resistance to efforts to base teacher certification upon demonstrated competency. They argue that no one has shown that a strong relationship between teacher and pupil performance exists. (Those of us who prepare reading teachers and offer specialist programs in reading believe that knowledgeable teachers of reading are more likely to produce better readers than are less knowledgeable teachers. If this were not so, how could we justify the expenditures that graduate reading specialist programs entail?) They also say that competency levels for someone entering the profession should be different from those possessed by practicing teachers, and these levels are yet to be developed, as are the strategies and tools required to focus on teacher competencies.

Then there is the question raised by the humanists in education who are concerned with such matters as adaptability, creativity, self-concept, values, attitudes, beliefs, feelings, and other affective results of learning. They ask, "Can you readily assess the internal meanings or changes that result from learning through specified and observable behaviors or competencies?" They argue that, except on the lowest levels, instruments for doing so do not exist. While the humanists do not deny the concept of accountability, they do reject the notion that all learning is discrete and observable. They would not reject the use of behavioral measures to assess skills learning. What they prefer to substitute for assessing other outcomes of learning is human judgment which, in their view, behavioristic tools cannot replace. While they recognize the possibility of fallibility, they do believe that, through inference, important educational outcomes can be weighed. Thus, they would recommend the use of both tools.

There is no question that valid arguments exist against the immediate and wholesale introduction of new teacher certification procedures. But these arguments do not negate the desirability of making changes in the way teachers are certified and, therefore, in the ways they are prepared for teaching. If professional educators do not respond to existing pressures for change and address themselves to the issues under review, change, like some fame, will be thrust upon them. In fact, such is already the case in some places. The State Education Department of New York is just beginning to address itself to the problems associated with competency based systems of preparation and will no longer approve any new teacher education programs unless it can be shown that they are competency based. Moreover, all existing teacher education programs must become competency based by 1980. The department has already issued a preliminary statement regarding basic competencies in reading for the classroom teacher, reading teacher, and reading consultant, and has commissioned the preparation of a test designed to serve as a college proficiency examination in reading instruction in the elementary school. However, it has yet to consider the requirements and logistics associated with field based education.

The International Reading Association (5), recognizing its role in improving teacher education for reading, has prepared a publication specifying "... the professional knowledge and instruction competencies which are the products of adequate programs for preparing teachers to teach reading in the schools of today and tomorrow." Seventeen modules have been identified, each consisting of five elements: a participation assessment plan to determine the learner's readiness to cope with the module's content, the teacher competencies to be realized, minimum performance levels for each competency, suggested learning experiences, and an assessment plan to determine how well performances have been realized. These modules, with changes where desirable, could become a basis for competency based teacher education programs in reading.

We already perceive changes in attitudes and actions which point in the direction of revised and, perhaps, more meaningful teacher education programs. That there are problems to be resolved cannot be denied. There are problems involving financial support for conducting field based education and offering creative learning experiences, problems growing out of associations among institutions of higher learning which still will be responsible for providing the basic education of prospective teachers and cooperating certifying agents, problems of reconciling tenure and competency, and problems associated with valid assessments of teacher behavior and appropriate behaviors as they relate to pupil performance. These problems cannot be ignored. How well competency based teacher education programs fare will certainly depend on the extent to which each can be satisfactorily resolved. Otherwise, like earlier movements for educational change, this effort will dissipate itself and there will be business as usual until new pressures force reexamination of what the profession is doing.

PROGRAMS FOR TEACHERS

Traditionally, prospective elementary school teachers in the United States have been exposed to reading instruction through a combined reading-language arts methods course or a one semester course in reading improvement. Until recently, prospective secondary school teachers have not even enjoyed this minimal exposure to reading concepts and methodologies. It is a fairly well-established fact that the typical newly appointed teacher has not been adequately prepared to teach reading, even though many are expected to devote a major portion of the school day to doing so. Instructors of courses in reading or reading-language arts have been relying mainly on lectures, textbooks, and discussions as media through which students acquire information about teaching reading. No doubt some have provided other meaningful experiences beyond these, but the fact remains that there is a wide gap between a teacher's ability to discuss reading concepts and his ability to translate them into viable teaching strategies. Talk to these young teachers about their preparation for teaching reading and you will understand why they feel so inadequate; of course, some of their weaknesses are within themselves (some should not become teachers because they simply don't have sufficiently high capabilities and dedication). But even among the more capable, there are many who lack real understanding about teaching reading and meeting children's reading needs. Rarely have teachers been required in courses to do more than verbalize about reading. When they have to face a class of 25 to 30 children they feel bewildered and lost; and unless they receive real help, they soon become discouraged. Perhaps, this is one reason why so many of our schools adopt basal readers with their accompanying manuals, for without the latter a large number of teachers wouldn't know where and how to begin and what directions to take.

There is no question but that changes in teacher preparation are long overdue, and preparation for teaching reading is a good place to start. Competency based preparation might not offer complete solutions to hard questions, for there are no panaceas; however, there is a reasonable chance that students who can demonstrate competency in teaching reading will become the better teachers of reading.

In a sense, we have always had competency based programs but generally at only one level. I prefer to view the requirements of such programs as consisting of three tiers: demonstration that basic knowledge of reading and reading instruction has been mastered; demonstration that, based upon such understandings, suitable strategies can be developed for teaching children; and demonstration that these strategies can be applied successfully in helping children to improve reading ability and in fostering appropriate attitudes toward reading.

We have always required students to show evidence (usually through written tests which sometimes probe deeply and at other times just scratch surfaces) that they have acquired information about reading. At times, we have required students to produce teaching plans that could be used for diagnostic teaching. But more often than not, and for a variety of reasons including time limitations and large numbers, these requirements have not been consistently applied. From the evidence at hand, I would suggest that rarely have we reached the tier that counts—the "show me" phase.

When the teacher-trainer decides to go the competency based route, it doesn't necessarily mean that he must discard every procedure he has been following in favor of innovative approaches. He can still adopt basic textbooks and reference sources, lecture, and hold group discussions. But since the main objective of the course or program is to help students develop competency in the fullest sense, there could be differences in the ways teachers would operate henceforth. For one thing, he will seek alternative ways of helping students acquire the content of reading and reading instruction. This effort results from the recognition that the classroom and books are not the only sources of information. Instead of a meeting three or four times a week as many undergraduate schedules require, a class might meet no more than once a week (and perhaps even less frequently in graduate sequences). When such reductions occur, it is assumed that students are involved elsewhere in activities such as observing a reading lesson being taught in a local school, discussing reading concepts with another faculty member, viewing taped reading lessons, meeting with the class instructor individually or in groups to clarify issues, preparing instructional materials for a prescribed lesson, administering diagnostic tests to children, helping one or more children overcome specific reading weaknesses, reviewing lessons taught by peers, meeting with parents to explain current reading practices, or reading professional literature evaluating suggestions in teaching manuals.

Naturally, students do not engage in any of these possible activities in a disorganized way. They know in advance what competencies they will be required to demonstrate and what possible avenues they might follow to prepare for such demonstrations. Thus, if the module or "the unit of study" were evaluation for diagnostic teaching, the student would be provided with a list of activities he could pursue in order to demonstrate his acquaintance with and use of appropriate diagnostic tools for analyzing reading behaviors and making recommendations for instructional programing. These competencies could be stated as follows:

1. Is familiar with reading tests
   - Can identify several oral and silent reading tests for elementary and secondary students
   - Is able to distinguish between a diagnostic and a survey test
   - Is able to assess a test's usefulness for measuring reading performances (discover word meaning in context, make inferences)
   - Can assess standardization procedures (validity, reliability, sampling)
   - Can prepare informal or teacher-made tests to measure specified skills
   - Is able to identify circumstances for using norm referenced tests

Competency Based Teacher Education

2. Can use reading test results
   - Groups children on basis of test results
   - Determines reading levels
   - Analyzes reading strengths and weaknesses
   - Plans appropriate lessons for different groups of children

In order to be able to acquire these kinds of competencies, students might select from a variety of activities.
   - Examine test files
   - Check Buros' *Reading Tests and Reviews*
   - Compare survey and diagnostic instruments
   - Observe live, or on videotape or film, how informal inventories are prepared and administered, and how their results are interpreted
   - Administer oral and silent reading tests and evaluate results
   - Discuss with a measurement expert the pros and cons of standardized vs. teacher-made tests
   - Select appropriate testing instruments for individual children
   - Plan instructional programs in word, comprehension, and study skills based on test evaluation
   - Read textbook and reference sources on test construction and evaluation
   - Make an item analysis of test items and classify them
   - Study test manuals

Some students might not have to engage in all the activities to develop necessary competence, while others could require more concentrated exposures. It might be useful to note that different levels of competencies (entry, advance, and specialized levels) could be identified for those preparing to teach, those seeking advanced standing, and those who are or will be assuming responsibilities for administering and supervising reading programs.

Under such an arrangement, students might not be pursuing identical areas of study at the same time since they would be progressing at different rates. Therefore, they will be demonstrating their mastery of knowledge and practice when they are ready to do so. Presumably, if the successful completion of one module depends upon the successful completion of an earlier one, students will not move ahead to new modules until they have satisfied the requirements which have been established for doing so. Instructors might prefer to group related modules of study and delay seeking evidences of competency until all have been completed.

Since competency in its truest sense involves doing more than talking, field based programs are more desirable than those limited to campuses and simulated conditions, since students can learn first-hand what good reading instruction is all about and put what they've learned into practice to develop their skills. The assumptions underlying this proposal are more easily identified than attained. One basic assumption is that resources, both material and human, are readily available. Another assumption is that suitable placements can be arranged. We know the problems associated with the placement of student teachers and how frustrated we can become in our efforts to provide quality experiences for them; but we should strive to meet the obstacles that might have to be overcome. If state departments of education mandate field based teacher education programs as a part of the certification process, then colleges and public schools will have to accommodate them.

What could happen if competency requirements were to become the rule and were administered in the interests of improved school practices? The typical four- and five-year programs might be extended over longer time periods for some students and reduced for others. More students than is presently the case, would likely be denied initial certification. And if the recommendations of some bodies are adopted, automatic permanent certification could become a thing of the past. Instead, teachers would have to demonstrate continuing professional growth, that is, show that they are better teachers of reading than they were when they received initial appointments and at subsequent time periods. The results of all this? Perhaps, improved instructional programs in reading, more children who can read well and do read more, and fewer children who require special reading services. Surely, these goals are worth striving for and competency based teacher education reading programs could be a vehicle for attaining them.

REFERENCES
1. Combs, Arthur W. "Educational Accountability From a Humanistic Perspective," *Educational Researcher,* 9 (September 1973), 19-21.
2. Elam, Stanley A. *A Resume of Performance-Based Teacher Education: What is the State of the Art?* Washington, D.C.: American Association of Colleges for Teacher Education, March 1972.
3. Gronlund, Norman E. *Stating Behavioral Objectives for Classroom Instruction.* New York: Macmillan, 1970.
4. Houston, Robert W. *Resources for Performance Based Education.* Albany, New York: Division of Teacher Education and Certification, New York State Education Department, March 1973.
5. Klein, Howard A. (Ed.). *The Quest for Competency in Teaching Reading.* Newark, Delaware: International Reading Association, 1972.
6. Rosner, Benjamin. "The Promise of Competency Based Teacher Education," *Education Quarterly,* 4 (Spring 1973), 2-6.

The Rationale for Competency Based Inservice Education

Betty Horodezky
University of British Columbia
Vancouver, British Columbia, Canada

If educational institutions, like automobile manufacturers, could afford the luxury of recalling their defective or minimal quality products as they pass through our educational assembly lines, reading specialists might well be spared the ominous task of rushing out to the scene of the accident in a last frantic effort to revive the intellectual and emotional remains of those who have had the misfortune of colliding with the hordes of teachers who fail in their daily task to develop literacy (9).

As Heilman (4) points out:

> Learning to read is probably one of the most important accomplishments that the child will achieve during his formal schooling . . . if he fails in reading, the frustrations and defeats which can beset him in the future are so numerous and varied that they have never been tabulated in one source.

Reading instruction in the United States and Canada has seldom been without its critics, yet it cannot be denied that considerable progress has been made over the years. As we review the current trends in educational institutions, however, we cannot help but concede that "improvement of reading instruction is still a major concern in education" (11).

WEAKNESSES IN CONVENTIONAL INSERVICE/PRESERVICE PROGRAMS

Among several of the shortcomings frequently cited against traditional training institutions, is the cry that teacher preparation is often too brief and too abstract. Because most teachers are able to graduate from our educational institutions with a minimum of exposure to reading—one or two courses—their limited knowledge of reading skills, diagnosis, methods, and materials prevents them from providing the instructional expertise required in solving the numerous reading problems which they encounter with children.

Complaints of theory oriented courses void of classroom involvement are not without foundation. Too frequently, students are shunted off to begin their practice teaching as late as their senior year, without ever having had previous on-the-job practice with children. Conventional preparation for this crucial phase of the program has failed to produce the essential teaching proficiencies needed later, since programs of this nature have not been based upon behavioral objectives toward which to focus instruction, demonstrate competency, and assess achievement (8).

We cannot hope to attain the high level of competency needed in our professional reading programs if we are to continue our instructional processes with traditional demands for cognitive skills without application to children. The earlier and more frequently the learner becomes involved in working with children in applying and assessing the theory he has learned, the better is his opportunity to grow in competence (7).

Inservice programs also have a growing responsibility for providing teachers of reading with more than the conventional facts and theories of reading that they may or may not have received in their earlier training "... for knowing about a problem or a solution to a problem is not equivalent to successfully applying that solution" (1).

WEAKNESSES IN CONVENTIONAL INSERVICE PROGRAMS

Unfortunately, the term *inservice education* is not likely to conjure up great bursts of enthusiasm, even among the most dedicated teachers. Although most inservice programs are desperately needed, they are severely inadequate. These inadequaces might be attributed to the fact that 1) activities are often selected without regard for purposes to be achieved; 2) programs fail to relate inservice programs to genuine needs of staff members; 3) program planners and directors who design and conduct inservice activities often lack the professional skills and knowledge to assure effectiveness; 4) planners fail to provide identifiable objectives and are unable to differentiate between activities and objectives; and 5) little or no assessment of teacher learning is provided, so teachers often sit passively with little incentive to learn.

These apparent weaknesses in our traditional inservice programs indicate that there is clearly a great "need to relate preservice and inservice education, not only more effectively, but to develop systematic teacher education programs that consider the training problems of teachers from the time they decide to become teachers to the time they retire from the profession" (5).

Clearly, there is a need to consider an alternate solution in our search to raise standards of reading instruction in our schools. It is for this reason that a competency based approach to inservice education is proposed in this paper.

WHAT IS A COMPETENCY BASED INSERVICE PROGRAM?

Perhaps one of the most vigorous and far reaching efforts in the seventies to raise the current standards of inservice and continuing education for those who teach reading was formulated by the IRA Commission on High Quality Teacher Education in the publication, *Modular Preparation for Teaching Reading.*

An examination of the IRA competency based teacher education model reveals that it is comprised of the following seventeen essential components identified by the Commission for program improvement (7):

1. Understanding the English Language as a Communication System
2. Interaction with Parents and the Community
3. Instructional Planning: Curriculum and Approaches
4. Developing Language Fluency and Perceptual Abilities in Early Childhood
5. Continued Language Development in Social Settings
6. Teaching Word-Attack Skills
7. Developing Comprehension: Analysis of Meaning
8. Developing Comprehension: Synthesis and Generalization
9. Developing Comprehension: Information Acquisition
10. Developing Literary Appreciation: Young Children
11. Developing Literary Appreciation: Latency Years
12. Developing Literary Appreciation: Young Adults
13. Diagnostic Evaluation of Reading Progress
14. School and Classroom Organization for Diagnostic Teaching
15. Adapting Instruction to Varied Linguistic Backgrounds
16. Treatment of Special Reading Difficulties
17. Initiating Improvements in School Programs

The seventeen components listed are referred to as resource modules, and can be divided into instructional modules for use in inservice, graduate, or undergraduate programs. Each resource module contains a developmental sequence of learnings at three levels to provide for individual differences. The most fundamental competencies, appropriate for the novice or inexperienced teacher, are found at the Professional Entry Level. The Advanced Level would apply to those persons who continue their graduate and inservice study. Emphasis here is on superior classroom performance. Research is used to support educational practices and decisions. The most sophisticated level of competency required by reading specialists, research personnel, and university teachers would be found at the Specialization Level.

Competencies at this level are directed toward experimentation for solutions to educational programs and leadership.

With the assistance of instructional leadership in schools, teachers can be guided in assessing their competencies so that appropriate portions of each module needed to improve individual capabilities in inservice programs can be implemented, thus assuring a more continuous improvement of reading instruction.

The five essential components of a module include: 1) a *preparticipation assessment plan*, used to identify the learner's proper placement or existing knowledge and skills for the module; 2) a list of *teacher competencies*, necessary for the acquisition of the module, written in precise behavioral statements on the objectives of the module; 3) a list of *criterion behaviors* used to measure the degree of achievement or attainment in a particular competency in terms of several kinds of behaviors, such as valuing, understanding, applying, analyzing-changing; 4) *learning experiences*, a suggested list of optional sources or means for use in acquiring the competency; and 5) *continuing assessment*, a means for determining whether a criterion behavior has been successfully mastered.

WHAT A COMPETENCY BASED PROGRAM CAN DO

Competency based models (7), when incorporated into ongoing inservice programs, can be of value insofar as they:

1. Assure the inclusion of all essential elements of an adequate reading education program
2. Assure that regular classroom teachers, as well as specialists, have a thorough grounding in the teaching of reading
3. Provide classroom performance competencies in teaching as well as knowledge competencies
4. Provide a variety of ideas for teaching teachers in assessing their mastery of desired competencies
5. Provide an approach to greater individualization of preservice and inservice programs
6. Provide detailed objectives of visible evidence of the need to increase the amount of time spent on the reading preparation of most elementary and secondary teachers

Since the preparation of excellent teachers of reading cannot be achieved in a short period of time, ongoing educational instruction must be planned into meaningful segments of experiences for inclusion in inservice programs.

The implementation of a modularized approach in a school setting requires that instructional leaders assist faculty members in assessing their own reading instruction competencies. This can be done through the use of self-assessment checklists based on modular content. Each member evaluates his own competency in relation to those listed. Faculty members then meet to identify and discuss their own professional needs in terms of the school's reading problems. Modules or modular segments are finally selected and assigned for the purpose of providing immediate solutions to existing problems and promoting professional growth and development in reading instruction. A series of concurrent inservice educational experiences would be included as a vital part of this program to insure the kinds of learning experiences suggested by the module.

If faculty members elect to participate, as a group, in selecting and working on a particular module, individual staff members would be appropriately assigned to work with groups commensurate with their educational experience and background. Here the emphasis would be on providing for continuous learning and professional development at every level of competence in joint effort to solving classroom problems (10). ". . . Not only should this process produce more effective teachers, but it should also encourage research into alternative approaches to inservice" instructional programs (2).

EXAMPLES OF COMPETENCY BASED INSERVICE PROGRAMS

The examples provided herein are designed to familarize the reader with the basic components of a module as described earlier in this paper.

1. *Preparticipation assessment.* Measurement of both knowledge and performance abilities. The inservice leader should include one or more techniques for assessment such as: oral tests, written tests, self-assessment checklists, videotape demonstrations, demonstration teaching, and other means as deemed appropriate.

2. *Teacher competencies.* Statements written in precise behavioral terms which identify the capabilities needed at each level of achievement, and which can be used for further development in inservice work and study. Examples of competencies at the advanced level might include (6):

   • Demonstrates a familiarity with several handwriting methods (including method currently taught). Describes differences in philosophy, letter formation, drills, and special features.
   • Knows provisions that should be made for left-handed child.

3. *Criterion behaviors.* The behaviors that provide evidence of competency attainment. Several criterion behaviors should be included for each competency. Any two of these examples would be appropriate for the competency listed previously.

- Presents a written summary.
- Shows models to inexperienced teachers and demonstrates.
- Prepares an illustrated bulletin.

4. *Learning Experiences.* Various sources or tasks listed where the learner can obtain knowledge and skill to fulfill the competency. Examples provided are appropriate for advanced competency listed previously.

- Reference reading.
- Study writing models.
- Study manuals for writing systems.
- Practice with left-handed pupils.

Other learning experiences appropriate for inservice programs might include:

- Prepare a detailed case study on one child.
- Try a recently learned instructional technique in the classroom and assess pupil growth.

5. *Continuing assessment.* The process of continuous measurement of the ongoing progress made by the learner in carrying out criterion behaviors.

Continuing assessment tools may include the same techniques as those used in preparticipation: tests, quizzes, observations of performance, analysis of preparation for performance, simulated teaching with peers as observed by instructor or peer evaluator, and other means.

SUMMARY

In light of demands from our rapidly changing society, the need is long overdue to revitalize and renovate teacher education through competency based programs. Educational institutions must be ready to reach beyond traditional programs of inservice and preservice instruction if we are to succeed in our thrust toward excellence in educational programs for our teachers of reading.

REFERENCES

1. Allington, Richard L. "A Rationale for Competency Based Education of Reading Teachers," *Journal of Reading*, 17 (April 1974), 517-523.
2. Austin, Mary. "Recommendations Drawn from Other Models," in H. Sartain and P. Stanton (Ed.), *Modular Preparation for Teaching Reading*. Newark, Delaware: International Reading Association, 1974, 22-28.
3. Harris, Ben M., and Wailand Bessent. *Inservice Education: A Guide to Better Practice*. Englewood Cliffs, New Jersey: Prentice-Hall, 1969, 3-15.
4. Heilman, Arthur W. *Principles and Practices of Teaching Reading*. Columbus, Ohio: Charles E. Merrill, 1961, 33.
5. Houston, Robert W., and Robert B. Howsam. *Competency Based Teacher Education: Progress, Problems, and Prospects*. Chicago: Science Research Associates, 1972, 79.
6. Horodezky, Betty. "Developing Perceptual Abilities and Language Fluency in Early Childhood," in H. Sartain and P. Stanton (Ed.), *Modular Preparation for Teaching Reading*. Newark, Delaware: International Reading Association, 1974, 92-93, 96.
7. Sartain, Harry W. "The Modular Content of the Professional Program," in H. Sartain and P. Stanton (Eds.), *Modular Preparation for Teaching Reading*. Newark, Delaware: International Reading Association, 1974, 31-59.
8. Sartain, Harry W. "Teacher Education: Preservice and Inservice," unpublished paper, University of Pittsburgh, 1971.
9. Sartain, Harry W., and Paul E. Stanton. "A Flexible Program for Preparing Teachers of Reading," in H. Sartain and P. Stanton (Eds.), *Modular Preparation for Teaching Reading*. Newark, Delaware: International Reading Association, 1974, 3-11.
10. Stanton, Paul E., and Harry W. Sartain. "Immediate Questions: The Teacher's Right to Know," in H. Sartain and P. Stanton (Eds.), *Modular Preparation for Teaching Reading*. Newark, Delaware: International Reading Association, 1974, 81.
11. Tiedt, Iris M., and Sidney W. Tiedt. *Contemporary English in Elementary School*. Englewood Cliffs, New Jersey: Prentice-Hall, 1967, 247-248.

Professional and Paraprofessional Roles in an Industrial Society

Ruth Love Holloway
U. S. Office of Education
Department of Health, Education, and Welfare
Washington, D.C.
United States of America

For many decades, schools and education were the domain of the professionally trained educator and prior to the 1960s in the United States, teachers and school administrators maintained a high degree of reserve relative to their particular roles and responsibilities for the education of children. But schools, like other institutions in society, have always been plagued by the fact of change and change in the public's awareness of need for human services and human resources has been accelerated in recent years. This change in awareness has taken place at a far more rapid rate than has the change in the social institutions designed to meet the needs which are now so apparent.

The educational enterprise is always known for the lag between conceptualization and implementation. Part of the cause relates to the rigidity of school systems throughout the country and their resistance to nontraditional ways of meeting the particular needs. However, the realization that there was a need for greater manpower, combined with the changed role and responsibility of teachers, brought a recognition of the vast reservoir of human potential ready to flow into the public schools of the United States and this has given rise to a new dimension in American education.

In the late 1960s, the need for and lack of availability of professional personnel, coupled with the intense questioning and protest regarding quality education for all schools, reached critical proportions. In addition, new dimensions in educational concepts and technology required a far more complex role for the classroom teacher.

The New Careers Movement as defined by Pearl and Reisman [1] was ignited by the recognition of the plight of uneducated persons and low income children. The movement called for a closer link between school and community and required a new entry level to careers in human services, with greater opportunity for upward mobility on the job. With this movement came a slow recognition of the school as an instrument of the community. During this period, new financial resources became available to school systems throughout the country. As a result, the War on Poverty of the Office of Economic Opportunity provided vast new resources for paraprofessionals to find their way into middle-class America. The concept related to the recognition that poor people, especially, must have the opportunity to help determine their destiny. The thrust opened up the schools in a new way. Additional resources were made available under the Manpower Development and Training Act and the Elementary and Secondary Education Act, especially Title I. Compensatory education became a major vehicle for employing teacher aides in the public schools.

The concept in this movement of new careers and upward mobility gave a degree of stature to individuals who were previously assigned to a lifestyle of unemployment and low level positions. This represents one of the essential innovative components—the whole thrust toward use of paraprofessionals in public service. While this movement related to institutions beyond the schools, it had a major impact upon American education. A number of categories established in the late sixties are now finding their way into educational institutions and are becoming almost traditional patterns of behavior. First, the teacher aide. While parents and individuals from middle-class backgrounds in the community have always served as volunteers in the schools, few served as real aides to teachers. Therefore, the movement toward paraprofessionals from low income backgrounds, with less than adequate education, became a phenomenon to be reckoned with. The aides came with a variety of backgrounds; in many instances they were parents of children who were the recipients of compensatory education. Now middle-class parents are seeking positions as teacher aides.

A number of studies indicate that the role development and the relationship of low income auxiliary personnel with other personnel made a major contribution to improvement in the teaching-learning process in the classroom. It was found that students benefited in terms of the actual technical skills received as well as the role models that were offered. While the essential role of the new careers concept was to provide occupations for paraprofessionals, it appears to have had a very positive impact upon the family and the community, as well as upon the individuals concerned, in terms of developing self-concept and skills needed to function in society.

Paraprofessionals from backgrounds similar to those of the pupils and parents served to bridge the gap between home and school. This ingredient helped to alleviate the adversary relationship which had created a loss of confidence in the schools. The impact of the teacher aide on the classroom teacher is one that must be dealt with. It was found that the initial installation of teacher aides in the classroom was met with a great deal of resistance. Classroom teachers, understandably, began to feel threatened by the new person in the room. At the same time, it was found that mutual teacher/aide training and opportunities to prepare and discuss activities jointly lead to what is now regarded as a high degree of acceptability on the part of professionally trained teachers. This resulted in the development of another role for the classroom teacher in meeting the individual needs of students in the classroom.

In their book, *New Careers and Roles in the American Schools*, Gordon Klopf and Garda Bowman indicate that the auxiliary personnel appeared to serve a catalytic function in the development of all other roles in the school system. The authors further indicate that training was identified as the essential element in effective use of auxiliary personnel. Employment without training appeared to present many problems, and there was no significant correlation between success in program and ethnicity or previous training of the auxiliary participants. Other studies have indicated that when teachers and other personnel participated in demonstration programs as trainees, the effectiveness of the training appeared to be facilitated.

Duties and responsibilities of teacher aides in the classroom have become more definitive as the new careers movement progressed. In the initial stages, the teacher aides or paraprofessionals were asked to perform many custodial functions for children. As the professionally trained teacher relaxed and as teacher aides became more comfortable and secure, we saw a widespread movement toward using the paraprofessional as an instructional aide. Paraprofessionals began to assist in reading, language, and mathematics, and persons with special skills were used in the arts. So the role definition was balanced with role development which gave variation and scope to the total program and concept.

Because of the need for training, institutions of higher education began to establish both preservice and inservice programs for paraprofessionals. School districts established a career ladder program in which assistants and aides began to find their way into the institutional setting.

Under an exciting program entitled "Career Opportunities," which was federally funded by the U.S. Congress, the concept of bringing into the school additional personnel who had previously gone into other job situations became a reality. From a variety of communities, the Career Opportunities Program selected individuals who could contribute significantly to the schools. This brought to the school system a new kind of person who had potential for becoming an exciting classroom teacher. So now we see a new cadre of young and exciting, and sometimes older individuals making their ways into the established school environment.

The idea of using unskilled workers in public service is not a new phenomenon. As early as the 17th century in England, the Elizabethan poor laws included a provision that those persons unable to find gainful employment and who were dependent upon the state should be placed in workhouses and trained to perform community improvement work. The workhouses were probably far from ideal settings and the nature of community improvement work was not likely to be dignified or meaningful, but the concept of training the unemployed to perform needed public service was apparent.

In the United States, an organized program based upon this concept was first developed three decades ago under the Works Progress Administration and the National Youth Administration. Particular emphasis was placed on the concept of NYA under which unemployed, out-of-school youth, as well as potential dropouts, were trained and placed in nonprofessional roles in human service. In 1953, the first major experiment in the use of auxiliary personnel in education was undertaken in Bay City, Michigan, with funds from the Ford Foundation. This program was designed to increase teacher effectiveness by freeing teachers from the necessity of devoting a disproportionate amount of time to nonprofessional functions. Another aim of this experiment was to assist administrators in preserving quality education in the face of a great shortage of professional personnel, the rising costs of education, and large class sizes. The teaching profession generally reacted negatively to this concept. However, in the mid 1960s when the new careers movement took hold with the combined resources of federal funds, there seemed to have developed a great deal of acceptance of the concept. A significant dimension of the new approach was the emphasis on the right of all individuals to essential human service. This was coupled with an increased awareness of the extent of human need and the paucity of existing services. The additional, and very important, ingredient related to a grave concern for the quality of education for all children in the community.

Traditionally, in American society, low income people have placed faith in the schools to solve their problems. It was only in the sixties that there emerged a large degree of unrest among this population. It is fair to say that the history of American education demonstrates that middle-class parents have always had a major impact on the quality and the quantity of education for their children. They have served on boards of education, they have been involved in parent-teacher associations, they have become volunteers in the schools, and they have used the instrumentation at their resources to demand quality education at all levels. When there was mass protest and mass unrest on the part of students and their parents, and when there seemed to have been a heightened disenchantment and alienation from the schools, the schools began to open up and to create new vehicles and avenues for both parents and teachers.

The paraprofessional movement in the United States brought with it other kinds of concepts. Tutoring, both in and out of school, became a major emphasis in the late 1960s. Here again, federal resources had a tremendous impact. Tutors were recruited from the community; generally from universities and colleges and from the vast middle class. Reading and language were major concerns for the tutors. The concept of peer teaching became a significant part of a school's program. Frequently, the formalized use of children within the classroom to help each other, as well as the use of older children to help younger children, became a reality. In fact, peer teaching has proven to be a major benefit to the individual giving help as well as to the individual receiving help. One of the major innovations and discoveries in the 1960s related to the use of students and pupils (who themselves were underachieving) as tutors to other children. It was found that many underachievers increased in achievement.

Another major component in the use of paraprofessionals was the increased emphasis on the use of volunteers. There are those who feel that the vast resources of the seventies and eighties in terms of manpower will be based upon a growing array of volunteers. There will be further efforts to call upon the public to give service to public institutions.

The volunteer movement has seen some interesting kinds of intervention from outside agencies. Major corporations and other employers have been willing to provide release time for individual volunteers to help children in the classroom. The activities do not always relate to reading, but a major emphasis is placed upon reading and language development. The activities included helping individual children in word attack skills and comprehension, reading to the children, and providing a near professional level of reading assistance.

The question arises as to how paraprofessionalism might be encouraged. In order to fully encourage and use the manpower resources of paraprofessionals, one must take a close look at what is expected of the professional and the school as a whole. There is a need to define clearly the emerging role of the professional educator. Teachers in the 1970s and the 1980s are expected to individualize and personalize instruction. They are expected to know more about individual learning styles and to provide instruction to match these particular styles. Teachers, as part of a team, are expected to diagnose accurately the educational, medical, social, and emotional needs of individuals in the classroom. Teachers are also expected to use the cultural heritage of a wide variety of children in designing the instructional program. Perhaps the greatest thing expected of teachers is that they should be accountable for the achievement or lack of achievement on the part of all children in their care.

There is an increased awareness in the United States and in other industrial societies that there is no place for second class education. All children are expected to learn and it is recognized that expectation has a great deal to do with achievement. This means then that teachers will perform as managers in the classroom, taking full advantage of their paraprofessional aides as well as acting as instructors themselves. As a team leader, the teacher has a much better chance of catering to the needs of every child.

To use paraprofessionals means that several factors must come into play and we can identify three factors of particular significance: 1) role definition and development; 2) inservice and preservice training; and 3) auxiliary personnel within the structure of the public school, with opportunities for advancement upon demonstration of effective service and educational growth.

The school as an institution must be flexible enough to allow those who wish to volunteer, those who wish to be employed, and those who wish to work part time only to come into the schools and make their contributions.

Finally, the new approach to using professionals and paraprofessionals means that team effort is to become a reality and that a concerted effort must be made to bring about the delivery of human resources to children. Its basic premise is that every child and youth has a right to learn.

The New Careers Movement, while still imperfect, is well on its way to becoming institutionalized. It offers a magnificent opportunity for both children and adults to realize their potential. Industrial societies cannot afford anything less than maximum use of its most precious resources—its people.

REFERENCE
1.   Pearl, Arthur, and Fran Reisman. *New Careers for the Poor: The Nonprofessional in Human Service.* London: Collier-Macmillan, 1965.

Professional and Paraprofessional Roles in Developing Countries

Morris Cutler
Columbia University
New York, New York
United States of America

In considering the question, "Do developing nations use paraprofessionals or volunteers?" I found that few developing nations presently employ paraprofessionals, teacher aides, or volunteer tutors in their efforts to improve the literacy levels of their people. With the exception of small numbers of peace corps type volunteers from industrialized nations, few educators of developing nations have initiated programs utilizing paraprofessionals to supplement and support the activities of the classroom teachers.

"Why don't developing nations employ paraprofessionals?" Not surprisingly, there are several reasons.

One major factor is the lack of a literate reservoir from which to draw. The limited numbers of people who can read and write and the great demand for their services, restrict their services to the schools. Functional literacy falls below 20 percent of the population of many developing nations of the world.

Another factor, which is a result of the literacy limitation, is the shortage of educated and professionally trained teachers. From a recent Unesco survey we find that in Afghanistan only 28 percent of the primary teachers have had a secondary education. In Laos, the figure is 30 percent; in Nepal, 34 percent; and in India, 52 percent. Only two nations in Asia had more than 76 percent primary teachers with a secondary education. The percentages of teachers with professional training is even lower in these and other nations.

Improving the quality and quantity of teachers requires much time and effort. The meager resources of developing nations limit their abilities to develop paraprofessional programs. In effect, a large percentage of teachers in developing nations are paraprofessional by comparison with the education and training of most teachers in industrialized nations.

In several cultures, females traditionally are not provided with opportunities for schooling and self-fufillment outside of the home. This is especially true in agricultural societies where women are needed to work in the fields to help produce food for survival. In Islamic societies, women are still secluded or only recently have been unveiled. This waste of human resources restricts large segments of the population from being available for service to children.

Another problem of developing nations is educational lag, the widening gap between existing educational systems and emerging changes in societal goals. Since most ministries of education are highly centralized and are staffed by men with classical educations, the bureaucracy is reluctant to change and to allow "outsiders" to enter their domains. Teachers and teacher organizations are also very concerned and many consider paraprofessionals as a movement to undermine their employment, status, and power.

If there are few paraprofessionals employed now, what are the prospects for their future use? Who might be used? How might they be used?

I believe that the overall possibility is very poor that developing nations will use paraprofessionals in normal school situations to supplement the work of the teacher of reading. The absence of financial resources, the paucity of literate personnel, and the rigidity of cultural traditions appear overwhelming at this time. Most nations are struggling to remain solvent and to meet, with undereducated and undertrained teachers, the rising demands for literacy. They do not see paraprofessionals as solutions to their problems. However, being an educator and an optimist, I do see some signs of hope.

A few of the developing nations actually have begun to encounter a temporary surplus of trained teachers. Young teachers leaving the training schools are finding few positions available; unqualified or untrained teachers with many years of experience are difficult to replace. Consideration is, therefore, being given by some agencies to the possibility of using these people in some educational capacity. There is the usual problem of finances and the additional problem of pride; these young people are not too willing to take positions as paraprofessionals since they feel that they are already qualified as teachers. If some systematic procedure can be developed to employ these young people as teachers following a year or two as a paraprofessional, it may point the way to establishing a paraprofessional internship as a required step in on-the-job training. This concept is different from that of the career paraprofessional envisioned in the literature today. However, for those nations whose children suffer from large classes and from poorly educated and trained teachers, this idea may prove to be practical as the national level of education is raised.

Regional Differences in Purposes and Standards for Teacher Education

Mathew L. L. Okot
Uganda Teachers Association
Kampola, Uganda

Over the ages, the primary function of education has been conceived as that of transmitting the accumulated body of knowledge from one generation to the next, and in imparting to the young an understanding of all aspects of culture to ensure society's stability, security, solidarity, and preservation. In this context, therefore, education has been expected to prepare the young for full membership in society. Vital as it is, this function is by nature static, for at best it can only be expected to reproduce "the type." As aspirations, knowledge, and population grew, this aim became narrower in scope and inadequate. Calling for a second aim for growth has become indispensable.

In making an independent survey of the prospects for development in the world's low income countries, the international Pearson Commission is reported as laying special emphasis on the vital need for trained manpower in Africa and has attributed this aspiration to education. Whether the system of education operating in both developing and developed countries can justify all this faith placed upon it and come up to expectations will, in my opinion, depend very largely on the quality or standard of teachers. It is of paramount importance that teachers should not only subscribe to the accepted educational goals, but should also possess the necessary attitudes, skills, and knowledge to make these aspirations a reality. I believe that if teachers are to succeed in translating the objectives of education into day-to-day classroom teaching, it will depend largely on the nature and quality of their training, since it is responsible for developing in them the attitudes, skills, and knowledge that will enable them to assist children in acquiring the necessary qualities to meet the expectations their societies place on education. These expectations are the philosophies each ethnic group adopts and is committed to follow.

Of all the educational problems that beset developing countries today, none appears to be as persistent or as compelling as the one related to the training of a competent teacher. The growing demands for more and better schools; the need to relate the curriculum to the child's environment; the need for appropriate textbooks and other instructional materials; the desirability of training in vocational and technical skills; and, indeed, the overall problem of preparing citizens who will be fully oriented to their environments, cannot be accomplished effectively without the aid of competent teachers. Nor can the demand for trained manpower be met adequately, for the success or failure of all these goals depends entirely on the pattern, the content, and objectives of teacher education programmes designed for these purposes. The concern for an adequate supply of high quality teachers forms a major preoccupation of educators the world over, but it is of particular interest to the developing countries, for they cannot affort waste. This school of thought was realized by Clarence Beeby in his book, *The Quantity of Education in Developing Countries*, when (in addition to dealing realistically with the problems militating against educational reform, such as financial stringency, lack of adequate resources, the level of general education and length of training of teachers, attitudes of parents and the public, and skill and liveliness of the administrators and professional leaders) he concluded: "There are many opinions in this essay that can, as yet, be expressed only tentatively; but of two things I am completely certain: more attention must be given to the quality of education in developing countries, and there must be closer professional cooperation between the educator and the economist in educational planning."

As far as I am concerned, the need for better quality teachers should be the ultimate concern of every state; but the type of education appears to be dictated by the aspirations adopted by each society.

Writing about American education, Henry J. Ehlers, in *Crucial Issues in Education*, lays special stress on freedom and excellence as democracy's most cherished goals, stating, "To transform these ideals into living realities, surely the most crucial educational issue of all has to do with the quality and adequacy of the teaching corps. How can we find or develop teachers who thereby can inspire American youth in the quest for liberty and the quest for excellence?" In this context, the roles and responsibilities of education grow more central and indispensable, and the function of teachers becomes of supreme importance.

In a situation of this nature, it seems to me that the level and content of teacher education in America has to take a different shape. Paul Woodring neatly epitomized the basic problem in *New Directions in Teacher Education, New York*:

> The truly liberally educated man is one who can make wise decisions independently. He can choose between good and bad, truth and falsehood, the beautiful and the ugly, the worthwhile and the trivial. His education will improve his ability to make ethical decisions, political decisions, decisions within the home and on the job. It will enable him to choose and appreciate a good work, a good painting, or a good piece of music. It will free him of provincialism and prepare him

to understand cultures other than his own. It will enable him to make the many decisions necessary in planning a good life and conducting it properly. This education should be common to all and independent of vocational choice.

From the quotation it is possible to sense that realization of Woodring's aspirations may be through competency in America's teacher education. The basic aims of professional education should be geared toward providing an adequate number of professionally educated entrants to the professions and maintaining or increasing the quality of entrants to satisfy society's needs. The first aim is quantitative and the second, qualitative.

For a long time, there has been a tendency in Africa to regard preschool and primary school teaching as areas in which the least qualified teacher should work. Consequently, well over 70 percent of Africa's uncertified and untrained teachers are to be found in the lower levels of primary schools. This assumption presupposes that every child would have an opportunity to reach the upper levels. Psychologists have sounded a warning by pointing out that the early years are the formative period of a child's existence and have advised that, unless the best teachers are employed at this level, the child may be intellectually and emotionally maimed for life through poor teaching. Against this background, underdeveloped or developing countries who share the same realization may well be advised to accept the fact that any would-be teacher, regardless of the level at which he intends to teach, should have the minimum qualification of full secondary school background as prerequisite professional training.

In this kind of situation, teacher education programmes should be designed to provide 1) a general education as a prerequisite for any profession, 2) the pursuance of subject matters, and 3) professional education. It seems to me that the nongraduate teacher earmarked for the preschool or elementary school should have a sound general educational background and his professional training should include the study of the social foundations of education, the history of education, elementary psychology, child study, curriculum and method, audiovisual aids, construction of instructional materials, and practical teaching.

Africa faces a great challenge in terms of its tremendous social, economic, and political problems; but it is imperative for the teacher in this constantly changing world of Africa to be better equipped than his European, American, or Russian counterparts because, for some time to come, both the teacher and the student in Africa will be living and working within two cultures—the traditional and the Western—and they must be able to maintain an equilibrium. This can be done only if teacher education programmes are designed to ensure flexibility. If this is to be done, educators might find it necessary to extend the period of training with a view to improving the quality of the teaching corps.

Personnel in teacher education programmes for graduate teachers in Africa are beginning to realize that an African bias must take precedence over any other cultural bias. This holds true in Europe, America, the USSR, and in other countries as well. A teacher has to appreciate the fact that any self-respecting nation must design its educational system to suit its own environment. He needs to know that there are as many systems of education as there are nations and that no system enjoys universality. But it should be realized that each of these systems shares the same concern for academic excellence in whatever they do or teach. Each also aims at the best for their pupils and at making their pupils good citizens of their respective countries. Each designs its own textbooks, prepares its teachers to be attuned to the country's aims, and expects the teachers to transmit the culture of the nation to the younger generation.

This approach calls for a drastic change in the cirriculum and syllabi of all nations and more so of underdeveloped nations. If this change is to become a reality, I would probably suggest that it can occur realistically and more effectively only if the teacher is fully involved in the process of change: he must be fully oriented as to the whys and wherefores of the change.

Comparing the African teacher and his European counterpart, one might sense that the latter is not faced with such a task but one may also say that the European continent is not faced with the same problems as the African continent. What is more, specialization is a common feature in most advanced countries, while the African countries are still faced with inadequate manpower.

As can be realized from the foregoing, various factors contribute to differences in purposes and standards for teacher education. Some of these differences are caused by the lack of manpower, forcing certain nations to employ expatriates to man secondary and university institutions, particularly. For instance, foreign aid programmes and organizations, such as the U.S. Peace Corps Volunteers and U.K. Voluntary Service Organization, are helping many African countries to staff secondary and post-secondary schools.

There is, however, a danger here, for some countries place too much reliance on these aids at the expense of planning for a gradual takeover from expatriate staff. Any self-respecting autonomous nation must staff its schools with its own nationals as soon as practicable and should do so with deliberate speed. It is politically, socially, and culturally unwise to entrust the education of the youth of a country largely to the nationals of another country, as education is the vehicle for the transmission of culture. And if the job of the school is to build into the personality of the young the selected aspects of the culture within which the school operates, it then stands to reason that an emerging nation must make every conscious effort to have its own nationals on its school staffs at all levels. This, of course, does not mean that nationals of other countries are not welcome; but it is a different thing entirely to rely on them exclusively without definite plans to change this state of affairs. Teacher education in Africa must bear the brunt of the responsibility for the training of graduate teachers for secondary, technical, and post-secondary schools, as well as the preparation of educational administrators and supervisors.

It might seem possible to generalize about the type of teacher education needed in underdeveloped or developing countries, but these areas vary widely in natural resources, climate, population, geography, and linguistic and cultural traditions. Such diversity makes it difficult to generalize about their physical, social, and educational needs. Regardless of their differences, however, most underdeveloped nations have demonstrated that they share an abiding faith in education as a major key to future happiness and economic security. Indeed, all nations should adhere to this aspiration or be reminded of the warning sounded by I. N. Thut in *Educational Patterns in Contemporary Societies:* "Education can contribute to the rapid development of a society, it can be used by a demagogue to warp the values of a people, or it can be an agent for preservation of the status quo."

I fully agree with Thut, for an education system could be designed which would assure neither progress nor retrogression and the same proportion of each generation would be enrolled in it. In other words, it might simply maintain the status quo. Teacher educators and those concerned with designing teacher education programmes the world over must have love and the aspirations of their respective countries at heart; but whether their undertaking should be done in absolute isolation from, and regardless of, what is happening next door, remains to be examined. One thing is certain, the planners have to guard against any destructive element in curriculum design as a result of unwarranted conflict in educational policies. The academic rubric used may differ from those adopted elsewhere in the world or from country to country, but the esteem accorded to the aims and the importance given to the curriculum objectives should be no less than that accorded to the meaningful deliberations of nations.

REFERENCES
1. Beeby, Clarence (Ed.). *Quantitative Aspects of Educational Planning.* Paris: Unesco, International Institute for Educational Planning, 1969.
2. Fafunwa, A. Babs. *New Perspectives in African Education.*

A Comparison of Australian and American Reading Teachers

Robert J. Tierney
University of Arizona
Tucson, Arizona
United States of America

There is a general consensus that efforts toward the ultimate improvement of educational systems are largely dependent upon teachers and their education. The teaching of reading is no exception and the crucial importance of the teacher in the reading process has been realized. Gray concluded in the 1956 report on a comparative study of fundamental education that, undoubtedly, the teacher was the most important factor in promotion of the general development of children and their progress in reading. One of the better known studies of recent years, "The Cooperative Research Program in First Grade Reading Instruction" (4), concluded that if reading instruction was to be improved it was necessary to prepare better reading teachers. Various researchers and writers have reiterated these sentiments (2, 5, 9, 13, 18).

The future directions of any sincere endeavor to improve the teaching of reading must be based on scientific evidence rather than on conjecture, and this can only be fully realized when an unbiased evaluation is made of what presently exists. An examination of teacher education programs in various nations reveals that there are marked differences between countries and even between institutions within the same country. Thus, these various groups may often be unaware of their own cultural biases concerning teacher education and teaching (7). It would seem, therefore, that there is need for a new frame of reference—that of evaluating teaching through an international frame of reference. Obvious advantages provided by a global perspective might be 1) a greater awareness of the assumptions and procedures of teaching, 2) better comprehension of various issues of teaching and teacher education, 3) solutions to common needs of the various countries to evaluate their practices, and 4) revelation of new insights concerning the pressing problems of improving teacher preparation programs. As Foshay (10) stated, "If custom and law define what is educationally allowable within a nation, the educational systems beyond one's national boundaries suggest what is educationally possible." Along this same line of reasoning, Douglass (8) stated:

It is sometimes instructive to take a look at the ways of other people as they work with children: not because they warrant being copied, but rather for purposes of contrast so that one may be helped to entertain ideas that could lead to useful modifications in ways of helping children learn.

It would seem clear that, if we are to improve reading instruction, empirical cross-national studies should be made of the teacher variable in reading.

PURPOSE

It was the purpose of this investigation to assess and compare the characteristics of distinct populations of Australian and American teachers at two grade levels. The teacher characteristics investigated were teacher knowledge of reading instruction and the frequency of the following behaviors during reading instruction: teacher direction, teacher initiation, teacher correction, cognitive questioning, broad questioning, narrow questioning, teacher acceptance, teacher praise, student responsiveness, oral reading, silent reading, directed activity, and nonfunctional behavior.

HYPOTHESES

In order to compare the teacher populations on the selected teacher variables, the following null hypotheses were tested at the .05 level of significance:

1. There is no statistically significant difference between the differences in grade level vectors of the mean teacher variable scores across countries.
2. There is no statistically significant difference between the vectors of the mean teacher variable scores across countries.
3. There is no statistically significant difference between the vectors of the mean teacher variable scores across grade levels.

If a significant multivariate F was found, a discriminant analysis would be used to determine the relative contribution of each measure to overall significance and univariate F-tests would be used to test each variable separately.

SAMPLING PROCEDURES

SUBJECTS

Subjects for this study consisted of 1) a random selection of 15 second grade teachers and 15 third grade teachers who were teaching at one of 30 preselected schools in the St. George Area (Australia) and who were willing to participate in this study, and 2) a random selection of 15 second grade teachers and 15 third grade teachers who were teaching at one of 30 preselected schools in DeKalb County (United States) and who were willing to participate.

RATIONALE FOR SELECTION

There were several reasons for the selection of the two countries, the single communities within these two countries, and the two grade levels specified. First, the investigator considered himself intimately acquainted with the cultures, communities, and education systems of both countries. Second, it was deemed necessary to study teachers from countries which were solely English speaking in order to avoid the difficulty of measuring teacher characteristics across countries of different languages. Third, as both the United States of America and Australia have over one-half of their populations residing in urban areas, urban areas were considered a suitable source for subjects in both countries. Fourth, the inclusion of teachers at two grade levels enabled the comparison of the characteristics of teachers at two consecutive grade levels. Within the Australian elementary school, the division into infant school and primary school occurs between second and third grade levels. Teachers who intend to teach in either of these two schools usually receive different teacher training experiences; therefore, for the Australian teachers this entailed the comparison of infant school teachers with primary school teachers. Fifth, teachers at these grade levels were teaching children at early stages of learning to read.

Every effort was made to select communities of similar size, location, function, and socioeconomic status and which were representative of the two countries. Given full particulars, approval for the study was granted by the necessary authority in each country, and the names of 30 schools within each community were sent to the researcher. Approval was obtained on the condition that a teacher's involvement would be voluntary.

DESCRIPTION OF THE COMMUNITIES

The two communities nominated to represent the two countries were the St. George area, Sydney, Australia, and DeKalb County, Georgia, United States of America.

St. George, one of six school areas in Sydney, operates 98 elementary schools and 21 high schools. The percentage of white-collar workers and professional men, as well as of partly skilled workers, is slightly above average for Australia.

The DeKalb County school system, in the northeastern section of Atlanta, operates 82 elementary schools and 21 high schools. As with St.

George, DeKalb County is dormitory in nature and its percentage of white-collar workers, professional people, and partly skilled workers is slightly above average for the United States.

DESCRIPTION OF TEACHER POPULATION

The teacher population to which the findings of this study may be generalized includes those second and third grade teachers who taught at one of the 30 designated schools in either DeKalb County or the St. George area and who were willing to participate in the study. In DeKalb County, a total of 34 second grade teachers and 35 third grade teachers indicated a willingness to participate; and in St. George, a total of 37 second grade teachers and 30 third grade teachers indicated a willingness to participate.

In an attempt to delineate the contextual framework of this comparison, a description of the teachers, their reading practices, and their pupils was obtained through teacher responses to data sheets.

INSTRUMENTATION

To assess teacher characteristics, the Test of Knowledge of Reading Instruction and the Reading Instruction Observation Scale were developed. The Test of Knowledge of Reading Instruction is a single form, 86-item, researcher-constructed, four-option, multiple-choice instrument designed to assess the knowledge of reading instruction of second and third grade teachers in Australia and the United States. The Reading Instruction Observation Scale incorporates 13 categories of behaviors and was designed to analyze cognitive and affective aspects of teacher behavior during reading instruction. Information on the reliability, validity, construction, and use of these instruments can be obtained from the author.

DATA COLLECTING PROCEDURES

The study was conducted during the 20th and 21st weeks of the school year. For the Australian schools, this occurred June 18, 1973 to June 29, 1973; for the American schools, January 7, 1974 to January 18, 1974. On each school day during this period, two, three, or four teachers were scheduled for observation and testing.

Each teacher's was observed during the teaching of a reading lesson; and each responded to the Test of Knowledge of Reading Instruction and completed data sheets. At a previously specified time, one of two observers, who had been randomly assigned to this class, spent 25-35 minutes observing a reading lesson. This observer used the Reading Instruction Observation Scale to categorize teacher behaviors every five seconds or every time the behavior changed into one of 13 categories. At no time was the teacher aware of the specific behavior being categorized. Teachers had been instructed to give the reading lesson planned for that day and they were asked to neither introduce the observer nor react to the presence of the observer in their class. These directions appeared to have been followed. Later the same day, while away from their classes, the teachers responded to questions on the Test of Knowledge of Reading Instruction and completed data sheets.

DESIGN OF THE STUDY

The research design was a 2 x 2 quasiexperimental design. This design is shown in Table 1. The following variables represent the sources of variation within the design. The independent variables are country and grade level. C represents countries: $c=2$. C_1 represents the Australian teachers; C_2 represents the American teachers. G represents grade levels: $g=2$. G_1 represents the second grade; G_2 represents the third grade.

There were 14 dependent variables in the design. The Reading Instruction Observation Scale was used to obtain each subject's measure on 13 of these variables and each subject's score was expressed as a transformed score through the use of an arc sine transformation. The variables included teacher direction, teacher initiation, teacher correction, cognitive questioning, broad questioning, narrow questioning, teacher acceptance, teacher praise, student responsiveness, oral reading, silent reading, directed activity, and nonfunctional behavior. The Test of Knowledge of Reading Instruction was used to obtain each subject's score on the 14th of these variables. Unlike the other 13 variables, the raw score of each subject was used.

Table 1. Experimental Layout of Teacher Comparison

		C_1				C_2			
G_1	$Y_{1,11,1}$	$Y_{1,11,2}$	. .	$Y_{1,11,14}$	$Y_{1,12,1}$	$Y_{1,12,2}$	. .	$Y_{1,12,14}$	$\overline{Y}_{.,1,.1}$
	$Y_{15,11,1}$	Y		Y	Y	Y		Y	$\overline{Y}$
G_2	$Y_{1,21,1}$	$Y_{1,21,2}$	. .	$Y_{1,21,14}$	$Y_{1,22,1}$	$Y_{1,22,1}$	. .	$Y_{1,22,14}$	$\overline{Y}_{.,2,.1}$
	$Y_{15,21,2}$	$Y_{15,21,2}$	. .	$Y_{15,21,14}$	$Y_{15,22,2}$	$Y_{15,22,2}$	. .	$Y_{15,22,14}$	$\overline{Y}_{.2..14}$
	$\overline{Y}_{...1,1}$				$\overline{Y}_{..2,1}$				$\overline{Y}_{....1}$
	$\overline{Y}_{...1,14}$				$\overline{Y}_{...2,14}$				$\overline{Y}_{.....14}$

STATISTICAL PROCEDURES

A multivariate analysis of variance was used as the major method of data analysis in this study because it was most appropriate for testing the significance of differences between comparison groups in terms of a number of dependent variables considered simultaneously (20). If a significant multivariate F was found, an a priori decision was made to use a discriminant analysis to determine the relative contribution of each measure to overall significance. Univariate F-tests would also be examined to locate the significance. The decision to refer to analyses of variance matrices was based on an empirical comparison of univariate and multivariate procedures by Hummel and Sligo (15). These researchers found the above procedure to be superior to either a series of univariate analyses or a completely multivariate approach.

RESULTS

The means and standard deviations of the teacher samples on the 14 variables is presented in Table 2. The Test of Knowledge of Reading Instruction measured teacher knowledge and the total possible raw score was 86. The Reading Instruction Observation Scale was used to obtain each teacher's measure on the other 13 variables. For each of these 13 variables, a teacher's score was expressed as a percentage of the total frequency of behavior for all 13 variables.

ANALYSIS OF THE TEACHER DATA
by MONOVA

The computer multivariate F statistic for the combined vectors of teacher variable scores produced a significant ($p < .001$) chi-square of 90.58 with 42 degrees of freedom. Since the results of the multivariate F test were significant, statistical hypotheses were tested relating to interactions of grade level and country and main effects of country and grade level. Table 3 summarizes the multivariate tests.

1. Interaction: country x grade

The multivariate test of significant interaction between country and grade reported indicates that the multivariate F statistic of .0000 was not significant ($p < .05$). Therefore, the null hypothesis that there is no statistically significant difference between the differences in grade level vectors of the mean teacher variable scores across countries was accepted.

2. Main effect of grade

The results of the multivariate test of significant main effect of grade indicate that the multivariate F statistic of 1.2717 was not significant ($p < .05$). Therefore, the null hypothesis was accepted that there is no

Table 2. Means and Standard Deviations of Australian and American Teachers on the 14 Variables at Two Grade Levels

Variable Name/Teacher Sample		Mean	Standard Deviation
Knowledge of Reading Instruction			
Australia	Grade Two	48.20	5.95
	Grade Three	48.93	7.39
United States	Grade Two	47.60	11.42
	Grade Three	48.33	12.57
Teacher Direction			
Australia	Grade Two	13.00	5.48
	Grade Three	9.70	3.44
United States	Grade Two	14.64	3.49
	Grade Three	12.38	4.75
Teacher Initiation			
Australia	Grade Two	6.34	2.68
	Grade Three	8.57	6.17
United States	Grade Two	4.43	4.56
	Grade Three	5.04	3.82
Teacher Correction			
Australia	Grade Two	6.86	4.28
	Grade Three	6.59	3.12
United States	Grade Two	4.74	4.17
	Grade Three	3.60	3.09
Cognitive Questioning			
Australia	Grade Two	4.47	2.37
	Grade Three	5.57	2.93
United States	Grade Two	7.34	3.41
	Grade Three	6.30	3.33
Broad Questioning			
Australia	Grade Two	1.72	1.23
	Grade Three	1.36	1.24
United States	Grade Two	2.61	2.01
	Grade Three	3.01	2.39
Narrow Questioning			
Australia	Grade Two	2.86	2.74
	Grade Three	2.44	1.56
United States	Grade Two	4.12	2.34
	Grade Three	4.13	2.15
Teacher Acceptance			
Australia	Grade Two	4.06	2.19
	Grade Three	5.40	3.41
United States	Grade Two	8.72	3.99
	Grade Three	7.26	2.47
Teacher Praise			
Australia	Grade Two	3.91	1.59
	Grade Three	1.75	1.86
United States	Grade Two	1.19	1.76
	Grade Three	1.48	1.61
Student Responsiveness			
Australia	Grade Two	14.88	4.86
	Grade Three	16.25	6.52
United States	Grade Two	19.85	7.76
	Grade Three	22.44	7.62
Oral Reading			
Australia	Grade Two	17.03	9.83
	Grade Three	14.89	13.49
United States	Grade Two	9.65	10.02
	Grade Three	8.41	7.12
Silent Reading			
Australia	Grade Two	.29	.97
	Grade Three	.34	.66
United States	Grade Two	4.43	9.58
	Grade Three	10.23	17.45
Directed Activity			
Australia	Grade Two	5.93	8.29
	Grade Three	6.82	8.27
United States	Grade Two	2.32	3.22
	Grade Three	2.36	3.16
Nonfunctional Behavior			
Australia	Grade Two	18.22	11.99
	Grade Three	20.75	10.22
United States	Grade Two	15.93	11.58
	Grade Three	13.78	8.52

statistically significant difference between the vectors of the mean teacher variable scores across grades.

3. Main effect of country

The results of the multivariate test of significant main effect of country indicate that the multivariate F statistic was significant ($p < .05$). Therefore, the null hypothesis that there is no statistically significant difference between the vectors of the mean teacher variable scores across countries was rejected. Instead, it was accepted that there was a statistically significant difference between the vectors of the mean teacher variable scores across countries.

The relative contribution of each measure to overall significance was examined to determine for which dependent variables significance occurred. To determine the relative contributions, a correlation between each original variable and the discriminant function for the main effect of country was computer and then examined to determine which dependent variables contributed most to the difference between factor level means. The correlations are reported in Table 4. The dependent variables which discriminated strongest and thus contributed most to the significant main effect of country were teacher initiation, teacher correction, narrow questioning, teacher acceptance, teacher praise, student responsiveness, oral reading, and silent reading. The univariate F-tests reported in Table 5 lend confidence to this interpretation. Significant main effects for country occurred on teacher initiation ($p < .05$), teacher correction ($p < .01$), narrow questioning ($p < .05$), teacher acceptance ($p < .001$), teacher praise ($p < .001$), student responsiveness ($< .01$), oral reading ($p < .05$), and silent reading ($< .01$). The Australian teachers displayed more teacher initiation, teacher correction, teacher praise and had more oral reading. American teachers displayed more narrow questioning, teacher acceptance and had more student responsiveness and silent reading.

Table 3.   Results of the Multivariate Analysis of Variance of the Teacher Data

Source of Variation	df Hypothesis	df Error	F-value
Country	14	43	6.2776***
Grade	14	43	1.2717
Country x Grade	14	43	.0000

***p < .001

Table 4. Main Effect of Country: Correlation between Discriminant Functions and Original Scores

Variable	Structure Correlation Coefficient
Knowledge of R.I.	.002
Teacher Direction	-.173
Teacher Initiation	.251
Teacher Correction	.282
Cognitive Questioning	-.203
Broad Questioning	-.205
Narrow Questioning	-.271
Teacher Acceptance	-.383
Teacher Praise	.379
Student Responsiveness	-.281
Oral Reading	.228
Silent Reading	-.302
Directed Activity	.183
Nonfunctional Behavior	.166

Table 5. Main Effect of Country: Univariate F-tests

Variable	Mean Square	$F_{(1,56)}$
Knowledge of R.I.	5.40	.05
Teacher Direction	.073	3.42
Teacher Initiation	.262	7.22*
Teacher Correction	.273	9.10**
Cognitive Questioning	.102	4.74
Broad Questioning	.002	4.83
Narrow Questioning	.162	8.42*
Teacher Acceptance	.295	16.75***
Teacher Praise	.288	16.40***
Student Responsiveness	.310	9.03**
Oral Reading	.727	5.95*
Silent Reading	1.273	10.43**
Directed Activity	.359	3.83
Nonfunctional Behavior	.290	3.16

*$<.05$

**$<.01$

***$<.001$

LIMITATIONS

Certain inherent limitations must be considered in the interpretation of the results.

1. This investigation was limited to the populations used herein and results may be generalized only to similar groups of teachers.

2. The investigation was limited to those variables measured by the instruments employed in this study and the degree to which these instruments were effective in measuring those variables.

3. The present study was subject to the usual limitations of a quasiexperimental design. While factors or circumstances which accompany certain phenomena can be isolated, the failure to schedule these variables makes difficult discernment of causal relationships.

DISCUSSION

In considering the rationale of cross national studies, Husén and Postlethwaite (16) suggested that countries contain far greater differences than can be found or created in any one system. As many writers have contended, this allows the global delineation of similarities and differences and provides a new frame of reference for the appraisal of education. The data of the present study supported this suggestion. When comparing the teachers across country and grade level, the multivariate F-test and the main effect of country were significant. Neither the interaction of grade level and country nor the main effect of grade was significant. The frame of reference of the present study provided a number of insights which afforded the following appraisals.

1. Australian teachers tended to be autocratic and their instruction was teacher-centered; whereas, American teachers appeared indirect and child-centered. Australian teachers exhibited more teacher correction, teacher initiation, teacher praise, and oral reading but less teacher acceptance, narrow questioning, silent reading, and student responsiveness. One might consider, therefore, that Australian teachers were less accepting, more corrective, and more reinforcing and their pupils less responsive than were the American teachers.

2. Insofar as the Australian and American teachers obtained mean scores on the Test of Knowledge of Reading Instruction, which were only slightly more than one-half the possible score for this test, the teachers in both countries were limited in their knowledge of reading instruction. Given that this finding coincides with the

results obtained in past studies of American teachers (1, 12, 14, 17, 19), and based upon the assumption that teachers with a limited knowledge will be unable to effectively teach reading, concerted efforts should be initiated to ensure the attainment of a higher level of knowledge of reading instruction and thus effective reading instruction.

3. With respect to questioning, the teachers in both countries dwelled on cognitive memory questioning; rarely elicited convergent, divergent, or evaluative questions; and many of the teachers, especially the Americans, asked questions requiring only "yes" or "no" responses. This same trend has been apparent from studies of American teachers (3, 6, 12, 21). Obviously, greater emphasis needs to be given to the development of the questioning techniques of the teachers in both countries if the ultimate goal of developing higher levels of thinking is to be attained among our pupils.

4. Oral reading, in lieu of silent reading, was the most frequent, directed, instructional activity in both the Australian and American classrooms. Although the acceptability of having children read aloud has varied through the years and while most educators would agree that oral reading should be included in a well-balanced reading program, most would consider its role to be secondary to that of silent reading. Most teachers appeared to be unaware of the appropriate role oral reading assumes in the total reading program. Furthermore, it seemed that silent reading was not considered a viable instructional mode, especially by the Australian teachers.

5. In both countries, effective reading instruction appeared hampered by inefficient teaching. Of the three variables which dealt with affective aspects of teacher behavior—teacher praise, teacher correction, and teacher acceptance—teacher praise is often assumed to be most effective in promoting learning. Nevertheless, teacher praise was rarely elicited by the teachers of either country. In fact, of the three affective teacher variables, teacher praise occurred least frequently.

Nonfunctional behavior, which referred to that category of behavior labelled confusion and irrelevant behavior, was the most frequently occurring behavior during the reading lessons in both countries. While some time must be spent organizing for instruction and managing extrinsic and intrinsic interruptions, the time spent by most teachers entails inefficient use of reading instruction time.

6. The logic of the present study prevents relating differences in the teacher characteristics across the two countries to the influence of specific variables; however, one can postulate that differences

arising from the contextual attributes within the two environments influenced the characteristics of teachers. Relative to the background of the teachers, differences were noted in their training, qualifications, and number of reading courses taken. Relative to the reading practices, differences were noted in their specification, the amount and type of support personnel, organization, pupil evaluation, and the time of day reading was taught. The actual influence of these variables can be assessed only through further experimentation.

RESEARCH RECOMMENDATIONS

1. To ensure the validity of the findings, the present study should be replicated using more sophisticated sampling procedures and other forms of teacher and pupil assessment.

2. The periodical study of teacher and pupil characteristics across several nations would be a significant step toward improving the quality of teaching throughout the world. By providing objective evidence, this method would enable the needs in certain areas to be discerned; by providing contrasts, it would allow for the suggestion of alternative means toward these ends.

3. Future cross national studies of teacher characteristics should also be broader in scope. Aspects including the teacher's philosophy, personality, role, and attitude should be assessed; and carefully delineated aspects of her affective and cognitive behavior should be compared.

4. The ultimate improvement of educational systems is dependent largely upon improved teacher preparation. For this purpose, cross national studies should be extended to include periodical, objective evaluations of teacher preparation programs.

REFERENCES
1. Aaron, I. E. "What Teachers and Prospective Teachers Know About Phonic Generalizations," *Journal of Educational Research*, 53 (1960), 323-330.
2. Artley, A. S. "The Teacher Variable in the Teaching of Reading," in C. J. Wallen and S. L. Sebesta (Eds.), *The First R: Readings on Teaching Reading*. Chicago: Science Research Associates, 1972, 263-278.
3. Austin, M. C., and C. Morrison. *The First R.* New York: Macmillan, 1963.
4. Bond, G. L., and R. Dykstra. "The Cooperative Research Program in First Grade Reading Instruction," *Reading Research Quarterly*, 2 (1967), 5-142.
5. Chall, J. *Learning to Read: The Great Debate.* New York: McGraw-Hill, 1967.
6. Davidson, R. L. "Teacher Influence and Children's Level of Thinking," *Reading Teacher*, 22 (1969), 702-704.
7. Dickson, G. E. "International Teacher Education Research: The New Frame of Reference for Teacher Education Reform," *Journal of Teacher Education*, 3 (1967), 277-284.
8. Douglass, M. P. "Beginning Reading in Norway," *Reading Teacher*, 23 (1969), 17-22.

9. Fay, L. "The Teacher and the Improvement of Reading," in N. B. Smith (Ed.), *Reading Methods and Teacher Improvement*. Newark, Delaware: International Reading Association, 1971, 113-123.
10. Foshay, A. W., et al. *Educational Achievements of Thirteen-Year-Olds in Twelve Countries*. Hamburg: Unesco Institute for Education, 1962.
11. Gray, W. S. *The Teaching of Reading and Writing*. New York: Unesco, Scott, Foresman, 1956.
12. Guszak, F. J. *Relationship between Teacher Practice and Knowledge of Reading Theory in Selected Classes*. Project Report No. 5-437. Washington, D.C.: United States Department of Health, Education and Welfare, 1966. ERIC ED 010191.
13. Harris. A. J., and C. Morrison. "The CRAFT Project: A Final Report," *Reading Teacher*, 22 (1969), 335-340.
14. Henriksen, E. G. "An Analysis of Teacher Knowledge of Word Recognition Skills," unpublished doctoral dissertation, University of Georgia, 1968.
15. Hummel, T. J., and J. R. Sligo. "Empirical Comparison of Univariate and Multivariate Analysis of Variance Procedures," *Psychological Bulletin*, 76 (1971), 49-52.
16. Husén, T., and N. Postlethwaite. "Intentions and Background of the Project," in T. Husén (Ed.), *International Study of Achievement in Mathematics*. New York: John Wiley and Sons, 1967.
17. McCollum, J. "Teachers' Knowledge of Word Analysis Skills and Linguistic Concepts," doctoral dissertation, University of California. Ann Arbor, Michigan: University Microfilms, 1964. No. 64-9051.
18. Ramsey, W. Z. "An Evaluation of Three Methods of Teaching Reading," in J. A. Figurel (Ed.), *Challenge and Experiment in Reading*, Proceedings of the International Reading Association, 7, 1962. New York: Scholastic Magazines, 151-153.
19. Spache, G. D., and M. E. Baggett. "What Do Teachers Know About Phonics and Syllabication?" *Reading Teacher*, 19 (1965), 96-99.
20. Tatsuoka, M. M. *Multivariate Analysis: Technique for Educational and Psychological Research*. New York: John Wiley and Sons, 1971.
21. Wolf, W., et al. *Critical Reading Ability of Elementary School Children*. Final Report Project No. 5-1040. Washington, D.C.: United States Department of Health, Education and Welfare, 1967.

Evaluating the Effectiveness of University Programs for Teacher Education

Mary C. Austin
University of Hawaii
Honolulu, Hawaii
United States of America

During the past twenty years in the United States, several studies have documented the need for improved teacher education in reading. Hester's 1953 survey (5) of 800 elementary school teachers, for example, disclosed that many of the teachers felt inadequately prepared to teach reading. In 1955, Robinson (9) cited the importance of establishing qualifications for remedial reading personnel. Following these publications, the Harvard-Carnegie reports of 1961 and 1963 described college programs for prospective teachers of reading and then examined the status of elementary school reading programs throughout the country. Perhaps the most significant among the 67 recommendations made by Austin and Morrison (2, 3) was their clarion call for upgrading the preservice and inservice training of teachers. In the latter half of the 1960s, the First Grade Studies focused national attention upon the methods and materials of reading instruction. Despite this shift of emphasis in research efforts from the teacher to the curriculum, there emerged, not unexpectedly, an increased recognition of the influence of the reading teacher.

Undoubtedly, the cumulative effect of these studies and others related to teacher preparation led many states to adopt certification standards for reading teachers and specialists. Furthermore, many colleges and universities strengthened their course offerings in reading for both elementary and secondary teachers. But, having accomplished these changes, educators could not rest complacently upon their laurels; nor could they afford to delude themselves or the public that these modifications would result in the quality education deemed essential for all children in the remaining years of the twentieth century. Had they seen fit to do so, however, innovative members of the profession, as well as verbal educational critics, would have continued to point to antiquated educational systems, unyielding to social and technological changes, and to traditional teacher education programs which did little more than perpetuate an already stagnant status quo (1).

Nevertheless, for a number of years, colleges and universities appeared to evaluate the effectiveness of their programs for teacher education by a single criterion: the production of an increasing number of graduates who found teaching jobs in the nation's schools. And then came the seventies with dwindling school enrollments and greater competition for teaching positions, accompanied by higher expectations for teacher performance and pupil achievement, and a general loss of public confidence in higher institutions of learning. Reformers began, in earnest, to exert social, political, and economic pressures on the schools, demanding accountability in every area of educational endeavor, including teacher preparation.

Many people believed that a fundamental restructuring of the entire educational system was in order. Some of them convinced the federal government to allocate several million dollars for the development of experimental models designed to create a new kind of teacher who would be "guaranteed" to get results in the classroom. Ten different models for teacher preparation from ten educational institutions across the United States offered especially bold, innovative approaches to elementary teacher preparation, their directions being away from the limiting, prescribed programs of the past toward those that were open-ended and process oriented with students' needs and interests as high priorities. The new programs rely generally upon objectives stated in behavioral or performance terms, opportunities for individualized instruction, and provisions for flexible curricular content through the use of instructional modules. The inclusion of varying levels of experiences with children in and away from elementary school classrooms, is also noteworthy.

ROLE OF THE UNIVERSITY IN TEACHER EDUCATION

The university has the responsibility for preparing teachers for the innovative practices and concepts they will encounter in the field. It can examine and analyze the many facets of effective teaching with the goal of setting standards for adequate preparation of prospective teachers, looking beyond ivied walls to the grassroots level of the classroom setting. As pointed out, teachers in the field are faced with educational problems with newly coined labels: cognitive and affective objectives, competency based education, criterion referenced vs. norm referenced tests, individually guided instruction, diagnostic prescriptive teaching, and accountability. Teachers in the field are also faced with newly devised approaches to 1) reading instruction; 2) programed materials; 3) new materials and equipment; and 4) new buildings constructed especially for such concepts as team teaching, library centers as the core of the curriculum, and open-spaced settings instead of walled classrooms. Teacher preparation colleges will need to make periodic evaluations of their programs in order to provide ones that are current and viable.

In order to prepare guidelines for evaluating their teacher education programs, the university can adapt the cybernetic principles of task analysis and instrument analysis; and it can focus upon the ultimate objective—the effective teacher. Each one of us engaged in the preparation of teachers must at some time have experienced at least a vague feeling of disquiet concerning our efforts. Is there something more or something different we could be doing to improve our program? Are we giving prospective teachers adequate preparation? Another line of questioning we might attempt to answer for our own program would include soul-searching questions such as: "What do we mean by a good teacher?" "What components of his education make him good?" In our analysis, we would look first at the responsibilities faced by the classroom teacher. We would analyze the tasks faced by him as he attempts to fulfill his responsibilities to the individual children assigned him. Then we would need to study the implications for his preservice instruction at the college level and for the continuing development of his career at the inservice level. These have been delineated in Table 1, which considers the accountability of both the college and the school system for the preparation of the effective teacher.

LEADS TO MARKED PROGRAM IMPROVEMENT

Just as some professions such as law and medicine have set certain standards which novices are expected to meet, a strong organization such as the International Reading Association can point out standards which novice teachers can be expected to meet—the knowledges and competencies which the effective teacher exhibits. In fact, through the IRA, Commission on High Quality Teacher Education, the Association developed and published a volume entitled *Modular Preparation for Teaching Reading (13)* which contains a well-developed program for preservice and continuing education. As Durr (4) states in the Foreword:

> ... this volume finally incorporates the principles of individual differences into teacher education in two dimensions. First, the modules provide for differences in both the previous learnings and mastery rate of those being trained to teach reading. Second, the modules provide a variety of delivery systems so that those responsible for the education of teachers may adapt the modules according to their own strengths and professional commitments.

Universities now use this volume to translate desired teaching competencies into objectives which, in turn, can be transformed into standards of excellence.

In addition to using IRA publications devoted to the improvement of the education of those who teach reading, each college or university undertaking evaluations of the effectiveness of its teacher education

Table 1. Accountability in Teacher Preparation

Teacher Responsibilities	Task Analysis	Implications for Teacher Training Institutions	Implications for School Systems
To produce readers capable of reading effectively for their own purposes	Individualization based upon ability and achievement levels	Developing courses which introduce Child Growth and Development Foundations of Education Children's Literature Reading Methods Reading in Content Areas Structure and Use of the English Language English as a Second Language Observations in Classroom Settings Internship experiences with children under supervision	Accepting only new teachers with the preparation indicated here or in accordance with IRA standards
To be knowledgeable concerning the embryo "good reader"—the child's abilities as well as his achievements to date	Diagnostic-prescriptive teaching Use of criterion-referenced instruction and testing	Offering demonstrations and experiences with tests—administering and interpreting informal and standardized instruments	Assigning the novice to an experienced teacher for one or more semesters
To be knowledgeable concerning the many facets of instruction—effective techniques and materials	Varied approaches to learning; hardware and software to implement instruction	Providing experiences in fitting materials to individuals, at their independent and instructional levels Formulating guidelines for continuous program evaluation and modification	Encouraging all teachers to keep up to date through observations, demonstrations, workshops, professional reading, graduate courses, and attendance at professional meetings

AUSTIN

553

program will probably take a number of steps. Three possibilities may be categorized under the general headings of surveys, assessment of goals, and examinations of innovative practices. Results obtained from these steps should lead to the formulation of guidelines for the institution's next decade of teacher preparation, with built-in provisions for earlier modifications, if they are needed.

Surveys often include carefully developed questionnaires and interviews of students who are enrolled in graduate programs, preferably first-year teachers and others whose teaching experiences cover a selected span of time such as three years and ten years. These individuals are asked to 1) identify specific teaching problems they have encountered, 2) react to the adequacy of their preparation, and 3) suggest needed changes for future programs. Examples of questions these teachers might be asked are, "How do you evaluate your undergraduate preparation? What would you like to see new teachers get in their preparation?" "What I found most useful was_____." When teacher college personnel analyze both objective and open-ended items, they should gain valuable information for program changes related to educational core requirements, content and conduct of methods courses, observation and participation activities in preservice programs, and student teaching experiences.

Surveys of course offerings can be helpful in determining adequacy of content according to the general and specific competencies that teachers are expected to acquire. To assure that students are being exposed to current philosophies and practices, a review can be made of the techniques, approaches, and materials introduced to prospective teachers. One such review revealed that new teachers were acquainted with only one approach to the teaching of reading. Periodic studies sometimes demonstrate the need to move from instructor-lecture type courses to 1) more classroom observations of good teachers in action, 2) demonstrations and discussions of new methods and materials, 3) videotape viewing and critiques, and 4) small group activities and presentations.

School systems expect to make contributions to the improvement of the preparation of the products they receive. They should be given ample opportunities to communicate their expectations and to explain any special conditions of their students and communities that should be taken into consideration by the universities preparing their new teachers.

In addition to surveys of various groups who should be involved in establishing the quality of teacher education programs, a second step in the evaluative process might be accomplished by an assessment of program goals. Questions such as the following can serve as guides: Are the institution's goals for its teacher education program readily available for study by all interested individuals and groups? Are the statements of these goals too limited? Too broad? Are they presented clearly in terms of competencies which specify desired teaching-learning acts or behaviors of prospective teachers? Do they include the objectives considered important in the development of both measurable outcomes of knowledges and skills and the less tangible outcomes of attitudes, appreciations, and values? Do the goals incorporate competencies identified as being essential for maximizing the emotional, cognitive, and social growth of children?

As a third step in the improvement of university teacher education, an examination of innovative programs should be anticipated. When carefully selected and tailored to the needs and resources of the institution, those programs and materials can greatly enhance the professional program.

Within the past five years in the United States, Competency Based Teacher Education (CBTE), also referred to as Performance Based Teacher Education (PBTE), has received much attention. Some 17 states have committed their teacher preparation institutions to competency/ performance based programs, either as the only route to certification or as a permissible alternative. Tennessee, on the other hand, has mandated competency based programs for school administrators but not for teachers. The movement continues to gain momentum from month to month, despite reactions which range from enthusiastic support to strong opposition.

Ideally, the long term goal of CBTE is to upgrade the quality of education in the nation's schools by means of improved teacher education. Impact of the movement probably will be felt in not less than ten years, a factor which may impede acceptance of the concept by many colleges and universities. An intermediate range goal (4-10 years) is "to prepare knowledgeable and skilled teachers in a curriculum whose elements have been tested for validity against criteria of school effectiveness" (12). Short range goals to be accomplished within four years include 1) identification of tentative teacher competencies, 2) preparation of instructional materials and evaluation procedures, and 3) establishment of conditions to validate the teacher education curricula and to promote teacher behavior research.

More immediate expectations, upon the implementation of CBTE, include 1) stronger relationships among teacher educators, public schools, and the organized teaching profession; 2) greater student satisfaction with skill-oriented teacher education programs; and 3) increased accountability of teacher education programs.

The Florida Center for Teacher Training Materials at the University of Miami in Coral Gables has an impressive collection of modules or training packages in reading and other curriculum areas. The Center collects, catalogs, reviews, and reports on competency based teacher education materials developed in the United States and offers its assistance in the implementation of these instructional resources.

May (8) has developed Mastery Performance Modules for Teachers in Training with accompanying tapes for *To Help Children Read*. Croft Educational Services has produced teacher education materials which may be helpful in the preparation of reading teachers.

Professional literature is replete with articles and books for the perusal of those who intend to embark upon an improved teacher education program. *Competency Based Teacher Education: Progress, Problems, and Prospects* (6) and *The Power of Competency Based Teacher Education: A Report* (11) are representative of recent publications.

Houston and his associates (7) have performed a Herculean task in providing access to a comprehensive annotated listing of instructional materials. Resources annotated in the collection include films, slide/tapes, modules, programed texts, and multimedia kits for training prospective or inservice educational personnel.

CONCLUSION

It is totally unrealistic to anticipate immediate outcomes from such a complex venture as the design and implementation of new teacher education programs. Even a 10-year projection before changes can be completed may be optimistic, but gradually improvements will be seen in classrooms of the seventies—especially in those rooms whose teachers are the graduates of colleges and universities devoted to quality preservice education programs. Every institution has the power to move rapidly from the traditional programs described by Smith (14) in *Research in Teacher Education*. These programs

> . . . have developed over the last hundred years, and especially since the beginning of the present century, on the basis of meager and inadequate knowledge acquired largely from the practical experience of teachers, general psychological principles, and studies in philosophy and the social sciences.

This paper has suggested a number of steps toward the evaluation of the effectiveness of teacher education, but the validity of a teacher education program is determined ultimately by the production of teachers who perform more effectively in classrooms than they would had they not received such training. At present, solid research evidence does not exist to support a direct relationship between teacher behavior and pupil learning (10). We must proceed, therefore, on the best bases we have for higher quality teacher preparation. Hopefully, educators will further develop habits of communication which enable all countries to benefit from ideas the profession generates. Future effective teacher education programs in reading depend a great deal upon the expertise of today's teachers.

REFERENCES

1. Allen, D. W., and R. A. Mackin. "A Revolution in Teacher Education," *Phi Delta Kappan*, 52 (May 1970), 485-488.
2. Austin, Mary C., and Coleman Morrison. *The First R: The Harvard Report on Reading in the Elementary Schools*. New York: Macmillan, 1963.
3. Austin, Mary C., and others. *The Torch Lighters: Tomorrow's Teachers of Reading*. Cambridge: Harvard University Press, 1961.
4. Durr, William K. "Foreword," in Harry W. Sartain and Paul E. Stanton (Eds.), *Modular Preparation for Teaching Reading*. Newark, Delaware: International Reading Association, 1974.
5. Hester, Kathleen B. "Classroom Problems in the Teaching of Reading," *Elementary School Journal*, 54 (October 1953), 84-87.
6. Houston, W. Robert, and Robert B. Howsam. *Competency Based Teacher Education: Progress, Problems, and Prospects*. Chicago, Illinois: Science Research Associates, 1972.
7. Houston, W. Robert, and others. *Resources for Performance Based Education*. Albany, New York: State University of New York, State Department of Education, 1973.
8. May, Frank B. Mastery performance modules for teachers in training and tapes to accompany *To Help Children Read*. Columbus, Ohio: Charles E. Merrill, 1973.
9. Robinson, Helen M. "Qualifications for Teachers of Remedial Reading," *School Review*, 43 (September 1955), 334-337.
10. Rosenshine, B., and N. Furst. "Research in Teacher Performance Criteria," in B. O. Smith (Ed.), *Research in Teacher Education*. Englewood Cliffs, New Jersey: Prentice-Hall, 1971, 40.
11. Rosner, B. *The Power of Competency Based Teacher Education*, report of the Committee on National Program Priorities in Teacher Education. Boston: Allyn and Bacon, 1972.
12. Rosner, Benjamin, and Patricia M. Kay. "Will the Promise of C/PBTE Be Fulfilled?" *Phi Delta Kappan*, 55 (January 1974), 290-295.
13. Sartain, Harry W., and Paul E. Stanton (Eds.), *Modular Preparation for Teaching Reading*. Newark, Delaware: International Reading Association, 1974.
14. Smith, B. O. (Ed.). *Research in Teacher Education*. Englewood Cliffs, New Jersey: Prentice-Hall, 1971, 1.

Evaluation and Accountability

Ira E. Aaron
University of Georgia
Athens, Georgia
United States of America

Accountability is a major concern of educators in the United States today. Of equal concern is the process of evaluation which must, of necessity, be a part of accountability. This article will review briefly the current concern about accountability and evaluation as they pertain to reading and will turn attention to four questions:

1. Who in the field of reading should be evaluated as a basis for accountability?
2. What should be evaluated?
3. Who should plan for and conduct the evaluation?
4. To whom should persons involved in reading instruction be held accountable?

INTRODUCTION

The 1970s will be known as the accountability decade in education in the United States. Educational historians, reflecting upon the period, will likely comment upon the heated and extensive debates generated among teachers and other educators by the accountability concept. Further, these historians will certainly refer to problems that arose because of inadequate evaluation.

Educational accountability refers to teachers and other educational workers being responsible for their performance in instruction. The reading teacher is responsible for teaching his or her students to read and to enjoy reading. The teacher is answerable for the effectiveness of his or her teaching.

Evaluation is the process of making decisions based upon information that has been gathered about whatever it is that is being evaluated—reading programs and reading achievement of students in this case. The strength of any system of accountability rests heavily upon an appropriate and adequate process of evaluation. Therefore, educational accountability and educational evaluation are interlocked, with evaluation being a necessary part of accountability.

Evaluation is one of the weakest areas in reading programs in the United States (and perhaps in the world). Most teachers would find it extremely difficult to document just how good or how bad their reading programs really are because they seldom have adequate data to support statements they make about the quality of their programs. Good evaluation is a necessary part of any workable system of accountability. An IRA publication, *Measuring Reading Performance* (1), presents papers that discuss some of the pertinent problems of measurement and accountability.

The concept of accountability in American education is quite old, as Lessinger (2) and Laffey (3) point out. In fact, Lessinger cites an 1817 law in which the accountability concept was used. Nevertheless, it was not until the late 1960s that educational accountability began to be a real concern of school personnel in the United States. Teachers and other educators always have been accountable to those who have financed education. Today, though, the accountability is more complex and forceful.

Many state departments of education have already moved, or are in the process of moving, toward statewide systems of accountability. In some instances, state legislatures have been active in working for statewide educational accountability.

Indicative of the opposition to the national movement toward educational accountability is a news report of the July 1974 convention of the National Education Association (a body of 1.4 million members). The executive secretary of that organization is quoted as follows:

> Teachers willingly accept their appropriate share of responsibility for the effectiveness of the nation's education programs. Teachers do not—and will not—accept the simplistic, bureaucratic approach to teacher accountability that is prevalent in America today. (*Atlanta Constitution*, July 6, 1974)

The article stated further that teachers will continue to fight accountability unless they are given more of a voice in establishing the accountability system.

Accountability definitely is a major issue today in American education. The ideas related to accountability, along with necessary evaluation, are equally applicable worldwide. The difference between the United States and other countries on this issue is merely one of intensity.

WHO IN THE FIELD OF READING SHOULD BE EVALUATED AS A BASIS FOR ACCOUNTABILITY?

Discussions of accountability often focus upon the teacher and the students, with the teacher being held accountable for the reading progress of students. This viewpoint is too narrow. Why should the reading teacher alone be held accountable for pupil progress in reading? Many persons are involved in and have responsibilities related to the teaching of reading in elementary and secondary schools, such as principals, content area teachers, supervisors, superintendents, librarians, aides, and parents. Students themselves also should be held accountable for their own participation in the program.

Most educators voice approval of some kind of accountability and a system of evaluation along with it. Too frequently, though, they tend to expect accountability to apply to other teachers or to administrators in another school district rather than to apply to themselves and their own schools. All educational workers should be involved in accountability and their performances should be evaluated.

WHAT SHOULD BE EVALUATED?

Although many factors should be evaluated to determine program effectiveness, student achivement in reading should be a major concern. Students are expected to gain in reading achievement from one assessment period to another. If students do not show progress, then a system of accountability calls for an explanation.

The usual measure of change has been attained through comparison of standardized from pre- and posttesting results from year to year. Such results do give useful information, if tests are keyed to program objectives. However, criterion referenced tests and informal procedures can supply valuable data. Criterion referenced tests are composed of items directly keyed to behaviors which the reading program is attempting to develop in students. Such tests establish the minimum level of performance, the criterion, which is considered to be satisfactory. Several states are now in the process of building criterion referenced tests for statewide use.

Assessment of change in reading achievement test scores is not easy to accomplish; assessment of attitudes toward reading (motivational and affective) is even more difficult to accomplish. And the affective area is an extremely important one. The instructional task is not complete if children have learned skills but have not learned to enjoy reading. Estimates must be made of how children feel about reading and of their interests in reading.

Evaluation in a system of accountability also must view the characteristics of the reading program in which the child has been taught. The reading program and instructional procedures must be studied to determine whether they develop readers who *can* and *will* read.

Somewhere in the evaluation related to accountability, responsibilities of teachers and others must be determined; and then, the instructional process and the total educational environment must be studied in terms of each group's responsibilities. The following rating scale is offered as an example of some specific responsibilities in reading instruction.

RATING SCALE FOR EVALUATING RESPONSIBILITIES IN READING INSTRUCTION

Directions: Many persons are involved in and have responsibilities related to the teaching of reading in elementary and secondary schools. Selected responsibilities of the teacher, principal, superintendent, reading supervisor, and parent are listed below. By circling the appropriate number, indicate the extent to which a given teacher, principal, superintendent, reading supervisor, or parent reflects each characteristic or meets each responsibility. Use the following ratings:

1. Almost always
2. Most of the time
3. Sometimes

4. Seldom or never
5. Undecided
6. Not applicable in program

Teacher's responsibilities: The teacher

1. Aims reading instruction toward the achievement of specific goals.   1 2 3 4 5 6

2. Understands children and adolescents and uses knowledge and development in teaching reading.   1 2 3 4 5 6

3. Adapts reading instruction to the individual levels, abilities, and needs of all learners.   1 2 3 4 5 6

4. Uses diagnostic-prescriptive approach in reading instruction.   1 2 3 4 5 6

5. Establishes a good working relationship with students.   1 2 3 4 5 6

6. Merges materials and equipment into a total program.   1 2 3 4 5 6

7. Knows the skills of reading and how to teach the skills.   1 2 3 4 5 6

8. Leads students toward enjoyment of reading.   1 2 3 4 5 6

9. Evaluates progress in reading in terms of instructional goals.   1 2 3 4 5 6

10. Organizes the classroom for effective management of reading instruction.   1 2 3 4 5 6

11. Keeps parents informed about the reading program and about individual progress of students.   1 2 3 4 5 6

Principal's responsibilities: The principal

12. Converses knowledgeably with teachers and parents about the school's reading program and practices.   1 2 3 4 5 6

13. Assists teachers in obtaining needed teaching materials.   1 2 3 4 5 6

14. Takes the lead in planning necessary staff development for teachers.   1 2 3 4 5 6

15. Taps all available resources for assistance for teachers.   1 2 3 4 5 6

16. Encourages teachers to move toward excellence in reading instruction.   1 2 3 4 5 6

17. Observes an atmosphere that encourages teachers to seek help.   1 2 3 4 5 6

18. Identifies leaders among the teachers who will assist in coordinating efforts in reading.   1 2 3 4 5 6

19. Recognizes the relationship of reading to the total curriculum and emphasizes reading in the school program.   1 2 3 4 5 6

Content area teacher's responsibilities: The content area teacher

20. Teaches students to use developmental skills in that content area.   1 2 3 4 5 6

21. Teaches the special reading skills of that content area.   1 2 3 4 5 6

22. Continues to work toward the development of each student's reading-study skills.   1 2 3 4 5 6

Reading supervisor's responsibilities: The reading supervisor

23. Assists in keeping teachers and principals abreast of new materials and new developments in the area of reading.   1 2 3 4 5 6

24. Assists principals in planning and conducting staff development in the area of reading for teachers and aides.   1 2 3 4 5 6

25. Prepares and works with leaders in each school who will in turn work with teachers.   1 2 3 4 5 6

26. Assists the superintendent in motivating principals and teachers to move toward excellence in reading instruction.   1 2 3 4 5 6

27. Assists the superintendent in motivating principals and teachers to try out new or different practices if they offer promise for improvement.   1 2 3 4 5 6

28. Creates an atmosphere that encourages teachers and principals to seek help when needed.   1 2 3 4 5 6

29. Observes instruction to locate "promising practices" and to assist in improving reading instruction.   1 2 3 4 5 6

3C. Provides leadership in evaluating the total reading program of the school and/or school system.   1 2 3 4 5 6

Superintendent's responsibilities: The superintendent

31. Sees that adequate staff development for reading instruction is planned for system schools.   1 2 3 4 5 6

32. Sees that all school personnel are motivated to move toward excellence in reading instruction.   1 2 3 4 5 6

33. Sees that adequate personnel and materials for teaching reading effectively are available.   1 2 3 4 5 6

34. Sees that persons involved in making systemwide decisions about reading are representative of the groups to be affected and are well qualified.   1 2 3 4 5 6

Parents' responsibilities: The parents

35. Work toward building concept backgrounds and meaning vocabularies in their children.   1 2 3 4 5 6

36. Encourage children to read.   1 2 3 4 5 6

37. Read to children and develop a reading atmosphere in the home.   1 2 3 4 5 6

38. Learn about the reading programs in the classrooms of their children.   1 2 3 4 5 6

As the performance of each educational worker is being evaluated in an accountability system, student performance alone should not be the basis for saying that a program, teacher, or other educational worker is successful. What happens in the instructional process is as important as the level of student performance. And all factors related to instruction—kind of students, materials available, and so on—should be considered.

WHO SHOULD PLAN FOR AND CONDUCT THE EVALUATION?

Accountability is much more palatable when those being held accountable helped to establish the system of accountability. Teacher representatives, therefore, should be involved in planning for teacher accountability. Setting up a system of accountability offers numerous opportunities for reading teachers to obtain a clearer picture of what they are trying to accomplish and how they are attempting to do the job. Within itself, it is a good inservice activity.

Every individual listed on the Rating Scale should be involved in self-evaluation and in the evaluation of those under supervision. Persons being supervised should assist, as well, in evaluating those who instruct or supervise them.

Sometimes, outside agencies or individuals are contracted to establish a system of accountability or evaluation for a school district. These outsiders often bring with them expert knowledge about evaluation that cannot be found locally; however, they do not have an understanding of the local setting in which the program has developed. They must depend upon local educators to supply this element.

TO WHOM SHOULD PERSONS INVOLVED IN READING INSTRUCTION BE HELD ACCOUNTABLE?

Who decides whether the teacher or other educational worker has met the test of accountability? Many voices have been raised in demanding that teachers be held accountable, but these voices seldom clarify the accountability hierarchy. Some teachers feel that they are expected to be accountable to everyone. On the other hand, some of the voices calling for accountability contend that American education through the years has not been accountable to anyone. The truth lies somewhere between these extremes.

Ultimately teachers and other educational personnel are responsible to boards of education; members of boards of education are responsible to their electors. However, teachers are accountable not only to boards of education and their representatives but to superintendents and principals as well. They are accountable to the children they teach and to the children's parents; and, perhaps even more important, teachers are accountable to themselves.

In a legal sense, teachers and other educational workers are accountable to both local and statewide boards of education. However, from a moral standpoint, the educator is accountable first to himself and then to all those who supervise him and who are served by him. Perhaps the first level of accountability should be how well children have been served.

SUMMARY

In summary, several precautions must be reviewed. The accountability system itself should be studied carefully to see if it is efficient, fair, and effective. An extremely important consideration is that the evaluation system be nonpunitive and nonthreatening, and that the system provide some help to those teachers and other personnel who are judged as inadequate.

The teacher, the individual students and their collective actions, the materials, the facilities, the principal, the supervisor, the school policies, and the community all influence growth in a given classroom. A finding of Thorndike's recent fifteen-country survey of comprehension (4) seems pertinent at this point. The best predictors of reading achievement appeared to be home and family backgrounds of the children. This conclusion does not mean that the teacher is unimportant. It does mean that many influences, other than the quality of instruction, are involved in the reading achievement of children. Any system of accountability and evaluation must reflect those influences.

Accountability can assist teachers and other educational workers to become more effective in their important job of helping children learn to read and to enjoy it. The factors referred to in this article—as well as many more—must be considered, however, in evaluating the effectiveness of an accountability system and its processes of evaluation.

REFERENCES
1. Blanton, William, Roger Farr, and J. Jaap Tuinman (Eds.). *Measuring Reading Performance.* Newark, Delaware: International Reading Association, 1974.
2. Laffey, James L. "Accountability: A Brief History and Analysis," in Robert B. Ruddell (Ed.), *Accountability and Reading Instruction: Critical Issues.* Urbana, Illinois: National Council of Teachers of English, 1973.
3. Lessinger, Leon. *Every Kid a Winner.* New York: Simon and Schuster, 1970.
4. Thorndike, Robert L. *Reading Comprehension Education in Fifteen Countries.* International Studies in Evaluation III, International Association for the Evaluation of Educational Achievement. Stockholm: Almqvist and Wiksell, 1973.

Author Index

Subject Index

Accessing
  information, 84
  materials, 222
Accountability, 558-564
Adult education, 39
Alphabet, 232, 275, 323, 371
Attitude
  contents of reading materials, 74
  identification of, 159
Audiovisual aids, 364
Bias in texts, 341, 352, 394
Bilinguals, 442
Blending, 231-232, 276
Breakthrough to Literacy, 83, 281
Class size, 413-418, 431, 514
Cloze
  procedure, 326-327, 338
  readability measures, 332, 354
  tests, 73
Cognitive confusion, 76, 253, 274, 281
Community involvement, 396
Comparative
  process, 37
  reading project, 251
  studies in reading, 39, 70-74
Competency based approach, 510-515,
    519-520
Comprehension
  cloze, 199
  creative, 233
  critical, 233
  cross-national studies, 500-507
  development of, 2
  evaluative, 46-47, 344
  goals, 12
  inference, 226
  in oral reading, 494
  interpretive, 46-47, 344
  levels of, 8
  literal, 8, 46-47, 233
  outcomes, 131-132, 226
  readability, 331
  reading rate, 28-35, 199
  recreational reading, 215
  reorganizaion, 226
  skills, 12, 221
  tables, 199
  teaching strategies, 125-139
  tests, 220
  textbook, 32
  translation, 226
Constraints
  syntactic and semantic, 90

Content
  areas, skills in, 234-235
  analysis, 346
Coordination, hand-eye, 456
Counselling of retarded readers, 435-438
Creative activities, 105-106
Cues
  context, 50, 231
  graphic, 16-17, 86
  graphophonic, 16-17
  information, 24
  phonic, 16-17, 86
  retrieval, 137-138
  semantic, 16-17, 20, 86
  syntactic, 16-17, 86
  typographical, 13
Cultural differences
  American Indian, 393
  bias in education, 535
  Cuban American, 393
  low socioeconomic groups, 393-394
Cursive writing, 275
Decoding, 252-253, 269, 285
Disadvantaged, 81, 375, 379, 464
Dyslexia, 96, 250, 253, 479
Education
  compensatory, 525
  compulsory (England), 278
  remedial, 422-424
Educational technology, 386-387
Electric Company, 364, 371, 377-380
Evaluation, 37, 215-219, 226
  procedures, 15, 208-209
  programs, 558, 565
  self-, 182
  textbook, 322
Eye movement, 28
Fairytales/fantasies, 305-307, 316
Feedback, 181-184
Film, 364-365
Flow diagrams, 147, 156
Fluency, 187, 236
Folklore, 54, 398
Graphemes, 270-271, 280, 286
Graphics, 18-22, 89
Headstart, 468-469
Hebrew, 274
Hiragana, 66, 244-248
Humanities, 327, 355
Illiteracy, 269, 278, 472-477
Individual reading inventory, 442
Initial teaching alphabet, 274, 375
Inservice education, 395, 517-518, 521-522

Interests, 217, 302-303, 312-315
  derivation, 312-315
  in reading subject, 302
Intervention programs, 464-471
Japan, 244-245, 255, 262, 269
Knowledge structures, 60
Language, 25, 133
  acceptance, 395
  acquisition, 90-91
  acquisition device, 80
  arts, 94
  development, 60
  experience approach, 63-64, 281, 396
  games, 102-109
  laboratory, 228, 389
  persuasive, 346
  process and skill, 280
  proficiency and reading success,
      102-103, 482-483
  related cognitive readiness, 4
Letter
  code, 83
  string, 285
Linguistics
  based materials, 127
  cultural variables, 75
  environment, 88-89
  perspective, 15-18
  processes, 18, 97, 279
Literacy
  functional, 27, 198-199, 278
  provision for adults in England and
      Wales, 476
  visual, 54
  pre-, 281
Literature, 52-57, 66, 304-305
  for children, 68
  for pleasure, 107-108
Look and Say, 298
Lure into Reading, 62-65
Maladjustment, 434
Media, 12, 224, 279
  function in reading, 60
  of instruction, 386
  printed, bias, 341, 343
  revolution, 198
Memory, 10, 37, 128-130, 226
Miscue
  analysis, 15, 86-93
  taxonomy, 16-19
Monitoring, 182, 187-189
Motivation, 80, 94, 108-109, 161-162, 222,
    325, 396
Nahuas Indians, 52
Newspapers, 347-350
Northern Ireland, 342
Ocular control, 454-457
Oracy, 102
Orthography, 23, 36, 285

Paraprofessionals, 524-530
Parent
  consultations, 237
  involvement, 82-83, 144
  teacher associations, 527
Perception, 449-450
Performance evaluation, 223
Phonemes, 75-76, 95, 244, 251, 271-280,
    297
Phonetics, 66, 83, 223, 230-231, 375
Phonic skills, 296-298
Picture clues and word cards, 230
Prejudice, 341-342
Prereading, 378-379
Preschool, 374
  children and television in Japan, 66-67,
      246, 255
Progress
  charts, 239
  evaluation of, 208-214
  measurement of, 217
Psycholinguistics, 18, 71, 128
  guessing game, 147
Puppets, 384
Purpose, 216
  resource grid, 227
  task-oriented, 32-33
  taxonomy, 156
Questions
  effective, 47
  interpretive, 145-146
  multiple-choice, 13, 338
  teacher's, 136-137
  type, 136-137
Readability, 321, 323
  developments in, 331-339
  elements of, 332-333
  formulae, 95-96, 323-324, 335-337, 354
  in languages other than English, 337
  measurement of, 326-327, 331-332
Readers
  advanced, 141
  backward, 496
  deficient, 25
  effective, 22, 147
  flexible, 27
  gifted, 141-146
  junior high school, 13
  poor, 202
  retarded, 293, 434-440
  skillful, 5-6
  unskilled, 130
Reader's diary, 217
Reader's passport, 65, 217
Reading
  accelerators, 158
  achievement factors, 479-492
  achievement test, 73
  activities, 515

Reading *(continued)*
affective elements, 126
aloud, 218
behaviour, 147, 185-186
bias, 341
bilingual, 446-447
comparative, 70-77
competence, 84, 511
comprehension *(see* Comprehension)
creative, 64
critical, 13, 198, 343
curriculum, 142, 222
deficiency in bilinguals, 442-448
development, 64, 292
development of interest, 215
disability, 248, 299
effective teaching, 12-13
efficient, 163
error analysis, 16
experience, 368
failure, 27, 434
flexibility, 28
functional, 189, 198
generative model, 147
goals, 226
group, 64
habit, 61-62, 66, 395-396
individual, 64, 218
instruction, 364, 538
interactive, 125, 138
interest in, 237
inventory, 210
level, 303
machines, 389-390
mechanics of, 198
media, 222
nature of, 10, 430
oral, 10
oral vs silent, 447, 547
outcome, 147-148, 154
pacers, 28
parent-child, 67
preferences, 502
primers, 72
process, 19-20, 97, 155
prodigies, 292
programs, 27, 383-384, 387-388
purpose, 29, 147-148, 154, 188, 222
readiness, 226, 277
records, 210
recreational, 216
research, 97
sex differentials, 313-314, 496, 501, 503
shared experience, 396
silent, 134
skills, 94, 155-156, 222
socioeconomic variables, 497, 501
specialist, 510
speed, 31-32, 62, 162-163, 216, 236

Reading *(continued)*
spurt, 297
standards (UK), 494-498
stimulation, 67
strategy, 147, 152-153, 222
study, 226
tasks, 221
techniques, 159
tests, 61-62, 200-201
Read record, 147-149
Received Pronunciation, 282
Repertory grid, 155
Research
design, 9-10
design and methodology, 72-73
Resource systems, 224
Response
construction, 129-130
expected, 19
factual, 10
oral, 15
Retentivity, 201
Reversals, 89, 90
Right to Read, 393, 395, 473, 477
Role play, 105
Scanning, 159-163, 226, 236
Schools
British primary, 98
as resource, 82
Segregation for remedial instruction,
422-427
Self
concept, 435
evaluation, 184
fulfilling prophecy, 83
image, 290
regulating systems, 183-185
Sentence
difficulty, 334-335
expanding and transforming game, 103
transformation, 366
Sequence, 273-278, 327
Sesame Street, 364, 371, 377-380, 384
Set, psychological, 34, 186
Sex differences, 75, 479-485
Skills, 88
adult, 46-48
appreciation, 281
communication, 39
comprehension, 281
derived, 46
development, 223
evaluation, 281
function, 181-182
fundamental reading, 234, 371
generic, 39, 47-48
goal setting, 222
hierarchy, 18, 25
higher level processing, 130-131